Displayed at the National Naval Aviation Museum at Pensacola, Florida is the only known Vought SB2U "Vindicator" in existence anywhere in the world. Captain Richard Fleming, U.S. Marine Corps Reserve, earned the sole Medal of Honor awarded for the Battle of Midway in 1942 in part for flying his Vindicator on a bombing run to attack a Japanese cruiser on June 5, 1942. (Author's photograph, 2015).

Pearl Harbor's Hidden Heroes

The Eighteen Medals of Honor
Awarded for Bravery in the Hawaiian Islands
During World War II (1941, 1942, and 1945)

Colonel Charles A. Jones
U. S. Marine Corps Reserve (Retired)

© 2017 Charles A. Jones

Disclaimer: This book is a private project completed by the author and represents his opinions and not those of the U. S. Government, National Park Service, Department of Defense, or any branch of the military service. Section 2-304 of the Joint Ethics Regulations (DoD 5500.7-R) permits the author's use of his military service and title in the book.

No part of this book may be copied or reproduced electronically or by any other means without the express written consent of the author excepting excerpts used in book reviews.

Front cover photographs:

    Top: The United States flag flying at half-mast over the memorial to U.S.S. *Utah* at "Carrier Row," Ford Island, Pearl Harbor, Oahu, Hawaii (why the flag was flying at half-mast is unknown). Part of the rusted hulk of the ship can be seen to the far left of the white portion of the Memorial extending to the left. The ship is one of two ships remaining in Pearl Harbor that were there on December 7, 1941. One *Utah* crewman earned a Medal of Honor (posthumously) for bravery on December 7: Chief Petty Officer Watertender Peter Tomich U.S. Navy. (Author's slide, 2004)

    Bottom: A Navy Medal of Honor. (Photograph courtesy of the Congressional Medal of Honor Society)

Published by CreateSpace

Available from Amazon.com

ISBN-13: 978-0692780749
ISBN-10: 0692780742
Library of Congress Control Number: 2016915293
Charles A. Jones, Greensboro, NC

Contact the author at cajonesdt@gmail.com

Contents

Dedication 10

Dramatis Personae 11

Reflections 12

Why and How I Wrote This Book 15

Introduction: Pearl Harbor's Hidden Heroes 33

Part I: Military Environment

Chapter 1: Ships, Terms, Grade, and Military Organization 43

Part II: Menace and Mess—History Written in Dark Ink

Chapter 2: The Attacks on December 7, 1941—Twenty-Five Minutes Late 65

Chapter 3: Aftermath of December 7 Attacks on Oahu—"The Yellow Peril" and "The Punch Below the Belt" 93

Part III: Men—Above and Beyond and Forcibly Removed

Section A: Medals of Honor Earned on December 7, 1941, at Pearl Harbor

Chapter 4: USS *California* (BB-44)—"The Prune Barge" 116

    Ensign Herbert Jones, U.S. Naval Reserve 117
    Warrant Officer (Gunner) Jackson Pharris, U.S. Navy 118
    Warrant Officer (Radio Electrician) Thomas Reeves, U. S. Navy. 119
    Petty Officer First Class (Machinist's Mate) Robert Scott, U. S. Navy 120

Chapter 5: USS *Oklahoma* (BB-37)—Not the Musical 127

    Ensign Francis Flaherty, U.S. Naval Reserve 128
    Seaman First Class James Ward, U. S. Navy 128

Chapter 6: USS *West Virginia* (BB-48)—"The Captain Is about Gone" 133

    Captain Mervyn Bennion, U. S. Navy 133

Chapter 7: USS *Arizona* (BB-39)—The Gunfight at Quay F-7 138

    Rear Admiral Isaac Kidd, U. S. Navy 139
    Captain Franklin Van Valkenburgh, U. S. Navy 139
    Lieutenant Commander Samuel Fuqua, U. S. Navy 140

Chapter 8: USS *Vestal* (AR-4)—The CO Swims Back to His Ship 157

    Commander Cassin Young, U. S. Navy 157

Chapter 9: USS *Nevada* (BB-36)—Gambling on a Short Run 165

    Chief Warrant Officer (Boatswain) Edwin Hill, U. S. Navy 166
    Warrant Officer (Machinist) Donald Ross, U. S. Navy 167

Chapter 10: USS *Utah* (AG-16)—The Battleship That Wasn't. 175

    Chief Petty Officer (Watertender) Chief Peter Tomich, U.S. Navy. 176

Section B: Medal of Honor Earned on December 7, 1941, at Kaneohe Bay

Chapter 11: Naval Air Station, Kaneohe Bay—Man to Man. 181

    Chief Petty Officer (Aviation Ordnanceman) John Finn, U. S. Navy 181

Section C: Medal of Honor Earned at Midway Atoll in 1941 and 1942

Chapter 12: Midway Atoll, 1941 and 1942—Marines, Ground and Air 187
    Midway 1941: First Lieutenant George Cannon, U.S. Marine Corps. 188
    Midway 1942: Captain Richard Fleming, U.S. Marine Corps Reserve. 191

Section D: Medal of Honor Earned at the West Loch of Pearl Harbor, 1945

Chapter 13: West Loch, Pearl Harbor—Death at Depth. 216

Petty Officer Second Class (Boatswain's Mate) Owen Hammerberg, U.S. Navy . . 219

PART IV: MEDALS—KIA, DOW, MIA, WIA

Chapter 14: Overview of Medals of Honor Earned in the Hawaiian Islands 235

PART V: MISSES AND MISTAKES-- OVERLY AWARDED AND "NON-AWARDED"

Chapter 15: Medals of Honor Not Earned—Rear Admiral Isaac Kidd, U.S. Navy, and Captain Franklin Van Valkenburgh, U.S. Navy, USS *Arizona* 276

Chapter 16: Medal of Honor "Non award"—Lieutenant Colonel Daniel Fox, U.S. Marine Corps, USS *Arizona* 295

Chapter 17: Medal of Honor Not Earned or Awarded—The Doris Miller Controversy . 301

Chapter 18: Errors and Omissions Concerning the Medals of Honor Earned in the Hawaiian Islands 333

PART VI: MAKEUP MEDALS

Chapter 19: The Jackson Pharris Medal of Honor (USS *California*)—Late and Lost . 364

Chapter 20: The Mitchell Medal of Honor—The Golden Apology. 395

PART VII: MEMORIES—LISTS OF NAMES

Chapter 21: Legacy—Men. 407

Chapter 22: Legacy—Ships and Stations. 417

Chapter 23: Legacy—Places. 420

Chapter 24: Conclusions and Observations—Clanging Halyards and the Last Light in the Turret 426

APPENDICES

Appendix A: Biographical Sketches of the Medal Recipients in the Hawaiian Islands . . . 437

Captain Mervyn Bennion, U.S. Navy. 437
First Lieutenant George Cannon, U.S. Marine Corps 437
Chief Petty Officer (Aviation Ordnanceman) John Finn, U.S. Navy 438
Ensign Francis Flaherty, U.S. Naval Reserve 439
Captain Richard Fleming, U.S. Marine Corps Reserve 439
Lieutenant Commander Samuel Fuqua, U. S. Navy 440
Petty Officer Second Class (Boatswain's Mate) Owen Hammerberg, U.S. Navy . . 441
Chief Warrant Officer (Chief Boatswain) Edwin Hill, U.S. Navy 442
Ensign Herbert Jones, U.S. Naval Reserve 442
Rear Admiral Isaac Kidd, U.S. Navy. 443
Warrant Officer (Gunner) Jackson Pharris, U.S. Navy 443
Warrant Officer (Radio Electrician) Thomas Reeves, U.S. Navy 444
Warrant Officer (Machinist) Donald Ross, U.S. Navy 445
Petty Officer First Class (Machinist's Mate) Robert Scott, U.S. Navy 446
Chief Petty Officer (Watertender) Peter Tomich, U. S. Navy. 446
Captain Franklin VanValkenburgh, U.S. Navy 447
Seaman First Class James Ward, U.S. Navy 448
Commander Cassin Young, U.S. Navy 448

Appendix B: Ships Named for the Hawaiian Islands Medal of Honor Recipients 450

USS *Bennion* (DD-662) 451
USS *Cannon* (DE-99) 451
USS *Flaherty* (DE-135) 451

USS *Fleming* (DE-32) 452
USS *Hammerberg* (DE-1015) 452
USS *Hill* (DE-141) 452
USS *Herbert C. Jones* (DE-137) 452
USS *Kidd* (DD-661) 452
USS *Kidd* (DDG-993) 453
USS *Pharris* (FF-1094) 453
USS *Reeves* (DE-156) 453
USS *Ross* (DDG-71) 453
USS *Scott* (DE-214) 453
USS *Tomich* (DE-242) 454
USS *Van Valkenburgh* (DD-656) 454
USS *J. Richard Ward* (DE-243) 454
USS *Cassin Young* (DD-793) 454
USS *General William Mitchell* (AP-114) 454

Appendix C: Visiting Graves, Memorials, and Museums Related to the Hawaiian Island Medal of Honor Recipients 457

Appendix D: A Brief History of the Medal of Honor and the Awards Process . . 496

Acknowledgments 507

Notes about Illustrations and Maps 514

Bibliography 515

Billy Mitchell Addendum 548

About the Author 555

DEDICATION

To

my late father,

Lieutenant Colonel Elmer Clinton Jones, US Air Force Reserve (Retired)

(August 11, 1924–April 5, 2014)

For his intelligence, intellect, inspiration, judgment, calm, support, and courage.

He flew twenty-nine combat missions in World War II as the radar operator of a B-29 Superfortress bomber.

Mission number 30 was flying over USS Missouri after the surrender document was signed on September 1–2, 1945.

He earned two Distinguished Flying Crosses.

After the Japanese attacked Oahu on December 7, 1941, he joined thousands of others who so courageously and without hesitation picked up their swords and marched off to a war that they won.

I wrote much of this book with one of his 1851 Navy Colts beside me (serial number 100321). Like my father, it never failed me in bringing good fortune.
And appropriate for this book, it was a Navy Colt.

DRAMATIS PERSONAE

(In alphabetical order)

Captain Mervyn Bennion, U.S. Navy
USS *West Virginia*, Pearl Harbor, Oahu, Hawaii

First Lieutenant George Cannon, U.S. Marine Corps
Battery H, Sixth Marine Defense Battalion, Midway

Chief Petty Officer (Aviation Ordnanceman) John Finn, U.S. Navy
Patrol Squadron 14, Naval Air Station, Kaneohe Bay, Oahu, Hawaii

Ensign Francis Flaherty, U.S. Naval Reserve
USS *Oklahoma*, Pearl Harbor, Oahu, Hawaii

Captain Richard Fleming, U.S. Marine Corps Reserve
Marine Scout Bombing Squadron 241, Midway

Lieutenant Commander Samuel Fuqua, U.S. Navy
USS *Arizona*, Pearl Harbor, Oahu, Hawaii

Petty Officer Second Class (Boatswain's Mate) Owen Francis Patrick Hammerberg
Salvage Unit, Commander Service Force, U.S. Pacific Fleet, Oahu, Hawaii

Chief Warrant Officer (Boatswain) Edwin Hill, U.S. Navy
USS *Nevada*, Pearl Harbor, Oahu, Hawaii

Ensign Herbert Jones, U.S. Naval Reserve
USS *California*, Pearl Harbor, Oahu, Hawaii

Rear Admiral Isaac Kidd, U.S. Navy
USS *Arizona*, Pearl Harbor, Oahu, Hawaii

Warrant Officer Jackson Pharris, U.S. Navy
USS *California*, Pearl Harbor, Oahu, Hawaii

Warrant Officer (Radio Electrician) Thomas Reeves, U.S. Navy
USS *California*, Pearl Harbor, Oahu, Hawaii

Warrant Officer (Machinist) Donald Ross, U.S. Navy
USS *Nevada*, Pearl Harbor, Oahu, Hawaii

Petty Officer First Class (Machinist's Mate) Robert Scott, U.S. Navy
USS *California*, Pearl Harbor, Oahu, Hawaii

Captain Franklin Van Valkenburgh, U.S. Navy
USS *Arizona*, Pearl Harbor, Oahu, Hawaii

Seaman First Class James Ward, U.S. Navy
USS *Oklahoma*, Pearl Harbor, Oahu, Hawaii

Chief Petty Officer (Watertender) Peter Tomich, U.S. Navy
USS *Utah*, Pearl Harbor, Oahu, Hawaii

Commander Cassin Young, U.S. Navy
USS *Vestal*, Pearl Harbor, Oahu, Hawaii

Brigadier General William Mitchell, U.S. Army

Reflections

"Never mind; it's a Jap."

—Commander Logan C. Ramsey, U.S. Navy, Operations officer, Navy Pacific Fleet Air Wing

Commander Ramsey said these words to a staff duty officer upon seeing the detonation of a bomb dropped from an aircraft onto Ford Island on December 7, 1941. He originally thought that the aircraft was American and was going to report the pilot for flat hatting, flying low and recklessly. When he saw the detonation, he knew the aircraft was Japanese.

"It was evident to one and all that 'the time' had arrived."

—Captain M. A. Tyler, U.S. Marine Corps, describing the feeling of Marines who knew that the Japanese were beginning their attack on Midway Atoll, June 4, 1942.

"Captain, they are here, bombing Hickam Field."

—Chief Gunner's Mate E. L. James's comment to his commanding officer, December 7, 1941 (destroyer USS Cassin)

"I saw no signs of fear on the ship [USS *Arizona* on December 7, 1941]. Everyone was surprised and pretty mad."

—Radioman's Mate Third Class G. H. Lane, crewman, USS *Arizona*, written statement submitted about the attack

"Only those who have felt the knife
Can understand the wound,
Only the jeweler
Knows the nature of the jewel."

—Mirabai

"It is not the same thing to talk of bulls as to be in the bullring."

—Spanish proverb

"If you don't enter the lion's den, you will never capture the lion."

—Seung Sahn

"One learns quickly when on the front against an enemy, and in a few months of actual war service one can pick up more than in a lifetime of theoretical study."

—General of the Armies John J. "Black Jack" Pershing (Retired), describing the value of experience over the value of study during war, August 7, 1935

"Every day serves to demonstrate more thoroughly that air power has been the determining factor in winning the European war and that if Gen. William Mitchell's repeated specific warnings had been heeded the disaster of Pearl Harbor would have been avoided and many lives lost in World War II would have been spared."

—Mr. E. G. B. Riley, speaking, while the war with Japan was ongoing, at the Hearings, HOUSE OF REPRESENTATIVES, SUBCOMMITTEE NO. 8 OF THE COMMITTEE ON MILITARY AFFAIRS, U. S. House of Representatives, First Session, 79th Congress, May 31, 1945.

The hearings concerned a MOH for Brigadier General William "Billy" Mitchell, U. S. Army.

"The bitterest cup a person has to drink out of is the cup of defeat."

—Former member of Congress, J. V. McClintic, speaking at the hearings just described

"The entire world is but a narrow bridge; the most important thing is not to be afraid."

—Mishkan T'Filah, Jewish prayer book

"There were several outstanding instances of coolness, high sense of duty, and bravery [including that of First Lieutenant George H. Cannon, who was mortally wounded and who later received a posthumous Medal of Honor]."

—Lieutenant Colonel H. D. Shannon, U.S. Marine Corps in his December 12, 1941, report describing action on Midway Atoll, December 7, 1941, after Japanese destroyers shelled Midway.

"The real glory of war is surviving."

—Motion picture director Samuel Fuller
"Honor the warrior, not the war."

"There was no one to hold the light for him."

—History Of World War II, referring to Seaman First Class James Richards (should be James Ward), who earned a Medal of Honor at the cost of his life by holding a flashlight in a turret aboard USS *Oklahoma*, which was capsizing on December 7, 1941, so that others could see to escape. He thereafter perished, trapped in the turret.

"Some heroes will unfortunately die unknown and unsung. But their deeds served to complete a magnificent demonstration of courage and fighting spirit that in spite of a treacherous surprise attack took heavy toll of the enemy."

—Rear Admiral Walter S. Anderson, Commander, Battleships, Battle Force, describing heroism during the attack on Oahu on December 7, 1941, in his December 19, 1941, report concerning "Distinguished Conduct" during the raid.

"I wear this [Medal of Honor],
I think every Medal of Honor recipient would say,
'We wear this [Medal of Honor] for those who can't.'"

—Colonel Leo Thorsness, U.S. Air Force (Retired), a pilot who earned a Medal of Honor in Vietnam, Dogfights (Season 1, Long Odds)

"War is an exceptionally horrible business[,] and the toll it takes on nations, societies, families, and individuals [is] incalculable. During World War II the combatant nations threw the entirety of their populations and industrial assets into a conflict that had as its outcome either total victory or utter annihilation."

—Will Dabbs, MD, Firearms News, Volume 70, Issue 11 (April 2016)

"Things are in the saddle, And ride mankind."

—Ralph Waldo Emerson, "Ode, Inscribed to William H. Channing"

"The whole sequence seemed like a bad dream. . . .

The thoughts of Lieutenant Matt Klemish, a Navy aviator who survived an aircraft crash in the ocean as he awaited rescue. "Do You Know Me?" ("approach Mech," September to October 1996), page 7.

"When we unleash the dogs of war…we must go where they take us."

—Maggie Smith as Lady Grantham in "Downton Abbey," Season 6, Part 5

"So was Pearl Harbor retaliation for us dropping the atomic bombs on Japan?"

—American college student

"Who is Pearl Harbor? Who is she?"

—American school girl

WHY AND HOW I WROTE THIS BOOK

"Awarded Medal of Honor with citation by the President."

That phrase is probably the most powerful phrase in this book, second only to the immortal, magisterial phrases found in President Franklin D. Roosevelt's December 8, 1941, speech in which he asked Congress for a declaration of war against Japan.

It is handwritten in block nine of the fitness report for then-Commander Samuel Fuqua, US Navy, for the period February 9, 1942, to December 11, 1942. The comment refers to the Medal of Honor (MOH) Fuqua was awarded on March 19, 1942, for his actions on December 7, 1941, amid the cataclysmic destruction of USS *Arizona* and most of her crew. Fuqua was the ship's damage-control officer and first lieutenant in charge of maintenance.

Any member of the military past or present knows or should know the power of those few words. Of the millions of military performance evaluations written in the history of the United States, only a small percentage contains words to that effect.

That phrase summarizes in great part why I wrote this book: I wanted to know what types of actions led and lead to that entry recorded in a formal report of performance evaluation. I also wanted to explore the actions that led to the MOHs awarded men in the Hawaiian Islands during World War II since they are to some extent a hidden part of the history of December 7, one of the most important dates in the history of the United States. Finally, I became interested in learning about the process by which these men were awarded MOHs.

The Fuqua fitness report can be found at the end of this section of the book. Page two comments that he was a calm and quiet officer, traits that will be apparent to the reader who reads about his personality and his MOH actions.

★ ★ ★ ★ ★ ★ ★ ★ ★ ★ ★ ★

"You do."

But another explanation for why I wrote this book is more prosaic and is summarized by those two words.

When I was on one of my brief tours of active duty on Oahu as a Marine Corps Reservist, I met Daniel Martinez of the National Park Service, who worked at what was then the USS *Arizona* Visitors Center. He is widely recognized as an expert on the attacks on December 7, 1941. I must have mentioned my distress at finding so little mention, in books or elsewhere, on Oahu of the men who earned MOHs for bravery on December 7, 1941. To fill the void of information, I had done my own research and learned that sixteen men had received MOHs for actions on that date. In my never-ending quest to learn about these men, I asked Dan who knew the most about them. He looked at me and to my great surprise said, "You do."

To prove the truth of his answer, I felt obliged to write a book about the December 7 MOH recipients.

★ ★ ★ ★ ★ ★ ★ ★ ★ ★ ★ ★

What should be understood from the outset is the connection of the men who are the subjects of this book to the Hawaiian Islands, primarily Oahu.

The book is about U.S. Marine Corps and Navy service members who were awarded MOHs for bravery at various locations in the Hawaiian Islands during World War II.

It is not about the MOH recipients who were from Hawaii (Hawaiian or Japanese-American natives of Hawaii) who were awarded MOHs. Twenty of these men were in the famous 442nd Regimental Combat Team or the famous 100th Infantry Battalion; these men fought in the European Theater of Operations (ETO) during World War II. Due to racism, only one member of the 442nd received a MOH close to the time of his action (1945); he received a posthumous MOH in 1946. As a remedial measure, the twenty men (and two more Asian Americans) received MOHs in 2000 for actions in World War II.

★ ★ ★ ★ ★ ★ ★ ★ ★ ★ ★ ★

Writing this book meant entering a certain environment. In effect, I felt as if I were directing a very bright light on a dark corner of the MOH universe; previous lights directed into that corner produced no, partial, or misdirected return beams of light. The environment was five parts for me.

Part 1

The first part of that environment was the lack of a good book about the MOH recipients in the Hawaiian Islands, which is one of the primary reasons I wrote this book. To my knowledge, only one other book covered the December 7 MOH recipients in toto, a book written by one of the recipients, Donald Ross. While laudable, it does not cover the subject matter in the detail or depth I thought necessary to honor these men or to inform the public about them. It also contains erroneous information.

Additionally, I could not find a book about the World War II sites on Oahu, a "single source" guide to places related to one of the most important dates in US history, December 7, 1941. So I found the sites on my own and wrote such a book myself: Hawaii's World War II Military Sites, published by Mutual Publishing in 2002.

Because of the lack of information on Oahu about the MOH recipients for December 7 and not yet knowing about the Ross book just mentioned, I devoted one chapter of the book to the December 7 MOH recipients to set the record straight. In other chapters about various World War II sites, I informed readers if any MOHs were earned at the sites.

But first I had to learn who had earned MOHs in the Hawaiian Islands in World War II; absent a book about the subject (I did not know about the Ross book at the time), I had to do my own research by sitting in the dank basement library at Camp Smith, Hawaii, and looking through an old book that was a collection of MOH citations. I looked for any citation with "Pearl Harbor" in it. I was expecting to find only MOHs for December 7, but in the book, I found the Hammerberg noncombat award for Pearl Harbor in 1945. Somehow I found the Finn MOH; his was earned on Oahu on December 7 but not at Pearl Harbor.

What I did not know is that another December 7 MOH recipient was out there. I did not find him in the book because I did not know that his MOH was for actions on the evening of 7 December 1941 on Midway, not Pearl Harbor. I do not know how I found this citation, the only one for a Marine for December 7. But I do remember how I found the other Midway MOH recipient.

When I was initially at Punchbowl and at the Honolulu Memorial, I had no idea that I was at the Honolulu Memorial or what it was. I looked up at one of the tablets and saw inscriptions in gold:

* O'HARE EDWARD H
LT COMMANDER
USN MISSOURI

The "asterisk" was a gold MOH symbol, so I knew I was at a place important (he was one of the most famous American heroes early in World War II, and the airport at Chicago was named for him). I then kept looking around and saw the gold Fleming inscription, and not knowing who he was, I found his citation and realized he was the only MOH recipient for the Battle of Midway in 1942.

Since space limitations precluded detailed accounts and summaries of each of the MOH recipients in Hawaii's World War II Military Sites, I wrote the present book to provide such accounts and summaries.

Although outdated and no longer in print, Hawaii's World War II Military Sites remains a good reference for readers who want to tour the World War II sites (including those where a MOH was earned) in person while visiting Oahu or who cannot go to Oahu but who want the best substitute for a tour in person. Copies of the book can be obtained via Internet search. I have, however, given the reader basic information about the MOH sites in Appendix C of this book.

Part 2

The second part of that environment was knowing that the general public's knowledge of December 7 was limited and that the degree of inaccurate information about the events of that day was great.

Part 3

The third part of that environment was knowing that if the public did not know about December 7 in general, then it certainly did not know that among the thousands of service members on Oahu during the December 7 attack, only sixteen MOHs were awarded for that day. Obviously, if the public did not know about the MOH awards, then it would not know the stories of the bravery or other factors leading to those MOHs.

Part 4

The fourth part of that environment was reading publications of all types about December 7 and finding the stories of the MOH recipients omitted or addressed partially or inaccurately. Publications included expensive books written by so-called experts on the December 7 attacks and even including books written with the collaboration of the Congressional Medal of Honor Society. The number of errors and omissions disturbed me, especially given the deeds that some of these men performed on December 7; I thought their deeds should be accurately portrayed.

But what could I expect from the public or from experts if (a) an editor of the major newspaper in Norfolk, Virginia, called me to ask if I was certain that December 7 was on a Sunday and (b) a child asked, "Who was Pearl Harbor?" as if "Pearl" were a given name and "Harbor" were a surname?

Part 5

What is important in the media concerning the MOH?

Pop culture and the media are the enemies of telling US about true heroes. Unbelievably, the Wall Street Journal, a conservative publication, is an example.

On July 20, 2015, its sports section devoted more than half a page to a positive story about Caitlyn (formerly Bruce) Jenner and his courage resulting in an ESPY award, an Excellence in Sports Performance Yearly Award, courage due, I suppose, to the well-publicized sex change that transformed the man Bruce Jenner, Olympic champion, to the woman Caitlyn Jenner. The headline was "Caitlyn Jenner and What Courage Means."

Well, the question is not so much what courage means but how much media covers true courage and what true courage means—courage in the face of battlefield bullets. So for two MOH recipients, the coverage was almost an afterthought, the coverage for each comprising his photograph, which could be measured in a small number of inches, and a caption: "Marine Corporal William Carpenter" (June 20, 2014, page A5) and Army Staff Sergeant Ryan Pitts (July 22, 2014, page A4). No story or citation accompanied the award stories.

To be fair, one must note the Journal ran a full page about the MOH on July 3, 2015 (page A-5), but no recipients were cited by name. And on November 13, 2015, the Journal ran a front-page photograph of President Barack Obama with Army Captain Florent Groberg, who had just received a MOH for bravery in Afghanistan, described in a short, three-paragraph story on page A-6.

But to put the MOH back in its true perspective, consider that the Journal ran a front-page photograph of the freak performer Prince on April 22, 2015, with a fifteen-paragraph story on page A-3. The punch line is that Prince received most of the coverage of the Arena section's front page, D-1, complete with a picture consuming approximately half the page and all of the space on page D-2. As if we needed more information about him, Prince received more Journal coverage (almost half a page) on page A-3 in the 23–24 edition. The tax man must know his worth: "What Is Prince Worth? The Tax Man Needs to Know" (page A-1, April 28, 2016). My answer is nothing compared to the story of a MOH recipient who has risked his life for country and comrade. And finally, this surprise headline on page A-3 on April 29: "Drugs Found on Prince at Death," with a narrative longer than any for a MOH recipient.

As my late father would have said, the whole thing makes me want to "spit up."

★ ★ ★ ★ ★ ★ ★ ★ ★ ★ ★

But this book is one place where the MOH does not share its story and recipients with pop culture and faux heroes; it is primarily about the men who earned the MOH on December 7, 1941, on Oahu, which was then the U.S. Territory of Hawaii, men who were repelling a sneak attack conducted by aircraft launched from aircraft carriers. The attack was the last link in a long chain of events involving diplomatic conflict between the United States and Japan.

Thus naval aviation made the attacks on December 7 possible. Naval aviation itself developed from two events occurring in Hampton Roads, Virginia, near where I lived in Norfolk from 1988 to 2012. Hampton Roads is the body of water connecting the Chesapeake Bay and the James, Nansemond, and Elizabeth Rivers. Norfolk, Portsmouth, Hampton, and Newport News are the major cities in the area.

The first event in Hampton Roads was the battle of the ironclads USS Monitor and CSS Virginia in 1862, a battle proving wooden ships obsolete. The second event was in 1910; the first flight of an aircraft from a ship was made when Eugene Ely flew a biplane off the cruiser Birmingham, anchored off Old Point Comfort near Fort Monroe at Hampton.

Ironclad plus flight from ship equals naval aviation. A question remained, however. Could aircraft, based on land or ship, sink ships? In the 1920s, aircraft flown by Billy Mitchell's army aviators sank derelict ships along the coasts of Virginia and North Carolina, my home state, proving to the Navy's dismay that aircraft could sink ships.

Thus naval aviation developed into a formidable force. Dive bombers, fighters, and torpedo bombers launched from aircraft carriers could sink other ships at sea or at harbor and could attack land targets. Naval aviation attacking Oahu on December 7, 1941, the date for which fifteen MOHs were awarded to men on Oahu, eviscerated many of the U. S. Navy's ships and Navy and Army installations on the island.

★ ★ ★ ★ ★ ★ ★ ★ ★ ★ ★

As just mentioned, during my research, I learned not only about the December 7 MOH recipients but also about two other MOHs, both posthumous, earned in the Hawaiian Island Archipelago during World War II, an archipelago including Midway Island. One of those MOHs was the sole MOH for the famous Battle of Midway in

1942. The other was a noncombat MOH earned in the West Loch of Pearl Harbor in 1945. I thought that since these MOHs were earned during a war beginning for the United States on December 7, they should be included in this book.

★ ★ ★ ★ ★ ★ ★ ★ ★ ★ ★ ★

All but one of the MOH recipients discussed in this book served in World War II and received their MOHs for actions in the Hawaiian Island Archipelago. Army Brigadier General Billy Mitchell, U.S. Army, was that sole recipient. He died in 1936.

Although not earned in the Hawaiian Island Archipelago or during World War II, for several reasons, I included the special MOH Congress authorized for Mitchell in 1946. Before World War II, he was the most vocal advocate in the United States for airpower. Years before his death in 1936, he predicted an attack on Oahu, an attack executed by naval aviation, a topic also related to Mitchell. The Battle of Midway in 1942 was primarily one of American naval aviation against Japanese naval aviation.

I thought the special MOH was important to the other MOH stories in this book not only because naval aviation executed that attack, bringing the United States into World War II, a war during which eighteen MOHs were awarded for actions in the Hawaiian Islands, but also because Mitchell had inspected Oahu before the war, found its defenses deficient, and predicted the attack on Oahu with uncanny accuracy.

Mitchell's MOH was not the classic combat MOH. It was a special MOH representing recognition and apology. First, it was recognition of the importance of airpower, Used against the United States beginning in December 1941 and Used by the United States so effectively during the war to achieve air supremacy. (Where were the German and Japanese air forces at Normandy in 1944 and at Iwo Jima in 1945?) Two, it was an apology for the way Mitchell was treated. His prewar advocacy of airpower development by the United States and his warnings that it would be used against the United States were ignored and ridiculed by the U.S. military, as are most new ideas and theories challenging conventional military thinking, strategies, tactics, and weapons. Mitchell was treated as a pariah rather than a wise man or a prophet. Prewar conventional thinking could not accept or envision aircraft sinking ships, notwithstanding Mitchell's successful ship sinking tests in the 1920s, tests the Navy opposed and obstructed.

Japan, more so than the United States, paid attention to Mitchell's ideas about airpower and used them in the form of naval aviation on December 7, 1941, ripping apart most of the U.S. military assets on Oahu. The attack led to World War II between the United States and Japan. While the Japanese were doing the ripping, fifteen men on Oahu were taking actions that would lead to their MOH awards. Although fifteen MOHs would be awarded for actions on Oahu that day, I question whether two of the fifteen were in fact earned. Later that evening, one more MOH would be earned on Midway Island, the last one for that day. And later in the war, as just noted, two more MOHs would be earned in the Hawaiian Islands, one at the Battle of Midway in 1942 and one in the murky waters of the West Loch of Pearl Harbor in 1945.

★ ★ ★ ★ ★ ★ ★ ★ ★ ★ ★

I wrote this book in basic terms and covered basic information. I learned in the Marine Corps that assumption was fatal, so I did not assume that either the average or advanced reader knew what I knew about December 7, the MOH recipients, or the MOH itself. Neither basic nor advanced knowledge can be assumed.

Also, basic knowledge is one weapon to counter the staggering amount of misinformation, errors, and misconceptions about the MOH. For example, one editor at a military magazine wrote that General Douglas MacArthur awarded a MOH to an aviator in World War II after Congress approved it. I wrote a letter to the editor, stating that Congress did not approve the average combat MOH award. The editor called me and demonstrated that he did not know the difference between the roles of Congress and the President in the MOH award process. He became irate when I told him that Douglas MacArthur's MOH was for World War II, not an earlier conflict. I knew I was right; a quick check on the Internet by this editor of a military publication while I was on the phone proved I was correct. If he did not know this basic fact, I wondered not only what other experts knew or did not know but what the general public knew or did not know.

★ ★ ★ ★ ★ ★ ★ ★ ★ ★ ★

One impediment to imparting correct information about the MOH recipients who are the subjects of this book is penetrating the wall constructed of inaccurate or partial information imparted by self-appointed experts, who I define as people in the general public who hold themselves out as experts on December 7, yet they lack formal academic training or they have done at best shoddy research. The person generally has no scholastic credentials, such as a baccalaureate or advanced academic degree. While someone can know much accurate information about a subject without having a degree, a degree is generally a minimal safeguard that the person can impart accurate information.

I make no pretense of being a self-appointed expert on the subjects covered in this book. The only safeguards readers have are my juris doctorate degree, my numerous visits to the historical sites on Oahu, the great degree of research I have conducted over the years, and my training and service (thirty years) as a judge advocate in the Marine Corps and its Reserve. I will add that I have a great desire to see that the stories of the men and events told in this book are done so accurately and completely.

★ ★ ★ ★ ★ ★ ★ ★ ★ ★ ★

One skill other authors have in writing about war-related topics is the ability to write verbatim conversations of men near or in combat. Sadly, I lack that skill, so readers will not find verbatim conversations in this book. They can be found in such famous books as To Hell and Back, which causes me to ask, "Unless someone was following the unit with a stenographer or a tape recorder, how can an author reproduce verbatim conversations, especially in combat conditions?" I think such conversations, absent a means of recordation, are fabricated or "best guesses" of what people said. The only quotations in this book from MOH recipients during their actions are short ones and thus easily remembered by witnesses. They are the words, and likely the last words, of two crewmen on December 7, ironically both from California, Ensign Herbert Jones and Petty Officer First Class (Machinist's Mate) Robert Scott. Their excited utterances are short, and memorable, and Jones's words were reported by a Marine near him who heard them. And to prevent the question of verbatim assertion, their MOH citations read that the words were to the effect of what is quoted.

★ ★ ★ ★ ★ ★ ★ ★ ★ ★ ★

The MOH remains a contemporary topic. I found interesting the degree to which MOHs can still cause disturbance in the military and can be influenced by political considerations (i.e., MOHs based on factors other than documented facts supporting a MOH). I wanted to explore this aspect of the MOHs for the recipients in the Hawaiian Islands during World War II.

One consideration is why some service members receive MOHs and others do not. For example, on the front page of Air Force Times for May 18–25, 2015, is this caption under a photograph of a forward controller who received an Air Force Cross, the second-highest decoration in the U.S. Air Force: "48 Hours Under Fire Yet No MoH? Is the Air Force being shortchanged for top valor award?" On page 24 is the story; on page 25 is this headline: "He saved 80 lives: Why not the Medal of Honor?" The story begins, "The Air Force is the only service that does not have a Medal of Honor in the Global War on Terrorism, and with another airman's heroic action in battle resulting in an Air Force Cross, experts are again asking: What does an airman have to do [to earn a MOH]?" On page 52 is an editorial under this headline: "Why no AF Medal of Honor?" The basic problem, at least as seen by Air Force Times, is that an Air Force member has, as of this writing, not received a MOH for the wars in Iraq and Afghanistan. The editorial, citing two airmen who received Air Force Crosses, asks if the Air Force "brass is holding an impossible standard for the MOH." The editorial quotes an expert on military awards:

"'What does it take to get a Medal of Honor?'" The expert asked the following question: "'Where is the Air Force MOH recipient for the next generation?'" "'I don't know why the air force isn't advocating for it.'"

The senior enlisted member of the Air Force, Chief Master Sergeant James Cody, addressed the subject in an article reported in Air Force Times (June 15, 2015). He thought that at least two cases of Air Force Cross awards should be discussed with an eye toward MOHs for the recipients. An opinion was also expressed that two posthumously awarded Air Force Crosses should be upgraded to MOHs.

Aside from the bravery of the airmen in question and whether they deserved MOHs, the tenor of the coverage of the subject was to the effect that each service was "entitled" to have at least one member receive a MOH. But the MOH is an award, not an entitlement or the subject of a quota for each service.

★ ★ ★ ★ ★ ★ ★ ★ ★ ★ ★

The Air Force's concern over an airman not having a MOH brings up the question of politics, another topic I wanted to explore in the MOH process. It proved to be a fascinating, enlightening one.

As most military veterans know, the awards process is often political, not in the sense of political party but in the sense that bestowing or denying awards is influenced by factors other than the merits of a service member's performance, such as recommending or approving or not recommending or disapproving an award because of factors unrelated to the award's criteria or the member's deeds.

Discretion by commanders or civilian officials can also influence awards. Discretion is the power of the commander to decide whether or not to grant a service member an award or to concur with or to oppose a recommendation for an award if he or she is not the final decision authority for the award.

Politics and discretion, since they may be based on factors other than facts or the merits, can produce skewed results—the deserving receive no or downgraded awards, and the undeserving receive prestigious awards when they should have received lower awards or no awards at all.

The author saw this phenomenon firsthand while serving in the military. These two factors are omnipresent and are discussed at length in Chapter 15 as they apply to the undeserved MOHs for Rear Admiral Isaac Kidd and Captain Franklin Van Valkenburgh and in Chapter 16 concerning the "non award" of a MOH for Lieutenant Colonel Daniel Fox, *Arizona*'s senior Marine, who was essentially in the same position as Kidd and Van Valkenburgh but was denied a MOH.

So, on the one hand, politics is the only explanation for the MOHs awarded to these two officers aboard USS *Arizona* who did not deserve MOHs. Their awards lack factual bases justifying MOHs. On the other hand is Jackson Pharris, who was awarded a Navy Cross in 1942, the second highest award in the navy, for his actions on December 7 when he clearly deserved a MOH. A hidebound Navy originally stated that the Navy Cross was sufficient recognition for his bravery, but fortunately, the system corrected itself, and he ultimately received the MOH he without question deserved and should have received ab initio. As explained in Chapter 17, Doris Miller's Navy Cross for December 7 was a political award directly ordered by none other than President Franklin Roosevelt.

The Washington Post reported about members of the military who did not receive MOHs for our most recent wars but should have or finally did receive them. In the case of a soldier who received a posthumous Silver Star for actions in Iraq, the soldier's commander did not realize the degree of bravery the soldier exhibited and decided to seek an upgrade of the Silver Star. Other members do not receive MOHs, at least promptly, because their commanders do not know about their bravery, because a lower award is made but new information surfaces to justify a MOH, or because a MOH recommendation is made but is lost and later found. The article referred to "lobbying" efforts or campaigns to obtain upgraded awards or MOHs. As will be seen in Chapter

19, such an effort or campaign was required to have the Navy Cross of Warrant Officer Jackson Pharris upgraded to a MOH to truly reflect his deeds on December 7. The Pharris case is at least one case where lobbying is not a dirty word; it achieved for him the MOH he deserved for saving his ship on December 7, 1941.

★ ★ ★ ★ ★ ★ ★ ★ ★ ★ ★ ★

I also like getting things right or setting the record straight. That is why I devoted an entire chapter in my book Hawaii's World War II Sites to the MOH. Neither the experts nor the amateurs could get it right, not even the simplest, most basic facts about these MOH recipients. By writing the present book, which expands the chapter in my previous book, I wanted not only to publicize the stories of these MOH recipients but also to find and correct the numerous errors contained in accounts of their MOH actions.

Finding and correcting so many errors and omissions was rewarding and intellectually challenging. The number of errors was disturbing, but what can we expect in today's world? For example, we live in a world that continues to bastardize and demean President Franklin Roosevelt's famous phrase, "a date which will live in infamy." Publications use "day in" or "day of" infamy. The headline on the May 31, 2015, front page of my own hometown newspaper, the Greensboro News and Record, was "A Day in Infamy." The story was about a killer and the day he killed himself to avoid arrest. The World War II magazine special edition for the sixtieth anniversary of the December 7 attacks has this on the cover: "The Day of Infamy." Life's Pearl Harbor: America's Call to Arms (2011) was a collector's edition for the seventieth anniversary of the attack. It made no reference to the MOH recipients for December 7, 1941. As mentioned earlier, an editor of the Norfolk, Virginia, newspaper called me concerning an article I had written for the newspaper about December 7 to ask me if I was sure that the day was a Sunday. Comment is unnecessary. Parade magazine had a feature on "National Treasures" in its May 31, 2015, edition. Martin Luther King, Junior, and actress Betty White were included, as was the famous Hollywood sign in Los Angeles, but no mention was made of the MOH or any of its recipients. The silence is deafening.

★ ★ ★ ★ ★ ★ ★ ★ ★ ★ ★ ★

I also wanted to explore the role of luck in the stories of these men. Some were lucky and survived; most were not and perished. The question revisits a common one for men who survive combat: Why was I allowed to live while my comrades were killed?

Bad luck haunts the story of two of these men. One earned a MOH at Pearl Harbor on December 7, 1941—he survived the day but was killed on a Friday the thirteenth in November 1942 at the Naval Battle of Guadalcanal.

The other earned a MOH at Pearl Harbor, survived the war, but died in 1966 after having a heart attack at, of all places, a MOH Society banquet. He is buried in Section 13 of Arlington National Cemetery in Arlington, Virginia. I found thirteen to be unlucky for me as I tried to find his grave. See Appendix C.

★ ★ ★ ★ ★ ★ ★ ★ ★ ★ ★

This subject matter is interesting from the standpoint of how each of the recipients receiving combat MOHs fits into a larger historical event, a big picture, or a historical development:

- **The December 7 MOH Recipients** participated in the defense of Oahu when the Japanese attacked it and led the United States into World War II. This attack was proof that airpower had surpassed sea power as the dominant weapon in naval warfare.

- **The Midway 1942 MOH** recipient participated in one of the most important battles in history, a battle again showing the dominance of airpower over sea power, as if another lesson of this nature need be repeated after the blistering lesson learned on December 7.

- **The Pearl Harbor 1945 MOH** recipient participated in the aftermath of the West Loch Disaster, commonly called the "Second Pearl Harbor," an obscure historical event.

Another interesting aspect of the stories of these MOH recipients is what they have in common: harrowing, ferocious, and unsettling experiences of varying lengths of time in the worst possible conditions of hardship and nightmare. For some, these conditions lasted only a short time. Rear Admiral Isaac Kidd and Captain Franklin Van Valkenburgh perished quickly at Pearl Harbor since their ship, *Arizona*, exploded catastrophically only minutes after the attack started. For others, these conditions lasted the entire duration of the attack (approximately two hours) and for various times thereafter. Examples include Warrant Officer Jackson Pharris and Lieutenant Commander Samuel Fuqua, who were at Pearl Harbor and survived the attack, dealing with it for days, if not weeks. For another, the agony of these conditions continued for eighteen hours. In 1945, Navy diver Petty Officer Second Class Owen Hammerberg remained alive underwater in the West Loch of Pearl Harbor for eighteen hours before dying—eighteen hours to die. For one Marine, Captain Richard Fleming at Midway, the conditions extended over two days.

★ ★ ★ ★ ★ ★ ★ ★ ★ ★ ★

Working on the book was a challenge in finding and assembling the pieces of the stories of the MOH recipients in the Hawaiian Islands in World War II. I found much interesting history and intrigue surrounding these MOHs that simply made the subject a great and enjoyable one about which to write. Examples include the following:

- I discovered undeserved awards. I found interesting uncovering the process by which two men, Rear Admiral Isaac Kidd and Captain Franklin Van Valkenburgh, both of USS *Arizona*, could receive MOHs without any facts to support the awards. I could do this for ninety dollars, the price I paid the

National Archives for the compact disc with the Kidd service record. And I could challenge their MOHs without challenging their characters as men or Navy officers; after all, they lost their lives in the service of their country. Doris Miller, who according to his late niece has a "silent" MOH, in no way deserves a MOH or even the Navy Cross he received in 1942, again an opinion that can be registered without attacking him as a person or service member.

- What does one do with an unclaimed MOH? Chief Petty Officer (Watertender) Peter Tomich's MOH went unclaimed for year

- Why do some recipients have two MOHs for the same action? Two cases come to mind: Captain Cassin Young and Petty Officer First Class (Boatswain's Mate) Owen Hammerberg.

- Why did Jackson Pharris, arguably the most deserving MOH recipient for December 7, have to wait until 1948 to receive his MOH? His story proved to be the most fascinating for me.

- Why did the media and authors state and continue to state, erroneously, that Warrant Officer Captain Donald Ross or Chief Petty Officer John Finn received the first December 7 MOH or the first MOH awarded in World War II? Surely the world will hear these canards from the media and the experts during the commemoration of the seventy-fifth anniversary of December 7, 1941, in December 2016.

★ ★ ★ ★ ★ ★ ★ ★ ★ ★ ★

A question related to why I wrote this book is the following: "Why did I write it the way I wrote it?" Due to the massive amount of material, organization was a problem, so I wrote the book in a somewhat encyclopedic manner rather than a narrative, which would have been unwieldy and confusing, given the number of men and events. The story simply involves too many men, ships, and stations to put in a coherent narrative. Also I wanted to give readers a how-to guide for finding and seeing the sites where the MOHs were earned and tell readers which sites were open to the public and which were not.

Thus the focus may at times in certain parts of the book appear to be on data and information rather than story. I tried in the individual chapters concerning the MOH recipients to use narrative rather than encyclopedic style. But often a lack of personal information prevented me from constructing a complete picture of these men as human beings; the result is that foremost their deeds are told rather than the details of their personalities or personal lives. Readers can surmise from those deeds what kind of people the recipients were.

★ ★ ★ ★ ★ ★ ★ ★ ★ ★ ★

For those interested in my methodology, I collected information by any number of methods: asking questions, consulting books and maps, being in the right place at the right time, being in the wrong place at the right time, being alert as I drove or walked around, good luck, and chance. As I mentioned earlier, by chance at the Honolulu Memorial on Oahu, I looked up at one tablet of the Courts of the Missing and saw the name O'Hare. I also saw the Fleming inscription—a Marine captain's name with a MOH symbol beside it. I knew nothing about him, which bothered me. So this chance glance led to me finding his MOH citation and learning that he was the sole MOH recipient for the famous Battle of Midway in 1942.

I am also naturally inquisitive, especially about coincidences and luck. For example, I wonder why I became a Master Mason in January 2015 and in September 2015 I saw by chance a book at a Masonic function, The Medal of Honor: The Letter G in Valor, about MOH recipients who were or are Masons. I found that Jackson Pharris was a Mason (see Chapter 19). And finding his grave, as related elsewhere in this book, was an act of Divine Intervention.

In another coincidence, I was sorting through my late father's World War II items when I found a manual marked "Jones, E.C." It was a manual he had in 1944 during his cadet training to become a member of the U.S. Army Air Forces. The manual was titled, Naval Forces, Ship Recognition, Restricted, Ellington Field, Texas, which is where he had training before appointment as a lieutenant. The manual has pages with ship silhouettes and blank spaces for the students to complete information about the ships, such as date, speed, guns, and primary recognition. I found three entries of interest: "Tennessee," "Pennsylvania," and *Nevada*." He made notes on the pages. So in 1944, these three ships, all at Pearl Harbor on December 7, were still in service, proving the durability of the battleship.

Coincidence again—I do not remember how or why I thought about doing so, but I compared the comments in the Lucky Bag, the United States Naval Academy (USNA) yearbook, with the actions of the five MOH recipients in this book who were USNA graduates. Many comments were incredibly predictive of the behavior of these men on December 7.

And again, good luck: I had written a note, a verbatim "transcript""of the portion of a 2008 NBC Nightly News program in which anchorman Brian Williams erroneously said that John Finn was at Pearl Harbor (he was at Kaneohe Bay) and received the first MOH of World War II (false). I typed the statement into the manuscript and then lost my note. Months later, as I was discarding some of my father's old VHS tapes (he would record the evening news), I noticed that some were from 2008. I wondered if the John Finn story was on one of them, so I reached into the pile to see if by chance the tape with the John Finn story was in the pile. Of the dozens of tapes I could have pulled out of the garbage can, the tape I reached for was marked 2008 and was the NBC Nightly News program with the John Finn story—more Divine Intervention.

And thanks, Dad.

★ ★ ★ ★ ★ ★ ★ ★ ★ ★ ★

A belated revelation occurred in 2016—years after I began researching and writing this book; the recipients were for the most part not actively engaged in combat with the enemy in the classic sense. Only Chief Petty Officer John Finn (Aviation Ordnanceman) and Captain Richard Fleming (pilot) were actively engaged in fighting the enemy in the sense of taking shots at him (ironically, both men were in aviation). The other men were reacting to attack (the December 7 recipients) or to disaster (the West Loch recipient); all of these men were rescuing men or mitigating or preventing damage, and many were exercising leadership. In this sense, their citations differ from MOH citations for men engaged in combat in the classic arenas or in set-piece battles where no surprise attack occurred as on December 7: standard ground (infantry and infantry support), ocean (undersea and surface navy and naval support), or the skies (aviation and aviation support). But Billy Mitchell flew combat missions during World War I.

★ ★ ★ ★ ★ ★ ★ ★ ★ ★ ★ ★

Another related topic is how I wrote this book. I often wonder how to answer this question. For the writing and grammar purists or experts, I will note that I realize that most chapters are written in the third person and some in the first. I used first person in the chapters in which I describe experiences and lessons that I personally endured and learned. Also, I write with an edge, particularly concerning the unearned MOHs discussed in Chapter 15, the "non award" of a MOH discussed in Chapter 16, and the Miller saga in Chapter 17. I am on edge in Appendix C; the hot spots are the lack of attention paid to the December 7 MOH recipients at the World War II Valor in the Pacific National Monument, formerly the *Arizona* Visitors' Center, and rules governing access to and photography on military bases. I do not apologize for the edge or my lack of political correctness.

★ ★ ★ ★ ★ ★ ★ ★ ★ ★ ★ ★

My goal was to write a book in the classic manner, including specific citations of authority registered by endnotes (rather than footnotes) at the end of each chapter.

What the reader will not find are two abominable practices. One is a bibliography in a nonstandard form. I use a traditional bibliography, not a bibliographic essay as found in Back from the Deep, where specific information is not cited by endnote to source but is identified by phrase and then is the subject of an explanatory essay and identification of the source. Second is referring to the main characters by their first names, as in Hanns and Rudolf, the story of the German Jew who captured the commander of the Auschwitz death camp. The author expresses a requirement that he must use first names to tell the story of the two men. I found this practice nauseating. I suppose I could have titled this book Teddy and Mitsuo to use Cassin Young's Naval Academy nickname and the first name of the Japanese officer who helped to plan the attack on Oahu (Mitsuo Fuchida); Cy and Minoru to use Young's other nickname (it must refer to his initials "C.Y.") and the first name of another Japanese officer who helped to plan the attack (Minoru Genda); or Mervyn and Hideki to use Mervyn Bennion's first name and the first name of Japan's wartime leader one notch below the Emperor. I thought about Cap and the Emperor with "Cap" an obvious reference to

Captain Kidd, the Naval Academy nickname for Isaac Kidd, but I do not know the Emperor's first name. Perhaps I should watch The Mikado.

★ ★ ★ ★ ★ ★ ★ ★ ★ ★ ★

Perhaps I am old-fashioned, but I would never call any of the subjects of this book studs, yet I find myself with a pop culture military, where on the front of the April 25, 2016, Air Force Times, I see a photograph of the man who will probably be the next chief of staff of the U.S. Air Force: "YOUR NEXT CHIEF: The top candidate is a battle-tested stud." No one would have called a Franklin Roosevelt or Harry Truman flag or general officer a "stud." Roosevelt would have reprimanded the editor, using good humor; Truman would have blown a gasket and excoriated the publication. No one in society, military or civilian, would have called Generals Marshall, Eisenhower, or MacArthur or Admirals Nimitz or Halsey "studs."

★ ★ ★ ★ ★ ★ ★ ★ ★ ★ ★

I hope that this book will land for direct hits in these grid squares.

- the location of the organization that can and will establish on Midway or Oahu a memorial for Captain Richard Fleming, U.S. Marine Corps Reserve, and the sole MOH recipient for the Battle of Midway in 1942

- the location of the organization that can put in places accessible to the public replicas of the two plaques at Naval Shipyard Pearl Harbor about the codebreakers whose efforts ensured victory at Midway in 1942, the battle in which Fleming earned the sole MOH for the battle

- the location of the arm of the United States Navy that can and will name a ship for Rear Admiral Samuel Fuqua, U.S. Navy, the only December 7, 1941, MOH recipient for whom a ship was never named

- the location of the arm of the National Park Service (NPS) or the U.S. Navy that can place a memorial accessible to the public dedicated to and listing all the MOH recipients for the Hawaiian Islands during World War II, the eighteen men who are the subject of this book

- the arm of the NPS that can and will place a replica wayside exhibit, possibly at the World War II Valor in the Pacific National Monument, about the West Loch Disaster and include on it mention of Petty Officer Second Class Owen Hammerberg, U.S. Navy, and his MOH

★ ★ ★ ★ ★ ★ ★ ★ ★ ★ ★

Readers may notice throughout this book groups or lines of 13 stars, either large (on divider pages) or small (to separate paragraphs in a section). The 13 stars represent the 13 stars on a MOH ribbon just above the point the MOH is attached to the ribbon that wraps around the recipient's neck. Thirteen is of course the number of original colonies in the United States.

★★★★★★★★★★

Given my chapter exposing the errors of others who have written about these MOH recipients, I am leaving myself vulnerable to others finding errors in this book. Also, I was in a sense my own editor, which is a dangerous situation. So anyone who thinks I have made an error or omission can contact me at cajonesdt@gmail.com.

★★★★★★★★★★

In summary, on page one of the April 2016 edition of the Tombstone Epitaph is this sentence: "All stories change with time and telling. They also vary from witness to witness but the outcome remained the same..." I never sensed that the stories of the men who are the subject of this book changed with time and telling or varied from witness to witness. These men died in circumstances well documented contemporaneously; what has changed over time is sloppy, careless historians omitting or butchering their stories, hence the need for my chapter 18 about errors in recounting the stories of these men.

★★★★★★★★★★

For whatever reason, "subtraction" seems to be the norm for these men. Not one of them appeared in the 2013 Forever stamp commemorative issue of World War II MOH recipients, yet sixteen MOHs were earned on one of the most famous dates in the history of the United States.

So I did some historical "addition" and found this population of largely overlooked MOH men who should have some publicity added to their stories: collective recognition for them and the telling of their stories is long overdue. Further addition—ironclad plus aircraft equals naval aviation—leads to a sum, when added to Billy Mitchell's ideas about and demonstrations of airpower, that was the weapon causing the destructive whirlwind on 7 December 1941 resulting in the MOHs discussed in this book, MOHs too frequently awarded to the families of men who had died in the process of earning their nation's highest award for combat bravery.

Charles A. Jones
Colonel, U.S. Marine Corps Reserve (Retired)
Greensboro, North Carolina, 2017

P.S. The "subtraction" continues. While writing this book, I bought, in November 2016, the Time Special Edition booklet commemorating the 75th anniversary of December 7, 1941. As predicted, Doris Miller had his obligatory sidebar, but only three of the MOH men (Reeves, Scott, and Tomich) are mentioned. And the usual error appears in the booklet: "A Day That Will Live in Infamy." Readers who do not already know so the correct word is "date," not "day," in the famous speech delivered by President Franklin Roosevelt when he addressed Congress to ask for a declaration of war against Japan. Looking back, I could have named this book "Pearl Harbor's Forgotten Heroes."

N. Nav. 448
(Revised Mar 1941)

REPORT ON THE FITNESS OF OFFICERS

(To be submitted in accordance with Section 5 of Chapter 2, U. S. Navy Regulations, 1920, and Bureau of Navigation Manual, Article C-1007)

(Before making out this report read latest Bureau of Navigation circular letter on the subject of fitness reports)

The following four questions to be made out by the officer reported on:

FUQUA, Samuel Glenn   DEC 18 1942   , Rank Commander   , U. S. N.
   (Surname first)

Ship or Station   U.S.S. TUSCALOOSA   Period from Feb. 9, 1942 to Dec. 11, 1942.
   (Ship aviation units enter ship to which attached)

1. Regular duties   Damage Control Officer and First Lieutenant. (10)

   Additional duties   Summary Court Martial (Senior Member) (4)
   (State watch duties, both deck and engineering. After each duty insert in parenthesis number of months this reporting period)

2. Present address of { wife (if married) 928 W. Main St., Jefferson City, Mo.
                      { next of kin (if unmarried)
   (Indicate above the best address at which the Bureau of Navigation may communicate with the wife or next of kin in an emergency. The above address does not relate to the usual residence (home) which is maintained to the Bureau. See Art. 185(2), U. S. N. R., 1920.)

3. Proficiency in foreign languages, stating which ones, and ability therein   Spanish 2.5

4. My preference for next duty is—

   (a) Sea   Battleship   Fleet   No Preference
   (b) Shore   Naval Academy   Location   Annapolis, Md.

                              Samuel Glenn Fuqua
                                 (Signature)

Following to be made out by Reporting Officer:

5. Reporting Officer: Name   Norman C. Gillette   , Rank   Captain   , U. S. N.

6. Reporting officer's official status relative to officer reported on   Commanding Officer

7. Employment of ship during period of this report   Operating with Cruiser Division SEVEN.

8. Assign marks on scale of 0-4 in appropriate subdivisions given below, and any other qualification on which observation has been sufficient to justify marking.
   (Staff officers to be marked with respect to required duties. Mark below 2.5 constitutes an unsatisfactory report)

   Present assignment 3.9   Ability to command 3.9   As executive or division officer 3.9   As deck watch officer

   In administration 3.9   Ship handling 3.9

9. Has the work of this officer been reported on either in a commendatory way or adversely during the period of this report? If so, state the subject, reference numbers, and substance of report. Clip copy to report. Comply with U. S. Navy Regulations, article 187 (11) with respect to commendatory reports. Any adverse comment constitutes an unsatisfactory report.

   Yes. Awarded Medal of Honor with citation by the President. Copy attached.

10. Considering the possible requirements in war, indicate your attitude toward having this officer under your command. Would you—
    (An alternative entry in item (4) constitutes an unsatisfactory report)

    (1) Particularly desire to have him? ✓   (2) Be pleased to have him? _____   (3) Be satisfied to have him? _____

    (4) Prefer not to have him? _____

11. Has he any weaknesses—mental, moral, physical, etc.—which adversely affect his efficiency? (If "Yes," give details.)
    (An inherited or stated defect constitutes an unsatisfactory report)

    No.

[OVER]

Introduction: Pearl Harbor's Hidden Heroes

Perspectives

At approximately 7:55 a.m. on December 7, 1941—a typical Sunday morning on Oahu, United States Territory of Hawaii—Japanese naval aviation began a surprise attack, a sudden, withering, devastating assault on the island paradise, lasting approximately two hours, leaving most of Oahu's military installations in shambles and eviscerating the ships and the men of the United States Pacific Fleet.[1]

One personal aftermath of this attack was eighteen Medals of Honor (MOHs) awarded to members of the Navy and Marine Corps and their Reserves in the Hawaiian Islands during World War II in 1942 and 1945, many of whom would be hidden heroes.[2]

On March 3, 1942, President Franklin Roosevelt signed fourteen Medal of Honor (MOH) citations for thirteen Navy members who resisted the morning attack on Oahu and one Marine who resisted a separate Japanese attack on Midway Island on the evening of December 7. Those men were from the following ships and stations.[3]

- Battleship USS *California* (BB-44)—Ensign Herbert Jones, Warrant Officer (Radio Electrician) Thomas Reeves, and Petty Officer First Class (Machinist's Mate) Robert Scott

- Battleship USS *West Virginia* (BB48)—Captain Mervyn Bennion

- Battleship USS *Oklahoma* (BB-37)—Ensign Francis Flaherty and Seaman First Class James Ward

- Battleship USS *Arizona* (BB-39)—Rear Admiral Isaac Kidd, Captain Franklin Van Valkenburgh, and Lieutenant Commander Samuel Fuqua

- Battleship USS *Nevada* (BB-36)—Chief Warrant Officer (Boatswain) Edwin Hill and Warrant Officer (Machinist) Donald Ross

- Repair Ship USS *Vestal* (AR-4)—Commander Cassin Young

- Target and Gunnery Ship USS *Utah* (AG-16)—Chief Petty Officer (Watertender) Peter Tomich,

- Midway Island, Battery H, Sixth Marine Defense Battalion—First Lieutenant George Cannon,

Four other MOHs would be approved for these ships and stations:

- Patrol Squadron 14, Naval Air Station Kaneohe Bay—In June 1942, the

President signed another MOH citation for a Navy member who fought on December 7, Chief Petty Officer (Aviation Ordnanceman) John Finn.[4]

- Marine Scout Bombing Squadron 241—On November 10, 1942, President Roosevelt signed a MOH citation for a Marine aviator who perished during the great Battle of Midway in June of that year, Captain Richard E. Fleming.[5]

- USS *California*—On June 3, 1948, President Harry Truman signed the last MOH citation for a Navy member for actions on December 7—Warrant Officer (Gunner) Jackson Pharris, US Navy.[6]

- Salvage Unit, Commander Service Force, U.S. Pacific Fleet—On November 26, 1945, President Harry Truman signed a noncombat MOH citation for a Navy diver who died in 1945 during a rescue operation in the West Loch of Pearl Harbor, Petty Officer Second Class (Boatswain's Mate) Owen Hammerberg.[7]

Another MOH related to the MOHs awarded for actions in the Hawaiian Islands is the posthumous MOH awarded in 1946 to Billy Mitchell, who was an Army aviator (Army aviation was not a separate service until 1947 when the U.S. Air Force was created) and as a civilian was the nation's foremost exponent of airpower, especially its superiority to sea power. An airpower advocate in a sea of sea power advocates, he predicted the attack on Oahu and advocated the development of airpower until his death in 1936. The Japanese paid attention to what he said and used naval aviation to attack Oahu on December 7. Just seven months later, however, the situation was reversed as U.S. naval aviators defeated Japan decisively at the Battle of Midway in June 1942.[8]

WHERE WERE THESE EIGHTEEN HIDDEN HEROES?

Fourteen men receiving MOHs for December 7 were on ships moored at Ford Island, the island in Pearl Harbor. Aviation Ordnanceman Chief John Finn and Marine First Lieutenant George Cannon were the only two December 7 recipients who were not at Pearl Harbor.[9]

Captain Richard E. Fleming, U.S. Marine Corps Reserve, fought at 1942's Battle of Midway.[10]

Boatswain's Mate Petty Officer Owen Hammerberg, U.S. Navy, received a noncombat MOH for bravery in the West Loch of Pearl Harbor in 1945.[11]

WHY ARE THEY *PEARL HARBOR'S* HIDDEN HEROES?

Pearl Harbor is used since the majority of the MOH recipients in this book earned their MOHs there. Of the seventeen combat and one noncombat MOHs mentioned in this book, fifteen were earned at Pearl Harbor—fourteen on December 7, 1941, and one on February 17, 1945.[12]

Why Are They *Hidden* Heroes?

For many reasons.

First, of all these men are hidden in numbers. Of the 473 MOHs awarded during and after World War II for actions during that conflict, only 18 were awarded for actions in the Hawaiian Islands.[13]

Second, from a macro or big-picture viewpoint, the general public's knowledge of the events leading to these MOHs is often hidden in that it is lacking or distorted to a remarkable degree. Those events include the attack on Oahu on December 7, 1941, the Battle of Midway in 1942, and the West Loch Disaster ("The Second Pearl Harbor") in 1944.

Third, from a micro or small-picture viewpoint, if the public does not fully know the big picture, then it probably will not know about a small but important subset of those events: the stories of the men awarded MOHs for actions on December 7, 1941, at the Battle of Midway or as a consequence of the West Loch Disaster.

Fourth, before anyone can know the picture, big or small, one must find the stories of the Hawaiian Island MOHs. Unfortunately, many of them are hidden or a sidebar in the overwhelming amount of information—accurate and inaccurate—concerning December 7 and the Battle of Midway in 1942. That information is found in the large number of published (books and magazines) and electronic (video, DVD, CD, and the Internet) accounts of December 7 and the Battle of Midway.

Fifth, the public may not know these stories not because they are hidden but because they are missing. The MOH stories are often partially or totally omitted in accounts of December 7, Midway, or West Loch.

Sixth, when the stories are told, the accounts are inaccurately or incompletely reported, often in piecemeal and abbreviated fashion and filled with errors. This observation is true even in official U.S. Government publications about battles and in books in which the Congressional Medal of Honor Society has collaborated.[14]

Seventh, the average person walking through or by a private or U.S. government cemetery or memorial would walk by the cemetery or memorial containing a grave or graves or memorial or memorials for one or more of these MOH men likely not knowing that he or they earned a MOH or MOHs, what was done to earn the MOH or MOHs, and if the action cost the recipient or recipients his or their lives.

Eighth, these men are in the shadow of more well-known MOH recipients. Francis Flaherty and James Ward, who perished on USS *Oklahoma* are unknowns compared to more prominent MOH recipients, such as Audie Murphy and Douglas MacArthur. Additionally, only four of the MOH recipients who are the subjects of this book survived the war. None of them are alive today.[15]

Ninth, more so than the other MOH recipients in this book, the two Midway

MOH recipients, both Marines, are hidden because they are not well known even in Marine Corps lore. All Marines know about John Basilone, one of the earliest and most popular World War II Marine Corps heroes, who earned a MOH on Guadalcanal in 1942 and died on Iwo Jima's D-Day, February 19, 1945. Few people, including Marines, know about Lieutenant George Cannon, that he earned a MOH at Midway in 1941, that he was the sole Marine MOH recipient for actions on December 7, or that his actions were the last on December 7 to earn a MOH (in the evening of that day). He was also the first Marine (officer or enlisted, aviator or ground officer) to earn a MOH in World War II. Although the famous 1942 Battle of Midway is well known, few people, including Marines, know that a Marine aviator, Captain Richard Fleming, earned the sole MOH awarded for that battle, the battle dooming Japan. While Japanese aircraft from carriers bombed Midway in 1942 (the Japanese never invaded Midway), the battle was essentially one of naval aviation based on aircraft carriers with aircraft attacking each other and each other's carriers. In that context, one would expect any MOHs would have been earned by Navy aviators based on carriers, yet Fleming was a Marine whose squadron was based on land on Midway, not on a carrier.[16]

Finally, a general public unfamiliar with military history beyond a superficial level (movies and television) will simply not know about one of the most important officers in United States military history: Brigadier General Billy Mitchell, U.S. Army, the leading exponent of airpower over sea power. Although he did not receive a MOH for combat service in either World War I or II, in 1946, Congress authorized for Mitchell a posthumous MOH (he died in 1936) to acknowledge his advocacy of military airpower. He is hidden because he is long dead, but his story is important because his ideas about airpower were very much alive in World War II and still are today. Mitchell was an outspoken advocate of airpower and based on his trip to the Far East, predicted that the Japanese would attack Pearl Harbor—specifically Ford Island, at 7:30 on a Sunday morning. He was only twenty-five minutes off. The attack began at 7:55 a.m., a meaningless margin of error for the attack directly leading to the United States entering World War II, during which occurred actions leading to the seventeen combat and one noncombat MOHs discussed in this book.[17]

Mitchell also conducted ship-sinking trials in the 1920s, proving that ships were vulnerable to air attack. In short, Mitchell demonstrated the offensive use of airpower and warned of its use against the United States. Most military and civilian leaders ignored him—until the Japanese proved him demonstrably correct on December 7.[18]

HISTORICAL CONTEXT:
TRANSITION AND THE MOST IMPORTANT NAVAL WEAPONS

The actions of most of the MOH recipients occurred in important historical contexts likely unknown to the general public.

The actions of the December 7 MOH recipients on Oahu occurred during an event marking the end of the era when battleships were the premier naval weapons. Before that day, battleships and naval guns were the most important ships and naval weapons. On December 7 and after, aircraft carriers and airplanes—naval aviation's components—became the most important ships and naval weapons. The proof of this transition from naval gun supremacy to naval aircraft supremacy was evident. The battleships' large guns, intended for surface combat with other ships at sea, were Useless against Japanese aerial attack.[19]

The Development of Naval Aviation

The three steps in this transition from battleship supremacy to aircraft-carrier supremacy are easily traced—as is the Navy's resistance to the suggestion that the battleship's days were numbered.

The first step was on March 9, 1862, the first battle between ironclads (USS Monitor and CSS Virginia) in Hampton Roads, Virginia, proving the supremacy of the iron ship to the wooden ship.[20]

The second step was proving the capability of aircraft to take off from and land on ships. On November 14, 1910, Eugene Ely made the first flight from a warship when he flew a biplane from the cruiser USS Birmingham, anchored off Old Point Comfort in Hampton Roads. On January 18, 1911, he made the first landing on a ship, landing an airplane on a platform on the cruiser USS Pennsylvania in San Francisco Bay.[21]

The third step was Mitchell proving aircraft could sink ships in the 1920s when land-based aircraft he commanded sank ships at sea off the Atlantic coast during his famous ship-sinking trials.

While Mitchell's tests were not in combat conditions, later combat engagements proved that aircraft, based aboard ships, could attack other ships, including ships in harbors. Such engagements include British planes attacking Italian ships in the harbor at Taranto, Italy, and of course Japanese planes attacking American ships in Pearl Harbor on Oahu. Unlike the Mitchell sinkings of derelict ships not defending themselves, attacks on Taranto and Oahu were in combat conditions, meaning targets were defending themselves against aerial attack.[22]

The battleship navy, however, remained dedicated to battleships, resisting Mitchell's efforts to prove the supremacy of airpower to sea power. Chapters 2, 3, and 20 describe in more detail Mitchell's conflicts with the "battleship Navy."

Mitchell, in addition to proving ship vulnerability to aerial attack, predicted the attack on Oahu and, after inspecting Oahu long before December 7, found its defenses inadequate. His finding and prediction were ignored. One result of ignoring his warnings was the December 7 attack on Oahu that riddled the island's U.S. military installations and devastated much of the Fleet, leaving many of its ships on the bottom of Pearl Harbor. The Fleet moored in Pearl Harbor that day was home for fourteen of the eighteen MOH recipients discussed in this book.[23]

While one can hardly ask for greater vindication of Mitchell than December 7, anyone requiring more proof that he was correct should consider the famous Battle of Midway in June 1942, during which the battle's sole MOH was earned in the airpower arena by a land-based aviator attacking a ship. The battle is considered one of history's great battles and also the turning point in the Pacific War. Japan's loss of four aircraft carriers at Midway—all sunk by U.S. Navy aviation—was catastrophic, shifting Japan's war machine into reverse and ultimately ensuring Allied victory.[24]

The following quotation is an important one from the 1945 Congressional hearings concerning recognition for Mitchell. At the time, Mitchell was dead and war with Japan was ongoing.

Every day [of World War II with Japan] serves to demonstrate more thoroughly that air power has been the determining factor in winning the European war and that if Gen. William Mitchell's repeated specific warnings had been heeded the disaster of Pearl Harbor would have been avoided and many lives lost in World War II would have been spared.[25]

Chapters 2, 3, and 20 more fully discuss Mitchell and his ship-sinking tests, his prediction of the attack on Oahu, and the special posthumous MOH Congress and the President authorized for him. His prediction of the attack on Oahu, made in a report in 1925 after he visited the Far East, and the MOH authorized by Congress in 1946 are, in a sense, the bookends haunting the story of the Hawaiian Island MOH recipients from beginning to end—a prediction ignored and an apology in the form of a MOH issued too late since Mitchell died in 1936 and did not live to see airpower's decisive role in Allied victory.

Airpower Versus Sea Power: Beginning, End, and Full Circle

Navies—particularly, battleships—and not air forces were seen as the primary military forces until World War II began both for Europe in 1939 and for the United States in 1941. German aircraft dropped bombs on Poland on September 1, 1939, the day World War II began between Germany and Great Britain.[26]

Likewise, Japanese aircraft started World War II for the United States by attacking Oahu on December 7 with aviation, leading to the Congressional declarations of war by the United States against Japan and then Germany.[27]

While the battleships' large guns were useless against Japanese aircraft on December 7, they were invaluable in supporting ground troops during Allied invasions in Europe and in the Pacific. Naval guns also remained important during battles in the Pacific between surface ships.

Although the Second World War in Europe ended in May 1945, the war continued in the Pacific until Japan ceased hostilities on August 15, 1945, after two aircraft showed the ultimate in American military might. A B-29 bomber dropped an atomic bomb on Hiroshima on August 6, and another B-29 dropped an atomic bomb on Nagasaki on August 9.[28] On August 6, 1945, President Harry Truman, who had the courage to authorize the two atomic bombings, issued a statement about the Hiroshima bombing, including these words, evidencing the long memory the United States had about December 7 and echoing the famous saying, "Remember the *Arizona*!": "The Japanese began the war from the air at Pearl Harbor. They have been repaid many fold [by the bomb just dropped, which had more power than 20,000 tons of TNT]."[29]

Ironically the battleship had the last word; the surrender ceremony ending World War II was held aboard the battleship USS Missouri in Tokyo Bay on September 1 or 2, 1945 (the date depends on one's location in reference to the International Date Line). The ceremony was simply one last symbolic gesture of the battleship's power. The aircraft carrier and naval aviation, not battleships and guns, were now the nation's most powerful naval weapons. One could argue that the role of the battleship had changed from surface combat to platforms for gunfire to support invasions or places on which to hold surrender or other ceremonies—or to floating museums.

But did the battleship really have the last word or just serve as a site for the penultimate gesture marking the end of the war? After the surrender ceremony ended, an armada of Allied aircraft (including a B-29 bomber of which the author's father was a crewman) flew over the battleship in a power show.

The new king of battle was again announcing his arrival.[30]

NOTES

1. Chapter 2.

2. Chapters 4 through 12 and 19.

3. Chapters 4 through 10 and 12.

4. Chapter 11 ("Kaneohe Bay").

5. Chapter 12 ("Midway").

6. Chapter 4 ("*California*").

7. Chapter 13 ("West Loch").

8. Chapter 3 ("Aftermath").

9. Chapters 4 through 12 and 19.

10. Chapter 12 ("Midway").

11. Chapter 13 ("West Loch").

12. Chapters 4; 6 through 13; 14 and 19.

13. Chapters 4 through 13 and 19. Congressional Medal of Honor Society Internet site (number of MOHs earned in World War II).

14. See Chapter 18 ("Errors").

15. Chapters 4 through 14, 19, and 21 and Appendix C.

16. Chapter 12 ("Midway"). During the author's thirty years of combined service in the Regular and Reserve Marine Corps, he learned about John Basilone and in fact found his grave by chance at Arlington National Cemetery, Arlington, Virginia. But during his career, he was never told about Lieutenant Cannon or Captain Fleming or their roles at Midway in 1941 or 1942, respectively. He only learned about them through his own research.

17. Chapters 2, 3, and 20.

18. Ibid.

19. Chapter 2 ("Attack").

20. James Tetris deKay, Monitor (Ballantine Books, New York, NY, 1997), 180–198.

21. "The Virginian Pilot," Hampton Roads Naval Aviation: A Centennial Retrospective (Norfolk, VA, 2011), 8–10.

22. Chapters 2, 3 and 20.

23. Ibid.

24. Chapter 14. Mitsuo Fuchida and Masatake Okumiya, Midway: The Battle That Doomed Japan, the Japanese Navy's Story (Naval Institute Press, Annapolis, MD, 1955, 1992), 218 (Akagi), 221 (Kaga), 224 (Soryu), and 234–35 (Hiryu).

25. Hearings [May 31, 1945] before HOUSE OF REPRESENTATIVES, SUBCOMMITTEE NO. 8 OF THE COMMITTEE ON MILITARY AFFAIRS, U.S. House of Representatives, Seventy-Ninth Congress, First Session on H.R. 2227 and Other Bills [authorizing the President to award a posthumous MOH in the name of Congress to William Mitchell] (U.S. Government Printing Office, Washington, DC, 1945), Statement by E. G. B. Riley, 25.

26. David E. Scherman, ed., Life Goes to War (Pocket Books, New York, NY, 1997), 50.

27. Chapter 2 ("Attack"). The United States declared war on Japan on December 8, 1941, and on Germany December 11, 1941.

28. Paul W. Tibbets, Flight of the Enola Gay (Mid Coast Marketing, Columbus, OH, 1989), 224, 236, and 238–39.

29. Statement by President Harry S. Truman, August 6, 1945, announcing the atomic bombing of Hiroshima, Japan (printed in Air Force Magazine (September 2006), 64).

30. William Manchester, American Caesar (Little, Brown and Company, Boston,

Toronto), 1978), 453 (discussion of the show of aerial force after the surrender document was signed). The author's father was the radar operator on the B-29 "Superfortress" bomber Double Trouble (Crew P-10, Thirty-Ninth Bomb Group, 314th Bomb Wing). The crew had twenty-nine combat and photo reconnaissance missions over Japan during the war, including the longest combat mission of the war. Mission 30 was flying over Missouri after the surrender instrument was signed. In the author's conversations with his father, Lieutenant Colonel Elmer C. Jones, U.S. Air Force Reserve (Retired), and his father's list of missions, written on the blank pages in his government-issue New Testament, he termed the Missouri flyover mission a "power show."

Part I

Military Environment

Chapter 1

Ships, Terms, Grade, and Military Organization

For the convenience of the reader, the following information is provided as an overview of the military in which the World War II MOH recipients served and lived and which was the subject of the attack on December 7. It focuses on the Navy and Marine Corps since Pearl Harbor and the ships therein were the main focus of the Japanese attack and since all the MOH recipients discussed in the book (except Billy Mitchell) were members of the Regular Navy, Naval Reserve (now Navy Reserve), regular Marine Corps, or Marine Corps Reserve.

Perhaps the two most important parts of the military environment for December 7 and the MOH recipients were leadership in combat and damage control. And the importance of the ship itself cannot be overstated. Of the seventeen classic combat and one noncombat MOHs that are the subject of this book, fourteen were awarded to officers and men assigned to ships: Rear Admiral Kidd; Captains Bennion and Van Valkenburgh; Commander Young; Lieutenant Commander Fuqua; Ensigns Flaherty and Jones; Chief Boatswain Hill; Warrant Officers Pharris, Reeves, and Ross; Chief Petty Officer Tomich; Petty Officer First Class Scott; and Seaman First Class Ward.

For perspective, the basic fighting unit or the center of the action in the infantry is the rifle company; in the artillery, it is the battery; and in aviation, it is the squadron. In a navy, it is the ship. She is the sailor's home and fighting unit.

Ships

Ship Names

Battleships were named for states, cruisers for cities, destroyers and destroyer escorts for Navy or Marine Corps heroes, and repair ships for Greek or Roman mythological figures. Aircraft carriers were often named for Revolutionary War battles and important older ships.[1]

This book uses two Navy traditions. One is omitting "the" before ship names ("*Arizona* sank," not "the *Arizona* sank"). The other is referring to ships in feminine terms, such as "she" and "her," for example, "She is a destroyer" and "Her bow was damaged."[2]

Ships Designations and Types

Ships have three designations. One is the type, an abbreviation of two to four letters, such as BB for battleship. Two is the hull number, such as "39." Three is the name of the ship, such as "*Arizona*." Altogether, the battleship is BB-39 USS *Arizona*.[3]

Battleships (BB)

Battleships were important for three reasons. First, before December 7, they were the primary naval fighting ship.[4] Second, as seen in Chapter 2, during the attack, they were priority targets, second only to aircraft carriers. Third, during the attack, twelve of the fourteen men earning MOHs at Pearl Harbor were on battleships on Battleship Row (Cassin Young was on a repair ship, and Peter Tomich was on a target ship).[5]

Designated "BB," battleships were the largest ships for surface combat and the principal ships of the fleet. They had the heaviest armor and guns of all ships. Their main weapons were large guns. Crew size was approximately 1,500.[6]

As seen in photographs, a battleship's distinguishing features include size, large guns mounted in turrets, and two large masts with fire-control stations atop the masts. The mainmast is at the center of the ship. The foremast is forward of the mainmast and near the bow (front). The masts were tripods, although some of the older ships had caged masts instead of tripod masts.[7]

Also seen in photographs of battleships are seaplanes stationed on the ship. The seaplanes, which could fly around the ship for observation, were mounted on catapults atop turrets and decks. They were launched from the catapults and recovered from the water by the crane at the ship's stern (rear). Seaplane squadrons were designated "VO"—heavier than air aircraft ("V") used for observation ("O").[8]

Other Ships

The followings ships are associated with the MOH recipients, although only two of the recipients were assigned to these types of ships; Cassin Young was on a repair ship (AR), and Peter Tomich was on an auxiliary ship (AG).

Aircraft carriers (CV), commanded by Navy pilots, carried the Navy's air force. Its weapon, unlike the battleship, was the aircraft, not the naval gun. Its main target was enemy aircraft carriers. Its aircraft could fly combat air patrols (CAPs), which protected ships in the fleet by looking for enemy threats.[9]

Cruisers (CA or CL) were next smaller in size to battleships. Heavy cruisers were designated "CA"; light cruisers were "CL." They were used as scouts of the fleet for long-range patrol; they could also be used to protect other ships, such as aircraft carriers, and to lead destroyers.[10] They had crews as large as approximately nine hundred Navy personnel and forty-one Marines.[11] As can be seen from photographs, cruisers, like battleships, could carry observation planes. One of the December 7 MOH recipients, Cassin Young, survived that day and was assigned in 1942 to command a cruiser (Chapter 8, *Vestal*).

Destroyers (DD) were smaller but faster than cruisers; one perspective is that destroyers are small cruisers or cruisers are large destroyers. Destroyers, which were originally designed as torpedo-boat destroyers, evolved into multipurpose ships that protected or screened larger ships from enemy aircraft and submarines ("picket" duty).

They also escorted convoys and attacked submarines. The slang for destroyers is "tin cans." Armament included guns for surface combat, guns for antiaircraft defense, torpedoes to attack ships and surfaced submarines, and depth charges for attacking submerged submarines. Crew size was approximately 200 to 350.[12]

Destroyer escorts (DE) were developed specifically for antisubmarine operations, which often meant convoy escort duty.[13] They were smaller, lighter, and slower than destroyers and lacked destroyer "speed, fire power, and armor."[14] They were, however, more maneuverable and thus better suited for antisubmarine warfare because a surface ship, in attacking a submarine, had to turn frequently and thus needed a small turning radius. Armament was similar to that of destroyers. Crew size was smaller than a destroyer and was approximately 170.[15] As indicated throughout this book and in Appendix B, destroyer escorts are important since so many were named for the MOH recipients.

Volume construction of DEs did not begin until mid-1943, as indicated by the large number of DEs commissioned in 1943 and named for the December 7 MOH recipients.[16] They made an invaluable contribution to destroying submarines when combined with aircraft carriers in hunter-killer teams. An example is in the history of USS Flaherty (Appendix B). The Enemy Below, a movie starring Robert Mitchum, is the story of a destroyer escort attacking a German U-boat.

Destroyer escorts are important since most ships built during World War II and named in memory of the MOH recipients in this book were destroyer escorts[17] (see Appendix B).

Classic destroyers, as well as DEs, are no longer made since they were made during a time when guns, torpedoes, and depth charges were primary weapons. After World War II, fighting other ships was no longer the destroyer's primary mission. Destroyers were developed to use helicopters for antisubmarine warfare and missiles for antiaircraft warfare. Thus the postwar version of the destroyer was the guided-missile destroyer (DDG). A ship that is, in effect, a small destroyer or a modern destroyer escort is the fast frigate (FF) or guided-missile frigate (FFG).[18]

Landing Ships Tank (LST) carried cargo and troops. Chapter 13 describes LSTs and the noncombat MOH awarded to a Navy diver who, in 1945, rescued two other divers salvaging around an LST sunk in 1944 during the West Loch Disaster in Pearl Harbor's West Loch.

Auxiliary ships perform various missions. The two auxiliary ships important for the MOH recipients were the repair ship *Vestal* (designation AR-4, Cassin Young MOH) and the auxiliary miscellaneous ship *Utah* (designation AG-16, Peter Tomich MOH).[19] Auxiliary ships, including tenders, repair ships, and oilers, supported combatant ships, such as battleships, cruisers, destroyers, submarines, and aircraft carriers. *Utah* was originally commissioned a battleship but was converted in the 1930s to a target ship and gunnery training ship with the corresponding change in designation from "BB" to "AG," meaning miscellaneous auxiliary ship (see Chapters 8 (*Vestal*) and 10 (*Utah*) of this book, respectively).

Placing Ships in or out of Service

Commissioning is the official ceremony placing a ship in active service in the Navy; logically, decommissioning is the official ceremony removing the ship from active service.[20] After decommissioning, ships are placed in permanent storage ("mothballs") for possible future use, sold to other governments, or scrapped. Most of the ships named for the Navy and Marine MOH recipients in this book were scrapped.

Shipboard Life

A ship is a floating city. She must be self-sufficient; be self-governing; carry essentials for life, such as fuel, ammunition, food, and water; and provide personal services and recreation.

The two most important officers, discussed in more detail later in this chapter, are the commanding officer (CO), who is in command, and the executive officer (XO or "exec"), who is second in command. The ship also has a senior enlisted sailor. The ship is organized into departments with each department having a department head, who may be a commander, lieutenant commander, or lieutenant. Important department heads include the chief engineer or "CHENG"; the supply officer; the first lieutenant; and damage-control officer (described in the next section). The first lieutenant is also in charge of maintenance. Departments are in turn divided into divisions led by "division officers."[21]

Damage Control

Each ship must have procedures for damage control, mitigating damage sustained in a combat or noncombat emergency, such as fire, collision, or hits from ordnance such as such as bombs or torpedoes. Damage control is so important that a battleship, cruiser, destroyer, and aircraft carrier had an officer who was the "damage control officer and first lieutenant."[22]

The crew practices damage-control procedures. Crewmen must know the location of emergency equipment, how to fight fires, and how to control damage, such as closing hatches and repairing holes in the hull to keep water out of the ship ("water-tight integrity").[23] A classic form of damage control is counterflooding. For example, if a ship is hit with torpedoes on the port (left) side, water rushes in the hull and causes the ship to tilt ("list") to port because of the weight of the water inside the ship's port side. The ship will capsize toward port if the crew does not counterflood (i.e., open valves on the starboard (right) side to permit water to enter that side of the ship, thus equalizing the weight on both sides of the ship).

As recounted in Chapter 7 (*Arizona*), Lieutenant Commander Samuel Fuqua, who earned a MOH aboard *Arizona*, described for an investigative body his duties as the ship's first lieutenant and damage control officer (DCO). As the DCO, he had to maintain watertight integrity of the ship and to keep it afloat notwithstanding battle damage. The damage-control section comprised him as section head, a lieutenant assistant, a chief boatswain, a carpenter, an ensign, and approximately thirty-five other crewmen.[24]

Marine Detachments Aboard Ships

In World War II, detachments of Marines were stationed aboard aircraft carriers, battleships, and cruisers. They were assigned to the ship just as Navy personnel were. Both the Navy and the Marines aboard the ship were ship's company. Marines provided security, manned guns, conducted ceremonies, and served as orderlies.[25]

Ship Terminology

The Navy has special terminology for ships.[26]

The front of a ship is the bow; the rear is the stern. Forward (heading toward the bow) and aft (heading toward the stern) are directions; bow and stern are positions.

When aboard ship looking at the bow, port is left and starboard is right.

A bulkhead is a wall; the overhead is the ceiling.

A door is a hatch. A hallway is a passageway.

Personnel

Grade Structure

Grade is a service member's position in the military hierarchy. Each step in the hierarchy is a grade, not a rank, the commonly used but improper term; the two terms are not interchangeable. Rank is seniority within a grade (each person in a certain grade has a date of rank that establishes the person's seniority within his or her grade).[27]

The President and Congress, via legislation, dictate the grade structure, which today is very similar to World War II's structure. For the modern military, Sections 5501 and 5502 of Title 10, US Code, govern the officer grades for the Navy and Marine Corps, respectively; Section 5503 governs the Navy and Marine Corps warrant and chief warrant officer grades.

Grades are in three categories: commissioned officer grades, warrant officer grades (warrant officers and chief warrant officers), and enlisted grades.

Navy grades are easily confused. For example, a chief boatswain's mate is a chief petty officer (CPO), an enlisted grade; a chief boatswain is a chief warrant officer who is a boatswain, an officer grade. The CPO but not the chief boatswain could be called "chief."

The following charts assist the reader in understanding the military status and seniority of the MOH recipients by giving a simplified overview of World War II's military hierarchy.[28] Congress created the five-star grade in 1944 for the Army and Navy but not the Marine Corps; the five-star grade is no longer authorized. Admiral Chester Nimitz, who ultimately assumed command of the Pacific Fleet after December

7, became a five-star admiral in December 1944.²⁹ During the war, the Marine Corps Commandant's grade changed from major general to lieutenant general to general.³⁰

Navy officers from ensign to fleet admiral and Marine officers from second lieutenant to general are called "commissioned officers," since they have formal appointments ("commissions") from the President, granting them military status as officers at certain grades.³¹ Officers above O-6 are, collectively, "flag officers" since they have personal flags with the number of stars for their grades (Marine Corps flag officers may also be called "general officers").³² For example, when a vice admiral is present, a blue flag with three white stars is flown, and when a marine lieutenant general is present, a red flag with three white stars is flown.³³ The correct collective terms are flag officers, not admirals, and general officers, not generals (admirals and generals are four-star officers).

The Navy grade immediately above captain was eliminated before World War II, so Navy officers promoted above captain were promoted directly to rear admirals (two stars). Thus Captain Isaac Kidd of *Arizona* was promoted from captain to rear admiral (two stars), the grade he held at his death. A one-star commodore grade was established for the navy and used from 1943 to 1947.³⁴ Today, the commodore grade is "rear admiral (lower half)" with one star; the next grade is rear admiral with two stars. Captains are now promoted to rear admiral (lower half), not directly to rear admiral.³⁵

A ship's commanding officer is the captain regardless of grade.³⁶ Most ship captains are captains or commanders; during the war, some were lieutenant commanders or even lieutenants. MOH recipient Cassin Young was a commander when he was the captain or commanding officer of the repair ship USS *Vestal*; after he was promoted to captain, he was the captain or commanding officer of the cruiser USS San Francisco.³⁷

Navy officers below the grade of commander may be called by their grade or by "mister."³⁸ A famous example is the movie Mr. Roberts, using "mister," referring to Lieutenant (junior grade) Doug Roberts (actor Henry Fonda).

Enlisted sailors junior to chief petty officers could be called bluejackets.³⁹ The famous navy manual for enlisted men is titled The Bluejackets' Manual.

COMMISSIONED OFFICER GRADES

Navy Grade	Army/Marine Corps Grade	Metallic Insignia
Fleet admiral (O–11)	General of the army (no five-star grade for the marine corps)	Five stars
Admiral (O–10)	General (highest grade in the marine corps)	Four stars
Vice admiral (O–9)	Lieutenant general	Three stars
Rear admiral (O–8)	Major general	Two stars
Commodore (O–7)	Brigadier general	One star
Captain (O–6)	Colonel	Eagle
Commander (O–5)	Lieutenant colonel	Silver leaf
Lieutenant commander (O–4)	Major	Gold leaf
Lieutenant (O–3)	Captain	Two silver bars
Lieutenant (junior grade) (O-2)	First lieutenant	One silver bar
Ensign (O–1)	Second lieutenant	One gold bar

Table 2-1. Commissioned officer grades, World War II.

Terminology

Component

Officers became officers by initial appointment as an officer in one of two components: the regular or the reserve component. Enlisted members became service members by enlistment in one of these two components. For the Navy, the components were the regular navy or naval reserve; for the Marines, the components were the regular Marine Corps or the Marine Corps Reserve.[40] The Regular component of a service is the permanent, professional force of officer and enlisted members who make the service a full-time career. A Regular in effect has tenure until he or she leaves the service. Departure can be voluntary, such as by retirement or for officers resigning, and enlisted members can decide not to reenlist. Involuntarily departure can be for disciplinary action or being passed over for promotion.

Graduates of the Naval Academy received appointments in the Regular Navy or Marine Corps. The December 7 MOH recipients who graduated from the academy were Kidd, Van Valkenburgh, Bennion, Young, and Fuqua.[41]

The Naval Reserve augmented the Regular Navy in World War II, just as the Navy Reserve augments the Regular Navy today.[42] One route to a reserve appointment as an officer was and still is the Navy Reserve Officers' Training Corps (NROTC). Another was the reserve midshipman (V-7) program, of which two December 7 MOH recipients were graduates: Ensigns Herbert Jones (Chapter 4, *California*) and Francis Flaherty (Chapter 5, *Oklahoma*).

Abbreviations may follow names. "U.S. Navy" or "USN" and "U.S. Marine Corps" or "USMC." indicate a regular member. "U.S. Naval Reserve" or "USNR" and "U.S. Marine Corps Reserve" or "USMCR" indicate a reserve member.

Line Officers and Staff Officers

All Marine officers are *line officers*, meaning that any officer can command any unit. Thus they wear the same grade insignia on each collar. For example, a major has a gold leaf on each collar of his or her shirt.[43]

The Navy, however, has *line officers* and *staff officers*. Line officers can command combat units, so they wear the same insignia on each shirt collar. In the Navy, shoulder boards across tops of shirts have the number of stripes indicating officer grade. A star on the shoulder board indicates the officer is a line officer. The classic examples of line officers are navy officers who are aviators or unrestricted surface officers.[44]

Navy staff officers are members of a staff *corps* and *restricted* in the sense that they cannot command any unit other than a unit of their own corps; they cannot command ships. Doctors, for example, are members of the medical corps (MC), and chaplains are members of the chaplains' corps (CHC). A doctor could command a hospital. These officers wear a grade insignia on the right shirt collar and a corps insignia on the left collar. On their shoulder boards, they have stripes indicating their grade, just as line

Commissioned Officer Grades

Grade	Number of Stripes
Fleet admiral (O–11)	One two-inch stripe with four one-inch stripes above it
Admiral (O–10)	One two-inch stripe with three one-inch stripes above it
Vice admiral (O–9)	One two-inch stripe with two one-inch stripes above it
Rear admiral (O–8)	One two-inch stripe with one one-half-inch stripe above it
Commodore (O–7)	One two-inch stripe
Captain (O–6)	Four one-half-inch stripes
Commander (O–5)	Three one-half-inch stripes
Lieutenant commander (O–4)	Two one-half-inch stripes with a one-fourth-inch stripe in between the stripes
Lieutenant (O–3)	Two one-half-inch stripes
Lieutenant (junior grade) (O-2)	One one-half-inch stripe and one one-fourth-inch stripe above it
Ensign (O–1)	One one-half-inch stripe
Chief warrant officer (W-2)	One one-half-inch stripe with tabs of blue thread around the stripe at intervals
Warrant officer (W-1)	One one-quarter-inch stripe with blue thread around the stripe at intervals

Table 2-2. Navy officer grades indicated by stripes.

officers do, but instead of the line officer star, they have a corps insignia.[45] None of the MOH recipients mentioned in this book were members of a staff corps.

WARRANT AND CHIEF WARRANT OFFICERS

Enlisted members who are experts in a particular field (such as gunnery or carpentry) could be appointed as officers and retain their enlisted specialties. They were called *warrant officers* since they were appointed by warrant from the Secretary of the Navy and not the president. They had titles such as boatswain, gunner, or machinist.[46]

During World War II, a warrant officer could be promoted to chief warrant officer. A chief warrant officer received an appointment from the President and thus was a commissioned officer, holding a grade below ensign or second lieutenant. They had the same titles as warrant officers with the preface "chief," such as chief boatswain, chief gunner, or chief machinist[47] (see Chapter 9 (*Nevada*) for examples). MOH recipient Edwin Hill was a chief warrant officer, specifically a chief boatswain; MOH recipient Donald Ross was a warrant officer, specifically a machinist.

Today, Section 5503 of United States Code establishes the warrant officer grades, starting with W-1 (warrant officer, the lowest warrant grade) and progressing from CWO-2 to CWO-5 (chief warrant officers, with CWO-5 the highest warrant grade). Thus the current grade system has three more warrant officer grades (CWO-3 through CWO-5) than did the grade system in World War II, which had only warrant and chief warrant officers.

OFFICER INSIGNIA

Depending on the uniform worn, grade may be indicated in several ways.

Marine and Navy line officers may wear a shirt with a grade insignia on each collar; these are the metallic insignia in table 2-1 (Navy and Marine corps metallic insignia are the same for each grade except warrant and commissioned warrant officers). A Navy staff officer may wear a shirt with a grade insignia on the right collar and the device representing his or her specialty on the left collar. Navy warrant and chief warrant officers wear specialty devices on both shirt collars.[48]

In addition to metallic grade insignia worn on shirts, one or more stripes on the cuffs of a navy officer's coat indicate his or her grade. Cuffs and shoulder boards have the same pattern of stripes to indicate grade (see table 2-2).[49]

Marine uniforms do not have stripes on the cuffs or have shoulder boards to indicate grade, although a metallic grade insignia may be worn at the edge of the outer shoulder loop of the Marine uniform jackets with shoulder loops.

Petty officers are equivalent to noncommissioned officers in other services (corporal and above).[51] In addition to grade, petty officers have a rating (occupational specialty), such as "electrician." Thus, a petty officer could be addressed by grade alone (Petty Officer First Class Smith) or, more precisely, by rating and grade, Boatswain's Mate Second Class Smith, with boatswain's mate being the rating.

Enlisted Grades

Unlike officer grades and insignia, which among the services were and remain similar, enlisted grades and insignia were much more varied and complicated; some changed during the war. The following chart gives the World War II grades in simplified form.[50]

Grade	**Army**	**Navy**	**Marines**
First	master sergeant	chief petty officer	sergeant major, master gunnery sergeant, first sergeant, master technical sergeant
Second	technical sergeant	petty officer first class	gunnery sergeant, technical sergeant
Third	staff sergeant	petty officer second class	platoon sergeant or staff sergeant
Fourth	sergeant	petty officer third class	sergeant, field music sergeant
Fifth	corporal	seaman first class	corporal, field music corporal
Sixth	private first class	seaman second class	private first class, field musician first class
Seventh	private	seaman third class	private

Table 2-3. Enlisted grades, World War II.

In the Navy, seaman third class (lowest grade), seaman second class, and seaman first class were called "nonrates" since they had no rating or specialty.[52] As can be seen from the table, the organization is from lowest to highest (without regard to rating):

- nonrated men—third class (lowest grade), second class, and first class
- rated men—petty officer third class, petty officer second class, petty officer first class, and chief petty officer (highest)[53]

After World War II, two more Navy enlisted grades were added senior to the chief petty officer grade: senior chief petty officer and master chief petty officer, the highest navy enlisted grade. Without the higher grades of senior and master chief before and during World War II, a chief petty officer could not advance beyond chief (unless he became an officer), so he may have been frozen at chief for many, many years before retirement.[54]

Enlisted members obtain military status via an enlistment, while officers, as indicated previously, do so by an appointment. Enlisted members were either in the Regular Navy or Naval Reserve or Regular Marine Corps or Marine Corps Reserve. Regular enlisted members formed the permanent nucleus of a military service while members of the reserve augmented the regular force when needed, such as in wartime.[55]

Enlisted Insignia

Enlisted Navy grade insignia was metallic collar grade insignia or cloth chevrons for sleeves of coats or shirts.[56] Enlisted Marine Corps grade insignia, likewise, was metallic collar grade insignia or cloth chevrons for sleeves of coats or shirts.[57]

Procurement

Procurement is the process by which civilians enter the service. Enlisted members generally signed up with recruiters or were drafted. Officers could also sign up with a recruiter. Officer graduates of the Naval Academy could join the regular component of the Navy or Marine Corps. As mentioned earlier in this chapter, officers could receive reserve appointments as officers via NROTC. They could also participate in the reserve midshipman (V-7) program. Finally, officers could come from the enlisted ranks. An enlisted member who became an officer was known in slang as a mustang.

Promotions and "Tombstone Promotions"

The normal promotion for an officer or enlisted member is based on documented performance. Depending on the member's grade, a promotion board may be required. Board members examine a candidate's record and vote for or against promotion.

Three officer MOH recipients included in this book who survived the war enjoyed special promotions known as "tombstone" promotions: Fuqua, Pharris, and Ross. Such promotions, awarded without board action, were recognition of the officer's combat record. Thus, while the members served until retirement in the last grade achieved by the normal promotion process ("terminal grade"), they were promoted upon retirement to the next grade to honor their combat record as indicated by the table below.[58]

Recipient	Final Grade Achieved by Promotion Process	Retirement Grade
Fuqua	Captain	Rear admiral (two stars)
Pharris	Lieutenant	Lieutenant commander
Ross	Commander	Captain

Table 2-4. MOH "Tombstone promotions"

These promotions are honorary and permit retirees who wear their uniforms to wear the insignia of the higher grade. Tombstone refers to the grade that will appear on the recipient's tombstone; the honorary higher grade appears on the tombstone, not the permanent grade reached via the normal promotion process before retirement.[59]

Military Structure: Organization

Two articles of the U.S. Constitution govern the military. Article II appoints the President as commander in chief. Article I grants Congress power to regulate the Army and Navy.

While those articles do not change, military organizations do. During World War II, it was unlike today's organization. In 1941, the structure at the Washington, DC, level was as follows.

Commander in Chief
The President

The War Department	**Department of the Navy**
Secretary of War	Secretary of the Navy
Chief of Staff	Chief of Naval Operations

The civilian Secretary of War superintended the War Department along with the Chief of Staff, the department's senior military advisor. The department comprised the army and the army air corps, which became the Army Air Forces. Thus during the war, what is now a separate service, the Air Force, was part of the Army (Navy and Marine aviation remained and remain under the control of those services). The civilian secretary of the navy superintended the Department of the Navy. The department comprised the Navy, headed by the Chief of Naval operations (CNO), and the Marine Corps, headed by the Commandant of the Marine Corps (CMC).[60]

After World War II, Congress created the Department of Defense (DOD), which comprised separate Departments of the Army (formerly the War Department) and the Navy (formerly the Department of the Navy), and the new Department of the Air Force, which made the Air Force a separate service and moved most of the Army's aviation from the Army to the Air Force. Under the DOD, the Department of the Navy comprised two separate, coequal services: the Marine Corps and the Navy.[61]

Military Structure: Command, Responsibility, Relationships, and Customs

Command

Military organizations above certain levels will have a commanding officer; the slang for the commanding officer is "CO" or "the old man." Ships, shore installations, and ground combat units may have a commanding officer. In the Navy, on larger ships, the CO will be captain. On smaller ships, his or her grade may be commander or lieutenant commander. A commanding officer for a ground combat unit may range from a captain to a colonel with higher grades for larger units. The CO commands the officers and enlisted members of the ship or unit. He or she is responsible for the safety and efficiency of his or her command and the lives of his or her subordinates and is responsible for everything the command does or fails to do.[62]

Second in command is the executive officer, who is generally one grade below the commanding officer but in some cases may be the same grade as the commanding officer (but junior to him or her with a date of rank later than the commanding officer's). He or she may be known as the "XO" or "exec." He or she is the commanding officer's representative and assists the commanding officer in maintaining discipline, organization, and administration aboard the ship. Reports or other projects destined for action or review by the CO are routed through the executive officer.[63]

Generally, the command will also have a senior enlisted member who is the senior enlisted advisor for the commanding and executive officers and who has the most hands-on overall senior management of the command's enlisted personnel. In the Navy in World War II, the senior enlisted member was most likely a chief petty officer; in today's Navy, the senior enlisted member would most likely be a senior chief petty officer or a master chief petty officer, grades that did not, as mentioned earlier, exist in World War II.

Responsibility

Commissioned officers have special trust and confidence, which means that the military entrusts them with great responsibilities and the power to command other service members and vessels as well as the power to make important decisions, many of which mean life or death for subordinates. Accordingly, "special trust and confidence" carries with it an expectation and requirement for the highest standards of conduct and performance by an officer. For a good officer, special trust and concept is a code by which he or she lives, not just meaningless words.[64]

Two other principles also guide officers. They must lead by example, setting the example for subordinates, and they must not ask subordinates to do what they themselves would not do.[65]

Leadership in garrison (i.e., out of combat) is sufficiently challenging, but leadership in combat is the ultimate challenge for the commander since his or her decisions, wise or unwise, can put his or her charges in harm's way and can get them killed or wounded. In short, the lives of the subordinates depend on many factors, one of which is the quality of the leadership of the commander of the unit in combat.

Officer and Enlisted Relationships

Based on his personal experiences in his career as a Marine Corps officer and judge advocate in the Regular and Reserve Marine Corps from 1981 to 2011 and his familiarity with military law and customs, he can provide the following summaries concerning officer and enlisted relationships and customs, traditions, and rituals, as well as the relationship between the Marine Corps and the Navy. His summaries are also shaped by extensive conversations with World War II veterans and studying the war for years.

The relationships between officers and enlisted were and are based on military law, regulations, and customs. Because of their status, officers are owed a special degree of respect. They are saluted and called "Sir" (male) or "Ma'am" (female). Subordinates generally stand when an officer enters a room, especially a commanding officer or a flag or general officer.

Enlisted members not only owe a duty of respect to officers; they also owe a duty of obedience to legal orders from officers. The duty is considered so important that disobeying, striking, or threatening an officer during time of war are capital (death penalty) offenses.

Officer and enlisted housing areas are separate on military bases. Flag and general officer housing is usually separate from housing for officers of lower grades. Aboard ship, officers live separately from enlisted members in "officers' country." The commanding officer of a ship has his or her own stateroom and in most cases his or her own galley (kitchen).[66]

Officers do not socialize with enlisted subordinates except at command functions, and they do not eat with subordinates except in limited circumstances, such as combat (officers are supposed to be last in the "chow" line). Officers and enlisted have separate messes (dining areas), and general and flag officers have their own messes. Similarly, junior enlisted members have a duty to treat senior enlisted members with respect and obedience.

Customs, Traditions, and Rituals

The military has unique customs, traditions, and rituals not found in civilian life. They may be written, such as codified into military law, or they may be unwritten and passed from senior service members to junior service members. An example of an unwritten custom is that in the field, Marine Corps officers eat last; they eat only after all their enlisted personnel are fed. Another custom is one enlisted member not calling another enlisted member "sir," except in training and other special circumstances. Honor toward and respect for a service and one's fellow service members are also unwritten customs. Customs can be strange. For example, officers are not supposed to carry umbrellas in the rain when in uniform.[67]

The penalties for violating various customs, traditions, and rituals are left to the reader's imagination.

The Relationship between the Marine Corps and the Navy

As noted previously above, after World War II, legislation made the Marine Corps and navy separate and coequal services within the Department of the Navy.

Until that legislation made the status of the Marine Corps absolutely clear—that the Corps was a separate service coequal with the Navy—the relationship between the Marine Corps and the Navy was, to say the least, undefined and murky at an institutional level. While the average Marine and average Navy member got along well (particularly Marines and corpsmen, who provided medical care to Marines), the relationship between senior Navy and Marine officers was at times strained; the tension could be palpable as the Marine Corps asserted its independence and needs and the Navy tried to limit it and them. The relationship worked well sometimes, but at other times, it was openly hostile with senior leaders arguing about various topics, such as how much naval gunfire would be provided before Marines landed on an island.

A key point—if not the key point—is that the Marine Corps never wanted to (or wants to, present tense) be referred to as "part of the Navy" or to be called "Naval infantry." To use a colloquial expression, "Them's fight'n' words." A speaker uttering those words to a marine should be beyond the reach of the marine's fist. Marines are never called "soldiers" or "troopers," which are Army terms. Marines can be called "troops"; they can be called "sea soldiers," appropriate since Marines are connected to ships on the seas.[68]

Legislation in 1798 established the Marine Corps. *"Nowhere in the Act is the Marine Corps described as part of the Navy, or of the Army. The working of the Act led to much argument for many years as to the legal status of the Marine Corps with respect to the other armed services of the Federal Government."* (Italics added for emphasis.)[69] Thus a compromise was reached during World War II; the Marine Corps was part of the "Naval Establishment," not part of the Navy or the Department of the Navy, but was supervised by that department.[69] Under this compromise, the head of the Marine Corps—the Commandant—reported to the Secretary of the Navy and not to the Chief of Naval Operations; also, the when reporting to the Secretary—and this is crucial—the Commandant reported to him directly and not via the chief of naval operations.

While the services were not, by law, separate and coequal during the war, the Marine Corps certainly acted, or tried to act, as if they were. Today, by law, they are coequal services under the Department of the Navy.

Notes

1. J. W. Bunkley, Rear Admiral, United States Navy, Retired, MILITARY and NAVAL RECOGNITION BOOK (D. Van Nostrand Company, Inc., New York, NY, 1943), 127–128 (hereafter "Bunkley, MILITARY and NAVAL RECOGNITION BOOK").

2. Colonel Charles A. Jones, U.S. Marine Corps Reserve (Retired), Hawaii's World War II Military Sites (Mutual Publishing, Honolulu, HI, 2002), 8 (hereafter "Jones, Hawaii's World War II Military Sites").

3. All the ships mentioned in this book are so designated. See also endnote 2: Jones, Hawaii's World War II Military Sites, 8–10.

4. Ibid., 8; Bureau of Naval Personnel, SEAMANSHIP ("NAVPERS 16118," U.S. Navy, Training, Standards and Curriculum Division, June 1944), 33 (hereafter "SEAMANSHIP").

5. See Chapters 4 to 7, 9, and 19 of this book ("Battleship Sailor" MOHs).

6. Endnote 4, SEAMANSHIP, 33; endnote 2, Jones, Hawaii's World War II Military Sites, 8.

7. Endnote 4, SEAMANSHIP, 58.

8. Endnote 1, Bunkley, MILITARY and NAVAL RECOGNITION BOOK), 130; endnote 2, Jones, Hawaii's World War II Military Sites, 9.

9. Endnote 1, Bunkley, MILITARY and NAVAL RECOGNITION BOOK, 123.

10. Endnote 4, SEAMANSHIP, 35–37.

11. Endnote 2, Jones, Hawaii's World War II Military Sites, 9.

12. Ibid.; endnote 4, SEAMANSHIP, 38–40.

13. Endnote 4, SEAMANSHIP, 40.

14. Theodore Roscoe, United States Destroyer Operations in World War II (United States Naval Institute, Annapolis, MD, 1953), 297 (hereafter, "Roscoe, United States Destroyer Operations in World War II.")

15. Ibid., 40.

16. Endnote 15, Roscoe, United States Destroyer Operations in World War II, 298.

17. Ibid.

18. James L. George, History of Warships (Naval Institute Press, 1998), 1–151 (discussion of post–World War II destroyer developments and modifications).

19. Endnote 4, SEAMANSHIP, 46 ("AG") and 47 ("AR").

20. Naval History and Heritage Command. "U.S. Navy Ships: Launching and Commissioning" (information sheet published January 6, 2015), printed from the Internet October 13, 2015.

21. Endnote 4, SEAMANSHIP, 120–129 (discussion of "Organization of the Ship).

22. Endnote 4, SEAMANSHIP, 122.

23. United States Naval Institute, The Bluejackets' Manual: United States Navy, 10th ed. (United States Naval Institute, Annapolis, MD, 1940), 215–234 (drills). See Chapters 4 (*California*) and 6 (*West Virginia*) concerning the importance of counterflooding. As noted in his MOH citation, Jackson Pharris ordered counterflooding of *California*, saving the ship from capsizing. As noted in the ship's after-action report, *West Virginia* also counterflooded. Each ship had torpedo holes in her port side hulls, allowing water to enter the ship, so the ships had to counterflood from the starboard sides.

24. Testimony of Lieutenant Commander Fuqua on January 2, 1942, before the Roberts Commission, included in the report of the 1945 Congressional investigation of the attack found in HEARINGS BEFORE THE JOINT COMMITTEE ON THE INVESTIGATION OF THE PEARL HARBOR ATTACK (U.S. Government Printing Office, 1946), Part 23, 632–633.

25. Colonel Robert D. Heinl, US Marine Corps (Retired), The Marine Officer's Guide (Naval Institute Press, 1977), 535–538 (hereafter "Heinl, The Marine Officer's Guide").

26. Endnote 4, SEAMANSHIP, 49; author's knowledge having served in the Regular Marine Corps from 1981 to 1992 and being deployed twice on Navy ships.

27. United States Code, Title 10, Section 101(b)(7) ("grade") and (8) ("rank").

28. Endnote 4, SEAMANSHIP, 9; the reference incorrectly Uses the term rank for grade; author's experience as a Marine officer.

29. Peter Grier, "The Highest Ranking," AIR FORCE MAGAZINE (March 2012): 50–54 (discussion of the five-star grade).

30. U.S. Marine Corps History Division, Biographies of General Thomas Holcomb, U.S. Marine Corps, and General Alexander Vandegrift, Marine Corps, accessed on the Internet October 6, 2015.

31. Endnote 4, SEAMANSHIP, 9.

32. Ibid.

33. Ibid.

34. Clark G. Reynolds, Famous American Admirals (U.S. Naval Institute Press, Annapolis, MD, 2002), vi–vii.

35. United States Code, Title 10, Section 5501 (4) and (5).

36. Endnote 2, Jones, Hawaii's World War II Military Sites, 10.

37. Chapter 8 (*Vestal*).

38. Dictionary.com, s.v. "Mister," accessed October 6, 2015.

39. Endnote 25, Heinl, The Marine Officer's Guide, 561.

40. Endnote 1: "Bunkley, MILITARY and NAVAL RECOGNITION BOOK"), 89–90. Endnote 25: Heinl, The Marine Officer's Guide, 60; author's military experience having been in both components of the Marine Corps, the Regular Marine Corps and the Reserve Marine Corps.

41. An example is Fuqua's acceptance of an appointment as an ensign in the Navy, not the Naval Reserve, upon his graduation from the Naval Academy. The National Personnel Records Center, St. Louis, Missouri, furnished military and personal information from Fuqua's Official Military Personnel File (OMPF) at the author's requests. One request was fulfilled by sending the author a compact disc with the entire (OMPF). The acceptance of his appointment as an ensign in the Navy can be found at Section 01: Service Documents, frames 2–4.

42. Endnote 43, Bunkley, MILITARY and NAVAL RECOGNITION BOOK, 90.

43. Endnote 25, Heinl, The Marine Officer's Guide, 279.

44. Ibid., 60; author's experience as a Marine officer serving with the Navy.

45. Ibid.

46. Endnote 4, SEAMANSHIP, 11.

47. Ibid.

48. Ibid.

49. Ibid., 10–11.

50. Gordon L. Rottman, U.S. Marine Corps World War II Order of Battle (Greenwood Publishing Group, Westport, CT, 2002), 578.

51. Endnote 2, Jones, Hawaii's World War II Military Sites, 11.

52. Ibid.

53. Endnote 4, SEAMANSHIP, 408.

54. Ibid.

55. Members not officers, chief warrant officers, or warrant officers, are called "enlisted" because they join the service via enlistments.

56. Endnote 4, SEAMANSHIP, 14–15, refer to an insignia chart.

57. Endnote 1, Bunkley, MILITARY and NAVAL RECOGNITION BOOK, Plate 23 (opposite page 201) shows Marine Corps chevrons.

58. Fuqua promotion, see Chapter 7 (*Arizona*); Ross promotion, see Chapter 9 (*Nevada*); Pharris promotion, see Chapter 19 (*California*); see also chapter 1.

59. Bruce D. Callandar, "When Is a Major Not (Exactly) a Major?" AIR FORCE MAGAZINE (November 1996), 56. The author has personally seen the grades of rear admiral and lieutenant commander, respectively, inscribed on the Fuqua and Pharris tombstones at Arlington National Cemetery (most recent visit in 2015). In 2015, the author saw a photograph of the Ross "In Memory Of" marker at Beverly, Kansas; his grade on the marker is captain.

60. United States Information Service, United States Government Manual (Executive Office of the President, Office of Government Reports, Washington, DC, March 1941), War Department, 213–214, and Department of the Navy, 243–244 and 262 (the Marine Corps).

61. Endnote 25, Heinl, The Marine Officer's Guide, 15.

62. Endnote 4, SEAMANSHIP, 120.

63. Ibid., 121.

64. Endnote 25, Heinl, The Marine Officer's Guide, 261. The phrase "special trust and confidence" is found in an officer's commission.

65. Ibid., 368 (setting an example).

66. Ibid., 687 ("officers' country").

67. Ibid., 375 (officers eat last).

68. Ibid., 689 and 692.

69. Rear Admiral Augustus Furer, U.S. Navy Retired, Administration of the Navy Department in World War II (U.S. Government Printing Office, Washington, DC, 1959), 547–548.

Part II

Menace and Mess– History Written in Dark Ink*

*Mr. Reed G. Landis, Regional Vice President, American Airlines, Inc., in a letter of June 21, 1941, to Mr. E. G. B. Riley, Hearings (May 31, 1945) before SUBCOMMITTEE NO. 8 OF THE COMMITTEE ON MILITARY AFFAIRS, HOUSE OF REPRESENTATIVES, SEVENTY-NINTH CONGRESS, FIRST SESSION on H. R. 2227 and Other Bills (authorizing the president to award a posthumoUS MOH in the name of Congress to William Mitchell) (Washington, DC: US Government Printing Office, 1945), [12]; Landis wrote that if Mitchell's ideas about aviation had been adopted and properly executed before World War II that they "might very well have resulted in a substantial change in world history from that which has been written in such dark ink since 1930."

CHAPTER 2
THE ATTACKS ON DECEMBER 7, 1941—
TWENTY-FIVE MINUTES LATE

INTRODUCTION

The attack on Oahu on December 7, 1941, cannot truly be understood, nor its effects felt, without visiting Pearl Harbor and the USS *Arizona* Memorial and the Pearl Harbor Visitor Center. All the movies, television specials, books, pamphlets, maps, and other media are for naught; a visceral understanding and experience are needed for complete comprehension of the attack and the actions for which the fifteen MOHs were awarded for actions on December 7. One can even get a feel for the other MOHs awarded for actions that evening on Midway—if one knows about the Midway MOH.

But since most Americans cannot or will not visit Oahu, words must suffice to describe the indescribable. Japanese naval aviation conducted a withering, unrelenting surprise attack, spraying all types of ordnance on Oahu on a peaceful Sunday morning, killing and wounding men and destroying and damaging ships and property. This attack had three primary aspects.

1) It prevented the U.S. Pacific Fleet from interfering with Japanese military aggression.

2) It answered a question that had been causing friction between the United States and Japan long before the attack, a question arising from the Japanese military aggression just mentioned: "Can we settle the diplomatic differences between the United States and Japan peacefully?" The attack was Japan's premeditated, well-planned, emphatic "No" to that question.

3) An attack with no warning was, without question, within the national character of Japan and individual Japanese combatants. The requirement in the Hague Convention that a signatory must give "previous and explicit warning" before commencing hostilities against another signatory was due to Japan's surprise attack on Russia in 1904 at the beginning of the Japanese-Russian War.[1]

In this context, what are the mechanics of the "date which will live in infamy"? What plans and weapons led to the circumstances sending eighteen World War II MOH citations across the desks of two different U.S. Presidents?

WHAT IS HAWAII?

People refer to Hawaii in a general sense, usually meaning "Oahu." The Hawaiian Islands or Hawaiian Island Archipelago comprises a group of many islands, including Oahu (Honolulu and Pearl Harbor are there), Hawaii ("the Big Island"), Maui, and Midway Atoll.[2]

Since Hawaii was, on December 7, a territory of the United State, the abbreviation "T.H." (Territory of Hawaii) is often seen. Hawaii became the fiftieth state on August 21, 1959.[3]

Political Context of the Attack
Japanese Aggression

The December 7 attacks bringing forth the sixteen MOH awards for that date were the culmination of a dizzying, complicated series of diplomatic, political, and military events occurring over many years that soured the relationship between the United States and Japan. Since numerous books, articles, movies, and documentaries have examined and debated, in detail, the reasons for war between the United States and Japan, only a general overview of the events leading to war will follow.

The basic source of friction was ongoing Japanese aggression and American measures, short of military response, to counter that aggression, particularly in China, where Japan progressively and brutally seized land and resources by military force.[4]

Three events are crucial in Japan's conduct in China. One, Japan invaded the Chinese region of Manchuria in 1931 after the Mukden Incident. Two, Japan invaded China full-scale after the Marco Polo Bridge Incident in July 1937, sparing no measure of brutality in its treatment of the Chinese. To say that the Japanese terrified the Chinese is a gross understatement. As a horrified but do-nothing world saw and heard, no atrocity or inhumane gesture was off limits. The Japanese bombed, raped, and executed by beheading, shooting, bayonetting, and burying or burning the living. Three, on December 12, 1937, Japanese naval aircraft sank the U.S. Navy gunboat Panay. Japanese aircraft even strafed the boats with Panay survivors headed ashore. Two sailors and one civilian passenger died of wounds. Eleven officers and men were seriously wounded. Japan avoided war by apologizing and offering reparations, claiming the attack was a mistake (the ship's American flag was purportedly mistaken for a Chinese flag), but the navy's investigation concluded the attack was deliberate. The United States, to avoid war, accepted Japanese reparations and falsehoods.[5]

Japanese aggression continued unchecked. Typical of Japan or any other aggressive country, it camouflaged truth by words and titles. A postwar U.S. Army Air Forces report incisively wrote the following about the reality of Japanese aggression before December 7, using blunt wartime language and tones with a refreshing lack of political correctness and no concern whatsoever that the language might offend the Japanese or anyone else. After an introduction, reading in part, "Critics scoffed, but air power beat Japan" is the following:

> The Japs had something which we didn't have. They had a scheme. It was a grandiose scheme that befitted true Sons of Heaven. We came to know of it as "The Greater East Asia Co-prosperity Sphere." *The name was illusory because it entailed a great deal more than Asia and had nothing whatever to do with co-prosperity.*[6] [Italics added for emphasis.]

In this atmosphere, the United States struggled with how to use diplomatic measures, such as embargoes, to deter Japan from aggression when those very measures deprived Japan of resources it needed. But depriving Japan of resources could backfire. Japan could decide to take resources by force anywhere, thus triggering war.

A key response to Japan's aggression was moving the Pacific Fleet from the West Coast to Pearl Harbor in April 1940 to impress Japan. In May 1940, the move became permanent.[7]

Some in the U.S. military questioned the move's wisdom and Fleet security in Pearl Harbor. Admiral Joseph Richardson, Commander-in-Chief, U.S. Pacific Fleet (CINPACFLT), disagreed with the move, believing Pearl Harbor was vulnerable to attack. The harbor had only one entrance, which was narrow; ships could not disperse in Pearl Harbor; and Pearl Harbor's defenses were inadequate. Oahu was far removed from supply sources, requiring slow transportation of supplies from the United States, and lacked adequate housing, recreation, and fleet support.[8] For expressing his concerns explicitly, Richardson was relieved of command and reverted from admiral (four stars) to his permanent grade of rear admiral; the grade of admiral was temporary and held only while acting as CINPACFLT. Rear Admiral Husband Kimmel was promoted from rear admiral to admiral and became CINPACFLT.[9]

Another concern was antitorpedo nets, which Navy commanders did not use since conventional thinking was that ships in shallow harbors (such as Pearl Harbor) were safe from torpedo attack because torpedoes dropped from airplanes traveled downward a hundred feet or more upon hitting the water before leveling off and heading toward their targets. Thus, torpedoes dropped in Pearl Harbor would hit bottom, rendering them useless.[10]

Basing the Fleet at Pearl Harbor had one advantage; it placed the Fleet closer to Japan in case of war, but proximity to Japan was a two-edged sword. The Fleet was now approximately 2,200 miles closer to Japan, making a Japanese attack much easier since the Japanese had less distance to travel to reach Oahu.[11] Japan's ability to attack the Fleet on the West Coast of the United States was doubtful. Sailing undetected from Japan to California was one thing; sailing undetected from Japan to Oahu was quite another—and quite possible. Few men in the U.S. military realized it was also quite probable. On December 7, that probability was realized via a nasty surprise.

Military Doctrine Context of the Attack: Conventional Versus Unconventional

Certain events and one prediction placed the U.S. military on notice that Pearl Harbor could be attacked successfully from the air, but conventional military doctrine and thinking rejected any indications that such an attack was possible. Conventional thinking rejected any event or theory, no matter the possibility or probability of the event or theory, inconsistent with that conventional thinking. Examples follow.

Conventional thinking was that Oahu would be attacked by submarine, not by air.[12] Japan used five midget submarines during the attack, but their effectiveness was minimal. In fact, the planners did not want submarines at all, but to prevent the submariners from being left out, Japan's navy insisted that they be part of the attack. They had no advantage worth the risk the attack planners feared; submarines would be discovered and thus compromise surprise. That compromise was almost realized when USS Ward sank a submarine before the attack in the channel leading to Pearl Harbor from the Pacific Ocean, but the sinking's report raised no alarm. The submarines backfired, giving America a public relations coup—the first prisoner of war. Soldiers captured one member of the two-man crew of a submarine after she beached at Bellows Air Station on Oahu's eastern shore, far from Pearl Harbor.[13]

As discussed in the following section, the most important event challenging conventional thinking was the British attacking Italian ships in port at Taranto, Italy, and the most important human aspect was Billy Mitchell's brain and mouth.

First, as mentioned earlier, conventional thinking was that ships were safe from torpedo attack in a shallow harbor, thinking persisting notwithstanding the British aerial attack against Italian ships in port at Taranto, Italy, in 1940.[15] The Navy's Chief of Naval Operations (CNO), Admiral Harold Stark, knew about Taranto; its implications for an attack on Pearl Harbor concerned him such that he wrote a letter for Secretary of the Navy Frank Knox to sign and to send to Secretary of War Henry Stimson, warning about the danger of attack facing Pearl Harbor and suggesting improvements in its defenses. The letter was dated January 24, 1941.[16]

Kimmel, the new Fleet commander, knew about the Taranto attack, but in a February 15, 1941, letter to the CNO explained why he did not think antitorpedo nets were necessary in Pearl Harbor, notwithstanding Taranto. He thought the harbor's shallow depth made nets unnecessary.[17] The Japanese certainly knew about the Taranto attack, although one attack planner, Minoru Genda, said "unequivocally" that Taranto did not influence Japanese planning for Pearl Harbor.[18]

Second, conventional thinking held that the surface ship, particularly the battleship, was superior to airpower, thinking persisting notwithstanding the actions and observations of Army aviator Brigadier General Billy Mitchell, airpower's great exponent in the 1920s and 1930s. Since the U.S. Air Force was not a separate service until after World War II, Mitchell and his pilots were Army officers. Mitchell flew in combat in World War I, earning a Distinguished Service Cross, the Army decoration second only to the MOH. As discussed in the Introduction, this chapter, and Chapters 3 and 20, his advocacy of airpower included ship-sinking trials in the 1920s, proving the vulnerability of ships to air attack. He also predicted the Japanese would attack Oahu, and he reported that Oahu's defenses were inadequate. His prediction and report were ignored. His sympathizers called him a "prophet without honor."[19]

Mitchell's first challenge to conventional thinking was to tell Congress in 1920 that his aircraft could sink any battleship in existence and to lobby for bombing trials during which his aircraft could attack ships to prove what he said. The Navy opposed the tests but could not stop them, especially with Congress urging the Navy to provide ships for testing. The Navy then agreed to joint testing with the Army, but the power of the "battleship admirals" (Navy leadership opposing airpower) made the test parameters as difficult as possible for Mitchell. Mitchell received as targets old American ships and ships taken from Germany after World War I. His aircraft sank the ships off the coasts of Virginia in 1921 and North Carolina in 1923, proving surface ships vulnerable to air attack. But in fairness to the Navy, one must acknowledge that the ships were derelicts not defending themselves against air attack. Mitchell was simply bombing old stationary ships.[20]

The Navy tried a sneak attack against Mitchell by conducting its own bombing test in 1920, bombing an old battleship. The report, kept secret until the Navy was forced to release it, concluded that aircraft sinking or crippling a battleship was improbable. In fact, the Navy had rigged the tests by bombing the ship with dummy bombs. Explosives placed on the ship were detonated to sink her.[21]

Mitchell's next challenge to conventional thinking was a report he wrote after his trip to the Far East during 1923–24, including visits to Japan and Hawaii. After studying Japanese progress in military aviation, he prepared the report of his trip, including a prediction that the Japanese would attack Ford Island at 7:30 a.m., a prediction off by only twenty-five minutes—the attack started at 7:55 a.m. The War Department suppressed his report, releasing it only after congressional "prodding."[22]

Mitchell visited Pearl Harbor, where he found the Army responsible for protecting the Pacific Fleet with Army fighter aircraft and antiaircraft guns. Mitchell believed the defense of the Hawaiian Islands against air attack inadequate. He recommended more aircraft for interception and defense, believing Oahu had too few fighters and that antiaircraft guns on the ground would be inadequate defense against massed air attack.[23]

The Navy continued to believe that battleships were the most important part of the fleet and that other ships were subordinate to and in support of it. This belief flew in the face of the success of the Mitchell ship-sinking tests; his prediction that Japan would attack Pearl Harbor; and his report about the inadequacy of Hawaiian defenses. Paradoxically, however, the Navy continued to develop naval aviation, but carriers were seen as ancillary to battleships.[24]

One wonders if Navy leaders noticed naval aviation's role in sinking Germany's behemoth Bismarck. Although not sunk by naval aviation, a torpedo launched by a British aircraft based on an aircraft carrier damaged her such that British ships could sink her. As one airpower advocate wrote, "Once a battleship is disabled, the manner of its final disposition is of relatively minor importance."[25]

Perhaps the high-water mark of the arrogance of the pre-December 7 "battleship navy" was a photograph and caption in, of all places, the program for the Army-Navy football game on November 29, 1941—just days before December 7. Ironically the photograph was of USS *Arizona*, which would soon be the unfortunate and ultimate nautical symbol of the end of battleship supremacy. The caption reads as follows:

Right—A bow on view of the USS *Arizona* as she plows into a huge swell. It is significant that despite the claims of air enthusiasts no battleship has yet been sunk by bombs.

The caption was insulting, to say the least. Only simpletons would not realize it was a slap at Mitchell and airpower advocates—"air enthusiasts" was the demeaning term for them. It was also misleading, since some of the ships Mitchell sank were battleships, although not sunk in combat conditions. A more accurate caption would read, "It is

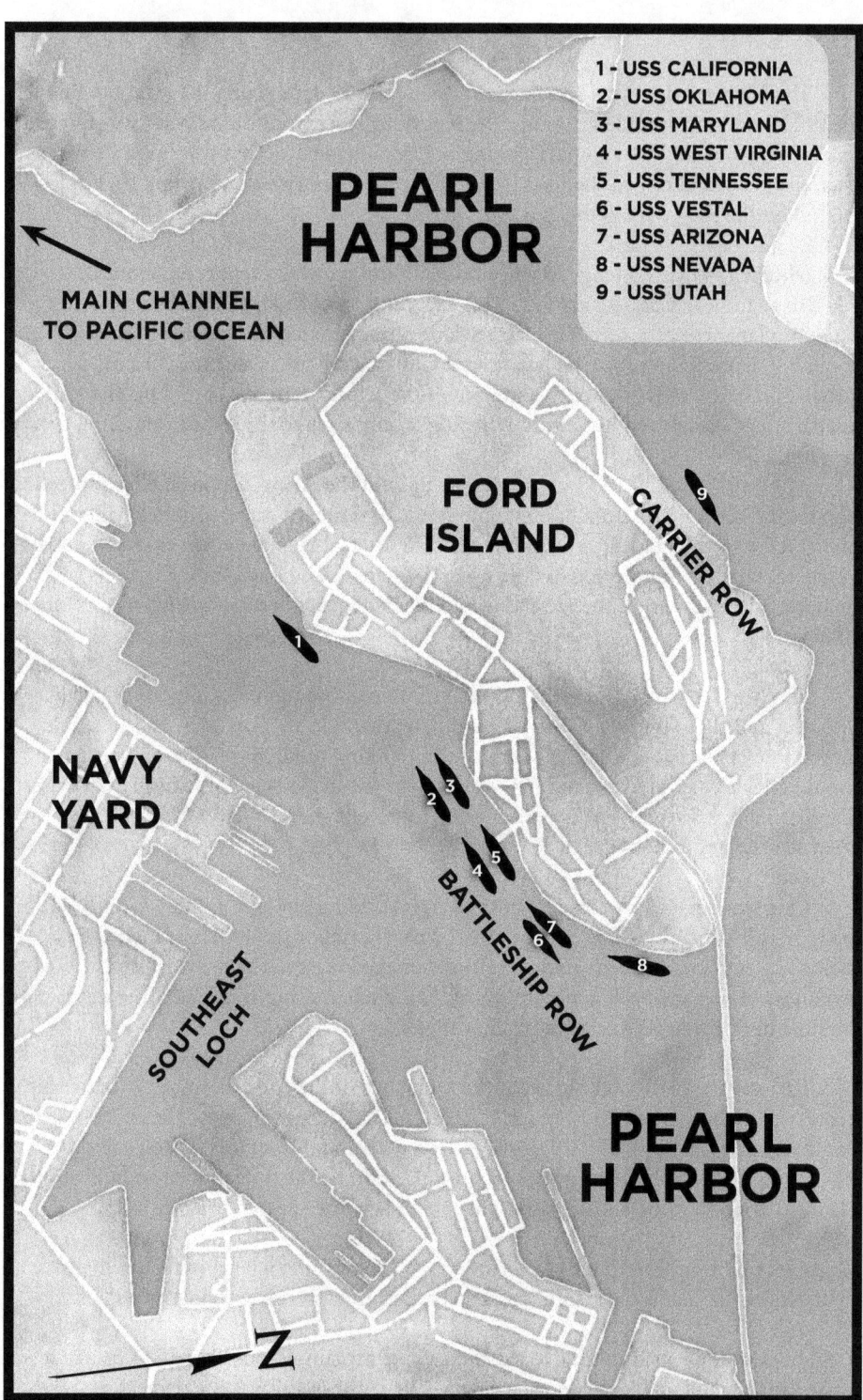

Ford Island and "Battleship Row" December 7, 1941

Ship	Type of Ship	Number	Berth	Mooring
USS California	Battleship	BB-44	F-3	Moored Alone
USS *Neosho*	Oiler	AO-23	F-4	Moored Alone
USS *Maryland*	Battleship	BB-46	F-5	Inboard of *Oklahoma*
USS *Oklahoma*	Battleship	BB-37	F-5	Outboard of Maryland
USS *Tennessee*	Battleship	BB-43	F-6	Inboard of *West Virginia*
USS *West Virginia*	Battleship	BB-48	F-6	Outboard of Tennessee
USS *Arizona*	Battleship	BB-39	F-7	Inboard of Vestal
USS *Vestal*	Repair Ship	AR-4	F-7	Outboard of Arizona
USS *Nevada*	Battleship	BB-36	F-8	Moored Alone

Table 2-1. Mooring plan for ships on December 7.

Berth	Inboard Ship	Outboard Ship
F-5	USS *Maryland*	USS *Oklahoma*
F-6	USS *Tennessee*	USS *West Virginia*
F-7	USS *Arizona*	USS *Vestal*

Table 2-2. Ships moored in pairs on December 7.

significant that despite the claims of Brigadier General Billy Mitchell and his followers that no battleship has yet been sunk by bombs in combat conditions." [Changes indicated in italics.] The photograph and caption are at the end of this chapter.

The bloodshed and sunken and damaged ships on December 7 in Pearl Harbor rendered both photograph and caption an interesting, inaccurate historic relic. The remainder of this chapter shows how Japan rewrote the caption such that—unfortunately—a new photograph of a destroyed *Arizona* would be required if the display were ever repeated.[26]

U.S. Military Installations on Oahu

While U.S. military installations were at various places throughout Hawaii, the installations at which the MOHs were earned on December 7 were on Oahu and Midway.

On Oahu, Pearl Harbor had three major installations—the Navy Yard, Submarine Base, and Luke Field, established in 1917 and named Luke Field for World War I ace Frank Luke, the first U.S. aviator earning a MOH. In 1923, Naval Air Station Pearl Harbor was established on Ford Island. The Navy Yard and shipyard were the primary installations supporting the fleet.[27]

Also on Oahu, Naval Air Station, Kaneohe Bay, had patrol squadrons flying PBY "Catalina" seaplanes (see Chapter 11).

Tandem mooring at Ford Island and "Battleship Row" December 7, 1941

One MOH was earned at Midway Atoll, which is part of the Hawaiian Islands. Midway had a naval air station and marines from the Sixth Defense Battalion assigned as a defensive force (see Chapter 12 (Midway)).

Ford Island as Ground Zero: Air Station and Ship Moorage

Primarily the story of the MOHs in the Hawaiian Islands on December 7, 1941, centers on Ford Island, an island inside Pearl Harbor and the attack's ground zero. Of the fifteen MOHs awarded for actions during the attack on Oahu, fourteen went to men in ships moored around Ford Island. Thirteen recipients were on Battleship Row, and one was on Carrier Row.

Ford Island was more than an air station. Ships could be moored around it, tied either to piers or to large white mooring quays (pronounced "keys" or "kways") in the water just off the island. These positions for mooring were called "berths," numbered such as "F-7" and called "Fox 7" with "Fox" representing the letter F.[28]

Ford Island was home to the famous Battleship Row since battleships were moored in an area running from approximately the southeast to the northeast corners of the island (berths F-2 to F-8). Battleship Row was across the channel from the Navy Yard and the shipyard (which later became a separate command), Southeast Loch, and Submarine Base.[29]

Lesser known was the side of Ford Island opposite Battleship Row, running from approximately the southwest corner to the northwest corner (opposite the Pearl City Peninsula). Berths F-9 to F-13 was here. It was called Carrier Row, since F-10 and F-11 were designated as carrier berths; carriers also used F-9.[30]

The Opposing Fleets

U.S. Pacific Fleet

While Kimmel was primarily CINCPACFLT, he assumed an additional duty as Commander-in-Chief, U.S. Fleet (CINCUS), an administrative organization comprising the Pacific, Asiatic, and Atlantic Fleets (for obvious reasons, "CINCUS" ("sink US") would later be changed).[31]

For operational purposes, Pacific Fleet was divided into task forces, each comprising various types of ships and commands. As of December 7, the Fleet had nine task forces, each with its own commander, and all under CINCPACFLT's overall command.[32]

For administrative purposes, Pacific Fleet was divided into three force commanders: battle force, scouting force, and base force. Each force had various "type commanders," who commanded all ships or aircraft of a certain type, such as battleships or cruisers. The commanders reported to a force commander, who reported to CINCPACFLT.[33]

Rear Admiral Claude C. Bloch, Commandant, Fourteenth Naval District, commanded all navy land facilities on Oahu, commanding installations, such as Pearl Harbor Navy Yard, instead of combat commands, such as the Fleet.[34]

BATTLESHIP ROW: BATTLESHIP ORGANIZATION

The battleships were grouped into three divisions (Battleship Division or "BatDiv"), numbered 1, 2, and 4 (no 3). A rear admiral (Commander, Battleship Division or "ComBatDiv") commanded each division, comprising three battleships, each of which had a captain (commanding officer) who was a captain (grade).[35] MOH recipient Isaac Kidd commanded Battleship Division One , and MOH recipients Mervyn Bennion and Franklin Van Valkenburgh commanded battleships. [36]

Ironically, the large battleship guns were useless on December 7 against aerial attack; intended for surface combat and shore bombardment, they could not fire on the attacking aircraft. Elevation was limited, and even if the guns could be raised to sufficient height to aim at aircraft and loaded with some kind of antiaircraft ammunition, the shot would risk hitting friendly forces, such as other ships and aircraft, and where such projectiles would fall at the end of their trajectories would be unpredictable.

BATTLESHIP MOORING ON DECEMBER 7

On December 7, Battleship Row presented the Japanese a dream target. Seven of eight battleships at Pearl Harbor—*California, Maryland, Oklahoma, Tennessee, West Virginia, Arizona, and Nevada*—were moored along Battleship Row. Pennsylvania was in Dry Dock 1 at the shipyard across the channel from Ford Island.[37]

The mooring of the ships on December 7 was crucial (see the tables on page 10 and the diagram on page 20).

Since the battleships were pointed toward the channel entrance so they could leave the harbor more quickly, their starboard sides faced Ford Island and thus were protected from torpedo attack. Unlike the battleships, however, repair ship *Vestal* was headed away from the channel and moored next to *Arizona*, so her port side was against *Arizona* and protected from torpedo attack, but her starboard side was exposed to torpedoes.[38]

Policy was to moor carriers, battleships, and cruisers singly, space permitting. On December 7, some ships had to be moored in pairs since much of the Fleet was in port. For ships moored in pairs or in tandem (table 5-2), the inboard ship was tied to the mooring quays just off Ford Island. Two features of inboard ship mooring protected inboard ships from torpedo attack. Ford Island protected their starboard sides, and the outboard ships protected their port sides. But such protection came at a price; the inboard ships were trapped between the outboard ships and Ford Island and, being unable to move, were at the mercy of aerial bombardment. *Vestal* and the tanker Neosho were the only ships on Battleship Row that were not battleships.[39]

Carrier Row

U.S. aircraft carriers meant luck because none were in Pearl Harbor on December 7. That was very good luck for the United States and very bad luck for Japan. Saratoga was at San Diego; Lexington sailing to Midway Atoll; and Enterprise sailing to Oahu. Moored at Carrier Row were the seaplane tender Tangier, the target and gunnery ship Utah, and cruisers Raleigh and Detroit.[40]

Marine Corps Role on Oahu

The army was primarily responsible for defending Oahu, but the Marine Corps provided security at three locations: the Navy Yard and Naval Air Stations at Ford Island and Kaneohe Bay. The Japanese eviscerated the one marine air station: Ewa at Barbers Point. Marines from defense battalions, whose mission was to defend navy installations, were also at Pearl Harbor. Finally, Marines were stationed in Marine detachments aboard various ships at Pearl Harbor—eight battleships, six cruisers, and Utah, an auxiliary ship used as a target and for gunnery training.[41]

The Japanese Fleet

In January 1941, Admiral Isoroku Yamamoto, Commander-in-Chief, Combined Fleet, conceived the idea of attacking the U.S. Pacific Fleet to prevent it from threatening future Japanese expansion in Asia.[42] Two officers of his staff, Lieutenant Commander Minoru Genda and Commander Mitsuo Fuchida, played crucial roles in attack planning and training.[43]

The hallmarks of the attack planning were great deliberation, superb attention to detail, and detailed intelligence gathering, providing golden knowledge of Pearl Harbor and the Fleet's operating and mooring procedures. A 1945 magazine article titled "The Japs Hear Things, Too" stated, "The Japanese intelligence service has long been smart, devious and effective."[44] The Japanese had great knowledge and judgment in selecting which weapons would be used to attack specific targets, knowledge obtained partially from a highly competent spy network on Oahu. As explained later, special attention would have to be given to ships moored in pairs around Ford Island; each ship would require a different type of weapon.

The Kido Butai—strike force—sent to attack Oahu comprised two elements.[45]

The first element, the First Air Fleet, comprised six aircraft carriers and supporting ships. The carrier Akagi was the flagship of Vice Admiral Chuichi Nagumo, who commanded the First Air Fleet and was overall task force commander.[46] Two destroyers forming the Midway Neutralization Force bombarded Midway on the evening of December 7.[47] The second element, the Advance Force, comprised a cruiser flagship and twenty-seven submarines, whose missions were to torpedo U.S. ships escaping Pearl Harbor and to protect Japanese carriers. Five submarines each carried a Type-A midget submarine, with two-man crews and two torpedoes, whose mission was attacking Pearl Harbor.[48]

Japanese Weapons

At Oahu, three types of naval aircraft flying from aircraft carriers figured prominently on December 7 in attacking ships and stations that were homes to the MOH recipients.[49]

Zeroes

Made by Mitsubishi (whose plant the author's father's B-29 probably bombed during the war) was the A6M Type 00 carrier-borne fighters, known as Zekes or Zeroes, the best naval aviation fighters early in the war. The Zero's mission was to protect dive and horizontal bombers; to strafe ground targets, particularly fighters; and to engage airborne U.S. fighters.

Vals

Made by Aichi were the D3A Type 99 bombers known as Vals. The Val's mission was to dive-bomb and to strafe ships and installations. Vals were vertical bombers or "dive bombers" because they dropped bombs while diving almost directly vertically at targets. A Val is easily identified by its large fixed two-wheel landing gear that could not be retracted during flight. The Val also has an aiming tube atop the fuselage in front of the canopy in front of the pilot.

Kates

Made by Nakajima was the B5N2 Type 97 horizontal bomber known as the "Kate." Kates could fulfill two roles while flying horizontally: dropping bombs and dropping torpedoes. They could carry one torpedo, one special armor-piercing bomb made from a naval shell (1,750 pounds), or one large bomb (550 pounds) and six small bombs (125 pounds). Their mission at Oahu was to attack battleships and aircraft carriers.

Which Weapon for Which Ship?

Pearl Harbor itself and the mooring plan of the battleships required special weapons for the Kates. As explained earlier, when ships were moored in pairs around Ford Island, one ship was inboard, the other outboard. If the bows of both ships were pointed toward the channel leading from Pearl Harbor to the Pacific Ocean, each ship's starboard (right) side would be facing Ford Island. The inboard ship would be protected from torpedo attack on her starboard side—the Japanese could not drop torpedoes on Ford Island to hit the starboard side of ships—and on her port side by the starboard side of the outboard ship. Thus the inboard ship, immune to hull attack, had to be attacked from above.

For ships—outboard or moored singly—pointing toward the channel leading to the Pacific Ocean, port sides were exposed to Pearl Harbor's waters and therefore to torpedoes.

Thus the attack plan required torpedoes for ships with hulls exposed to the water, so torpedoes would be dropped in Pearl Harbor or Southeast Loch, conveniently located, for the Japanese, directly across from Battleship Row, and aimed at the port sides of *Oklahoma* and *West Virginia* and the starboard side of *Vestal* (she alone had a bow pointing away from the channel). Also, torpedoes could be used against the port sides of *California* and *Nevada* since they were moored singly. Bombs from Vals or Kates would be used for inboard ships with hulls protected from torpedo attack: Maryland beside *Oklahoma*; Tennessee beside *West Virginia*; and *Arizona* beside *Vestal*.[50]

Torpedoes and bombs had problems, however.

The torpedo problem was due to the shallow waters of Pearl Harbor, which, as explained earlier, excluded conventional torpedo attack. Previously the Japanese dropped torpedoes from heights exceeding three hundred feet; the torpedoes sank from one hundred to three hundred feet before leveling, so if dropped in Pearl Harbor, they would stick in the bottom—until Genda's solutions: launching torpedoes from lower altitudes and adding wooden fins to torpedoes that limited the depth they sank after hitting water.

The bomb problem was due to the thick deck armor on battleships—until the Japanese developed a weapon specifically for the inboard ships: a 1,750-pound armor-piercing bomb that was a naval shell converted for the horizontal aerial bombing of battleships, a bomb sufficiently powerful to penetrate the deck armor of battleships that could not be hit by torpedoes.[51]

THE JAPANESE ATTACK PLAN

The Japanese attack had a lot of moving parts and required detailed and extensive planning, good intelligence, deception, and luck. The plan also involved two basic military concepts that generally ensure success: surprise and, despite so many variables, simplicity. Surprise in warfare is devastating for those who are surprised. Surprise cannot be underestimated on the macro scale of a December 7 attack or the micro scale of an infantry platoon ambush. The following is the step-by-step recipe for the attack.[52]

First, sail six aircraft carriers from Japan to Oahu under radio silence to prevent detection.

Second, launch two waves of aircraft toward Oahu with the first wave undetected.

Third, accomplish the following objectives with an aerial attack force comprising two attack units:

1) Dive bombers attack land installations and ships.

2) Torpedo bombers attack aircraft carriers and ships with exposed hulls.

3) High-level bombers attack inboard battleships.

4) Fighters protect dive and horizontal bombers by engaging airborne American fighters and destroying American fighters on the ground.

First Attack Unit

Lieutenant Commander Fuchida, commanding all air groups in the First Air Fleet, commanded the first attack units, the first wave. The first attack unit had three groups with 183 aircraft:

- First Group—forty-nine Kates with the 1,750-pound armor-piercing bombs for high-level bombing and forty Kates with torpedoes; objectives: aircraft carriers and battleships

- Second Group—fifty-one Vals with 250-pound bombs; objectives: to bomb hangars and grounded aircraft at Ford Island and Wheeler Field

- Third Group—forty-three Zeroes; objectives: to protect the Kates and Vals from US aircraft in the air and to prevent aircraft on the ground from taking off, so their targets were flying and grounded aircraft in and around Naval Air Stations at Ford Island and Kaneohe Bay, the Army Air Fields at Hickam and Wheeler, and Marine Air Corps Air Station Ewa at Barbers Point.[53]

Second Attack Unit

Lieutenant Commander Shigekazu Shimazaki commanded the second attack unit, the second wave. The second attack units also had three groups with 167 aircraft.

- First Group—fifty-four Kates, each with one 250-pound bomb and six 125-pound bombs; objectives: high-level bombing of targets such as hangars and aircraft at Ford Island, Barbers Point, Kaneohe, and Hickam. All torpedo bombing was in the first wave because torpedo bombers had to make slow runs directly at ships. Kates with torpedoes would be too vulnerable to antiaircraft defenses alerted by the first attack wave.

- Second Group—seventy-eight Vals with 250-pound bombs; objectives: aircraft carriers, cruisers, and battleships

- Third Group—thirty-five Zeroes; objectives: aircraft in the air and aircraft at the air stations and airfields previously mentioned[54]

Executing the Attack on December 7

Attack Phases or Waves

The February 15, 1942, report by Admiral Nimitz divided the attacks into phases:

Phase I—from 7:55 to 8:25 a.m.: torpedo and dive bombers

Phase II—from 8:25 to 8:40 a.m.: horizontal and dive bombers

Phase III—from 8:40 to 9:15 a.m.: horizontal and dive bombers

Phase IV—from 9:15 to 9:45 a.m.: dive bombers

Phase V: 9:45 a.m.: by this time, all enemy aircraft gone from Oahu[55]

The attack can also be divided into two waves (see the diagram on page 18, showing the paths of the two attack waves).

The First Wave

Fuchida's first wave, with 143 planes, left their carriers, flying to northern Oahu and then along its western side.[56]

The first-wave attack lasted from approximately 7:55 to 8:25 a.m. The time at which the first bombs fell at Pearl Harbor—approximately 7:55 a.m.—was easily remembered since a signal is routinely given five minutes before colors, the ceremony for raising the U.S. flag at 8:00 a.m.[57] The first bombs are believed to have hit Ford Island's seaplane ramps.[58]

Since the most important ships—U.S. aircraft carriers—were absent, the battleships became the primary targets.[59]

As indicated by the Japanese plan for and organization of this wave, Vals, Kates (with bombs and torpedoes), and Zeroes hit various targets on or around Ford Island and the Navy Yard. Roughly, the sequence was dive bombing, torpedoing, dive bombing, and high-level bombing.[60] Torpedoes did the most damage. Kates flew over Merry Point and Merry Loch and over Dry Dock 1 toward Battleship Row, launching torpedoes and hitting every outboard battleship: *California*, *Oklahoma*, *West Virginia*, and *Nevada*.[61]

Along Carrier Row, Japanese pilots were ordered to attack only aircraft carriers. The pilots, however, launched torpedoes that capsized *Utah* and severely damaged the cruiser Raleigh, which was moored in front of *Utah*.[62]

The most catastrophic event at Pearl Harbor that day occurred at approximately 8:05 a.m. *Arizona* suffered a cataclysmic explosion when one of the special 1,750-pound naval shells converted into a bomb penetrated her forward deck and caused a fire, igniting the ship's powder magazines. *Arizona* sank upright and burned until the following Tuesday. *Arizona* suffered the most casualties of any ship or station in the raid: 1,177 crewmen killed or missing in action.[63]

The Japanese lost three Zeroes, one Val, and five Kates. Fuchida's own plane was hit several times by antiaircraft fire.[64]

The Second Wave

Shimazaki's second wave, with 167 planes, left their carriers about an hour after Fuchida's wave and flew to northern Oahu and then along the eastern side of Oahu.[65] This attack began at approximately 8:40 a.m. and ended at approximately 9:45 a.m.[66]

As indicated by the Japanese plan for this wave, Vals, Kates (with bombs), and Zeroes hit various targets on or around Ford Island and the navy yard.[67] The Kates also hit Kaneohe and Hickam. Zeroes again hit the various air stations and airfields.[68]

Shimazaki returned to the carrier Zuikaku safely. He lost six Zeroes and fourteen dive bombers.[69]

Fuchida returned to Akagi safely; as leader, he waited until all planes left Oahu.[70] Only one item remained: the attack on Midway on the evening of December 7 (see Chapter 12).

Effectiveness of Japanese Weapons

On December 7, the Japanese aircraft and weapons exacted a terrific toll on Oahu, decimating the Fleet, damaging, sinking, or capsizing ships, some of whose crewmen earned MOHs—*Arizona, Oklahoma, California, Nevada, West Virginia, Vestal*, and *Utah*—and destroying installations on Ford Island and at Kaneohe Bay. The attack led to the sixteen MOH citations signed at various times by two different U.S. presidents for actions on December 7.

Bombs
The cataclysmic explosion sinking *Arizona* in place was just described. The explosion affected the repair ship *Vestal*, which was also hit by bombs.[71]

Torpedoes
Oklahoma and *Utah* capsized when torpedoes ruptured their hulls.[72] Torpedoes also hit *California* and *West Virginia*, but fortunately, unlike *Oklahoma* and *Utah*, crewmen ordered counterflooding, which flooded the side of the ship opposite the side hit by torpedoes, leveling the ship and preventing capsizing. Counterflooding sank the ships in place, but sinking in place was most preferable to the nightmare of capsizing. *Nevada* received one torpedo hit but did not sink at her berth.[73]

Machine Gun and Cannon Fire
Zeroes strafed various aircraft installations, destroying and damaging aircraft and hangars.[74]

Evaluation of the Attack

Overall, the Japanese attack was a great tactical success.

First of all, the Japanese fleet reached Oahu undetected. Warnings of attack as aircraft approached Oahu—detection of incoming aircraft by radar and the sinking of a midget submarine in the channel leading to Pearl Harbor—raised alarm but for various reasons led to no alert.

Second, the Japanese destroyed and heavily damaged various ships of the Pacific Fleet. Of seven battleships on Battleship Row, three sank upright in place and were heavily damaged: *California*, *West Virginia*, and *Arizona*. *Oklahoma* capsized. *Nevada* had sailed from her berth, was heavily damaged, beached at Hospital Point at the Navy Yard and then moved to Waipio Peninsula. The permanent losses were *Arizona*, *Oklahoma*, and *Utah*. Maryland, Tennessee, *West Virginia*, *Nevada*, and *California* were repaired and returned to service.[75]

Third, only three ships on Battleship Row left their berths and got underway: *Nevada*, Neosho, and *Vestal*. The two most important movements were by *Nevada* and Neosho.

JAPANESE ATTACK ROUTES ON DECEMBER 7, 1941

FORD ISLAND ON DECEMBER 7, 1941

BATTLESHIP ROW ON DECEMBER 7, 1941

Although damaged during the first wave, *Nevada* got underway and sailed past Battleship Row, headed for the narrow channel leading from Pearl Harbor to the Pacific Ocean. Planes from the second wave attacked and damaged the moving ship, knowing that the narrow harbor channel would be blocked if *Nevada* sank in it. Blocking passage to and from Pearl Harbor would make a nightmarish situation even worse. To prevent blocking the channel, *Nevada* was ordered to run aground at Hospital Point, a point on the navy yard. She was moved again, this time across the channel to Waipio Peninsula to a place later named "*Nevada* Point."[76]

Nevada attracted so much attention that the Japanese did not attack Neosho, which had unloaded fuel at Ford Island and was docked in front of Maryland and *Oklahoma*. During the attack, Neosho moved without being hit from Ford Island to the Submarine Base.[77] Had Neosho been hit while near Battleship Row, the explosion could have been catastrophic.

To escape the horrific fires and debris from the explosions on *Arizona*, *Vestal* moved and grounded on Aiea Shoal near Aiea.[78]

Fourth, Japanese losses were minimal. Most important, Japan lost no aircraft carriers. While all five midget submarines were lost, only 29 of 350 aircraft were shot down, a loss rate of only 8 percent and acceptable under any standard, given what was achieved in return: the nearly complete evisceration of the fleet and Oahu's military installations.[79]

But one instance of bad luck and several errors would haunt the Japanese.

The bad luck was the absence of the fleet's carriers, Saratoga, Lexington, and Enterprise. In 1942, the carriers would participate in crucial battles at Coral Sea and Midway.[80]

One of the major errors, if not the major error, was that Fuchida wanted to launch a third strike but Nagumo—who opposed the December 7 attack from the beginning—forbade it; he was satisfied with what the first two waves had accomplished. Also, he did not know where the American carriers were and feared they, as well as submarines or land-based aircraft, could attack his force.[81]

The problem an astute Fuchida recognized was that the first and second strikes focused on ships and aircraft, not on key shore installations, such as the Navy Yard with its Shipyard, Submarine Base, and oil tanks. The focus on combatant vessels and aircraft was necessary to destroy the fleet and to protect Japan's attacking force. With the combatants destroyed or damaged, a third strike could have focused on the other targets.[82]

But those three facilities would remain in action. The Shipyard would play a key role in repairing and salvaging the fleet. Since Hawaii produced no oil, all the fleet's oil had to be imported, so the oil tanks the Japanese left intact provided fuel for Fleet operations. Rear Admiral Kimmel, testifying before Congress after the attack, emphasized the oil's importance. In answering a question about the attack, he stated, "If they had destroyed the oil which was all above ground at that time and which could have been destroyed, it would have forced the withdrawal of the fleet to the [U.S. West Coast] because there wasn't any oil anywhere else out there to keep the fleet operating." He added later, "Well, I am saying that if they had destroyed the base and the facilities in the base and destroyed the oil there, it might have been even worse than it was." Another factor, mentioned after the war by then-Vice Admiral Anderson, was that ruptured oil tanks could have spilled burning oil into Pearl Harbor, making "a complete mess."[83]

Submarines would take a terrific toll of Japanese shipping, playing a critical role in defeating Japan.

Effect of the Attack on the Individual

This book is primarily about thirteen men who earned MOHs for actions on December 7 on Oahu; the Kidd and Van Valkenburgh MOHs are excluded because what they did to earn MOHs is unknown (see Chapter 15). The personal roles of those thirteen men in combat that day are of prime importance. Their actions distinguished them from all other men on December 7. The historical context of the attack is clear; it was firsthand proof, via an excruciating and unnerving experience, that airpower had replaced sea power as the dominant force in warfare. But what about the personal context of the battle, the personal hell far removed from the attack's historical implications?

Each arena of combat (air, ground, surface navy, and subsurface navy) has its own horrors. Combat on or under the sea, however, has a unique, particularly nightmarish quality. Water is an unforgiving, brutal battleground. A ship or submarine is a large confined space comprised of smaller confined spaces, and those aboard may have limited options for escape in the face of fire, explosion, or flooding. An explosion aboard ship or near a ship may send pieces of metal into the guts of crewmen, it may kill by concussion, or it may simply vaporize their bodies. Thus, for many of the men discussed in this book, death was particularly nightmarish and, in some cases, prolonged because they bled to death, suffocated or drowned in a ship's compartment, or drowned aboard capsized ships that slowly flooded.

Standing at Oahu's historical sites, particularly at Pearl Harbor, one can only imagine the horror unleashed on December 7 and the effect on the average officer or enlisted member or civilian, who had to quickly transition without warning from the peace of a lazy Sunday morning to a sky and harbor filled with ordnance and destruction, from routine flag raisings at 8:00 a.m. to fighting on the sea or in the air and to caring for dying and wounded comrades.

Minutes before a ship had been a peaceful home for crewmen; now she was barely floating, sinking, or capsizing. She was a hazard filled with death, injury, darkness, debris, chaos, smoke, gas, and fire. Shipboard fuel and ammunition fed explosions and fires aboard ship; oil fires floated on the water. Oil and water entered ships through holes caused by bombs and torpedoes. A crew faced dangers not only from its own ship but from surrounding ships, such as the oil fire from *Arizona* drifting toward *West Virginia* and *Vestal*.

How did the men react to such conditions? In short, the finest traditions of loyalty and leading by example prevailed, motivated by anger at the attack.

Pennsylvania's commander wrote, "The conduct of all officers and men was of the highest order. There was no flinching. There was no necessity of urging men to action… There were, however, a number of cases of wounded men insisting on continuing on station, serving guns, until ordered to battle dressing stations to have the wounds attended." [84] His language was typical of command reports; many stated that singling men out for commendation was difficult since so many acted so bravely.

Radioman's Mate Third Class G. H. Lane of *Arizona* wrote that he "saw no signs of fear on the ship. Everyone was surprised and pretty mad."[85] The commander of destroyer Cassin wrote, "The conduct of the men was superb, particularly the quiet over all supervision by the Chief Boatswain [sic] Mate, J. T. Stratton, who seemed to be everywhere at the same time directing closure and abandoning. At no time was there any fear or panic, but merely rage not only at enemy attack but at inability, after months of training, to be able to return the fire."[86] Likewise, the commander of destroyer Downes wrote that his crew "showed that they were real shipmates with a concern for each other's safety. They were loyal and determined. Their primary concern during the engagement was to get the guns in action, *and their biggest regret was that they couldn't meet the enemy in a fair fight at sea. I am proud to have commanded the USS Downes.*" The executive officer's memorandum to the commanding officer stated in paragraph 8, "The determination of the Downes crew to avenge the loss of their ship will make them valuable members of any crew. *It is extremely regrettable that they could not have had the chance to prove their worth under more favorable circumstances.*"[87] [Italics added for emphasis in both quotations.]

The desire to be with comrades and to continue the fight was strong. Ensign H. W. Sears was ashore when the attack started but could not reach his ship, *West Virginia*. He reached Phoenix, however, and asked the ship's commanding officer if he needed his services. When the commanding officer declined the offer, Sears dove over the side of Phoenix as she passed *West Virginia* and swam to his own ship.[88]

An *Oklahoma* sailor, D. L. Westfall, wrote that he was shaving when the attack began. He felt three hits on the ship. When he reached his station in radio central the ship was listing to port. He saw water and oil "bubbling up along the junction of the bulkhead and deck of the electrical work shop" and "many pieces of [radio] equipment knocked over or dangling by wires." On the third deck, "all lights were out and only a few flashlights were available."

Westfall heard the order to abandon ship, helped a partially incapacitated man, and then helped pass injured men along to a ladder. He "lost all knowledge of time while here." He then saw men collapsing around him. He himself collapsed, feeling paralyzed and having difficulty breathing. He reached the ladder and climbed a couple of steps before "collapsing completely." He recovered in a Ford Island dispensary. He wrote, "The action of everyone I observed was cool and purposeful as soon as they fully realized we were actually under attack…My life itself is proof of the courage and disregard of personal danger on the part of unknown shipmates."[89]

The actions of seniors or leaders, whether officers or enlisted, greatly affected subordinates in these conditions. Good seniors or leaders embodied the time-honored military principles of leading by example and of having the ability to function and to lead in wartime chaos. They had to control their own fear while being mindful of the fear of subordinates. They had to focus on problems as they were in real time and to move forward without dwelling on how or why the attack happened. These principles were crucial as was the ability of these men to restore order from that chaos if restoration of order is possible.

Another perspective comes from Audie Murphy, who earned a MOH as an Army lieutenant in Europe in 1945. In his famous autobiography To Hell and Back, he wrote, "Again I see the war as it is: an endless series of problems involving the blood and guts of men."[90] For example, those endless problems on December 7 included how to prevent his ship from capsizing (Warrant Officer Jackson Pharris aboard *California*), how to restore order and command at his command post (First Lieutenant George Cannon on Midway), and how to resist the enemy (Chief Petty Officer John Finn at Kaneohe Bay).

Examples of such leadership also occurred on a rapidly deteriorating *Arizona* after the attack.

Corporal E. C. Nightingale, a Marine on *Arizona*, wrote that "badly burned men were heading for the quarterdeck, only to fall apparently dead or badly wounded… Charred bodies were everywhere."[91] He and Alan Shapley, the Marine major and former commander of *Arizona*'s marines, jumped overboard. Nightingale reached the mooring quay but found himself suddenly in the water, apparently blown off the quay from a bomb concussion. Due to his wet clothing and shock, he started sinking. Shapley grabbed him. Seeing that Shapley's strength was ebbing, Nightingale tried to leave him and told him to swim on alone. Shapley refused to let him go. "I would have drowned but for the Major."[92] Shapley received a Silver Star for his actions.[93] Years ago, the author saw Shapley's sword, salvaged from *Arizona*, displayed at the Pearl Harbor exhibit at Parris Island at the Marine Corps Recruit Depot's museum.

A sailor on *Arizona*, Petty Officer First Class (Aviation Machinist's Mate) D. A. Graham, wrote the following about Lieutenant Commander Samuel Fuqua, the ship's damage-control officer.

> [Fuqua] was the senior officer on deck and set an example for the men by being unperturbed, calm, cool, and collected, exemplifying the courage and traditions of an officer under fire. It seemed like the men painfully burned, shocked, and dazed, became inspired and took things in stride, seeing Mr. Fuqua, so unconcerned about the bombing and the strafing, standing on the quarterdeck…
>
> Courage and performance of all hands was of the highest order imaginable, especially being handicapped by adverse conditions and shipmates being blown up beside alongside them. These was no disorder non tendency to run around in confusion. *The coolness and calm manner of Lieutenant Commander Fuqua and Ensign J. D. Miller installed [sic] confidence in the surviving crew.* [Italics added for emphasis.][94]

Fuqua wrote the following in the enclosure he submitted for *Arizona*'s after-action report:

> The personnel of the antiaircraft and machine gun batteries on the *Arizona* lived up to the best traditions of the Navy. I could hear guns firing on the ship long after the boat deck was a mass of flames. I can not [sic] single out any one individual who stood out in the acts of heroism above the others, as all of the personnel under my supervision conducted themselves with the greatest heroism and bravery.[95]

Fuqua earned a MOH for his actions on *Arizona* (see Chapter 7 (*Arizona*)).

In such circumstances, one can understand why only five of the fifteen MOH recipients for Oahu on December 7 survived the day. Fuqua was one of those lucky brave men.[96]

Summary
The Tragedy of Dark Ink and the Twenty-Five Minutes

In the hearings described in chapter 20, concerning a special MOH for Billy Mitchell, a 1945 Congressional subcommittee received a letter from Reed G. Landis, a regional vice president with American Airlines, Inc. Landis wrote that men who agreed with Mitchell's ideas about aviation, although not agreeing with his "methods of selling his ideas," could see in 1945 how Mitchell's ideas, had they been properly implemented, "might very well have resulted in a substantial change in world history from that which has been written in such dark ink since 1930."[97]

And dark ink would record that Mitchell was off only twenty-five minutes; he predicted the attack on Oahu would be at 7:30 a.m.; the first bomb fell at 7:55 a.m.[98]

Notes

1. Hague Convention No. III, "Relative to the Opening of Hostilities," (1907) Article 1, Headquarters, Department of the Army, International Law (Department of the Army Pamphlet 27-161-2, Washington, DC, October 1962), 36.

2. Colonel Charles A. Jones, US Marine Corps Reserve (Retired), Hawaii's World War II Military Sites (Mutual Publishing, Honolulu, HI, 2002), 13 (hereafter "Jones, Hawaii's World War II Military Sites").

3. "This Day in History," History.com, accessed October 12, 2015.

4. Vice Admiral Homer N. Wallin, U.S. Navy (Retired), Pearl Harbor: Why, How, Fleet Salvage, and Final Appraisal (Washington, DC: Naval History Division, United States Government Printing Office, Washington, DC, 1968), 14–22 (hereafter, "Wallin, Pearl Harbor").

5. Ibid., 14–17; Samuel Eliot Morison, History of United States Naval Operations in World War II, Vol. 3 (Little, Brown and Company, Boston, 1948) 16–18 (Panay incident); endnote 2, Jones, Hawaii's World War II Military Sites, 15–17; Iris Chang, The Rape of Nanking (BasicBooks, New York, NY, 1997) (overall description of Japanese conduct in China).

6. Editorial Staff, U.S. Army Air Forces, Air Victory Over Japan ("Impact," September to October 1945), 3.

7. Endnote 2, Jones, Hawaii's World War II Military Sites, 17.

8. Ibid.

9. Endnote 2, Jones, Hawaii's World War II Military Sites, 17–18; Commander Roger D. Scott, Judge Advocate General's Corps, U.S. Navy, "Kimmel, Short, McVay: Case Studies in Executive Authority, Law, and the Individual Rights of Military Commanders," Military Law Review, Department of the Army Pamphlet 27-100-156, Volume 156 (June 1998), 67 (discussion of admiral grade and Richardson's relief); Rear

Admiral Augustus Furer, U.S. Navy Retired, Administration of the Navy Department in World War II (U.S. Government Printing Office, Washington, DC, 1959), 83–85 (discusses the reasons for Richardson's relief) (hereafter, Furer, Administration of the Navy Department in World War II).

10. Ibid., 18.

11. Endnote 9, Furer, Administration of the Navy Department in World War II, 85.

12. PEARL HARBOR ATTACK: HEARINGS BEFORE THE JOINT COMMITTEE ON THE INVESTIGATION OF THE PEARL HARBOR ATTACK, SEVENTY-NINTH CONGRESS, FIRST SESSION, Part 26 (U.S. Government Printing Office, Washington, DC, 1946), pages 453–455 (testimony of Rear Admiral Joel W. Bunkley, U.S. Navy (Retired), June 5, 1944, before the Hart Inquiry)(hereafter "PEARL HARBOR ATTACK HEARINGS"); endnote 2, Jones, Hawaii's World War II Military Sites, 22–23.

13. Gordon W. Prange, At Dawn We Slept (Penguin Books, New York, NY, 1982), 337–338; Leatrice R. Arakaki, and John R. Kuborn, December 7, 1941: The Air Force Story (Pacific Air Forces, Office of History, Hickam Air Force Base, Hawaii,1991), 42–46.

15. Endnote 2, Jones, Hawaii's World War II Military Sites, 17.

16. Ibid.

17. Ibid.

18. Paul Stillwell, ed. Air Raid: Pearl Harbor! RECOLLECTIONS OF A DAY OF INFAMY (Naval Institute Press, Annapolis, MD, 1981), 74 (hereafter, Stillwell, Air Raid: Pearl Harbor!

19. Hearings [May 31, 1945] before SUBCOMMITTEE NO. 8 OF THE COMMITTEE ON MILITARY AFFAIRS, HOUSE OF REPRESENTATIVES, SEVENTY-NINTH CONGRESS, First Session on H.R. 2227 and Other Bills [authorizing the President to award a posthumous MOH in the name of Congress to William Mitchell] (Washington, DC: U.S. Government Printing Office, 1945) (hereafter "Mitchell Hearings"), 35–37 (Mitchell's World War II service and decorations) and page 30 (discusses ship-sinking tests and Uses the phrase "prophet without honor").

20. John T. Correll, "Billy Mitchell and the Battleships," AIR FORCE MAGAZINE (June 2008): 62–68 (hereafter "Correll, 'Billy Mitchell and the Battleships'").

21. Ibid., 64–65.

22. John L. Frisbee, "Warrior, Prophet, Martyr," AIR FORCE MAGAZINE (September 1985), 162 (predictions, report suppressed); National Museum of the U.S.

Air Force, "Gen. Billy Mitchell," U.S. Air Force fact sheet, accessed from the Internet May 11, 2008) (prediction) (hereafter, "Mitchell Air Force Fact Sheet").

23. Alfred Hurley, BILLY MITCHELL: Crusader for Air Power (Indiana University Press, Indianapolis, IN, 1975), 86–88.

24. Endnote 20, Correll, "Billy Mitchell and the Battleships," 68.

25. Major Alexander P. de Seversky, Victory Through Airpower (Simon and Schuster, 1942), 96–98.

26. Endnote 22, Mitchell Air Force Fact Sheet. Photograph and caption on page 180 of the 1941 Army-Navy game program provided by the United States Naval Academy.

27. Endnote 2, Jones, Hawaii's World War II Military Sites, 65–107.

28. Endnote 2, Jones, Hawaii's World War II Military Sites, 107; author's viewing of mooring quays during visitations of and boat tours around Ford Island.

29. Ibid.

30. Ibid.

31. Ibid., 17–18; endnote 12, PEARL HARBOR ATTACK HEARINGS, SEVENTY-NINTH CONGRESS, SECOND SESSION, Part 21, note at page 4556.

32. Ibid., 4556–4562.

33. Ibid., First Session, Part 1, 29.

34. Ibid., Second Session, Part 21, 4556.

35. Ibid., 4556–4557.

36. Ibid., Chapters 6 (*West Virginia*) and 7 (*Arizona*).

37. Information about ship mooring is from the author's personal view of Battleship Row and its mooring quays; the report by Rear Admiral W. S. Anderson, Commander Battleships, Battle Force (subject: "Attack at Pearl Harbor by Japanese Planes on December 7, 1941") of December 19, 1941, paragraph three; and diagrams and photographs in this chapter.

38. Bess Altfield, publisher, Air Raid, Pearl Harbor. This Is Not Drill! (O.S.B. MapMania, Phoenix, AZ, 1999) (map and pamphlet showing moorings on December 7) (hereafter, Altfield, Air Raid, Pearl Harbor. This Is Not Drill!).

39. See Chapters 4 (*California*, Neosho was a tanker) and 8 (*Vestal*, a repair ship).

40. Endnote 2, Jones, Hawaii's World War II Military Sites, 19–34.

41. Robert J. Cressman and J. Michael Wenger, Infamous Day: Marines at Pearl Harbor December 7, 1941, History and Museums Division, Headquarters, U.S. Marine Corps (Washington, DC, 1992). This pamphlet discusses Marine Corps action on December 7.

42. Endnote 2, Jones, Hawaii's World War II Military Sites, 19; endnote 18, Stillwell, Air Raid! Pearl Harbor!

43. Ibid.

44. "The Japs Hear Things, Too," Collier's Weekly (August 11, 1945), 82.

45. Endnote 2, Jones, Hawaii's World War II Military Sites, 20.

46. Ibid., 21.

47. Chapter 12 (Midway).

48. Endnote 2, Jones, Hawaii's World War II Military Sites, 20.

49. Ibid.; endnote 12, PEARL HARBOR ATTACK HEARINGS, SEVENTY-NINTH CONGRESS, FIRST SESSION, Part 1, 239–241 (Fuchida described the aircraft and the targets in a 1945 postwar questionnaire).

50. Endnote 2, Jones, Hawaii's World War II Military Sites, 20–21.

51. Ibid.

52. Ibid., 19–26.

53. Ibid., 21.

54. Ibid., 21.

55. Report from Commander-in-Chief, Pacific Fleet (Subj: Report of Japanese Raid on Pearl Harbor, December 7, 1941) of February 15, 1942), Part III.

56. Endnote 2, Jones, Hawaii's World War II Military Sites, 23.

57. Ibid.

58. Ibid.; Attack on Naval Air Station, Pearl Harbor: Report from Commander Patrol Wing Two (Subject: Operations on December 7, 1941) of December 20, 1941, paragraph 3 (first bomb hit near a hangar at 7:57 a.m.).

59. Ibid., 24.

60. Ibid.

61. See Chapters 4 (*California*), 5 (*Oklahoma*), 6 (*West Virginia*), and 9 (*Nevada*).

62. Chapter 10 (*Utah*).

63. Chapter 7 (*Arizona*).

64. Endnote 2, Jones, Hawaii's World War II Military Sites, 25–30.

65. Ibid., 25–26.

66. Ibid., 25.

67. Ibid., 25.

68. Ibid., 26.

69. Ibid.

70. Ibid., 26.

71. Chapter 8 (*Vestal*).

72. Chapters 5 (*Oklahoma*) and 10 (*Utah*).

73. Chapter 9 (*Nevada*).

74. Endnote 2, Jones, Hawaii's World War II Military Sites, 25–26.

75. Chapters 4–7 and 9 and 10.

76. Chapter 9 (*Nevada*).

77. Chapter 4 (*California*).

78. Chapter 8 (*Vestal*).

79. Endnote 2, Jones, Hawaii's World War II Military Sites, 30.

80. Lexington (lost) and Yorktown were at Coral Sea; Yorktown (lost) and Enterprise were at Midway.

81. Endnote 2, Jones, Hawaii's World War II Military Sites, 27.

82. Ibid., 33–34.

83. PHA Hearings, Seventy-Ninth Congress, Second Session, Part 6 (1946), 2812 (Kimmel); endnote 18, Stillwell, Air Raid: Pearl Harbor!, 131 (Anderson).

84. Report from USS Pennsylvania (Subject: USS Pennsylvania's Report of Action during Enemy Air Attack Morning of Sunday, December 7, 1941, of December 16, 1941), paragraph 9 Distinguished Conduct.

85. Endnote 4, Wallin, Pearl Harbor, 305.

86. Report from USS Cassin (Subject: Report of Action with Japanese Aircraft During Attack on Pearl Harbor, T. H., December 7, 1941, of December 13, 1941), paragraph 25.

87. Report from USS Downes (Subject: Report of Action with Japanese Aircraft during Attack on Pearl Harbor, T. H., December 7, 1941, of December 17, 1941), paragraph 18; Executive officer's memorandum to the commanding officer of December 17, 1941.

88. Report from USS *West Virginia* (Subject: "Action of December 7, 1941—Report of") of December 11, 1941.

89. Endnote 4, Wallin, Pearl Harbor, 300.

90. Audie Murphy, To Hell and Back (Holt, Reinhardt and Winston, New York, Chicago, San Francisco, 1949), 179.

91. Endnote 4, Wallin, Pearl Harbor, 307.

92. Endnote 15, Wallin, Pearl Harbor: Why, How, Fleet Salvage, and Final Appraisal, 306–307 (description of factual basis for Shapley's Silver Star: preventing a Marine corporal from drowning as the two men moved from *Arizona* to Ford Island).

93. Jane Blakeney, Heroes: U.S. Marine Corps 1861 * 1955 (Guthrie Lithograph Co., Inc., Washington, DC, 1957), 228.

94. Endnote 4, Wallin, Pearl Harbor, 307–309.

95. Report from USS *Arizona* (Subject: Action Report of USS *Arizona*, December 7, 1941) of December 13, 1941; enclosure (H) is Fuqua's statement.

96. See chapters 7 (*Arizona*) and 14 (Overview).

97. Endnote 19, Mitchell Hearings, 12.

98. Endnote 22, Mitchell Air Force Fact Sheet.

Photographs: The Attack on Oahu

The infamous photograph and caption on page 180 of the program for the Army-Navy football game held on November 29, 1941. The caption reads, "Right—A bow on view of the USS *Arizona* as she plows into a huge swell. It is significant that despite the claims of air enthusiasts that no battleship has yet been sunk by bombs." (Photograph courtesy of the late Gary Lavalley of the U.S. Naval Academy.)

Chapter 3
Aftermath of December 7
Attacks on Oahu—"The Yellow Peril" and "The Punch Below the Belt"

What Happened on December 7, 1941?

After the attack, the immediate question was "What happened?" What environment was created leading to the award of sixteen MOHs for December 7, 1941? In what type of circumstances were the MOH recipients acting such that they would be awarded MOHs?

The environment leading to the awards is important in understanding the nature of the actions by the recipients and just how desperately the nation needed heroes in the days after the treacherous, devastating attack on Oahu. And knowing the enemy is important in judging just what conditions he created, leading to the MOHs awarded for December 7.

As will be seen, the recipients, except for John Finn, were not fighting the enemy. They were not combatants in a set-piece battle; they were responding and reacting to an unprovoked, surprise attack that created numerous types of disaster and casualties. Damage control was a crucial activity so that ships, such as *California* and *Vestal*, could remain stable and survive. Unstable ships, such as *Arizona*, *Oklahoma*, and *Utah*, did not.

And because it was a surprise attack, the recipients had no chance to prepare their commands or themselves for the horrors that befell them. In short, they not only had to overcome the aftermath of the attack but also the initial shock of an attack that was unexpected. As can be seen from comments in this chapter and Chapter 2, no one saw the attack as a fair fight. To use a cliché, the day was no movie in which the cavalry had time to prepare for an expected charge by the Indians. The MOH recipients had to react in the worst of circumstances, thus making the deeds of the men who truly earned MOHs all the more heroic.

With apologies to the writing gods who detest adjectives, the attack on December 7 can be described many ways:

- character—despicable, infamous, treacherous, and backstabbing
- execution—sudden, savage, unrelenting, daunting, harrowing, heart-stopping, unnerving, volatile, tense, ruthless, unyielding, and vicious
- result—ignominious

Deception, Surprise, and Treachery

Without the adjectives, the what was apparent fairly quickly. As Billy Mitchell predicted, Japanese aviation attacked Oahu. What was also clear was that it was not just a ferocious, unrelenting attack; it was catastrophic and overwhelming, beyond belief, leaving much of Oahu and its military assets devastated.

The December 7 attack shattered the quiet serenity and beauty of Oahu, especially Pearl Harbor. Japanese bombs, torpedoes, and bullets churned the still waters of Pearl Harbor, ripping the Pacific Fleet apart. The result was to turn paradise into a portrait of hell, much like the portraits of hell painted by the famous Dutch painter Hieronymus Bosch, making his vision of the underworld come alive with US military members the characters in the painting—tortured, twisted, sad, suffering figures inhabiting Bosch's view of hell as a burning place of unequalled misery. The pleasant existence in the paradise of Oahu had become a Gothic experience in hell in approximately two hours; in a suddenly Gothic world, everything comforting had changed to everything excruciating as waves of bullets ripped men and machines on Oahu.

Compounding the damage was Japan using two classic elements of warfare: deception and surprise. Their use can be devastating, whether a platoon-sized ambush on the ground or a large attack, such as Japan executed on December 7 or such as the United States executed in June at Midway.

As noted in Chapter 2, deception was the superficial appearance of diplomacy before December 7. The United States and Japan were conducting diplomatic talks to achieve a peaceful resolution of the disagreements between them. Below the surface, however, Japan was planning to attack Oahu. The United States, particularly the Pacific Fleet in Oahu, was the only major threat that could stop the years of unchecked Japanese aggression in the Pacific, and the threat posed by any force that dared impede what Japan wanted to do had to create seething anger in Japan against the that force, in this case, the United States. Thus the appearance was Japanese interest in negotiations; the reality was planning for a secret attack to eliminate the threat posed by the Pacific Fleet at Oahu, planning so exceptional and deliberate that it had to have been ongoing for months under the cover of the negotiations.[1]

As will be seen, the attack without formal warning violated international law.

The result of deception and surprise was to infuriate American service members on Oahu and the American public. To say that it created hard feelings and animosity between the United States and Japan is a gross understatement. They also created a universal reputation of Japanese treachery since it was a sneak attack executed in an atmosphere of sincere diplomacy—or what appeared to be sincere diplomacy. What Japan did was like a misdirection football play in which a player appears to be carrying the ball one way when in fact another player is carrying the ball another way.

The Japanese penchant for treachery demonstrated on December 7 would continue throughout the war, causing the Allies to adopt a "No quarter asked, no quarter given" policy to protect them from such perfidy as feigned surrenders. When a Marine came forward in good faith to accept purported surrender, Japanese grenades or bullets met him. Thus, some Americans refused to take prisoners. The Japanese were seen as diabolical subhumans and treated accordingly. To "Jap" someone meant to trick them. The Japanese were called "Japs" and "Nips" (for "Nipponese") and rightly so after the barbarity they exhibited in China before the war (burning and burying Chinese alive, beheading and shooting them, and using babies for bayonet practice).

Documents and books referred to treachery. The first paragraph of the December 19, 1941, report by Commander Battleships, Battle Force, U.S. Pacific Fleet, began, "On the occasion of the treacherous surprise attack on Pearl Harbor on December 7, 1941, battleship ready guns opened fire at once."[2] A book on seamanship stated, "We all know the how the Japs' sneak attack on Pearl Harbor put almost half of our battleships and also other types of ships out of service, at least temporarily."[3]

Japanese treachery even became the exclusive subject of an August 1, 1945, War Department pamphlet: THE PUNCH BELOW THE BELT: Japanese Ruses, Deception Tactics, and Antipersonnel Measures. It was published "especially for the individual combat soldier" and included this direction: "SHARE THIS COPY." The introduction begins, "The favorite Jap punch is below the belt. Probably no army in the history of warfare has equaled the Japs in treachery and craftiness." Pearl Harbor could not be overlooked: "From the sneak attack at Pearl Harbor [throughout the war] the Japs have used every trick, every deceit to gain advantage." The pamphlet warned, "The first things any soldier who is to fight against the Japs must learn is that under no circumstances are they to be trusted." The pamphlet shows side-by-side photographs, one of a Japanese child dressed as a soldier (caption "Cunning, isn't he?") and one of a Japanese soldier (caption "Still cunning—after 20 years of 'thought control.' Cunning as a rattlesnake."). [4]

The treachery theme continued without end. John Ford's film December 7 features such phrases as Japanese Prime Minister Hideki Tojo having "done a good job of stabbing [us] in the back." The Axis brand of war was "a stab in the back Sunday morning." In describing a captured Japanese midget submarine, the narrator said, "This piece of underwater perfidy won't be forgotten." He described the attack as "[o]ne hour and fifty minutes of perfidy."

Disgust ranged from the lowest enlisted ranks to the highest officer ranks. Radioman's Mate Third Class G. H. Lane, an *Arizona* crewman mentioned in Chapter 2, wrote about men being surprised and angry. "Everyone was surprised and pretty mad."[5] Service members on Oahu wanted a "return engagement" in which the two sides could meet in the open without a surprise attack. They wanted the "fair fight" as a chance to avenge the "unfair fight" that they felt the December 7 attack had been. Rear Admiral W. S. Anderson, Commander, Battleships, Battle Force, opened his report concerning distinguished conduct on December 7 with this sentence: "In the treacherous surprise attack by the Japanese on the ships in Pearl Harbor on December 7, 1941, the conduct of all officers and men of the battleships was distinguished by courage and an instant response to the need to take prompt action against the attackers."[6]

Even the officer supervising the salvage efforts at Pearl Harbor, Homer Wallin, wrote the following in his book about salvage operations: "The enemy achieved much of his goal in the perfidious air raid of 7 December 1941."[7]

The sneak attack effect cannot be overstated, although the US military, like other militaries, had used or would use them. The Confederates executed a surprise attack at Chancellorsville in 1863, once again catching the U.S. military by surprise. And, based on an intercepted Japanese message decoded by U.S. codebreakers—ironically Navy personnel working at the Navy Yard in Pearl Harbor—U.S. Army Air Forces fighters ambushed and killed, of all people, Yamamoto, shooting down his aircraft in a well-planned aerial ambush on April 18, 1943. And only in America could that event lead to litigation, a court case in which one of the American pilots sought to claim sole credit for downing Yamamoto's aircraft.[8]

But Americans thought surprise attacks were unfair—if directed at them. Even in 1964, the idea of a sneak attack caused "tremors" in the U.S. military if one is to believe the following interchange in the movie Fail-Safe reflected U.S. military thinking. When a professor, portrayed by actor Walter Matthau, suggested to military officials that the U.S. launch a first strike against the Soviet Union, a flag officer recoiled. "We don't go in for sneak attacks. We had that done to U.S. at Pearl Harbor."

Matthau replied, "And the Japanese were right to do it. From their point of view, we were their mortal enemy. As long as we existed, we were a deadly threat to them. Their only mistake was that they failed to finish US at the start…and they paid for that mistake at Hiroshima."

Many would agree with Matthau's character.

The fear of treachery continued until war's end. A headline for an Associated Press newspaper article for August 11, 1945, read, "Danger of Treachery after Jap Surrender Stressed by Nimitz." His message was to beware of Japanese treachery even for "some time" after surrender. The history of the Seventy-Third Bomb Wing reproduced this August 14 message from Nimitz:

> CEASE OFFENSIVE OPERATIONS AGAINST JAPANESE FORCES X CONTINUE SEARCHES AND PATROLS X MAINTAIN DEFENSIVE AND INTERNAL SECURITY MEASURES AT HIGHEST LEVEL AND BEWARE OF TREACHERY OR LAST MOMENT ATTACKS BY ENEMY FORCES OR INDIVIDUALS X[9]

And another that would become clearer later to the Japanese and to the Americans is that the attack was a mistake by Japan that would return to haunt it just as Matthau's character had observed. While the attacks were a brilliantly executed tactical way to open a war and to gain advantage in the short run, in the long run, the Japanese would regret December 7 and the fears of some of Japanese leaders about war with the United States would come all too true. For example, the Japanese failure to destroy the Navy's repair facilities and oil supply was probably one aspect of what Matthau's character meant by failing "to finish us at the start."

The why of the attack was answered in Chapter 2. Japan wanted to eliminate the U.S. Pacific Fleet so Japanese aggression in the Pacific would be unstoppable.

In summary, the atmosphere just described led to the MOHs that are the subject of this book.

The Immediate Consequences of the Attack

U.S. Casualties and Losses

Human Casualties: Numbers

Service Members or Civilians	Killed, Missing, Died of Wounds	Wounded
Navy	1,998	710
Marine Corps	109	69
Army	233	364
Civilians	45	35
Totals	2,388	1,178

Table 3-1. Casualties by branch of service and civilians.[10]

Casualties: Practical Problems

War triggers a timeless practical problem: what to do about the wounded and dead. The immediate concerns are treating the wounded, recovering the bodies or body parts of the dead that can be recovered, accounting for the missing, and notifying the families of the dead, wounded, and missing.

The dead may be buried at sea or on land near where they fell. If they died on land, their remains may later be moved to a national or private cemetery.

One must go back in time to understand how families were notified of death or injury. In today's world, technology, such as television, satellites, computers, e-mail, and cellular phones are everywhere, making communication fast or even instantaneous. Such communication was unavailable during World War II, when the primary means of communication were letter, telephone, and telegrams. With so many dead and wounded, personal notification by a service member visiting the home was impractical. Accordingly, families were notified impersonally by telegrams delivered by civilians, unwanted pieces of paper telling them that a family member was dead, wounded, or missing.

For example, the widow of *Arizona*'s commanding officer, Captain Franklin Van Valkenburgh (one of the MOH recipients in this book), was sent such a telegram. Dated December 11, 1941, it informed her that he was lost in action and, after expressing condolences, cautioned her to prevent aiding the enemy by not revealing his ship or duty station. It advised that if his remains were recovered that they would be interred temporarily in the area where he was killed. The telegram was from Rear Admiral C. W. Nimitz, Chief of the Bureau of Navigation. Nimitz was a rear admiral and Chief of the Bureau until he was promoted to admiral and assumed duty as Commander-in-Chief of the Pacific Fleet in December 1941.[11]

Ship Casualties

Since the ships were moored, often together, in Pearl Harbor and thus stationary, they were not "moving targets." Moving targets would have been somewhat more difficult to hit, but maybe not; the Japanese, as was seen with *Nevada*—the only battleship to get underway—still pounded her mightily as she moved a short distance in Pearl Harbor. She was moving slowly though, and the slow speed counteracted any advantage or defense offered by faster sailing.

Fate of the Battleships

Of the seven battleships on Battleship Row, only two were lost permanently: *Oklahoma* (capsized) and *Arizona* (sunk in place by catastrophic explosion). These were the only two battleships the United States lost in World War II, both damaged beyond repair on December 7. *Arizona* was left at Pearl Harbor in place and later became a memorial. *Oklahoma* was sold for scrapping but sank in 1947 while being towed to the United States. Each ship had crewmen who earned MOHs on December 7 (see Chapters 5 (*Oklahoma*) and 7 (*Arizona*)).

All other battleships on Battleship Row were repaired and served during the war: Maryland, Tennessee, *West Virginia*, *Nevada*, and *California*. Battleship durability was crucial; the ships could take terrific punishment and—except for *Arizona* and *Oklahoma*—be repaired and return to service.

After returning to service, these five Battleship Row ships served in the Atlantic and Pacific. Warfare had changed, however. Battles between carrier strike forces replaced classic surface actions with battleships blasting each other. The slow old battleships could not keep pace with the faster carrier battle groups; newer fast battleships could. After repair and return to service, however, the older battleships repaid Japan by pre-invasion battleship firepower as Marines invaded Pacific islands. Here, the firepower of the ships' big guns was more important than speed. Also, their durability again showed itself during the war; incredibly, all survived hits by kamikaze planes. Their post-attack service is especially interesting given their ages, based commissioning dates:

- 1916 - USS *Nevada*
- 1920 - USS *Tennessee*
- 1921 - USS *California* and USS *Maryland*
- 1923 - USS *West Virginia*

After the war, all five ships were scrapped or sunk—none were saved as memorials or "floating museums" as were battleships Missouri, Alabama, Wisconsin, Iowa, and North Carolina, all of which now are open to the public.[12]

Ship Damage, Salvage, and Repairing Ford Island

With so many ships damaged and Ford Island itself a wreck, the horror of the attack did not end on December 7. A massive salvage and repair effort was required, an effort that was a difficult, grim, ghastly, dangerous, and sometimes fatal undertaking, as workers encountered live ordnance, fumes, and bodies. The salvage and repair effort was so extensive that the Navy captain superintending it, Homer Wallin, wrote the definitive book about the salvage operations: Pearl Harbor: Why, How, Fleet Salvage, and Final Appraisal. He retired as a vice admiral.[13]

Ship	Damage	Killed / Missing (Navy and Marine)	Disposition
USS Arizona	Sunk in Place	1,177	Memorial at Pearl Harbor
USS California	Sunk in Place	102	Returned to Service; Scrapped 1959
USS Maryland	Moderate	4	Returned to Service; Sold for scrapping 1959
USS Nevada	Sunk (Ran Aground)	57	Retunred to Service; Sunk 1948
USS Neosho	None	0	Scuttled after attack by Japanese 1942
USS Oklahoma	Sunk (Capsized)	429	Never returned to service; scrapped, sank in 1947 under tow
USS Tennessee	Moderate	5	Returned to Service; Scrapped 1959
USS Vestal	Severe	7	Returned to Service; Sold for Scrapping 1950
USS West Virginia	Sunk in Place	106	Returned to Service; Sold for Scrapping 1959

Table 3-2. Fate of ships on Battleship Row.

Pennsylvania also returned to service but was sunk after the war.[14]

HUMAN TRAGEDY

The human tragedy was ghastly and overwhelming; it either happened to the MOH recipients, or they saw it. Bodies, including some of three of the December 7 recipients, were lost in overturned ships. When water was pumped from flooded compartments, bodies and body parts were encountered, so pumping had to cease when two or three feet of water remained in the compartments so that bodies and parts could be placed in bags. Aboard *West Virginia* salvagers found sixty-six bodies. They also found evidence that three crewmen trapped on the ship had survived by eating emergency rations but had perished due to lack of oxygen. A calendar found with them showed they had lived from December 7 to December 23, the last date marked on the calendar.[15]

Under the heading "Removal Of Human Bodies," Wallin wrote about a particularly gruesome task, salvaging ships with large numbers of bodies in various compartments.

A scheme was developed for handling these without the knowledge of the men who comprised the working parties. Two or three feet of water were left in each compartment so that the bodies could be floated into canvas bags. The bags were tightly tied and transported to the Naval Hospital for proper identification and burial. The method was very effective and was undisturbing to the salvage crew.[16]

Salvage was also dangerous. Two survivors of *Nevada* were killed after breathing hydrogen sulfide gas aboard the ship.[17]

The two capsized ships, *Oklahoma* and *Utah*, presented difficult challenges. Cables were attached to their hulls to connect them to winches on Ford Island that could pull the ships upright. *Oklahoma* was successfully righted, but *Utah* was only partially righted and remains today at her berth partially capsized.[18]

In addition to salvaging the ships, land installations had to be repaired.

JAPANESE CASUALTIES AND LOSSES

Mission	Number Killed
Midget Submarines	9
Large Submarines	121
Airmen	55
Total	185

Table 4-3. Japanese losses: Casualties.[19]

Type	Number Downed
Fighters	9
Dive Bombers	15
Torpedo Bombers	5
Total	29

Table 4-4. Japanese losses: Aircraft.[20]

SHORT-TERM CONSEQUENCES OF THE ATTACK

Declaration of War

Under Article II, Section 2 of the U.S. Constitution, the President is the "commander in chief of the army and navy of the United States" but lacks constitutional authority to declare war. Article I, Section 8 of the Constitution grants that power exclusively to Congress (the Senate and the House of Representatives). Thus on December 8, 1941, President Franklin Roosevelt delivered his famous "date of infamy" speech, asking Congress to declare war on Japan. Congress agreed.[21]

Relief of Admiral Kimmel

On December 16, 1941, Secretary of the Navy Frank Knox relieved Admiral Husband Kimmel of his duties as Commander-in-Chief, U.S. Pacific Fleet, but Kimmel was not formally punished, although the Chief of naval operations did give him an adverse fitness report (report of performance). Kimmel held the grade of admiral only while serving as the Fleet commander, so he reverted to his permanent grade of rear admiral after he was relieved as CINCPACFLT. His retirement in 1942 in his permanent grade of rear admiral, rather than admiral, remains a source of controversy to this day. Notwithstanding attempts by Kimmel supporters to vindicate him and a law permitting officer retirement grades to be in the highest grade held, the Navy will not support restoration to admiral, so his terminal and retirement grade remains rear admiral.[22]

An interim successor held the post until December 31, 1941, when Rear Admiral Chester Nimitz assumed permanent command of the Pacific Fleet and thus the grade of admiral. Since he was a submariner, the ceremony was aboard the submarine USS Grayling, which was lost in 1943. Nimitz would be a major commander in the Pacific throughout the war and ultimately earn five stars in 1944, becoming a fleet admiral and one of the few men in the Army and Navy achieving five-star grade.[23]

The Effect on the American Public

Shot in the Back by the "Yellow Peril" or the "Yellow Sneaks"

Perhaps no event in the history of the United States aroused the public as did the attacks on December 7. The arousal was immediate and remained in high gear for most of the war, although the public, as did the military, tired of the war as it continued. The date the war ended is known today, but during the war, the ending date could not be predicted. As an Iwo Jima veteran told the author, one saying expressing the uncertainty was "Golden Gate in '48."

But the hatred of the Japanese never subsided. Anger and treachery are the two best words capturing the feeling of the public about the Japanese after hearing of the attack on Oahu. As mentioned earlier, the public was not only angry at the attack itself but also at its treacherous nature; it was a surprise or sneak attack delivered while the United States and Japan were ostensibly engaged in diplomacy. It violated America's notion of fair play in which two gunfighters from the Old West faced off in a street, each knowing the other was there. To shoot someone in the back was bad form and a sign of cowardice.

On December 7, Japan shot the United States in the back. Ironically, one man knew well the danger of that shot—Yamamoto. Yamamoto, who conceived the attack, knew about the vast industrial base of the United States. He knew that fighting a country with such an industrial base—larger than his and protected from outside attack—was dangerous. He saw that base when he was in the United States as a naval attaché and studied at Harvard. The old saying is, "If you punch the king, you better kill him." The attacks on December 7 did not and could not kill the king.[24] And as recounted earlier, the United States—ironically—shot Yamamoto in the back, ambushing his aircraft in flight and killing him.

Thus Yamamoto's fear of "awaking a sleeping tiger" or not killing the king came true. The attack simply infuriated and united the American public, setting its military machinery in overdrive. Recruiting offices filled with men eager to join the military. While talking to the author, Jack Hankins of Martinsville, Virginia, who would be a Navy pilot in the war, best summarized the initial reaction: *"I wanted to fight any son of a bitch that bombed my country."* [italics added for emphasis]. At the end of the section of a 1942 Army infantry training manual one finds this language:

> [58]. **Conclusion.** No one act by our enemies could have united the people of the United States better than [the] treacherous attack on Pearl Harbor by Japan. With one dissenting vote the Congress voted [on December 8] for war against Japan and without a single one for war against Germany and Italy…The Axis group [Japan, Germany, and Italy] consists of power-mad nations bent on ruling the world at the expense of the other countries which are made up of peace-loving people who are determined that the Axis and all that it stands for will be driven from the earth. [Bold in original][25]

Yamamoto was upset that proper warning was not provided as required by treaty. Japan and the United States signed the 1907 Hague Convention No. III, "Relative to the Opening of Hostilities." Article 1 of the Convention stated that "hostilities" could not begin "without previous and explicit warning, in the form either of a reasoned declaration of war or of an ultimatum with conditional declaration of war." The treaty did not specify how far in advance of commencement of hostilities the warning had to be given. Ironically the warning requirement was made part of the treaty due to the Japanese sneak attack on the Russian fleet at Port Arthur in 1904.[26]

Because of problems Japanese diplomats had in Washington decoding the message about the attack, the Japanese did not deliver the warning until after it had begun, which "threw gas on the fires" already burning at the White House and State and War Departments because Washington officials already knew about the attack before the Japanese diplomats could tell them.[27]

The Japanese reputation for treachery, their brutal treatment of prisoners of war, and their fight-to-the-death mentality permeated the entire Pacific war, causing a hatred of the Japanese generally not found in feelings toward the other enemies of the United States—Germany and Italy. Numerous references to treachery can be found, and the possibility or reality of treachery and brutality was the basis for the "no prisoners" policy adopted by many American combatants.

References to the treachery aspect continued from the beginning to the end of the war. Rear Admiral W. S. Anderson mentioned treachery in the two reports cited earlier in this chapter.[28]

The 1942 infantry training manual previously mentioned was brutally direct. It began Chapter 11, "The United States and World War II," with these sentences: "Japan treacherously attacked the United States on December 7, 1941. The next day Congress declared war." Paragraph 56 of the manual stated,

> **56. Attack by Japan.** *A. Against the United States.* On the morning of December 7, 1941, Japan, without warning[,] struck by air and sea at our Pearl Harbor Naval Base and adjacent establishments in the Hawaiian Islands. The attack surprised our forces with the result that in addition to numerous casualties in personnel, three warships were sunk, several damaged, and many airplanes destroyed. [Bold and italics in the original][29]

Although the number of ships sunk was incorrect, the point was made.

President Roosevelt's famous address to Congress on December 8 noted that the distance from Japan to Hawaii indicated the attack had been planned over many days or weeks; he alleged that during this time when Japan was planning the attack, Japan deceived the United States by false expressions of hope for peace. He also mentioned in his address the overriding theme discussed extensively in this chapter—treachery—when he said that the United States "will make it very certain that this form of treachery shall never again endanger us."[30]

The official biography of the sole Marine Medal of Honor (MOH) recipient for December 7, First Lieutenant George Cannon, states that he was killed "during the sneak attack by Japanese forces."[31]

Treachery is mentioned even in personnel records. *Arizona*'s commanding officer on December 7, Franklin Van Valkenburgh, is one of the MOH recipients in this book. His Official Military Personnel File (OMPF) has this entry, dated December 7, 1941, under the title "Record of Officers, U.S. Navy":

> While Japanese envoys were in Washington, DC, in an avowed attempt to reach an amicable settlement of controversies between the United States and Japan, aircraft of the latter nation, without warning and without a declaration of war, on this date attacked US forces in Hawaii and in other Pacific areas by aerial torpedoes, aerial bombs, and machine guns. The USS *Arizona*, at Pearl Harbor, T.H., to which ship Captain Franklin Van Valkenburgh was attached, was destroyed by bombs, and Captain Van Valkenburgh was lost. Under date of December 27, 1941, the Secretary of the Navy declared [him] officially dead as of December 7, 1941.[32]

The OMPF of Rear Admiral Isaac Kidd has a similar entry; he was aboard *Arizona* on December 7 as the Commander, Battleship Division One . He also perished when the ship exploded. His OMPF contains a tribute from the ARMY AND NAVY

REGISTER of March 7, 1942. The unnamed author wrote,

> ...bombs from Japanese aircraft treacherously flown in a "surprise" attack. These yellow sneaks did not surprise Admiral "Cap" Kidd. I think he knew that the Japs would do this some day [sic]...Just 40 years earlier he had a boyish premonition of the danger inherent in Japanese treachery. The theme he chose for his high school graduation address was "The Yellow Peril."

The author noted that the Japanese were bombing a navy with whom they were at peace and that "Ike (Kidd) knew their yellow color. Had he not though long about the Yellow Peril?" He closed with the famous words that would become a rallying cry for the United States: "Remember Pearl Harbor!"[33]

Battle reports submitted by Marine commanders who fought the Japanese on Iwo Jima comment on Japanese treachery, such as booby-trapping bodies, poisoning sake or water, feigning surrender, and wearing Marine uniforms or uniform parts and carrying Marine weapons and equipment.[34]

The word "Jap" was not only short for someone who was Japanese. President Roosevelt was not politically correct in at least one sense; he used "Jap" and "Japs." "Jap" also became a verb: to "jap" someone was to surprise them or to display treachery. The author's grandfather was named Jasper and nicknamed Jap, and his family knew a man named "Jap" Sizemore. Men named Jasper might have had the nickname "Jap"—but not after December 7.[35]

And no one had any compunction about killing "Japs."

The treachery theme continued even as war's end approached. A newspaper headline read, "Danger of Treachery after Jap Surrender Stressed by Nimitz." The article began,

> GUAM, Aug. 11. [1945]—Admiral Nimitz today warned against Japanese "treachery" even after a complete surrender. He emphasized that vigilance against possible further enemy attacks and "treachery" should be exercised for some time [sic] after the surrender.[36]

Even toilet paper provided a chance to condemn Japan. In 1942, the commanding officer of the submarine USS Skipjack wrote a letter about the difficulty of obtaining toilet paper via supply channels, noting that the supply system's failure to deliver made the situation "acute, particularly during depth-charge attacks by the '*back stabbers*.'"[37] [Italics added for emphasis.]

In summary, the political correctness of today did not exist during World War II during which President Roosevelt said "Jap" or "Japs" publicly and few Americans, whether in the military or members of the public supporting the military, had any compunction about killing the enemy, regardless of what he was called. This included the author's father, who was the radar operator on a B-29 with twenty-nine combat missions during the war, both bombing and photographic reconnaissance. The author detected a sentiment that killing "Japs" was a job his father was required to do to prosecute the war, and while not a source of enjoyment, killing was done without hesitation.

"Too Little, Too Late": Beware of Sundays and Holidays

In what can only be irony or black humor, on December 28, 1941, Vice Admiral W. S. Pye, the immediate and temporary replacement for Kimmel, sent a message to the Fleet titled "Subject: Surprise Attack, Sunday and Holidays." The message recited that Pye had caused all ships and stations "to assume a constant state of readiness against surprise attack." It continued, "…it should be especially noted that the Japanese and German tactics and psychology make Sundays and holidays likely days for attack." The message directed special vigilance on "Sundays and holidays to guard against surprise attacks."[38]

Collecting Information about the Attack; Investigations

Commanders on Oahu (or senior surviving officers, if commanders were dead, wounded, or missing) submitted reports about December 7. For the purposes of this book, these reports are termed "after-action reports." These reports usually include "enclosures," documents supporting comments in the letter reports or otherwise providing information. Generally enclosures are statements from witnesses.

Admiral Nimitz submitted a comprehensive report dated February 15, 1942.[39]

The U.S. Government conducted eight formal investigations of December 7 between 1942 and 1946.[40]

Awards

Numerous personnel earned various awards for conduct on December 7, including the nation's highest award for combat valor, the MOH. In March 1942, President Franklin Roosevelt approved fourteen MOHs for actions on December 7. Thirteen were for Navy officers and men at Pearl Harbor: twelve on Battleship Row and one on Carrier Row. The fourteenth was a Marine MOH for actions on Midway. In June 1942, he approved a MOH for December 7 actions at Kaneohe Bay. In 1948, President Harry Truman approved the last MOH for December 7 actions for Pearl Harbor and Battleship Row, increasing the total to thirteen MOHs for "battleship sailors." The majority of this book (Chapters 4–12 and 19) is about these MOH recipients.

Long-Term Consequences of the Attack: The Fate of the Japanese Commanders

As noted earlier, Yamamoto was assassinated in an aerial ambush.

As was typical of wartime publications expressing no sympathy for the enemies of the United States, Time magazine, near an article with a subtitle "Jap in a Trap," sarcastically announced Nagumo's death under a headline "Admiral's Week" that recounted the deaths or demotions of several Japanese commanders, beginning with "It was a bad fortnight for Japanese brass hats[.]" For Nagumo, the magazine wrote,

> On Saipan, Vice Admiral Chuichi Nagumo made his honorable exit. Onetime hero of the Empire, Nagumo commanded the carriers in the Pearl Harbor attack [and] lived to see his fame dimmed when he lost four of five carriers in the Battle of Midway. After Saipan fell, US soldiers found his corpse. He had, quite obviously, committed hara-kiri.[41]

In fact, Nagumo lost only four carriers at Midway, four of the six that had sailed from Japan to Oahu to attack on December 7.[42]

Revenge or Payback

Did the United States achieve revenge for December 7? A broader question could be asked: Did the nations in the Pacific suffering brutality spanning the 1930s and up to 1945 achieve revenge? One finds "yes" in several places.

The first "yes" is a review of the newspaper coverage of the war. The author's late father, a veteran of World War II, wondered about the lack of news coverage of the modern war in Afghanistan and asked, "What happened to the war?" That question was not asked during World War II. The American government and people took the Pacific war seriously. The population was invested in the war with so many families having a member or members in the armed forces. The U.S. military did not play or hand-wring over rules of engagement and the media. Some headlines will affirm that assertion, headlines one would never see today about enemies of the United States.[43]

"Air Force Gives Japan List of 11 Cities Next In Line For Attack
(continued on another page: Air Force Hands Japan List of Cities To Die)"

★ ★ ★ ★ ★ ★ ★ ★ ★ ★ ★

"Atomic Bombs Exterminate At Least 70,000 Japs"

The second "yes" is this observation in a newspaper: "That Jap officer on Okinawa who made a final banzai charge armed only with a cap pistol is just a symbol of what's going to happen to Nippon."[44]

The third "yes" is Yamamoto's fate: assassination by bullets from American fighter planes. Fuchida and Genda were luckier; they survived the war.

The fourth "yes" is the Doolittle Raid, described in the conclusion of this book, which was a psychological defeat for Japan early in the war.

The fifth "yes" is the U.S. victory at Midway, a catastrophic military defeat for Japan early in the war and turning point in the war in the Pacific.

The sixth "yes" is the ceremony on USS Missouri in September 1945 and knowing (1) who signed what sections of the surrender document ending the war and (2) who stood where. The men standing in front of General of the Army Douglas MacArthur were the clear losers.

For the seventh "yes," one need only reread President Truman's observation about the Hiroshima bombing mentioned in chapter 2—the answer always returns to Pearl Harbor:

The Japanese began the war from the air at Pearl Harbor. They have been repaid many fold [by the bomb just dropped, that had more power than 20,000 tons of TNT].

LESSONS LEARNED: WEAPONS AND THINKING

One casualty of the attack was the various forms of conventional thinking described in chapter 2. A good summary of that thinking is found in a postwar interview with Rear Admiral W. S. Anderson, who on December 7 was Commander, Battleships, Battle Force. In the interview, he reaffirmed the belief that most naval officers had before December 7: torpedo attack in a shallow harbor, such as Pearl Harbor, was impossible. He noted that the modified Japanese torpedoes worked well and did the greatest damage. He did not think the modified bombs designed to hit the inboard ships were very effective.[45]

Many lessons can be learned from the attack on December 7. Two are particularly important.

One was the transition of the aircraft carrier to the position of primacy in naval warfare, putting the battleship in second place. The battleship and naval gun gave way to the aircraft carrier and naval aviation. The lesson would be demonstrated dramatically by American victory at the Battle of Midway, where the majority of fighting would be between aircraft carriers and their aircraft; the battle did not involve classic naval surface ship combat featuring naval guns. And ironically the four Japanese carriers lost at Midway (Akagi, Hiryu, Kaga, and Soryu) were four of the six carriers executing the attack on December 7.[46]

Two is the importance of a defensive mind-set and preparation. The following passage is from a government book about the Navy in World War II:

The most important [lesson] is, perhaps, that in making plans for defense in a period of international tension a prospective aggressor should be considered capable of resorting to any course of action that is a possibility no matter how illogical and contrary to his own interests that course may seem to be. Possibilities should not be ignored because they are improbabilities. This, however, may not be as simple as it sounds. The means for resistance are seldom so abundant as to permit planning, training, and full commitment against all possibilities without impairing the effectiveness of defense measures that can be planned for use against the probable.[47]

Conventional Thinking Still Lives on Life Support

Conventional thinking existing before December 7 died a prolonged, excruciating death on December 7. Mitchell's warnings forecasted that death, and his advocacy of airpower would find continuing validation at the Battle of Midway and other World War II battles in which airpower dominated sea power.

Or it *appeared* to die. Despite the dead bodies and burning ships on Oahu, readers find the following statements in a book written by, of all people, J. W. Bunkley, who as a Navy captain commanded *California* on December 7. Japanese aircraft, using torpedoes and bombs, sank his battleship in place on Battleship Row. *Four of his men earned MOHs, three of them dying in the process.*

He retired during the war as a rear admiral and wrote a book published in 1943 about military organization, uniforms, and insignia. In his chapter on ships are these stupefying sentences about battleships:

"[Battleships] are the backbone of the world's navies."

"[They] are the heavyweight in our battle forces."

He then discusses aircraft carriers, placing them a distinct "second," by writing, "[They have] come into prominence during this war and as a fighting ship holds the number two position, *being next to the battleship in importance*"[48] [Italics added for emphasis]. He still did not "get it."

To recap basic, simple historical facts, on December 7, Japanese aircraft—flying from Japanese aircraft carriers, not from battleships—eviscerated the Pacific Fleet, including its battleships, including Bunkley's own ship, *California*. No surface naval combat between battleships or any other ships occurred that day except for a minor engagement: destroyer USS Ward sinking a Japanese midget submarine before the attack. Conclusion—the aircraft carrier dominated naval warfare from December 7 forward.

And in the Wings: Brigadier General Billy Mitchell, U.S. Army

No pun intended.

The Introduction described Billy Mitchell's advocacy of airpower and the unpopularity of and resistance to his ideas. Chapter 20 more fully discusses Mitchell and the special posthumous MOH awarded him and presented to his son. At this point, all that needs to be noted is that the attack confirmed two aspects of what Mitchell had been saying. One, it proved that he was correct in predicting a Japanese attack on Oahu and observing that its defenses were deficient. Two, it proved he was correct in in stating that airpower was superior to sea power. Japanese aircraft battered the ships of a U.S. Pacific Fleet helplessly moored in Pearl Harbor.

Pearl Harbor Today

What is left from December 7? What changes were made?

After the war, the Navy Yard became two commands: Pearl Harbor Naval Station and Pearl Harbor Naval Shipyard. The Submarine Base closed, becoming part of the Naval Station. The Naval Air Station on Ford Island closed in 1962, but Ford Island remains an active military base and is part of Naval Station Pearl Harbor.[49]

Around Ford Island, small plaques mounted on white stones (or on the front of the firehouse for Maryland and *Oklahoma*) are memorials to the ships, but none of the plaques mention MOH recipients.

In the water around Ford Island, the large white mooring quays used in 1941 remain to mark the positions or berths of most ships on Battleship Row. The quay for Maryland and *Oklahoma* no longer exists; that berth is now for Missouri, which was not present in Pearl Harbor on December 7. The large lettering on the remaining quays reads as follows, with the quays in this order, as they were in 1941 (F-3 closest to the channel leading to the Pacific Ocean, F-8 closest to the bridge connecting Ford Island and the mainland). The positions were called, for example, "Berth Fox 3" with "Fox" being the word for "F" in the phonetic alphabet:

F-3: USS *CALIFORNIA* BB 44 (two quays, one lettered)

[USS *MISSOURI*] (no quays at the former F-5 berth)

F-6: USS *WEST VIRGINIA* BB 44 (one quay)

F-6: USS *TENNESSEE* BB 43 (one quay)

F-7: USS *VESTAL* AR 4 (one quay)

[USS *ARIZONA* MEMORIAL]

F-7: USS *ARIZONA* BB 39 (one quay)

F-8: USS *NEVADA* BB 36 (two quays, one lettered)

None of the ships on Battleship Row—*Nevada, Oklahoma, Tennessee, California,* Maryland, *West Virginia*, Neosho, and *Vestal*—survive today (see Chapter 22 ("Legacy—Ships and Stations")).

Only two ships from December 7 remain off Ford Island, both wrecks frozen in time and commemorated by white memorials over which fly U.S. flags. *Arizona* is where she sank in place and is well known; *Utah* is where she was partially righted and is, tragically, not as well-known as *Arizona*. *Arizona*'s dead rest among ceaseless tourist visitation; *Utah*'s dead rest in silence broken only by noises from occasional visitors or by the flapping of her American flag in the breezes over Pearl Harbor.

NOTES

1. Franklin D. Roosevelt, "Address to Congress Requesting a Declaration of War with Japan" (December 8, 1941), printed from the Franklin D. Roosevelt Presidential Library and Museum Internet site October 9, 2015 (hereafter "Roosevelt Declaration of War Speech").

2. Report by Rear Admiral W. S. Anderson, Commander Battleships, Battle Force (Subject: "Attack at Pearl Harbor by Japanese Planes on December 7, 1941") of December 19, 1941, 1, (paragraph 1).

3. SEAMANSHIP ("NAVPERS 16118," U.S. Navy, Training, Standards, and Curriculum Division, June 1944), 6.

4. War Department, Military Intelligence Division, THE PUNCH BELOW THE BELT: Japanese Ruses, Deception Tactics, and Antipersonnel Measures (Washington, D.C., August 1, 1945); the photographs precede page 1.

5. Vice Admiral Homer N. Wallin, U.S. Navy (Retired), Pearl Harbor: Why, How, Fleet Salvage, and Final Appraisal (Naval History Division, United States Government Printing Office, Washington, 1968), 305 (hereafter, "Wallin, Pearl Harbor").

6. Report by Rear Admiral W. S. Anderson, Commander Battleships, Battle Force (Subject: "Distinguished Conduct—report of—Pearl Harbor Raid, December 7, 1941") 1 (paragraph 1).

7. Endnote 5, Wallin, Pearl Harbor, 282.

8. Barber v. Sheila Widnall (U.S. Ninth Circuit Court of Appeals, No. 93-36200, 1996); Rex Barber was one of the pilots on the mission flown to intercept Yamamoto; Sheila Widnall was the Secretary of the Air Force at the time of the court decision.

9. The Story of the 73rd: The Unofficial History of the 73rd Bomb Wing (Reprinted by The Battery Press, Nashville, TN, 1980), no page number.

10. Colonel Charles A. Jones, U.S. Marine Corps Reserve (Retired), Hawaii's World War II Military Sites (Mutual Publishing, Honolulu, HI, 2002), 27 (hereafter "Jones, Hawaii's World War II Military Sites").

11. The National Personnel Records Center, St. Louis, Missouri, furnished military and personal information from Van Valkenburgh's Official Military Personnel File (OMPF) at the author's requests. The telegram was on a compact disc containing the OMPF at page 45 of Section 04, "Service Documents" (hereafter "Van Valkenburgh OMPF (CD)"); see endnote 16 in Chapter 7 (*Arizona*) and the bibliography for more OMPF details.

12. See Chapter 22, "Legacy—Ships and Stations"; the commissioning dates are from Dictionary of American Naval Fighting Ships (written by either the Naval History

Division or the Naval Historical Center, Department of the Navy, Washington, D.C., 1976) (hereafter "DANFS"); dates of commissioning: *Nevada*, Vol. V, 52; *Tennessee*, Vol. VII, 88; *California*, Vol. II, 14; Maryland, Vol. IV, 257; and *West Virginia*, Vol. VIII, 222. James L. Mooney was the editor for Volumes VII and VIII of DANFS.

13. Endnote 5, Wallin, Pearl Harbor.

14. Endnote 9, Jones, Hawaii's World War II Military Sites, 28; see Chapters 4–10 and 22.

15. Endnote 13, DANFS, Vol. VIII, 224 ; endnote 5, Wallin, Pearl Harbor, 238.

16. Endnote 5, Wallin, Pearl Harbor, 280–281.

17. Ibid., 218.

18. Ibid., 253–262 (*Oklahoma*) and 262–267 (*Utah*).

19. Endnote 9, Jones, Hawaii's World War II Military Sites, 29.

20. Ibid., 30.

21. Endnote 1, Roosevelt Declaration of War Speech.

22. Endnote 9, Jones, Hawaii's World War II Military Sites, 31; Commander Roger D. Scott, U.S. Navy, "Kimmel, Short, McVay: Case Studies in Executive Authority, Law, and the Individual Rights of Military Commanders," (Military Law Review, Department of the Army Pamphlet 27-100-156, Department of the Army, Washington, DC, June 1998), 52–53, 103, and 115–119.

23. Endnote 9, Jones, Hawaii's World War II Military Sites, 31; Loss of Grayling: Theodore Roscoe, United States Submarine Operations in World War II (Naval Institute Press, Annapolis, MD, 1949), 273 (hereafter, "Roscoe, Submarine Operations in World War II"); Nimitz as a fleet admiral: Peter Grier, "The Highest Ranking," AIR FORCE MAGAZINE (March 2012), 50–54 (discussion of the five-star grade with Nimitz mentioned on page 54).

24. Gordon W. Prange, At Dawn We Slept (Penguin Books, New York, NY, 1982), 337–338; the author has heard the expression, "If you punch the king, you better kill him."

25. Tactics And Technique Of Infantry (The Military Service Publishing Company, Harrisburg, PA, 1942), 66 (hereafter "Tactics And Technique Of Infantry").

26. Endnote 9, Jones, Hawaii's World War II Military Sites, 21–22 and 27.

27. Ibid., 27.

28. Endnotes 2 and 6 (Anderson reports).

29. Endnote 27, Tactics And Technique Of Infantry, 56–65.

30. Endnote 1, Roosevelt Declaration of War Speech.

31. Official U.S. Marine Corps biography, First Lieutenant George H. Cannon, USMC (September, 1949) (hereafter "Cannon U.S. Marine Corps biography"); see Chapter 12 concerning Lieutenant Cannon.

32. Endnote 10, Van Valkenburgh OMPF (CD).

33. The National Personnel Records Center, St. Louis, Missouri, furnished military and personal information from Kidd's Official Military Personnel File (OMPF) at the author's requests. The tribute was on a compact disc containing the OMPF at page 3 of Section 08, "Newspaper Clippings"; see endnote 7 in chapter 9 (*Arizona*) and the bibliography for more OMPF details.

34. Examples include Regimental Combat Team 21 (Subject: Action Report, Iwo Jima Operation) of April 10, 1945, 13 (faking surrender and wearing Marine uniforms); Action Report of Combat Team 28, Iwo Jima (no subject, undated), Annex Baker, 12 (live Japanese hiding among the dead playing possum); Commanding Officer, Third Battalion, Twenty-First Marines, Third Marine Division, (Subject: Action Report) of April 11, 1945, paragraph 7, page 13 (booby-trapped saki [sic] bottles and direction to put acid in water left behind).

35. The author heard the expression "to Jap" someone in law school (1977 to 1980); it would not be said today. His family's lore mentioned "Jap" as short for the surname "Jasper."

36. Associated Press item (in newspaper with no identification) of August 11, 1945.

37. Endnote 9, Roscoe, Submarine Operations in World War II, 145.

38. Pacific Fleet Notice 45N-41 (Subject: "Surprise Attack, Sundays and Holidays") of December 28, 1941.

39. Report from Commander-in-Chief, U.S. Pacific Fleet (Subject: "Report of Japanese Raid on Pearl Harbor, December 7, 1941") of February 15, 1942.

40. Endnote 9, Jones, Hawaii's World War II Military Sites, 30–31.

41. "Admirals' Week," Time (July 24, 1944), 28.

42. Endnote 9, Jones, Hawaii's World War II Military Sites, 33.

43. Murlin Spencer (Associated Press), July 28, 1945, (cities headline); Greensboro Daily News (United Press, August 23, 1945) (atomic bomb headlines).

44. Greensboro Daily News ("Paragrahics"), June 28, 1945.

45. Paul Stillwell, ed. Air Raid: Pearl Harbor! Recollections of a Day of Infamy (Naval Institute Press, 1981), 129–131

46. Endnote 9, Jones, Hawaii's World War II Military Sites, 33.

47. Rear Admiral Augustus Furer, U.S. Navy Retired, Administration of the Navy Department in World War II (U.S. Government Printing Office, 1959), 101.
48. J. W. Bunkley, Rear Admiral, United States Navy, Retired, MILITARY and NAVAL RECOGNITION BOOK (D. Van Nostrand Company, Inc., 1943), 122–123.

49. Information about Pearl Harbor today is from the author's numerous visits to Pearl Harbor in 1999, 2004, and most recently in 2015.

Part III

MEN–
ABOVE AND BEYOND AND FORCIBLY REMOVED

Section A:
Medals of Honor Earned on December 7, 1941, at Pearl Harbor

Chapter 4
USS California (BB-44)
"The Prune Barge"

Ensign Herbert Jones, U.S. Naval Reserve

Warrant Officer (Radio Electrician), Thomas Reeves, U.S. Navy

Petty Officer First Class (Machinist's Mate) Robert Scott, U.S. Navy

Warrant Officer (Gunner) Jackson Pharris, U.S. Navy

USS California, December 7, 1941

USS *California* was called "the Prune Barge" because of California's export of prunes.[1]

On December 7, *California* was, like *Nevada*, moored by herself along Battleship Row, with her starboard side facing Ford Island and her port side facing the waters of Pearl Harbor. *California* was at Berth F-3 at the opposite end of Battleship Row from *Nevada*. In short, they were the "bookends" of Battleship Row on December 7. With the exception of USS Pennsylvania, which was at the shipyard at the Navy Yard, all battleships were between *California* at berth F-3 and *Nevada* at Berth F-8 along with the repair ship *Vestal* (beside *Arizona*) and the tanker Neosho (behind *California* and in front of Maryland and *Oklahoma*).[2]

Oiler Neosho (AO-23) survived December 7 and was attacked and damaged in 1942 during the Battle of the Coral Sea. Neosho remained afloat for four days until the crew was rescued and American gunfire sank the ship. One crew member, Chief Watertender Oscar Peterson, received a posthumous MOH for performing damage control during the attack.[3]

California was closest to the entrance to the channel leading from Pearl Harbor to the Pacific Ocean. This entrance was between the Waipio Peninsula and Hospital Point. *Nevada*, at Berth F-8, was farthest from the mouth of that channel.[4]

Mooring alone along Ford Island was dangerous since the side of the ship facing the waters of Pearl Harbor and Southeast Loch was vulnerable to torpedoes dropped from the air into Southeast Loch or the waters of Pearl Harbor surrounding the ships.[5] The port sides of *California* and *Nevada* were thus exposed. *California* was particularly vulnerable since she was closer to Southeast Loch, which was called "Torpedo Alley" for a reason; torpedoes dropped in Southeast Loch could travel directly toward the heart of Battleship Row.[6]

That danger became reality when *California* suffered three torpedo hits on her port side. One bomb hit her; four just missed her but spewed fragments. She sank upright in place.⁷

California's commanding officer, Captain J. W. Bunkley, spent the night ashore and did not return to the ship until 9:00 a.m.; at 10:02, he ordered abandon ship but cancelled the order at 10:15.⁸

The ship's casualties were five officers and forty-eight men killed and forty-five men missing.⁹

As explained in this Chapter, on December 7, three *California* crewmen—Warrant Officer (Gunner) Jackson Pharris, Ensign Herbert Jones, and Warrant Officer (Radio Electrician) Thomas Reeves—assisted in an essential task: organizing ammunition supply to the antiaircraft guns by hand after mechanical ammunition hoists were disabled. And as will be seen in Chapter 19, Pharris, despite his own injuries, saved numerous shipmates and took decisive, critical actions to save the ship. His most important action was to order counterflooding so the ship would not capsize, thus saving the crew from the dreadful, ghastly consequences suffered by a crew of a capsized vessel: the agony, fear, and disorientation of being trapped in the dark, flooded compartments of an overturned ship. Thus *California* remained upright, and her crew did not suffer the horrors of the two ships that did capsize: USS *Oklahoma* and USS *Utah*.¹⁰

These three men, along with *California* crewman Machinist's Mate First Class Robert Scott, received MOHs. Only one of them survived December 7.

Ensign Herbert Jones, U.S. Naval Reserve

Background

Jones was born on January 21, 1918, in Los Angeles, *California*, and enlisted in the naval reserve on May 14, 1935, as an apprentice seaman. He was discharged on November 30, 1937, under honorable conditions. On July 8, 1940, he reenlisted as an apprentice seaman. He had active-duty training on USS Wyoming from July 15 to August 9, 1940. On August 10, 1940, he was appointed a midshipman in the U.S. Naval Reserve Midshipman's School aboard USS Illinois (later Prairie State), graduating from the first class (the V-7 program) on November 13, 1940. He was appointed an ensign on November 14, 1940, and reported to USS *California* on December 1, 1940.¹¹

Actions on December 7

On December 7, Jones organized and led a party in supplying antiaircraft ammunition by hand after the electric and hand-powered hoists failed.¹²

Private A. E. Senior, probably a member of the ship's Marine detachment, went below deck to assist in passing ammunition by hand. He saw Jones at the foot of a ladder, directing the supply chain. Senior worked under his direction for about fifteen to twenty minutes, after which a bomb explosion disrupted the effort, darkened the compartment, and filled it with smoke. The bomb fatally wounded Jones. Senior turned his flashlight on Jones and saw blood on his face and white uniform jacket. He and another man evacuated Jones up the ladder until Jones stopped them from carrying him any farther, saying, and "Leave me alone! I am done for. Get out of here before the magazines go off."[13]

In his report of December 13, 1941, the ship's commanding officer mentioned Jones under the heading "DISTINGUISHED CONDUCT PERSONNEL[.]" He wrote, "Ensign H. C. JONES and Ensign I. W. JEFFREY (both deceased)…organized a party and were attempting to get ammunition up by hand when killed."[14]

In his revised report of December 22, 1941, the commanding officer wrote about a group organized to supply ammunition to the antiaircraft guns. He continued, "In the meantime an additional group was organized, Ensigns H. C. Jones, W. F. Cage, and I. W. Jeffrey, to assist further in the ammunition supply." Under "DISTINGUISHED CONDUCT—PERSONNEL" he included "JONES, N. C. [sic], USNR (Deceased)" following this sentence: "The following named men and officers were outstanding in their work during battle in the ammunition supply and in removing wounded."[15]

In a letter of January 10, 1942, the ship's commanding officer recommended Jones, Pharris, and Scott for awards. In recommending Jones for an award, he described the same actions reported in his two reports of the attack and by Private Senior. In the January 10 letter, he concluded, "His body was recovered the next day…[B]y his action Ens. Jones displayed initiative, leadership, devotion to duty, and courage of the highest order."[16]

Warrant Officer (Gunner) Jackson Pharris, U.S. Navy

Because Pharris was for some unknown reason awarded a Navy Cross for December 7 while Jones, Reeves, and Scott received MOHs and because of the prolonged process required by the Navy for the Pharris Navy Cross to be upgraded to a MOH, his background and his actions on December 7 are discussed in detail in Chapter 19. He did not receive his MOH until 1948 while the posthumous awards to Jones, Reeves, and Scott were made in 1942.

Aftermath of December 7

After-Action Reports and Awards Recommendation Letter

Captain Joel W. Bunkley, the commanding officer of *California* on December 7, submitted three documents reporting the bravery of the four *California* crewmen who would receive MOHs. They were mentioned earlier in this Chapter—two after-action reports (original and revised) addressed to the Commander-in-Chief of the U.S. Pacific Fleet. His initial report is dated December 13.[34] His revised report is dated December 22.[35] both reports mentioned Reeves, Jones, and Pharris. Neither report letter mentioned Scott.

The third document was a letter Bunkley wrote dated January 10, 1942, to the "Commander in Chief [sic], U.S. Fleet." The exclusive purpose of the letter was to recommend "appropriate awards" for Pharris, Jones, and Scott for their conduct on December 7. The letter summarized the action of each man on December 7 justifying the awards, with the summary for Pharris being the longest. The letter does not mention Reeves.[36]

Ensign Herbert Jones, Warrant Officer (Radio Electrician) Thomas Reeves, and Petty Officer First Class (Machinist's Mate) Robert Scott would be three battleship sailors from *California* on Battleship Row to earn MOHs on December 7, all posthumous awards. President Franklin D. Roosevelt signed each of the three MOH citations on March 4, 1942.

As just noted, Warrant Officer Jackson Pharris would be the fourth *California* crewman to earn a MOH and the only living *California* MOH recipient, but he would not receive his MOH until 1948 (see Chapter 19).

Warrant Officer (Radio Electrician) Thomas Reeves, U.S. Navy

Background

Reeves were born on December 9, 1895, at Thomaston, Connecticut. He enlisted in the Navy on July 21, 1917, at New York City and released from active duty in 1919. He was recalled and transferred to the regular navy on April 16, 1920. He was discharged on August 21, 1921, but he reenlisted on October 12, 1921, and remained in the Navy thereafter, reaching the grade of chief radioman. On November 13, 1941, he was appointed a warrant officer (radio electrician) to rank from October 2, 1941.[17] A warrant officer radio electrician assists the communications officer or, if the ship has no communications officer, the engineering officer. He or she also stands watches.[18]

Actions on December 7

Reeves, as were Jones and Pharris, was mentioned in the commanding officer's reports of the action on December 7.

In his report of December 13, 1941, the commanding officer mentioned Reeves under the heading "DISTINGUISHED CONDUCT PERSONNEL." He wrote, "REEVES, T.J., CRM (PA), deceased, was outstanding in his conduct in that upon being forced to abandon Main Radio, at the request of Gunner PHARRIS, he assisted in a burning ammunition passageway, attempting to continue the flow of ammunition until overcome by smoke and fire."[19]

In his revised report of December 22, 1941, under "DISTINGUISHED CONDUCT PERSONNEL," he wrote, "The following named men and officers were outstanding in their work during battle in the ammunition supply and in removing wounded." Included in the names under that sentence was "REEVES, T.J., C.R.M.

(PA) USN (Deceased)."[20]

His MOH citation notes that Reeves continued to assist with passing ammunition by hand until he was overcome by smoke and fire that "resulted in his death."[21]

Reeves is not mentioned in the commanding officer's letter of January 10, 1942, concerning awards for Jones, Pharris, and Scott.[22]

PETTY OFFICER (MACHINIST'S MATE) FIRST CLASS ROBERT SCOTT, U.S. NAVY

Background

Scott was born on July 13, 1915, in Massillon, Ohio. He is one of three Ohio natives who earned MOHs on December 7. The other two are Ward (USS *Oklahoma*) of Springfield and Kidd (USS *Arizona*) of Cleveland.[23]

Scott graduated from Washington High School and attended Ohio State University (OSU) from 1936 to 1937. A residence hall at OSU was named for him because of his death at Pearl Harbor: Scott House.[24]

Scott enlisted in the Navy on April 18, 1938, at Cleveland, Ohio, and eventually became a machinist's mate first class.[25] The duties of a machinist's mate included operating, maintaining, and repairing main and auxiliary engines, auxiliary machinery, and the steering and anchor engines. He also operated machine shop machinery and repaired machine equipment and small boats.[26]

Actions on December 7

On December 7, Scott went to his battle station, a compartment that had an air compressor. The compartment was flooded because of a torpedo hit. Everyone in the compartment evacuated it but Scott, who refused to leave. His words were to this effect: "This is my station and I will stay and give them air as long as the guns are going."[27]

A statement from Gunner's Mate Third Class V. O. Jensen confirmed what Scott had done and continued:

> During the air raid Sunday morning, December 7, 1941, Robert Scott of the "A" Division[28] was in waist deep water and fuel oil and refused to leave his station after we had gotten word to abandon our compartment. I called to him and told him everyone else had abandoned the compartment but he insisted on standing; "As long as I can give these people air, I'm sticking." His station was on the Forward Air Compressor by Main G.S.K. Things were blacking out for me so I was forced to leave the compartment and I never saw him afterwards.[29]

Although the commanding officer's reports of December 13 and December 22 do not mention Scott, in his letter of January 10, 1942, the commanding officer recommended Scott for a medal, describing actions similar to those in Jensen's statement, noting Scott said, "This is my station and I'll stay and given them air as long as the guns are going" or words to that effect. He noted that Scott's compartment was flooding because of a torpedo hit and again observed that Scott refused to leave the compartment although everyone else had evacuated it. He concluded,

His body has not as yet been recovered[,] and it is believed that he died at his post by drowning. The devotion to duty and disregard of his own safety displayed by Scott in staying at his post in the face of almost certain death is considered to be in keeping with the highest traditions of the service and [worthy] of the highest award.[30]

Scott was killed in action, and his body was recovered.[31]

His hometown newspaper article noted that Scott was the town's first "victim of World War II."[32]

Another newspaper article about Scott titled "Service Held for War Hero" reports that a memorial service was held for him on a Sunday at Wesley Methodist Church, where he was a member. The article stated that family, "former members of his Sunday school class," and many relatives and friends attended to honor "the only Massillon man ever to receive the [C]ongressional [M]edal of [H]onor." Also attending were members of the "'Victory Mothers'" club of Massillon, a group whose sons were serving in the armed forces. The article stated that Scott received the MOH because he refused to leave his air compressor as "water poured into his ship through a hole blasted in its side by a Jap torpedo."[33]

MOH Citations

Ensign Herbert Jones

For conspicuous devotion to duty, extraordinary courage, and complete disregard of his own life, above and beyond the call of duty, during the attack on the fleet in Pearl Harbor, by Japanese forces on December 7, 1941. Ens. Jones organized and led a party, which was supplying ammunition to the antiaircraft battery of the USS *California* after the mechanical hoists were put out of action when he was fatally wounded by a bomb explosion. When 2 men attempted to take him from the area, which was on fire, he refused to let them do so, saying in words to the effect, "Leave me alone! I am done for. Get out of here before the magazines go off."

Warrant Officer (Radio Electrician) Thomas Reeves

For distinguished conduct in the line of his profession, extraordinary courage, and disregard of his own safety during the attack on the fleet in Pearl Harbor, Territory of Hawaii, by Japanese forces on December 7, 1941. After the mechanical ammunition hoists were put out of commission in the USS *California*, Reeves, on his own initiative, in a burning passageway, assisted in the maintenance of an ammunition supply by hand to the antiaircraft guns until he was overcome by smoke and fire, which resulted in his death.

Machinist's Mate First Class Robert Scott

For conspicuous devotion to duty, extraordinary courage, and complete disregard of his own life, above and beyond the call of duty, during the attack on the fleet in Pearl Harbor, Territory of Hawaii, by Japanese forces on December 7, 1941. The compartment, in the USS *California*, in which the air compressor to which Scott was assigned as his battle station, was flooded as a result of a torpedo hit. The remainder of the personnel evacuated that compartment, but Scott refused to leave, saying words to the effect, "This is my station, and I will stay and give them air as long as the guns are going."

The Reeves MOH citation submitted to the President for signature refers to him as a "chief radioman," and the ship's reports refer to him as a "C.R.M.," which must mean "chief radioman." While his Navy biography states he progressed to chief radioman, it also states that he was appointed a "Radio Electrician" on November 13, 1941 ("appointment" implies officer status).[37]

Why the *California* MOHs Are Unique

The four *California* MOHs are unique for four reasons.

First, four was the largest number of MOHs for any ship or station on December 7. Only one other ship, the cruiser USS San Francisco at the Naval Battle of Guadalcanal, had four MOH recipients for one action during the war. Ironically, Cassin Young, commanding officer of San Francisco, was killed during that battle after surviving December 7 and receiving a MOH for bravery as commanding officer of USS *Vestal* on December 7 (see Chapters 8 (*Vestal*) and 14).

Second, one of the recipients, Pharris, was the last MOH recipient to receive his MOH for bravery on December 7. His MOH was not approved until 1948; the other three from *California* were approved in 1942.

Third, Pharris is the only December 7 recipient to have originally received a Navy Cross for December 7, a Navy Cross that was upgraded to the MOH awarded in 1948.

Fourth, the only two MOH citations for December 7 including words spoken, verbatim or approximately, by recipients during the MOH actions are both from *California* crewmen: Jones and Scott.

Notes

1. Homer N. Wallin, Vice Admiral, U.S. Navy (Retired), Pearl Harbor: Why, How, Fleet Salvage, and Final Approach (Naval History Division, U.S. Government Printing Office, 1968), 222 (hereafter "Wallin, Pearl Harbor").

2. Information about ship mooring is from the author's personal view of Battleship Row and its mooring quays; the report by Rear Admiral W. S. Anderson, Commander

Battleships, Battle Force (Subject: "Attack at Pearl Harbor by Japanese Planes on December 7, 1941") of December 19, 1941, paragraph 3 (hereafter Anderson, "Attack at Pearl Harbor by Japanese Planes on December 7, 1941"); and diagrams and photographs in Chapter 2.

3. Dictionary of American Naval Fighting Ships (Naval History Division, Department of the Navy, Washington, DC, 1976), Vol. V, 42 (hereafter "DANFS"). The MOH citation for Peterson can be found by searching the Internet for "Army MOH site" and accessing the citation by choosing the correct icon for World War II at the "Medal of Honor Recipients: Center of Military History" Internet site.

4. Author's knowledge of mooring of ships on December 7; endnote 2, Anderson, "Attack at Pearl Harbor by Japanese Planes on December 7, 1941"); diagrams and photographs in Chapter 2.

5. Author's knowledge of mooring of ships on December 7; diagrams and photographs in Chapter 2.

6. Ibid.

7. Report from USS *California* (Subject: "Report of Raid, December 7, 1941") of December 13, 1941 (hereafter "*California* report"); Report from USS *California* (Subject: "Report of Raid (Revised), December 7, 1941") of December 22, 1941 (hereafter "*California* report (revised)"); endnote 1, Wallin, Pearl Harbor, 222.

8. Endnote 7, *California* report (revised).

9. Ibid.

10. Chapter 5 (*Oklahoma*) and Chapter 10 (*Utah*) of this book.

11. The National Personnel Records Center, St. Louis, Missouri, furnished military and personal information from Jones's Official Military Personnel File (OMPF) at the author's request; Karl Schuon, U.S. Navy Biographical Dictionary (Franklin Watts, Inc., New York, NY 1964), 128.

12. Jones MOH citation in this chapter and at appendix A of this book; endnote 7, *California* report, *California* report (revised).

13. Endnote 1, Wallin, Pearl Harbor, 145–146; Jones MOH citation.

14. Endnote 7, *California* report.

15. Endnote 7, *California* report (revised).

16. Letter from Commanding Officer, USS *California*, to Commander-in-Chief, U.S. Fleet (Subject: Awards of medals for heroic conduct during the raid on Pearl Harbor, December 7, 1941, recommendations concerning) of January 10, 1942, paragraph 2

(hereafter "*California* awards letter").

17. Endnote 3, DANFS, Vol. VI, 58; Official U.S. Navy biography, "Radio Electrician Thomas James Reeves, United States Navy, Deceased" (June 15, 1949) (hereafter "Reeves, U.S. Navy biography").

18. J. W. Bunkley, Rear Admiral, United States Navy, Retired, MILITARY and NAVAL RECOGNITION BOOK (D. Van Nostrand Company, Inc., 1943); a description of the duties of radio electricians is on page 138 (hereafter "Bunkley, MILITARY and NAVAL RECOGNITION BOOK").

19. Endnote 7, *California* report.

20. Endnote 7, *California* report (revised).

21. Reeves MOH citation in this chapter and at Appendix A of this book.

22. Endnote 16, *California* awards letter.

23. Official U.S. Navy biography, "Robert R. Scott, Machinist's Mate First Class, United States Navy, Deceased" (March 3, 1949) (hereafter "Scott, U.S. Navy biography"); Chapter 5 (Ward) and Chapter 7 (Kidd).

24. "Gave His Life to Keep Guns Firing" (Massillon Independent newspaper, author and date unknown) sent to the author from the Ohio Military Museum in 2006; "Hall Names [at Ohio State University] reflect honor of past students" (The Lantern, story posted November 13, 2001, at http://www.thelantern.com and printed by the author February 21, 2007)—the Lantern is the student newspaper at Ohio State.

25. Endnote 23, Scott, U.S. Navy biography.

26. Endnote 18, Bunkley, MILITARY and NAVAL RECOGNITION BOOK; the duties of a machinist's mate are at page 141.

27. Scott MOH citation in this chapter and at Appendix A of this book.

28. A ship is divided into departments, which are divided into divisions assigned a letter or letters or a number—"A" Division is under the Engineering Department and comprises machinist's mates (as was Scott), water tenders, metalsmiths, molders, and firemen; Bureau of Naval Personnel, SEAMANSHIP ("NAVPERS 16118," U.S. Navy, Training, Standards, and Curriculum Division), 126.

29. Endnote 1, Wallin, Pearl Harbor, 317; Scott MOH citation.

30. Endnote 16, *California* awards letter, paragraph 4.

31. Endnote 23, Scott U.S. Navy biography; the author visited his grave at Arlington National Cemetery, most recently in 2015.

32. Untitled newspaper article caption printed in the Massillon Independent for a photograph of Scott's mother unveiling a memorial during the war (author and date unknown, sent to the author from the Ohio Military MUSeum in 2006). One of the onlookers at the ceremony was the last nurse to be evacuated from Corregidor.

33. "Service Held for War Hero," Massillon Independent, date and author unknown, sent to the author from the Ohio Military Museum in 2006.

34. Endnote 7, *California* report.

35. Endnote 7, *California* report (revised).

36. Endnote 16, *California* awards letter.

37. The Roosevelt approval of MOH citations is based on documents provided to the author by the Franklin D. Roosevelt Presidential Library and Museum. As noted in the background section for Reeves in this chapter, on November 13, 1941, he was appointed a warrant officer (radio electrician) to rank from October 2, 1941; see endnote 17, Reeves U.S. Navy biography; see also endnote 18, Bunkley, MILITARY and NAVAL RECOGNITION BOOK, which describes the duties of a chief radio electrician and radio electrician (but not radiomen) under the section "Duties of Officers" (133–138); under the section "Duties of Enlisted Men," the book describes the duties of a radioman (139–142).

Photographs
USS *CALIFORNIA* MOH Recipients

Ensign Herbert Jones, U.S. Naval Reserve. (Photograph NH 92307 from the Naval History and Heritage Command.)

Warrant Officer (Radio Electrician) Thomas Reeves, U.S. Navy. (Photograph NH 101649 from the Naval History and Heritage Command.)

Petty Officer First Class (Machinist's Mate) Robert Scott, U.S. Navy. (Photograph NH 92308 from the Naval History and Heritage Command.)

Chapter 5
USS Oklahoma (BB-37)
Not the Musical

Ensign Francis Flaherty, US Naval Reserve

Seaman First Class James Ward, U.S. Navy

USS Oklahoma, December 7, 1941

The two most unfortunate ships on December 7, 1941, were USS *Arizona* and USS *Oklahoma*. Each ship suffered a different hellish fate caused by different weapons.

An aerial bomb hit *Arizona*, causing a catastrophic explosion of her fuel and ammunition, toppling her foremast and causing her to drop or to sink in place without capsizing.[1] Torpedoes hit *Oklahoma* almost immediately after the attack began, ripping open the port side of her hull. She simply turned over, turning away from Ford Island and Maryland and toward Southeast Loch, turning to approximately 150 degrees in the waters of Pearl Harbor. Eventually, she stopped turning, leaving exposed the starboard propeller, her hull, and her keel. Her masts hitting the shallow bottom of Pearl Harbor prevented a complete 180-degree capsize. Although she did not completely capsize, the damage from capsizing to such a degree was irreparable.[2]

As far as casualties, the number of dead and missing crewmen (Navy and Marine) on *Oklahoma* (429) is second only to the number of dead and missing crewmen on *Arizona* (1,177).[3]

The capsizing was possible because of the ship's positon on December 7: *Oklahoma* was the outboard ship at Berth F-5, moored next to Maryland along Battleship Row. Behind *Oklahoma* was *West Virginia*; behind Maryland was Tennessee.[4] Maryland, the inboard ship moored next to Ford Island, received moderate damage from two bomb hits. Four crewmen were killed.[5]

Being the outboard ship, *Oklahoma*'s starboard side faced Maryland and Ford Island; her port side faced the waters of Pearl Harbor. As with any outboard ship, one side (in this case, *Oklahoma*'s port side) was exposed to the waters of Pearl Harbor and Southeast Loch. Such mooring was dangerous since the exposed side could be hit by torpedoes dropped from the air into the waters of Pearl Harbor, especially if dropped around Southeast Loch since the mouth of Southeast Loch was directly opposite the center of Battleship Row. That danger became a reality when three to five torpedoes hit her port side, making holes that permitted water to enter and to flood the ship; more torpedoes hit her, and she began to capsize. The result was the capsizing just described.[6]

Capsizing was a nightmare, causing numerous problems, one of which was it trapped terrified survivors in water in the dark in the bottom of the ship. The men were disoriented because the ship was almost completely upside-down. Some survivors signaled their location to rescuers by tapping on the hull, which was now partially exposed to the sky. The initial rescue efforts killed some of the survivors—torches used to cut through the hull to reach them caused deadly fumes and consumed oxygen in the compartments holding the survivors. Rescuers solved the problem by using air-powered tools. Navy Yard workers, led by Navy Yard Worker Julio DeCastro, and other men rescued thirty-two crewmen by cutting holes in the hull, with the last man's rescue on December 9; the work by the Navy Yard was key to the rescue efforts. Lieutenant Commander William M. Hobby, Jr., was the senior officer from the ship supervising salvage.[7]

On December 7, two of *Oklahoma*'s crewmen would act in the most selfless of ways to save their shipmates, taking actions that would take their lives.

ENSIGN FRANCIS FLAHERTY, U.S. NAVAL RESERVE

Background

Flaherty was born in Charlotte, a city in Eaton County, Michigan, on March 15, 1919, and graduated from Charlotte High School in 1936. An undated wartime newspaper item, with no source given and titled "Francis Flaherty Ensign on the *Oklahoma*," announced that he had graduated from the University of Michigan in 1940 and then had Navy training at Northwestern University.

Flaherty had enlisted in the Naval Reserve on July 6, 1940, as an apprentice seaman. That summer, he had training aboard USS Wyoming. On September 15, 1940, his enlistment ended, and on the next day, he was appointed a midshipman in the Reserve. After additional training, he accepted an appointment as an ensign on December 12, 1940. He was assigned to USS *Oklahoma*, reporting there on January 12, 1941.[8]

Actions on December 7, 1941

The Flaherty MOH citation is short and almost identical to the citation for the other *Oklahoma* MOH recipient, Seaman First Class James Ward. Although the order to abandon ship had been given when the ship was about to capsize, Flaherty—as did Ward—remained in a turret, holding a flashlight so the remainder of the turret crew could see to escape. Staying behind so others could escape cost Flaherty his life.[9]

SEAMAN FIRST CLASS JAMES WARD, U.S. NAVY

Background

Ward was born on September 10, 1921, at Springfield, Ohio. He is one of three Ohio natives who earned MOHs on December 7. The other two are Scott of Massillon (USS *California*) and Kidd (USS *Arizona*) of Cleveland.[10]

Ward graduated from Springfield High School on June 15, 1939. He played baseball as a young man and when he was in the Navy. At one time, he held the batting championship of the Pacific Fleet.[11]

Ward enlisted in the Navy in Springfield on November 25, 1940. Since he was only nineteen, his father had to consent to the enlistment. Ward was assigned to the Pacific in January 1941 and ultimately reported to USS *Oklahoma*.[12]

In a data sheet completed by his parents (see following discussion), they stated that Ward seemed to be "perfectly satisfied in the Navy, and very proud to be a member of the baseball team of the USS *Oklahoma*."[13]

Actions on December 7

Although the order to abandon ship had been given, Ward—at the cost of his life—held a flashlight in a turret so other men in the turret could escape.[14]

One cannot tell from the citations if the men were in the same turret or a different turret. Their citations have only minor differences, which are indicated by brackets in the Ward citation (the citations are found at the end of this chapter).

One book about the ship, Trapped at Pearl Harbor: Escape from Battleship *Oklahoma*, gives contradictory information. The author states in one place that Flaherty was the assistant First Division officer and turret officer for Number 1 turret, which was the turret closest to the ship's bow. He writes that Seaman Ward was in the Number 2 turret, immediately behind the Number 1 turret such that Number 2's guns extended over the top of Number 1's turret. Later, however, he writes, "In turret no. 1 Ensign Flaherty and Seaman Ward remained at their stations despite the order to abandon ship, continuing to hold their flashlights so the rest of the turret crew could see to escape."[15] The same undated wartime newspaper item cited earlier in this chapter, "Francis Flaherty Ensign on the *Oklahoma*," announced that he was on *Oklahoma*, which was believed to have been hit by Japanese bombers. The article also stated that he was stationed on the ship since January 1941 and that "his battle station was in the No. 1 turret[,] foremost turret in the ship."

Aftermath of December 7

After-Action Report

The ship's report for December 7 does not mention Flaherty or Ward.[16]

Ensign Francis Flaherty and Seaman First Class James Ward were two of the battleship sailors on Battleship Row to receive posthumous MOHs for sacrificing their lives to save their shipmates on December 7. President Franklin D. Roosevelt signed each of the MOH citations on March 4, 1942.

MOH Citations

Ensign Francis Flaherty

For conspicuous devotion to duty and extraordinary courage and complete disregard of his own life, above and beyond the call of duty, during the attack on the fleet in

Pearl Harbor, by Japanese forces on 7 December 1941. When it was seen that the USS *Oklahoma* was going to capsize and the order was given to abandon ship, Ens. Flaherty remained in a turret, holding a flashlight so the remainder of the turret crew could see to escape, thereby sacrificing his own life.

SEAMAN FIRST CLASS JAMES WARD

For conspicuous devotion to duty, extraordinary courage, and complete disregard of his own life, above and beyond the call of duty, during the attack on the fleet in Pearl Harbor, by Japanese forces on 7 December 1941. When it was seen that the USS *Oklahoma* was going to capsize and the order was given to abandon ship, Ward remained in a turret holding a flashlight so the remainder of the turret crew could see to escape, thereby sacrificing his own life.

NOTES

1. Chapter 7 of this book for details concerning the attack on *Arizona*.

2. Report from USS *Oklahoma* (Subject: "Action Reports") of December 18, 1941, concerning the attack on the ship on December 7, 1941, (hereafter "*Oklahoma* report").

3. The number of dead and missing from *Oklahoma* is from the National Park Service brochure "USS *Oklahoma* Memorial" (obtained online in 2010) and from the author's visitation of the memorial in 2015; Chapter 7 gives the number of *Arizona* dead and missing.

4. Information about ship mooring is from the author's personal view of Battleship Row and its mooring quays; the report by Rear Admiral W. S. Anderson, Commander Battleships, Battle Force (Subject: "Attack at Pearl Harbor by Japanese Planes on December 7, 1941") of December 19, 1941, paragraph 3; and diagrams and photographs in Chapter 2.

5. The information about Maryland damage and casualties during the attack is from Dictionary of American Naval Fighting Ships, (Naval Historical Center, Department of the Navy, Washington, DC, 1969), Vol. IV, 25, and the report from USS Marilyn (Subject: "Attack of December 7, 1941"), paragraph 1C(1).

6. Endnote 2, *Oklahoma* report.

7. Endnote 2, *Oklahoma* report (paragraph 4 describes the rescue effort); additional information about the rescue can be found in Dictionary of American Naval Fighting Ships, Vol. V, 148, and in Vice Admiral Homer N. Wallin, U.S. Navy (Retired), Pearl Harbor: Why, How, Fleet Salvage, and Final Appraisal (Naval History Division, United States Government Printing Office, Washington, 1968), 132–135 and 136–178.

8. The National Personnel Records Center, St. Louis, Missouri, furnished military and personal information from Flaherty's Official Military Personnel File (OMPF) at the author's request (hereafter "Flaherty OMPF"); information also came from Don

Colizzi, "Charlotte's Medal of Honor Recipients" (May 7, 1999), a copy of an essay sent to the author by Michigan's Own Military and Space Museum.

9. The Flaherty and Ward MOH citations are in the text of this chapter and in appendix A.

10. Official U.S. Navy biography, "James Richard Ward, Seaman First Class, U.S. Navy (Deceased)" (April 27, 1944) (hereafter "Ward, U.S. Navy biography"); the stories of the other two Ohio MOH recipients are in Chapters 4 (Scott) and 9 (Kidd) of this book.

11. Recipient Data Sheet for Ward completed by the Ward family (hereafter "Recipient Data Sheet"); paragraph 11 gives the date of high school graduation; letter of March 7, 1974, from Mr. Howard J. Ward and Mrs. Nancy M. Ward to Mr. Carl A. Robin, North Carolina State Director, Medal of Honor History Roundtable (baseball interest); program "Dedication of Ward Field" (April 7, 1953), which mentions his batting championship of the Pacific Fleet (hereafter "Dedication of Ward Field").

12. Letter of March 7, 1974, from Mr. Howard J. Ward and Mrs. Nancy M. Ward to Mr. Carl A. Robin, North Carolina State Director, Medal of Honor History Roundtable (enlistment date); official U.S. Navy biographical sheet for Seaman First Class James Ward, U.S. Navy (enlistment date).

13. Endnote 11, Recipient Data Sheet for Ward, paragraph 13 (satisfaction with Navy and being a member of the ship's baseball team).

14. Ward MOH citation in the text of this chapter and in Appendix A.

15. Stephen Bower Young, Trapped at Pearl Harbor: Escape from Battleship *Oklahoma* (Naval Institute Press, 1991), 54 (Flaherty and Ward in separate turrets) and 70 (Flaherty and Ward in the same turret).

16. Endnote 2, *Oklahoma* report.

Photographs
USS *Oklahoma* MOH Recipients

Ensign Francis Flaherty, U.S. Naval Reserve. (Photograph NH 92305 from the Naval History and Heritage Command.)

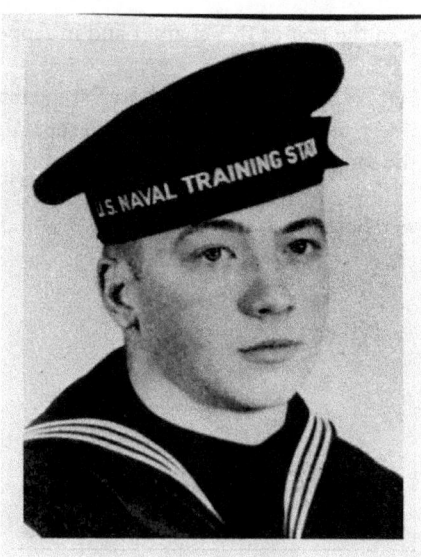

Seaman First Class James Ward, U.S. Navy. (Photograph NH 92309 from the Naval History and Heritage Command.)

CHAPTER 6
USS WEST VIRGINIA (BB-48)

"THE CAPTAIN IS ABOUT GONE"

CAPTAIN MERVYN BENNION, US NAVY
USS WEST VIRGINIA, DECEMBER 7, 1941

On December 7, *West Virginia* was moored at Berth F-6 alongside USS Tennessee, the inboard ship next to Ford Island. Each ship's starboard side faced Ford Island. Behind *West Virginia* was *Vestal*; behind Tennessee was *Arizona*.

Tennessee, as the inboard ship, received moderate damage from two bomb hits and was surrounded and hit by burning oil and debris from *West Virginia* and *Arizona*. Three of her crew were killed; one crewman died aboard ship of his wounds, and two crewmen were missing in action.[1]

As with any outboard ship, one side (in this case, *West Virginia*'s port side) was exposed to the waters of Pearl Harbor and Southeast Loch. Such mooring was dangerous since the exposed side could be hit by torpedoes dropped from the air into the waters of Pearl Harbor, especially if dropped around Southeast Loch since the mouth of Southeast Loch was directly opposite the center of Battleship Row. That danger became a reality on December 7 when she was hit by perhaps as many as seven torpedoes and two of the special armor-piercing bombs made from naval gun shells; both bombs were duds. The ship listed so heavily at one point that walking aboard her was impossible without holding on to something. Acting on orders from Bennion, prompt action by the damage-control officer and another officer in ordering the counterflooding of the ship saved her from the fate *Oklahoma* suffered: capsizing caused by water entering the ship through holes made by torpedo hits. Instead, the ship sank upright in place, wedging Tennessee against the mooring quays, thus preventing Tennessee from moving. *West Virginia* lost 106 crewmen.[2]

West Virginia had one MOH recipient: Captain Mervyn Bennion, the ship's commanding officer.

CAPTAIN MERVYN BENNION, U.S. NAVY

Background

Bennion, who was born on May 5, 1887, at Vernon, *Utah*, graduated from the Naval Academy in 1910 but was not appointed an ensign until 1912. Ironically, in addition to serving on *West Virginia* on December 7, Bennion had served on four other ships that were on Battleship Row on that date: Maryland, Tennessee, *California*, and as executive officer of *Arizona* from June 1936 to June 1937. He became a captain in the regular Navy in June 1938. On August 12, 1941, he reported for duty as the commanding officer of *West Virginia*.[3]

Comments about Bennion from The Lucky Bag for the Class of 1910 were incredibly prophetic. In showing concern only for his ship and protesting being removed from the bridge on December 7, a mortally wounded Bennion gave life to these The Lucky Bag observations about him as a midshipman nicknamed "Mary."

> He usually gets the class jobs which require much labor and return little glory, but Mary goes into everything he does with the same heartiness of purpose, and invariably performs a little more than he has to.
>
> However, if from this description you gather that you can bluff Mary into doing anything, you are sadly wrong. Like most quiet, good-natured men, he has his limits, and they are absolutely inflexible. Come as a friend and he will do all in his power for you, but try to force him and you'll find that you have been monkeying with the buzz-saw.[4]

Actions on December 7

On December 7 as *West Virginia* was listing to port, Bennion went to the ship's signal bridge. He was with Lieutenant Commander T. T. Beattie out on the starboard side of the bridge (the side facing Tennessee) when, according to Beattie, Bennion "doubled up with a groan and stated that he had been wounded. I saw that he had been hit in the stomach probably by a large piece of shrapnel and was very seriously wounded. He then sank to the deck, and I loosened his collar." The shrapnel was fragments of a bomb that had hit the center gun of Tennessee's forward "high" turret (the ship had two large forward turrets with the top one over the bottom one).

The story at this point becomes a struggle between crew members and their commanding officer; they are trying to save him while he simultaneously resists their efforts, exhibiting more concern with the welfare of the ship and crew than his own wounds. He did not want to be moved from the conning tower, which was his battle station.

Lieutenant Commander D. C. Johnson and Lieutenant (junior grade) F. H. White were ordered to bring Bennion down from the signal bridge, which is above the main deck. Johnson went to the signal bridge, writing that he took "a colored mess attendant with me—a very powerfully built individual, having in mind that he might pick the Captain up and carry him below." This man was Mess Attendant Second Class Doris Miller, a black sailor. White wrote that he found Bennion lying on the deck. "The Captain's abdomen was cut apparently by a fragment of bomb, about three by four inches, with part of his intestines protruding. The Captain deserves the highest praise, for although he was in great pain, his only concern was for the ship and crew. The Captain did not want to be moved…" Lieutenant C. V. Ricketts wrote that Bennion "had a serious abdominal wound, a large piece of metal or other similar object apparently having passed through his abdomen." Ricketts also noted that Chief Pharmacist's Mate L. N. Leak "dressed the wound as best he could."

Initially, Ricketts and Leak thought they should leave Bennion where he was because of the nature of his wound. With fire and smoke approaching, however, Ricketts decided Bennion had to be moved. They first carried him on a cot, which almost broke, to the ladder leading down from the signal bridge. They returned him to the bridge since he could not be lowered down the ladder. Due to the pain involved with movement, Bennion asked to be left on the signal bridge. The crewmen lashed him to a ladder with the intention of lowering him to safety, but fire, smoke, and flame—even the life jackets and signal flags were burning—defeated their efforts. He was still partially conscious when they cut him loose from the ladder and moved him to the navigation bridge. Leak, the chief pharmacist's mate, finally told one of the officers that "the Captain is about gone."

While this ordeal was occurring, *West Virginia* was incurring battle damage, primarily from torpedo hits, as well as smoke and fire from an oil fire that had drifted alongside *West Virginia* from *Arizona*.[5]

Aftermath

After-Action Report

The after-action report of December 11, 1941, was written by the senior surviving officer, who was the executive officer, R. H. Hillenkoetter. His report and its enclosures contain numerous mentions of Bennion's actions on December 7 and the actions of the men trying to help him. In his report, he wrote,

> …throughout the entire action, and through all the arduous labors which followed, there was never the slightest sign of faltering or of cowardice. The actions of the officers and men were all wholly commendable; their spirit was marvelous; there was no panic, no shirking nor flinching, and words fail in attempting to describe the truly magnificent display of courage, discipline, and devotion to duty of all officers and men.

He then cited some of the officers and men mentioned above, including Miller, for "outstanding performance of duty."[6]

On December 13, Commander Battleships, Battle Force, Rear Admiral W. S. Anderson endorsed the executive officer's report, writing,

> [The crew] did their best to fight and save their ship under terrifically hard and hazardous conditions beyond anything ever before experienced.
>
> That they failed was because they were beset beyond human capacity. This is to be noted particularly in the case of the Commanding Officer, Captain M. S. Bennion, who although mortally wounded and helpless continued to be concerned only with fighting and saving his ship. He was a gallant exemplification of the highest traditions of the Service and is recommended for posthumous commendation and official recognition.[7]

Captain Mervyn Bennion would be one of twelve "battleship sailors" at Pearl Harbor to receive a MOH for December 7. President Franklin D. Roosevelt signed the

MOH citation on March 4, 1942.

MOH Citation

For conspicuous devotion to duty, extraordinary courage, and complete disregard of his own life, above and beyond the call of duty, during the attack on the fleet in Pearl Harbor, by Japanese forces on December 7, 1941. As Commanding Officer of the USS *West Virginia*, after being mortally wounded, Capt. Bennion evidenced apparent concern only in fighting and saving his ship, and strongly protested against being carried from the bridge.

Notes

1. Report from USS Tennessee (Subject: "Narrative of Event of Action in Japanese Air Raid on Pearl Harbor, December 7, 1941") of December 11, 1941.

2. Report from USS *West Virginia* (Subject: "Action of December 7, 1941—Report of") of December 11, 1941 (hereafter "*West Virginia* Report"); Lieutenant Commander J. S. Harper's statement is Enclosure (A)—he ordered counterflooding; Lieutenant C. V. Ricketts's statement is Enclosure (F)—degree of listing and ordering counterflooding with Bennion's consent); Vice Admiral Homer N. Wallin, U.S. Navy (Retired), Pearl Harbor: Why, How, Fleet Salvage, and Final Appraisal (Naval History Division, United States Government Printing Office, Washington, 1968), 233 (number of torpedo hits). Information about ship mooring is from the author's personal view of Battleship Row and its mooring quays; the report by Rear Admiral W. S. Anderson, Commander Battleships, Battle Force (subject: "Attack at Pearl Harbor by Japanese Planes on December 7, 1941") of December 19, 1941, paragraph 3; and diagrams and photographs in chapter 3.

3. The National Personnel Records Center, St. Louis, Missouri, furnished information from Bennion's Official Military Personnel File (OMPF) at the author's request (hereafter "Bennion OMPF").

4. The Lucky Bag, (U.S. Naval Academy, Class of 1910), 66.

5. Endnote 2, *West Virginia* report; the information about Bennion's wounds and the efforts to aid and to evacuate him comes from the Enclosures (witness statements) that are a part of the report; Lieutenant Commander Beattie's statement is Enclosure (B); Lieutenant Johnson's statement is enclosure (D); Lieutenant Ricketts's statement is Enclosure (F); Lieutenant (junior grade) White's statement is Enclosure (H); see Chapter 16 for more information about Mess Attendant Second Class Doris Miller, Dictionary of American Naval Fighting Ships (Naval Historical Center, Department of the Navy, 1976), Vol. VII, 89 (explains origin of the shrapnel hitting Bennion).

6. Endnote 2, *West Virginia* report.

7. First Endorsement dated December 13, 1941, to *West Virginia* BB48/A 16-3 of December 11, 1941, by Commander Battleships, Battle Force, Rear Admiral W. S. Anderson.

Photograph
USS *West Virginia* MOH Recipient

Captain Mervyn Bennion, U.S. Navy. (Photograph NH 56151 from the Naval History and Heritage Command.)

CHAPTER 7
USS ARIZONA (BB-39):
THE GUNFIGHT AT QUAY F-7

REAR ADMIRAL ISAAC KIDD, U.S. NAVY

CAPTAIN FRANKLIN VAN VALKENBURGH, U.S. NAVY

LIEUTENANT COMMANDER SAMUEL FUQUA, U.S. NAVY

USS ARIZONA, DECEMBER 7, 1941

Perhaps no other U.S. military site attracts more attention, interest, or visitors than USS *Arizona* in Pearl Harbor, Oahu, Hawaii. It remains a popular tourist site for Americans and foreigners, especially Japanese tourists.

On December 7, *Arizona* was moored alongside USS *Vestal*, a repair ship (AR-4), at Berth F-7. *Arizona* was the inboard ship, with her starboard side facing Ford Island and her port side facing *Vestal*, the outboard ship. *Vestal*'s port side faced Ford Island and *Arizona*. *Arizona*'s bow pointed toward the channel connecting the Pacific Ocean and Pearl Harbor; *Vestal*'s bow was pointed in the opposite direction.[1]

The exact number of bombs that hit *Arizona* cannot be determined because of the extensive damage the ship suffered, but a good estimate is four; some report that a torpedo also hit her.[2]

At approximately 8:10 a.m., a bomb pierced the forward deck, probably one of the 1,760-pound armor-piercing bombs that was actually a sixteen-inch naval gun projectile converted to an aerial bomb.[3] This bomb, which hit on the starboard side and just forward of Turret 2 (the second large turret back from the bow), ignited the forward ammunition magazines.[4]

The explosion of the magazines was catastrophic and fatal, causing the ship to sink in place and the ship's forward mast (foremast) to bend down as if a ghastly creature in a death pose.[5]

The resulting number of dead and missing—1,177 of the 1,514 sailors and Marines assigned to the ship—was the highest number of dead and missing for any one command on December 7 or for any ship in US Navy history. Only 337 men assigned to the ship survived; only [15] of the ship's [88] Marines survived.[6]

Three *Arizona* officers were awarded MOHs for December 7, two of them posthumously. Unquestionably, Fuqua deserved his MOH, as can be seen by reading the citation. Whether Kidd and Van Valkenburgh deserved their MOHs is the subject of Chapter 15.

Rear Admiral Isaac Kidd, U.S. Navy

Background

Kidd was born in Cleveland, Ohio, on March 26, 1884.[7] He is one of three Ohio natives who earned MOHs on December 7. The other two are Scott of Massillon (chapter 6, *California*) and Ward of Springfield (Chapter 7, *Oklahoma*).

Kidd was in the Navy from September 23, 1902, until his death on December 7, 1941.[8] He graduated from the Naval Academy in 1906. His entry in The Lucky Bag for the Class of 1906 has his nickname as "Cap," an apparent reference to the infamous pirate Captain Kidd; it also disparagingly refers to him as a "fat blond with an appetite."[9]

In addition to serving at various shore stations—including the Naval Academy—he served aboard and commanded various ships.[10]

Two of his assignments are of note because they involve the only two ships from December 7 remaining in Pearl Harbor: *Arizona* and *Utah*.[11] Kidd was the executive officer of *Utah* from April 27, 1925, to November 19, 1926, when she was a battleship (Chapter 10 explains her conversion to a target and gunnery training ship). As a captain, Kidd was the commanding officer of *Arizona* from September 9, 1938, to February 3, 1940. At that time, Rear Admiral Chester Nimitz, Kidd's friend, was Commander, Battleship Division One and *Arizona*, his flagship.[12] After Kidd was appointed a rear admiral on July 1, 1940, and assigned as Commander, Battleship Division One on January 7, 1941, he returned to *Arizona*, his flagship and place of duty, where he was killed on December 7, 1941.[13]

Actions on December 7

Kidd's actions on December 7 are unclear. His MOH citation, unlike Fuqua's, cites no specific deeds of heroism. It is a short citation, merely stating that Kidd went to the bridge and "courageously discharged his duties," without explaining how he did so, until his death from the explosion that "killed" the ship.[14]

Paul Stillwell's book about the ship, the definitive history of *Arizona*, notes that Van Valkenburgh was on the bridge at the time of the catastrophic explosion aboard the ship and that Kidd was nearby.[15]

Kidd's actions or lack of actions are discussed in more detail in Chapter 15.

Captain Franklin Van Valkenburgh, U.S. Navy

Background

The correct name is Franklin (first name) Van Valkenburgh (last name); the "Van" is not a first name, as is so often seen.

Van Valkenburgh was born on April 5, 1888, in Minneapolis, Minnesota, but grew up in Milwaukee, Wisconsin.[16]

Van Valkenburgh served in the Navy from April 5, 1905, until his death on December 7.[17] He graduated from the Naval Academy in 1909. His entry in The Lucky Bag for the Class of 1909 listed his nicknames as "Van" and "Dutch." It lists his hometown as Milwaukee, Wisconsin, noting that "His name and native city signify that Van indulges in the beverage that made Milwaukee famous." It stated that he "[a]lways greets you in the pleasant way that shows his comfortable, optimistic view of life." It also commented on his "warm, affectionate nature."[18]

Apparently, he had big ears. According to The Lucky Bag, he was "easy-going but very sensitive, those big ears will turn red at the slightest provocation. He manages to get by without much worry." It closes with, "Van, feather those ears." A cartoon at the bottom of the page shows his back and him facing four women; his ears are prominently sticking out.[19]

During his career, he served at various shore stations—including the Naval Academy—and aboard various ships, one of which was, ironically, at Battleship Row on December 7, USS Maryland. He reported as *Arizona*'s commanding officer in February 1941 and served in that capacity until December 7.[20]

Actions on December 7

As with the actions of Kidd on December 7, the actions of Van Valkenburgh on that date are unclear. And, as with Kidd, the MOH citation, unlike that of Fuqua, cites no specific deeds of heroism. It is a short citation, merely stating that he "gallantly fought his ship," without explaining how he did so, until his death from the explosion that destroyed the ship.[21]

Stillwell's book about *Arizona* notes that Van Valkenburgh was on the bridge at the time of the catastrophic explosion that destroyed the ship.[22]

As with Kidd, Van Valkenburgh's actions or lack of actions will be discussed in more detail in Chapter 15.

LIEUTENANT COMMANDER SAMUEL FUQUA, U.S. NAVY

Background

As will be seen, Fuqua had one of the more interesting and at times "bumpy" careers of all the men mentioned in this book. His military career saw him go from Army private to Navy rear admiral. The "bump" is included here to show that a junior officer can in some, but not all, cases make a mistake and then later as a midlevel or senior officer excel in the worst of circumstances and, for his efforts, go from admonished officer to MOH recipient.

Fuqua was born on October 15, 1899, in Laddonia, Missouri, and was a private in the Army during World War I. He was in the Navy from 1923 to 1953, holding a wide variety of assignments on ships and at bases, but, most important, he experienced Japanese hostilities before and during the war.[23]

He entered the Naval Academy in 1919 and graduated in 1923. Ironically, his first ship assignment after graduating the Naval Academy was *Arizona*, where he served from graduation in 1923 to 1924. Before December 7, he served at various shore commands and aboard various ships.[24]

From 1937 to 1939, he served aboard USS Peary and USS Bittern. As noted here, Peary sailed in Chinese waters during hostilities between China and Japan. These hostilities, discussed in Chapter 2, included the 1931 invasion of Manchuria after the Mukden Incident and the full-scale invasion of China in 1937 after the Marco Polo Bridge Incident, the latter incident resulting in outright war between China and Japan. The hostilities also included the "accidental" sinking of a U.S. Navy river gunboat, Panay, by Japan in 1937, a foreshadowing of war between the United States and Japan.

The Commander-in-Chief (CINC) of the Asiatic Fleet sent a letter dated March 10, 1939, to Peary's commanding officer, J. C. Hubbard; the subject was "Commendation." The letter noted that Peary had executed her regularly assigned missions in Chinese waters during the Sino-Japanese hostilities, which had commenced at Shanghai, China, on August 13, 1937. The mission required "investigation of, and reports on, disturbed conditions in Chinese ports within the zone of hostilities, necessitating close cooperation with consular authorities of the United States, and independent operations requiring sound judgment, tact and initiative for their successful accomplishment in the interests of American citizens and their property."

The letter stated that the CINC considered that Peary executed her missions "under difficult conditions in an efficient manner, for which you are herewith commended." The letter also authorized the ship's commanding officer to forward a copy of the letter to "any officer who served under your command during this period, whose performance of duty in connection with the accomplishment of your mission as outlined above appropriately merits such recognition."

A copy of the CINC letter of March 10 is in Fuqua's official service record, which must mean that his performance was deserving of the recognition mentioned in the letter. Additionally, in a first endorsement dated December 9, 1937, Hubbard forwarded a copy of "the basic letter" to Fuqua; that letter must be a copy of the March 10, 1937, letter of commendation. The endorsement reads, "In accordance with the basic letter it is considered that you were one of the officers attached to this vessel [Peary] who did good work in the evacuations."[25] The "evacuations" must have referred to evacuations conducted by American Navy craft ("gunboats"), of civilians, diplomats, and journalists in China in the face of Japanese hostilities against the Chinese as was described in chapter 2; one example was evacuations performed by USS Panay, just mentioned and recounted in chapter 2.[26] A fictional portrayal of these evacuations can be found in the 1966 Steve McQueen movie The Sand Pebbles.

On December 9, 1937, then-Lieutenant Fuqua was ordered to detach from Peary to assume command of USS Bittern, a minesweeper (AM [36]); on January 21, 1938, he was also given the additional duty of Commander, Mine Division 3.[27]

A July 15, 1938, "NOTATION OF INSPECTION," concerning the annual inspection of the ship contained this comment: "The condition of the BITTERN was found to be very good to excellent except for Battle Problem." Beside "REMARKS" is "Special discredit."[28]

What followed was a letter of August 26, 1938, from the Commander-in-Chief of the Asiatic Fleet to Fuqua, "Subject: Admonition." In summary, the problem was two projectiles fired from ships landing on Philippine soil. Bittern and Finch, the two ships comprising Mine Division 3, were firing their guns on that date, "creating a definite presumption that the projectiles in question were fired from the ships operating under your command." The letter stated that the commander in chief was embarrassed by having to express his regrets to the Philippine Government through the U.S. High Commissioner. The letter admonished Fuqua for poor judgment during the firing exercise.[29]

Fuqua submitted a rebuttal dated October 10, 1938, explaining that he thought that the ships were sufficiently distant from land such that no shells would land ashore.[30]

While such an incident can end a career in what can be at times a modern "zero defect" Navy, the admonition did not end Fuqua's Navy career or prevent his promotion; he was promoted to lieutenant commander on March 15, 1939.[31]

When assigned to *Arizona* in 1941, he was the ship's First Lieutenant and Damage Control Officer (DCO). The First Lieutenant and DCO leads the ship's construction and repair department. In peacetime, he must coordinate damage control among all the ship's departments and supervise training to ready the ship in condition for combat, controlling damage and defending against gas attack. He is also responsible for the ship's appearance and cleanliness and any repair and construction. In battle, he makes emergency repairs and maintains list and trim to keep the ship afloat.[32]

As will be seen later in this chapter, Fuqua had to discharge damage-control duties as best he could on December 7 amid the chaos on the flaming wreck that *Arizona* had become. Fuqua's "amazingly calm and cool manner" (the phrase used in his MOH citation) while directing rescue, firefighting, and evacuation of the wounded under these circumstances on December 7 proved the accuracy of his entry in the Naval Academy's The Lucky Bag for the Class of 1923. The Lucky Bag observed the following about "Ben," his nickname, and his ability to look after his shipmates, a time-honored tradition in the military:

> Ben in normalcy has the Sphinx snowed under, but once in a while we get wise to him. Ask "Jenny" or any of the boys about the night before the Penn State game in Philly and they will tell you how he brought them all back to the hotel safe and sound.[33]

While he must have been knowledgeable and decisive, Fuqua must also have been soft-spoken and self-effacing, as can be inferred from his testimony, discussed below, before the Roberts Commission in January 1942. The Commission was one of eight investigations of the events of December 7.[34] Two members of the commission had to ask him to speak more loudly when he answered their questions.[35]

Actions on December 7: "Fall Apart Like a Pack of Cards"

Numerous sources record specific actions Fuqua took on December 7, and he is by far the most deserving of the MOH recipients for *Arizona*. What he experienced can only be described as harrowing.

While the record of the activities of Kidd and Van Valkenburgh on December 7 is sparse and their MOH citations are brief with no detail, the record for Fuqua is much more detailed, probably in part because he survived the catastrophic explosion or explosions sinking the ship and because, as senior surviving officer, he was very visible directing rescue efforts, meaning numerous witnesses could testify concerning his bravery on December 7.

Much of the information about Fuqua's responsibilities aboard ship and actions on December 7 comes from his testimony on January 2, 1942, before the Roberts Commission.[36]

Fuqua stated that he was the ship's First Lieutenant and Damage Control Officer (DCO). He described his role as the DCO: to maintain the watertight integrity of the ship and to keep it afloat notwithstanding battle damage. The damage-control section comprised him as the section head, a lieutenant assistant, a chief boatswain, a carpenter, an ensign, and approximately thirty-five other crewmen.[37]

He was on the ship from the evening of December 6 to the morning of December 7 since he was on duty during that time. That morning began with Fuqua in the wardroom (officers' dining room) eating breakfast when at approximately 7:55 a.m., he heard a blast of the ship's air-raid siren. He told the antiaircraft control officer to man the antiaircraft guns. The officer thought the alarm was just a test, but Fuqua—even though he thought that someone may have inadvertently hit the siren switch—insisted, saying that the siren sounded like an air-raid alarm.[38]

He tried to reach the officer of the deck by telephone from the wardroom to tell him to man the antiaircraft batteries but could not contact him. He then went to the port side of the quarterdeck, the area where ship personnel leave and board the ship. There he saw an aircraft approximately fifty feet above him, firing its machine guns as it passed the ship. When he looked at the aircraft, he realized it was Japanese.[39]

Fuqua went to the number 4 turret, the turret closest to the ship's stern. There he found the officer of the deck (OOD), a different officer chosen daily to be the commanding officer's representative and to ensure the ship operated correctly. He told the OOD to sound "general quarters," the signal sounded to send crewmen to their battle stations. He also told him to set "material condition ZED as final damage control condition for battle, which means that all hatches and openings are closed except for those that have to remain open for combat purposes."[40]

In reading his testimony about the following events, one can imagine his calm, stoic demeanor not only before the Commission as he recounted his experiences but also on December 7:

> About this time I heard a plane overhead. I glanced up. I saw a bomb dropping which appeared to me was going to land on me or close by.
>
> The next thing I remember I came to on deck in a position about six feet aft the starboard gangway. I got to my feet and looked around to see what it was that had knocked me down. Then I saw I was lying about six feet from a bomb hole in the deck. This bomb had hit the face plate of No. 4 [the aft-most] turret, had glanced off that and gone through the deck and had exploded in the captain's pantry…
>
> Then I glanced up forward and saw the whole midship a mass of flames in that section of the ship.[41]

He noted that no water was coming out of the fire hoses. He fought the fire with a fire extinguisher and by obtaining water by dipping buckets over the side of the ship.[41]

Arizona then received her deathblow: a bomb hit the forward part of the ship, exploding the forward magazines. At about 8:15 a.m., Fuqua realized that "the ship had apparently broken in two…" He estimated that at 8:15 or 8:20, he

> saw a tremendous mass of flames, the height of 300 feet, rising in the air forward, and shook the ship aft as it would fall apart like a pack of cards.
>
> It was then I realized that the forward magazine had exploded. I then directed that the after magazine be flooded [to prevent fire or explosion]. This was done, but the man who flooded the after magazine was not saved.[42]

When asked by a commission member about the sailor who flooded the magazine, Fuqua said, "He was not saved. He is missing."[43]

Despite the terrific explosions and enemy bombing and strafing, Fuqua continued directing rescue and firefighting.

His obituary quotes him as saying, "I saw men on fire burning to death, and they fought the fire until they fell dead at their battle stations. When we picked them up, flesh fell from their hands."[44]

By then, Fuqua saw that all the ship's antiaircraft guns had ceased firing, which meant the ship could no longer defend herself or her crew. He now had only two rational options available: first, to order abandon ship and second to transfer the wounded and burned, "who were running out of the flames, to Ford Island."[45]

After boats helped to move the wounded to Ford Island, Fuqua searched the areas of the aft that were accessible for any personnel, wounded or not.[46]

At approximately 8:45 a.m., he ordered that *Vestal*'s forward lines, which were tied to *Arizona*, be cut; the two ships were moored to each other. He thought *Vestal* had cut her own after (rear) lines. *Vestal* then drifted clear.[46]

Fuqua did not leave his ship until approximately 9:15 a.m., when he reported in at a barracks on Ford Island.[47]

After the fire aboard ship stopped burning—it burned for two days—Fuqua went aboard to look for bodies. He found a body believed to be that of Kidd at the foot of the ladder to the flag bridge, the area from which a flag officer directs operations. He found Kidd's Naval Academy ring and some coat buttons on the flag bridge.[48]

As explained in Chapters 4 and 6 respectively, Jackson Pharris of *California* and the crew of *West Virginia* could save their ships from fatal damage—capsizing—by counterflooding them. The ships sank in place but could be repaired and could fight another day, unlike the capsized *Oklahoma* and *Utah*, both of which proved unfit for further service. Also, *California* and *West Virginia* were badly damaged but did not suffer a catastrophic explosion caused by an aerial bomb as did *Arizona*. Fuqua, however, through no fault of his own, could not save his ship; the damage was just too great because of the catastrophic explosion of the forward magazines. Fuqua told the Roberts Commission that the ship had no time to counterflood.[49]

Chapter 2 described the mooring of the ships on Battleship Row. *Arizona* was an inboard ship and thus a target for Japanese horizontal bombing since *Vestal*, moored beside *Arizona*, protected *Arizona* from torpedo attack. Since the Japanese could not reach inboard ships with torpedoes, *Arizona* was bombed, with one bomb hitting forward near turret 2, igniting the magazines and setting off the catastrophic explosion, causing her to simply sink or to drop in place, an action Fuqua could not prevent.

As his MOH citation reflects, Fuqua could and did, however, as senior surviving officer, take charge, ameliorate the suffering of the dying and wounded, and give the command to abandon ship. Moreover, he could and did set an example of calm that inspired confidence in the remaining crew in the worst of circumstances—smoke, fire, and casualties all over the ship—and restored whatever degree of control, order, and discipline was possible in such circumstances.

Fuqua's MOH citation also notes that his performance was "in such an amazingly calm and cool manner and with such excellent judgment that it inspired everyone who saw him and undoubtedly resulted in the saving of many lives." Chapter 3 provides an account of his conduct, drawing the attention of two of the ship's enlisted men— one Marine and one Navy—who later remarked on how calm Fuqua was under fire: Corporal E. C. Nightingale and Aviation Machinist's Mate First Class D. A. Graham.

Perhaps the best summary of his action and personality prepared by the military, other than that found in his MOH citation, is in the narrative of his fitness report for October 1, 1941, to January 18, 1942, written by the officer who replaced Van Valkenburgh as commanding officer of *Arizona* after his loss on December 7:

> A thoroughly reliable conscientious hard working officer. He is calm, eventempered [sic] and completely in possession of his faculties. Practical common sense and sound judgement. His performance of duty has been outstanding. A survivor from the destruction of the *Arizona* his presence of mind, initiative and resourcefulness at the time and subsequently in rescue, salvage, and organization as acting executive officer is worthy of the highest praise. I would like to have this officer under my command in action. Strongly recommend this officer for promotion.[50]

AFTERMATH OF DECEMBER 7

After-Action Report

The ship's after-action report was dated December 13, 1941. Enclosure (H) to the report is Fuqua's statement.[51]

Three officers from *Arizona* received MOHs for bravery on December 7. The actions of the only officer who lived to receive his MOH, Lieutenant Commander Samuel Fuqua, were described in this chapter. Chapter 15 describes the actions of Rear Admiral Isaac Kidd and Captain Franklin Van Valkenburgh, who received posthumous MOHs. President Franklin D. Roosevelt signed all three MOH citations on March 4, 1942.

MOH CITATIONS

REAR ADMIRAL ISAAC KIDD

For conspicuous devotion to duty, extraordinary courage, and complete disregard of his own life, during the attack on the fleet in Pearl Harbor, by Japanese forces on December 7, 1941. He immediately went to the bridge and as Commander Battleship Division One, courageously discharged his duties as Senior Officer Present Afloat until the USS *Arizona*, his flagship, blew up from magazine explosions and a direct bomb hit on the bridge, which resulted in the loss of his life.

CAPTAIN FRANKLIN VAN VALKENBURGH

For conspicuous devotion to duty, extraordinary courage, and complete disregard of his own life, during the attack on the fleet in Pearl Harbor, by Japanese forces on December 7, 1941. As Commanding Officer of USS *Arizona*, Captain Van Valkenburgh gallantly fought his ship until the USS *Arizona* blew up from magazine explosions and a direct bomb hit on the bridge, which resulted in the loss of his life.

Lieutenant Commander Samuel Fuqua

For distinguished conduct in action, outstanding heroism, and utter disregard of his own safety, above and beyond the call of duty during the attack on the fleet in Pearl Harbor, by Japanese forces on December 7, 1941. Upon the commencement of the attack, Lieutenant Commander Fuqua rushed to the quarterdeck of the USS *Arizona* to which he was attached where he was stunned and knocked down by the explosion of a large bomb, which hit the quarterdeck, penetrated several decks, and started a severe fire. Upon regaining consciousness, he began to direct the fighting of the fire and the rescue of wounded and injured personnel. Almost immediately there was a tremendous explosion forward, which made the ship appear to rise out of the water, shudder, and settle down by the bow rapidly. The whole forward part of the ship was enveloped in flames, which were spreading rapidly, and wounded and burned men were pouring out of the ship to the quarterdeck. Despite these conditions, his harrowing experience, and severe enemy bombing and strafing, at the time, Lieutenant Commander Fuqua continued to direct the fighting of fires in order to check them while the wounded and burned could be taken from the ship, and supervised the rescue of these men in such an amazingly calm and cool manner and with such excellent judgment, that it inspired everyone who saw him and undoubtedly resulted in the saving of many lives. After realizing that the ship could not be saved and that he was the senior surviving officer aboard, he directed that it be abandoned, but continued to remain on the quarterdeck and directed abandoning ship and rescue of personnel until satisfied that all personnel that could be had been saved, after which he left the ship with the (last) boatload. The conduct of Lieutenant Commander Fuqua was not only in keeping with the highest traditions of the Naval Service but characterizes him as an outstanding leader of men.

Later Life: Samuel Fuqua

During the remainder of his career, Fuqua served at numerous ships and bases.

In 1942, Fuqua was assigned to the cruiser USS Tuscaloosa (CA-37), which escorted Murmansk convoys; the ship engaged German aircraft and submarines on July 4, 1942. He was also in the battle of Casablanca (November 8, 1942). He was later assigned to Navy Operating Base, Guantanamo, Cuba, and to the Naval War College. He finished the war on the staff of the commander of Service Force Seventh Fleet in the Southwest Pacific, where he earned a Legion of Merit as the Force Operations Officer.[52]

Upon retirement on July 1, 1953, he was promoted to rear admiral by a "tombstone promotion" that advanced officers one permanent grade upon retirement if they had been "specifically commended for his performance of duty in actual combat..." The quoted language comes from Fuqua's retirement certificate[53] (see also Chapter 1 concerning tombstone promotions).

After retirement, he was a teacher.[54].

Perhaps the most interesting aspect of his postwar life was his 1958 guest appearance on the television show This Is Your Life.[55] Host Ralph Edwards reviewed each guest's life and often brought family members and friends on stage to reunite them with the guest.⁵⁶

After the show with Fuqua, Edwards appealed to the public to send contributions for a memorial for those who died aboard *Arizona*. The public contributed $275,869; Congress and the Hawaiian legislature added $250,000. The memorial, as it exists today, was dedicated in 1962.⁵⁷

Fuqua died at the Veterans Administration Medical Center in Decatur, Georgia, on January 27, 1987. He had a wife and a daughter.⁵⁸

Fuqua was one of five of the December 7 MOH recipients surviving that day and one of four surviving the war. He outlived Pharris, who died in 1966, but the other two survivors outlived him; Ross died in 1992, and Finn died in 2010.⁵⁹

Why *Arizona* Is Unique

The ship is unique in many ways.

The official presiding at her keel laying on March 16, 1914, was Franklin D. Roosevelt, who was then Assistant Secretary of the Navy.⁶⁰ As mentioned earlier in this chapter, in 1942, he would, as President of the United States, approve MOHs for three of the ship's officers for actions on December 7, 1941.

Arizona was the only ship on Battleship Row to have been in a Hollywood feature movie: Here Comes the Navy (1934).⁶¹

She was the only ship on December 7 to have a flag officer (officer above the grade of Navy captain) aboard at the time of the attack: Rear Admiral Kidd, Commander, Battleship Division One . He was the first flag or general officer killed during the war and the only flag officer killed on December 7; the attack on Oahu was the first combat of World War II for the United States, and no other flag or general officer was killed on that date.⁶²

Ironically, Kidd had been the ship's commanding officer from 1938 to 1940, and while so serving, a friend of his, Rear Admiral Chester Nimitz, was Commander, Battleship Division One . In 1938, *Arizona* became the flagship for Battleship Division One , which comprised *Arizona*, *Oklahoma*, and *Nevada*.⁶³ Kidd succeeded Nimitz as the Battleship Division One commander and held that position on December 7 when he was killed aboard *Arizona*.⁶⁴

Chapter 3 of this book noted that *Arizona*—of all the ships in Pearl Harbor on December 7—became the focus of a rally to defeat the Japanese. "Remember the *Arizona!*" became a familiar cry among military members and civilians alike. The fear and reality of Japanese treachery fueled the American desire to defeat Japan. That treachery was the sneak attack on December 7 as symbolized by the vessel suffering the greatest loss on that date: *Arizona*. Chapter 3 also explains that the fear and reality of Japanese treachery on December 7 fueled the American desire to beat the Japanese. *Arizona* embodied that fear and reality.

The attack on December 7, as symbolized by *Arizona*, was similar to another important event in the military history of the United States, the Battle of Gettysburg in 1863. Each event gave rise to a memorable speech by the President of the United States. President Abraham Lincoln delivered the famous Gettysburg's Address following the battle, and President Franklin Roosevelt delivered a speech on December 8, 1941, asking Congress to declare war on Japan, using a phrase that would become famous in describing December 7: "a date [not "day"] which will live in infamy."

She is one of only two ships—the other is USS *Utah*—that was at Pearl Harbor on December 7 that remains there today. She is the only ship remaining on Battleship Row that was there on December 7.[65]

WHY *ARIZONA'S* MOHS ARE UNIQUE

The *Arizona* MOH awards are unique for five reasons.

One, all three of the ship's MOH recipients were graduates of the U.S. Naval Academy—Kidd in 1906, Van Valkenburgh in 1909, and Fuqua in 1923.[66]

Two, Kidd was the first of three Navy rear admirals to receive MOHs during World War II, all posthumously. The other two were Norman Scott and Daniel Callaghan, both killed in the Naval Battle of Guadalcanal.[67]

Three, Fuqua was the only one of the three *Arizona* MOH recipients to survive the attack and was the first living December 7 MOH recipient to receive his MOH, which was presented to him in person at Newport, Rhode Island, on March 19, [194268] (see also Chapter 14).

Arizona's MOHs are also unique for a fourth reason: the process by which the Kidd and Van Valkenburgh awards originated. And they are unique for a fifth reason: of the sixteen MOHs awarded for December 7, the Kidd and Van Valkenburgh MOHs are the only two MOHs that were undeserved. The author writes that sentence knowing full well that *Arizona* is sacred and that any questioning of the MOHs awarded to the commanding officer and the flag officer killed aboard her on December 7 could be considered heresy. But truth is more important than heresy. Chapter 15 describes at length the process by which the Kidd and Van Valkenburgh MOH recommendations originated and were approved and why they are undeserved MOHs since they are unsupported by any facts sufficient to warrant a MOH. Chapter 16 also concerns their MOHs in light of the "non award" of a MOH to another *Arizona* officer: Lieutenant Colonel Daniel Fox.

NOTES

1. Information about ship mooring is from the author's personal view of Battleship Row and its mooring quays; the report by Rear Admiral W. S. Anderson, Commander Battleships, Battle Force (Subject: "Attack at Pearl Harbor by Japanese Planes on December 7, 1941") of December 19, 1941, paragraph 3; and diagrams and photographs in Chapter 3.

2. James L. Mooney, editor. Dictionary of American Naval Fighting Ships (Naval Historical Center, Department of the Navy, Washington, DC, 1991), Vol. I (Part A), 381 (hereafter "DANFS"); Paul Stillwell, Battleship *Arizona* (Naval Institute Press, Annapolis, MD, 1991) 273 (torpedo) and 274 (bomb hits) (hereafter "Stillwell, Battleship *Arizona*").

3. Endnote 2, Stillwell, Battleship *Arizona*, 233 (time of bomb hit) and 275 (nature of converted projectile).

4. Ibid., 276–278.

5. Ibid., text at 278, diagram at 262–63, and photographs at 238, 239, and 243.

6. Ibid., 255.

7. The National Personnel Records Center, St. Louis, Missouri, furnished military and personal information from Kidd's Official Military Personnel File (OMPF) at the author's request. The material came in two formats; initially, it was in selected pages copied from his OMPF (hereafter "Kidd OMPF initial request"); later it came in the form of a compact disc with his entire OMPF (hereafter "Kidd OMPF (CD)"). His birthday is on the compact disc, section 04 (Service Documents), record of service, 31.

8. Ibid., Kidd OMPF initial request.

9. The Lucky Bag, Class of 1906, 107.

10. Endnote 7, Kidd OMPF (CD), section 04 (Service Documents), record of service, 31–35.

11. Author's numerous visitations to the Memorials for *Arizona* and *Utah*, the most recent in 2015.

12. Endnote 7, Kidd OMPF (CD); Kidd's time as *Arizona*'s commanding officer is in section 04 (Service Documents), record of service, 34; Potter, E. B. Nimitz (U.S. Naval Institute Press, 1976), 13 (friendship and *Arizona* as Nimitz's flagship) (hereafter "Potter, Nimitz").

13. Endnote 7, Kidd OMPF (CD), section 04 (Service Documents), 118, records Kidd's position as commander, Battleship Division One , and *Arizona* as Kidd's flagship.

14. The Kidd MOH citation is in this chapter and in appendix A.

15. Endnote 2, Stillwell, Battleship *Arizona*, 268.

16. The National Personnel Records Center, St. Louis, Missouri, furnished military and personal information from Van Valkenburgh's Official Military Personnel File (OMPF) at the author's request. The material came in two formats; initially, it was in selected pages copied from his OMPF (hereafter "Van Valkenburgh OMPF, initial request"); later, it came in the form of a compact disc with his entire OMPF (hereafter "Van Valkenburgh OMPF (CD)"). His birthday is on the compact disc, section 04 (Service Documents), record of service, 54. Meg Jones, "Milwaukee's Forgotten Hero" (Milwaukee Journal Sentinel, December 7, 2006), states that Van Valkenburgh grew up in Milwaukee (hereafter "'Milwaukee's Forgotten Hero'").

17. Endnote 16, Van Valkenburgh OMPF, initial request.

18. The Lucky Bag (U.S. Naval Academy, Class of 1909).

19. Ibid.

20. Endnote 16, Van Valkenburgh OMPF (CD), section 04 (Service Documents), record of service, 54–55.

21. The Van Valkenburgh MOH citation is in this chapter and in Appendix A.

22. Endnote 2, Stillwell, Battleship *Arizona*, 268.

23. The National Personnel Records Center, St. Louis, Missouri, furnished military and personal information from Fuqua's Official Military Personnel File (OMPF) at the author's request. The material came in two formats. Initially, it was in selected pages copied from his OMPF (hereafter "Fuqua OMPF, initial request"); later, it came in the form of a compact disc with his entire OMPF (hereafter "Fuqua OMPF (CD)"). His birthday is on the compact disc, section 04 (Service Documents), news release information, 28. His Army service and dates of his Navy service are from the initial OMPF request.

24. Ibid., Fuqua OMPF, initial request.

25. Endnote 23, Fuqua OMPF, initial request (basic letter); Fuqua OMPF, section 04 (Service Documents), 37.

26. Iris Chang, The Rape of Nanking (BasicBooks, New York, NY, 1997), 106–107.

27. Endnote 23, Fuqua OMPF, section 03 (Service Documents), 36–38.

28. Ibid., 46.

29. Ibid., 49.

30. Ibid., 53.

31. Ibid., 41.

32. Endnote 23, Fuqua OMPF, initial request; J. W. Bunkley, Rear Admiral, United States Navy, Retired, MILITARY and NAVAL RECOGNITION BOOK (D. Van Nostrand Company, Inc., 1943) (hereafter "Bunkley, MILITARY and NAVAL RECOGNITION BOOK); page 136 summarizes the duties of the First Lieutenant and Damage Control Officer.

33. The Lucky Bag (U.S. Naval Academy, Class of 1923), 167.

34. Colonel Charles A. Jones (USMCR Retired), Hawaii's World War II Military Sites (Mutual Publishing, Honolulu, HI, 2002), 30–31.

35. Testimony of Lieutenant Commander Fuqua on January 2, 1942, before the Roberts Commission, included in the report of the 1945 Congressional investigation of the attack found in PEARL HARBOR ATTACK: HEARINGS BEFORE THE JOINT COMMITTEE ON THE INVESTIGATION OF THE PEARL HARBOR ATTACK, SEVENTY-NINTH CONGRESS, FIRST SESSION, Part 23 (U.S. Government Printing Office, 1946), 633.

36. Endnote 35, Roberts Commission included in Joint Committee Report, 632–637.

37. Ibid., 632–633.

38. Ibid.

39. Ibid., 633.

40. Ibid., 634.

41. Ibid.

42. Ibid., 634–635.

43. Ibid., 635.

44. Tom Bennett, "Adm. Samuel Fuqua, 87, Honored for Heroism at Pearl Harbor, Dies," Atlanta Constitution, January 28, 1987, page C-11 (hereafter, "Fuqua obituary").

45. Endnote 35, Roberts Commission included in Joint Committee Report, 635.

46. Ibid.

47. Ibid.

48. Ibid.

49. Ibid., 635.

50. Endnote 23, Fuqua OMPF (CD), section 09 (Efficiency Reports), 132.

51. Report from USS *Arizona* (Subject: "Action Report of USS *Arizona*, December 7, 1941") of December 13, 1941 (hereafter "*Arizona* report").

52. Endnote 23, Fuqua OMPF, initial request.

53. Endnote 23, Fuqua OMPF (CD), section 06 (Service Documents), 55–56 and 61 (retirement certificate).

54. Endnote 44, Fuqua obituary.

55. Ibid.

56. Author has memories of the show, which was broadcast when he was a child.

57. Endnote 44, Fuqua obituary.

58. Ibid.

59. See Chapter 9 (Ross), Chapter 11 (Finn), and Chapter 19 (Pharris).

60. Endnote 2, Stillwell, Battleship *Arizona*, 3. Ironically, as President, Roosevelt would deliver one of the most famous speeches given in the history of the United States—his address to Congress, asking that it declare war on Japan after the attack on Oahu on December 7, which destroyed *Arizona*. The speech was famous for the label he gave December 7: "a date which will live in infamy."

61. Endnote 2, Stillwell, Battleship *Arizona*, 133–142.

62. Endnote 2: Of the many references consulted in writing this book, none mentioned the presence of any flag officer aboard any ship in Pearl Harbor on December 7 other than Rear Admiral Kidd aboard *Arizona*, DANFS, Vol. I (Part A), 381 (first flag officer killed during the war). Kidd was also the first of three Navy rear admirals to receive a MOH, all posthumously, during World War II. The other two were Daniel Callaghan and Norman Scott at the Naval Battle of Guadalcanal. See Chapter 8 of this book.

63. Endnote 2, DANFS, Vol. I (Part A), 381. The first two of these three ships would be sunk and damaged beyond repair on December 7. *Arizona* would remain in Pearl Harbor as explained in this chapter. *Oklahoma* would sink in the Pacific Ocean while being towed (Chapter 5). *Nevada* (Chapter 9) would be repaired to fight another day.

64. Endnote 2, Stillwell, Battleship *Arizona*, 197–211 (Kidd as commanding officer

of the ship); E. B. Potter, *Nimitz* (Naval Institute Press, Annapolis, MD, 1976), 13 (Nimitz as Commander, Battleship Division One when Kidd commanded *Arizona*). Nimitz would be promoted to admiral and appointed as Commander-in-Chief, U.S. Pacific Fleet, after Admiral Husband Kimmel was relieved of that billet after the December 7 attack. Nimitz would also achieve fame and five stars as one of the most famous American commanders of World War II.

65. Author's numerous visits to Pearl Harbor and the memorials for *Arizona* and *Utah*. Each ship rests where she sank (*Arizona*) or capsized (*Utah*).

66. Charles A. Jones, "Men of Honor: Pearl Harbor, December 7, 1941," Shipmate (December 2001), 11–13 (hereafter "Jones, 'Men of Honor'"). Shipmate is the magazine for Naval Academy alumni.

67. The Scott and Callaghan MOH citations can be found by searching the Internet for "Army MOH site," which will lead to the Army's master list of MOH recipients. The citations can be found under the sections for World War II MOH recipients.

68. Endnote 66, Jones, "Men of Honor," 13 (Fuqua as the sole survivor); see discussion of first MOHs in chapter 14 of this book.

Photographs
USS *Arizona* MOH Recipients

Rear Admiral Isaac Kidd, U.S. Navy, as a captain and Commanding officer, USS *Arizona*, circa 1939; the four stripes on his coat sleeves indicate the grade of captain. The ship's name and affiliation with Battleship Division One can be seen on the lifesaver. (Photograph NH 97385 from the Naval History and Heritage Command.)

Captain Franklin Van Valkenburgh, U.S. Navy; the fours stripes on his shoulder board indicate the grade of captain. (Photograph NH 75840 from the Naval History and Heritage Command.)

Commander Samuel Fuqua, U.S. Navy wearing his MOH (the MOH itself cannot be seen and is hanging from the ribbon around his neck). (Photograph NH 92306 from the Naval History and Heritage Command.)

The Fuqua MOH on display (circa 1999) at what was formerly the Arizona Visitors' Center. (Photograph from U.S. Navy Internet site.)

Chapter 8
USS Vestal (AR-4)
The CO Swims Back to His Ship

Commander Cassin Young, U.S. Navy
USS Vestal, December 7, 1941

Vestal was originally built as a collier (coal ship) and placed in service in 1909. She was converted to an auxiliary ship—specifically, a repair ship with the designation AR—and commissioned as such in 1913.[1]

On December 7, *Vestal* was moored alongside USS *Arizona* at Berth F-7 with *Arizona* the inboard ship and *Vestal*, the outboard ship. *Vestal*'s port side faced Ford Island and *Arizona* so that *Vestal*'s bow was near *Arizona*'s stern and thus pointed away from the opening to the channel leading from Pearl Harbor to the Pacific Ocean.[2]

Arizona suffered the catastrophic damage explained in chapter 7. Two bombs hit and damaged *Vestal*; she was also endangered by fires started on *Arizona*. Because of the threat posed by *Arizona*, *Vestal*'s commanding officer, Commander Cassin Young, decided to move the ship away from *Arizona* and to ground her, which he did on Aiea Shoal.[3] The ship's crew lost six identified dead, three unidentified dead, and seven missing.[4]

Vestal had one MOH recipient: Commander Cassin Young.

Commander Cassin Young, U.S. Navy

Background

Young was born in Washington, DC, on March 6, 1894. He entered the Naval Academy in 1912 and graduated in 1916.[5]

His nicknames at the Academy were "Cy" (perhaps from the first letters of his first and last names) and "Teddy." Young's tenacity and calm under fire aboard USS *Vestal* proved the accuracy of these insights found in The Lucky Bag for the Class of 1916:

> TEDDY is a cute little devil but the last is far more appropriate than the first, for ever since his early days here Teddy has been getting into trouble at pretty regular intervals, but he has, however, managed to get out of trouble at equally regular intervals, and it is a safe bet he will take out his clearance papers with the rest of US. Lack of size is one of the things—in fact, the only thing—that kept Ted from doing more in athletics. But he has done enough for the average man and *he possesses plenty of spunk*. [Italics added for emphasis.]
>
> Teddy isn't brilliant; he's too irresponsible to be considered as one of the more capable men in the Class, *but he's got his nerve with him, and that alone should pull him through many a situation* ... [Italics added for emphasis.]

Teddy was made to enjoy life—that is, while he is young—but some day he'll grow up and his abilities, which in here were at times obscured by his indifference to mere matters such as regulations, etc., will come to the surface, and Ted will then get the confidence that his abilities deserve.[6]

He accepted an appointment as an ensign in 1916 upon his graduation from the Naval Academy. He was promoted to lieutenant junior grade in 1917 and to lieutenant in 1918. He was promoted to lieutenant commander in 1927 and to commander in 1937. He held a variety of billets during his career, including service aboard surface ships and submarines. He also was an instructor at the Naval Academy. He became the commanding officer of USS *Vestal* on October 8, 1941, reporting to the ship on November 19, 1941; he remained the commanding officer of the ship until November 7, 1942.[7]

Actions on December 7

The ship had sounded general quarters (battle stations) at approximately 7:55 a.m. At approximately 8:05 a.m., two bombs hit *Vestal*. One hit the starboard side, piercing three decks, and the other hit the port side, piercing several spaces and exiting the hull. Because of fire ignited by the bombing, the crew had to flood the forward magazines to prevent them from burning or exploding.[8]

At approximately 8:20, a bomb hit *Arizona*'s forward magazine, causing an explosion that started fires on *Vestal*. The fuel oil between the two ships ignited. The force of the explosion on *Arizona* cleared *Vestal*'s decks, blowing men overboard, including Young. He swam back to the ship and countermanded an order someone gave to abandon ship. He regained control of the ship and knew he had to get underway to move away from *Arizona*, the ship to which his own ship was moored. At 8:30, the orders were given to make preparations for getting underway although the ship had to do so without having any steering gear; a tug had to pull the ship's bow away from *Arizona*. *Vestal* got underway and because of her damage anchored near McGrew's Point. Because of the damage to and the instability of the ship—she was listing and was on fire in several places—and the possibility of additional attacks, Young decided to ground her and did so at Aiea Shoal.[9]

During the attack, the ship's antiaircraft guns were in action. The blast from *Arizona* cleared one gun station, killing one man.[10]

Young survived December 7 and signed the ship's December 11, 1941, report of the attack, in which he reported the ship's losses: six identified dead and three unidentified dead. Seven men were missing. Nineteen men were hospitalized.[11]

Young's action in moving his ship accomplished a critical task; by moving his ship away from *Arizona*, he ensured *Vestal* would not sustain further damage from explosions aboard and debris from *Arizona*.

Aftermath of December 7

After-Action Reports

Vestal's report of the action on December 7 was dated December 11, 1941, addressed to the Commander-in-chief, US Pacific Fleet (Nimitz), and signed "C. Young." It described what happened to the ship and is in part the basis of the section "Actions on December 7" previously in this chapter. Young concluded his own after-action report thus, offering the highest praise for his crew one can offer in the military—the desire to serve with the crew members again in combat: "The conduct of all officers and enlisted personnel was exemplary and of such high order that I would especially desire to have them with me in future engagements."[12]

Commander Cassin Young was one of five living MOH recipients to receive a MOH for actions on December 7 and one of thirteen officers and men on Battleship Row receiving MOHs for actions on that date. President Franklin D. Roosevelt signed the MOH citation on March 4, 1942.

MOH Citation

For distinguished conduct in action, outstanding heroism and utter disregard of his own safety, above and beyond the call of duty, as commanding officer of the USS *Vestal*, during the attack on the fleet in Pearl Harbor, Territory of Hawaii, by enemy Japanese forces on December 7, 1941. Comdr. Young proceeded to the bridge and later took personal command of the three-inch antiaircraft gun. When blown overboard by the blast of the forward magazine explosion of the USS *Arizona*, to which the USS *Vestal* was moored, he swam back to his ship. The entire forward part of the USS *Arizona* was a blazing inferno with oil afire on the water between the two ships; as a result of several bomb hits, the USS *Vestal* was a fire in several places, was settling and taking on a list. Despite severe enemy bombing and strafing at the time, and his shocking experience of having been blown overboard, Comdr. Young, with extreme coolness and calmness, moved his ship to an anchorage distant from the USS. *Arizona*, and subsequently beached the USS. *Vestal* upon determining that such action was required to save his ship.

Later Life: Cassin Young

After surviving the hell of December 7, Cassin Young suffered a tragic, sad fate.

Young was appointed a temporary captain on March 4, 1942.[13] He received his MOH on April 18, 1942, from Admiral Chester Nimitz.[14] On November 9, 1942, Young reported as commanding officer of the cruiser San Francisco, an ironic assignment for several reasons.[15] The ship was at Pearl Harbor on December 7 under the command of San Francisco native Captain Daniel Callaghan.[16] After Callaghan was promoted to rear admiral in 1942, he commanded a task group, operating around Guadalcanal. Callaghan chose San Francisco as his flagship.[17]

Callaghan's task group was part of Task Force 67, which included a task group under Rear Admiral Norman Scott, whose flagship was the cruiser Atlanta.[18]

On November 12, 1942, the Japanese attacked Callaghan's task group as it protected ships delivering supplies to Guadalcanal, beginning the Naval Battle of Guadalcanal. A Japanese aircraft crashed into San Francisco, damaging the ship, killing and wounding many crewmen.[19]

The worst was yet to come. On November 12, Callaghan was ordered to strike Japanese ships near Guadalcanal. A battle with Japanese ships began at approximately 2:00 a.m. on Friday, November 13.[20]

Friday the thirteenth proved to be bad luck for Cassin Young. Chaos reigned as ships battled in darkness. One of the first casualties was Atlanta, hit either by friendly fire from San Francisco or by enemy fire, killing Scott.[21] Japanese shells hitting San Francisco killed Callaghan and Young.[22]

Notwithstanding the damage done to its ships and the loss of men and ships, the U.S. Navy won the battle and achieved its objective—protecting Henderson Field, a very important Marine airfield on Guadalcanal. Victory was largely due to the bravery of many men, including five receiving MOHs. After the battle, the American ships sailed to the New Hebrides.[23]

Four men on San Francisco earned MOHs, matching the highest number received by one ship for December 7 (four for USS *California*) and the highest number for any U.S. Navy ship during the war. The four San Francisco MOH recipients were as follows:[24]

- Callaghan received a posthumous MOH for tactical skill and coordination of his units.
- Boatswain's Mate First Class Reinhardt Keppler died in the Naval Hospital, New Hebrides, and received a posthumous MOH for assisting casualties after the Japanese plane hit the ship on November 12 and for damage-control actions and assisting the wounded—while mortally wounded himself—on November 13.
- Two San Francisco officers lived to receive their MOHs. Largely because of the actions of these officers, the ship kept moving and fighting and survived to fight another day. Lieutenant Commander Bruce McCandless, seriously wounded and knocked unconscious, recovered and, finding himself the senior surviving officer on the navigating and signal bridges, assumed command of the ship. Lieutenant Commander Herbert Schonland was senior to McCandless but left McCandless in command so that Schonland could continue supervising damage control elsewhere on the ship.

The fifth MOH recipient was Scott, whose posthumous MOH citation commended his leadership in October and November 1942.[25] He and Callaghan thus became two of three navy flag officers receiving MOHs during the war. Both men were rear admirals, and both were killed in the same battle on the same day, November 13, 1942.[26] The third rear admiral to receive a MOH was Isaac Kidd, who perished aboard his flagship, USS *Arizona*, on December 7.[27]

Cassin Young—who had survived December 7, earned a MOH, and commanded San Francisco for such a brief time—earned a Navy Cross posthumously for his actions on November 13. The citation reads as follows:

For extraordinary heroism in the line of his profession during action with enemy forces on the night of November 12–13, 1942, on which occasion the force to which he was attached engaged at close quarters and defeated a superior enemy force. His daring and determination contributed materially to the victory, which prevented the enemy from accomplishing their purposes.[28]

All MOH recipients mentioned in this chapter (except Keppler, who was enlisted) were Naval Academy graduates.[29]

Where do these men rest today?

Young's remembrance is discussed in the following section.

Like Young, Callaghan and Scott have no graves since they were lost or buried at sea; their names appear on the Tablets of the Missing at Manila American Cemetery.[30]

Keppler is buried in National Golden Gate Cemetery and McCandless at the Naval Academy.[31] A final irony is the date of death appearing on Schonland's tombstone at Arlington National Cemetery. While the day of death was not a Friday, the date remains a haunting coincidence and reminder: "13 NOV 84."[32]

NOTES

1. James L. Mooney, editor. Dictionary of American Naval Fighting Ships, (Naval Historical Center, Department of the Navy, Washington, DC, 1981), Vol. VII, 494 (hereafter "DANFS"); SEAMANSHIP ("NAVPERS 16118," U.S. Navy, Training, Standards, and Curriculum Division), 47 (AR means "Repair Ship").

2. Information about ship mooring is from the author's personal view of Battleship Row and its mooring quays; the report by Rear Admiral W. S. Anderson, Commander Battleships, Battle Force (Subject: "Attack at Pearl Harbor by Japanese Planes on December 7, 1941") of December 19, 1941, paragraph 3; and diagrams and photographs in Chapter 2.

3. Report from USS *Vestal* (Subject: "Report of action on December 7, 1941, in accordance with references (a) and (b)) of December 11, 1941 (hereafter "*Vestal* report").

4. Ibid., paragraph 5.

5. Official U.S. Navy biography, Captain Cassin Young, U.S. Navy (Deceased), February 20, 1946 (hereafter "Young U.S. Navy biography").

6. The Lucky Bag, (U.S. Naval Academy, Class of 1916), 221.

7. The National Personnel Records Center, St. Louis, Missouri, furnished military and personal information from Young's Official Military Personnel File (OMPF) at the author's request (hereafter "Young OMPF").

8. Endnote 1, DANFS, Vol. VII, 495; endnote 3, *Vestal* report.

9. Ibid.

10. Endnote 3, *Vestal* report.

12. Ibid.

13. Endnote 7, Young OMPF.

14. Chapter 14, table 5-1.

15. Endnote 7, Young OMPF.

16. Pearl Harbor Attack: Hearings Before The Joint Committee On The Investigation Of The Pearl Harbor Attack, Seventy-ninth Congress, Second Session, Part 21 (1946), 4558.

17. Samuel Eliot Morison, History Of United States Naval Operations In World War II, Vol. V (Atlantic Monthly Press, Little, Brown, and Company, 1949), 231.

18. Ibid., 232, 237.

19. Ibid., 231.

20. Ibid., 236, 242.

21. Ibid., 243, 247.

22. Ibid., 247.

23. Lieutenant Colonel Frank O. Hough, USMCR, Major Verle E. Ludwig, USMC, and Henry I. Shaw, Jr., Pearl Harbor to Guadalcanal: HISTORY OF THE U.S. MARINE CORPS OPERATIONS IN WORLD WAR II, Vol. I (Historical Division, Headquarters, U.S. Marine Corps, Washington, DC, 1958, reprinted by the Battery Press, Inc., Nashville, TN, 1993), 353; endnotes 23 and 24 describe the five MOHs.

24. Chapters 4 (USS *California*) and 14 (Overview). The San Francisco MOHs were as follows:

    a) Callaghan
His posthumous citation refers to leading "his forces into battle against tremendous odds, thereby contributing to the rout of a powerful invasion fleet and to the consequent frustration of a formidable Japanese offensive."

    b) Boatswain's Mate First Class Reinhardt Keppler
He received a posthumous MOH for assisting casualties after the Japanese plane hit the ship on November 12 and for damage-control actions and assisting the wounded—while mortally wounded himself—on November 13. His death in the New Hebrides can be explained by the American ships sailing there after the battle as noted in the text.

    c) Lieutenant Commander Bruce McCandless
He was seriously wounded and knocked unconscious, recovered, and, finding himself the senior surviving officer on the navigating and signal bridges, assumed command of the ship.

    d) Lieutenant Commander Herbert Schonland
He was senior to McCandless but left McCandless in command so that he could continue supervising damage control elsewhere on the ship.

McCandless and Schonland survived to receive their MOHs. The MOH citations for Callaghan, Schonland, McCandless, and Keppler can be found by searching the Internet for "Army MOH site" and accessing the citations by choosing the correct icon for World War II at the "Medal of Honor Recipients: Center of Military History" Internet site.

25. Ibid.; the Scott MOH citation can be found at the Army MOH citation site.

26. The MOHs for Callaghan and Scott are posthumous awards for actions on November 12–13, 1942.

27. Chapter 7.

28. Endnote 5, Young US Navy biography.

29. Callaghan, Class of 1911; Scott, Class of 1911; McCandless, Class of 1932; and Schonland, Class of 1925.

30. Printings from the American Battle Monuments Commission Internet site—Callaghan (2000) and Scott (2002)—show that Callaghan and Scott are missing in action or buried at sea and are commemorated with their names on the Tablets of the Missing at Manila American Cemetery, Manila, Philippines.

31. The Keppler death and burial information is from George Lang (MOH), Raymond

L. Collins, and Gerald F. White (compilers), Medal of Honor Recipients 1863–1994 Vol. II (World War II to Somalia) (Facts on File, Inc., New York, NY), 516 (hereafter "Lang, Medal of Honor Recipients 1863–1994").

32. Author's view of the Schonland tombstone at Arlington National Cemetery.

Photography
USS *VESTAL* MOH Recipient

Commander Cassin Young, U.S. Navy; the three stripes on his shoulder boards indicate the grade of commander. (Photograph NH 92310 from the Naval History and Heritage Command.)

Obverse (front, top photograph) and reverse sides of the Cassin Young MOH. (Photographs courtesy of the holder of the MOH, the National Museum of the Pacific War, 2008.)

Chapter 9
USS Nevada (BB-36)
Gambling on a Short Run

Chief Warrant Officer (Boatswain) Edwin Hill, U.S. Navy

Warrant Officer (Machinist) Donald Ross, U.S. Navy

USS Nevada, December 7, 1941

On December 7, *Nevada* was, like *California*, moored by herself along Battleship Row at Berth F-8 at the opposite end of Battleship Row from *California*. As noted in Chapter 4 (*California*), they were the bookends of Battleship Row on December 7; all other battleships, with the exception of USS Pennsylvania at the shipyard, were between *California* and *Nevada*, along with the repair ship *Vestal* and tanker Neosho. *California*, at berth F-3, was closest to the entrance to the channel leading from Pearl Harbor to the Pacific Ocean, with that entrance between Hospital Point at the Navy Yard and the Waipio Peninsula. At Berth F-8, *Nevada* was farthest from the mouth of that channel. Immediately ahead of *Nevada* were two ships moored at Berth F-7: *Vestal* and *Arizona*. No ships were immediately behind *Nevada*.[1]

Like *California*, *Nevada*'s starboard side faced Ford Island. Such mooring was dangerous since it exposed her port side to the waters of Pearl Harbor and thus to torpedoes dropped from the air into the water.[2]

That danger became reality on December 7 when *Nevada* suffered one torpedo hit on her port side. She also suffered at least six bomb hits, some while at her berth and some while, as described in this chapter, she was underway. She may have received up to ten bomb hits, but the precise number could not be determined; only six bomb hits were accounted for in the December 15, 1941, report of the ship's commanding officer.[3]

Although mooring alone was a disadvantage since the ship was exposed to torpedo attack, it had one advantage. *Nevada* could move freely away from her berth without concern for a ship beside her. In reality, no other battleship could move. As explained in chapters 4, 6, and 7 of this book, *California*, *West Virginia*, and *Arizona* sank in place and could not move. Two inboard ships were trapped by outboard ships: Maryland, inboard of *Oklahoma*, was blocked when *Oklahoma* capsized (Chapter 5), and Tennessee, inboard of *West Virginia*, was blocked when *West Virginia* sank in place (Chapter 6).

So, unlike *California*, which was also moored alone but sank in place, *Nevada* could and did exploit the advantage of being able to move. She had the distinction of being the only battleship to get underway during the attack.

Although damaged while stationary at F-8, *Nevada* left her berth, passing by Battleship Row on her starboard side and the Navy Yard on her port side, and headed for the channel leading out of Pearl Harbor to the Pacific Ocean.[4]

But as *Nevada* moved from her berth and sailed the route just described, she became the target of Japanese dive bombing. The Japanese knew that a ship sunk in the narrow channel leading from Pearl Harbor to the Pacific could stop or greatly impede movement to and from Pearl Harbor. To prevent the ship from being sunk in the channel, she was ordered to run aground near Hospital Point at the Navy Yard, which she did. Later in the day, she was moved across the water and grounded off Waipio Peninsula at a place that later became known as "*Nevada* Point."[5]

She lost fifty of her crew.[6]

On December 7, two of *Nevada*'s crewmen would take actions resulting in awards of MOHs: Warrant Officer (Machinist) Donald Ross and Chief Warrant Officer (Boatswain) Edwin Hill. Only one survived the day.

Chief Warrant Officer (Boatswain) Edwin Hill

Background

Hill was born in Philadelphia, Pennsylvania, on October 4, 1894. He enlisted in the Navy on February 14, 1912. He was discharged on October 2, 1915, but immediately reenlisted. He accepted a temporary appointment as a warrant officer (boatswain) on November 3, 1918. On August 5, 1920, he received a warrant as a boatswain. On February 25, 1925, he was appointed a regular chief boatswain to date from October 21, 1924.[7] Warrant or chief warrant officers are boatswains who assist the ship's First Lieutenant; they care for the basic equipment of the ship, such as "boats, anchors, cables, and rigging" and any other equipment for which they are responsible.[8]

During his career, he served on numerous ships and at numerous shore duty stations. Ironically, he served on two ships that would be at Pearl Harbor on December 7: USS Maryland, on Battleship Row, and USS Pennsylvania, at the Shipyard.[9]

From late 1939 to July 1940, he was involved with the transfer of a floating drydock from New Orleans to Pearl Harbor. He remained with the drydock until ordered to USS *Nevada* at Pearl Harbor on October 31, 1940.[10]

He had a wife and three children.[11]

Actions on December 7

Although his MOH citation does not provide clear context, Hill received a MOH for two separate actions. The report of the ship's commanding officer describes Hill's actions on December 7 and must be the basis for the MOH citation.[12]

The first action necessarily occurred during the initial stage of the attack when the ship was bombed and strafed while moored and while the ship was getting underway. According to the commanding officer's report, under enemy fire and at "the height of the enemy attack," Hill led his men to the quays at F-8 and, under fire, cast off the lines.[13] Apparently the ship began leaving the berth, or had left the berth, without him since the MOH citation and the commanding officer's report note that he had to swim back to the ship.[14]

The second action necessarily occurred when the ship was underway but in the process of grounding near Hospital Point. He was on the forecastle (area of the ship's deck forward of the foremast) trying to release the anchors when he was blown overboard and killed by the explosion of several bombs. He was obviously trying to assist in grounding the ship; as previously noted, the ship had been ordered to ground at Hospital Point so that she would not be sunk in the channel leading from Pearl Harbor to the Pacific Ocean, thus blocking entrance to and exit from Pearl Harbor. The report summarized Hill's conduct as follows: "His performance of duty and devotion to duty was [sic] outstanding."[15]

WARRANT OFFICER (MACHINIST) DONALD ROSS

Background

Ross was born on December 8, 1910, in Beverly, Kansas.[16]

He enlisted in the Navy on June 3, 1929, and was in the Navy from that date until retirement on July 1, 1956, serving on a variety of ships and at a variety of bases.[17]

He began recruit training on June 6, 1929, as an apprentice seaman and was the honor man of his training company, receiving a letter of commendation from his commanding officer.[18] He progressed in grade as follows: from apprentice seaman to fireman third class (F3c) to machinist's mate (MM) to MM second class (MM2c) to MM first class (MM1c), which is one grade below chief petty officer.[19]

Most of his career was aboard ships.[20] He accepted an appointment as a warrant officer (machinist) on October 7, 1940, and reported to *Nevada* in November 1940.[21] Warrant or chief warrant officer machinists assist the chief engineer and maintain and repair machinery; they also stand watches.[22]

Actions on December 7

On December 7, Ross forced his men to leave their station when smoke, steam, and heat made presence in the station almost unbearable. He, however, remained at his post and performed his duties alone until he was rendered unconscious and blind. Rescued and resuscitated, he secured his station and proceeded to another, where he was again rendered unconscious due to exhaustion. He regained consciousness and returned to his station where he remained until ordered to abandon it.[23]

AFTERMATH OF DECEMBER 7

After-Action Report

The basis for the text of the Hill MOH citation is obviously the ship's "Report of December 7, 1941 Raid" dated December 15, 1941, given the similarity in wording in the Hill MOH citation and the report. Paragraph 4a3 of the report,

"DISTINGUISHED CONDUCT OF PERSONNEL," describes Hill's actions on December 7 and was cited previously in this chapter. Paragraph 4a3 of the report stated that Hill was "deserving of the highest commendation possible to be given for his skill, leadership and courage." The report concluded that his "performance of duty and devotion to duty was [sic] outstanding." The report does not mention Ross.

Chief Boatswain Hill and Warrant Officer Ross would be two of the "battleship sailors" to receive MOHs for December 7; Hill's was a posthumous award while Ross lived to receive his MOH. President Franklin D. Roosevelt signed both MOH citations on March 4, 1942.

MOH Citations

Chief Warrant Officer (Chief Boatswain) Edwin Joseph Hill, U.S. Navy

> For distinguished conduct in the line of his profession, extraordinary courage, and disregard of his own safety during the attack on the fleet in Pearl Harbor by Japanese Forces on December 7, 1941. During the height of the strafing and bombing, Chief Boatswain Hill led his men of the line handling details of the USS *Nevada* to the quays, cast off the lines and swam back to his ship. Later, while on the forecastle attempting to let go the anchors, he was blown overboard and killed by the explosion of several bombs.

Warrant Officer (Machinist) Donald Kirby Ross, U.S. Navy

> For distinguished conduct in the line of his profession, extraordinary courage, and disregard of his own life during the attack on the fleet in Pearl Harbor, Territory of Hawaii, by Japanese forces on December 7, 1941. When his station in the forward dynamo room of the USS *Nevada* became almost untenable due to smoke, steam, and heat, Lieutenant Commander Ross forced his men to leave that station and performed all the duties himself until blinded and unconscious. Upon being rescued and resuscitated, he returned and secured the forward dynamo room and proceeded to the after dynamo room where he was later again rendered unconscious by exhaustion. Again recovering consciousness he returned to his station where he remained until directed to abandon it.

Later Life: Donald Ross

Ross became an ensign on June 15, 1942, served on *Nevada* for the first three years of the war, and participated in action in the Aleutians and in the landings in 1944 at Normandy and Southern France. In 1945, he rejoined *Nevada* for a short time since in 1946 the ship was selected as a target ship for the atomic bombings of ships at Bikini Islands.[24]

He retired on July 1, 1956. Although he was a commander, he was advanced to captain based on of his combat record.[25]

Ross settled in the Glenwood area of South Kitsap County, Washington, near the city of Port Orchard.[26]

In 1988, he and his wife wrote a book about the men who had received various decorations for December 7, 0755: The Heroes Of Pearl Harbor.[27]

Ross died on May 27, 1992, at Bremerton, Washington.[28] He had a wife, two sons, and two daughters.[29] His ashes were scattered over the site of *Nevada* (eighty-five miles southwest of Pearl Harbor) by the crew of the submarine USS *Nevada* (SSBN-733).[30] He has an "In Memory of" tombstone at Beverly Cemetery, Beverly, Kansas, the town of his birth.[31]

NOTES

1. Information about ship mooring is from the author's personal view of Battleship Row and its mooring quays; the report by Rear Admiral W. S. Anderson, Commander Battleships, Battle Force (Subject: "Attack at Pearl Harbor by Japanese Planes on December 7, 1941") of December 19, 1941, paragraph 3; and diagrams and photographs in Chapter 2.

2. Ibid.

3. Report from USS *Nevada* (Subject: "Report of December 7, 1941 Raid") of December 15, 1941, paragraph 3 (hereafter "*Nevada* report").

4. Dictionary of American Naval Fighting Ships, Vol. V (Naval History Division, Department of the Navy, Washington, DC,1981), 52 (hereafter "DANFS"). DANFS states that being moored "singly" gave *Nevada* "a freedom of maneuver denied the other 8 battleships present during the attack." The "singly" and "freedom of maneuver" are correct, but DANFS is incorrect in stating that no other ship had such freedom. *California* was also moored "singly" but could not get underway; see Chapter 4 of this book. Also, the inference from the "other eight battleships present during the attack" is that nine battleships were in Pearl Harbor. The correct number is eight (seven on Battleship Row and USS Pennsylvania at the Shipyard); *Nevada* report, paragraph 2a3; Vice Admiral Homer N. Wallin, U.S. Navy (Retired), Pearl Harbor: Why, How, Fleet Salvage, and Final Approach (Naval History Division, US Government Printing Office, Washington, DC, 1968), 150–213 (hereafter "Wallin, Pearl Harbor").

5. Ibid.; endnote 3, *Nevada* report (paragraph 2a5); endnote 4, Wallin, Pearl Harbor, 150–213.

6. Endnote 4, DANFS, Vol. V, 52.

7. Official U.S. Navy biography, "Chief Boatswain Edwin Joseph Hill, U.S. Navy (Deceased), February 19, 1946 (hereafter "Hill, U.S. Navy biography"); the National Personnel Records Center, St. Louis, Missouri, furnished military and personal information from Hill's Official Military Personnel File (OMPF) at the author's

request (hereafter "Hill OMPF").

8. J. W. Bunkley, Rear Admiral, United States Navy, Retired, MILITARY and NAVAL RECOGNITION BOOK (D. Van Nostrand Company, Inc., New York, NY, 1943); a description of the duties of warrant and chief warrant officer boatswains is on page 138 (hereafter "Bunkley, MILITARY and NAVAL RECOGNITION BOOK").

9. Endnote 7, Hill OMPF and Hill, U.S. Navy biography.

10. Ibid.

11. Endnote 7, Hill OMPF.

12. Endnote 3, *Nevada* report (paragraph 4a3, "Distinguished Conduct Of Personnel").

13. Ibid.

14. Ibid.; Hill MOH citation in Appendix A of this book.

15. Endnote 3, *Nevada* report (paragraph 4a3).

16. Official U.S. Navy biography, "Captain Donald K. Ross, United States Navy, Retired," March 17, 1967 (hereafter "Ross, U.S. Navy biography").

17. Ibid.

18. Ibid.; the National Personnel Records Center, St. Louis, Missouri, furnished military and personal information from Ross's Official Military Personnel File (OMPF) at the author's request (hereafter "Ross OMPF").

19. Ibid.

20. Ibid.

21. Endnote 18, Ross, U.S. Navy biography.

22. Endnote 8, Bunkley, MILITARY and NAVAL RECOGNITION BOOK; a description of the duties of warrant and chief warrant officer machinists is on page 138.

23. Ross MOH citation at Appendix A of this book.

24. Endnote 16, Ross, U.S. Navy biography.

25. Ibid.

26. Document appearing to be a typed obituary of Donald Kirby Ross (undated and with no source) provided to the author by the crew of USS Ross; the public relations department of Litton Ingalls Shipbuilding had telefaxed the document to the ship's

PCO (Prospective Commanding Officer) on March 24, 1995 (hereafter "Litton Ingalls obituary (Ross)"). Litton Ingalls built USS Ross.

27. Ibid.; Donald K. and Helen Ross, "0755," The Heroes Of Pearl Harbor (Rokalu Press, 1988).

28. Endnote 26, Litton Ingalls obituary (Ross).

29. Ibid.

30. George Lang, Raymond L. Collins, and Gerald F. White, Medal of Honor Recipients 1863–1994, World War II to Somalia, Vol. II (Facts on File, Inc., New York, NY, 1995), 567 (hereafter "Lang, Medal of Honor Recipients 1863–1994"; electronic mail from Carol Cepregi, Congressional MOH Society, to the author (December 21, 2005). His "In Memory Of" marker states "Buried at Sea."

31. Appendix C.

PHOTOGRAPHS
USS *NEVADA* MEDAL OF HONOR RECIPIENTS

Chief Boatswain Edwin Hill, U.S. Navy. (Photograph NH 49196 from the Naval History and Heritage Command)

Warrant Officer (Machinist) Donald Ross, U.S. Navy, as a lieutenant circa 1944; he is wearing his MOH ribbon above his left pocket, but the ribbon is inverted. (Photograph NH 97461 from the Naval History and Heritage Command)

Nevada's historic "run" on December 7, 1941, began when she departed her mooring quays, one of which is shown here (to the left is the *Arizona* Memorial). To the rear of the quay is Ford Island. (Author's photograph, 2015)

Nevada, moored behind *Arizona*, first passed *Arizona* during her historic run. (Author's photograph, 2015)

After passing *Arizona* (the Memorial is the white structure in the upper center of the picture), *Nevada* passed *West Virginia* and *Oklahoma*; their berths now occupied by USS *Missouri*, the stern of which can be seen at the center of the picture. The white awning on the stern protects crew and visitors from the sun. Ford Island is to the left. (Author's photograph, 2015)

After passing *Oklahoma*, *Nevada* would have passed this area and grounded here at what is now *Nevada* Point; the stone in the foreground is the *Nevada* Memorial. Chief Boatswain Edwin Hill was killed by bombs falling near here while trying to let go the ship's anchors. (Author's photograph, 2015)

Nevada first grounded here at *Nevada* Point (the *Nevada* Memorial is in foreground with flagpole) and was later moved across the channel to the Waipio Peninsula to what would become *Nevada* Point (center of the green area in the distance across the channel from the Memorial). (Author's photograph, 2015)

CHAPTER 10
USS UTAH (AG-16)
THE BATTLESHIP THAT WASN'T

CHIEF PETTY OFFICER (WATERTENDER) PETER TOMICH, US NAVY

USS UTAH, DECEMBER 7, 1941

Utah has been called "Pearl Harbor's forgotten ship" since she today rests in the shadow of USS *Arizona*.[1] And she is frequently but mistakenly included as a battleship present on December 7; although she had been a battleship, on that date she was an auxiliary ship,.

Utah was a battleship (BB-[31]) commissioned in 1911. She landed navy and marine personnel in 1914 during operations at Vera Cruz, Mexico. In 1920, she was assigned hull number 31, making her designation "BB-31."[2]

In 1931, she was converted to a mobile target ship, requiring a change in her designation from "BB-31" to "AG-16," with AG meaning "miscellaneous auxiliary ship." In 1935, she also became the home of a fleet machine gun school and served as an antiaircraft gunnery training ship. Her designation remained AG-16.[3] She is often mistakenly counted as a battleship when the number of battleships lost on December 7 are counted or listed.

On December 7, *Utah* was moored on Carrier Row, the side of Ford Island opposite Battleship Row. The term Carrier Row is used because aircraft carriers often moored on the side of Ford Island farthest from the Navy Yard and Shipyard.[4]

Utah was moored at Berth F-11 ("Fox-11") at two mooring quays, F-11-S and F-11-N (the bow was at F-11-N). Her starboard side faced Ford Island. USS Raleigh, a cruiser, was at Berth F-12, ahead of *Utah* with *Utah*'s bow behind Raleigh's stern. USS Tangier, a large seaplane tender, was at F-10, with her bow to the stern of *Utah*.[5]

The senior officer aboard at the time of the attack, Lieutenant Commander S. S. Isquith, reported seeing aircraft with "brilliant red Rising Sun insignia on fuselage [sic] and red wing tips..." He also reported sequential "underwater hit[s]" causing the ship to list to port or away from Ford Island. After the second hit, he realized the ship would capsize, so he ordered that all prisoners be released from the brig and that all hands abandon ship by going to the starboard side, the side facing Ford Island and the highest side since the port side was submerging because of the torpedo hits allowing water inflow. Japanese aircraft strafed the men as they abandoned ship. As the listing (tilting) of the ship increased, the lines holding the ship to the mooring quays (the mooring lines) broke. The last line broke, and the ship capsized at approximately 8:12 a.m.[6]

Survivors reaching the shore of Ford Island heard knocking from inside the overturned hull. Firemen Second Class John Vaessen had removed a manhole and climbed to the bottom of the ship. Vaessen was famous for the way he was rescued;

while the area was being strafed, volunteers used a torch to cut a hole in the hull and rescue him. He received a Navy Cross for remaining at his post, notwithstanding an order to abandon ship, and for keeping lights burning as long as possible.[7]

The ship's dead and missing numbered fifty-eight men and six officers.[8]

Utah had one MOH recipient: Chief Watertender Peter Tomich.

CHIEF PETTY OFFICER WATERTENDER PETER TOMICH, U.S. NAVY

Background

Born on June 3, 1893, in the village of Prolog (in Yugoslavia), Tomich first enlisted in the Army on June 6, 1917, in New York and was sent to serve in North Carolina. He was naturalized at Charlotte, North Carolina, on October 19, 1918, and honorably discharged on January 13, 1919.[9]

He enlisted in the Navy on January 23, 1919, in Newark, New Jersey, as a fireman third class. He had used the name Tonich until the time of his Navy enlistment, when he changed the name to Tomich. He initially served on a destroyer, USS Litchfield. He maintained his Navy career via a series of reenlistments, achieving the grade of chief petty officer (watertender) on June 4, 1930, which was a permanent appointment.[10] A watertender's duties included supervising, maintaining, and operating the ship's boiler room and repairing its equipment; he also supervised the ship's "firemen" (engine-room workers, not firefighters). His final assignment was *Utah*.[11]

Actions on December 7

Although realizing that his ship was capsizing, Tomich ignored the order to abandon ship and remained at his post in the engineering plant to ensure that the boilers were secured (Navy terminology in this case meaning "turned off") and that all fire-room personnel had left their stations. By remaining inside the ship, he lost his life.[12]

The importance of securing the boilers was to prevent a catastrophic explosion; hot boilers could rupture and explode if engulfed by the cold water of Pearl Harbor entering the ship because of capsizing or flooding. His actions could not prevent the ship from capsizing, but they prevented the boilers from exploding.[13]

AFTERMATH OF DECEMBER 7

After-Action Report

The ship's report of the action, "USS *Utah*—Loss by Enemy Action," was dated December 15, 1941. In it, the ship's commanding officer, J. M. Steele, recommended that seven crewmen (officers and men), including Tomich, be awarded posthumous Navy Crosses for sacrificing their lives to ensure that other crew members escaped. He also recommended Vaessen for a Navy Cross.[14]

An enclosure to the report is the statement of the senior surviving line officer on the ship at the time of the attack, Lieutenant Commander S. S. Isquith. Among those he singled out for "exceptional conduct under fire" was Tomich, "for insuring that all fireroom personnel had left the ship and the boilers were secured prior to his abandoning the ship which resulted in the probable loss of his own life."[15]

Chief Petty Officer (Watertender) Peter Tomich would be the only MOH recipient whose ship was moored at Carrier Row; his would be one of ten posthumous awards for officers and men on ships moored around Ford Island. President Franklin D. Roosevelt signed his MOH citation on March 4, 1942.

MOH Citation

For distinguished conduct in the line of his profession and extraordinary courage and disregard of his own safety during the attack on the fleet in Pearl Harbor by the Japanese forces on December 7, 1941. Although realizing that the ship was capsizing, as a result of enemy bombing and torpedoing, Tomich remained at his post in the engineering plant of the USS *Utah*, until he saw that all boilers were secured and all fireroom personnel had left their stations, and by so doing lost his life.

Why the Tomich MOH Is Unique

One, it was the only December 7 MOH awarded for a ship crewman on Ford Island's Carrier Row. All other December 7 MOHs were for men on Battleship Row, at Kaneohe Bay, or on Midway.[16]

Two, the Tomich MOH was unclaimed for years due to difficulty in locating Tomich family members to accept it. Its journey from Presidential approval in 1942 to family presentation in 2006 (sixty-four years) is, to say the least, winding and interesting, with the MOH being transferred from one entity and place to another until finally presentation could be made to a family representative.

Three, Tomich would, for reasons explained in this chapter, become an honorary citizen of *Utah*. Interestingly, another December 7 MOH recipient from Ford Island also had ties to *Utah*; Captain Mervyn Bennion of USS *West Virginia* was a *Utah* native.

Chapter 14 explains the MOH presentation process and his honorary citizenship.

Notes

1. Thomas O'Brien, "Pearl Harbor's Forgotten Ship," *Naval History* (August 2001), 24 (hereafter "O'Brien, 'Pearl Harbor's Forgotten Ship'").

2. James L. Mooney, editor. Dictionary of American Naval Fighting Ships, Vol. VII (Naval Historical Center, Department of the Navy, Washington, DC, 1981), 421–22 (hereafter "DANFS").

3. Ibid., 423; SEAMANSHIP ("NAVPERS 16118," U.S. Navy, Training, Standards, and Curriculum Division), 46; AG means "auxiliary miscellaneous."

4. Information about *Utah*'s mooring is from the author's personal view of Carrier Row and diagrams and photographs in Chapter 2; Vice Admiral Homer N. Wallin, U.S. Navy (Retired), Pearl Harbor: Why, How, Fleet Salvage, and Final Approach (Naval History Division, U.S. Government Printing Office, 1968), 55 (hereafter "Wallin, Pearl Harbor"); Bess Altfeld, publisher, Air Raid, Pearl Harbor. This Is Not Drill! (O. S. B. MapMania Publishing, Phoenix, AZ, 1999), which is a map of Pearl Harbor, complete with ship locations and various narratives concerning December 7.

5. Ibid.; Endnote 2, DANFS, Vol. VII, 424; author's knowledge of mooring of ships on December 7; diagrams and photographs in Chapter 2.

6. Commanding Officer's report, "USS *Utah*—Loss by Enemy Action," dated December 15, 1941, paragraph 2 of Lieutenant Commander Isquith's report, which is Enclosure (A) to this report (hereafter, "*Utah* report").

7. Ibid., paragraph 10; paragraphs 5 and 6 note that Japanese planes were still strafing the ship; endnote 2, DANFS, Vol. VII, 424, also notes that the Japanese were still strafing the ship during the Vaessen rescue; Endnote 1, O'Brien, "Pearl Harbor's Forgotten Ship," mentions Vaessen's Navy Cross at page 29; the author obtained and read a copy of Vaessen's Navy Cross citation.

8. Endnote 2, DANFS, Vol. VII, 424.

9. Official U.S. Navy biography, Peter Tonich (Tomich), Chief Water Tender, U.S. Navy (Deceased), June 12, 1947 (hereafter "Tomich, U.S. Navy biography"); the National Personnel Records Center, St. Louis, Missouri, furnished military and personal information from Tomich's Official Military Personnel File (OMPF) at the author's request (hereafter "Tomich OMPF").

10. Ibid.

11. J. W. Bunkley, Rear Admiral, United States Navy, Retired, MILITARY and NAVAL RECOGNITION BOOK (D. Van Nostrand Company, Inc., New York, NY, 1943); the duties of a water tender are found at page 144; the duties of firemen are found at page 141.

12. Tomich MOH citation is in the text of this chapter and in Appendix A of this book; Endnote 2, DANFS, Vol. VII, 424.

13. O'Brien, "Pearl Harbor's Forgotten Ship," 27; the Congressional Record, U.S. Senate (March 21, 1963), 4435.

14. *Utah* report, paragraphs 7a and 8.

15. *Utah* report (Isquith's Enclosure (A), paragraph 11).

16. Chapters 4–9, 11, and 12.

Photograph
USS Utah MOH Recipient

Chief Petty Officer Watertender Peter Tomich, U.S. Navy. (Photograph NH 79593 from the Naval History and Heritage Command)

Section B:
Medal of Honor Earned on December 7, 1941, at Kaneohe Bay

Chapter 11
Naval Air Station, Kaneohe Bay: Man to Man

Chief Petty Officer (Aviation Ordnanceman) John Finn, US Navy

Kaneohe Bay

Kaneohe Bay is between the eastern shore of Oahu and Oahu's Mokapu Peninsula, which extends northeast into the Pacific Ocean; if one were looking at Kaneohe Bay, the peninsula would be to the right and the eastern shore would be to the left. Before the war, Kaneohe Naval Air Station (NAS) was on the Mokapu Peninsula[1] The base was a seaplane base for PBY "Catalina" airplanes. "PBY" meant the plane was for patrol (P) and bombing (B) and was manufactured by Consolidated-Vultee (Y). The Catalina was used throughout the war for patrol, rescue, and other operations.[2]

On December 7, the Japanese attacked Kaneohe, heavily damaging the base and its Catalinas: twenty-six of thirty-five seaplanes were destroyed.[3]

The Naval Air Station had one MOH recipient for December 7, a chief petty officer who was an aviation ordnanceman, Chief Petty Officer John Finn.

Background

Finn was born on July 24, 1909, in Los Angeles, California. He joined the Navy on July 19, 1926. After basic training in San Diego, California, he ultimately went to Naval Station Great Lakes, Illinois, for general aviation training. He eventually became an aviation ordnanceman. He had one tour aboard the aircraft carrier USS Lexington. After that tour, he served on various ships and with various aviation units.[4]

On December 7, the Pacific Fleet was organized into various task forces. Rear Admiral P. N. L. Bellinger commanded Task Force (TF) 9, known as Battle Wing 2 or "BatWing 2." The TF comprised two elements: Patrol Wing 1, commanded by Commander K. McGinnis at Kaneohe NAS, and Patrol Wing 2, commanded by Bellinger himself at Pearl Harbor NAS. Each element comprised several ships and several patrol squadrons.[5] Finn was a member of a heavier-than-air (V) patrol (P) squadron, VP-14, which was one of three patrol squadrons in Patrol Wing 1 commanded by McGinnis at Kaneohe.[6]

Actions on December 7

As Japanese aircraft strafed the Naval Air Station ramps where aircraft were parked, Finn was in the open without cover, firing at Japanese planes with a fifty-caliber machine gun mounted on an instruction stand rather than the tripod that would be used when the weapon was fired in ground combat. He continued firing at the aircraft notwithstanding several wounds. His citation states, "It was only by specific orders that he was persuaded to leave his post to seek medical attention." After receiving first aid, he returned to the squadron area and rearmed aircraft notwithstanding his wounds, pain, and difficulty moving.[7]

Finn's actions are consistent with those reported by Bellinger, who commanded Patrol Wing 2 at NAS Pearl Harbor. He noted that during the first attack, his men fired at Japanese planes using machine guns mounted in the Catalinas parked on the base. This mode of firing was ineffective since the structure of the Catalinas limited the movement of the machine guns, which were meant for use when the Catalinas were in the air. Bellinger reported that many men "removed these guns from the planes and set them upon benches in vises and opened up an effective fire against the second attack." He estimated that men firing this way shot down four Japanese planes.[8]

Finn was at Kaneohe but not mentioned in the report of McGinnis, the Kaneohe commander, but Finn's improvised method of firing aircraft machine guns—using an instruction stand as a mount—was similar to the method used by Bellinger's men at Pearl Harbor.[9] McGinnis twice wrote that the conduct of his personnel was "magnificent." In one case, he wrote,

…magnificent, in fact too much so. Had they not, with no protection, deliberately set themselves up with machine guns right in line with the drop of the attacking and straffing [sic] planes and near the object of their attack, we would have lost less [sic] men. It was, however, due to this reckless resistance that two enemy planes were destroyed and six or more were sent away with heavy gas leaks.[10]

The McGinnis report's description of men standing in the open and firing with no protection is consistent with what Finn did according to his MOH citation.[11]

Other noteworthy aspects of the McGinnis report were the following events. One, his aircraft (an OS2U-1 Kingfisher observation and scout aircraft) was the first aircraft attacked as it sat on the landing mat. Two, the attack destroyed the base fire truck. Three, all bombsights were accounted for and undamaged since they were in a vault that was not attacked. Bombsights were essential and thus were accorded great security.[12]

Chief Petty Officer (Aviation Ordnanceman) John Finn was one of five living MOH recipients to receive a MOH for actions on December 7. President Franklin D. Roosevelt signed the MOH citation in June 1942.

MOH Citation

For extraordinary heroism, distinguished service, and devotion above and beyond the call of duty. During the first attack by Japanese airplanes on the Naval Air Station, Kaneohe Bay, on December 7, 1941, Lieutenant Finn promptly secured and manned a fifty-caliber machine gun mounted on an instruction stand in a completely exposed section of the parking ramp, which was under heavy enemy machine-gun strafing fire. Although painfully wounded many times, he continued to man this gun and to return the enemy's fire vigorously and with telling effect throughout the enemy strafing and bombing attacks and with complete disregard for his own personal safety. It was only by specific orders that he was persuaded to leave his post to seek medical attention.

Following first-aid treatment, although obviously suffering much pain and moving with great difficulty, he returned to the squadron area and actively supervised the rearming of returning planes. His extraordinary heroism and conduct in this action were in keeping with the highest traditions of the United States Naval Service.

Later Life

Finn remained a chief petty officer until he received an officer's appointment during the war. He retired as a lieutenant in 1956; whether his lieutenancy is a regular or a tombstone promotion is unclear from the service record provided to the author by the National Personnel Records Center.[13]

Finn died on May 27, 2010, at age one hundred. He was the oldest MOH recipient at the time of his death and the last December 7 MOH recipient to die. Pharris died in 1966, Fuqua in 1987, and Ross in 1992.[14]

Thus when this book was started in the early to mid-2000s, Finn was not only the last December 7 MOH recipient alive but was also the oldest living MOH recipient.

Why the Finn MOH Is Unique

Finn's MOH award is unique among the December 7 recipients in six respects.

One, he was the only MOH recipient for Kaneohe Bay.

Two, of the fifteen Navy MOH recipients for December 7 on Oahu, his MOH was the only one earned outside Pearl Harbor.

Three, he was the only December 7 recipient receiving a MOH for directly engaging the enemy in "man-to-man" combat; as seen in his MOH citation, he shot directly at Japanese aircraft strafing the Naval Air Station.

Four, he was the only Navy MOH recipient for December 7 who did not earn a MOH for an action aboard a ship.[4]

Five, as just mentioned, he was the last December 7 recipient to die.

Six, he was and is erroneously cited as being the first man to receive a MOH for actions on December 7 or during World War II (see Chapters 14 and 18).

Notes

1. Vice Admiral Homer N. Wallin, US Navy (Retired), Pearl Harbor: Why, How, Fleet Salvage, and Final Approach (Naval History Division, US Government Printing Office, 1968), 44 (hereafter "Wallin").

2. Kenneth Munson, Aircraft of World War II (Doubleday & Company, Inc., New York, NY, 1962), 32–33 and 53 (hereafter "Munson, Aircraft Of World War II").

3. Endnote 1, Wallin, 101–102.

5. The date and place of birth are from Finn's MOH citation at Appendix A; the National Personnel Records Center, St. Louis, Missouri, furnished military and personal information from Finn's Official Military Personnel File (OMPF) at the author's request (hereafter "Finn OMPF").

6. PEARL HARBOR ATTACK: HEARINGS BEFORE THE JOINT COMMITTEE ON THE INVESTIGATION OF THE PEARL HARBOR ATTACK, SEVENTY-NINTH CONGRESS, SECOND SESSION, Part 21 (1946), 4562.

7. Ibid., concerning command of VP-14; Finn's assignment in VP-14 can be found in George Lang (MOH), Raymond L. Collins, and Gerald F. White (compilers), Medal of Honor Recipients 1863–1994 Vol. II, World War II to Somalia (Facts on File, Inc., New York, NY), 486 (hereafter "Lang, Medal of Honor Recipients").

8. Finn MOH citation in this chapter and at Appendix A of this book (hereafter "Finn MOH citation").

10. Attack on Naval Air Station, Pearl Harbor: Report from Commander Patrol Wing Two (Subject: "Operations on December 7, 1941") of December 20, 1941, paragraph 3.

10. Endnote 8, Finn MOH citation.

11. Attack on Naval Air Station Kaneohe Bay: Report for Kaneohe Bay from Commander Patrol Wing One ("Subject: Report of Japanese Air Attack on Kaneohe Bay, T. H. [Territory of Hawaii]—December 7, 1941"), paragraph 5 (hereafter "Kaneohe Attack Report").

12. Endnote 9, Finn MOH citation.

13. Endnote 11, Kaneohe Attack Report; the OS2U-1 "Kingfisher" was an observation and scout plane; Munson, Aircraft of World War II, 33 and 231; the "O" represented "observation," the "S" represented "scouting," and the "U" represented the manufacturer (Chance Vought), the "2" represented the design sequence, and the "1" represented the modification number; author's knowledge about bombsights.

14. Endnote 6, Finn OMPF.

15. T. Rees Shapiro, "Lt. John W. Finn, Medal of Honor Recipient, Dies at 100," Washington Post, May 29, 2010, B5 (hereafter "Shapiro, Finn Death"); see Chapters 6 (Pharris), 9 (Fuqua), and 11 (Ross).

16. See Chapters 4–10 and 12.

Photograph
Kaneohe Bay and Its MOH Recipient

Chief Petty Officer Aviation Ordnanceman John Finn, U.S. Navy, wearing his MOH. (Photograph NH 95448 from the Naval History and Heritage Command)

Section C:
Medals of Honor Earned at Midway Atoll in 1941 and 1942

CHAPTER 12
MIDWAY ATOLL, 1941 AND 1942
MARINES, GROUND AND AIR

FIRST LIEUTENANT GEORGE HAM CANNON, U.S. MARINE CORPS

CAPTAIN RICHARD E. FLEMING, U.S. MARINE CORPS RESERVE

MIDWAY 1941 AND 1942

Midway's connection to Hawaii is that it is an atoll that is part of the Hawaiian Island Archipelago, which comprises various islands and atolls, including Oahu with its Pearl Harbor. Midway Atoll, approximately 1,130 miles northwest of Oahu, comprises Sand, Eastern, and Spit Islands.[1]

The United States annexed Midway in 1867. Before World War II, the United States and Japan realized Midway's strategic importance. A 1938 report by an American concerning naval bases in the Pacific noted that Midway, "the outer rampart of the Hawaiian chain," was second in importance only to Pearl Harbor. After a reconnaissance mission to Midway in 1939, the Chief of Naval Operations ordered that a Marine detachment be established on Midway. Marines began preparing defensive positions on Midway in 1940. On August 1, 1941, the United States commissioned Naval Air Station, Midway. Also in August, an advance element of the Sixth Defense Battalion arrived, commanded by Lieutenant Colonel H. D. Shannon, the battalion's executive officer, who soon became the commanding officer. A brief glimpse of Shannon, as well as the colors of the battalion, can be seen in the 1942 documentary The Battle of Midway, which won an Academy Award. As will be seen later in this chapter, he was the commanding officer of Lieutenant George Cannon, who earned a MOH on Midway on December 7, 1941. Marine aircraft from Oahu would soon augment Marine ground defense.[2]

The Japanese attacked Midway in 1941 and 1942 but never captured it.[3] Two Marines assigned to Midway earned MOHs helping to ensure that it never fell; one was an infantry officer, the other an aviator. They were the only MOHs earned on or near Midway. No navy officers or enlisted men earned MOHs for Midway in 1941 or 1942; this fact is particularly noteworthy for the Battle of Midway in 1942 since the battle was primarily between aircraft carriers and naval aviation of the navies of the United States and Japan. Midway was never the site of a land battle although the Japanese attacked it using naval guns in 1941 and naval aviation in 1942.

As noted in Chapters 4 through 12 and 19 of this book, sixteen men earned MOHs for actions on the "date which will live in infamy," December 7, 1941. Fifteen were Navy officers and enlisted men on Oahu. The sixteenth recipient, Marine First Lieutenant George Cannon, was based on Midway's Sand Island, where he commanded a battery in Midway's defense battalion.

In June 1942, Marine pilot Captain Richard Fleming, based on Midway's Eastern Island, earned the only MOH awarded for combat during the famous Battle of Midway in 1942. As discussed in Chapter 18, accounts of Fleming's MOH actions are filled with errors.

Part I: Midway, December 1941

First Lieutenant George Ham Cannon, U.S.Marine Corps

Background

Born November 5, 1915, in Webster Groves, Missouri, Cannon initially entered the Army but resigned so he could accept an appointment as a second lieutenant in the Marine Corps. He accepted that appointment on June 27, 1938, and was assigned to The Basic School in Philadelphia, a "finishing school" for new Marine lieutenants. His next duty station was USS Boise, where he was a member of the ship's Marine Detachment. A Marine Detachment or "Mar Det" comprises Marines assigned to a ship for various duties. In 1940, he was assigned to Marine Barracks, Quantico, Virginia. In December 1940, he was assigned to the Marine Base in San Diego, where he was Commanding Officer, Battery H, Machine Gun Group, Sixth Defense Battalion, Second Marine Division.[4] Defense battalions provided Marines to defend islands and bases overseas.[5]

In July 1941, he and the battery arrived at the Marine Barracks at the Pearl Harbor Navy Yard. He was promoted to first lieutenant on August 13, 1941. He accepted the appointment and executed the oath of office on August 29. Cannon went with the battalion to Midway, arriving there on September 11, 1941.[6]

Actions on December 7

On Midway's Sand Island, Cannon continued to command Battery H, a part of the Sixth Defense Battalion defending Midway. His command post (CP) was in Sand Island's power plant.[7]

As part of their strike on Oahu on December 7, the Japanese also dispatched ships to attack two secondary targets: Midway Island and Wake Island. Two Japanese destroyers comprised the ominous-sounding Midway Neutralization Unit, the mission of which was to bombard Midway's air station on the evening of December 7 as the main force that had attacked Oahu left the Hawaiian Islands. The Ushio was one of the destroyers. The other was Akebono, according to Commander Mitsuo Fuchida, who helped plan the December 7 attack. Gordon Prange, however, writes that the second ship was Sazanami.[8] In any event, the two ships left Tokyo approximately December 1 (Japanese date) and sailed to Midway, not Oahu, arriving there on the evening of December 7.[9]

At approximately 2135 hours (9:35 p.m.) on December 7 (U.S. date) the destroyers shelled Midway, the mission being as just noted: to neutralize its air base to prevent it from threatening the force returning from the attack on Oahu earlier on December 7. The shelling hit Cannon's CP, disrupting its communications and wounding two Marines. Cannon himself sustained mortal wounds almost immediately after the shelling began. His official Marine Corps casualty report states that at 2135 hours, he suffered a fractured "left fibula & tibia, when struck by shell fragment[s]…"[10]

Cannon refused to leave his CP because he wanted to ensure communications were reestablished and to ensure evacuation of other wounded men before his own evacuation (two other Marines were seriously wounded and one was "shell shocked"). Only after his communications chief restored communications did Cannon consent to evacuation, although of note is the wording in his MOH citation, stating that he was "forcibly" removed.[11]

The casualty report documenting his wounds states that Cannon was evacuated to the Naval Air Station Dispensary and that he "expired [there] before further treatment could be rendered." The time of death was 2205 hours (10:05 p.m.).[12]

The December 12, 1941, report of the Sixth Defense Battalion noted that Cannon, "after having received wounds [fracturing] both legs and pelvis, when 'H' Battery CP in the second deck of the new power house was hit, refused to be evacuated before his men wounded by the same shell. He died from loss of blood." The MOH citation, consistent with the Battalion's report, also states that he died from blood loss.[13]

On Christmas Day 1942, his remains were shipped to Oahu, where he was initially buried at Halawa Cemetery in Honolulu.[14]

On January 12, 1942, he was selected for promotion to captain, but his death precluded the promotion.[15]

Aftermath of December 7

After-Action Report

Lieutenant Colonel H. D. Shannon was the senior Marine on Midway, commanding officer of the Sixth Defense Battalion or the "Defense Garrison." His report of the Japanese naval bombardment shelling is dated December 12, 1941, and titled "Report of Action on Night of December 7, 1941." He noted the moon was bright, which unfortunately for the Marines illuminated their "new white construction." In paragraph 6, he wrote the following:

> The conduct of the personnel of this battalion was highly satisfactory. All hands proceeded about their duties in a cool, calm and businesslike manner. There were several outstanding instances of coolness, high sense of duty, and bravery. First Lieutenant George H. Cannon, Battery Commander of Battery "H", after having received wounds that fractured both legs and pelvis, when "H" Battery CP in the second deck of the new power house was hit, refused to be evacuated before his men who were wounded by the same shell. He died from loss of blood.[16]

First Lieutenant George Cannon was the only December 7 MOH who was a Marine and was the only recipient whose MOH actions were not on Oahu. His actions were also the latest in the day. As noted earlier in this chapter, he was mortally wounded during the night of December 7, and the attack on Oahu was as too well known on the morning of December 7. President Franklin D. Roosevelt signed the MOH citation on March 4, 1942.

MOH Citation

For distinguished conduct in the line of his profession, extraordinary courage, and disregard of his own condition during the bombardment of Sand Island, Midway Islands, by Japanese forces on December 7, 1941. First Lt. Cannon, Battery Commander of Battery H, 6th Defense Battalion, Fleet Marine Force, U.S. Marine Corps, was at his command post when he was mortally wounded by enemy shellfire. He refused to be evacuated from his post until after his men who had been wounded by the same shell were evacuated, and directed the reorganization of his command post until forcibly removed. As a result of his utter disregard of his own condition he died from loss of blood.

Noteworthy Aspects of the Cannon MOH

Cannon's MOH is noteworthy in seven respects.

First, his is the earliest action during the war by a Marine leading to an approved MOH citation for a Marine—officer or enlisted.[17] One could, however, argue that his action occurred before World War II, not during World War II, since at the time the Japanese attacked Midway and Oahu on December 7, Congress had not declared war against Japan. But Cannon is universally included in World War II awards, as are the other December 7 recipients, which is logical and practical, especially since President's Roosevelt's request to the House of Representative for a declaration of war contains the following language, in effect backdating the beginning of the war:

> I ask that the Congress declare that since the unprovoked and dastardly attack by Japan on Sunday, December 7th, 1941, a state of war has existed between the United States and the Japanese empire.[18]

Second, Cannon's was the first MOH presented to a Marine in World War II, living or posthumously. Two dates lead to this conclusion: the date President Roosevelt signed the citation (March 4, 1942) and the date of the thank-you letter Cannon's mother sent to the President (March 22, 1942).[19]

Third, he is the sole Marine recipient among the sixteen MOH recipients for December 7. As stated earlier in this chapter, the other fifteen MOH recipients for December 7 were Navy officers and men.[20]

Fourth, his was the sole MOH awarded for December 7 for actions not on Oahu. All Navy recipients for December 7 earned their MOHs on Oahu.[21]

Fifth, his MOH was the only MOH earned on Midway for December 7, 1941.[22]

Sixth, he is one of only two MOH recipients—both Marines—who earned MOHs at Midway during the war.[23]

Seventh, since he was wounded and died during the evening of December 7, his MOH was the latest and last for December 7.

Part II: Midway, June 1942

Captain Richard E. Fleming, U.S. Marine Corps Reserve

The story of Captain Fleming is different from the stories of the other MOH recipients in this book because he is the only pilot among the recipients. His war was the war fought in the air. John Finn's shots at Japanese aircraft were antiaircraft warfare, not aerial warfare, since he was on the ground. The December 7 Navy MOH recipients fought a naval war, though not classic battles at sea. First Lieutenant Cannon was the only December 7 MOH recipient fighting a ground war, though the shells that killed him on land were fired by destroyers at sea.

Captain Fleming's story is fascinating, a story of three aerial combat missions that can only be described as harrowing, which in true Marine Corps fashion featured the Marine Corps flying with inferior equipment and weapons into the face of an enemy with better equipment and weapons; in this case, Marines flew obsolete Wildcat and Buffalo fighters and obsolete Vindicator and Dauntless dive bombers into torrents of antiaircraft fire from Japanese ships and against Japanese pilots flying the best naval fighter at the time: the dreaded Japanese Zero, one of three types of Japanese aircraft giving a sleeping US Pacific Fleet a startling awakening on Oahu on the morning of December 7, 1941.

Any Japanese advantage in equipment was, however, outweighed by U.S. aviators who were not only lucky but skilled. And Japanese indecisiveness and poor tactics worked against the Japanese fleet that was supposed to produce a decisive victory.

So in this circumstance of disadvantage and advantage at Midway in 1942, Captain Fleming, a land-based not a carrier-based pilot, would emerge with the only MOH awarded for the Battle of Midway, one of the most famous and crucial battles in history.

Background

Born on November 2, 1917, in St. Paul, Minnesota, Richard Fleming "was the highest ranking cadet officer at St. Thomas Military academy," where he graduated in the Class of 1935. As a senior, he was chosen "top student officer." He attended the University of Minnesota, "where he was a campus leader" and president of Delta Kappa Epsilon fraternity. In 1939, he received a bachelor of arts degree.[24]

The November 24, 1942, edition of the St. Paul Dispatch wrote that the Navy reported that Fleming became an aviator "largely by accident." In December 1938, a fraternity friend asked Fleming to go to a location where the Army was administering physical examinations for prospective air corps candidates. Fleming went "[o]n the spur of the moment"; of two hundred applicants, he was one of nine who passed examination.[25] He served in the Army from March 4, 1939, to December 14, 1939.[26]

He was an enlisted Marine on inactive duty from December 15, 1939, to January 25, 1940. He was an aviation cadet on inactive duty from January 25 to February 23, 1940; he was an aviation cadet on active duty from February 24 to December 5, 1940. Upon graduating flight training at Naval Air Station, Pensacola, Florida, where he finished first in his class, he became an officer on December 6, 1940.[27]

In January 1941, Fleming joined Scouting Squadron 2 of the Second Marine Aircraft Group (MAG), which in August changed to MAG-21. In May 1941, the squadron traveled aboard USS Enterprise to Marine Corps Air Station Ewa on the southern part of Oahu. In July, the unit's designation was changed to Marine Scout-Bombing Squadron 231. On September 12, 1941, he received minor abrasions in an aircraft crash and was in the Pearl Harbor Naval Hospital from September 12 to 24.[28]

From December 5 to 9 and 17 to 31, he was on a "Classified mission," which probably involved the movement of the squadron to Midway.[29] On December 17, 1941, he successfully flew with seventeen "Vindicator" aircraft (described later in this chapter) from Oahu to Midway, "a distance of 1137 nautical miles over water with no surface vessels assigned as 'plane guards.'" Plane guards are ships stationed along the path of a flight over the ocean that rescue aviators who have to parachute from, or to ditch, their aircraft.[30]

From January 12 to 31, 1942, he was with the squadron on a classified mission. On January 10, 1941, the designation of the unit was changed again, this time to Marine Scout-Bombing Squadron 231, Marine Aviation Detachment, probably to reflect its presence on Midway.[31]

April 1942 was noteworthy for Fleming in two respects. First, he accepted an appointment as a first lieutenant in the Marine Corps Reserve on April 16. Second, he received a letter of commendation on April 18 for the December 17 flight from Oahu to Midway.[32]

On March 1, 1942, Fleming joined VMSB-241 a Marine Scout-Bombing Squadron based on Midway. "V" indicated "heavier than air" to distinguish it from lighter-than-air squadrons, such as blimp squadrons. "M" indicated "Marine"; "S" indicated "scouting"; and "B" indicated "bombing."[33] The next highest level of command in aviation above the squadron is the group, which comprises squadrons. VMSB-241 was a subordinate squadron in Marine Aircraft Group [22] ("MAG-[22]"), along with a headquarters and service squadron and a fighter squadron. MAG-[22], the parent unit for VMSB-241, flew four types of obsolete aircraft organized into two squadrons: the SBD Dauntless and the SB2U-3 Vindicator, which were dive bombers comprising the Scout-Bombing Squadron commanded by Major Lofton Henderson, and the F2A-3 Buffalo and the F4F Wildcat, which were fighters comprising the fighting squadron commanded by Major Floyd Parks. The aircraft involved in the Fleming MOH actions were the Dauntless and the Vindicator.³⁴

Douglas ("D") manufactured SBD-2 "Dauntlesses." As with the unit designation, "S" represented "scouting" and "B" represented "bombing." The "2" indicated the second major variation of the aircraft. The squadron had eighteen Dauntlesses.³⁵

Vought-Sikorsky ("U") manufactured SB2U-3 "Vindicators." The "2" indicated the second aircraft of its kind; the "3" indicated the third major variation of the aircraft. The squadron had sixteen Vindicators.³⁶

Major Lofton Henderson, VMSB's commanding officer, divided his squadron into two attack units; his eighteen Dauntlesses were in a unit he commanded and twelve of his sixteen Vindicators in a unit commanded by Major Benjamin Norris, the squadron's executive officer (second in command).³⁷

The MAG ²² commander, Major L. Kimes, wrote a June 7, 1942, report about the Battle of Midway, the most famous battle in the Pacific War, which turned the tide against the Japanese. In the report, the commander commended the conduct of his command during the battle but leveled withering criticism at its aircraft. The "secret sign" at Naval Shipyard Pearl Harbor has a very good summary of the battle and the crucial role played by cryptography (see Appendix C of this book). As of the report's date (June 7, 1942), Fleming had performed the actions that would lead to his MOH (June 4 and 5).³⁸ One can determine from the report's comments about the Vindicator, which will be quoted in the text of this chapter, that Fleming was literally and figuratively flying a deathtrap during his MOH action on June 5.

The MAG commander noted that the two types of fighters he had, the Brewster F2A-3 "Buffalo" or "Flying Coffin" and the Grumman F4F "Wildcat," were "markedly inferior" to the Japanese Zero "in speed, maneuverability, and rate of climb." Unfortunately for MAG-²², the Japanese Zero was the best naval fighter at the beginning of the war and one of the types of Japanese aircraft that had attacked Oahu on December 7. The bases for his negative opinion about the Buffalos and the Wildcats were statements by pilots flying them in combat. Kimes stated in his report that the Buffalo and Wildcat should be used only for training—not for combat—hardly a confidence-inspiring opinion for his pilots. And he noted that his criticism stood notwithstanding the "excellent" performance of his squadron, which was due to his pilots and to the vulnerability of enemy bombers.³⁹

His assessment of the Vindicator was harsher, but he was less harsh concerning the Dauntless. Again his opinions would not inspire confidence in either aircraft:

The SB2U-3 [Vindicator] type airplane is inferior in all phases of performance. Furthermore those in this Group were, and those yet remaining are, in such deplorable condition as regards fabric covering because of long exposure to rain and sun[,] and the performance of the power plant has been so unsatisfactory[,] as to render them valueless except for training or used as "drones." The SBD-2 [Dauntless] airplanes, while being far superior to the SB2U-3 type, are deficient in performance to such a degree as to indicate that their only practical usefulness is for training purposes.[40]

Vindicators were nicknamed "Vibrators" or "Wind Indicators" because of the flapping of loose panels on the exterior of the aircraft.[41]

Thus before the Battle of Midway in 1942, Henderson faced a challenging situation. First of all, his squadron comprised obsolete, inadequate aircraft with the deficiencies just cited by his own commanding officer—the MAG commanding officer. Second, Henderson had a large number of pilots new to the squadron—ten who had arrived only a week before the battle. Finally, he had insufficient fuel and time for training: only two hours for the Norris group and one hour for the Henderson Group.[42]

Also, because of pilot inexperience in dive bombing and since the squadron had only practiced glide bombing in the Vindicators, Henderson decided to use only glide bombing when attacking the Japanese.[43] In horizontal bombing, such as the Japanese Kates used when attacking Oahu on December 7, bombs are dropped while the aircraft flies over the target horizontally. As Commander Fuchida observed after the war when questioned about the Oahu attack, horizontal bombing is "relatively inaccurate."[44]

Glide bombing and dive bombing were used rather than horizontal bombing when more accuracy was needed. They were more accurate than horizontal bombing in part because the aircraft flew down at the target, not horizontally over it, until the bomb was released. In dive bombing, the angle of attack (angle between target and diving aircraft) was 60 to 90 degrees. In glide bombing, the angle was not as steep, being between 30 and 55 degrees, but to ensure accuracy in glide bombing, the altitude for dropping the bomb had to be lower (often as low as 500 feet or lower). The disadvantage of the lower altitude meant exposure to antiaircraft fire from the target being attacked.[45] The MAG executive officer noted the danger of antiaircraft fire because of the lower dropping altitude in his June 7, 1942, report of the battle under the heading "Remarks of Pilots": "Glide bombing is more hazardous than dive bombing in the absence of [our] own protective VF [fighters]."

Translation—glide bombing is more hazardous than dive bombing unless the aircraft executing glide bombing are protected by fighters. As noted before, in VF, the "V" is heavier than air; the "F" is "fighter."[46]

On missions, the squadron was often divided into divisions, and divisions were divided into sections.[47]

MOH Actions on June 4 and 5

Fleming's MOH citation reflects actions on two days: June 4 and 5, 1942. At the time, he was a captain, having accepted an appointment as a captain in the Marine Corps Reserve on May 25, 1942.[48]

Actions on June 4

On June 4, VMSB-241 was ordered to attack enemy aircraft carriers.

The reader should understand that such attacks were dangerous for several reasons. One, aircraft carriers did not travel alone; they generally had a screen of ships, such as cruisers, destroyers, or submarines to protect them. Two, the carrier and the surface ships had antiaircraft guns. Three, a combat air patrol ("CAP") of fighters flew around a carrier to protect it from incoming enemy aircraft.[49]

On June 4, VMSB-241 was divided by aircraft type into two groups for the mission. Major Henderson, flying a Dauntless, led two divisions of Dauntlesses (one division had four sections, the other two sections). Henderson, Fleming (in an SBD), and one other pilot were in a command section. Major Norris led two groups of Vindicators. All the aircraft were armed with five-hundred-pound bombs. The target turned out to be the Japanese aircraft carrier Hiryu, one of four Japanese aircraft carriers later sunk at Midway; they were four of the six aircraft carriers executing the attack on Oahu on December 7. The other three lost at Midway were Akagi, Kaga, and Soryu.[50]

The MAG-22 executive officer's report of June 7, 1942, noted that the aircraft met "violent AA [antiaircraft] fire" and heavy attacks by enemy fighters, several of which were Zeroes that attacked Henderson's aircraft, setting his plane on fire. He wrote, "It was apparent that he [Henderson] was badly injured and out of action, so Captain Glidden, leader of the second section took over and committed the squadron to the attack."[51] The official casualty report for Henderson reads, "Shot down in plane during approach to dive on target."[52] The VMSB report of June 12 also mentions that Henderson's actions indicated that he was "seriously wounded" and that Captain Glidden took the lead.[53] These statements conflict with Fleming's MOH citation, which states that after Henderson went down, Fleming "led the remainder of the division…"[54]

The aerial battles were harrowing with the Americans suffering several disadvantages: inferior aircraft, superior Japanese aircraft, withering antiaircraft fire, and expert Japanese airmanship and tactics. The MAG-22 executive officer's report describes the ferocity of the fighting, which showed how well the Japanese fought, how much the Zero was superior to American fighters, and how the Americans had to "make do" with aircraft whose deficiencies were described in excruciating detail by one of their own group commanders (the MAG-22 commander's withering comments previously cited concerning the Vindicator and Dauntless):

> All VMF [Marine fighter pilots] of various degrees of experience and capability were awed by the performance of the [Zero] fighter, claiming it has 20% more speed climb and maneuverability than does the [Buffalo] and the [Wildcat]. The claimed victories which follow, do not tell the whole story. Each pilot made only one or two passes at the [Japanese] bombers, and then spent the remainder of the time trying to shade from one to five Jap fighters off his tail. Most succeeded by using cloud cover, or, in two cases, by leading the Japs into fire from light AA [antiaircraft guns] and on PT [patrol torpedo] boats.[55]

The "claimed victories" were aerial victories, which he reported as three Zeros shot down and one damaged and eight Aichi Type 99 Navy dive bombers ("Vals") shot down and three damaged.⁵⁶ He also noted "very heavy" fighter attacks and that "[e]nemy antiaircraft fire was heavy and accurate, but of little importance compared to fighter opposition." The "[e]nemy fighters operate at two or three levels, work in pairs with excellent teamwork, and their attacks on formation leaders are heavy and persistent."⁵⁷

The Executive Officer's report and the VMSB Commanding Officer's report reported two direct hits on a battleship.⁵⁸

Eight of the sixteen VMSB aircraft failed to return after the morning mission.⁵⁹ Fleming returned, his aircraft a testament to antiaircraft fire. It had 179 hits from Japanese fighters and antiaircraft guns. He suffered two minor wounds.⁶⁰

Guadalcanal's famous Henderson Field was named for Major Henderson, who received a Navy Cross posthumously.⁶¹

Major Norris, the VMSB-241 executive officer, assumed command upon the loss of Major Henderson.⁶² The evening of the day of Henderson's loss—June 4—the squadron flew a night mission under the command of Norris to attack what was thought to be burning aircraft carriers. The MAG-22 Executive Officer reported that Norris went into a steep right turn and was thought to have hit the water since his aircraft lights could no longer be seen.⁶³ Captain Tyler of VMSB-241 reported that the Norris aircraft disappeared into a "violent tight spiral" after Norris apparently became disoriented.⁶⁴ His casualty report reads, "Lost returning from the night attack, evidently going down out of control in inclement, overcast weather. All of the pilots 'lost him [.]'"⁶⁵ Norris also received a Navy Cross posthumously.⁶⁶ Fleming flew his own aircraft (a Vindicator) back to base in total darkness and hazardous weather.⁶⁷

ACTIONS ON JUNE 5

At 0700 hours on June 5, Marine aircraft were sent to attack Mikuma and Mogami, which were initially thought to be battleships, one of which was crippled or thought to be crippled.⁶⁸

The plan was for six SBDs, led by Captain Marshall A. Tyler of the squadron, to attack Mogami by dive bombing at ten thousand feet. Six Vindicators, led by Fleming (who had had fewer than four hours of sleep), were to attack Mikuma by glide bombing at five thousand feet.⁶⁹

The VMSB aircraft took off at 7:00 a.m. and flew for forty-five minutes before finding an oil slick left by a damaged ship. VMSB found the ships at 8:05 a.m.⁷⁰ As would be learned later and as Japanese officers would explain in postwar interviews, the VMSB aviators had found not two battleships but two cruisers, escorted by two destroyers, lagging behind the Japanese cruiser division since Mikuma and Mogami were damaged when Mogami collided with the port quarter of Mikuma while they were taking evasive action to avoid an American submarine. According to the Japanese interviewed after the war, Mikuma suffered minor damage; Mogami's bow was damaged; some of it was missing, and some of it was bent to port, reducing the ship's speed. One Japanese officer noted that VMSB attacked the ships flying out of the sun, which is standard procedure to protect the aircraft since they are more difficult to see for observers looking into the sun for or at them.[71]

Tyler's dive bombers first attacked one of the ships, Mogami, in the face of withering antiaircraft fire and the ship's evasive action. Tyler observed no hits.[72]

Fleming's Vindicators then attacked. His was the first to attack the other ship, Mikuma. Again the aircraft met withering antiaircraft fire. Fleming continued his attack although his Vindicator had been hit and was burning. He dropped his bomb at five hundred feet, barely missing the ship's stern, and then Fleming's aircraft crashed in flames. Tyler wrote in his report that one VMSB bomb hit the forward third of the ship. When VMSB departed, the ship was listing to starboard and turning in sharp circles to starboard. On the afternoon of June 6, she finally sank after suffering deadly aerial attacks from SBDs.[74]

Did Fleming's Vindicator Hit Mikuma on June 5?

A question arose concerning Fleming's attack: Did his Vindicator crash on one of Mikuma's aft (rear) turrets, or did it crash into the sea without hitting the ship? The question is unimportant for the battle's outcome but certainly was important for Fleming and Mikuma. Aircraft crashing into or on a warship is no small matter, either for the aircrew or for the ship—fire and damage at sea are critical factors in the ship's seaworthiness.

Evidence that Fleming's Vindicator Hit Mikuma

The commonly held belief, repeated in various publications and in at least one photograph's caption, is that Fleming's Vindicator crashed or probably crashed into a turret on the aft of Mikuma. The following eight sources support that consensus, showing just how firmly an erroneous conclusion entrenched can be. The next section of this chapter will prove that in all likelihood, Fleming's Vindicator did not hit the ship.

First, In Midway: The Battle That Doomed Japan, the Japanese Navy's Story (1992 edition), Japanese authors Mitsuo Fuchida and Masatake Okumiya write on page 262:

The pilot[1] of the leading dive bomber [Captain Fleming], however, after being hit by antiaircraft fire, attempted a daring suicide crash into Mikuma's bridge. He missed the bridge but crashed into the after turret, spreading fire over the air intake of the starboard engine room. This caused an explosion of gas fumes below, killing all hands working in the engine room. This was a damaging blow to the cruiser, hitherto unscathed except for the slight hull damage received in the collision with [the cruiser] Mogami.

The passage's note 1 states, "Editor's Note: This brave sacrifice hit was made by Capt. R. E. Fleming, USMC." The Japanese account given here indicates that his action caused much greater damage to Mikuma than hitherto believed.[75]

As discussed later in this chapter, the authors of the book Shattered Sword discredit this passage and its conclusions.

Second, Robert Heinl's Marines at Midway writes on page 41 that Fleming's Vindicator "dropped his bomb. Just at the moment of pull-out, his plane burst into flames[.]" Heinl does not state whether Fleming hit Mikuma but adds this quotation from Rear Admiral Akira Soji, Mogami's commanding officer at Midway: "I saw a dive bomber dive into the last turret (of the Mikuma) and start fires. [The dive bomber pilot] was very brave."[76]

The source of this quotation is Soji's interrogation for the U.S. Strategic Bomb Survey (Pacific) since Heinl cites the Soji interrogation elsewhere on page 41. In his interview, Soji, then a rear admiral, states that during Fleming's attack, no bombs hit Mikuma but that "I saw a dive-bomber dive into the last turret and start fires. He was very brave."[77] The authors of Shattered Sword also discredit this account and Soji's observation.

Third, in Marines At Midway, the caption for the famous photograph of the heavily damaged Mikuma states that "wreckage" atop one of the aft turrets "may well be the remains of the Marine SB2U-3 Captain Fleming deliberately dived in after sustaining mortal hits."[78] How would one know he deliberately flew into the turret?

Fourth, the first volume (Pearl Harbor to Guadalcanal) of a six-volume official Marine Corps World War II history states that the Vindicator crashed into the cruiser's after turret, citing text from page 226 of Fuchida's and Okumiya's book (page 262 in the 1992 edition of the book).[79]

Fifth, in Miracle At Midway, Gordon Prange writes on page 325 that "either by design or by accident, Fleming crashed his fiery aircraft on Mikuma's aft turret" with the ensuring catastrophic damage described by Fuchida and Okumiya.[80]

More important than Prange's text, however, is the footnote (number 20, page 325) supporting the conclusion. The footnote's text, at page 425, is a lengthy review of both sides of the question; in the footnote, Prange concludes that the Vindicator hit Mikuma.

Prange's analysis, however, about Fleming hitting Mikuma is incomplete and sloppy. His text and footnote omit a key phrase found in the Fleming MOH citation—"released his bomb to score a near miss on the stern of his target, then crashed to the sea in flames." The citation contains no language indicating Fleming's Vindicator hit Mikuma.[81]

Sixth, "A Marine at Midway" is an interview in World War II magazine (July 2002) of Sumner Whitten, a former SB2U-3 pilot at Midway. The interviewer notes that early in the morning of June 5, Mogami collided with Mikuma, making them targets for the Americans on June 6. Whitten agrees and states that the squadron attacked the cruisers, but he does not give the date of the squadron's attack, initially leading the reader into believing the attack was on June 6. He also states that he did not fly the mission, that another pilot flew his aircraft. He must have been referring to June 5, since, in the same paragraph, he describes the attacks by Tyler and by Fleming on Mogami and Mikuma. Again, although he was not on the mission, Whitten makes the categorical statement that Fleming "flew his plane into the ship [Mikuma]." He also states that Mikuma's executive officer said, "Fleming was a very brave man," for hitting the ship, but that quotation, as discussed earlier, is from then Captain Akira Soji, commanding officer, not executive officer, of Mogami, the cruiser sailing with Mikuma. He finally states that Mikuma was sunk on the afternoon of June 6. Calling further into question the article's accuracy is the caption of the photograph for Captain Fleming, misidentifying him as "Captain Francis M. Fleming" and stating that he "flew his doomed plane into Mikuma and caused critical damage to the cruiser…"

Seventh, in Incredible Victory, Walter Lord writes that Fleming made a glide-bombing run on Mikuma, "but on the way in, Fleming's plane began to burn. Somehow he kept his lead, made his run, dropped his bomb. Then—a blazing comet—he plunged into the after turret of his target." He added that Captain Akira Soji of Mogami thought "[v]ery brave" upon seeing the aircraft crash into the turret.[83]

Eighth, even the famous writer Robert Sherrod followed the "company line" here. In his book about the history of Marine Corps aviation, he wrote about Midway, "Although none of the pilots accompanying him [Fleming] reported the action that way, Fleming's plane apparently dived into Mikuma." He relied on the Soji comment mentioned earlier in this section.[84]

Evidence that Fleming's Vindicator Did Not Hit Mikuma

An equally compelling and more persuasive argument can be made that the MOH citation is correct. Fleming's Vindicator did not hit Mikuma. Three sources support the conclusion that Fleming's aircraft did not hit the ship.

First, the wording of the MOH citation itself must be considered; Fleming's bomb missed Mikuma and his Vindicator "crashed to the sea in flames."[85]

Second, in Shattered Sword: The Untold Story of the Battle of Midway, Jonathan B. Parshall and Anthony P. Tully convincingly assert that Fleming did not hit Mikuma. On page 362, the authors contradict Prange's conclusion with persuasive proof that Fleming's aircraft did not hit Mikuma.[86]

Just as Prange's footnote purportedly proves that Fleming hit the ship, Shattered Sword's footnote 38 more persuasively proves that it did not hit the ship. The three key pieces of evidence that he did not hit the ship were that Soji's "brave pilot" comment concerned another incident, not Fleming's attack, the famous Mikuma photograph cited earlier with the caption stating that debris atop a Mikuma turret could be from Fleming's Vindicator shows it was not in fact aircraft debris, and official reports (MAG-22 and VMSB-241) and witnesses who participated in the attack do not mention Fleming hitting the ship. Caption 20-3 for the photograph at page 380 of Shattered Sword, the photograph purporting to show wreckage of Fleming's Vindicator atop a Mikuma turret, is also informative in this regard.[87]

As to reports, the VMSB-241 squadron report of June 12, 1942, is from the "Commanding Officer." The report is signed "M. A. Tyler"; apparently because of the loss of senior officers, Captain Tyler had to sign the report, which was addressed to his next senior commander, the commanding officer of MAG-22. After stating in paragraph 41 of the VMSB report that no hits were observed from the dive bombing attack on Mogami, Tyler stated in paragraph 42 in part the following:

> Immediately following this [dive bombing] attack, Captain Fleming commenced his glide bombing attack from 4,500 feet amid heavy anti-aircraft opposition. He pressed home his attack even after being hit and while his plane was burning. He dropped his bomb, scored a very close miss on the stern of the ship and then went down in flames.[88]

The report simply states that the aircraft "went down in flames" without stating whether it hit the ship. If it had hit the ship, one would think that the report would have so stated.

In the end, whether Fleming's Vindicator hit Mikuma does not detract from two aspects—beyond challenge—of Fleming's MOH flight.

First, he exhibited great bravery, skill, and dedication in leading and pressing his attack in the face of enemy antiaircraft fire.

Second, Fleming may not have sunk or damaged Mikuma on June 5, but he probably scared the wits out of the crew. Fleming's attack must have adversely affected crew morale—shaken it badly—that day. The crew was subjected to an aerial attack, although an ineffective one, but one during which Fleming's bomb and aircraft just barely missed the ship.[89]

Fleming's Fate

Fleming and his gunner in the Vindicator, Marine Private First Class George Toms, were both lost in the June 5 attack. The casualty reports for Fleming and Toms read the same:

> "Shot down in flames***";
> "Body not recovered*"; and
> "*Determined nonrecoverable by field board 6/22/49 (vah)."[90]

Fleming's casualty card accounts for his fate clinically by stating, "Missing in action at Midway Island," "shot down in flames," and "determined nonrecoverable by field board 6/22/49." It also records that the Secretary of the Navy officially declared him dead as of June 6, 1943. The notation "field board" is important in the context of identifying and recovering remains. During World War II, not all remains could be identified or recovered. Thus in 1947, the Board of Review system was created. A Board of Review (or field board) was a panel of not fewer than three commissioned officers who made determinations concerning remains that could not be identified and the nonrecoverability of remains. Thus the casualty cards of Marines whose remains could not be recovered will have a note that on a certain date a "field board" determined that the remains could not be recovered.[91]

Aftermath of June 4 and 5

After-Action Reports

As noted previously, the Commanding Officer, MAG-22, (the Group commander) wrote a report for the Battle of Midway dated June 7, 1942. The heart of the report is Enclosure (A), the June 7, 1942, report of the Group Executive Officer, which included five annexes or components in addition to the Executive Officer's report itself. The two most important annexes are Annex (A), the casualty report, and Annex (E), the report of Fleming's squadron, VMSB-241.

The Executive Officer's report of June 7, 1942, lists Fleming's participation on June 4 and 5 as follows: the day flight on June 4 flying a Dauntless (SBD), the night flight on June 4 flying a Vindicator (SB2U-3), and the day flight on June 5 flying a Vindicator.[93]

As explained earlier, Captain M. A. Tyler signed the VMSB report, dated June 12, an indication of the high casualty rate and the loss of senior VMSB-241's pilots. Ordinarily the squadron commander (Major Henderson) would have signed the report, but he was missing in action; in his absence, the executive officer (Major Norris) would have signed the report, but he too was missing in action. For Captain Tyler to sign the report, he must have been the squadron's senior surviving officer.[94]

The VMSB report covers the missions on June 4 and 5. Fleming's roles were as follows:

Date	Target	Element	Aircraft
June 4 (morning)	Carriers	Major Henderson	SBD Dauntless
June 4 (evening)	Burning carriers	Major Norris	SB2U-3 Vindicator
June 5 (morning)	Battleships	Captain Fleming	SB2U-3 Vindicator

The target for the June 4 morning attack was on what would later be determined to be the Japanese aircraft carrier Hiryu. The June 4 evening mission was the mission during which Major Norris was lost. The target for the June 5 morning attack was the two cruisers Mogami and Mikuma. The VMSB report noted that on June 5, Fleming pressed his attack amid heavy antiaircraft fire and even after his plane was hit. His bomb barely missed the stern of the ship; Fleming's plane "then went down in flames."[95]

None of the reports single out Fleming for bravery, but in paragraph 7 of the

Group Commander's report, he writes that he had recommended personnel "deserving of praise and special mention...in accordance with [a Pacific Fleet Letter]." He did not mention Fleming by name in this paragraph.[96]

President Franklin D. Roosevelt signed the MOH citation on November 10, 1942. As the author (a retired Marine Reservist) well knows, November 10 is ironic since it is the date of the U.S. Marine Corps Birthday, the date on which two battalions of Marines were formed in 1775.

MOH Citation

For extraordinary heroism and conspicuous intrepidity above and beyond the call of duty as flight officer, Marine Scout-Bombing Squadron 241, during action against enemy Japanese forces in the battle of Midway on June 4 and 5, 1942. When his squadron commander was shot down during the initial attack upon an enemy aircraft carrier, Captain Fleming led the remainder of the division with such fearless determination that he dived his own plane to the perilously low altitude of 400 feet before releasing his bomb. Although his craft was riddled by 179 hits in the blistering hail of fire that burst upon him from Japanese fighter guns and antiaircraft batteries, he pulled out with only two minor wounds inflicted upon himself. On the night of June 4, when the squadron commander lost his way and became separated from the others, Captain Fleming brought his own plane in for a safe landing at its base despite hazardous weather conditions and total darkness. The following day, after less than four hours' sleep, he led the second division of his squadron in a coordinated glide-bombing and dive-bombing assault on a Japanese battleship [cruiser]. Undeterred by a fateful approach glide, during which his ship was struck and set afire, he grimly pressed home his attack to an altitude of 500 feet, released his bomb to score a near miss on the stern of his target, then crashed to the sea in flames. His dauntless perseverance and unyielding devotion to duty were in keeping with the highest traditions of the United States Naval Service.

Noteworthy aspects of the Fleming MOH

As with Cannon's, Fleming's MOH is unique.

First, Fleming was the sole MOH recipient for the 1942 Battle of Midway, the Pacific War's pivotal naval battle.[97]

Second, the battle was, for the most part, fought by aircraft squadrons based on aircraft carriers attacking the enemy's carriers—the Japanese attacked Midway Island by naval aviation but never invaded or captured it. Fleming's squadron, however, was not based on an aircraft carrier; his squadron was based on land, on Midway itself.[98]

Third, Fleming participated in a battle that was an outstanding example of the new way of naval warfare. In his chapter "The End of Sea Power," Alexander P. DeSeversky, an enthusiastic disciple of aviation advocate Billy Mitchell, wrote about how ships could no longer sail out from under their "umbrella of air power" and that naval "contempt" for airpower resulted in ships sunk by aircraft. The sea battles taken for granted in the past, during which ships would fight "face to face," were the battles of yesterday. About Midway, he wrote,

> The pattern of the new type of "naval engagement" was set by the battle of Midway in June, 1942. Though touted to this day as a great naval battle, it was strictly an air battle, in which aircraft did the fighting and ships provided the targets. At no time in the three days' action did surface vessels make direct contact. Japanese carrier planes fought for control of the skies against American carrier planes and aircraft based on Midway Island [as were VMSB-241 and Fleming]. When Japan lost four carriers, its Imperial Fleet retired.[99]

And despite the adverse opinion of the SBD Dauntless, found in the MAG-22 commander's report of June 7, 1942, the obsolete Dauntlesses proved to be workhorses and the keys to victory; they sank all four of the Japanese carriers and "changed the course of World War II."[100]

Fourth, Fleming was the first Marine aviator in the war to be awarded a MOH (albeit posthumously), but his actions leading to the MOH were not the earliest leading to a Marine aviator MOH. The earliest actions by a Marine aviator in the war ultimately leading to a MOH were those of Captain Henry Elrod, a pilot at Wake Island, whose bravery at Wake in December 1941 resulted in a posthumous MOH awarded in 1946.[101]

NOTES

1. The Roberts Commission investigation of December 7, 1941, included in the report of the 1945 congressional investigation of the attack found in PEARL HARBOR ATTACK: HEARINGS BEFORE THE JOINT COMMITTEE ON THE INVESTIGATION OF THE PEARL HARBOR ATTACK, SEVENTY-NINTH CONGRESS, FIRST SESSION, Part 39 (U.S. Government Printing Office, 1946), 3.

2. Lieutenant Colonel Robert D. Heinl, Jr, USMC, Marines At Midway (The Historical Section, Division of Public Information, USMC, Washington, DC, 1948), 1–9 (hereafter "Heinl, Marines At Midway").

3. Lieutenant Colonel Frank O. Hough, USMCR; Major Verle E. Ludwig, USMC; and Henry I. Shaw, Jr., Pearl Harbor To Guadalcanal: History Of The U.S. Marine Corps Operations In World War II, Vol. I (Historical Division, Headquarters, US Marine Corps, Washington, DC, 1958, reprinted by the Battery Press, Inc., Nashville, TN, 1993), (hereafter "Hough, Pearl Harbor To Guadalcanal: History Of The US Marine Corps Operations In World War II"); the 1941 attack is described on pages 78–81, and the 1942 attack is described on pages 214–231. Neither attack resulted in a Japanese victory.

4. Official US Marine Corps biography, First Lieutenant George H. Cannon, USMC, September 1949, (hereafter "Cannon, US Marine Corps biography"); the National Personnel Records Center, St. Louis, Missouri, furnished military and personal information from Cannon's Official Military Personnel File (OMPF) at the author's

request (hereafter "Cannon OMPF").

5. Major Charles D. Melson, USMC (Retired), Condition Red: Marine Defense Battalions In World War II (History and Museums Division, Headquarters, US Marine Corps, 1996).

6. Endnote 4, Cannon US Marine Corps biography; Endnote 4, Cannon OMPF.

7. Endnote 4, Cannon OMPF; Cannon MOH citation at Appendix A (hereafter "Cannon MOH citation"); the Roberts Commission investigation of December 7, 1941, included in the report of the 1945 Congressional investigation of the attack found in PEARL HARBOR ATTACK: HEARINGS BEFORE THE JOINT COMMITTEE ON THE INVESTIGATION OF THE PEARL HARBOR ATTACK, SEVENTY-NINTH CONGRESS, FIRST SESSION, Part 24 (U.S. Government Printing Office, 1946), 1560 (Cannon command post)(hereafter "Shannon December 12, 1941 report").

8. Endnote 3, Hough, Pearl Harbor To Guadalcanal: History Of The US Marine Corps Operations In World War II, 78; at page 79, Hough writes that the destroyers were Akebono and Ushio; Commander Mitsuo Fuchida wrote that Akebono and Ushio were the two destroyers in answering questions addressed to him after the war; PEARL HARBOR ATTACK: HEARINGS BEFORE THE JOINT COMMITTEE ON THE INVESTIGATION OF THE PEARL HARBOR ATTACK, Part 1 (US Government Printing Office, Washington, DC,1945), 239, question 25 (hereafter "Fuchida, question 25"); Prange writes that they were Akebono and Sazanami in Gordon W. Prange, At Dawn We Slept (Penguin Books, New York, NY, 1982), 435–436; endnote 2, Heinl, Marines at Midway at page 10 names the two ships as Akebono and Ushio.

9. Endnote 8, Fuchida, question 25; Fuchida gives the arrival date as December 8, the date of the day on the Japanese calendar.

10. Endnote 7, Shannon December 12, 1941, report, 1559–1560; casualty report for First Lieutenant George Ham Cannon, USMC, for December 7, 1941 (hereafter "Cannon casualty report").

11. Endnote 7, Cannon MOH citation; endnote 7, Shannon report, 1560.

12. Endnote 10, Cannon casualty report; Cannon is also listed as killed in a message from Commanding Officer, Naval Air Station, Midway. to the Commander in Chief of the Pacific Fleet; see page 1558 of Part 24 of the PEARL HARBOR ATTACK HEARINGS cited at endnote 7.

13. Endnote 7, Cannon MOH citation; endnote 7, Shannon December 12, 1941, report, 1560.

14. Endnote 10, Cannon casualty report.

15. Endnote 4, Cannon OMPF.

16. Endnote 7, Shannon December 12, 1941, report, 1560.

17. Hough, Pearl Harbor to Guadalcanal: History Of the U.S. Marine Corps Operations in World War II, 79–80; see discussion of first MOHs earned and awarded in Chapters 5 and 18.

18. Franklin D. Roosevelt, "Address to Congress Requesting a Declaration of War with Japan" (December 8, 1941), printed from the Franklin D. Roosevelt Presidential Library and Museum Internet site October 9, 2015 (hereafter "Roosevelt Declaration of War Speech").

19. See discussion of first MOHs earned and awarded in Chapter 14.

20. See Chapters 4–11 and 19 of this book.

21. Ibid.

22. Ibid.

23. Ibid.

24. Official U.S. Marine Corps biography, Captain Richard E. Fleming, USMC [sic] (Deceased) (undated) (hereafter "Fleming U.S. Marine Corps biography"). He was USMCR (the Reserve Marine Corps, not USMC, the Regular Marine Corps).

25. "Slain St. Paul Hero Given Highest Tribute," St. Paul Dispatch, November 24, 1942, 1.

26. The National Personnel Records Center, St. Louis, Missouri, furnished military and personal information from Fleming's Official Military Personnel File (OMPF) at the author's request (hereafter "Fleming OMPF").

27. Ibid.; endnote 31, Fleming U.S. Marine Corps biography.

28. Endnote 33, Fleming OMPF.

29. Ibid.; endnote 2, Heinl, Marines At Midway, 9.

30. Endnote 26, Fleming OMPF; author's knowledge about a common practice—ships serving as lifeguards for aircraft flying over the ocean. His father flew combat missions during World War II in the Pacific with and without lifeguards.

31. Endnote 26, Fleming OMPF.

32. Ibid.

33. Ibid.; Kenneth Munson, Aircraft of World War II (Doubleday & Company, Inc., New York, NY, 1962), 32–33 (hereafter "Munson, Aircraft of World War II"); e-mail of May 18, 2015, from Curt Lawson, Library Research Volunteer, National Naval Aviation Museum.

34. Author's knowledge of the organization of Marine aviation into groups comprising squadrons, having served in a helicopter squadron; report of Marine Aircraft Group 22 (Subject: "Battle of Midway Islands, Report of") of June 7, 1942, page 1, paragraph 1 (hereafter "MAG-22 Commanding Officer's report"); the MAG-22 commander writing the report was Major Ira L. Kimes.

35. Endnote 33, Munson, Aircraft of World War II, 67; endnote 34, MAG-22 Commanding Officer's report, page 1, paragraph 1.

36. Endnote 33, Munson, Aircraft of World War II, 232; endnote 34, MAG-22 Commanding Officer's report, page 1, paragraph 1.

37. Report of Marine Scout-Bombing Squadron 241 (Subj[ect]: "Report of Activities during June 4 and June 5, 1942") of June 12, 1942, page 1, paragraph 1 (hereafter "VMSB-241 commanding officer's report"). Captain M. A. Tyler signed the report; ordinarily, the squadron commanding officer or executive officer (lieutenant colonels or majors) would sign a report, but both the commander (Henderson) and executive officer (Norris) had been lost in action.

38. Endnote 34, MAG-22 Commanding Officer's report, page 1 (date); page 3, paragraph 7 (praise); and page 4, paragraph 8 (a) and (b) (aircraft criticism). The MOH action dates for Fleming are from his citation at Appendix A of this book.

39. Ibid., page 4, paragraph 8(a); author's and common knowledge about the Zero and its role on December 7.

40. Ibid., paragraph 8(b).

41. Hill Goodspeed, "Always Faithful," Naval Aviation News (May–June 2003), 22.

42. Endnote 37, VMSB-241 Commanding Officer's report, page 1, paragraph 2.

43. Ibid., page 1, paragraph 4.

44. Author's knowledge of the Japanese attack plan and tactics for the attack on Oahu; HEARINGS BEFORE THE JOINT COMMITTEE ON THE INVESTIGATION OF THE PEARL HARBOR ATTACK, Part 1 (U.S. Government Printing Office, Washington, DC, 1945), 239, question 26.

45. Endnote 37, VMSB-241 report, page 1, paragraph 4, and page 7, paragraph 52; Jonathan B. Parshall and Anthony P. Tully, Shattered Sword: The Untold Story of the Battle of Midway (Potomac Books, Washington, DC, 2005), 178, at which the authors condemn glide bombing (hereafter "Parshall and Tully, Shattered Sword: The Untold

Story of the Battle of Midway").

46. Report of Executive Officer, MAG-22 (Subject: "Marine Aircraft Group Twenty-Two, Second Marine Aircraft Wing, Midway Islands T.H.") of June 7, 1942, 10 (hereafter "MAG-22 Executive Officer's report").

47. Ibid.; page 6 of the report shows the division-section organization for Dauntlesses.

48. Endnote 26, Fleming OMPF.

49. Author's knowledge.

50. Endnote 46, MAG-22 Executive Officer's report, 4 and 6; endnote 51, Parshall and Tully, Shattered Sword: The Untold Story of the Battle Of Midway, 176–178, which identifies the target as Hiryu and also discusses the VMSB attack; Colonel Charles A. Jones, USMCR. Hawaii's World War II Military Sites (Mutual Publishing, Honolulu, HI, 2002), in which the list of the six Japanese aircraft carriers attacking Oahu on December 7 and the list of Japanese aircraft carriers lost at Midway can be found at page 33.

51. Ibid., 9.

52. Official Marine Corps casualty report for Major Lofton Henderson.

53. Endnote 37, VMSB-241 Commanding Officer's report, paragraph 14.

54. Fleming MOH citation at the end of this chapter and at Appendix A of this book (hereafter "Fleming MOH citation").

55. Endnote 46, MAG-22 Executive Officer's report, page 9.

56. Ibid.; author's knowledge that the Type 99 Japanese Navy dive bomber, which played a major role in the attack on Oahu on December 7, was called the "Val."

57. Ibid., 10.

58. Endnote 46, MAG-22 Executive Officer's report, 10; VMSB-241 Commanding Officer's report, 10, paragraph 24.

59. Endnote 47, VMSB-241 Commanding Officer's report, 3, paragraph 18.

60. Fleming MOH citation.

61. Jane Blakeney, Heroes: US Marine Corps 1861 * 1955 (Guthrie Lithograph Co., Inc., Washington, DC, 1957), 102 (Navy Cross) (hereafter "Blakeney, Heroes: U.S. Marine Corps 1861 * 1955"); endnote 3, Hough, Pearl Harbor To Guadalcanal: History Of The U.S. Marine Corps Operations In World War II, 224–25 (footnote 8 notes that the Japanese airfield on Guadalcanal, later captured by the Marines, was

named by then in Major Henderson's honor).

62. Endnote 46, MAG-22 Executive Officer's report, 11.

63. Ibid.

64. Endnote 47, VMSB-241 Commanding Officer's report, page 4, paragraph 34.

65. Official Marine Corps casualty report for Major Benjamin Norris.

66. Endnote 61, Blakeney, Heroes: US Marine Corps 1861 * 1955, 108.

67. Fleming MOH citation.

68. Endnote 46, MAG-22 Executive Officer's report, 10; endnote 37, VMSB-241 Commanding Officer's report, page 5, paragraph 35.

69. Endnote 37, VMSB-241 Commanding Officer's report, page 5, paragraph 37; Fleming's MOH citation mentions his lack of sleep.

70. Endnote 37, VMSB-241 Commanding Officer's report, page 5, paragraph 40.

71. U.S. Strategic Bombing Survey [Pacific] (Naval Analysis Division, Washington, DC, 1946); In volume 2, at page 361, Rear Admiral Akira Soji is identified as Mogami's commanding officer at Midway. His interrogation, which is number 83, was November 13–14, 1945; his description of the action at Midway involving the ship collision and the VMSB attack is at page 363. In volume 1, at page 269, Lieutenant Commander Nishikawa is identified as the Mogami's gunnery officer at Midway. His interrogation, which is number 66, was November 7, 1945; his description of the ship collision and the action at Midway is at page 271 (hereafter, "U.S. Strategic Bombing Survey [Pacific]).”

72. Endnote 37, VMSB-241 Commanding Officer's report, page 5, paragraphs 40 and 41.

73. Ibid., page 5, paragraph 42; endnote 45, Parshall and Tully, Shattered Sword: The Untold Story of the Battle of Midway, discusses the sinking of Mikuma at pages 367 to 380.

74. Mitsuo Fuchida and Masatake Okumiya, Midway, The Battle That Doomed Japan: The Japanese Navy's Story (Naval Institute Press, Annapolis, MD, 1992), 262.

75. Ibid., 262, note 1.

76. Endnote 2, Heinl, Marines At Midway, 41.

77. Endnote 71, U.S. Strategic Bomb Survey [PACIFIC], Volume II, Interrogation 83, 363.

78. Endnote 2, Heinl, Marines At Midway, 40.

79. Hough, Pearl Harbor To Guadalcanal: History Of The U.S. Marine Corps Operations In World War II, 229, text for footnote 13 and text of footnote 13.

80. Gordon W. Prange, Donald M. Goldstein, and Katherine V. Dillon, Miracle At Midway (McGraw-Hill Book Company, New York, NY, 1982), 325.

81. Endnote 54, Fleming MOH citation.

82. Jon Guttman, "A Marine at Midway," World War II (July 2002). The article, which begins on page 48, is an interview of a Marine who served on Midway, Sumner H. Whitten. The relevant pages are 51 (Fleming's name incorrect) and 52 (incorrect date of VMSB attack on cruisers, Whitten stating he did not fly the mission, and confusing Mikuma's commanding officer with her executive officer).

83. Walter Lord, Incredible Victory (Harper & Row, Publishers, New York, NY, 1967), 123.

84. Robert Sherrod, History of Marine Corps Aviation in World War II (Washington, DC: Combat Forces Press, 1952), 58–62.

85. Endnote 54, Fleming MOH citation.

86. Endnote 51, Parshall and Tully, Shattered Sword: The Untold Story of the Battle of Midway, 362.

87. Ibid., 573 (footnote 38).

88. Endnote 37, VMSB-241 Commanding Officer's report, page 5, paragraphs 41 and 42.

89. Endnote 45, Parshall and Tully, Shattered Sword: The Untold Story of the Battle of Midway, 367–380.

90. Official Marine Corps casualty reports for Captain Richard E. Fleming and Private First Class George A. Toms.

91. Official Marine Corps casualty report for Captain Richard E. Fleming; for information on Boards of Review, see Edward Steere and Thayer M. Boardman, Final Disposition of World War II Dead 1945–51 (Historical Branch, Office of the Quartermaster General, Washington, DC, 1957), QMC Historical Studies, Series II, No. 4, 625–626.

92. Endnote 34, MAG-22 Commanding Officer's report; endnote 46, MAG-22 Executive Officer's report; endnote 37, VMSB-241 Commanding Officer's report.

93. Endnote 46, MAG-22 Executive Officer's report, pages 6 (June 4 day flight with Henderson leading the first division and Henderson and Fleming in the command section); page 11 (June 4 night flight with Fleming in the unit commanded by Norris), and 13 (June 5 flight with Tyler with Fleming leading the Vindicator unit).

94. Endnote 37, VMSB-241 Commanding Officer's report (Tyler signed on page 8). The losses of Majors Henderson, the original VMSB Commanding Officer, and Norris, the original VMSB Executive Officer, were discussed earlier in this chapter. To author's knowledge, the senior surviving officer signing a report is consistent with military protocol: if the senior officers are dead, wounded, or missing, the senior surviving officer signs the report even if he is a junior officer, such as a captain.

95. Endnote 37, VMSB-241 Commanding Officer's report lists Fleming as follows:

- June 4 day flight with Henderson, page 2, paragraph 10; Fleming flew a SBD, page 1, paragraph 6.
- June 4 night flight with Norris, page 4, paragraph 28; Fleming flew a Vindicator, 4, paragraph 28
- June 5 day flight with Tyler, page 5, paragraph 36 shows two units, one under Tyler and one under Fleming. Fleming flew a Vindicator; page 5, paragraph 39 discusses the Dauntlesses and dive bombing. By implication, Fleming was flying a Vindicator since his unit performed glide bombing after the dive bombers attacked by dive bombing (page 5, paragraph 42). Paragraph 42 describes Fleming's fatal flight.

96. Endnote 39, MAG-22 Commanding Officer's report.

97. All other MOH recipients in this book, receiving classic combat MOHs for combat or noncombat, were on Oahu; Lieutenant Cannon was on Midway, but his MOH action was in 1941; Chapters 4–14.

98. Alexander P. DeSeversky, AIR POWER: KEY TO SURVIVAL (Simon and Schuster, New York, NY, 1950), 87–88 (hereafter "DeSeversky, AIR POWER: KEY TO SURVIVAL"); endnote 26, Fleming's OMPF notes that VMSB was on Midway Island, not aboard an aircraft carrier.

99. Endnote 109, DeSeversky, AIR POWER: KEY TO SURVIVAL.

100. Endnote 34, MAG-22 Commanding Officer's report, page 4, paragraph 8(b) (Dauntless criticism); Zaur Eylanbekov, "Airpower Classics" (SBD Dauntless), AIR FORCE MAGAZINE (October 2009), 80.

101. Heinl, Marines at Midway, 41, footnote 54; copy of Fleming MOH citation received from the Franklin D. Roosevelt Presidential Library and Museum; author's knowledge of the Marine Corps' Birthday celebration having served in the Marine Corps and its Reserve from 1981 to 2009. Fleming can be determined to be the first Marine aviator to receive a MOH during World War II by reference to a monograph: Commander Peter B. Mersky, US Naval Reserve, Time of the Aces: Marine Pilots in the Solomons, 1942–1944 (History and Museums Division, Headquarters, US Marine

Corps, Washington, DC, 1993), 14. One must read the page carefully to discern that Fleming's was the first MOH received, although his was not the first action to result in a MOH to an aviator. (Captain Henry Elrod's MOH action was earlier, but he did not receive his posthumous MOH until after the war. His widow received it on November 8, 1946, Who's Who in Marine Corps History, "Major Henry Talmage Elrod, USMC (Deceased), a fact sheet produced by the Marine Corps History Division and accessed by Internet on April 9, 2008 (his MOH was for actions on Wake Island).

Photographs
Midway and Its MOH Recipients

First Lieutenant George Cannon, U.S. Marine Corps, wearing his dress blue uniform with the US Marine Corps emblem (eagle, globe, and anchor) seen at his right collar. (Photograph NH 105688 from the Naval History and Heritage Command)

Lieutenant Cannon's command post as seen in 2008 on Midway. (Photograph courtesy of Barry Christenson of the Fish and Wildlife Service, 2008)

Captain Richard Fleming, U.S. Marine Corps Reserve. (Photograph from the U.S. Marine Corps History Division)

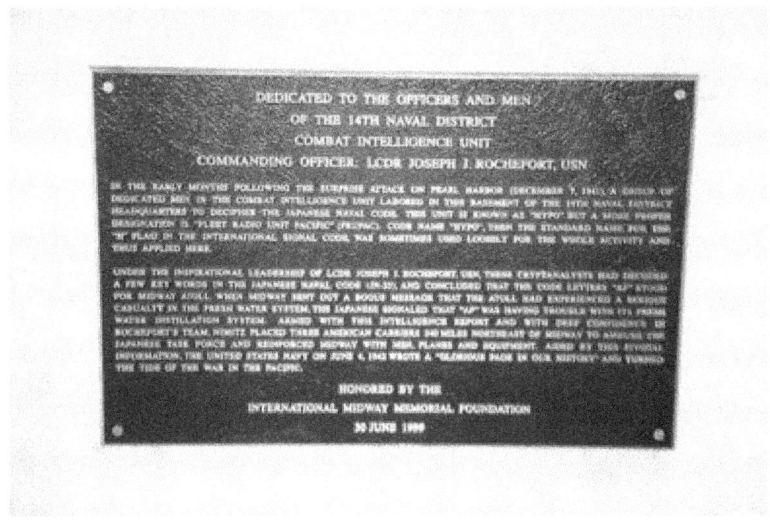

One of two "secret signs" attached to the outside of an administrative building at the Naval Shipyard at Naval Station Pearl Harbor. It is an excellent summary of the 1942 Battle of Midway. See Appendix C for the text typed so it can be read easily. (Author's slide taken with permission from Mr. George Royce, then–head of security at the Shipyard, 1999.)

A Douglas SBD-2 Dauntless dive bomber, similar to the SBD that Captain Richard Fleming flew on the morning of June 4, 1942. This aircraft, at the National Naval Aviation Museum, was at Ford Island during the Japanese attack and was used for missions early in the war before being assigned to Fleming's squadron (VMSB-241) at Midway. Note the 500-pound bomb under the center of the aircraft and the 250-pound bomb under the wing. Also note the perforated dive flaps used to slow the aircraft during a dive. (Author's photograph, 2015. Information from Deej Kiely at the National Naval Aviation Museum, where the Dauntless is displayed.) A photograph of a Vindicator is at the front of this book.

West Loch, Pearl Harbor, February 17, 1945

Section D:
Medals of Honor Earned at the West Loch of Pearl Harbor, 1945

Chapter 13
West Loch, Pearl Harbor
Death at Depth

Petty Officer Second Class (Boatswain's Mate)
Owen Francis Patrick Hammerberg, U.S. Navy

The ghosts of the Second Pearl Harbor haunt Oahu just as the ghosts of the First Pearl Harbor do. This chapter is about the ghost of the last victim of the Second Pearl Harbor.

Most of the time when writing this book, the subject matter presented the author no emotional difficulties. This chapter, about the Second Pearl Harbor, is an exception, especially when reading and mentally processing the powerful, poignant letter from the immediate commander of the deceased MOH recipient to the recipient's mother. Although the MOH was earned in 1945, it was most likely a MOH awarded because of thoughtlessness in 1944 when someone smoked in an area where smoking was forbidden. Such thoughtlessness, leading to that MOH in 1945, cost the life of the junior sailor who earned it.

Most MOH actions have two components. One is ghastly conditions of conflict, chaos, suffering, death, and wounds or injuries the average citizen never sees and cannot envision. The other is the action or reaction of the recipient, such as bravery, decisive action, or sacrifice, in those conditions.

One would be hard pressed to find more outright horror and frightening, dangerous, and ghastly circumstances than that endured by Navy diver and Petty Officer Second Class (Boatswain's Mate) Owen Hammerberg in 1945 in the West Loch of Pearl Harbor, circumstances prolonging his death for eighteen hours. One would also be hard pressed to find a greater degree of suffering than that he endured.

His MOH is different from the other MOHs awarded for bravery in the Hawaiian Islands in that it was awarded for noncombat bravery: the site of the action was one not of aerial, sea, or land combat. The site was Oahu, a Hawaiian Island filled with many beautiful sights and waters. For Hammerberg, on February 17, 1945, Oahu's beauty was transformed into a nightmare. The recipient of a combat MOH faces an enemy and his ordnance; Hammerberg faced dark water and the hazards of diving around the wreckage of a submerged ship.

The Second Pearl Harbor: The 1944 West Loch Disaster

The stage for the Hammerberg MOH was set not on December 7, 1941, but on May 21, 1944, the date of the infamous West Loch Disaster, also called "the Unknown Pearl Harbor," "the Second Pearl Harbor," or "the Other Pearl Harbor." The story is one of the lesser-known disasters in U.S. Navy history, unknown even to knowledgeable World War II historians. The likelihood of average tourists visiting Oahu knowing or learning about the West Loch Disaster is low; the likelihood they will know or learn about the Hammerberg MOH is even lower.

The 1944 West Loch Disaster is a long and complicated story, the subject of a Navy Court of Inquiry (investigation) in 1944 and a book, The Second Pearl Harbor: The West Loch Disaster, May 21, 1944. A brief description of the disaster is required as background for the Hammerberg MOH. The description of the disaster is from the Navy Court of Inquiry and the book just mentioned. The information is also based on an investigation report by Fourteenth Naval District and the author's familiarity with the area, having twice visited Naval Magazine Pearl Harbor at West Loch (the site of the disaster) and having visited Pearl Harbor and the surrounding area numerous times.[1]

Coincidentally, the Second Pearl Harbor occurred on a Sunday, as did the Japanese attack on December 7, although during May, not December.

It occurred in a part of Pearl Harbor that saw no conflict on December 7, 1941: West Loch. As described in Chapter 2, Pearl Harbor comprises several lochs: Southeast, Quarry, Merry, Magazine, and East Lochs are the most important for December 7. Southeast Loch was the infamous "Torpedo Alley," leading directly from the Navy Yard to Battleship Row. Japanese torpedoes dropped in the loch had a "straight shot" at Battleship Row's ships.

The main channel connecting Pearl Harbor to the Pacific Ocean meets the ocean at the southern edge of Oahu. Traveling north from that opening up the main channel toward Pearl Harbor, one passes Hickam Air Force Base (Hickam Field in World War II) on the right. Continuing north, one enters Pearl Harbor and finds Ford Island in the center. Sailing around Ford Island, one would find the previously described lochs that were important on December 7.

As can be seen on the map on page 200, Pearl Harbor has another loch, West Loch, the location of the Hammerberg MOH action. Sailing north in the main channel from the Pacific, one can—before reaching Ford Island—veer left and enter West Loch Channel at Waipio Point, the southernmost point of the Waipio Peninsula. As an analogy, Waipio Point marks an intersection: continuing north (straight) in the main channel leads to Ford Island, but veering left at Waipio Point leads into West Loch Channel, leading approximately northwest into West Loch. The western side of Waipio Peninsula, which continues north toward Ford Island, forms West Loch's eastern or right side. Running along the eastern side of the peninsula is the main channel leading to Ford Island.

To the left inside West Loch are Naval Magazine Pearl Harbor and its wharves and warehouses. At the Magazine is Powder Point, and beyond Powder Point is the wharf. In 1931, the Magazine, known as the Naval Ammunition Depot (NAD) Oahu, was commissioned, comprising several branches, including one in Lualualei (near Schofield Barracks), the site of the headquarters, and one at West Loch. In 1999, the headquarters moved from Lualualei to West Loch and the organization's name changed from Naval Magazine Lualualei to Naval Magazine Pearl Harbor.

To the right inside West Loch is Walker Bay, which extends eastward a limited distance from West Loch into the Waipio Peninsula and toward Pearl Harbor, but it stops short of and does not completely cross the Peninsula, so Walker Bay does not connect West Loch with the main section of Pearl Harbor. Two points define the opening to Walker Bay. Sailing north up the West Loch Channel, one first encounters Intrepid Point, which is across West Loch Channel from Powder Point. After passing Powder Point and crossing the mouth of Walker Bay, one reaches the second point defining Walker Bay: Hanaloa Point.

On Sunday, May 21, 1944, West Loch was filled with more than one hundred ships loaded for the invasion of Saipan, a major operation in the Marianas. Twenty-nine were LSTs (landing ship tanks), which were cargo ships carrying troops, fuel, ammunition, and supplies. Because of their cargo, size, and slow speed, LSTs were often called "large (or long) slow targets." The LST was a cargo ship whose bow could land on a beach; the doors could then be opened so that men, vehicles, and cargo could unload directly ashore.[2]

Numerous LSTs were berthed together around the entrance to Walker Bay, across West Loch from the NAD wharf at Powder Point and in the area between Hanaloa and Intrepid Points—the opening to Walker Bay. The ships were "combat loaded" with men, ammunition, fuel, explosives, and other supplies. Ships were also moored around Intrepid Point in the channel leading toward Pearl Harbor.

Other LSTs, including LST-480 and LST-353, were moored inside Walker Bay. LST-480 was in a row of ships to the northeast of Hanaloa Point; LST-353 was in a row of ships beside LST-480's row and farther into Walker Bay.

The Second Pearl Harbor began at approximately 3:05 p.m. with an explosion aboard LST-353. Several explanations for the cause of the explosion were offered and examined. One was sabotage, but neither the Court of Inquiry nor the Fourteenth Naval District Investigation Report found any evidence of sabotage.[3] Another was an untoward event involving the handling of mortar ammunition (smoking or dropping a mortar shell).[4] A third and the most likely cause was the ignition of gasoline fumes seeping from fuel tanks mounted topside on LST-353's deck. Although no definitive source of ignition was found, crewmen or workers smoking near the area most likely caused the ignition.[5]

A series of fires and terrific explosions spread quickly and easily among the ships since they were moored so closely, some side by side, making a bad situation worse. The explosions and fires ended approximately twenty-four hours later. Six LSTs sank; several were damaged. Twenty or more buildings were damaged. Personnel losses were 163 dead and missing and 396 injured. LST-480, whose rusting hulk is today the sole visible reminder of the West Loch Disaster, caught fire, exploded, and ultimately moved toward Hanaloa Point and grounded. Two days after the initial explosions, the ship was still burning.

The final chapter in this tragedy did not occur until 1945, when West Loch would claim a brave sailor's life.

BOATSWAIN'S MATE SECOND CLASS OWEN HAMMERBERG, US NAVY

Background

Hammerberg was born on May 31, 1920, in Daggett, Michigan. He enlisted in the Navy on July 16, 1941, and attended boot camp at Naval Training Station, Great Lakes, Illinois, graduating on September 12, 1941. He served on three ships and at various shore commands. He was a boatswain's mate, a sailor responsible for ship maintenance and general seamanship duties, such as loading and unloading stores and equipment.[6]

He was promoted to boatswain's mate second class in October 1943. He graduated from Deep Sea Diving School at the Navy Yard, Washington, DC, in August 1944.[7]

He joined Commander Service Force, US Pacific Fleet, on October 5, 1944, and was assigned to the Salvage Unit.[8]

Action on February 17, 1945

The MOH action occurred on February 17, 1945, when Navy divers were diving on one of the ships that sank during the West Loch Disaster. The bases for the following account of the MOH action are the MOH citation and a typed letter dated March 8, 1945, addressed to Hammerberg's mother and signed by Commander Henry Foss, U.S. Naval Reserve, who was the Deputy Fleet Salvage Officer and apparently Hammerberg's immediate officer supervisor. Because of the power and poignancy of the letter, its full text appears at the end of this chapter.[9]

On February 17, a diver was trapped when a steel plate collapsed on him as he was making a tunnel, using jet nozzles, under a LST sunk in forty feet of water and twenty feet of mud. A second diver, working on the other side of the ship, attempted to rescue the first diver but also became trapped when steel wreckage caved in.[10]

Without hesitating, Hammerberg went overboard to attempt rescue in the face of great dangers, including possible additional collapse of metal, mud, darkness, and having his lifeline caught on jagged steel from the sunken ship.[11]

Hammerberg cleared a passage and freed one diver, Fuller, from the steel plate trapping him, but he could not free Fuller's lifeline. He passed Fuller to accomplish two tasks—one, to free Brown (the other diver), and two, to free Fuller's lifelines. Unfortunately, Hammerberg became trapped as the plate trapping Brown fell on him, which somehow freed Fuller. When the plate fell, it fell on Hammerberg such that he protected Brown, who was directly under him. Fuller's lifelines remained fouled (tangled), so new lines were sent to him and attached, allowing Fuller to surface.[12]

The rescue was made difficult, according to Foss, by steel fragments embedded in the mud around the LST, fragments from the explosion that sank her. Divers removed many fragments to release the weight on Hammerberg, but removing the fragments did not release the pressure on Brown or Hammerberg. After Fuller surfaced, Foss used a pump to remove mud so that Brown and Hammerberg could be freed. Foss described the removal of the mud as "heart-breakingly slow" in part due to debris "continually clogging the pump and suction."[13]

Brown was somehow freed since the MOH citation states that Hammerberg saved "two comrades."[14]

No men or equipment were spared to save Hammerberg. Foss had at his disposal three derricks, one salvage tug, other divers, physicians, and three "specially skilled civilian divers."[15]

While Hammerberg was trapped, his close friends as well as Foss talked to him via a diver's telephone. Foss wrote that men gave Hammerberg as much "comfort and encouragement as was possible under the circumstances. This was a most arduous task. Many a message transferred was sent at my request. At these times I tried to express what I thought would be best for him and silently saying what I knew would be in your hearts."[16]

According to his MOH citation, Hammerberg "succumbed in agony eighteen hours after he had gone to the aid of his fellow divers…"[17]

A Catholic priest (a navy lieutenant chaplain) officiated at the burial, held on February 27 at Halawa Naval Cemetery on Aiea Heights near the Naval Hospital at Halawa. The Salvage Unit attended the burial. The chaplain held a Mass at "special services." The amount collected for flowers was $266.00; since only $90.00 were spent for flowers, the remainder of the money was sent to Hammerberg's mother.[18]

Aftermath of February 17: Notifying the Family

Secretary of the Navy James Forrestal's letter of March 30, 1945, to the father, Mr. Jonnes Hammerberg, stated he had learned "with deep regret" about Hammerberg's death. He wrote, "I express to you my sincere sympathy in your great sorrow and assure you that the Navy shares in your sense of bereavement."[19]

The Bureau of Naval Personnel sent the father a letter dated May 4, 1945, referencing the telegram it had already sent him, advising him of his son's death. The Bureau's letter added that the date of death was February 17, 1945, but explained that no further details were available. The letter again extended sympathy for the loss.[20]

Letters No Family Wants to Receive

Anyone familiar with the U.S. military knows that in modern times the commanding officer of a member of his or her command who is killed in combat or dies by other means traditionally writes a letter of condolence to the family of the deceased.

In World War II, the practice of commanders sending letters could not always be followed since so many officers were killed or wounded and evacuated; in some cases, those evacuated never returned to the command. The classic example was Iwo Jima, where the officer casualty rate was so high that families often did not receive letters from commanders because the commanders themselves were killed or wounded and removed from the command.

Families are generally obsessed with knowing the circumstances of the death and, in particular, if the dead family member suffered. The letter from the commander can explain the circumstances of death to ease family members' anxiety. If the commander cannot write a letter, the family is left in the dark unless a successor commander or a comrade writes the family. Chaplains often wrote letters to families. In addition, the family can on its own affirmatively seek the details of the death by contacting members of the command.

Hammerberg's family received the March 8 letter from Foss previously mentioned as well as the letters from the Secretary of the Navy and the Bureau of Naval Personnel. The Foss letter is extraordinary—especially for military correspondence—for its remarkable degree of detail, explanation, and poignancy. It is not written in the uncaring military bureaucratic style one finds in typical military writing. It is clearly the product of a humane, empathetic man, trying his best to console a family for the loss of a son.

Foss, whether justified or not, took responsibility for the unsuccessful attempts to rescue Hammerberg: "It was my responsibility to effect the rescue of your son. In this I failed." But he assured the family that the lack of success was not for want of trying or lack of equipment, men, or specialists. The letter is at the end of this chapter.

Petty Officer Second Class (Boatswain's Mate) Owen Hammerberg would receive the only classic MOH for noncombat bravery on Oahu during World War II. President Harry S. Truman signed the citation on November 26, 1945.

MOH Citation

For conspicuous gallantry and intrepidity at the risk of his life above and beyond the call of duty as a Diver engaged in rescue operations at West Loch, Pearl Harbor, February 17, 1945. Aware of the danger when two fellow divers were hopelessly trapped in a cave-in of steel wreckage while tunneling with jet nozzles under an LST sunk in 40 feet of water and 20 feet of mud, Hammerberg unhesitatingly went overboard in a valiant attempt to effect their rescue despite the certain hazard of additional cave-ins and the risk of fouling his lifeline on jagged pieces of steel imbedded in the shifting mud. Washing a passage through the original excavation, he reached the first of the trapped men, freed him from the wreckage, and, working desperately in pitch-black darkness, finally effected his release from fouled lines, thereby enabling him to reach the surface. Wearied but undaunted after several hours of arduous labor, Hammerberg resolved to continue his struggle to wash through the oozing, submarine, subterranean mud in a determined effort to save the second diver. Venturing still further under the buried hulk, he held tenaciously to his purpose, reaching a place immediately above the other man just as another cave-in occurred and a heavy piece of steel pinned him crosswise over his shipmate in a position which protected the man beneath from further injury while placing the full brunt of terrific pressure on himself. Although he succumbed in agony eighteen hours after he had gone to the aid of his fellow-divers, Hammerberg, by his cool judgment, unfaltering professional skill, and consistent disregard of all personal danger in the face of tremendous odds, had contributed effectively to the saving of his two comrades. His heroic spirit of self-sacrifice throughout enhanced and sustained the highest traditions of the United States Naval Service. He gallantly gave his life in the service of his country.

WHY THE HAMMERBERG MOH IS UNIQUE

The Hammerberg MOH is of interest in four aspects.

First, it was for a noncombat action. Chapter 14 and Appendix C explain how the Navy MOH created in 1942 could be awarded for combat or noncombat bravery.

Second, for perspective, it was one of only six MOHs awarded to Navy divers. Five were earned when the nation was not at war; Hammerberg's was the only one earned during wartime. The other five were as follows.[21]

- Gunner's Mate Thomas Eadie in rescuing a diver during rescue operations for the submarine S-4, sunk off Massachusetts in 1927.

- Machinist's Mate Chief William Badders, Boatswain's Mate Chief Orson Crandall, Metalsmith Chief James McDonald, and Torpedoman First Class John Mihalowski, all four of whom assisted in rescuing crewmen from the submarine USS Squalus when she sank near Portsmouth, New Hampshire, in 1939.

Third, the Hammerbergs received two MOHs since the mother and father were divorced. The presentation was by Captain G. R. Fairbanks on February 16, 1946, at Grosse Ile Naval Air Station, at Gross Ile, Michigan, to his father and mother (JonnesHammerberg and Elizabeth Moss). The original MOH was presented to his father. The family requested and received a second MOH for his mother and eventually donated both to a museum in Michigan, Michigan's Own, Incorporated Military and Space Museum. Since the museum had no need for both MOHs, it kept the MOH presented to the father and donated the MOH presented to the mother to the Congressional MOH Society when it was aboard USS Intrepid in New York; the Society later moved aboard USS Yorktown at Mount Pleasant, near Charleston, South Carolina. The author saw the Hammerberg Medal displayed there in 2000.[22]

Fourth, the Hammerberg MOH donated to the Congressional MOH Society was stolen in 2004. While working on this book in April 2008, the author discovered a story reporting the theft of seven MOHs from Yorktown in 2004. One was the Hammerberg MOH, and, ironically, another was that of another diver, John Mihalowski, one of the four divers who earned a MOH for the Squalus rescue. The MOHs have not been recovered, and the Federal Bureau of Investigation inquiry into the thefts remains open.[23]

The stolen Hammerberg MOH is essentially worthless to the thief or thieves unless he or they derive intrinsic pleasure in possessing it. First, selling it would pose the danger of discovery and arrest. Second, unlike unidentifiable, generic, or fungible stolen goods that can be sold easily without fear of tracing the goods to the thief, the Hammerberg MOH is easily identified due to the engraving (including his name) on the reverse (assuming the mother's MOH was engraved on the reverse).

The Hammerberg family was lucky, however, because it had two MOHs because of the parents' divorce, so at least one Hammerberg family MOH (the one presented to the father) remains at Michigan's Own in Frankenmuth, Michigan.

COMMANDER SERVICE FORCE
UNITED STATES PACIFIC FLEET

8 March 1945

Mrs. Elizabeth ███████ Hammerberg,
2634 Carter Street,
Detroit, Michigan.

Mother

Owen Francis Patrick Hammerberg,
BM2c, 311-77-40, U.S. Navy.

Dear Mrs. Hammerberg:

Even though I have been in a number of Naval attack operations during the past year, this is the first time I have found it necessary to report a loss of a Salvage man under my command. Although I do not know you, I feel a close kinship; you were with him at his birth, I was present at his passing.

Letters and words do not console nor can they convey depth of feelings that are most personal. They can, however, render conveyance of thoughts and acts. From these we must come to full appreciation of your own son.

Even though oft repeated, I say, "No man renders greater service than he who lays down his life for his fellow man". Your son did just that.

One diver had become embedded in mud under a sunken vessel and a second diver – one who had been working on the opposite side – went down to release him. In so doing, he too was trapped and a third man descended in emergency outfit while additional gear and personnel were being secured. Upon arrival of this aid, which included your son, he was sent to clear the two men who were caught.

He efficiently cleared one, named Fuller, in such a manner as to release him from the steel plate, but could not free his life line. However, he pressed by Fuller to secure release of Brown and to effectuate clearance of Fuller's lines. In so doing, the plate that was holding Brown came to rest against Hammerberg, firmly pinning him.

By his efforts, he released Fuller and literally took his place. Also, when plate came to rest, Hammerberg took weight of steel, protecting Brown, who was now directly under him. On account of Fuller being free, except for life lines, new life lines were sent down, old ones cut off, allowing Fuller to come to surface.

The difficulty in rescue was caused by the mud being impregnated with steel fragments that became embedded in the bottom from the explosion, which originally sank the LST. During the long hours of the first night many such

The Foss Letter (page 1)

COMMANDER SERVICE FORCE
UNITED STATES PACIFIC FLEET

- 2 -

However, we were only jeopardizing Fuller in the narrow tunnel-way and the pieces removed were not releasing pressure on Brown or Hammerberg. With Fuller "surfaced", the plan of rescue resolved itself down to the removal of mud by pump, thus securing safe access to tunnel under vessel where men were trapped. This operation was heart breakingly slow on account of heavy equipment, requiring derrick to handle from top-side and a diver on the bottom. Debris continually clogged the pump and suction.

It was my sole responsibility to effect the rescue of your son. In this I failed. I wish to assure you, however, that every facility of men and equipment of the Navy was placed at my disposal. Among other pieces of equipment we had three derricks, one salvage tug, Navy Yard divers and special submarine doctors standing by during entire effort. Also, Commander Service Force, Pacific Fleet, placed at my disposal three specially skilled civilian divers.

During these trying hours, every man performed his individual duties in a most willing and indefatigable manner. Various close friends of your son stood by his telephone giving him such comfort and encouragement as was possible under the circumstances. This was a most arduous task. Many a message transferred was sent at my request. At these times I tried to express what I thought would be best for him and silently saying what I knew would be in your hearts.

I too have a son of same age over whom I have spilled many tears and endured hours of sad contemplation. I know a little of your bitter anguish and irreparable loss. I know that tears are a great relief for such hours of sad recollection. Some think it is a weakness to weep, but I have come to know refreshment in such silent tribute.

Lieutenant W. A. Czajkowski, USNR, Padre at Aiea Barracks, officiated at burial ceremonies. The grave was blessed, services were held at Halawa Naval Cemetery on 27 February at 2:30 p.m. with Salvage Unit attending. Mass was said by Padre at special services. Pictures taken at service will be sent you as soon as available.

When individuals at Salvage Base contributed to fund for flowers it was found to contain $266.00. $90.00 was spent for flowers and the balance is being sent to you as beneficiary. The thought in mind of Salvage boys was that you would find better use for surplus than would come from additional flowers, that last but a fleeting moment.

May I express to you the heart-felt sympathy of the men of the Pacific Fleet Ship Salvage Unit. They held your son in highest esteem as a shipmate and friend.

The Foss Letter (page 2)

COMMANDER SERVICE FORCE
UNITED STATES PACIFIC FLEET

- 3 -

Having lived is one of God's great gifts. Having lived well is his law. Having made friends along the way, having lived unselfishly, having performed service for his fellow man, having the indomitable courage to face the dangers of the deep unafraid - these are the measure of full life, rather than length of years.

May our words and his acts carry to you comfort and consolation in your great grief. May his mode of life make you proud of his efforts. May your memory of him be always one of affection. May your mother's love be with him always.

Sincerely,

Henry Foss

HENRY FOSS,
Commander, USNR,
Deputy Fleet Salvage Officer.

The Foss Letter (page 3)

The Foss Letter, Transcribed

COMMANDER SERVICE FORCE
UNITED STATES PACIFIC FLEET

8 March 1945

Mrs. Elizabeth (REDACTED) Hammerberg,
2634 Carter Street,
Detroit, Michigan.

Mother

    Owen Francis Patrick Hammerberg,
    BM2c, 311-77-40, U.S. Navy.

Dear Mrs. Hammerberg:

Even though I have been in a number of Naval attack operations during the past year, this is the first time I have found it necessary to report a loss of a Salvage man under my command. Although I do not know you, I feel a close kinship; you were with him at his birth, I was present at his passing.

Letters and words do not console nor can they convey depth of feelings that are most personal. They can, however, render conveyance of thoughts and acts. From these we must come to full appreciation of your own son.

Even though oft repeated, I say, "No man renders greater service than he who lays down his life for his fellow man". Your son did just that.

One diver had become embedded in mud under a sunken vessel and a second diver - one who had been working on the opposite side - went down to release hm. In so doing, he too was trapped and a third man descended in emergency outfit while additional gear and personnel were being secured. Upon arrival of this aid, which included your son, he was sent to clear the two men who were caught.

He efficiently cleared one, named Fuller, in such a manner as to release him from the steel plate, but could not free his life line. However, he pressed by Fuller to secure release of Brown and to effectuate clearance of Fuller's lines. In so doing, the plate that was holding Brown came to rest against Hammerberg, firmly pinning him.

By his efforts, he released Fuller and literally took his place. Also, when plate came to rest, Hammerberg took weight of steel, protecting Brown, who was now directly under him. On account of Fuller being free, except for life lines, new life lines were sent down, old ones cut off, allowing Fuller to come to surface.

The difficulty in rescue was caused by the mud being impregnated with steel fragments that became embedded in the bottom from the explosion, which originally sank the LST. During the long hours of the first night many such pieces were removed hoping to effectuate release of weight on your son.

COMMANDER SERVICE FORCE
UNITED STATES PACIFIC FLEET

- 2 -

However, we were only jeopardizing Fuller in the narrow tunnelway and the pieces removed were not releasing pressure on Brown or Hammerberg. With Fuller "surfaced", the plan of rescue resolved itself down to the removal of mud by pump, thus securing safe access to tunnel under vessel where men were trapped. This operation was heart breakingly slow on account of heavy equipment, requiring derrick to handle from top-side and a diver on the bottom. Debris continually clogged the pump and suction.

It was my sole responsibility to effect the rescue of your son. In this I failed. I wish to assure you, however, that every facility of men and equuipment of the Navy was placed at my disposal. Among other pieces of equipment we had three derricks, one salvage tug, Navy Yard divers and special submarine doctors standing by during entire effort. Also, Commander Service Force, Pacific Fleet, placed at my disposal three specially skilled civilian divers.

During these trying hours, every man performed his individual duties in a most willing and indefatigable manner. Various close firends of your son stood by his telephone giving him such comfort and encouragement as was possible under the circumstances. This was a most arduous task. Many a message transferred was sent at my request. At these times I tried to express what I thought would be best for him and silently saying what I know would be in your hearts.

I too have a son of same age over whom I have spilled many tears and endured hours of sad contemplation. I know a little of your bitter anguish and irreparable loss. I know that tears are a great relief for such hours of sad recollection. Some think it is a weakness to weap [sic], but I have come to know refreshment in such silent tribute.

Lieutenant W.A. Czajkowski, USNR, Padre at Aiea Barracks, officiated at burial ceremonies. The grave was blessed, services were held at Halawa Naval Cemetery on 27 February at 2:30 p.m. with Salvage Unit attending. Mass was said by Padre at special services. Pictures taken at service will be sent you as soon as possible.

When individuals at Salvage Base contributed to fund for flowers it was found to contain $266.00. $90.00 was spent for flowers and the balance is being sent to you as beneficiary. The thought in mind of Salvage boys was that you would find a better use for surplus than would come from additional flowers, that last but a fleeting moment.

May I express to you the heart-felt sympathy of the men of the Pacific Fleet Ship Salvage Unit. They held your son in highest esteem as a shipmate and friend.

COMMANDER SERVICE FORCE
UNITED STATES PACIFIC FLEET

- 3 -

Having lived is one of God's great gifts. Having lived well is his law. Having made friends along the way, having lived unselfishly, having performed service for his fellow man, having the indomitable courage to face the dangers of the deep unafraid - these are the measure of full life, rather than length of years.

May our words and his acts carry to you comfort and consolation in your great grief. May his mode of life make you proud of his efforts. May your memory of him be always one of affection. May your mother's love be with him always.

Sincerely,

HENRY FOSS
Commander, USNR,
Deputy Fleet Salvage Officer.

NOTES

1. Report of US Navy Court of Inquiry ("Subject: Destruction of Six LSTs by Explosions and Fire, West Loch, Oahu, T. H. [Territory of Hawaii]") of May 21, 1944 (hereafter "Court of Inquiry"); "Investigation Report," Fourteenth Naval District, U.S. Intelligence Service ("Subject: Destruction of Six LSTs by Explosions and Fire, West Loch, Oahu, T.H., May 21, 1944") of July 24, 1944 (hereafter Fourteenth Naval District Investigation Report); Gene Eric Salecher, The Second Pearl Harbor: The West Loch Disaster, May 21, 1944 (University of Oklahoma Press, Norman, OK, 2014) (hereafter "Salecher, The Second Pearl Harbor"); Colonel Charles A. Jones, U.S. Marine Corps Reserve (Retired), Hawaii's World War II Military Sites (Mutual Publishing, 2002).

2. Endnote 1, Salecher, The Second Pearl Harbor, 28; Bureau of Naval Personnel, SEAMANSHIP ("NAVPERS 16118," US Navy, Training, Standards, and Curriculum Division), 43.

3. Endnote 1, Court of Inquiry, 16, paragraph 13; Fourteenth Naval District Investigation Report (opinion stated under "Deductions").

4. Endnote 1, Court of Inquiry, 13, paragraph D (smoking while unloading ammunition), and 15, paragraph E (ammunition cases smashed); Fourteenth Naval District Investigation Report, paragraphs 2 C (smoking while unloading ammunition) and 2 D (ammunition cases smashed).

5. Endnote 1, Court of Inquiry, 7, paragraph B (emphasis on leakage or fumes from gasoline drums on the bow that was used by ship's personnel to clean weapons and equipment); Fourteenth Naval District Investigation Report, paragraph 2 B (gasoline on bow used for cleaning). While the Court of Inquiry and the Fourteenth Naval District Investigation mentioned the gasoline drums, neither gave an opinion as to the source of ignition. Each mentioned welding, but the welding had ceased before the explosion; Court of Inquiry, 10, paragraph C; Fourteenth Naval District Investigation Report, paragraph 2 D; Salecher, The Second Pearl Harbor, 65–69 (the source of ignition was most likely cigarette smoking).

6. Official U.S. Navy biography, "Owen Francis Patrick Hammerberg, Boatswain's Mate Second Class, United States Navy" (hereafter "Hammerberg, U.S. Navy biography").

7. Endnote 6, Hammerberg, US Navy biography.

8. The National Personnel Records Center, St. Louis, Missouri, furnished military and personal information from Hammerberg's Official Military Personnel File (OMPF) at the author's request.

9. Letter from Commander Henry Foss, U.S. Naval Reserve, of March 8, 1945, to Mrs. Elizabeth Hammerberg (hereafter "Foss letter"). The MOH citation is at Appendix A of this book (hereafter "Hammerberg MOH citation").

10. Hammerberg MOH citation in this chapter and in Appendix A.

11. Ibid.

12. Endnote 9, Foss letter, page 1.

13 Endnote 9, Foss letter, pages 1 and 2.

14 Hammerberg MOH citation, which in light of the Foss letter must have referred to Fuller and Brown as the two freed comrades; the Foss letter does not mention Brown being freed.

15. Endnote 9, Foss letter, page 2.

16. Ibid., 2.

17. Hammerberg MOH citation; the only time period the Foss letter mentions is "during the long hours of the first night…"

18. Endnote 9, Foss letter, 2.

19. Letter from Secretary of the Navy James Forrestal of March 30, 1945, to Mr. Jonnes Hammerberg.

20. Letter from Lieutenant W. J. McNicol, Jr. (Navy Department, Bureau of Naval Personnel) of May 4, 1945, to Mr. Jonnes Hammerberg; McNicol was the Assistant Officer in Charge of the Casualty Notification and Processing Section.

21. The MOH citations for the divers can be found by searching the Internet for "Army MOH site," which will lead to the Army's master list of MOH recipients. The divers can be found at the section titled "Interim 1920–1940."

22. E-mail of October 7, 2015, from the Congressional Medal of Honor Society to the author; Stan Bozich (director/curator, Michigan's Own, Inc., Military and Space

Museum) letter of November 27, 2000, to the author (hereafter "Bozich letter").

23. Story from America's Most Wanted Internet site: "Congressional Medals of Honor Stolen" (February 12, 2007); e-mail of October 7, 2015 from the Congressional Medal of Honor Society to the author.

Photographs of West Loch and Its MOH Recipient

Petty Officer Second Class (Boatswain's Mate) Owen Francis Patrick Hammerberg, U.S. Navy. (Photograph courtesy of Mr. Stan Bozich, Michigan's Own Military and Space Museum)

One of two MOHs presented to the Hammerberg family. The MOH, displayed at the Congressional Medal of Honor Society, was stolen in 2004, along with other MOHs on display there. (Author's slide, 2000.)

The reverse of the Hammerberg MOH. (Photograph courtesy of Stan Bozich.)

The remains of transport ship LST-480 (landing ship tank) in the West Loch of Pearl Harbor at the Naval Magazine, Pearl Harbor. She is the sole ship remaining from the West Loch Disaster, also called "the Second Pearl Harbor." (Author's slide, 2004.)

Attendees at ceremony marking the sixtieth anniversary commemoration of the West Loch Disaster. (Author's slide, 2004.)

Firing party at the ceremony marking the sixtieth anniversary commemoration of the West Loch Disaster. Its members are armed with M-14 rifles. (Author's slide, 2004.)

Part IV

Medals–
KIA, DOW, MIA, WIA

CHAPTER 14
OVERVIEW
THE MEDALS OF HONOR
EARNED IN THE HAWAIIAN ISLANDS

Knowledge of the attack on Oahu on December 7, 1941, its aftermath, and World War II in the Pacific Theater of Operations (PTO) is incomplete without an overview of the eighteen men who were awarded MOHs—the nation's highest award for combat bravery—for actions in the Hawaiian Islands. Chapters 4 through 13 and 19 of this book recounted the backgrounds and deeds leading to these MOHs. In summary, sixteen MOHs were awarded for actions on December 7—fifteen for Oahu and one for Midway Atoll, which is a part of the Hawaiian Islands. One was awarded for the Battle of Midway in 1942, which is part of the Hawaiian Island Archipelago. In 1945, one MOH was awarded for noncombat action on Oahu in the West Loch of Pearl Harbor.

The nineteenth recipient was Brigadier General Billy Mitchell, U.S. Army, who received a posthumous MOH or Congressional Gold Medal, authorized in 1946 by Congress and the President; the award was not for combat bravery but for foresight in the field of military aviation, which was a key factor in the Hawaiian Islands in World War II not only on December 7, 1941, but also at the Battle of Midway in June 1942.

This chapter is an overview of the MOH recipients as seen from many directions. Much of the information was taken from previous chapters so basic information could be consolidated in this chapter.

For the convenience of the reader and because of the massive amount of process and material presented in this chapter, it is divided into the ten sections listed here. The author's visitation to various sites and memorials is noted in the text of Section 9 ("Burial and Remembrance for the Hawaiian Island MOH Recipients") and Section 10 ("Commemorating the MOH Recipients") to show personal familiarity with the topics in those sections and familiarity with the major commemorations of the MOH recipients. The author could not visit all sites of remembrance and commemoration because of their number and their locations. Finding all such sites and commemorations would probably be impossible.

- Section 1—Summary: MOH Awards for Actions in the Hawaiian Islands during World War II
- Section 2—The Process of Awarding MOHs: In General
- Section 3—The Process of Awarding the Hawaiian Island MOHs during World War II
- Section 4—The Process of Presenting or Transmitting the Hawaiian Island MOHs during World War II
- Section 5—The Process for Awarding the Special MOH for Foresight in Aviation
- Section 6—Interesting Aspects of the Hawaiian Island MOHs
- Section 7—Hawaiian Island MOH "Firsts"
- Section 8—The Hawaiian Island MOHs Themselves
- Section 9—Burial and Remembrance for the Hawaiian Island MOH Recipients

- Section 10—Commemorating the MOH Recipients

★ ★ ★ ★ ★ ★ ★ ★ ★ ★ ★ ★

Section 1—Summary: MOH Awards for Actions in the Hawaiian Islands during World War II

For reader orientation, the following summary of the seventeen combat and one noncombat awards is provided in this section along with note of the special MOH awarded to Billy Mitchell. An asterisk indicates a posthumous award.[1]

Fifteen MOHs for Actions on December 7, 1941, on Oahu

USS *Arizona*
    Lieutenant Commander Samuel Fuqua, U.S. Navy
    Rear Admiral Isaac Kidd, U.S. Navy*
    Captain Franklin Van Valkenburgh, U.S. Navy*

USS *California*
    Ensign Herbert Jones, U.S. Naval Reserve*
    Warrant Officer (Radio Electrician) Thomas Reeves, U.S. Navy*
    Warrant Officer (Gunner) Jackson Pharris, U.S. Navy
    Petty Officer First Class (Machinist's Mate) Robert Scott, U.S. Navy*

USS *Nevada*
    Chief Warrant Officer (Boatswain) Edwin Hill, U.S. Navy*
    Warrant Officer (Machinist) Donald Ross, U.S. Navy

USS *Oklahoma*
    Ensign Francis Flaherty, U.S. Naval Reserve*
    Seaman First Class James Ward, U.S. Navy*

USS *Utah*
    Chief Watertender Peter Tomich, U.S. Navy*

USS *Vestal*
    Commander Cassin Young, U.S. Navy

USS *West Virginia*
    Captain Mervyn Bennion, U.S. Navy*

Naval Air Station Kaneohe Bay
    Aviation Chief Ordnanceman John Finn, U.S. Navy

One MOH for Actions on December 7, 1941, on Midway
Sixth Marine Defense Battalion, First Lieutenant George Cannon, U.S. Marine Corps*

One MOH for Actions on June 4 and 5, 1942, Near Midway

Marine Scout-Bombing Squadron 241, Captain Richard Fleming, U.S. Marine Corps Reserve*

One MOH for Actions on February 17, 1945, on Oahu

Commander, Service Force, U.S. Pacific Fleet (Salvage Unit), Petty Officer Second Class (Boatswain's Mate) Owen Francis Patrick Hammerberg, U.S. Navy*

One Special MOH Awarded to Recognize "Pioneer Service and Foresight" in Military Aviation (1946)

Brigadier General William Mitchell, U.S. Army*2

★ ★ ★ ★ ★ ★ ★ ★ ★ ★ ★ ★

Section 2—The Process of Awarding MOHs: In General

The Historical and Legal Bases for the MOH

Appendix D is a detailed history of the MOH and other awards. The following sections are provided at this point so readers will know the basics of the historical and legal framework for the MOH before reading about individual awards of the MOH.

The key points are the creation of the MOH, how and when various members of the military became eligible for a MOH, and the different roles of Congress and the President in the MOH awards process.

As an analogy, the process is somewhat like a court case involving two steps. First, advocates trying to prove their cases must present facts to the trier of fact—judge or jury. Two, the trier of fact must judge those facts against a certain threshold called the "standard of proof" to determine if the evidence is of sufficient quantity or strength to support the case. In a civil case, the standard is a preponderance of the evidence; in a criminal case, the standard is beyond a reasonable doubt.[3]

Thus, a commander or a board recommending someone for a MOH must present facts meeting a standard of proof such that the facts are judged sufficient to support a MOH award. The statutes do not provide a standard of proof, but as is seen in the Jackson Pharris case in Chapter 19, the standard of proof imposed by the Board of Review for Decorations and Medals, without any citation of authority establishing the standard, was very high; the facts supporting the Pharris MOH had to be "incontestable" or "incontrovertible."[4]

The Roles of Congress and the President

The primary role of Congress, the legislative branch, is enacting legislation creating

MOHs. Its secondary role is enacting legislation governing them, such as establishing time limitations between action and award of a MOH for that action and the action to be rewarded and submitting the report of the action with a recommendation for a MOH.

The primary role of the executive branch (the military and the President) is processing and approving or disapproving MOH recommendations. MOH recommendations approved by the military are forwarded to the president for his or her final approval. After final approval, the President or his or her designee awards a MOH to a service member in the name of Congress. In short, Congress delegated to the president the authority to award MOHs in the name of Congress, and in the vast majority of cases, MOHs are awarded via this delegated power, not by Congress itself enacting legislation to award MOHs to specific individuals. This general procedure of Presidential approval of MOH awards for individuals in the name of Congress, however, does not deprive Congress of certain powers concerning the MOH.[5] Three cases will serve as examples of congressional involvement in individual MOHs.

One, Congress, although giving the President the power to award MOHs in its name, retained the authority itself to award MOHs to specific individuals by legislation. By such legislation, MOHs were awarded for achievement in exploration to Lieutenant Commander Richard E. Byrd[6] for flying over the North Pole and awarded for achievement in travel to Charles Lindbergh for flying nonstop from New York City to Paris.[7] Congress also enacted legislation authorizing the Billy Mitchell MOH award discussed throughout this book.[8]

Again, however, Congress, as a general rule, is uninvolved in the awarding of MOHs to specific individuals. The mistaken belief that Congress is involved in individual awards is probably based on the frequent but erroneous inclusion of "Congressional" before "Medal of Honor," thus giving rise to the erroneous title "Congressional Medal of Honor." The correct title is "Medal of Honor" (the term used in current statutes is "medal of honor" without the "Congressional" modifier or without capitalization).[9] The only place the author has seen "Medal of Honor" in the statutes is in the header for the special MOH for Billy Mitchell (see Chapter 20 and the title and text of the Mitchell MOH).

MOH Legislation

Congress created the first MOH in 1861; it was only for enlisted members of the Marine corps and Navy. This MOH was the first MOH created.

Over the years, Congress created other MOHs and revised its MOH statutes. Two important statutes concern the men who are the subject of this book.

One was Congressional legislation in 1919 creating a Naval service MOH for officers and enlisted members of the Navy, Marine Corps, and Coast Guard, modeled after the MOH Congress created in 1918 for the Army. The criteria are as follows: the President presented the MOH in the name of Congress to any officer or enlisted member of the Naval service who, in action involving actual conflict with an enemy, distinguished himself conspicuously by gallantry and intrepidity at the risk of his life above and beyond the call of duty without detriment to the mission. The "without detriment to the mission" criterion was not in the Army MOH legislation of 1918.

The other was Congressional legislation in 1942 creating a Navy MOH (or more specifically, a Naval service MOH) with the same criteria as the 1919 Navy MOH, but the legislation made the MOH an award for both combat and noncombat bravery by adding the phrase in italics, "…*in action involving actual conflict with the enemy, or in the line of his profession,* distinguish himself conspicuously by gallantry and intrepidity at the risk of his life above and beyond the call of duty…" The phrase "in the line of his profession" allowed for a noncombat Navy MOH; this language is not in the statute for the Army MOH Congress created in 1918.

Again the correct term then and now is "Medal of Honor," not the commonly used but erroneous "Congressional Medal of Honor." The MOH statutes never used or use the term "Congressional Medal of Honor."

What was noted earlier is that the legislation establishing the criteria for a MOH does not include a standard of proof against which facts supporting a MOH recommendation must be judged to determine if they warrant a MOH. The question here is not the action that may deserve a MOH but the strength of evidence proving the action. For example, how strong must the facts be to support a MOH recommendation: mere assertions by one or more witnesses (e.g., Soldier A says that Soldier B stopped a bayonet charge by himself); some facts; a preponderance of the evidence (civil court cases); or beyond a reasonable doubt (civil and military criminal cases)? The only award in this book for which a standard was mentioned was the Pharris MOH, which is the subject of chapter 19.[10] In addition to the absence of a standard of proof in the MOH statutes, a plain reading of the statutes reveals no requirement concerning the number or status of witnesses to the action for which the MOH is recommended.

Section 3—The Process of Awarding the Hawaiian Island MOHs during World War II

This chapter discusses process in the context of MOHs that saw little or no deviation from the standard process of awarding MOHs. Some of the discussion will be repeated as necessary in two chapters: chapter 15, which concerns a MOH process that led to two MOHs (Kidd and Van Valkenburgh) that were undeserved because they lacked factual bases, and chapter 19, which concerns a MOH (Pharris) that was more than deserved yet withheld from the recipient via a prolonged, well-documented process of ensuring that every "i" was dotted and every "t" crossed—not only dotted and crossed but precisely so, a process foreign to the undeserved Kidd and Van Valkenburgh MOHs that were "shoehorned" into the process without regard to factual basis.

But returning to the average MOH award, one will see that the process is fairly well established but, again, like every governmental process, not completely immune to political considerations.

First, the recipient had to meet the statutory requirements for a MOH; he must have displayed, while engaged in action with the enemy, conspicuous gallantry above and beyond the call of duty. During World War II, the Navy MOH—due to the addition in 1942 of the "in the line of his profession" language just noted—could be awarded for noncombat action that met the remainder of the statutory requirements. The Hammerberg MOH for actions in 1945 in the West Loch of Pearl Harbor is such a case.[11]

Second, the action had to be known to the person's command.

Third, the individual had to be recommended for a MOH. The recommendation could originate from the commanding officer or an awards board; some commands have awards boards in the field to determine who should be recommended for what award.

Fourth, the recommendation had to be submitted via the chain of command to the member's department (War or Navy) for review.

Fifth, MOH recommendations approved by the department were sent to the president for his action, either final approval or disapproval of the recommendations.

The Fleming (Midway) and Hammerberg (West Loch) MOH recommendations followed this process without any complexity or delay.

The December 7 MOH recommendations are a different story. The primary differences from the typical process were two. One was the large number of number of MOH recommendations originally considered—twelve, with that number increasing to fourteen with the inclusion of two "add-ons" (Kidd and Van Valkenburgh). Two was the omission, for whatever reasons, of two men from this group of fourteen. One was Finn, whose MOH was approved in June 1942 soon after the original fourteen were approved (March 4, 1942). Two was Pharris, suffering a process that went horribly sideways and involved, to say the least, extraordinary delay in processing and presentation, culminating in his 1948 MOH award for actions on December 7.

The original twelve MOH recommendations were likely the recommendations of the awards board mentioned by Admiral Chester Nimitz in his February 15, 1942, report of the December 7 attack. Near the report's end, he wrote that a "Board of Awards, headed by Rear Admiral Robert A. Theobald, US Navy, is currently in session for the purpose of making recommendations for awards incident to the Pearl Harbor attack." The author believes this board to be the "Fleet Board of Awards" mentioned in the Navy's Permanent Board of Awards "Third Endorsement," discussed here and found by chance in the service record of Rear Admiral Isaac Kidd, obtained from the National Personnel Records Center. Repeated attempts to obtain any information about the "Board of Awards" mentioned by Nimitz or any report of its recommendations were unsuccessful.[12] Thus the Third Endorsement is the closest one can get to the report by the Fleet Board of Awards.

Next, the recommendations had to be reviewed in the field as would any MOH recommendation submitted for Presidential presentation in the name of Congress.

Review of the Fleet Board recommendations would most likely have been in this order:

The Commander in Chief of the U.S. Pacific Fleet, Admiral Chester Nimitz, would have made the first endorsement on the Fleet Board's report. The second endorsee is unknown.[13]

The Navy Department Permanent Board of Awards, whose review and action were addressed to the Secretary of the Navy, made the third endorsement on the Fleet Board's report.

The Permanent Board, established by the Secretary of the Navy in 1927 to review award recommendations, comprised three members; it also had a Navy lieutenant commander as recorder (administrative assistant).[14] The Senior Member was Rear Admiral J. O. Richardson, whom President Roosevelt had relieved of command of the Pacific Fleet because Richardson objected to moving the Fleet from the United States West Coast to Oahu (his replacement was Rear Admiral Husband Kimmel, who commanded the Fleet on December 7). The other two members were Navy Rear Admiral A. C. Pickens and one Marine, Brigadier General W. N. Hill (Retired).

The Board wrote a Third Endorsement of the report of the Fleet Board of Awards, submitted by Admiral Nimitz to the Secretary of the Navy; the endorsement contained numerous recommendations for awards, including MOHs and added two MOH recommendations to the twelve recommended by the Fleet Board. A Third Endorsement means that two other officers or agencies had reviewed the report before the third endorsee (the Permanent Board) reviewed it, but those officers and agencies are unidentified in the Third Endorsement, although as just noted, Admiral Nimitz, the Commander in Chief of the U.S. Pacific Fleet, would almost certainly have been the first officer to review and endorse the Fleet Board's report—after all, he created the board of awards in his February 15, 1942, report of the attack.[15]

The Secretary of the Navy, Frank Knox, approved the Permanent Board's endorsement on February 27, 1942. By his memorandum of March 3, 1942, Knox forwarded the fourteen MOH recommendations to the President for his action.[16]

The President, who had the final-approval authority for MOH recommendations, signed the fourteen MOH citations on March 4, 1942, thus approving all fourteen.[17]

Congressional absence in this process is clear. While Congressional legislation created and governed the MOHs, the process of recommending, reviewing, and approving individual cases occurred solely within the executive, not the legislative, branch of the federal government, meaning action exclusively by the military and by the President.[18]

The Original Navy and Marine MOH Recommendations for December 7

To backtrack, as can be determined by the Third Endorsement, the Fleet Board of Awards recommended only twelve men for MOHs for December 7. All were at Pearl

Harbor except for Cannon, who was on Midway.[19]

- Bennion
- Cannon
- Flaherty
- Fuqua
- Hill
- Jones
- Reeves
- Ross
- Scott
- Tomich
- Ward
- Young

As explained in detail in Chapter 15, the Fleet Board of Awards did not recommend Kidd or Van Valkenburgh, officers who perished on *Arizona*, for any award; the Fleet Board did not even mention their names in its report. The Navy Department Permanent Board of Awards, in its report to the Secretary of the Navy, noted the Fleet Board's omission of these officers and wrote that "acting on the directive of the Secretary," it recommended that these two officers be awarded posthumous MOHs and included proposed MOH citations for each officer. As proven in Chapter 15, the two awards must have been the results of political considerations; they certainly were not based on facts or the merits of what the officers did in just a few minutes on December 7. Thus, the President was finally presented fourteen, not twelve, recommendations for MOHs for December 7.[20]

THE FIRST MOH RECOMMENDATIONS APPROVED FOR DECEMBER 7

With the inclusion of Kidd and Van Valkenburgh, Secretary of the Navy Frank Knox forwarded to President Roosevelt the fourteen MOH citations for his signature. In his March 3, 1942, cover memorandum to the President, Knox stated that the fourteen citations were for men exhibiting "conspicuous conduct" on December 7; the wording of the Secretary's cover letter clearly implies he recommended the President approve all fourteen MOH recommendations.[21]

President Franklin D. Roosevelt approved the MOH recommendations by signing the citations on March 4, 1942, for the fourteen men (asterisks indicate the two names the Permanent Board added):[22]

- Bennion
- Cannon
- Flaherty
- Fuqua
- Hill
- Jones
- Kidd*
- Reeves

- Ross
- Scott
- Tomich
- Ward
- Young
- Van Valkenburgh*

All awards were posthumous except those of Fuqua, Ross, and Young.[23] As already mentioned and as discussed in more detail to follow, Finn and Pharris had survived December 7 and would receive MOHs after these fourteen recipients.

Cannon, a Marine lieutenant, was the only Marine MOH recipient for December 7. He earned his MOH on Midway and was the only Midway MOH recipient for December 7. The remaining thirteen men earned their MOHs at Pearl Harbor proper (twelve on Battleship Row, one on Carrier Row).[24] Finn was the only Oahu recipient who was not at Pearl Harbor; Pharris, who would receive his MOH in 1948, was at Pearl Harbor.

ADDITIONAL HAWAIIAN ISLAND MOH AWARDS: DECEMBER 7

The names of two men, John Finn and Jackson Pharris, were not among the list of fourteen names of men the Third Endorsement recommended for MOHs. The Secretary of the Navy submitted no MOH citations for these two men to the President for approval in March 1942 when he submitted the fourteen names the Board, in the Third Endorsement, recommended for MOHs. Each, however, ultimately received a MOH for December 7.

President Roosevelt signed a MOH citation for Finn in June 1942. Why Finn was not on the original list of MOH recommendations submitted by the Fleet or Permanent Boards is unknown. Perhaps the omission was due to him being stationed at Kaneohe Bay's Naval Air Station rather than Pearl Harbor; Kaneohe was farther north and more isolated than Pearl Harbor, the headquarters and nerve center of Fleet activity.[25] The copy of the citation provided by the Franklin D. Roosevelt Presidential Library to the author does not have the date of signature but states that it was prepared "June 6, 1942," and that the original signed copy of the citation was sent to the Navy Department on June 20, 1942.

Warrant Officer (Gunner) Jackson Pharris of USS *California* (on Battleship Row) was omitted from the MOH recommendation list because the Navy Department Permanent Board of Awards concurred in the Fleet Board's recommendation that he receive a Navy Cross; thus Pharris is under the heading of men recommended for Navy Crosses. Because of the initiative of J. W. Bunkley, Pharris's commanding officer on December 7 (the captain of USS *California*), his Navy Cross was upgraded to a MOH after the war. In 1948, President Truman both approved the MOH recommendation and presented the MOH to Pharris, making him the last December 7 MOH recipient to receive his MOH, approximately six and one-half years after the actions supporting the MOH. Chapter 19 discusses the long, arduous effort expended to have the Pharris Navy Cross upgraded to a MOH.[26]

Additional Hawaiian Island MOH Awards:
Midway and West Loch

On November 10, 1942, President Roosevelt signed the citation for a posthumous MOH for Captain Richard Fleming, U.S. Marine Corps Reserve, for his actions during the Battle of Midway in June 1942. November 10 is celebrated annually by Marines as being the "birthday" or founding of the U.S. Marine Corps.[27]

By an undated memorandum, Secretary of the Navy Forrestal transmitted to President Harry Truman's Naval aide a citation for a MOH for Petty Officer Second Class (Boatswain's Mate) Owen Hammerberg, requesting that the President sign it. President Harry S. Truman was the vice president who became president after the death of President Roosevelt on April 12, 1945.[28] On October 3, 1945, President Truman signed the citation for a posthumous noncombat MOH for Hammerberg, but a second memorandum dated November 23, 1945, transmitted to the Naval aide a citation "rewritten in accordance with the attached letter" (the author did not receive the "attached letter" from the Truman Library and Museum). The President signed the revised citation on November 26, 1945.[29]

Hammerberg is the only recipient in this book to have a classic MOH for noncombat bravery; as explained in this Chapter and in Appendix D, in 1942, Congress revised the Navy MOH legislation such that it authorized MOHs for noncombat bravery. The recipient's actions still had to meet the criteria of the statute, but it could occur in one of two cases: in conflict with an enemy or "in the line of [the recipient's] profession." Hammerberg obviously qualified under the "line of profession" category. The author cannot imagine an objection to a noncombat MOH for Hammerberg given his actions in the circumstances in West Loch on February 17, 1945, and given the noncombat MOHs Congress itself had directed for other men.

MOH Citations and Medals

The citations can be found in Chapters 4 through 13 and 19 and in Appendix A. Sections 4 and 8 in this chapter discuss the MOHs themselves and the engraving on the reverse of the MOHs known to the author.

Time Required from Action to MOH Approval and Presentation: World War II Versus Modern War

In a time of war, the MOH approval process could be expeditious. For example, the president approved the original fourteen MOH recommendations for December 7, 1941, on March 4, 1942, just short of three months between MOH actions and Presidential approval of the MOH recommendations. The exact period between action and approval was eighty-seven days in this time of war—the remainder of December (twenty-four days), January (thirty-one days), February (twenty-eight days), and March (four) days.

The next process, which involved various time periods, was the time after

MOH recommendation approval and transmitting the MOH to the next of kin for posthumous awards or presenting MOHs to living recipients. The time of receipt could range from March 1942, when some of the posthumous MOHs approved in March were sent by registered mail to the next of kin, to presentation to living recipients as shown in Table 14-1, with Fuqua receiving his first (March 19, 1942) and Pharris receiving his last (June 25, 1948); as noted earlier, the time between action and award was slightly more than six and one-half years. Thus the wartime awards were processed and presented fairly quickly, with the Pharris award an aberration, requiring a longer time because of his initial receipt of a Navy Cross and because of the time required after the war to upgrade his Navy Cross to a MOH.

Today, eighty-seven days would be the aberration and the time required for the Pharris award would be the norm. In other words, the time from action to award today is extreme compared to the time from action to award in World War II. For example, the action in Afghanistan leading to a MOH for Army Staff Sergeant Ryan Pitts was on July 13, 2008. He did not receive his MOH from President Barack Obama until July 21, 2014, six years and eight days from action to award.[30]

While some delay is inherent in the process because of time required to uncover and to investigate the facts justifying a MOH award, one wonders why that delay was so short in World War II and so long today or, in World War II, so long for Jackson Pharris. Such delay, in World War II or today, is an inexcusable embarrassment for the U.S. military and is no way to treat the bravest of the brave. Much can happen in six years, including loss of documents, dimming of memories, and disappearance or deaths of witnesses—or the death of the proposed MOH recipient. One would think that expeditious processing would be the norm, not the exception. Delay due to "lost" or "misplaced" recommendations is yet another slap in the face for the member who ultimately receives a MOH. Only two excuses for delay seem acceptable. One is commanders not learning of MOH actions until months or years after they occurred; they cannot submit recommendations for MOHs or any award if they do not know what members did in combat to justify a MOH. The other excuse is difficulty in locating witnesses.

Delay in awarding MOHs to minorities is regrettable but understandable given the way minorities were treated long ago—as second-class citizens. Only when society, Congress, and the military evolved and treated minorities and majorities equally did former minority service members receive MOHs they should have received during or shortly after a war. As can be seen by Congressional action, Congress attempted to address racial disparity in MOH awards and in many cases succeeded.

In summary, the United States is not now and has not been in a world war since 1945, yet the Pitts MOH took an absurdly long processing time when few MOH recommendations were being processed. Yet when the United States was in World War II and perhaps thousands of awards were being processed, including MOHs, one should consider that a famous MOH recipient, Audie Murphy, who earned his MOH based on his actions on January 26, 1945, received his MOH in the field on June 2, 1945.[31]

Section 4—The Process of Presenting or Transmitting the Hawaiian Island MOHs during World War II

This section provides details concerning the MOHs presented to living recipients and presented or transmitted to the next of kin of posthumous recipients where information about presentation or transmission is known (such information is unavailable for some recipients).

An overview shows that MOHs (the MOHs and their corresponding paper citations) were presented or transmitted in three ways.

Living recipient presentation at a ceremony—Table 14-1 shows that MOHs were presented in person to these men: Fuqua, Young, Ross, Finn, and Pharris.[32]

Posthumous awards presented to family members in person—the following posthumous MOHs are known to have been presented in person to the recipient's family: Fleming, Hammerberg, and Tomich. The presentations are discussed later in this chapter.

Posthumous awards sent by registered mail—The following posthumous MOHs are known to have been sent to the recipient's next of kin by registered mail: Bennion, Cannon, Kidd, Scott, Van Valkenburgh, and Ward.[33] While on the surface sending the MOH to the next of kin by registered mail may seem callous, one must remember that world wars were ongoing in the Pacific and in Europe when the MOHs were approved; wartime exigencies thus made personal presentation by the President to every recipient or to his next of kin impractical in wartime. President Roosevelt did, however, make some wartime presentations, such as the presentation to Captain Fleming's mother described in this chapter.

Some additional details about the process of presentation or transmission of the MOHs as well as about the MOHs themselves are offered in the following paragraphs.

Presenting the December 7 MOHs to Living Recipients

Recipient	Date of Presentation	Presentation Details
Samuel Fuqua	March 19, 1942	Presented by Vice Admiral Royal Ingersoll, Naval Training Station, Newport, RI
Cassin Young	April 18, 1942	Presented by Admiral Chester Nimitz aboard USS Enterprise, Pearl Harbor, TH
Donald Ross	April 18, 1942	Presented by Admiral Chester Nimitz aboard USS Enterprise, Pearl Harbor, TH
John Finn	September 15, 1942	Presented by Admiral Chester Nimitz aboard USS Enterprise, Pearl Harbor, TH
Jackson Pharris	June 25, 1948	Presented by President Harry Truman, White House, Washington, DC

Table 14-1

Detail: West Virginia MOH Recipient Captain Mervyn Bennion

The Bennion MOH arrived in Salt Lake City by mail on March 17, 1942, and was delivered to Bennion's widow. A newspaper article described the delivery and had a photograph of the MOH and its citation signed by President Roosevelt. It also described the inscription on the reverse of the MOH, an inscription that would be similar for the December 7 MOHs. Curiously, the inscriptions used the "in the line of his profession" language in the 1942 Navy MOH statute rather than a reference to gallantry and intrepidity above and beyond the call of duty.

> CAPT. MERVYN S. BENNION, US NAVY DECEASED.
> FOR DISTINGUISHED CONDUCT
> IN THE LINE OF HIS
> PROFESSION ON OCCASION
> JAPANESE ATTACK ON
> PEARL HARBOR,
> TERRITORY OF HAWAII,
> DECEMBER 7, 1941

The article included testimonials from those who knew him, stating that he was a "fine gentleman, respected by all, a good example to all his juniors" and a man of "marvelous character."[34]

Detail: Oklahoma MOH Recipients Ensign Francis Flaherty

The Flaherty MOH was presented or sent to his brother, John J. Flaherty, on March 6, 1946.[35]

The brother gave the MOH to his sister, Frances Dolores Perry, who donated it to Michigan's Own, Incorporated, Military and Space Museum in Frankenmuth, Michigan. The reverse of the MOH is engraved as follows.[36]

> ENSIGN
> FRANCIS C. FLAHERTY,
> US NAVAL RESERVE,
> DECEASED
> FOR DISTINGUISHED CONDUCT
> IN THE LINE OF HIS
> PROFESSION ON OCCASION
> JAPANESE ATTACK ON
> PEARL HARBOR,
> TERRITORY OF HAWAII,
> DECEMBER 7, 1941

SEAMAN FIRST CLASS JAMES WARD

The Ward MOH was sent to his parents by registered mail with a cover letter signed by the Secretary of the Navy.[37] The reverse of the Ward MOH reads as follows.[38]

> SEAMAN FIRST CLASS
> JAMES R. WARD,
> US NAVY, DECEASED
> FOR DISTINGUISHED CONDUCT
> IN THE LINE OF HIS
> PROFESSION ON OCCASION
> JAPANESE ATTACK ON
> PEARL HARBOR,
> TERRITORY OF HAWAII,
> DECEMBER 7, 1941

A one-page handwritten letter of March 17, 1942, from Ward's parents to President Roosevelt thanked him for the MOH and citation. The second paragraph reads as follows:

> This is an honor and blessing not given to everyone. Neither is the privilege to live in a country where such things are recognized and honored, and we are very proud that we are a part of the United States of America.[39]

By letter dated March 23, 1942, the President's Naval aide, Captain John L. McCrea, wrote the Wards a short message: "The President has directed that I acknowledge with appreciation the receipt of your letter of March 17, 1942."[40]

In March 1942, Ward's parents, Nancy and Howard, received the letter noted previously, the letter signed by Secretary of the Navy Frank Knox dated March 14, 1942, that the Wards reproduced by hand in a data sheet they completed when writing a man in North Carolina who had requested information about their son and his MOH (see discussion following). The Knox letter as reproduced by the Wards is as follows.[46]

> Mr. dear [sic] Mr. Ward:
>
> I deem it an honor to transmit to you the Congressional Medal of Honor and citation awarded your late son James R. Ward, Seaman First Class, United States Navy, by the President of the United States in the name of Congress for his conspicuous conduct in the line of his profession.
>
> The Medal of Honor is being forwarded this date under separate cover by registered mail.
>
> Sincerely yours,
> Frank Knox

At some point, confusion and error arose when Ward was thought to be a North Carolina native. In 1951, the Wards received a letter from the navy's director of medals and awards, advising them that they would receive a book about Navy MOH recipients. In the book the Wards received, they read that Ward's enlistment site was erroneously listed as North Carolina, not Ohio, the state of his birth and enlistment.[42]

The Wards notified the Navy of the error, but since the book had been printed, the Navy informed the Wards that the error could not be corrected. The Navy assured them, however, that the error would be corrected in future books and that both Ohio and North Carolina would be notified. The Wards assumed that the error had been corrected "in all other military records" and that both states were notified of the error.[43]

On March 7, 1974, Ward's parents wrote Carl A. Robin, the North Carolina state director of the Medal of Honor History RoundTable, providing information about their son since Robin had written them asking for information about him. Robin apparently thought that Ward was from North Carolina or had enlisted there; a copy of Ward's citation in the book Medal of Honor the Navy had sent them erroneously stated Ward's enlistment was "Accredited to: North Carolina." The Wards explained the error and continued,

> Please know that we have nothing against the great State of North Carolina. We only know, or feel, if our son had his choice, he would rather be remembered by, and along with, those of his classmates and others who he had known most of his life. Some who also gave their lives in W.W.2.[44]

The Wards completed for the RoundTable a "Recipient Data Sheet" with information about their son, cited in endnotes 37 and 41.

On March 9, 1974, the Wards wrote the Navy, forwarding a copy of their March 7 letter to Robin, expressing their frustration that apparently their son was still thought to have enlisted from North Carolina rather than Ohio; in substance, they were wondering why they received a letter from North Carolina asking about their son as if he were a North Carolina MOH recipient. They recited the assurances the Navy had given them in 1951 that the error would be corrected. They continued as follows:

> When we received this assurance [from the Navy we] were confident the error had been corrected, especially in the US Senate records. And now, February 1974, 23 years later, comes this letter from [Mr. Robin in] North Carolina asking for the complete history and giving the enlistment site as North Carolina. We feel strongly that this correction should have been made a long time ago.
>
> If James Richard Ward is to be remembered, we would prefer, and we are very sure he would prefer to be remembered by, and align with, those whom he had known most of his life; young men, some to serve and return home, others who also gave their lives in W.W.2.

We would appreciate it very much if you would decide if his enlistment site is Ohio, and if not, why not?⁴⁵

Detail: Arizona MOH Recipients

Rear Admiral Isaac Kidd

The Kidd MOH was sent to Mrs. Inez Kidd, the widow, by registered mail, addressed to Annapolis, Maryland. Accompanying it was a letter of March 11, 1942, signed by Secretary of the Navy Frank Knox.⁴⁶

Captain Franklin Van Valkenburgh

The Van Valkenburgh MOH was sent to Mrs. Marguerite Van Valkenburgh, the widow, by registered mail, addressed to Long Beach, California. Accompanying it was a letter of March 11, 1942, similar to the letter sent to Mrs. Kidd.⁴⁷

Detail: Nevada MOH Recipients

Chief Boatswain Edwin Hill

The author was unable to find presentation data for the Hill MOH.

Warrant Officer (Machinist) Donald Ross

Admiral Chester Nimitz, Commander in Chief, U.S. Pacific Fleet, presented Ross his MOH on April 18, 1942, aboard USS Enterprise.⁵³

Detail: California MOH Recipients

Ensign Herbert Jones

The author was unable to find presentation data for the Jones MOH.

Warrant Officer (Gunner) Jackson Pharris

See Chapter 19; an entire chapter had to be devoted to the Pharris MOH because of the protracted ordeal leading to the Pharris MOH. Details about his MOH are in that chapter.

Warrant Officer (Radio Electrician) Thomas Reeves

The author was unable to find presentation data for the Reeves MOH.

Petty Officer First Class (Machinist's Mate) Robert Scott

As indicated earlier in this chapter and in Chapter 4 (*California*), the Scott MOH was sent to his next of kin (mother) by registered mail. The reverse of the Scott MOH reads as follows.⁴⁹

> MACHINIST'S MATE FIRST CLASS
> ROBERT R. SCOTT,
> US NAVY,
> DECEASED
> FOR DISTINGUISHED CONDUCT
> IN THE LINE OF HIS
> PROFESSION ON OCCASION
> JAPANESE ATTACK ON
> PEARL HARBOR,
> TERRITORY OF HAWAII,
> DECEMBER 7, 1941

Detail: Vestal MOH Recipient

Commander Cassin Young

Admiral Chester Nimitz presented Young his MOH on April 18, 1942, aboard USS *Vestal*. By this time, Young had been promoted to captain, as can be seen by the four stripes on each of his uniform shirt's shoulder boards.[50]

Two Cassin Young Medals of Honor

Cassin Young has two MOHs, as explained here. What cannot be determined is why he or his family obtained two MOHs, one of which is at the National Museum of the Pacific War and the other at the Naval Academy Museum. The reverse of the Young MOH held by the National Museum of the Pacific War reads as follows.[51]

> COMMANDER CASSIN YOUNG
> US NAVY
> FOR DISTINGUISHED CONDUCT
> IN THE LINE OF HIS
> PROFESSION ON OCCASION
> JAPANESE ATTACK ON
> PEARL HARBOR,
> TERRITORY OF HAWAII,
> DECEMBER 7, 1941

As just noted, the National Museum of the Pacific War (formerly the Nimitz Museum) in Fredericksburg, Texas, has a Cassin Young MOH that appears to the original since the reverse was inscribed as noted, as are original MOHs.

In 1943, Young's widow sponsored the destroyer named for him and loaned the ship a plaque with a MOH complete with ribbon. Because this MOH is mounted, the viewer cannot see the back of the MOH and thus cannot see if it has an inscription. The family later requested the return of the mounted MOH. After receiving it, the family donated it to the Naval Academy Museum.[52]

Detail: Utah MOH Recipient

Chief Petty Officer (Watertender) Peter Tomich

If readers think that two MOHs for Cassin Young causes confusion, they will find true confusion and intrigue in the one Tomich MOH, which traveled the most bizarre but most interesting path from approval to ultimate presentation to next of kin.

A MOH can generate great interest and controversy, as can be seen from Chapter 20, which discusses the Billy Mitchell MOH; the controversy there was issuance. The Tomich MOH has an interesting history, indicated by a flurry of letters demonstrating the level of interest and controversy a MOH can generate. The controversy with the Tomich MOH is receipt: Who gets the MOH?

Tomich had named a cousin as next of kin, John Tomich of Los Angeles, California, but the cousin could not be found.[53] Thus, the questions in Tomich's case were simple. What does a military service do with an unclaimed MOH? What person or institution would receive the Tomich MOH?

The following chronology follows the odyssey of the Tomich MOH.

- 1944—Presentation of MOH to USS Tomich

Unable to locate the cousin, Navy Rear Admiral Monroe Kelly presented the MOH to the destroyer escort named for Tomich, USS Tomich, on January 4, 1944.[54]

- 1946—Decommissioning USS Tomich

When the ship was decommissioned in 1946, the MOH was returned to the Navy Department.[55]

- 1946—Steele Letter

Mr. J. M. Steele wrote the Navy's Director of Public Relations on October 30, 1946, noting that he had recently dedicated a plaque in Salt Lake City honoring men who died on *Utah*. He also stated that during his address, he had mentioned Tomich and his MOH. After the ceremony, he told *Utah* Governor Herbert Maw that he understood that the Navy could not find any next of kin to whom to present the MOH. The Governor suggested to Steele that if Steele's understanding were true, the Governor would be glad to place the MOH beside the plaque dedicated by Steele. Steele asked the Navy to send the MOH to the governor if the MOH had not already been presented elsewhere.[56]

- 1947—Honorary Citizenship and Delivery of MOH to *Utah*

On May 25, 1947, the Governor of *Utah* formally made Tomich an honorary citizen of *Utah*. At a ceremony on that date with full military honors in the *Utah* Capitol rotunda, the Navy presented the MOH and its citation to *Utah* with the state being Tomich's official guardian.[57]

- 1986—Letter to VFW Magazine

A letter to the editor of the VFW (Veterans of Foreign Wars) magazine, printed in the February 1986 issue mentioned Tomich. The author of the letter had met Tomich during his own Navy career, served with him on Litchfield (a four-stack destroyer), and had read the article "USS *Utah*: The Forgotten Memorial," published in the VFW magazine's December 1985 issue. He wrote that Tomich was a "dedicated Navy man" and that he knew of "no one more deserving" of the MOH Tomich received.[58]

- 1985—Vaessen Letter

In 1985, then *Utah* Senator Jake Garn wrote Vaessen, the crewman mentioned in Chapter 10, who was rescued through a hole cut in *Utah*'s hull, about the location of the Tomich MOH. He informed Vaessen that *Utah*, his "home state," had accepted the MOH in 1947 but that it was now at the Navy Historical Center in Washington, DC.[59]

- 1997—Bucha Letter

On June 23, 1997, Paul W. Bucha, president of the Congressional MOH Society, wrote a navy rear admiral in the New York Naval Militia, stating that in the twentieth century, only one MOH had gone unclaimed—the Tomich MOH. He stated that a proper recipient could not be found after the President approved the MOH. He noted that Tomich's birthplace on the citation was listed as Prolog, Austria. He requested that the rear admiral, who was about to visit Croatia, assist in finding a next of kin who could receive the MOH.[60]

- Don Chvarak Correspondence

Mr. Chvarak, a retired Army chief warrant officer, expressed great interest in the Tomich MOH.

On October 15, 1997, the Public Affairs Officer at the Naval Education and Training Center in Newport, Rhode Island, wrote Mr. Chvarak that the reverse of the Tomich MOH displayed at the Center to honor Tomich was not inscribed with Tomich's name.[61]

On November 4, 1997, Chvarak, by letter, expressed concern that the Tomich MOH displayed at Naval Education and Training Center in Newport, Rhode Island, was not the original since Tomich's name was not on the reverse and the MOH may have been made by a company that had been cited for making "contraband medals."[62]

On November 3, 1997, a senior chief petty officer representing the Service School Command at Great Lakes, Illinois, wrote Chvarak that the reverse of the MOH displayed at Great Lakes to honor Tomich had "Display" on the reverse, indicating it was a copy. He noted that the original Tomich MOH was "donated to the Navy Museum in Washington, DC, on 28 November 1978."[63]

On November 13, 1997, Chvarak wrote the Congressional MOH Society, noting he was involved in Croatian genealogy. He stated that the original MOH was at the Navy Historical Center and that Great Lakes and Newport had display copies of the MOH. He claimed to have found the Tomich next of kin in Croatia and recommended that the next of kin be presented the original MOH. He also asked for a display MOH for the Croatian Fraternal Union Museum in Pittsburgh, Pennsylvania.[64]

On November 19, 1997, the Naval Historical Center wrote Chvarak, informing him that the Center had the Tomich MOH. Attached with the letter was a brief description of the Tomich MOH, which in part reads, "Navy Medal of Honor W/10" Neck Ribbon Inscr. [sic] On Back & [sic] Watertender Peter Tomich, USN, Jap. P. H. Attack, 5-Point Star…"[65]

- MOH presentation in 2006

The MOH remained at the Naval Historical Center until 2006. On May 18, 2006, Admiral Harry Ulrich, commander of U.S. Forces Europe, presented the Tomich MOH to a retired Croatian army lieutenant colonel, Srecko Tonic, on behalf of the Tomich family; the lieutenant colonel was the grandson of Tomich's cousin, John Tomich, who as earlier noted in this chapter, Tomich had indicated as his next of kin but who could not be found. The ceremony occurred aboard the aircraft carrier USS Enterprise.[66]

The reverse of the Tomich MOH, the MOH that traveled such an interesting path from issuance to final presentation, can be seen on the Naval History and Heritage Command website; its wording is as follows:

CHIEF WATER TENDER
PETER TOMICH
US NAVY, DECEASED
FOR DISTINGUISHED CONDUCT
IN THE LINE OF HIS
PROFESSION ON OCCASION
JAPANESE ATTACK ON
PEARL HARBOR,
TERRITORY OF HAWAII,
DECEMBER 7, 1941

Detail: Kaneohe MOH Recipient

Chief Petty Officer (Aviation Ordnanceman) John Finn

Admiral Nimitz presented Finn his MOH on September 15, 1942, aboard USS Enterprise.[67]

Detail: Midway MOH Recipients

First Lieutenant George Ham Cannon

Cannon's mother, by a one-page handwritten letter dated March 22, 1942, thanked President Roosevelt, writing in part, "Thank you for the wonderful citation and the

Medal of Honor which you caused to be sent to me..." She continued, "I accept this, the greatest of honors to him and for him." She closed, "He would and I do cherish both [MOH and citation] and shall do so, so long as I shall live."[68]

Captain Richard Fleming

As noted previously, President Roosevelt approved the Fleming MOH citation on November 10, 1942, the U.S. Marine Corps' "birthday" or date on which the founding of the marine corps is traditionally celebrated, making Fleming the first Marine aviator in World War II to receive a MOH, posthumously or living.[69]

The original citation listed Fleming's unit as "Marine Scout-Bombing Squadron TWO FORTY-ONE." At the bottom of the copy of the citation the author obtained from the Franklin D. Roosevelt Presidential Library and Museum is this typewritten note: "IN LINE THREE OF CITATION, DELETE 'TWO FORTY-ONE,' FOR PUBLICITY PURPOSES [AND] CHANGE TO 'A MARINE FIGHTING SQUADRON.'" The intended deletion must have been meant to delete the entire unit designation ("Marine Scout-Bombing Squadron TWO FORTY-ONE") for the substituted words to make a sensible unit designation. Otherwise the citation would read nonsensically: "Scout-Bombing Squadron A Marine Fighting Squadron."[70]

Secretary of the Navy Frank Knox telephoned the White House to report that Captain Fleming's mother was in town to receive the MOH and asked if the President would present it to her. The President agreed, and on November 24, 1942, he presented the MOH to her at a ceremony attended by Fleming's two brothers: Ward, an Army Air Corps lieutenant, and James, a student. Also attending were Marine Corps Commandant Major General Thomas Holcomb, the Marine Corps Director of Aviation, and a lieutenant colonel identified as Fleming's commanding officer at Midway.[71]

Appropriately, a Minnesota newspaper, the St. Paul Dispatch, reported the ceremony's details. Fleming was from St. Paul, Minnesota. President Roosevelt read the citation, presenting the MOH to Mrs. Fleming (Richard Fleming's father was dead). The President noted that his own son Jimmie was a marine major who went to Midway and was there briefly during the battle, replacing a major who had been killed (a brief shot of Major Roosevelt can be seen in the 1942 documentary The Battle of Midway, which won an Academy Award in 1943 for Best Documentary). Referring to Fleming's brothers, the president waved his hand toward the MOH saying, "This is for you boys, too.'" He asked Ward about his military service. The Commandant told the President that James Fleming wanted to become a Navy pilot. The newspaper printed the MOH citation the President read, noting that "Fleming was one of the Marine Corps pilots who went down through almost solid walls of anti-aircraft fire to lay their bombs on the very decks of Jap aircraft carriers at Midway." In fact, as stated previously in Chapter 12, none of the VMSB bombs hit a ship. The citation printed in the newspaper refers to Fleming's command as "a Marine scout-bombing squadron" not as "VMSB-241." The substitution was perhaps for wartime security.[72]

For some reason, the citation correctly records the June 4 action as attacking an aircraft carrier but erroneously records the June 5 action as attacking a battleship, not a cruiser (Mikuma). The error is due possibly to erroneous observations during the battle that one of the cruisers was a battleship or that both were battleships. It may have been due to pilot disagreement over ship identification. Some thought Mikuma a battleship; others thought her a cruiser. Also, the reports from the Executive Officer of Fleming's group (Marine Aircraft Group 22) and from the Commanding Officer of Fleming's squadron (Marine Scout-Bombing Squadron 241) referred to the cruisers as "battleships."[73] Apparently no one realized the error at the time the MOH citation was prepared and presented.

Detail: West Loch MOH Recipient

Petty Officer Second Class (Boatswain's Mate) Owen Hammerberg

A Navy captain presented the MOH in 1946 to the father by placing it around his neck.[74]

After the MOH had been presented in 1945, an undated article in the Free Press described the return of Hammerberg's body to Michigan for final burial as is explained at the end of this chapter. Approximately three thousand people attended the ceremony at which Hammerberg's flag-draped coffin was displayed. Present were his father and his mother, Mrs. Elizabeth Moss (the parents were divorced and the mother remarried).[75]

The reverse of the MOH has a summary of his citation engraved on it; the reverse had insufficient space to permit engraving the entire citation. The words are so closely engraved that reading the inscription is difficult. Why the date is 1946 is unknown.

OWEN HAMMERBERG
BM2C
US NAVY
FOR CONSPICUOUS GALLANTRY
AND INTREPIDITY AT THE COST
OF HIS LIFE ABOVE AND BEYOND
OF DUTY AS A DIVER ENGAGED
IN RESCUE OPERATIONS AT PEARL HARBOR
17 FEBRUARY 1946. BY HIS CONSISTENT
DISREGARD OF ALL PERSONAL DANGER HE CON-
TRIBUTED EFFECTIVELY TO SAVING TWO COMRADES.
HIS HEROIC SPIRIT OF SELF-SACRIFICE WAS IN
KEEPING OF THE HIGHEST
TRADITIONS OF THE
UNITED STATES
NAVAL SERVICE

A photograph of the reverse of the MOH appears at the end of this chapter.[76]

Purple Heart Awards

Awarded with the December 7 and 1942 Midway MOHs presented posthumously were Purple Hearts, which are awarded to those who, while engaging the enemy, are wounded, killed, or who die of wounds. The authority for the Purple Heart award is General Order 186 of January 21, 1943, which authorized the Secretary of the Navy to award a Purple Heart posthumously, in the name of the president, to anyone in the Navy, Marine Corps, or Coast Guard who, since December 6, 1941, was killed in action or who died of wounds received in action with an enemy of the United States.

Living recipients who were wounded also received Purple Hearts.

Purple Hearts: Posthumous Awards for MOH Recipients

Due to death in combat on December 7, 1941, the following officers and men received Purple Hearts: Bennion (*West Virginia*); Flaherty and Ward (*Oklahoma*); Kidd and Van Valkenburgh (*Arizona*); Tomich (*Utah*); Cannon (Midway); Jones, Reeves, and Scott (*California*); and Hill (*Nevada*).[77]

Fleming earned a Purple Heart due to death in combat at Midway on June 5, 1942; he perished when his Vindicator crashed into the sea after its diving attack on the Japanese cruiser Mikuma.[78]

Purple Hearts: Wounded Living MOH Recipients

Men who are wounded in combat are "wounded in action or "WIA" and receive a Purple Heart to indicate wounded status. The only living December 7 MOH recipients to receive Purple Hearts were Finn and Pharris.[79] Young had only one Purple Heart; his service record has no indication of injury on December 7, so the Purple Heart must be for his death in combat on USS San Francisco during the Naval Battle of Guadalcanal.[80]

In photographs, Ross is seen wearing a Purple Heart, but documentation from the National Personnel Records Center does not list a Purple Heart among his awards; his official U.S. Navy biography does not mention a Purple Heart.[81]

Section 5—The Process for Awarding the Special MOH for Foresight in Aviation

Chapter 20 discusses the MOH awarded posthumously to Billy Mitchell. A summary is provided here for reader convenience.

On August 8, 1946, the President approved Congressional legislation requesting that the President honor the late Brigadier General Billy Mitchell, US Army, by having a gold medal struck to honor him for his "outstanding pioneer service and foresight in the field of American military aviation." President Truman approved the legislation.

As explained in various chapters in this book, Mitchell and his MOH are relevant because he had been an outspoken and, to many, a (very) irritating and unpopular advocate of airpower, particularly its supremacy over sea power. More specifically, the attack on December 7, 1941, which he had predicted and which was executed by naval aviation, vindicated his belief that airpower was essential to winning wars and was superior to sea power. The importance of airpower during World War II also vindicated Mitchell's ideas.

The medal was a special MOH, not a classic combat MOH; in the heading of the legislation, it is described as a "Medal of Honor," but in the body of the legislation, it is described as a "gold medal." It should also be considered a Congressional Gold Medal. Because Mitchell died in 1936, the MOH was to be presented to his son "in the name of the people of the United States."

Section 6—Interesting Aspects of the Hawaiian Island MOH Awards

Recipients Having Command

Four of the MOH recipients held command as noted in the chapter covering each of the four recipients. Kidd was a senior commander as the commander of Battleship Division One. His flagship was *Arizona*; he had previously been the ship's commanding officer. Battleship Division One comprised *Arizona*, *Nevada*, and *Oklahoma*.

Kidd's loss is noteworthy in three regards. One, as can be seen from the grades of the men lost on December 7, 1941, Kidd was the only U.S. flag or general officer killed on December 7 (any officer serving above the grade of Army, Air Force, or Marine colonel is a "general officer" and above Navy captain is a "flag officer").[82] Two, he was the first flag or general officer killed in the war since the attack on December 7, 1941, was the first World War II combat action for the United States. Third, he was one of only three Navy flag officers to receive a MOH in the war. All three were rear admirals, and all three were killed in combat. As noted in Chapter 4, the other two earned Medals of Honor in the same battle in which they died.

Three of the recipients were commanding officers of their ships: Bennion (*West Virginia*), Van Valkenburgh (*Arizona*), and Young (*Vestal*).

MOH Recipients: Naval Academy Graduates

Of the eleven Navy officers receiving MOHs for actions during the attack on Oahu, five were graduates of the U.S. Naval Academy at Annapolis, Maryland, founded in 1845 as a college preparing students to become officers in the Navy and Marine corps. Listed here are the Academy graduates with their class years, class nicknames, and ships on December 7.

Officer	Class Year	Nickname	Ship
Rear Admiral Isaac Kidd	1906	"Cap"	USS *Arizona*
Captain Franklin Van Valkenburgh	1909	"Dutch" or "Van"	USS *Arizona*
Lieutenant Commander Samuel Fuqua	1923	"Ben"	USS *Arizona*
Captain Mervyn Bennion	1910	"Mary"	USS *West Virginia*
Comannder Cassin Young	1916	"Ted" or "Cy"	USS *Vestal*

These five men, all Naval Academy graduates, were serving aboard ships along Battleship Row on December 7; of these five officers, two survived the attack (Fuqua and Young) and one the war (Fuqua).[83]

The Academy's yearbook is The Lucky Bag.[84] The Lucky Bag comments about Bennion, Fuqua, and Young were incredibly prophetic in predicting their conduct on December 7 if one overlooks the sarcastic, humorous, and biting parts. The comments were snapshots of the character of each man, and that character would manifest itself in the bravery and actions of these three men on December 7. The specific comments from The Lucky Bag for these three men were mentioned in the chapters devoted to the ships on which they were serving on December 7.

Senior and Junior Recipients

The recipients spanned the grade structure from a low enlisted grade, Seaman First Class James Ward, through the middle grades (chief petty officers, lieutenant commander, commander, and captains) to a low-grade flag officer, Rear Admiral Isaac Kidd.

The Most MOHs for December 7

California had the most MOH recipients for any ship on December 7 (four); *Arizona* was next with three. *California*'s MOHs are considered earned in World War II although the attack on December 7 was before the United States was at war with Japan. President Roosevelt's request for a declaration of war, approved by Congress, however, effectively "backdated" the start of the war with Japan to December 7, the date of the unwarned attack beginning hostilities.[85] Only one other ship had four MOHs for one action during the war: San Francisco, which is discussed in the next section.

December 7 MOH Recipients Surviving the Attack

As noted previously, the five men who survived December 7 to receive MOHs were Finn, Ross, Pharris, Fuqua, and Young. All survived the war except Young.

As explained in more detail in Chapter 8, Young was promoted to captain and in 1942 assigned as the commanding officer of the cruiser San Francisco. He was killed aboard ship on November 13, 1942 (a Friday the thirteenth) during the Naval Battle of Guadalcanal. Since he was buried as sea, his name is on the Tablets of the Missing at Manila American Cemetery, Manila, Philippines. Four MOH recipients for San Francisco all received their MOHs for November 13, 1942: Rear Admiral Daniel Callaghan, Lieutenant Commanders Herbert Schonland and Bruce McCandless, and Petty Officer First Class Reinhardt Keppler.[86] Thus the most MOHs for one action for one ship went to both *California* and *San Francisco*. With the death of Rear Admiral Norman Scott, also killed on November 13 during this battle, the navy lost three rear admirals during World War II; all three received posthumous MOHs.[87]

December 7 MOH Recipients Surviving the War

Chapters 4 (*California*), 7 (*Arizona*), 9 (*Nevada*), 11 (Kaneohe Bay), and 15 (Pharris) discuss the four December 7 MOH recipients who survived the war—Finn, Fuqua, Pharris, and Ross, all of whom retired from the Navy. Pharris, Fuqua, and Ross each retired at his terminal grade achieved, but each was given a "tombstone promotion," which was explained in Chapter 1. In short, the person reaches his or her terminal (final) grade by the normal promotion process and retires but is retired in the next highest grade as an honor based on his or her war record.

Pharris was a lieutenant before retirement but was promoted to lieutenant commander as his retirement grade. He died in 1966 and is buried in Arlington National Cemetery. Fuqua was a captain before retirement but was promoted to rear admiral (two stars) as his retirement grade. He died in 1987. He is also buried in Arlington National Cemetery. The author has seen the tombstones for both officers inscribed with their grades of lieutenant commander and rear admiral, respectively.

Ross was a commander before retirement but was promoted to captain as his retirement grade. He died in 1992; his ashes were scattered over the sunken battleship *Nevada* off the coast of Hawaii by the crew of the submarine USS *Nevada*.

Finn was appointed an officer during the war and retired as a lieutenant. He appeared at Kaneohe in 1999 for the dedication of a building named for him. He died in 2010.

Section 7—Hawaiian Island MOH Firsts

Two questions arise concerning firsts: one, who was the first MOH recipient in World War II, and two, who was the first December 7 MOH recipient?

But who received the first MOH in World War II is irrelevant. The first man to receive a MOH during the war is no different from the man who received a MOH during the war or who was the last man to receive a MOH for action in World War II, either just before the war ended or after the war. They all are MOH recipients; when they received their MOHs does not confer upon them additional honor.

The United States, however, is, for better or worse, a nation obsessed with firsts, so the question of first inevitably arises in the context of December 7 MOHs since it was the earliest combat action for the United States in World War II and thus the first event presenting opportunities to earn a MOH in that war.

The author's initial interest in who received the first World War II MOH arose when by chance he saw a footnote reference to the first MOH recipient in World War II in the book his father had during the World War II to teach him how to be an Army officer: *The Officer's Guide*.[88]

Myths die hard, and the prevailing myth or canard, for whatever reason, is that John Finn or Donald Ross received the first MOH for World War II or for December 7. For example, on NBC Nightly News on July 24, 2008, anchorman Brian Williams narrated a story about the ninety-ninth birthday of John Finn. Williams, since disgraced for embellishing stories about his coverage of news about the Iraq War, said the following:

> As a young Navy man at Pearl Harbor, for his actions on the day of the Japanese attack, he was awarded the very first Medal of Honor given out for combat actions in World War II.[89]

By now, readers should immediately recognize the first error: Finn was at Kaneohe Bay, not at Pearl Harbor. And as will be proven in this section, he was not the first MOH recipient for World War II (or for December 7).

The question of first recipient appears again in the biography of John Finn in the program for the dedication of the John W. Finn Building in 1999 at Marine Corps Base Hawaii, Kaneohe Bay. The last sentence of his biography is as follows:

> It is believed that John is the first Medal of Honor recipient of World War II and he is the last surviving Medal of Honor winner from the day of infamy.[90]

The "It is believed" structure should immediately cause a high index of suspicion: no belief is relevant—the question of the first MOH award is a matter of fact, not "belief." And one wonders about a Navy that cannot even determine which of its own members received the first Navy MOH in World War II.

The sentence contains two errors. First, the belief is incorrect. Using the same information and analysis mentioned later in this section proving that Ross was not the first MOH recipient for World War II or for December 7, one can determine that Finn, likewise, was not the first MOH recipient for World War II or December 7. As noted earlier in this chapter, Finn's MOH citation was prepared on June 6, 1942, long after March 4, 1942, the date President Roosevelt signed the initial fourteen MOH citations for the December 7 recipients (including Ross). The program states that Finn received the MOH from Admiral Chester Nimitz on September 15, 1942, which was after Fuqua, Young, and Ross had received their MOHs. Second, the term used by President Roosevelt was "date of infamy,"[91] not "day of infamy."

An Associated Press obituary for Finn states erroneously that he "was the first man to receive the nation's highest military award for heroism during the Japanese attack on Pearl Harbor on Dec. 7, 1941." Another Associated Press obituary states that he was "the first American to receive the nation's highest military award for defending sailors under a torrent of gunfire during the Japanese attack on Pearl Harbor…" Again, as must be repeated ad nauseam, Finn was at Kaneohe Bay, not at Pearl Harbor, and as will be shown, he was not the first December 7 MOH recipient.[92]

A 2008 printing from the Public Broadcasting System's Internet site for American Valor states, "Of Note: John Finn received the first Medal of Honor awarded for WWII."[93]

A 1992 newspaper article (unfortunately, the source is missing) has this title: "1st Pearl Harbor Medal of Honor recipient dies." The article announces the Ross death, beginning, "Captain Donald K. Ross, US Navy, retired, the first World War II recipient of the Medal of Honor…" It continues, "Ross was the first of 16 Pearl Harbor heroes who received the Medal of Honor, twelve of them awarded posthumously."

The article is incorrect in two respects. As noted repeatedly in this book, only fourteen of the sixteen MOH recipients for December 7 were at Pearl Harbor. Of the other two, one was at Kaneohe Bay (Finn) and the other at Midway (Cannon). Unfortunately, this simple fact must be repeated "a-gain and a-gain" (to paraphrase President Roosevelt's pronunciation) throughout this book. Second, eleven, not twelve, of the MOHs for December 7 or "Pearl Harbor" were posthumous. Also, one could ask this question in the face of the paragraph's ambiguity: Which recipient? Was he the first Pearl Harbor recipient, the first Oahu recipient, or the first World War II recipient?

Similarly, another article about Ross, written shortly after he died, contains the same error about him being the first World War II recipient. The article has a photograph of Ross; the caption reads in part, "Capt. Ross won the first Medal of Honor awarded in World War II…" He did not "win" anything; a MOH is earned, not won in a contest.[94]

So, how does one navigate in the fog created in this universe of misinformation and myths and superficial and faulty analysis and fact finding? Fortunately, correct navigation via simple and accurate fact gathering, research, and analysis can lead to the answers about MOH firsts.

To be accurate, the question of firsts must be subdivided into various firsts:

- Action—Whose actions in the war were the first to lead to a MOH?
- Approval—Whose MOH recommendation was the first MOH recommendation the President approved?
- Receipt—Who was the first recipient, for any MOH or a December 7 MOH, to receive his MOH? Two questions must be asked here. One, who was the first living recipient to receive his MOH, any MOH or a December 7 MOH? Two, whose family was the first to receive a MOH awarded posthumously, any MOH or a December 7 MOH?

First Action

As far as first action leading to a MOH, no definitive answer can be given. Fact: the earliest combat for the United States leading to entry into World War II was on December 7 1941. But the author has uncovered no indication that anyone on Oahu was running around with a watch noting the times the MOH recipients took the actions leading to their MOHs.

The easiest and most rational way to address the first action question is to conclude that the fourteen men whose MOH citations President Roosevelt signed on March 4, 1942, for actions on December 7 were jointly the first men whose actions led to MOHs in World War II. To be accurate, however, Cannon should be excluded from the fourteen men since his MOH was earned during an evening attack on Midway on December 7; the MOH actions by the other thirteen men were hours earlier during the morning attacks on Oahu (in a world where some think that "Pearl Harbor" is the name of a woman, the author, with some hesitancy, assumes that most readers know that the Japanese attack was in the morning).

To close the loop, one can write with certainty that the last action on December 7 leading to a MOH was the action involving the only Marine MOH recipient for that day: First Lieutenant George Cannon on Midway. As described in Chapter 12, the Japanese ships fired the rounds mortally wounding him at approximately 2135 hours, and he died at 2205 hours (9:35 p.m. and 10:05 p.m., respectively).

First Approval

As far as the first approval of a MOH recommendation in World War II, two questions can be asked. One, whose MOH recommendation, regardless of date of action leading to the MOH, was the first MOH recommendation approved during the war? Second, whose recommendation for a MOH based on actions on December 7 was the first MOH approved during the war?

The first MOH award approved by President Roosevelt during the war for any recipient was the MOH for Army Lieutenant Alexander R. Nininger, Jr., for action in the Philippines on January 12, 1942. His posthumous MOH was awarded "By the direction of the President" as reflected in "General Orders No. 9" of the War Department dated February 5, 1942.[95]

The first MOH award approved by President Roosevelt during the war for a December 7 recipient must be considered to be the collective approval of awards for the fourteen men listed earlier in this chapter. That approval was March 4, 1942, and no MOH based on actions on December 7 was approved before that date.[96]

The date of the President's direction of the Nininger award is not given, but common sense dictates that the Nininger MOH approval was before the President approved any of the December 7 awards since February 5, 1942, the date of General Orders No. 9 concerning Nininger, precedes the dates of approval of any of the December 7 MOHs, with the first fourteen MOHs for December 7 being approved on

March 4, 1942. Also, the Nininger MOH was presented on February 10, 1942, which precedes March 4, 1942.[97]

First Award

Nininger's MOH was the first MOH awarded or received in World War II by any recipient, living or posthumous; the date of presentation was, as just stated, February 10, 1942. Thus Nininger is the first posthumous MOH recipient of the war. The first living MOH recipient of the war was Fuqua, who received his MOH (which happened to be for actions on December 7) on March 19, 1942, at U.S. Naval Training Station, Newport, Rhode Island, by Vice Admiral Royal E. Ingersoll, Commander in Chief of the Atlantic Fleet (see table 14-1).

As far as the first award or receipt for the December 7 recipients, as noted earlier, more subdivision is required: first award to a living recipient and first award to the family of a posthumous recipient.

First, the first award to a living December 7 recipient was, as just stated, to Fuqua, who received his MOH on March 19, 1942. Contrary to popular belief, neither Finn nor Ross, as stated in various sources noted in this Chapter and in Chapter 18, was the first December 7 recipient. The other surviving December 7 recipients received their MOHs as indicated by the dates in table 14-1; all these dates were after the date Fuqua received his MOH. Thus the date of Fuqua's presentation made him the first living December 7 MOH recipient to receive his MOH.

Second, the first award to a posthumous December 7 recipient's family cannot be determined, but the time of receipt of the MOHs by four families (Kidd, Van Valkenburgh, Ward, and Cannon) can be estimated, leading to the conclusion that one of the families was the first to receive a posthumous MOH, but one must also allow for the possibility that one or more families received a MOH on the same date. As noted earlier in this chapter, letters dated March 11, 1942, from the Secretary of the Navy to the widows of Kidd and Van Valkenburgh advised that the MOHs were being forwarded by registered mail; the date of receipt of the MOHs is unknown, but assuming regularity of mail service, they must have received the MOHs in March. What is known is that the Wards and Mrs. Cannon had to receive the MOHs between the time of approval (March 4, 1942) and the dates of their thank-you letters to the President; the Ward letter was dated March 17, 1942, and the Cannon letter was March 22, 1942.

Section 8—The Hawaiian Island MOHs Themselves

Today the MOHs earned in the Hawaiian Islands during World War II are in various places, some of which were mentioned earlier in this chapter.

One of the two Hammerberg MOHs and the Flaherty MOH are in Michigan's Own Military and Space Museum in Frankenmuth, Michigan. The Hammerberg family received two MOHs since the parents were divorced (the original was awarded to his father). The MOH awarded his mother was donated to the Congressional Medal of Honor Society Museum at Mount Pleasant, South Carolina, where it was stolen in 2004 with other MOHs on display there.[98]

Two Kidd MOHs are at the floating museum complex for USS Kidd in Baton Rouge, Louisiana.[99]

As explained earlier in this chapter, the Naval Historical Center had the Tomich MOH until the MOH could finally be presented to Tomich's family in 2006. The author saw a duplicate Tomich MOH at Tomich Hall at Naval Station, Newport Rhode Island.

The Naval Academy Museum and the National Museum of the Pacific War each have a Young MOH; the Young family donated the MOHs to each institution. The National Museum of the Pacific War seems to have the original MOH since it has engraving on the reverse.

The author saw a duplicate of the Finn MOH at the John W. Finn Building on Marine Corps Base Hawaii.

Section 9—Burial and Remembrance for the Hawaiian Island MOH Recipients

Chapter 21 ("Legacy—Men") and Appendix C discuss burials and memorials in detail and include photographs.

Section 10—Commemorating the MOH Recipients

Ships, Boats, Buildings, and Other Commemorations

Chapter 21 ("Legacy—Men") and Appendix C discuss commemorations in detail and include photographs.

Notes

1. Chapters 4–13 and 19.

2. Chapter 20 (Mitchell).

3. Author's knowledge and experience as a lawyer.

4. Chapter 19 (*California*, Jackson Pharris MOH award process).

5. Hearings [May 31, 1945] before Subcommittee No. 8 of the Committee on Military Affairs, House of Representatives, Seventy-Ninth Congress, First Session on H.R. 2227 and Other Bills [authorizing the President to award a posthumous MOH in the name of Congress to William Mitchell] (Washington, DC: U.S. Government Printing Office, 1945); statement by Representative John J. Sparkman, 8 (hereafter "Mitchell Hearings"). The modern MOH statutes listed at endnote 12 follow the same scheme: Congress authorizes the President to present a medal of honor in the name of the

Congress.

6. The Roosevelt approval of MOH citations is based on documents provided to the author by the Franklin D. Roosevelt Presidential Library and Museum (hereafter "Roosevelt approval").

7. The Truman approval of MOH citations is based on documents provided to the author by Harry S. Truman Library and Museum (hereafter "Truman approval").

8. Endnote 5, Mitchell Hearings, 8.

9. The original, amended, and modern statutes are consistent in using "medal of honor" rather than "Congressional Medal of Honor." Historically, "medal of honor" in lowercase has been used in statutes. For example, the statute creating the first MOH used that term (Section 7 of Chapter I of the public acts of the Thirty-Seventh Congress). The modern statutes in title 10 of US Code for the MOH use "medal of honor"; US Air Force, Section 8741; US Navy and Marine Corps, Section 6241; and US Army, Section 3741.

10. Author's knowledge and experience as a lawyer.

11. Chapter 13 (West Loch) and Appendix D (Graves and Memorials).

12. Admiral Chester W. Nimitz, "Report of Japanese Raid on Pearl Harbor, December 7, 1941" (February 15, 1942). Part IV(D) is "Recommendation for Awards." It reads, "A Board of Awards, headed by Rear Admiral Robert A. Theobald, US Navy, is currently in session for the purpose of making recommendations for awards incident to the Pearl Harbor attack." A letter of September 29, 2014, from the National Archives and Records Administration (NARA) advised that NARA could not satisfy the author's request to find a copy of the Report of the Fleet Board of Awards.

13. Military custom and protocol require Admiral Nimitz to endorse the Fleet Board's report; author's knowledge and experience with military protocol and correspondence.

14. Jane Blakeney, Heroes: US Marine Corps 1861 * 1955 (Guthrie Lithograph Co., Inc., Washington, DC, 1957), 4.

15. Third Endorsement QB-4-OS from the Senior Member, Navy Department Permanent Board of Awards to the Secretary of the Navy, "Subject: Japanese Attack on U.S. Pacific Fleet in Pearl Harbor 7 Dec. 1941—Recommendations for Awards for Gallant Conduct in Action of Naval and Civilian Personnel," 5, paragraph 4 (hereafter "Third Endorsement"). The endorsement is unsigned, but "J. O. Richardson" appears at the end of it on page 5. Chapter 3 (Attacks) describes Richardson's relief from command of the U.S. Pacific Fleet.

Also found with the endorsement was a one-page summary, unsigned by the recorder but with indication that the recorder prepared it, noting that the Permanent Board had met from 9:00 a.m. to 1:10 p.m. on February 23, 1942, in Washington, DC, and that the three members and the recorder were present. The summary also noted that the Fleet Board of Awards had made no recommendations for Kidd or Van Valkenburgh but that the Permanent Board, "action on the directive of the Secretary of the Navy," recommended that MOHs be awarded posthumously to the next of kin of Kidd and Van Valkenburgh. The summary was essentially a cover letter for the Third Endorsement. The Third Endorsement was found on page 41 of the "Awards, Decorations, and Correspondence" section (Section 06) on the compact disc (CD) containing the Official Military Personnel File (OMPF) of Rear Admiral Isaac Kidd (see endnote 7 of Chapter 7 (*Arizona*)).

The Third Endorsement and its accompanying summary are in Section 06 ("Awards, Decorations, and Correspondence") of the CD on pages 40 to 45 of the OMPF CD (CD page numbers). The twelve MOH recommendations are in paragraph 2 of page 1 (endorsement page number). The comment about Kidd and Van Valkenburgh is in paragraph 4 of page 5 (endorsement page number) (hereafter "Third Endorsement").

16. At the bottom of page 5 (endorsement page number) of the Third Endorsement under "APPROVED" is "Feb. 27, 1942" in handwriting above the typed title "Secretary of the Navy." Endnote 6 gives the source of the Secretary's March 3, 1942, memorandum forwarding the MOH citations to the President.

17. Endnote 6, Roosevelt approval.

18. Endnote 5, Mitchell Hearings; none of the documentation for the December 7 MOH awards mentions any involvement by Congress in the awards process.

19. Endnote 19, Third Endorsement, 1; Chapters 4–10, 12, and 19.

20. Endnote 6, Roosevelt approval; missing from the Third Endorsement list of men recommended for MOHs were Warrant Officer Jackson Pharris and Chief Aviation Ordnanceman John Finn. Thus the Secretary submitted no MOH citations for them to the President via his March 3, 1942, memorandum. Endnote 6 cites documentation for Finn's MOH approval in June 1942 after the approval of the fourteen MOH recommendations submitted in March. For whatever reason, the Third Endorsement had no MOH recommendation for Pharris or Finn. The text explains the MOH awards for these two recipients. In the Third Endorsement Finn is not mentioned; Pharris was mentioned, but the board recommended him for a Navy Cross, not a MOH.

21. Ibid.

22. Ibid.

23. Chapters 4–10, 12, and 19.

24. Ibid., Third Endorsement.

25. Endnote 6, Roosevelt approval.

26. Endnote 6; Pharris is listed on page 2 of the Third Endorsement as recommended for a Navy Cross.

27. Endnote 6, Roosevelt approval; "Slain St. Paul Hero Given Highest Tribute," St. Paul Dispatch, November 24, 1942, 1; author's knowledge of the Marine Corps' birthday having served in the Marine corps and Marine Corps Reserve from 1981 to 2011.

28. Death certificate for President Franklin D. Roosevelt with a date of death of April 12, 1945, accessible at the Internet site for the Franklin D. Roosevelt Presidential Library and Museum.

29. Endnote 7, Truman approval.

30. Dan Lamothe, "Modern Medals of Honor and the Time They Take to Award," Washington Post, July 21, 2014.

31. Audie Murphy's MOH action was January 26, 1945, at Holtzwihr, France; he was presented a MOH on June 2, 1945, after President Harry S. Truman approved it on April 23, 1945 (Secretary of War Henry L. Stimson signed the citation); Harold B. Simpson, Audie Murphy, American Soldier (The Hill Jr. College Press, 1975), 153–160, 175, and 190.

32. Fuqua—Fuqua OMPF (CD), section 04 (Service Documents), frame 43, orders of March 16, 1942, from R. E. Ingersoll order Fuqua to report to Newport, Rhode Island, at 1200 hours, March 19, 1942, for presentation of his MOH. Vice Admiral Royal E. Ingersoll was the commander in chief, US Atlantic Fleet. Young—George Lang, Raymond L. Collins, and Gerald F. White, Medal of Honor Recipients 1863–1994, World War II to Somalia, Vol. II (Facts on File, Inc., New York, NY, 1995), 602–603, 567 (hereafter "Lang, Medal of Honor Recipients 1863–1994").
Ross—Ibid., 567. Finn—Ibid., 486. Pharris—see Chapter 19.

33. Letters transmitting the MOHs for Kidd and Van Valkenburgh can be found in their Official Military Personnel Files (OMPFs), described in detail in endnotes 7 (Kidd) and 16 (Van Valkenburgh) of Chapter 7 (*Arizona*). The letters are cited in this chapter in endnote 51 (Kidd) and 52 (Van Valkenburgh).
Bennion—see endnote 39.
Cannon—Letter of March 22, 1942, from Mrs. Estelle Ham Cannon to President Franklin D. Roosevelt.
Scott—"He Gave His Life to Keep Guns Firing," Massillon Independent (author and date unknown) sent to the author from the Ohio Military Museum in 2006) (hereafter "He Gave His Life to Keep Guns Firing"). The article reported that Scott's mother received the MOH but does not report how she received it; the inference that the Scott MOH was mailed to the family can be drawn from this sentence in the newspaper article: "The box containing the [M]edal of [H]onor has not yet been opened by his grief stricken mother."
Ward—see the section following in this Chapter concerning a letter Ward's parents

received from the Secretary of the Navy.

34. E-mail from Doug Misner (Research Center of the *Utah* State Archives and *Utah* State History) to the author of October 14 and 15, 2015 (delivery of the Bennion MOH); article furnished by Doug Misner to the author, "Congressional Medal Arrives in S. L. [Salt Lake] for Late Captain Bennion, Deseret News, March 17, 1942), 11–13.

35. E-mail from Mr. Stan Bozich, Director, Michigan's Own Military & Space Museum, April 21, 2009; endnote 32, Lang, Medal of Honor Recipients 1863–1994," 487.

36. "A Day Americans Will Never Forget," Michigan History (July/August 2001), 30 (story and MOH inscription); e-mail to the author from Mr. Stan Bozich, April 21, 2009.

37. [MOH] Recipient Data Sheet for James R. Ward completed by his parents, Howard and Nancy Ward, paragraph 7 (hereafter "Ward Recipient Data Sheet").

38. Ibid., paragraph 9.

39. Letter of March 17, 1942, from Mr. Howard J. Ward and Mrs. Nancy M. Ward, obtained from the Franklin D. Roosevelt Presidential Library and Museum.

40. Letter of March 23, 1942, from Captain John L. McCrea, Naval aide to the President, to Mr. Howard J. Ward and Mrs. Nancy M. Ward, obtained from the Franklin D. Roosevelt Presidential Library and Museum.

41. Endnote 42, Ward Recipient Data Sheet, paragraph 7.

42. Letter of March 7, 1974, from Mr. Howard J. Ward and Mrs. Nancy M. Ward to Mr. Carl A. Robin, North Carolina state director, Medal of Honor History Round Table, describes the letter they received from the Navy, advising they would receive a MOH book, and their discovery when receiving the book that their son's enlistment was accredited to North Carolina.

43. Ibid.

44. Ibid.

45. Letter of March 7, 1974, from Mr. Howard J. Ward and Mrs. Nancy M. Ward to the Department of the Navy.

46. See endnote 38; the letter is found on page 48 of Section 06 of the Kidd OMPF on the CD; section 06 is "Awards, Decorations, and Commendations."

47. Ibid.; the letter is found on page 21 of Section 06 of the Van Valkenburgh OMPF on the CD; section 06 is "Awards, Decorations, and Commendations."

48. Endnote 40, Lang, Medal of Honor Recipients 1863–1994, 567.

49. Photograph of the reverse of the Scott MOH provided by Mike Bardin of the Ohio Military Museum in 2006.

50. Endnote 40, Lang, Medal of Honor Recipients 1863–1994, 602.

51. The information about the Young MOH at the National Museum of the Pacific War is from various e-mails, dated 2008–2010, from Reagan Grau at the Museum. On July 28, 2015, Mr. Mike Lebens, curator of collections, confirmed by electronic mail to the author that the National Museum of the Pacific War still had a Cassin Young MOH. On October 7, 2015, Laura Jowdy, the archivist at the Congressional Medal of Honor Society, stated in an e-mail to the author that the Young family had donated the MOH to the National Museum of the Pacific War.

52. The information about the Young MOH at the U.S. Naval Academy is from e-mails of May 26, 2015, and October 8, 2015, to the author from Mr. James Cheevers, senior curator, U.S. Naval Academy Museum; the author also saw the Young MOH when visiting the Museum in 2014.

53. The National Personnel Records Center, St. Louis, Missouri, furnished information from Tomich's Official Military Personnel File (OMPF) at the author's request (hereafter "Tomich OMPF").

54. Endnote 53, Lang, Medal of Honor Recipients 1863–1994, 584; Tomich OMPF.

55. Ibid.

56. Letter of October 30, 1946, from Mr. J. M. Steele to Vice Admiral A. S. Carpender, USN.

57. Endnote 40, Lang, Medal of Honor Recipients 1863–1994, 584; endnote 58, Tomich OMPF.

58. "USS *Utah*: The Forgotten Memorial," VFW Magazine (December 1985), 18; the letter to the editor is from the February 1986 issue of the magazine at page 8.

59. Letter of February 11, 1985, from then-Senator Jake Garn (*Utah*) to Mr. J. B. Vaessen.

60. Letter of June 23, 1987, from Mr. Paul Bucha to Rear Admiral J. Robert Lunney, NYNM (New York Naval Militia).

61. Letter of October 15, 1997, from David Sanders, Public Affairs Officer at the Naval Education and Training Center in Newport, Rhode Island, to Chief Warrant Officer Donald H. Chavark, U.S. Navy (Retired).

62. Letter of November 4, 1997, from Chief Warrant Officer Donald H. Chavark, U.S.

Navy (Retired) to the Naval Historical Center in Washington, DC.

63. Letter of November 3, 1997, from Senior Chief Machinist Mate Richard Moore, U.S. Navy, to Chief Warrant Officer Donald H. Chavark, U.S. Navy (Retired).

64. Letter of November 13, 1997, from Chief Warrant Officer Donald H. Chavark, U.S. Navy (Retired) to the Congressional Medal of Honor Society.

65. Letter of November 19, 1997, from Mr. Normal M. Cary, Jr., head, Curator Branch, Naval Historical Center, Washington, DC, to Chief Warrant Officer Donald H. Chavark, U.S. Navy (Retired).

66. Jason Thompson, Journalist Second Class (Surface Warfare), US Navy, Navy Newsstand (May 19, 2006), printed from the Internet June 26, 2006.

67. Endnote 40, Lang, Medal of Honor Recipients 1863–1994, 486.

68. Letter of March 22, 1942, from Mrs. Estelle Ham Cannon to President Franklin D. Roosevelt.

69. Copy of Fleming MOH citation received from the Franklin D. Roosevelt Presidential Library and Museum; author's knowledge of the Marine Corps' "birthday," having served in the Marine Corps and its Reserve from 1981 to 2011. Fleming can be determined to be the first Marine aviator to receive a MOH during World War II by reference to a monograph: Commander Peter B. Mersky, U.S. Naval Reserve, Time of the Aces: Marine Pilots in the Solomons, 1942–1944 (History and Museums Division, Headquarters, U.S. Marine Corps, Washington, DC,1993), 14. One must read the page carefully to understand that Fleming's was the first MOH received, although his was not the first action to result in a MOH to an aviator. Captain Henry Elrod's MOH action was earlier, but he did not receive his posthumous MOH until after the war. His widow received it on November 8, 1946. His MOH was for actions on Wake Island; Who's Who in Marine Corps History, "Major Henry Talmage Elrod, USMC (Deceased)," a fact sheet produced by the Marine Corps History Division and accessed by Internet on April 9, 2008.

70. Ibid.

71. Documents received from the Franklin D. Roosevelt Presidential Library and MUSeum.

72. St. Paul Dispatch, November 24, 1942, 1–2.

73. Report of Executive Officer, MAG-22 (Subject: "Marine Aircraft Group Twenty-Two, Second Marine Aircraft Wing, Midway Islands T.H.") of June 7, 1942, 12; Report of Marine Scout-Bombing Squadron 241 (Subj[ect]: "Report of Activities during June 4 and June 5, 1942") of June 12, 1942, 5, paragraph 35; Captain M. A. Tyler signed the report; ordinarily, the squadron commanding officer or executive officer (lieutenant colonels or majors) would sign a report, but both the original commander (Henderson)

and original executive officer (Norris) had been lost in action.

74. Undated photograph showing a Navy captain placing the MOH around the neck of Mr. Jonnes Hammerberg; e-mail of October 8 from the Congressional Medal of Honor Society to the author; Mr. Stan Bozich, director/curator, Michigan's Own, Inc., Military and Space Museum, letter of November 27, 2000, to the author (hereafter "Bozich letter").

75. Florence Allen, "Detroit Salutes Hero in Tribute to War Dead," Detroit Free Press, undated; endnote 74, Bozich letter.

76. Photograph from Mr. Stan Bozich of the Hammerberg MOH inscription.

77. The following paper copy OMPFs document awards of Purple Hearts: Bennion, Flaherty, and Scott. The following CD OMPFs document awards of Purple Hearts: Kidd at section 06 ("Awards, Decorations, and Commendations"), 49; and Van Valkenburgh at section 06 ("Awards, Decorations, and Commendations"), 23. The following U.S. Navy biographies document awards of Purple Hearts: Hill, Reeves, Tomich, and Ward. Cannon's U.S. Marine Corps biography documents an award of a Purple Heart. No record of the Jones Purple Heart can be found in the OMPF provided the author, although he would certainly be eligible for one under General Order 186 (authorizing Purple Hearts for death in combat) mentioned in this chapter.

78. The Fleming OMPF (see endnote 33 in chapter 12) documents the award of a Purple Heart.

79. The Finn OMPF (see endnote 5 in Chapter 11) documents the award of a Purple Heart. The Pharris OMPF documents a Purple Heart with a Gold Star (second award); the second award was for wounds sustained at another command later in the war (see Chapter 19).

80. The Young OMPF (see endnote 7 in Chapter 8) documents the award of one Purple Heart.

81. Neither the Ross U.S. Navy biography nor the Ross OMPF documents a Purple Heart (see endnotes 16 and 18, respectively, in chapter 9).

82. Author's knowledge as a Marine officer from 1981 to 2011.

83. Colonel Charles A. Jones, USMCR (Retired), "Men of Honor: Pearl Harbor, December 7, 1941," Shipmate (U.S. Naval Academy Association, December 2001), 11–13.

84. Ibid.; a "lucky bag" is a bag in which stray, found, or unclaimed clothing is kept, The Bluejackets' Manual United States Navy (United States Naval Institute Press, Annapolis, MD, 1940), 20.

85. Franklin D. Roosevelt, "Address to Congress Requesting a Declaration of War with

Japan" (December 8, 1941), printed from the Franklin D. Roosevelt Presidential Library and MUSeum October 9, 2015 (hereafter "Roosevelt Declaration of War speech").

86. Jack Zanger, "A Perspective in Leadership: Rear Adm. Herbert E. Schonland," Surface Warfare 23, no. 6 (November/December 1998), 34–37. The MOH citations for Callaghan, Schonland, McCandless, and Keppler can be found by searching the Internet for "army MOH site" and accessing the citations by choosing the correct icon for World War II at the "Medal of Honor Recipients: Center of Military History" site.

87. Endnote 89, the Scott MOH citation can be found by searching the Internet for "army MOH site" and accessing the citations by choosing the correct icon for World War II at the "Medal of Honor Recipients: Center of Military History" site.

88. The Officer's Guide, 9th edition (The Military Service Publishing Company, Harrisburg, PA, 1943), 166 (footnote 2); the reference in the Guide's footnote to Nininger's MOH being the first MOH in World War II was the author's first indication that the Nininger MOH was the first MOH approved in World War II.

89. Author's notes from and viewing of a tape of NBC Nightly News for July 24, 2008.

90. Program from Commander, Patrol and Reconnaissance Force, U.S. Pacific Fleet, for the dedication ceremony of the John W. Finn Building, "John W. Finn Building Dedication Ceremony."

91. Endnote 88, Roosevelt Declaration of War speech.

92. The Associated Press obituaries were posted on May 27, 2010, on the Internet. One was by Julie Watson; the other listed no author.

93. "American Valor: John Finn," Public Broadcasting System, WETA Internet site (August 24, 2008), printed September 28, 2015.

94. Vorina Palmer, "It's Taps for the Captain," Port Orchard Independent, June 3, 1992, 1; the general rule is to refer to a MOH recipient as just that, a "recipient," not a winner since a MOH award is not a contest; author's knowledge and experience.

95. War Department General Orders Number 9 (February 5, 1942), Section V; see also endnote 88.

96. The information provided the author by the Roosevelt Presidential Library and Museum revealed no MOH approvals for December 7 actions before the fourteen approvals on March 4, 1942.

97. Endnote 40, Lang, Medal of Honor Recipients 1863–1994, 549.

98. Information about the Flaherty and Hammerberg MOHs is from Mr. Stan Bozich, director, Michigan's Own Military and Space Museum, e-mail to the author April 21, 2009; Chapter 5 (*Oklahoma*, Flaherty MOH) and Chapter 13 (West Loch,

Hammerberg MOHs); the thefts of the MOHs were reported on various Internet sites, including America's Most Wanted.

99. Information about the Kidd MOH replicas is from e-mail of July 16, 2015, from Mr. Tim Nesmith, Ship Superintendent, USS Kidd Veterans Memorial, Baton Rouge, Louisiana.

Part V

Misses and Mistakes– Overly Awarded and Non Awarded

Chapter 15
Medals of Honor Not Earned—Rear Admiral Isaac Kidd and Captain Franklin Van Valkenburgh, U.S. Navy, USS Arizona (BB-39)

Rear Admiral Isaac Kidd, U.S. Navy

Captain Franklin Van Valkenburgh, U.S. Navy

USS Arizona, December 7, 1941

Any questioning of any aspect of USS *Arizona* is likely to trigger controversy and to be considered heresy; she is the Holy Grail of December 7, 1941, and memories of her remain strong.

But truth is more important than heresy, and if one is to be objective about the MOHs that are the subject of this book, then one must examine the MOHs awarded posthumously to Rear Admiral Isaac Kidd and Captain Franklin Van Valkenburgh. What triggered the author to question these two MOHs was the discovery of the manner in which the MOH award recommendations were proposed. Documentation definitively shows that they did not originate in the field at Pearl Harbor as did the initial twelve MOH recommendations made by the Field Board of Awards; rather, they were added at the Navy Department level, far removed from the on-scene knowledge of the awards board at Pearl Harbor.

Chapters 7 (*Arizona*) and 14 (Overview) told the story of the ship and her three MOH recipients. Chapter 7 also mentioned five reasons why the ship's MOH recipients are unique and referred readers to this chapter for an examination of the fourth and fifth reasons for the uniqueness. The fourth reason was the process by which two of the three *Arizona* MOH recommendations originated. The fifth reason was of the sixteen MOHs awarded for December 7, the Kidd and Van Valkenburgh MOHs are the only two that were undeserved.

As will be seen, merely because the men were recommended for MOHs and the President approved the recommendations does not mean the MOHs were in fact deserved.

The Process by which Arizona MOHs Were Awarded

Chapter 14 is an overview of the MOHs that are the subject of this book. It covered in general terms the process by which the MOHs were approved. More focused and specific information will be offered here as well as important questions.

The assertion that the Kidd and Van Valkenburgh MOHs are undeserved begins with the original report of the Fleet Board of Awards, which submitted the names of these twelve officers and men recommended for MOHs, including Fuqua of *Arizona* (these names are found in the Third Endorsement of the Permanent Board described here).

- Bennion
- Flaherty
- Reeves
- Tomich
- Hill
- Fuqua
- Ross
- Ward
- Cannon
- Jones
- Scott
- Young

Of critical importance and as seen in this section, the report of the Fleet Board of Awards at Pearl Harbor, the entity closest to the site where the MOH actions occurred, did not recommend Kidd or Van Valkenburgh for any award or even mention their names.[1]

The Navy Department Permanent Board of Awards reviewed the Fleet Board's recommendations and wrote as follows in its endorsement of the Fleet Board report (the endorsement was essentially the cover letter from the Permanent Board forwarding the Fleet Board of Awards' report to the Secretary of the Navy):

> While the Fleet Board of Awards submitted no recommendations in the case of the following named officers, this [B]oard, acting on the directive of the Secretary of the Navy, recommends that the Medal of Honor be awarded posthumously to the next of kin in each case.[2]

The Permanent Board then added MOH recommendations for Kidd and Van Valkenburgh and included a proposed citation for each officer without any reference to witnesses. The Fleet Board did not reference witnesses for the twelve men it recommended for MOHs, but one must assume that the Fleet Board had already examined witness statements at Pearl Harbor since the Fleet Board was reporting men recommended for MOHs, and recommendations would not have been made without reference to witness statements (the basis for a classic combat MOH is statements of fact from witnesses attesting the actions of the recipient). The Pharris case (Chapter 19) is an excruciating example of the requirement that witnesses provide verifiable facts to support a recommendation for a MOH.

In any event, these two officers, both aboard *Arizona*, were the only two MOH recommendations the Permanent Board added to the Fleet Board's original list of twelve MOH recommendations. A crucial point is that the Permanent Board recommended no additional crewmen from the ship or from any other ship or station for MOHs except for Kidd and Van Valkenburgh.[3]

At the bottom of the Third Endorsement's page 5 under "Approved" is "Feb. 27, 1942," in handwriting above the typed title "Secretary of the Navy."[4]

Thus the letter of March 3, 1942, signed by Secretary of the Navy Frank Knox forwarding fourteen MOH citations to President Roosevelt with a recommendation that he sign them included MOH citations not for one *Arizona* officer, as recommended by the Fleet Board, but for three: Kidd, Van Valkenburgh, and Fuqua. The President signed all fourteen citations on March 4, 1942.[5]

ARIZONA MOHS: TWO QUESTIONS

With Fuqua the only *Arizona* officer among the list of twelve men originally recommended by the Fleet Awards board for MOHs, the obvious questions are one, why the Fleet Board omitted Kidd and Van Valkenburgh from the list of officers and men recommended for MOHs, and two, why the Permanent Board added their two names to that list. Those questions will be examined in detail in the following sections of this chapter. Later, another question will be asked: Were the two additional MOHs deserved?

As to the first question, the obvious answer is that the members of the members of the Fleet Board of Awards did not think that either officer deserved a MOH.

As to the second question, the author's conclusion is that Kidd and Van Valkenburgh were added to the list of men recommended for MOHs because of political reasons unrelated to the merits of the conduct of the two men on December 7. That political reason was probably an unwritten policy to recommend senior commanders killed in action on December 7 for MOHs since all those killed were in fact recommended for MOHs: Bennion, Kidd, and Van Valkenburgh. Bennion was already included among the twelve men recommended since facts supported a MOH for him, but as will be seen later, no facts supported the Kidd and Van Valkenburgh recommendations.

In reaching this conclusion, the author makes no judgment about the addition of Kidd and Van Valkenburgh to the list of men recommended for MOHs; he makes no judgment of them as officers or people. As a general rule, officers were (and are) not given commands such as the commands they had, especially commands of battleships, unless they had proven to be good officers. A newspaper article about Kidd's death and a tribute to him, both included later in this chapter, reflect favorably on Kidd as a decent man and good officer. But character and officership are not the questions; good character and good officership are not criteria for a MOH.

Thus the question remains: Why did the Permanent Board add Kidd and Van Valkenburgh to the list of twelve officers and men the Fleet Board recommended for MOHs if the Fleet Board did not recommend these two officers for MOHs or any other awards?

ARIZONA MOHS: THE DOUBLE STANDARD, PART I—POLICY OVER MERITS

One way to determine why Kidd and Van Valkenburgh were added to the list of men recommended for MOHs is to examine each way a MOH can be awarded. By using the process of elimination, one can deduce why Kidd and Van Valkenburgh were added to the list.

1) MOHs awarded by Congressional legislation

No evidence of Congressional action (legislative or otherwise) is found in the Third Endorsement of the Permanent Board or elsewhere, so action by Congress to mandate the MOHs can be eliminated. Chapter 14 and Appendix D discuss the authority of Congress to award MOHs by legislation.

2) Combat MOH recommendations originating from a field command or commander with the recommendation, subjected to the rigorous vetting process required of a MOH recommendation

Facts must be produced and judged by a high or rigorous standard of proof. As will be seen later in this chapter, this process can be eliminated because it was not the process leading to the Kidd or Van Valkenburgh awards.

3) Some other reason

The only remaining explanation is some reason other than Congressional action or the typical command recommendation process leading to a MOH. In looking for that reason to replace Congressional or the typical recommendation process, the author concludes that the reason is an implicit policy not based on the merits of the men's actions but based on their status as senior commanding officers killed in the line of duty.

One clue that such a policy existed and was the reason the officers were added to the list of men recommended by the Field Board for MOHs is the phrase "Secretarial directive" in the Permanent Board's endorsement; as stated in the Third Endorsement, the Permanent Board added the two names "acting on the directive of the Secretary of the Navy." Does this phrase mean that the Secretary of the Navy personally ordered the board to include Kidd and Van Valkenburgh on the list of MOH nominees, or does it mean a general affirmation that the Permanent Board had the power from the Secretary to add, on the Board's own initiative, nominees for awards to the list of nominees submitted by the Fleet Board and did so with these two officers? No answer to this question can be found.[6]

A policy of awarding MOHs to commanders killed on December 7 must have been established by the Permanent Board, the Department of the Navy (perhaps by the Secretary of the Navy himself), or the White House. After all, President Roosevelt had been the Assistant Secretary of the Navy earlier in his career, and he and the Secretary of the Navy had to know about the losses of *Arizona* and Kidd and Van Valkenburgh. To add to the intrigue, when President Roosevelt was the Assistant Secretary of the Navy he was the presiding official at the laying of *Arizona*'s keel in 1914.[7]

While policy as an explanation for the Kidd and Van Valkenburgh MOH awards is based on circumstantial evidence, circumstantial evidence is acceptable evidence and is used in all aspects of life; it is valid if the facts support it. The facts here prove the existence of an unwritten policy for awarding MOHs based on reasons other than facts supporting the award of a classic combat MOH meeting MOH criteria. In short, replacing the Congressional or the command recommendation processes was the policy of a MOH for any senior commander killed on December 7.

In judging the soundness of this conclusion, one must consider the factual reality of the awards process and who received awards: Bennion, Kidd, and Van Valkenburgh were all commanders (Bennion and Van Valkenburgh were ship commanding officers, and Kidd was commander of Battleship Division One). At least in Bennion's case—the classic case of a combat MOH awarded to a mortally wounded man who refused evacuation—the existence and strength of facts proving Bennion's resistance to evacuation were overwhelming. For Kidd and Van Valkenburgh, MOHs were awarded regardless of the presence of facts supporting a MOH, facts judged by the high standard of proof required in the usual process of awarding combat MOHs.

Also to be considered are the comments of Commander Battleships, Battle Force, Rear Admiral W. S. Anderson, in his December 13, 1941, endorsement of the action report submitted by the Senior Surviving Officer of *West Virginia*. Anderson commented about Bennion's concern only for his ship and wrote that he "is recommended for posthumous commendation and official recognition."[8]

Interestingly, Anderson also described the atmosphere of the awards process by placing even more stress on seniority in his December 19, 1941, report Distinguished Conduct—Report of—Pearl Harbor Raid, December 7, 1941. Although he mentioned officers of lower grade, such as Jones (ensign, *California*) and Hill (chief boatswain, *Nevada*), he wrote the following about *Arizona*:

> Rear Admiral Isaac C. Kidd and Captain F. Van Valkenburgh were in the *Arizona* when the attack began and were on the bridge when the destruction of the *Arizona* occurred which resulted in losing their lives in action while in the full discharge of their duties. Inasmuch as they have paid the supreme sacrifice it is recommended as suitable and fitting that some posthumous official recommendation and recognition be extended.[9]

What is noteworthy is Anderson included no other *Arizona* crewmen by name in his report—not even Fuqua, who without doubt deserved a MOH (one need only read Fuqua's MOH citation to reach that conclusion). Even if the conclusion of policy as the basis for the two MOHs is circumstantial, it is strongly circumstantial, especially when the Kidd and Van Valkenburgh citations and purported deeds are compared to the citations and specific, proven deeds of the other December 7 MOH recipients, such as Fuqua. And importantly, if one considers the entire MOH process for the December 7 recipients, policy as the basis for these two MOHs cannot be excluded. The appropriate awards for Kidd and Van Valkenburgh, as will be stated at the end of this section, were Purple Hearts for death in combat, not MOHs for death in combat or for simply discharging their duties without any facts indicating that such discharge warranted a

MOH. In fact, the wording of Anderson's summary reads like a summary justifying Purple Hearts, not MOHs, for men killed in action.

Also of importance is the Permanent Board relying on policy, not facts, in its action in another case related to *Arizona*: its recommendation to disapprove a MOH recommendation for Marine Lieutenant Colonel Daniel Fox, the senior Marine aboard *Arizona* who perished on the ship; he was a member of Kidd's staff and on December 7 similarly situated as Kidd and Van Valkenburgh. Chapter 16 discusses the Fox case in detail; what is important here is the policy aspect of the Board's recommendation. The basis of the Board's recommendation in the Fox case was policy, not an absence of facts; the Board stated in the Fox case that it did not want to set a precedent of presenting awards for everyone for doing what is expected and getting killed for doing so.[10] While not setting such a precedent is laudable, the Board did just that—set a precedent, but only for Kidd and Van Valkenburgh, who were essentially rewarded for going to their battle stations. Additionally, it should have disapproved the Fox recommendation, as well as the other two recommendations, for the lack of a factual basis supporting it; no provable facts supported the criteria of a MOH for the actions of Kidd, Van Valkenburgh, or Fox for December 7. And if the board were acting fairly and consistently, it would never have added the Kidd and Van Valkenburgh MOH recommendations since their recommendations were as objectionable setting a wrong precedent as was the Fox recommendation objectionable for setting the wrong precedent. Thus the reason undermining the Fox MOH recommendation also undermined the Kidd and Van Valkenburgh recommendations—not establishing a precedent for rewarding mere death in the line of duty.

And one can find support in arguing counterfactually that a policy existed to favor commanders. As a matter of common sense and military reality, in no case would Seaman First Class William Smith of USS *Arizona* or any other ship or station have been awarded a MOH, or even recommended for one, with citations similar to the citations for Kidd and Van Valkenburgh. Such an award to an average crew member of the ship would be unthinkable, especially in light of the specific heroic deeds cited in the other December 7 award citations. Such a generic MOH was not awarded to any other December 7 recipient. The Kidd and Van Valkenburgh citations are unlike the other citations in this book—the combat MOH citations and the Hammerberg noncombat citation—all of which recited some specific conduct, other than manning a battle station, justifying a MOH.

Certainly, other MOHs have been presented for policy or political reasons. Obviously the MOH presented to General Douglas MacArthur in 1942 after President Roosevelt ordered him out of the Philippines was to save face upon the withdrawal of a highly important senior commander from the battlefield so that he would not be captured or killed; the citation reveals no valor in the face of engaging an enemy in combat although it shows that he was clearly in a situation of danger presented by the Japanese attacks in the Philippines.[11]

The MOH presented to Major Adolphus Greely, U.S. Army, by Congress in 1935 would be risible if it did not demean the MOH to such a degree. The citation is as follows:

For his life of splendid public service, begun on March 27, 1844, having enlisted as a private in the US Army on July 26, 1861, and by successive promotions was commissioned as major general February 10, 1906, and retired by operation of law on his 64th birthday. [Italics added for emphasis.][12]

The award was an inappropriate award to acknowledge public service; the MOH is not a lifetime achievement award but an award for specific instances of combat or noncombat bravery. But such political MOHs are no justification for the Kidd and Van Valkenburgh MOHs—two wrongs do not make a right. And at least the MacArthur award had some basis in fact.

In summary, a policy of issuing MOHs for combat deaths based merely on status is the only reason explaining why the Navy Department Permanent Board of Awards added Kidd and Van Valkenburgh to the list of men recommended for MOHs, especially when the Fleet Board did not recommend them for MOHs. The Permanent Board, the Secretary, and even the President focused on Kidd's status as a flag officer and commander and Van Valkenburgh's status as a ship commanding officer. The general rule in the military is to defer to the commander or agency closest to the action; in this case, the Fleet Awards Board was the closest agency to the scene of the awards, Oahu, yet the Navy Department Permanent Board of Awards in Washington, DC, acting on its own or at the direction of a higher authority, added two names to the list of the twelve MOH recommendations submitted by the Fleet Board, names the Fleet Board had not included in its report. Thus a double standard is created when a MOH is based on policy, not facts. Then, inevitably, some men receive the award and some do not. In either case, all-important facts are irrelevant.

ARIZONA MOHS: THE DOUBLE STANDARD, PART II—NO FACTUAL BASIS

The typical combat or noncombat MOH must have a factual basis (i.e., it must be based on merit, meaning facts exist to support the MOH and such facts are judged by a high standard of proof). The requirement that facts be produced to support a MOH can be found in the ordeal Jackson Pharris endured in the process of trying to upgrade his Navy Cross to a MOH. This process is explained in the next section of this chapter and in Chapter 19 (Pharris).

But the Kidd and Van Valkenburgh MOHs were based on policy, not facts, so factual basis for the awards is irrelevant to the approval process since the president was presented their names as being recommended for MOHs and he approved the recommendations. But facts are relevant if one is to determine whether the awards, like most other MOHs, were in fact deserved. Policy tells the reader why the MOHs were awarded but tells the reader nothing about whether the MOHs were deserved.

Thus after one answers the question about why Kidd and Van Valkenburgh were added to the list of officers and men recommended for MOHs, one can then ask a second question: Were their MOHs deserved? The Permanent Board, as seen by the language of its Third Endorsement just cited in the text of this chapter, simply cited a brief reference to a Secretarial directive for adding Kidd and Van Valkenburgh to the list of names of those recommended for MOHs without citing facts supporting their inclusion on that list. Did facts exist unmentioned in the Third Endorsement, supporting awards of MOHs to Kidd and Van Valkenburgh?

The requirement that facts support a MOH recommendation exists for combat MOHs—at least for all combat MOHs except those approved for Kidd and Van Valkenburgh. As will be shown, since the Kidd and Van Valkenburgh awards lack factual bases, the MOHs were undeserved.

Anyone reading the Kidd and Van Valkenburgh citations, as approved by President Roosevelt, who has also read the other December 7 MOH citations should immediately have a high index of suspicion regarding the MOH awards for these two officers.

On the one hand, of *Arizona*'s three MOH recipients, Fuqua unquestionably deserved a MOH. His citation contains specific deeds warranting a MOH, deeds proven by his own statements and the statements of others. The record of Fuqua's actions as described Chapter 7 and in his MOH citation are very detailed, probably because he survived and because, as senior surviving officer, he was very visible directing rescue efforts, meaning numerous witnesses could testify concerning his bravery on December 7.[13]

On the other hand, the record of the activities of Kidd and Van Valkenburgh on December 7 is sparse, and their MOH citations are brief with no detail. Both cite the men for "conspicuous devotion to duty, extraordinary courage, and complete disregard of his own life." Kidd's citation adds that he "courageously discharged his duties" but does not explain how he did so; Van Valkenburgh's adds that he "gallantly fought his ship" but does not explain how he did so.[14] In short, the factual bases for these two awards are nonexistent. The MOH citations are short and lack recitation of specific deeds warranting a MOH. The citations are essentially conclusions with only one fact cited in one citation: the Kidd citation, which states that he immediately went to the bridge. The citations are placed here for reader convenience:

Rear Admiral Isaac Kidd

For conspicuous devotion to duty, extraordinary courage, and complete disregard of his own life, during the attack on the fleet in Pearl Harbor, by Japanese forces on December 7, 1941. *He immediately went to the bridge* and as Commander Battleship Division One, courageously discharged his duties as Senior Officer Present Afloat until the USS *Arizona*, his flagship, blew up from magazine explosions and a direct bomb hit on the bridge, which resulted in the loss of his life. [Italics added for emphasis.]

Captain Franklin Van Valkenburgh

For conspicuous devotion to duty, extraordinary courage, and complete disregard of his own life, during the attack on the fleet in Pearl Harbor, by

Japanese forces on December 7, 1941. As Commanding Officer of USS *Arizona*, Captain Van Valkenburgh gallantly fought his ship until the USS *Arizona* blew up from magazine explosions and a direct bomb hit on the bridge, which resulted in the loss of his life.

In fact, as will be made clear, of all the MOHs discussed in this book, combat and noncombat, only these two lack factual bases and are thus undeserved.

In asking if the Kidd and Van Valkenburgh MOHs were deserved, two additional questions must be asked. What did Kidd and Van Valkenburgh do between the time the first bomb fell on Oahu and the time *Arizona* suffered the catastrophic explosion that most likely killed these two officers? That time is approximately between 7:55 (just before "morning colors," when US flags are raised at 8:00 a.m.) and 8:10, the approximate time at which the forward powder magazine exploded cataclysmically.[15] More specifically, did their activities during this time warrant MOHs? As will be demonstrated, the answers to these two questions is that little is known about what they did during this time or what they did to earn MOHs. The answers are that few provable facts about what they did can be found and those that can be found do not warrant MOHs.

What are the facts concerning the actions of Kidd and Van Valkenburgh aboard *Arizona* before the ship exploded?

The persons supplying the most information and most reliable information about Kidd and Van Valkenburgh were Fuqua and Ensign D. Hein, a junior officer aboard *Arizona* during the attack. As senior surviving officer who took charge of the ship in the absence of Kidd and Van Valkenburgh, Fuqua would have been in an excellent position to have firsthand or secondhand knowledge about the two men's activities aboard ship during the attack. Fuqua had little information, from his own observations or those of others, to report about what Kidd and Van Valkenburgh did during the attack. Hein was in the best position to report on Van Valkenburgh's activities before and after the catastrophic explosion that killed the ship because Hein, as explained, was on the navigation bridge with Van Valkenburgh when the explosion occurred.

The information provided by these officers about the precise activities and fates of Kidd and Van Valkenburgh is found in the following formats: each officer submitted statements that were included as enclosures to the ship's after-action report dated December 13, 1941.[16] Additionally, Fuqua personally testified concerning December 7 before the Roberts Commission in 1946, one of the eight investigations of the attack on Oahu.[17]

When asked by a member of the Roberts Commission if he was the senior officer aboard *Arizona*, Fuqua replied, "I was the senior survivor. The captain and the admiral were on board." If those two officers were aboard and alive, then Fuqua would not have been the senior officer.[18]

Fuqua's testimony before the Roberts Commission was essentially the same as his statement in the enclosure to the ship's report concerning December 7. In summary,

Fuqua thought he had been knocked out temporarily by a bomb blast. After he revived, he did not see Kidd or Van Valkenburgh. In his statement, he said he sent two junior officers to look for them in their cabins; in his testimony, he said he sent one junior officer to their cabins. In any event, the officer or officers did not find Kidd or Van Valkenburgh in the cabins. Fuqua then asked those around him if they had seen either officer; no one had. Later, however, the officer of the deck told Fuqua that he had seen Van Valkenburgh "proceed to the bridge." Fuqua wrote in his statement in the enclosure, "By this time [when he dispatched the officer or officers to look for Kidd and Van Valkenburgh] the Captain's cabin and Admiral's cabin were about waist deep in water. A search of the two cabins revealed that the Admiral and Captain were not there."[19]

Fuqua told the Commission that the fire on the ship amidships burned for two days. After it was extinguished or burned out, Fuqua went aboard ship to look for the bodies of Kidd and Van Valkenburgh. Fuqua stated that the crew found Kidd's body, or what was thought to be his body, at the foot of the ladder leading to the flag bridge, the area from which a flag officer directs operations. Fuqua said that Van Valkenburgh's body was never found, although he said that his ring and some coat buttons were found on the flag bridge. He did not identify the type of ring.[20]

Fuqua also told the Commission that about two days after the attack, he found Ensign Hein from the ship in the Naval Hospital at Pearl Harbor. Fuqua testified as to what was in Hein's statement, but he did not clarify if the statement was what Hein may have said to Fuqua in the hospital or if it was the statement the ensign made that was included as an enclosure to the ship's after-action report. In any event, the ensign stated that he was on the bridge (he did not specify which bridge) with the Captain Van Valkenburgh and a quartermaster. The quartermaster told Van Valkenburgh that a bomb hit on or near Turret Number 2. The ensign recounted that the "ship was sinking like an earthquake had struck it, and the bridge was in flames." The ensign ran off the bridge, down the flag bridge, and then fell onto the boat deck. Fuqua testified that the ensign told him, "The boat deck was a mass of flames, and the men were dying all around." The ensign thought about lying down and dying with them, but he went from the boat deck to the quarterdeck to lie down there. Fuqua thought the ensign was one of the wounded men he put in the boats.[21]

In Hein's statement, included as an enclosure to the ship's after-action report, he stated that he saw Kidd on the signal bridge, then he (Hein) went to the navigation bridge, where he found only Van Valkenburgh and the quartermaster, who asked Van Valkenburgh if he wanted to go into the conning tower. Van Valkenburgh declined and made phone calls. He confirmed Fuqua's version of Hein's statement. Hein reported that the bridge "shook like it was in an earthquake" and that flames came through the broken bridge windows. Hein then described how the three men tried to escape from the bridge; apparently Hein was the only one who escaped. He ultimately made his way to a barge. He added that just before the shaking, the quartermaster had reported a bomb hit near Turret Number 2.[22]

In addition to Hein and Fuqua, other officers made statements that were enclosures for the ship's after-action report. Ensign J. D. Miller wrote that soon after the attack began, he went to Van Valkenburgh's cabin to obtain keys for the magazine, but Van Valkenburgh was not there; this visit to the cabin preceded the visit he later made at the direction of Fuqua. When Fuqua later asked Miller if he had Kidd or Van Valkenburgh, Miller said no. Fuqua told him to search Van Valkenburgh's cabin again, and Miller, accompanied by a boatswain's mate, went to the cabin but did not find Van Valkenburgh; they did not go into Kidd's cabin.²³ Ensign H. D. Davidson stated that he had sounded the air-raid alarm after seeing bombs fall from an aircraft with "red dots" on its wings. He told Van Valkenburgh about the alarm; Van Valkenburgh then went to the bridge.²⁴

Flying in the face of Fuqua's testimony and statement and the statements of the junior officers is a 2006 article in the Milwaukee Journal Sentinel newspaper purporting to tell in detail of Van Valkenburgh's actions on December 7. The article states that when the ship's air-raid siren sounded, he went to the bridge; he died within minutes when the ship suffered a catastrophic explosion at 8:06 a.m. The article continued thus:

> Van Valkenburgh was on the phone directing his men when he was wounded in the abdomen by shrapnel. When the explosion ripped open the ship, Van Valkenburgh refused to be carried to safety and ordered sailors who tried to move him to save themselves, according to newspaper accounts. He received the Medal of Honor posthumously.
>
> Only Van Valkenburgh's Naval Academy ring was found.²⁵

The only part of this section of the article Fuqua corroborates is his testimony that Van Valkenburgh's ring was found, although Fuqua did not say it was a Naval Academy ring. Neither Fuqua nor any other office ever mentioned directly or indirectly that Van Valkenburgh was wounded by shrapnel in the abdomen and then refused evacuation. The statements of the junior officers do not give this account of Van Valkenburgh's purported actions, although Hein mentions Van Valkenburgh being on the bridge and using the phone. Hein mentions nothing about Van Valkenburgh being wounded on the bridge and refusing assistance. The author has seen no other information or evidence stating that Van Valkenburgh was wounded in the abdomen or anywhere else and refused evacuation, ordering other crewmen to leave him alone, although an author reported in a book published in 1945 Van Valkenburgh's purported resistance to evacuation, writing that "Captain Bennion [aboard *West Virginia*], as had Captain Van Valkenburgh on the *Arizona*, refused to be moved and ordered his subordinate officers to save the men and themselves."²⁶

In fact, this description of Van Valkenburgh's purported activities is suspiciously similar to the MOH citation for Captain Bennion of *West Virginia*, whose MOH action has strong corroboration. For comparison, the Bennion MOH is placed here:

> For conspicuous devotion to duty, extraordinary courage, and complete disregard of his own life, above and beyond the call of duty, during the attack on the fleet in Pearl Harbor, by Japanese forces on December 7, 1941. *As Commanding Officer of the USS West Virginia, after being mortally wounded,*

Capt. Bennion evidenced apparent concern only in fighting and saving his ship, and strongly protested against being carried from the bridge. [Italics added for emphasis.]

Although the citation does not describe the wound or its cause, the evidence is undisputed that shrapnel hit Bennion in the abdomen and mortally wounded him. Chapter 6 of this book describes in detail how Bennion was wounded. Readers must conclude that the Journal Sentinel writer or the "newspaper accounts" were confused, attributing Bennion's specific action (resistance to evacuation) to Van Valkenburgh as well.

Another factor calling into question the credibility of the Journal Sentinel's account is timing. The bomb that destroyed the ship hit on the starboard side near Turret Number 2, which was the forward turret closest to the bridges. Given the power of the explosion—it was caused by a bomb piercing the deck and hitting powder magazines or fuel or both—Van Valkenburgh and anyone on the bridge would have been immolated by the flames quickly. As Ensign Hein reported, the bridge was in flames when he escaped from it. In those conditions and in that brief time period, the events as described by the newspaper could not have occurred: a wounded Van Valkenburgh refusing to be evacuated and urging sailors trying to help him to save themselves. Also, according to Hein, only Van Valkenburgh, the quartermaster, and Hein were on the bridge, so who were the "other sailors" trying to rescue Van Valkenburgh? Unlike the purported actions aboard *Arizona* described by the Journal Sentinel, the actions described on *West Virginia* are consistent with reality. Although the conditions on *West Virginia*'s bridge and ship were atrocious, they were not as catastrophic as on *Arizona*, thus affording crewman time and opportunity to try to save Bennion. Again, Chapter 6 of this book describes the Bennion ordeal.

One final source will be mentioned. The Kidd Official Military Personnel File (OMPF) contains a tribute in the Army and Navy Register of March 7, 1942. The unnamed author wrote that on December 7, Kidd "was on hand and on duty, directing in person the anti-aircraft [sic] gun crews in the vicinity of the battleship's bridge."[27] No sources reviewed in writing this book revealed any evidence whatsoever supporting the assertion that Kidd personally directed antiaircraft fire.

So one must return to the two questions asked previously: What did Kidd and Van Valkenburgh do between the time the first bomb fell on Oahu and the time the *Arizona* suffered the catastrophic explosion that most likely killed them, and did their activities during this time warrant MOHs? The answers to these two questions remain the same as earlier stated. Little is known about what they did during this time and what activities are known did not warrant MOHs.

The deduction from the answers is that their MOHs lack factual bases and their MOHs should not have been awarded based on broad, nonspecific statements, unsupported by facts, about acting gallantly (Van Valkenburgh) or courageously (Kidd). The MOHs appear to have been awarded for the same reason Kidd's and Van Valkenburgh's names were added to the fleet board's list of men recommended for MOHs: policy based on status as senior commanders killed manning their battle stations. Certainly no facts have been discovered supporting a MOH. In fact, as will be seen in the discussion in Chapter 16 about Marine Lieutenant Colonel Daniel Fox, who perished aboard the ship, the Permanent Board of Awards recommended that the Secretary of the Navy deny him a MOH; to paraphrase the Board's reasoning, it recommended denial because to award him a MOH would set a precedent for giving awards for simply manning battle stations, which is, ironically, the only actions in the citations supporting the Kidd and Van Valkenburgh awards. The Secretary concurred with the Board and disapproved the Fox MOH recommendation.

If the Kidd and Van Valkenburgh MOH awards were not based on facts, one may ask, "Who cares?" The question is important since each MOH award made without factual basis demeans other MOH awards earned with factual bases and often at the cost of the recipients' lives. One wonders how Lieutenant Commander Fuqua felt knowing he had on the merits earned a MOH and that his Commanding Officer and Battleship Division Commander had received the same award without demonstrating sufficient actions to justify MOH awards. One may regret that the two officers were killed, but death in the line of duty alone does not justify a MOH. As just noted, the Navy's own Permanent Board of Awards denied a MOH for just that reason for Lieutenant Colonel Daniel Fox of *Arizona* while adding to the list of those recommended for MOHs two senior *Arizona* officers who had simply died in the line of duty.

Finally, the Kidd and Van Valkenburgh MOH awards are the only generic MOH awards for December 7. As seen in Chapters 4 through 13 and 19 of this book, all the other MOH citations cite specific actions by the recipients justifying their MOHs. The Kidd and Van Valkenburgh MOH awards are the only generic awards in the sense that the citations simply cite generalities. The key language of the Kidd citation cited in this chapter states that he went to the bridge and "courageously discharged his duties as Senior Officer Present Afloat…" What duties, and how did he discharge them in a way justifying a MOH? Mere courage does not qualify an action for a MOH. The key language of the Van Valkenburgh citation cited in this chapter states that he gallantly fought his ship…" How did he do so, and how did he do so in a way justifying a MOH? Mere gallantry does not qualify an action for a MOH. What is interesting is that no other officer or enlisted man receiving a MOH in the Hawaiian Islands in World War II received one with a citation containing such vague language describing what the recipient did.

In summary, the hypocrisy and double standard are easily seen. Of four MOH recommendations for *Arizona* officers, Fuqua received a MOH supported by facts, Kidd and Van Valkenburgh received MOHs based on no facts, and Fox received no MOH with no reference to facts, although he was apparently in the same position as Kidd and Van Valkenburgh. So twelve of the fourteen MOH recommendations made by the Permanent Board were based on facts. Two were not. On their faces, the language in their citations did not meet the requirements of a MOH.[28]

Arizona MOHs: The Double Standard, Part III—Facts and the Standard of Proof

To revisit the second question about whether the facts supported MOHs for Kidd and Van Valkenburgh and the "no" answer, one can ask how the "no" answer was reached. If facts were irrelevant, then judging them against any standard of proof is a wasted act. If no facts existed to support MOHs, then the standard of proof is irrelevant—no facts exist to be judged against any standard of proof.

But at least a few facts indicated what Kidd and Van Valkenburgh did on December 7. What was the strength of those facts, and did they warrant MOHs?

The specters of hypocrisy and double standard arise again, this time in the area of the degree or standard of proof required by the Navy in World War II to support a MOH recommendation. In this regard, one should read Chapter 19 concerning the Jackson Pharris MOH and notice the high, stringent evidentiary standards the Navy required before it would recommend upgrading the his Navy Cross to a MOH— "incontestable justification" and "incontrovertible facts." The reader should then compare the Pharris MOH citation to the Kidd and Van Valkenburgh citations. The comparison is embarrassing to the Navy, to say the least. Two men receive MOHs for generic actions while one man, enduring substantial physical abuse that plagued him for years, initially received a Navy Cross and finally a MOH for saving shipmates and preventing his ship from capsizing.

What has been established is that with just a few clacks of typewriter keys, the Permanent Board of Awards added Kidd and Van Valkenburgh to the list of MOH recommendations and added proposed citations in its endorsement of a Fleet Board of Awards report that did not recommend either officer for a MOH or any other award or even mention their names. The process of typing their names and citations should have taken only minutes, especially since the citations are short and the actions supporting the MOHs are generic. Additionally, no standard of proof is mentioned.[29]

The facts that do show what Kidd and Van Valkenburgh did on December 7 were obviously not evaluated against the high standard of proof required for the approval of a combat MOH. Not only must a MOH have a factual basis, but those facts must be evaluated against a stringent standard of proof—at least for all combat MOHs except those approved for Kidd and Van Valkenburgh. Again, the requirement of judging facts supporting a MOH against a high standard of proof can be found in the ordeal Jackson Pharris endured in the process of trying to upgrade his Navy Cross to a MOH. As will be shown, the few facts proving what Kidd and Van Valkenburgh did on December 7 were judged by a very low standard of proof to the extent that they were judged against any standard of proof.

The result is an inescapable conclusion: double standards. One was a double standard in the existence of facts supporting a MOH. The Navy required the Pharris MOH recommendation to be supported by facts; it did not require the Kidd and Van Valkenburgh MOH recommendations to be supported by facts other than manning their battle stations. The other double standard was in the standard of proof required for the facts supporting a MOH; in other words, what degree of factual proof was needed? Chapter 19 explains that "incontestable justification" and "incontrovertible facts" were the standard by which the facts were judged during the process of upgrading the Navy Cross Pharris had received in 1942 to a MOH he finally received in 1948. He was not only required to furnish numerous witness statements attesting to the existence of facts, but also the facts in the statements were held to the very high standards of proof just mentioned. Apparently no or a very low standard was required of the facts, if any existed, supporting the Kidd and Van Valkenburgh MOH recommendations.

As an analogy, in the law, civil cases require a standard of proof known as "the preponderance of the evidence." The side having 51 or more percent of the proof wins. In a criminal case, the standard of proof is higher: "beyond a reasonable doubt." No number attaches to beyond a reasonable doubt.[30] Jackson Pharris appears to have been held to a standard close to beyond a reasonable doubt when terms such as incontestable justification and incontrovertible facts are used; those terms leave no room for doubt.

Although the general rule is, as noted above, deference to the commander or agency "closest to the action," exceptions exist. The Fleet Board was wrong in recommending Pharris for a Navy Cross instead of a MOH. Why the Fleet Board did not have in 1942 the witness statements supporting a MOH that could and would be obtained after the war to support a MOH for Pharris is unknown.

SUMMARY
THE KIDD AND VAN VALKENBURGH MOHS

The conclusion stated earlier in this chapter bears repeating: of all the MOHs discussed in this book, combat and noncombat, only the Kidd and Van Valkenburgh MOHs lack sufficient factual bases to warrant MOHs, and the few facts demonstrating their activities on *Arizona* on December 7 were not judged by the high standard of proof by which facts are evaluated in the process of awarding combat MOHs.

And what bears repeating is that the Fleet Board at Pearl Harbor, the site of the actions leading to 10 of the 12 MOH recommendations it made (it also recommended Finn for Kaneohe and Cannon for Midway), did not recommend Kidd or Van Valkenburgh for MOHs—or even mention them in its report. The absence of recommendation by the Fleet Board and the absence of facts supporting the MOH recommendations are perhaps the most damning pieces of evidence in this matter. Another crucial factor is the lack of evidence indicating that Admiral Nimitz, the Fleet Commander, recommended either officer for a MOH.

In Chapter 14 and in this chapter, the MOH process was analogized to a court case. The advocate trying to prove his case must present facts to the trier of fact—judge or jury—and those facts must meet a certain threshold or standard of proof before the advocate can win. In a civil case, the standard is a preponderance of the evidence; in a criminal case, it is beyond a reasonable doubt.

Likewise, the commander or a board recommending someone for a MOH must present facts, and those facts must meet a threshold such that they are judged sufficient to support a MOH award.

Thus if an advocate presented to a court the case for the Kidd or Van Valkenburgh MOHs, the case would be dismissed for failure of proof. No standard of proof has been met—whatever that standard was for them—either because of no facts or a paucity of facts supporting a MOH for either officer. If those putting forth the Kidd and Van Valkenburgh awards had few or no facts supporting their MOHs from the beginning, then the standard of proof would be irrelevant since the advocate would have no facts to be judged by any standard of proof. All that is known is that in the Pharris case, the advocates—Bunkley and Pharris—not only had to produce facts but also had to produce facts meeting a high standard, which was, according to the Board of Review for Decorations and Medals, "incontestable justification" and "incontrovertible facts."

The Kidd and Van Valkenburgh recommendations simply escaped the requirement imposed for other combat MOHs: a recommendation supported by facts—facts supplied by more than one witness and judged or evaluated against a stringent standard of proof. The Pharris MOH recommendation, however, was held to that requirement, almost to an extreme degree. Only one fact was cited in the Kidd and Van Valkenburgh citations—Kidd going to the bridge. The fact of Van Valkenburgh making phone calls from the bridge was not even included in his citation. What is remarkable is that the Third Endorsement makes no reference to witness statements; it simply includes proposed citations for Kidd and Van Valkenburgh, citations adopted almost verbatim and sent to the President for his approval; he approved them on March 4, 1942. Witness statements, however, were the heart and soul of the effort to upgrade the Pharris Navy Cross to a MOH. No question existed that the Navy Board required Pharris to produce them if the upgrade were to occur.

But, after all, Pharris was merely a warrant officer on December 7. He was not a rear admiral or a captain and did not command a battleship division or even his own ship—rather, he simply saved her from capsizing and saved the lives of many of his crewmen.

By proposing the Kidd and Van Valkenburgh MOHs and by processing them the way it did, the Navy did the following.

First, it made a MOH into an award bestowed to Kidd and Van Valkenburgh merely because they were senior officers killed at their battle stations. The MOH is not an award for being killed in action; the Navy made that point clear when the recommendation for a MOH for Lieutenant Colonel Fox was disapproved. An award specifically designed to recognize death in combat exists: a Purple Hear, which each officer received in addition to the MOH. Absent factual support for a MOH for Kidd or Van Valkenburgh, they should have received only Purple Hearts. So, in effect, the MOHs are Purple Hearts in the guise of MOHs, and the Navy had its cake and ate it too: undeserved MOHs for two Navy officers, Kidd and Van Valkenburgh, and no MOH for the ship's senior Marine officer, Lieutenant Colonel Fox.

Second, it made a mockery of the customs, traditions, and rituals of the service by demeaning the MOH, which is sacred within the military, by removing the honor associated with it. A MOH is not honorable if it has no factual basis to support its award.

Third, it permitted the gravamen of the MOHs to be conclusions, opinions, and general statements rather than supportable facts that are cited in the typical MOH citation.

Finally, without any apparent justification other than Kidd and Van Valkenburgh being senior officers killed in action—certainly no facts proving bravery were proffered—it ensured the two men would receive MOHs easily while putting Jackson Pharris, one of four *California* MOH recipients and the final December 7 recipient to receive his MOH, through administrative hell in his effort to upgrade his MOH, which was more than supported by facts that could be proven.

Thus Kidd and Van Valkenburgh were commended not once but twice posthumously by receiving MOHs and Purple Hearts for being killed at their battle stations. No additional facts exist to prove they took any actions other than manning those battle stations. Their Purple Hearts were the only award appropriate for these two officers. As the Navy's own Permanent Board of Awards wrote in recommending that the request for a MOH for Fox be disapproved, the Navy cannot set a precedent for rewarding every member who is killed at his battle station.

That may be the rule, and a sound one, but unjustified exceptions were made to it for Kidd and Van Valkenburgh such that they were awarded MOHs that were in effect "super" Purple Hearts. The only logical reason for these exceptions is status and death; each officer was a senior officer killed in action. The award for such circumstance—the Purple Heart, just described—was the only award justified for either officer in this case.

Notes

1. The National Personnel Records Center, St. Louis, Missouri, furnished military and personal information from Kidd's Official Military Personnel File (OMPF) at the author's request. The material came in two formats. Initially, it was in selected pages copied from his OMPF (hereafter "Kidd OMPF initial request"); later, it came in the form of a compact disc with his entire OMPF (hereafter "Kidd OMPF (CD)"). In the Kidd OMPF (CD) is the Third Endorsement QB-4-OS from the Senior Member, Navy Department Permanent Board of Awards to the Secretary of the Navy. "Subject: Japanese Attack on U.S. Pacific Fleet in Pearl Harbor Dec. 7, 1941, Recommendations for awards for gallant conduct in action of naval and civilian personnel." The Third Endorsement and its accompanying summary are in section 06 ("Awards, Decorations, and Correspondence") of the CD on pages 40–45 of the OMPF CD (CD page numbers). The twelve MOH recommendations are in paragraph 2 of page 1 (endorsement page number). The comment about Kidd and Van Valkenburgh is in paragraph 4 on page 5 (endorsement page number) (hereafter "Third Endorsement"). Attempts to obtain a copy of any report the Fleet Board may have written were unsuccessful, but the absence of any Fleet Board report is not fatal; the

Third Endorsement is the operative, crucial document here because it shows how Kidd and Van Valkenburgh were recommended for MOHs.

2. Endnote 1, Third Endorsement, 5, paragraph 4 (endorsement page number).

3. Ibid.

4. Ibid.

5. The Roosevelt approval of MOH citations is based on documents provided to the author by the Franklin D. Roosevelt Presidential Library and MUSeum.

6. Ibid., 5, paragraph 4.

7. Paul Stillwell, Battleship *Arizona* (Naval Institute Press, Annapolis, MD, 1991) 3 (hereafter "Stillwell, Battleship *Arizona*").

8. First Endorsement of December 13, 1941, by Commander Battleships, Battle Force Rear Admiral W. S. Anderson on *West Virginia* BB48/A 16-3 [report] of December 11, 1941.

9. Report from Rear Admiral W. S. Anderson (Subject: "Distinguished Conduct—Report of—Pearl Harbor Raid, December 7, 1941") of December 19, 1941; paragraph 4(b), Bennion, paragraph 4(d); Jones, paragraph 4(f)(2)(Hill); Kidd and Van Valkenburgh, paragraph 4(e).

10. Letter from the Senior Member of the [Navy] Board for the Award of Medals of Honor, Distinguished Service Medal, Navy Cross, Distinguished Flying Cross, and Life Saving Medals ("Subject: Recommendation for the posthumous award of the Medal of Honor in the case of the late Lieutenant Colonel Daniel R. Fox, U.S. Marine Corps") of June 3, 1942 (hereafter "Fox MOH Rejection Letter"); the National Personnel Records Center, St. Louis, Missouri, furnished military and personal information from Fox's Official Military Personnel File (OMPF) at the author's request. The material that came was pages copied from his OMPF (hereafter "Fox OMPF"); Robert J. Cressman and J. Michael Wenger, Infamous Day: Marines at Pearl Harbor December 7, 1941 (Marine Corps Historical Center, Washington, DC,1992), 12 (Fox on Kidd's staff and the senior Marine aboard *Arizona*).

11. William Manchester, American Caesar (Little, Brown and Company, Boston, Toronto, 1978), 275; the MacArthur MOH citation can be found by searching the Internet for "army MOH site," which will lead to the army's master list of MOH recipients. The citation can be found under the section "World War II (M–S)."

12. The Greely MOH citation can be found by searching the Internet for "army MOH site," which will lead to the Army's master list of MOH recipients; the citation can be found under the section "Interim 1920–1940."

13. Chapter 7 and Appendix A of this book have the full citation of the Fuqua MOH.

14. The operative language of the Kidd and Van Valkenburgh MOH citations appears in this chapter, respectively. The full citations are in Chapter 7 and Appendix A of this book.

15. The first Japanese bomb hit Ford Island at approximately 7:55 a.m., just before morning colors occurred.

16. Report from USS *Arizona* (Subject: Action Report of USS *Arizona* December 7, 1941) of December 13, 1941 (hereafter "*Arizona* report"); Enclosure (H) to the report is Fuqua's statement (hereafter "*Arizona* report, Fuqua enclosure"); Enclosure (C) is Hein's statement (hereafter "*Arizona* report, Hein enclosure").

17. Testimony of Lieutenant Commander Fuqua on January 2, 1942, before the Roberts Commission, included in the report of the 1945 Congressional investigation of the attack found in PEARL HARBOR ATTACK; HEARINGS BEFORE THE JOINT COMMITTEE ON THE INVESTIGATION OF THE PEARL HARBOR ATTACK, SEVENTY-NINTH CONGRESS, FIRST SESSION, Part 23 (U.S. Government Printing Office, Washington, D.C., 1946), 632–637.

18. Ibid., 635–636.

19. *Arizona* report, Fuqua enclosure (paragraph 2).

20. Endnote 17, Roberts Commission included in Joint Committee Report, 636.

21. Ibid., 636.

22. Endnote 16, *Arizona* report, Hein enclosure.

23. Endnote 16, *Arizona* report; enclosure (A) is Miller's statement.

24. Endnote 16, *Arizona* report; enclosure (F) is Davidson's statement.

25. Meg Jones, "Milwaukee's forgotten hero," Milwaukee Journal Sentinel, December 7, 2006, states that Van Valkenburgh grew up in Milwaukee.
26. Francis Trevelyan Miller, History of World War II (The Publisher's Guild, New York, NY, 1945), 329.
27. Endnote 11, Kidd OMPF (CD), section 08 ("Newspaper Clippings"), 3.

28. The statute governing the Navy MOH at the time (enacted in 1919) required conspicuous by gallantry and intrepidity at the risk of the recipient's life above and beyond the call of duty (see Chapter 14 and Appendix D of this book).

29. Endnote 1, Third Endorsement, 5, paragraph 4.

30. Author's knowledge of the different standards of proof learned in law school.

Chapter 16
Medal of Honor "Non Award"—Lieutenant Colonel Daniel Fox, U.S. Marine Corps, USS *Arizona* (BB-39)

Chapters 14 and 15 recounted how Rear Admiral Isaac Kidd and Captain Franklin Van Valkenburgh, both of *Arizona*, received posthumous MOHs after the Permanent Board of Awards, for whatever reason or reasons, added their names to the list of men recommended by the Fleet Board for MOHs although no facts supported the two recommendations.

But the Permanent Board, in a classic instance of military hypocrisy and double standards, recommended disapproval of a MOH recommendation for the senior Marine Corps officer aboard *Arizona* on December 7, who perished with Kidd and Van Valkenburgh and who was apparently in the same position as Kidd and Van Valkenburgh: Lieutenant Colonel Daniel Fox, who was on Kidd's staff as the Battleship Division One Division Marine officer. He was one of the most if not the most decorated men aboard the ship: his Official Military Personnel (OMPF) file records his enlisted service during World War I, during which he received a Navy Cross (second to the MOH) and a Purple Heart.

On March 27, 1942, the Commanding General of Marine Forces, Fourteenth Naval District (encompassing the Navy base and Pearl Harbor), recommended Fox for a MOH, noting that he thought that Fox was on the ship's bridge with Kidd and Van Valkenburgh when all were killed by the same explosion. He wrote that in light of Kidd and Van Valkenburgh being cited posthumously that Fox should receive the same consideration as the other two officers.[1] After all, in the absence of facts demonstrating what any of the three officers did to earn a MOH and if the Marines believed that Fox had gone to the bridge with Kidd and Van Valkenburgh, the Marines were justified in recommending Fox for a MOH. If simply going to their battle stations warranted a MOH for the two Navy officers, then it should warrant a MOH for a Marine officer who took the same action as the Navy officers. In short, the Marines, and rightly so, detected hypocrisy and took action to address it.

In the first endorsement of the letter, Headquarters, U.S. Marine Corps, requested that Major Alan Shapley submit a statement concerning the activities of Fox on December 7. Shapley, who had been the Commanding Officer of the Marine Detachment, aboard *Arizona*, was aboard *Arizona* on December 7.[2]

Shapley submitted an endorsement dated April 20, 1942, stating that he had seen Fox on December 7 on his way to the flag bridge, which was his battle station. He continued,

> Since he was never seen again it must be assumed that he met his death at his battle station with Rear Admiral I. C. Kidd. To the best of my knowledge all hands in this vicinity of the ship were killed.
>
> *It is strongly recommended that Lieutenant Colonel Fox be cited posthumously as were Rear Admiral Kidd and Captain Van Valkenburgh.*[3] [Italics added for emphasis.]

The Commandant of the Marine Corps favorably endorsed the request on May 4, 1942, writing the first two paragraphs of his as follows:

> It is recommended that the Medal of Honor be posthumously awarded the late Lieutenant Colonel Daniel R. Fox, USMC., who was killed on the Flag Bridge or on his way to the Flag Bridge which was his battle station aboard the USS *Arizona* the morning of the attack on Pearl Harbor, 7 December 1941.
>
> Rear Admiral Isaac C Kidd, USN., and Captain Franklin Van Valkenburgh, USN., were posthumously awarded the Medal of Honor. They both were killed when the USS *Arizona* blew up from magazine explosions and a direct bomb hit on the bridge.[4]

But on June 3, 1942, the Permanent Board of Awards recommended that the Secretary of the Navy disapprove the recommendation, writing, "to award the Medal of Honor in this case would establish a precedent for awards to every one [sic] who has lost or subsequently may lose his life while at his battle-station…"[5]

The Commandant, contrary to his earlier favorable endorsement, recommended by endorsement of the Board's June 3 letter that the Board's action be approved. The subject line of the Commandant's June 18, 1942, letter was, "Non Award of the Medal of Honor in the case of the late Lieutenant Colonel Daniel R. Fox, USMC."[6] The Secretary of the Navy approved the Board's action on June 29, 1942.[7]

The Board's recommendation in the Fox case is correct as a matter of policy; the MOH should not be awarded to men who simply man their battle stations and die while doing so without additional actions justifying MOHs. So the double standard is that manning battle stations and being killed while so doing, which is precisely the nature of the MOH awards for Kidd and Van Valkenburgh, was sufficient basis for their MOHs but not for Fox's.

What the Board failed to do was to decide the case based on the facts or really a lack of facts supporting the Fox recommendation for a MOH; were it to do so, it would again display hypocrisy and a double standard. No facts are cited or known to support a MOH award for either Navy officer or the Marine officer. The Permanent Board cited no facts supporting a MOH for Kidd or Van Valkenburgh for actions they took between the short time the attack began (approximately 7:55 a.m.) and the time of the catastrophic explosion of *Arizona* (approximately 8:05 a.m.), the explosion thought to have taken the lives of Kidd, Van Valkenburgh, and Fox. But as can be seen from the record, the presence or absence of facts was irrelevant in all three case; the facts were unimportant in the case of two officers who received MOHs and were unimportant in the case of one officer who did not. Policy, not presence or absence of facts, ruled the day.

So the hypocrisy and double standard of the Board and Secretary in recommending MOHs for Kidd and Van Valkenburgh—while denying a recommendation to Fox—are apparent; essentially, Kidd was cited explicitly and Van Valkenburgh cited implicitly for going to their battle stations and doing what was expected of them rather than taking actions that were extraordinary or above and beyond the call of duty. In fact, the Permanent Board's addition of Kidd and Van Valkenburgh to the list of those recommended for MOHs contradicted its very reason for denying a MOH to Fox. The Navy cannot set a precedent of giving awards to everyone killed at his battle station, but that is precisely what the Permanent Board did in including Kidd and Van Valkenburgh for MOHs. In this regard, the following is the operative language from the Kidd MOH citation found in Appendix A of this book:

> Rear Adm. Kidd immediately went to the bridge and, as commander Battleship Division One, courageously discharged his duties as senior officer present afloat until the USS *Arizona*, his flagship, blew up from magazine explosions and a direct bomb hit on the bridge which resulted in the loss of his life.

The following is the operative language from the Van Valkenburgh MOH citation found in Appendix A of this book:

> As commanding officer of the USS *Arizona*, Capt. Van Valkenburgh gallantly fought his ship until the USS *Arizona* blew up from magazine explosions and a direct bomb hit on the bridge which resulted in the loss of his life.

Since the Kidd and Van Valkenburgh awards were awards based on policy rather than facts, one could argue that Billy Mitchell should not have received a MOH that was in essence an award based on policy. The stated reason for the award was the legitimate recognition of his foresight in the field of military aviation, not for combat heroism. The unstated reason for the award, however, was an apology for the shabby, disrespectful way Mitchell was treated, in and out of the military, as a pariah, someone whose ideas were dismissed at the time because they challenged conventional thinking, but his ideas about airpower proved decisive during World War II. He was correctly called "a prophet without honor." Chapter 20 of this book discusses the Mitchell award in detail.

What should be noted here, however, is that no pretense was made that the Mitchell award was for combat heroism, and other men—such as Charles Lindbergh—had received MOHs for noncombat heroism. Overwhelming evidence supported an award for both Lindbergh and Mitchell. Lindbergh flew from the United States to Paris nonstop, and Mitchell's actions and pronouncements advocating airpower are a matter of public record. They are noncombat awards with bases in fact while, as has been repeatedly stated, the Kidd and Van Valkenburgh awards were awards with no bases in fact.[8]

Also, Mitchell's award is not a traditional MOH; it is a special gold medal that should never have been termed a "Medal of Honor." In fact, it can be considered a Congressional Gold Medal although "Medal of Honor" is in the title of the legislation authorizing the Mitchell award.

In short, Mitchell had earned, the hard way, recognition for his advocacy of airpower, and Congress and the President believed that that recognition should be in the form of a special gold medal presented to his son—a medal that was not, however, a classic combat MOH and did not reference combat bravery. It was an award deserved since so many of Mitchell's predictions and ideas about airpower came true; airpower was a major factor in the Allied defeat of Japan and Germany in World War II.

Summary: The Fox MOH "Non Award"

Unfortunately, the conversations and discussions—and possibly arguments—concerning the Marine's action in recommending Fox for a MOH are not recorded. Were they recorded in writing or audibly, they would in all likelihood make for very, very interesting reading or listening. They, unlike official documents, may have revealed the true motivation for the marine recommendation. That motivation, in the author's opinion and in laymen's terms, was that the Marines smelled a rat and took steps to mitigate the smell.

The Marine recommendation was dated March 27, 1942; President Roosevelt approved the Kidd and Van Valkenburgh MOH recommendations on March 4, 1942, so the Marines had to know about the MOHs for these two Navy officers. The correspondence cited earlier in this chapter proves that the Marines did know about the two Navy MOHs. Knowing that the two Navy officers had received MOHs, the Marines tried, in true Marine Corps fashion and tradition, to obtain a MOH for one of their own officers similarly situated as the Navy officers.

But the Marines failed in their efforts to eliminate the smell of politics or the smell of MOHs awarded without factual basis. The problem was not the failure to award a MOH to Fox; the problem was awarding MOHs to Kidd and Van Valkenburgh. As with Kidd and Van Valkenburgh, no facts of record supported a MOH for Fox. But for some reason, the requirement for factual support was dispensed with for the two Navy officers but not for the Marine officer.

And those who were or are Marines are left wondering why their Commandant recommended approval of the Fox MOH recommendation on its way up the chain of command but shifted into reverse and recommended approval of the Permanent Board's recommendation that the Fox MOH recommendation be disapproved.

In any event, the Board undercut its own decision in the Kidd and Van Valkenburgh cases by deciding the Fox case based on policy. Fox received no MOH for merely manning his battle station while Kidd and Van Valkenburgh received MOHs for doing exactly that. And the board could not decide the case on the facts. If it decided that no facts supported the Fox MOH, then how could it justify the Kidd and Van Valkenburgh awards, which were also unsupported by facts?

So history leaves the military with two December 7 MOHs that were undeserved. Nothing can be done about the awards, and no sane person, military or civilian, would advocate that they be revoked. And the Fox OMPF notes that he received a Gold

Star in lieu of a second Purple Heart for his death aboard *Arizona*; Kidd and Van Valkenburgh should have likewise received only Purple Hearts for death aboard the ship.

If two wrongs do not make a right, then denying Fox a MOH was the correct decision, leaving December 7 history scarred with that awkward term in the Fox case that is probably unique in the annals of the MOH and bureaucratic military writing: "Non award of the Medal of Honor…"

Notes

1. The National Personnel Records Center, St. Louis, Missouri furnished military and personal information from Fox's Official Military Personnel File (OMPF) at the author's requests. The material came was pages copied from his OMPF (hereafter "Fox OMPF"); one of the pages was the Letter from Headquarters, Marine Forces, Fourteenth Naval District, Navy Yard, Pearl Harbor, T. H. (Subject: "Lieutenant Colonel Daniel R. Fox, Report of") of March 27, 1942.

2. Ibid.; First Endorsement from Headquarters, US Marine Corps (Subject: "Information Regarding the Service of the Late Lieutenant Colonel Daniel R. Fox, USMC, on December 7 1941") of April 14, 1942.

3. Ibid.; Third Endorsement from Major Alan Shapley (Subject: "Information Regarding the Service of the Late Lieutenant Colonel Daniel R. Fox, USMC, on December 7 1941") of April 14, 1942.

4. Ibid.; Fifth Endorsement from Major General Thomas Holcomb (Subject: "Recommendation for the Posthumous Award of the Medal of Honor in the Case of the Late Lieutenant Colonel Daniel R. Fox, USMC, on December 7, 1941") of May 4, 1942.

5. Ibid.; "Senior Member of the Board for the Award of Medals of Honor, Distinguished Service Medal, Navy Cross, Distinguished Flying Cross and Life Saving Medals" of June 3, 1942." This is the letter by which the Board recommended disapproval of the recommendation that Fox receive a MOH.

6. Ibid.; Second Endorsement from Major General Thomas Holcomb (Subject: "Non award of the Medal of Honor in the Case of the Late Lieutenant Colonel Daniel R. Fox, USMC") of June 18, 1942.

7. Ibid.; below Holcomb's signature is "Approved" and the signature "Frank Knox" over the titled "Secretary of the Navy"; the date of his signature is June 29, 1942).

8. The Mitchell MOH citation can be found by searching the Internet for "army MOH site," which will lead to the army's master list of MOH recipients; the citation can be found under the section "Special Legislation." The Lindbergh award can be found under "Interim 1920–1940."

Photograph
Lieutenant Colonel Daniel Fox, USMC

Lieutenant Colonel Daniel Fox, U.S. Marine Corps. His senior ribbon is the Navy Cross he earned during World War I.

Chapter 17
Medal of Honor Not Earned or Awarded—The Doris Miller Controversy

Introduction: The "Silent" Medal of Honor

No story of the MOHs awarded for December 7 would be complete without mentioning Doris Miller, whose niece wrote the book Doris Miller: A Silent Medal of Honor Winner. One could ask many questions here, such as "Who is a silent MOH winner?" or "What is a silent MOH?"

One could inquire why Doris Miller is the first American hero of World War II; the first hero of World War II, period; or a "World War II Icon."

What is more productive is to penetrate the wall surrounding Miller that comprises myths, hero worship, speculation, political correctness, and hyperbole. Only by penetrating this wall can one obtain clear access to the facts about his actions on December 7 at Pearl Harbor and place those facts in context and perspective. After the facts are known and Miller's actions placed in perspective and context, one can then reach an informed, intelligent opinion about whether his actions on December 7 aboard USS *West Virginia* warranted a MOH, which he did not receive although many thought he should have, or the Navy Cross he received, as directed by President Franklin D. Roosevelt himself, for political reasons.

The story of Miller's life, his actions on December 7, and the political and personal intrigue regarding his Navy Cross and lack of a MOH has been told in many publications. The result is two versions of the Miller story: an accurate one and an inaccurate one. The bases of the accurate version are demonstrable facts, context, and perspective. The bases of the inaccurate, politically correct version are distortions, errors, omissions, hyperbole, fabrication, and myth. Disregarded or ignored are facts, context, and perspective. The politically correct version also includes opinions lacking factual bases. In the politically correct world, where the extreme is normal, authors feel comfortable anointing Miller as "the first American hero of World War II" or even the "first hero of World War II"—the entire war—as if heroes are numbered in order of precedence, if that precedence can be determined in the scope and chaos of a world war.

This chapter gives the accurate version, examining the factually baseless assertions that Miller is either such hero. From the accurate version, one will see that Doris Miller is, realistically with context and all facts and circumstances considered, one of the least important service members present at Pearl Harbor on December 7, 1941. His importance derives solely from being the first black sailor to receive a Navy Cross, which he received for his actions on December 7. Were he Caucasian with or without a Navy Cross, he would not rate a footnote in the story of December 7.

Most important, the politically correct version does not examine the MOH question in three contexts. One, it does not examine in detail what Miller did on December 7. Two, it does not compare his actions with the statutory criteria for a MOH. Three, it does not compare what he did with the actions of the men who did receive MOHs for December 7. Unfortunately, the two authors examining the Miller story in detail (Richard E. Miller and Neil Sapper) do not examine the contexts of the MOH; they do not even mention the December 7 MOH recipients.

The MOH question, as does his importance in general, exists for only one reason: Miller's race. Miller was black, and all the December 7 MOH recipients were Caucasians. If Miller were a Caucasian sailor named "Tom Smith," a controversy over a Navy Cross or MOH would never have arisen if Smith's actions were the same as Miller's on December 7.

Previous chapters of this book discussed men who received the MOH for actions on December 7, at Midway in 1942, or at Pearl Harbor in 1945. This chapter focuses on a man who did not receive the MOH—Doris Miller. Various campaigns have been initiated over the years to obtain a MOH for him; some began while he was alive, others after he died. The controversy and attempt to obtain a MOH for him remains very much alive for some people.

Three points should be understood at the outset of this chapter.

One, Miller's life history will not be recounted here since the focus of this chapter is his military career. The story of his entire life can be found in other sources.

Two, this chapter does not question Miller's bravery or his dedication to duty to his ship, to his shipmates, and to his commanding officer in the horrid circumstances of December 7.

Three, the question in this chapter is not whether segregation and racism existed in the armed forces or society during World War II or whether they were humane or appropriate ways to treat people; while they existed and certainly were inhumane and inappropriate ways to treat people and would not be tolerated today, they were facts of American life on December 7, 1941, and during World War II. Condemning them today merely states the obvious and is of no value other than to wallow in victimhood.

Doris Miller on December 7
The Facts behind a Name Etched in Stone and History

A factual basis of the events on December 7 involving *West Virginia* and Doris Miller can be found in a reliable source that does not contain the factual errors or unfounded opinions found in other writings about Doris Miller discussed later in this chapter. That source is the ship's after-action report written by *West Virginia*'s senior surviving officer, which contains supporting statements ("enclosures") from officers present during the attack who gave firsthand, contemporaneous accounts of the events of December 7. They discuss efforts of officers and enlisted men, including Miller, to move and to save the gravely wounded commanding officer of the ship, Captain Mervyn Bennion. Only those facts necessary to determine whether Miller's actions warranted a MOH or even a Navy Cross will be recited again in the following section of this chapter, which establishes a correct record, based on facts, of Miller's actions on December 7. That record can later be compared to the mythical, erroneous, politically correct record. The correct record can be comprised by answering two questions:

What happened to USS *West Virginia* on December 7? Chapter 6 recounts in detail the attack on the ship on December 7. A summary is provided here for reader convenience.

Several torpedoes hit *West Virginia*'s port side (she was an outboard ship moored beside Tennessee), causing her to list but prompt counterflooding saved her from capsizing. She sank upright in place amid smoke and fire, losing 106 crewmen.

Bomb fragments flew into Bennion's abdomen while he was standing outside the bridge, mortally wounding him. An officer ordered that Bennion be taken from the bridge to the lower part of the ship.

A poignant drama occurred as a small group of crewmen, including Miller, tried in vain to lower the captain from the bridge to safety on a lower deck. Smoke and fire were not the only factors opposing them. Bennion himself resisted evacuation, exhibiting more concern for his ship and crew than for his own welfare. He died aboard ship and received a posthumous MOH, the only member of the ship to receive a MOH.

The most crucial question: What did Doris Miller in fact do on December 7? Again *West Virginia*'s after-action report must be consulted here. Lieutenant Commander D. C. Johnson, responding to the call to help Bennion, wrote that he went to the captain's location taking "a colored mess attendant [Doris Miller] with me—a very powerfully built individual, having in mind that he might pick the Captain up and carry him below." They joined other crewmen in aiding and trying to move Bennion. As materials to construct a stretcher to move Bennion were obtained, Miller and Lieutenant (junior grade) F. H. White manned two machineguns forward of the conning tower.[1] At some point, White and Miller were "instrumental in hauling people along through oil and water to the quarterdeck, thereby unquestionably saving the lives of a number of people who might otherwise have been lost."[2] In summary, Miller's actions were assisting Bennion as did other crewmen, manning a machinegun, and helping to retrieve men from the water onto the ship at the quarterdeck, the area where crewmen enter and exit the ship.

DORIS MILLER AFTER DECEMBER 7: A NAVY CROSS AND A NAME ETCHED IN STONE

After December 7, the focus was not so much on what Miller did that day but the process of identifying him and obtaining official recognition for his actions. What follows is a step-by-step account of that process based on facts found in the two sources cited in the endnote by authors mentioned earlier: Sapper and Miller.[3] These two sources, as was the ship's after-action report, are reliable, reporting facts without basic errors or without opinions unfounded in fact as found in sources discussed later in this chapter. For example, they, unlike other authors, place Miller on the correct ship.

The December 22, 1941, New York Times mentioned a "Negro mess attendant" firing a machine gun on December 7. He was unnamed.

The mention of the mess attendant triggered dissatisfaction in the black community since, early in the war, Caucasian heroes were identified and recognized but the mess attendant was not.

On March 5, 1942, the navy finally revealed the name of the mess attendant, Doris Miller, and summarized his actions at Pearl Harbor. It also announced that he would receive a Letter of Commendation.

After he was identified, the black community pressured Washington to award Miller a decoration.

A congressman called for Miller to receive a MOH. Black journalists supported the congressman.

A Representative and a Senator introduced Congressional legislation recommending a MOH.

On March 30, 1942, Secretary of the Navy Frank Knox issued a Letter of Commendation to Miller.

Knox informed Congress in April 1942 that the Pacific Fleet Awards Board and the Pacific Fleet commander, Admiral Chester Nimitz, thought that the Letter of Commendation was sufficient recognition. With no Navy support for a MOH for Miller, the bills in Congress recommending the MOH died in committee.

President Roosevelt, however, decided in May 1942 to award Miller a Navy Cross. An official Navy record with Miller's name on it has this typed entry lined out:

"Commended by Secretary of the Navy."

Beside it in handwriting is "Cancelled." Under the entry in handwriting is "Awarded Navy Cross by Sec Nav by direction of the President" ("Sec Nav" is the "Secretary of the Navy"). The card also notes the Navy Cross and citation were sent to Pacific Fleet by airmail on May 7, 1942, and that they were presented May 27, 1942. His Navy Cross citation is as follows:

> For distinguished devotion to duty, extraordinary courage and disregard for his own personal safety during the attack on the fleet in Pearl Harbor, Territory of Hawaii, by Japanese forces on December 7, 1941. While at the side of his captain on the bridge, Miller, despite enemy strafing and bombing and in the face of serious fire, assisted in moving his captain, who had been mortally wounded, to a place of greater safety, and later manned and operated a machine gun directed at enemy Japanese attacking aircraft until ordered to leave the bridge.[4]

Nimitz personally presented the award to Miller on April 27, 1942, at a Pearl Harbor awards ceremony, making Miller the first black sailor to receive a Navy Cross.

For several reasons, the Miller Navy Cross was a political award not based on merit or facts. First of all, the ship's command (as reflected in the after-action report) did not recommend Miller for a Navy Cross.[5] Second, none of the other crewmen assisting Bennion received Navy Crosses. The Navy Department Permanent Board of Awards' Third Endorsement (official commentary) on the Fleet Board of Awards list of recommendations for awards does not mention Miller or the other crewmen who assisted Bennion. The Fleet Board did not recommend Miller for a Navy Cross or any commendation.[6] As noted in the text and at endnote 9 of appendix D, the criteria for the Navy Cross created in 1919 is "extraordinary heroism or distinguished service in the line of his profession, such heroism or service not being sufficient to justify the ward of a medal of honor or a distinguished service medal." Chapters 14 and 15 discussed the Fleet Board of awards and Third Endorsement in depth.

Third, the black community's pressure to reward Miller was just described and obviously had some effect on the Navy Cross award. Fourth, the President's direction to award a Navy Cross was unusual; in typical cases, the Secretary of the Navy approved Navy Cross recommendations while the president approved MOH recommendations. Thus, in the context of community pressure, Roosevelt's decision can only be seen as based on politics, not on the merits of Miller's actions.

Miller transferred from *West Virginia* and eventually served at sea on USS Liscome Bay (CVE-56), an escort carrier. A Japanese submarine sank the ship in 1943; Miller was one of the crewmen lost.[7]

From loss at sea, the story moves to the Honolulu Memorial, adjacent "Punchbowl," the National Memorial Cemetery of the Pacific on Oahu. Appendix C of this book describes the cemetery and the memorial. The Honolulu Memorial contains large stone tablets, "Courts of the Missing," with names of those missing in action.

In Section 1, the name "DORIS MILLER" is inscribed in stone among the names of Navy personnel missing in action in World War II.[8]

This section of this chapter and the preceding section establish a factual record of Miller's actions on and after December 7, a record that collides directly with the politically correct, erroneous record that gives him unwarranted hero status, erroneously credits him with doing more than he did to assist Bennion, and erroneously credits him with shooting down Japanese aircraft.

Doris Miller after December 7: Creating a Hero Using Baseless Opinions and Erroneous Information

The mythical Doris Miller comprises two components, one opinion and one "factual." One is opinions of his status with no regard to perspective. The opinions assert that he is not only the first American hero of World War II but the first hero of World War II. Two is the "factual" account of his actions on December 7, based on distortion, speculation, or error. The accounts of his actions on December 7 place him on the incorrect ship and credit him with shooting down Japanese aircraft.

OPINION:
DORIS MILLER AS THE FIRST *AMERICAN* HERO OF WORLD WAR II

Part one of the Doris Miller myth begins with unfounded, ridiculous opinions.

One should imagine a Caucasian male author writing these words: "The first American hero of World War II was Caucasian." Outcry and backlash would be immediate. To say the least, the author would be excoriated and condemned. If the author gave a lecture, the lecture hall would be picketed; demonstrators would disrupt the lecture.

One should now imagine a black female author, Gail Buckley, writing in her 2001 book American Patriots the following about Doris Miller. In the chapter "World War II," she writes, "The first American hero of World War II was black."[9]

No one calls this assertion what it is: ludicrous, inaccurate opinion—and it is opinion, not fact—unsupported by fact. No outcry is heard. Buckley's statements apparently escaped scrutiny, question, and criticism, at least in public. This opinion stands unchallenged in the popular press and probably in the minds of most people who read them, especially people preoccupied with popular culture and who lack the ability, power, or energy to think critically and who accept as fact any information disseminated by the media or found in publications.

Interestingly, the Washington Post book review of American Patriots, written by a Rutgers history professor, did not question Buckley's assertion that Miller was the war's first American hero or any of the other errors or unsupported opinions in her book.[10]

What is defective about this assertion or opinion—again, that is what it is, assertion or opinion and not fact—is the writer's disregard or ignorance of the context of the facts of Miller's conduct on December 7 and the broader context of World War II. "Anointing" someone as "the first American hero of World War II" presents several problems.

First, what is the importance of determining the identity of the first hero of the war? In the author's opinion, the question is of limited if any importance. Of what importance is the time differential between heroism on day 1 of a war and on day 10 of the war?

Second, how does one determine who is a hero? No universal standards or criteria defining hero exist. Hero is a subjective term. For many people, a hero is someone who exhibits bravery. For many people in our sports-crazy culture, an athlete or racecar driver can be a hero; for many people in our popular culture, an administrator who shuffles papers competently can be a hero.

Third, what are the criteria or standards for determining first? As Chapter 14 of this book observes concerning the question of MOH "firsts," no one was running around Oahu on December 7 with a watch recording whose heroic acts occurred first or keeping a chronological record of heroic acts. Thus, "first" cannot be determined based on facts.

Fourth, to appoint one person as the "first American hero of World War II" lacks perspective. It insults everyone, regardless of race, on Oahu on December 7 in harm's way, defending against or suffering from the Japanese attack. Everyone includes Americans of all races as well as native Hawaiians, who were not Americans at the time. (Hawaii was an American territory.) To choose a "first American hero" for December 7 from the hundreds of military members from all branches of the US military on Oahu and from civilians assisting the military is literally impossible given the chaos of the attack and the number of combatants and civilians and military installations on Oahu on December 7. The term is a slap in the face to those who exhibited as much or more bravery than did Miller and who were not accorded the title "first American hero" of the war and did not, as Miller did, receive an award for actions that day. Their deeds were either unrecognized or the men received awards of lesser standing than a Navy Cross, such as Silver Stars, Bronze Stars, or letters of commendation.

Opinion: Doris Miller as the First Hero of World War II

One now jumps from Doris Miller being the first American hero of World War II to the first hero of World War II without regard to nationality. In the introduction of American Patriots, she writes, "You would never know from the movies that the very first hero of World War II was Dorie Miller, a Navy messman at Pearl Harbor who became the first black winner of the Navy Cross."[11] In a story about the movie Miracle at St. Anna in the August 17, 2008, Washington Post, she was quoted to the same effect: "He [Miller] was actually the first hero of World War II[.]"[12]

Even the Sapper article previously discussed—an article concerned with the historical inaccuracies about Miller—states the following: "The keepers of the historical record have done less well for this country's first hero of World War II."[13]

Buckley is not alone in naming Miller as the first hero of World War II. In the book Negro Medal of Honor Men, the author writes that "a colored seaman [Miller] became the first hero of World War II."[14]

Ordinarily the author would write that no citation of authority is necessary to support the statement that World War II began on September 1, 1939, with the German invasion of Poland, long before the U.S. Congress declared war on Japan on December 8, 1941; however, given the number and nature of errors discussed in this chapter and in chapter 18 ("Errors and Omissions Concerning the Medals of Honor earned in the Hawaiian Islands"), such citation seems not only necessary but mandatory.[15] Thus Buckley's anointment of Miller as the "first hero of World War II" excludes from consideration as "the first hero of World War II" any soldiers from countries such as Poland, Great Britain, and France, who were in the war from the beginning, September 1, 1939. And one assumes she means "Allied" and not "Axis" heroes, thus excluding a German soldier in Poland whose heroism may have made him "the first hero of World War II" even if he were the enemy.

Buckley's statements in the introduction to her book ("the very first hero of World War II was Dorie Miller") and in the Post article ("He was actually the first hero of World War II") are even troubling and ludicrous by implying a nonsensical belief that someone other than an American could be the "first hero" of World War II. A Pole, an Englishman, or a Frenchman could have been the "first hero of World War II" before the attack on Oahu on December 7, 1941, generated American heroes; the US Congress did not declare war until December 8.[16] One would think that historians of European countries would laugh at the assertion that Miller was the first hero of World War II, a war that started in their theater of the world.

In short, the concept of identifying or naming "the first hero of World War II" is as ludicrous as the concept of naming "the first American hero of World War II." Such anointing of hero status for the war from its true beginning presents the same problems as anointing someone as the first American hero of the war.

This opinion is arrogant, demeaning, and insulting to all Allied service members who risked their lives in World War II. One assumes that those appointing Miller the first hero of the war have appointed him without regard to nationality, so he is the first hero of the war without regard to heroism by any service members of the Allied nations.

After Miller's heroism is placed in perspective by removing his status as the first hero of World War II or the first American hero of World War II, one can then examine recurring factual errors exacerbating the myth of Doris Miller and can judge the type and degree of his heroism.

FACT: MILLER'S DUTY STATION ON DECEMBER 7, 1941

Part 2 of the Doris Miller myth comprises erroneous factual information.

Various authors cannot even place Miller on the correct ship, *West Virginia*, a fact that should not need restating at this point. The most frequent error is naming his ship as *Arizona*. Such a basic fact would seem to be easy to report, but apparently it is not.

Buckley first places him on the burning deck of *West Virginia* and then states that only when "the ammunition was exhausted and the *Arizona* was sinking beneath him did he abandon ship." If *Arizona* were not his ship, then one wonders how he could abandon her.[17]

Buckley is not alone in placing Miller aboard *Arizona*. In the magazine America's War Heroes: Unsung and Legendary, military history expert Rod Paschall wrote that Miller "ignor[ed] the disaster aboard USS *Arizona*…" Ironically, Paschall was, of all people, the editor of Military History Quarterly. One can "explain away" the error by attributing it to ambiguity and assume the author knew that Miller was on *West Virginia* and that his statement meant that Miller ignored the conflagration aboard *Arizona*, moored behind *West Virginia*. The logical, commonsense interpretation of his sentence, however, is that the author thought that Miller was aboard *Arizona*. He also wrote that Miller was credited with shooting down two Japanese planes while manning a machine gun, a claim discredited later in this chapter.[18]

An Internet printing in 2000 from the Arlington National Cemetery site titled "Historical Information, Black History at Arlington National Cemetery" stated, "In 1941, Dorie Miller, a messman aboard the USS *Arizona*, was awarded the Navy Cross for shooting down four enemy airplanes during the attack on Pearl Harbor."[19]

In a 1945 book about World War II, the author writes, "Dorris [sic] Miller, negro [sic] mess attendant second class, had never fired a gun in his life until he came out of the *Arizona*'s galley."[20]

FACT: MILLER ASSISTING HIS MORTALLY WOUNDED COMMANDER

Another impression left by some authors is that Miller was the only crewman assisting the mortally wounded commanding officer of the ship.

Buckley's book erroneously implies that Miller alone carried *West Virginia*'s mortally wounded captain to safety. In fact, as the after-action report and its enclosures report, Miller was simply one of several crewmen assisting Bennion. The Navy Cross citation recited earlier in this chapter states that he "assisted in moving his Captain who had been mortally wounded, to a place of greater safety..."[21] It does not state that he solely moved Captain Bennion.

In Negro Medal of Honor Men, the author writes that Miller could not stop the captain's bleeding "so he decided to move the captain to a safer place and look for the medic. Lifting the man carefully, he started across the bridge and down a ladder." The implication is that Miller alone moved the captain; no mention is made of the officers and other enlisted men helping to move the captain. The after-action report for the ship makes no mention of Miller administering first aid to the captain; as explained in Chapter 6, a chief pharmacist's mate was the person tending to Bennion medically. In the Navy, the correct term is "corpsman," not "medic."[22]

In the dreadful, historically inaccurate movie Pearl Harbor (2001), Miller helps Bennion but also talks with him alone amid the wreckage, an event not reported in the after-action report and unlikely given Bennion's condition (mortally wounded) and the presence of other crewmembers.

FACT: THE NUMBER OF JAPANESE AIRCRAFT MILLER DOWNED

Perhaps the most inquiry-resistant and "bulletproof" (pun intended) assertion is that Miller purportedly shot down Japanese aircraft while manning a fifty-caliber machine gun on the ship. Most authors accept and repeat this assertion rather than questioning it. The question is not manning the machine gun—the after-action report described earlier reports that Lieutenant (junior grade) White and Miller manned two machine guns forward of the conning tower—but how many, if any, Japanese aircraft he shot down.

The number of planes he downed varies depending on source, and no details are offered concerning the airplanes' locations or what they were doing (maneuvering, bombing, or flying by or around the ship) when he allegedly downed them.

Buckley writes that Miller shot down four Japanese aircraft according to witnesses but "officials listed two[.]"[23]

The Internet printing from Arlington National Cemetery about "Black History" cited earlier in this chapter credits Miller with downing four enemy airplanes.[24]

America's War Heroes: Unsung and Legendary states that Miller "was credited with bringing down two Japanese planes."[25]

Negro Medal of Honor Men states that Miller shot down at least four aircraft.[26]

For six reasons, the number of aircraft Miller purportedly shot down is irrelevant because the great likelihood is that he did not and could not down any aircraft. First of all, the after-action report cited in chapter 6 (*West Virginia*) and earlier in this chapter (including the statement of White, the officer manning machine guns with Miller) did not mention Miller shooting down any Japanese aircraft. Second, the following factors support the conclusion that he did not shoot down any Japanese aircraft while manning a fifty-caliber machine gun on the ship.

One, he had no formal training as a machine gunner. Although he attended Secondary Battery Gunnery School in July 1940, he was not trained to use the fifty-caliber machine gun.[27]

Two, one must consider the speeds of the Japanese aircraft and whether an untrained gunner could shoot down any aircraft flying at attack speed in combat conditions in the fog of war, discussed as reason number 5.[28] The Zero fighter had a maximum speed of approximately 330 miles per hour and cruising speed of approximately 200 miles per hour. The Val dive bomber had a maximum speed of approximately 240 miles per hour and cruising speed of approximately 180 miles per hour. The Kate horizontal bomber had a maximum speed of approximately 235 miles per hour and cruising speed of approximately 160 miles per hour;

Three, the Navy Cross citation does not mention that he downed any planes.[29]

Four, a study of Japanese planes downed during the attack leads to the conclusion that Miller did not down any of them. The Messman Chronicles includes a discussion of this study.[30]

Five, one must consider the fog of war, the chaos and confusion experienced on the ground caused by Japanese aircraft attacking all over Pearl Harbor at various altitudes in "combat conditions" (smoke, explosions, debris, burning ships and oil, noise, and numerous activities taking place simultaneously). Hitting an aircraft flying at hundreds of miles an hour with one or even a battery of machine guns in the combat conditions just described would be difficult even for a trained gunner. In fact, one of the selling points authors emphasize in enhancing Miller's deeds is that Miller lacked gunnery training. This fact reflects discrimination (whites but not blacks received gunnery training) as well as marksmanship. If he lacked extensive gunnery training, what is the likelihood that he shot down fast-moving Japanese aircraft? A day of attack would be the worst possible day for someone to man a machine gun for the first time and to down any aircraft with it.

Six, the Japanese lost only twenty-nine aircraft on December 7.[31] The number of planes Miller purportedly downed generally ranges from two to four. Two planes is 6 percent of the Japanese losses; four is 13 percent. To conclude that an untrained, inexperienced crewman, such as Miller, shot down any Japanese aircraft, whether measured by number or percentage, in combat conditions and with no gunnery training or experience is preposterous and unsupported by demonstrable facts reported by the ship's surviving officers.

In summary, Miller shooting down planes was possible, meaning he could have done so; in fact, Miller shooting down airplanes was highly improbable, meaning the likelihood of him shooting down any aircraft was minimal. Shooting down enemy aircraft are simply a part, and a large one, of the myth surrounding Doris Miller.

A Compendium of Miller Errors

An observer may be sufficiently fortunate to find one account that has all Miller errors and adds some. One is a 1982 Waco Tribune-Herald article stating the following, which the reader by now will know to be inaccurate or false.[32] The story is simply risible.

Miller is the first hero of World War II.

Miller was aboard USS Virginia.

Miller ran for his battle station and "stumbled over the ship's captain who had been seriously injured [the correct term is wounded]."

"After dragging the officer to a safe spot, he saw one of the gunners killed and he grabbed the man's gun and shot down five Japanese planes, despite never having received training on the gun" (no mention is ever made of him replacing a killed gunner).

"One year later, Adm. Chester W. Nimitz awarded Miller the Navy Cross as he stood on the deck of the USS Virginia. Miller was promoted to First Class Petty Officer." (He was never promoted to first class petty officer.)

FACT: DID MILLER RECEIVE A NAVY CROSS AND FROM WHOM?

In reviewing the movie Pearl Harbor, critic Gregory Epps, a writer for Port Folio (formerly a weekly newspaper in Norfolk, Virginia) went so far as to write that due to "relentless racism" Miller never saw his Navy Cross, a statement that would have puzzled Miller or Admiral Nimitz, who personally presented Miller the award in 1942.[33]

In the movie, Miller's character receives a Navy Cross from a navy officer wearing the uniform of a commander (three sleeve stripes), not Admiral Nimitz, who would have four stars on his collar or one large and three stripes on his sleeve.

Even Pearl Harbor experts make mistakes concerning Miller. Three—Gordon W. Prange, Donald W. Goldstein, and Katherine V. Dillon—wrote the famous book At Dawn We Slept. In their book 7 December, 1941: The Day the Japanese Attacked Pearl Harbor, they write that Lieutenant Commander D. C. Johnson of *West Virginia* "was so impressed with Miller's courage, coolness, and initiative that he recommended him for the Navy Cross." The footnote supporting this assertion is 51, which cites to pages 131 to 132 of Walter Lord's book Day of Infamy. Lord's pages mention Miller but nothing about Johnson or a Navy Cross recommendation. Johnson's statement in the ship's after-action report, mentioned at the beginning of this chapter, contains no such recommendation.[34]

DORIS MILLER: NO MOH AWARDED, NO MOH DESERVED

As can be seen from the preceding sections, the various opinions unsupported by fact and the numerous factual errors create an environment that obfuscates the facts concerning Miller's actions on December 7. With Miller's hero status placed in perspective and with the factual errors identified, one can examine the facts and context of his actions on December 7. That examination will lead to two conclusions.

First, the facts do not support a MOH or even a Navy Cross, the award in the Naval service second only to the MOH, for Miller for his actions on December 7.

Second, he does not warrant a MOH as "compensation" for all the December 7 MOH recipients being white or as a political or social gesture, making him a representative of his race who received the MOH as redress for past injustices, such as blacks who deserved but did not receive MOHs. As explained in Chapter 14 (Overview) and in Appendix D, various minorities who deserved but were denied MOHs due to racism belatedly received MOHs, but redress of racism was only one aspect of the belated awards. What must be considered is that Congress and the military attempted to correct MOH injustices by examining cases of minorities who had, due to racism, received either lesser awards or no awards when they deserved MOHs. In 1997, seven black soldiers received Army MOHs after a study the army commissioned concluded that they deserved MOHs but did not receive them due to racial prejudice; the study is irrelevant to Miller since it was a study under Army auspices. A reading of their citations reveals deeds and sacrifices far greater than those exhibited by Miller on December 7. After a review of records directed by Congress, twenty-two Japanese-American soldiers serving in the war received MOHs in 2000 after the review found MOHs not awarded because of racial prejudice. Again, the citations reveal deeds and sacrifices far greater than Miller's. The important points are that the MOH awards not only were redress for discrimination but also that they had factual bases meeting the statutory criteria for MOH awards. In other words, their MOHs were not awarded to them simply because they were minorities without regard to whether the facts supported MOHs. A MOH awarded to Miller would be based on race alone and not on facts sufficient to warrant a MOH.

Other factors should be considered in assessing whether he earned a MOH.

As discussed at length in Chapters 7 (*Arizona*) and 19 (the Pharris MOH), the Jackson Pharris Navy Cross was inadequate recognition for his actions on December 7 and was upgraded after the war to a MOH. One may ask why the Miller Navy Cross was not upgraded to a MOH.

The two cases are radically different. First of all, the activity of Pharris on December 7 was of far greater scope and importance than that of Doris Miller. In short, Pharris not only saved the lives of many shipmates, but he saved the ship itself by preventing her from capsizing. Second, while the Pharris Navy Cross "underrewarded" him, the Miller Navy Cross "overrewarded" Miller. No Navy Crosses were awarded to the other crewmen assisting Bennion, and no Navy Cross was awarded to the officer (Lieutenant (junior grade) White for manning a machine gun.

A comparison of Miller's actions with the actions of December 7 MOH recipients, such as Pharris and Fuqua, is instructive.

As discussed in Chapter 11 of this book, John Finn was the only MOH recipient cited for manning a machine gun and directly engaging the enemy; his MOH citation can be found in Appendix A of this book. Finn fired at oncoming Japanese planes at Kaneohe from a fifty-caliber machine gun mounted on a parking ramp outside a hangar; during this action, he was completely exposed to enemy fire. Although wounded, he refused to leave the gun until ordered to seek medical help. After receiving first aid, he returned to his command to rearm aircraft although he was in pain and moving with difficulty. The essential differences between Finn and Miller are Finn's complete exposure to enemy fire for a prolonged time and his continued service notwithstanding painful wounds (Miller was not wounded).

A comparison of Miller's actions with the actions of his shipmates on December 7 is instructive. The key point made repeatedly is that that none of the other *West Virginia* officers or sailors assisting Bennion received Navy Crosses or MOHs. If their conduct—far more crucial overall to the ship's survival than Miller's conduct—did not warrant Navy Crosses, then Miller, in fairness to them, should not have received a Navy Cross and certainly should not receive a MOH.

The only MOH for USS *West Virginia* was the posthumous MOH awarded to Bennion, who, while mortally wounded, resisted evacuation, showing disregard for his own welfare and only concern for his ship. He kept asking about the ship and insisting that the others leave him and evacuate the bridge. Such conduct is well above that expected of a mortally wounded man and certainly dedication beyond Miller's given Bennion's degraded state.

As noted in Chapter 15 of this book, the brevity and lack of detail in the nearly identical MOH citations for Rear Admiral Kidd and Captain Van Valkenburgh (both lost on *Arizona*) raise questions about factual support for their MOH awards. A MOH award to Miller, however, cannot be justified based by this logic. Two other MOHs were awarded with little or no factual bases, so a MOH should be awarded to Miller with little or no factual basis. The criteria in the legislation governing the MOH includes no requirement that the MOH be awarded based on comparison with MOHs awarded to other recipients in the same or similar action. In other words, a MOH award to Miller based on insufficient facts to support a MOH cannot be justified by MOHs awarded to Kidd and Van Valkenburgh that were also based on insufficient facts. When one looks at the December 7 MOH citations for MOHs that were based on demonstrable facts clearly warranting MOHs, Miller's deeds fall far short of the deeds in those citations. They fall far short of actions by Pharris (he prevented *California* from capsizing), Fuqua (he supervised *Arizona*'s rescue efforts and evacuation from the death blow to the abandonment of the ship, whose conditions were untenable). They fall short of the actions of Cannon, Scott, Tomich, Ward, and Flaherty, all of whom perished while consciously deciding to refuse to abandon station or ship.

Thus the bases for the conclusion that a Miller MOH is undeserved are detailed research and an appreciation for context. Such research and context are in contrast to poor or missing research and disregard of context that the popular press and media have historically demonstrated and demonstrate to this day. In fact, when media members or politicians write or speak about Doris Miller, their shallow or missing research and their lack of facts and context are apparent to anyone who has studied Miller's actions on December 7 as reported by officers on the ship.

Yet Miller's supporters launched a noble but misguided attempt by federal legislation to redress the alleged unfairness of not awarding Miller a MOH. In 2001, Congressional Representative Eddie Bernice Johnson of Texas reintroduced a bill in the House of Representatives waiving the MOH time limitation. With the time limitation waived, Miller could receive a MOH. A resolution by the U.S. Conference of Mayors supported Johnson's bill. Neither action indicates concern for or knowledge of the facts or context of the December 7 MOHs as related to Doris Miller; for example, the Mayors' Conference resolution stated that "Miller distinguished himself above all others by aiding wounded fellow sailors and the mortally wounded captain of the ship…" as if no other crewmen assisted the wounded, including Bennion. The bill never became law.[35]

Finally, an important point is that concluding that Miller does not deserve a MOH can be made without questioning his bravery or that of anyone of any race and without denying or justifying the deplorable treatment accorded blacks in the military in the past, even during time of war when they, like anyone else, simply wanted to serve their country.

A Military View of Doris Miller: The Army Staff Ride Runs off the Road

How was and is Miller treated compared to MOH and other Navy Cross or DSC recipients?

As has been emphasized repeatedly, the other *West Virginia* Navy crewmen assisting Bennion did not receive Navy Crosses.

The focus now shifts to the Army, which conducts staff rides, tours of battlegrounds to study the battles. In what can only be labeled as political correctness and racism, Miller is mentioned after a listing of the December 7 MOH recipients in an appendix to the Army's guide for a Pearl Harbor staff ride. After the MOH citation for Cassin Young, who is last alphabetically, the appendix has a long paragraph about Miller, discussing his actions on December 7, reciting the wording of his Navy Cross citation. The paragraph begins, "Another hero from Pearl Harbor was Mess Attendant Second Class Doris Miller."[36][Bold in original.]

The discerning reader, aware of the facts and circumstances of the actions of the MOH and Navy Cross recipients for December 7, may ask why Miller alone was included as a "[a]nother hero" and why other recipients of awards, such as Navy Crosses and Silver Stars, were not included as "other heroes." Omitted was *Nevada*'s Ensign Joseph Tausig, who was white and whose citation reveals that he did as much or more than Miller to earn his Navy Cross. Although seriously wounded (his leg was shattered), he refused to leave his station as senior officer in the ship's antiaircraft battery. He continued controlling the battery's fire until he was forcibly removed.[37]

One wonders why the Army did not list two of its own aviators as "heroes": Lieutenants Kenneth Taylor and George Welch, both white, who were not mentioned as "other heroes" for December 7. The irony is that the staff ride book is an Army publication, and at the time, Taylor and Welch, even though they were fighter pilots who engaged Japanese aircraft in aerial battle, were Army officers since an independent Air Force did not exist during World War II and Army aviation was under Army command. They did much more to earn their Distinguished Service Crosses (DSC) on December 7 than Miller did to earn his Navy Cross. Taylor and Welch, greatly outnumbered, flew P-40 fighters, which were inferior to the Japanese Zero fighters attacking Oahu. Welch shot down four Japanese aircraft; Taylor shot down three Japanese aircraft and was wounded in aerial combat. Each man received a DSC, the army equivalent of the Navy Cross. Unlike the assertions made concerning Miller downing Japanese aircraft, no question exists that these two pilots downed Japanese aircraft.[38]

The staff ride did not list as another hero Marine Major Alan Shapley, who had been relived as commanding officer of *Arizona*'s Marine Detachment (his tour of duty had expired) but had stayed on the ship overnight from December 6 to 7. He was therefore present during the attack. He received a Silver Star for entering the water between the ship and Ford Island to save, under enemy fire, a Marine corporal from drowning as he tried to swim from the ship to Ford Island.[39]

DEPICTING DORIS MILLER TODAY: EXCESSIVELY REMEMBERED

The inaccurate depiction of Miller in the 2001 movie Pearl Harbor was discussed earlier in this chapter. The incoherent and inaccurate accountings from his niece, Vickie Gail Miller, are mentioned in the next section of this chapter.

Appendix C of this book describes the author's 2015 visitation of the World War II Valor in the Pacific National Monument (formerly the USS *Arizona* Visitors' Center), where he toured two exhibit halls, the first labeled "Road to War" and the second labeled "Attack."

What is truly objectionable at the site is the focus on Doris Miller in the exhibition halls as if he were one of the most important sailors at Pearl Harbor on December 7. He simply was not that important among the hundreds of service members and civilians fighting the Japanese that day.

The focus on Miller begins with a large photograph of him at the entrance to "Road to War" and ends with the large photograph of him at the exit of "Attack."

Thus the exhibit halls are politically correct in that they give inordinate attention to a minority—Miller was black—who did nothing outstanding on December 7. The focus on him continues in the "Valor" section of "Attack" as the first black to receive a Navy Cross. A large photograph of him receiving the Navy Cross from Nimitz is displayed. Knowledgeable visitors are dumbfounded, by comparison, by the lack of a listing or photographs of the MOH recipients.

And one would think that the focus of "Valor" would be on the MOH recipients who received the nation's highest award for combat bravery. While "Valor" has an easily overlooked sign stating that fifteen MOHs were earned during the attack, it does not list the names of the recipients. The only other MOH information is a partial citation for Jackson Pharris with a Navy MOH and ribbon above the citation, but the MOH and ribbon are unidentified, so viewers do not know if it is the Pharris MOH and ribbon. Pharris is the only MOH recipient identified by name.

Although the MOH is the country's highest military honor, the display's focus is not the MOH but Doris Miller, who received the country's second highest honor for bravery by members of the Naval service. Tourists not knowing the stories of the December 7 MOHs and an accurate account of Miller's performance on that date could easily, and incorrectly, conclude that Miller was the, or one of the, most important sailors at Pearl Harbor on December 7.

VICKIE GAIL MILLER:
INTRODUCTION

A discussion of Doris Miller is incomplete without comment on the incoherent writings of the late Vickie Gail Miller, Doris Miller's niece, who died in 2014. She was perhaps the strongest exponent and advocate for Doris Miller receiving a MOH. On the one hand, her motivation and loyalty to family are admirable; on the other hand, her book Doris Miller: A Silent Medal of Honor Winner and her website dedicated to Doris Miller indicate that her knowledge about December 7 and her judgment about the appropriateness of a MOH for her uncle indicate a woefully inadequate understanding of December 7, the MOH, and the Navy Cross.[40]

An important point is that Richard E. Miller, mentioned at the beginning of this chapter, cites Vickie Miller's book in his own book, The Messman Chronicles: African Americans in the US Navy, 1932–1943 but does not note in its chapter on Doris Miller the numerous errors of fact, style, and grammar found in her book and noted in this chapter.[41]

Also important is that she made a cottage industry around Doris Miller, selling all kinds of Doris Miller paraphernalia, including her book. The errors in the book are just one indication of the inaccurate information in the public domain about Doris Miller. One can only hope that that anyone reading her book will recognize the errors in it.

Book: Doris Miller - A Silent Medal of Honor Winner

The initial red flag indicating problems in the book Doris Miller: A Silent Medal of Honor Winner is that the title misleads the reader into thinking he received a MOH when he did not. Second, in the phrase "Silent Medal of Honor Winner," what does "silent" modify, the MOH or the MOH "winner"? Does the term mean a MOH recipient who does not or cannot talk? Third, the term "winner" is inappropriate since it implies that the award of a MOH is a contest one "wins." The correct term is recipient. Fourth, since Doris Miller did not receive a MOH, the title is a slap in the face to the men who did earn MOHs on that date, in particular men such as Jackson Pharris, who saved his ship; Samuel Fuqua, who supervised the evacuation of *Arizona* in the worst of circumstances; George Cannon on Midway, who died after refusing to be moved until other wounded marines were moved before him; and Peter Tomich, Robert Scott, Francis Flaherty, and James Ward, all of whom died because they refused to abandon their duty stations. Fifth, one need not have a doctorate to know that no such award as "Silent Medal of Honor" exists.

The book lacks the basics of a professionally or competently written and edited book; it lacks a bibliography and index. It also lacks endnotes or footnotes. The writing is awkward and at best at the junior high school level. The poor quality of the writing, in style, grammar, and content, indicates that the book either had no editor or had an editor who lacked basic editorial skill, and apparently it had no fact checker or proofreader. Problems include inconsistent facts, absence of facts, facts incorrectly recited, inattention to detail, confusion of terms, misunderstanding of military awards and the awards systems, incorrect or fabricated terms, poor grammar, and unclear writing. The result is a book with tortured, confusing, and bad writing. Reading it is painful for anyone who knows the basics of the December 7 attacks and the December 7 MOH recipients.

Since the chapters in the Miller book concerning December 7, the Navy Cross, and the MOH (Chapters 7 through 11) are the only chapters relevant to those topics, only the major errors in those chapters will be noted below.

Chapter 7: A Hero at Pearl Harbor

The problems begin in Chapter 7 (pages 45–52). The poor writing and questionable substance in the chapter almost defy commentary.

To prevent repetition at each mention of the following topics, the following two observations, discussed in detail earlier in this chapter, are placed here. One, the ship's after-action report for December 7 and the Navy Cross citation do not credit Miller with downing any aircraft. The Navy Cross citation found in the text earlier simply states that he "later manned and operated a machine gun directed at enemy Japanese attacking aircraft until ordered to leave the bridge." Two, much is made about his lack of weapons training in the Navy and his manning the machine gun on December 7 being the first time he manned a machine gun. If the attack were his first experience shooting a machine gun, what is the likelihood that he downed any Japanese aircraft with no training or practice with a machine gun? Another observation must be made: Vickie Miller cannot inform readers of Miller's thoughts or mental state, as she frequently does, unless she was clairvoyant, an unlikely possibility.

Most of the factual errors can be recognized by reference to the correct factual accounts, given earlier in this chapter, of actions on *West Virginia* on December 7 and of the actions of Miller on that date.

Page 45: "On 7 December, 1941, on a Sunday morning, Japanese diplomatic representatives were meeting with the United States government in Washington, DC." In fact, the Japanese and U.S. government officials did not meet until the afternoon of December 7.[42]

Page 45: "The naval base [at Pearl Harbor] failed to identify several warnings of the approaching Japanese raid, which was a declaration of war upon the United States." What was a declaration of war: the warnings or the raid itself? A raid or attack is not a formal declaration of war. As noted in chapter 3 of this book, Article 1 of Hague Convention Number III Relative to the Opening of Hostilities (October 18, 1907) prohibits the signatories from commencing hostilities without "previous and explicit warning, in the form either of a declaration of war or of an ultimatum with conditional declaration of war." The requirement is a "warning," not a declaration of war. One can see easily from the Hague Convention that a raid or attack and a formal declaration of war are separate concepts.

Page 46: "There were [in addition to *West Virginia*] also cruisers, targets, and destroyer ships in port." "Ships" is superfluous. By definition, cruisers, and destroyers are ships. "Targets" is also superfluous since all ships in the harbor were targets. Perhaps the reference is to *Utah*, a target in two senses. She was a target ship used for American bombing and gunnery practice, and she was a target on December 7 for the Japanese.

Pages 46–47: "The alarm for general quarters sounded aboard the *West Virginia*, piercing through the sounds of repeated blasts. It pronounced that Japanese raiders had struck Pearl Harbor." The alarm "piercing through the sounds of repeated blasts" is senseless writing. The correct word is warned not pronounced.

Page 47: "Captain Bennion of the USS Virginia…" Captain Bennion was aboard *West Virginia*, not Virginia.

Page 47: "Torpedo damage had already rendered the battle station in total destruction." Which battle station?

Page 48: "[Doris Miller's] constellation of thought allowed his body and soul to jump into action quickly." What is a "constellation of thought" and how can the author know what Miller was thinking at the time?

Page 48: "[After aiding other sailors Miller] then spotted the mortally wounded commanding officer, Mervyn Sharp Bennion, lying in a pile of debris on the deck." Miller did not "spot" the captain. As noted in Chapter 6 of the present book, Johnson was ordered to bring Captain Bennion down from the signal bridge. He went there, taking Miller with him, since he thought Miller's strength would help the men move the captain.

Page 48: "A 'flying shotgun,' a field artillery projectile, had struck the captain in the stomach." This sentence is an example of the confusing, senseless writing found in Chapters 7 through 11. The term flying shotgun is meaningless. No "field artillery projectile" is known as a "flying shotgun," although "beehive" rounds exist for artillery (rounds filled with multiple small projectiles, making the artillery piece in effect a huge shotgun). A shotgun is a small arm used for hunting, recreational shooting, or self-defense. One can hardly imagine a shotgun flying around during the attack. The Japanese used only machine guns, torpedoes, bombs, and specially modified naval projectiles to attack Battleship Row; they did not use field artillery ammunition. Bennion was hit not by a "flying shotgun" but by a metal fragment or fragments.

Page 49: "The assistant pharmacist, Leakand, bandaged [Captain Bennion's] wound in an effort to maintain the bleeding." The pharmacist was a chief petty officer (a chief pharmacist's mate) whose last name was "Leak," not "Leakand." And he would have been trying to stop the bleeding from the captain's wound, not to maintain it. To "maintain" the bleeding would be to hasten death from loss of blood.

Pages 49–50 describe Miller's purported downing of Japanese aircraft. This Chapter has already discussed this topic, but again the essential paradox is that the book notes that Miller had no machine gun training yet purportedly downed as many as four Japanese fighters.

Page 49: "Doris was aware that blacks were prohibited from using machine guns. And he knew that he had no combat training. Shunning these negative thoughts, and overwhelmed with awe, he decided he could do better elsewhere. Observing the surrounding conditions, courage pushed him into action. A dead gunner lay beside an unmanned machine gun. Doris moved the dead gunner aside and took over the machine gun. With aim and coordination, he began blasting away at the planes. He aimed at one Japanese plane and fired. His first round of rapid fire was a precise hit. The plane crashed into the harbor, plunging head first." The after-action report mentions nothing about Miller moving a dead gunner away from the machine gun he (Miller) used. Again, the downing of aircraft is part of the Doris Miller myth. How does the author know that Miller "shunned negative thoughts"?

Paragraphs on page 50 discuss Miller's good marksmanship as a hunter and that Miller "surmised that the machine gun wasn't too big of a problem to handle. It was much like a rifle, but the machine gun had more firepower, a continuous rapid rate. Doris was a pro at just about any task. So aiming and firing the machine gun at his targets was no challenge to him." Marksmanship skills with different weapons are not necessarily interchangeable; someone can be an expert shot with a pistol but a poor shot with a rifle. A hunting rifle and a machine gun are radically different weapons, and skill with one does not necessarily mean that the shooter is skilled with the other. In other words, a fifty-caliber machine gun aboard *West Virginia* is simply not the equivalent of a hunting rifle. A hunting rifle is not capable of fully automatic fire, and no sane hunter would hunt deer with a fifty-caliber machine gun.

Page 50: "A pernicious smile of enlightment [sic] prevailed upon Doris's face… With aim and precaution, he fired away at the attacking planes. He proved himself successful in the ordeal, as he watched the planes crash from his attacking fire. One set ablaze, spun out of control, and crashed into the water. It was a glory Doris marveled… Doris was ecstatic as more planes crashed from his fire as they zeroed in. He continued to fire, until he was ordered to abandon the bridge." "Pernicious" seems an inappropriate modifier since it means deadly or destructive. "Enlightment" is not a word. How did the author know that he smiled? How did she know that he "marveled" or "was ecstatic"? "Precaution" also seems to be an inappropriate noun. Again, to repeat ad nauseam, the likelihood of him downing any aircraft was negligible.

Page 51: "Isorok [sic] Yamamoto planned the Japanese raid on Pearl Harbor. He escaped after achieving the successful, well planned mission. There were 350 Japanese planes reported to be involved in the attack. Thirty-six were verified shot down, or failed to return to their carriers. Doris saw four crash before him as he fired. To uphold his proclaimed deed, he was credited with eyewitness accounts of fellow sailors to have shot down four Zero fighter Japanese planes." The first name of the admiral who planned the attack was "Isoruku," not "Isorok." Twenty-nine, not thirty-six, Japanese aircraft were lost. And the implication from "escape" is that Yamamoto was present with the Japanese task force; in fact, he was not with the task force—the on-scene commander aboard one of the aircraft carriers in the Japanese task force was Vice Admiral Chuichi Nagumo.[43]

Page 51: "That was Doris's first experience with a machine gun." Page 52: The last paragraph of the chapter states in part that Miller "had watched others practicing with the weapons before, but he had never practiced with them himself. He had no real knowledge of their power until the day of the attack. And his efforts proved successful." The same comment can be made again about Miller not downing any aircraft of he had no experience with the fifty-caliber machine gun.

Chapter 8: "The Navy Cross"

Problems with writing and substance continue in chapter 8 (pages 53–59).

Page 53: The newspaper publishing Miller's name was the Pittsburgh Courier, not the Pittsburgh Observer.[44]

Page 54: "Day of Infamy" is "a date which will live in infamy." Chapter 18 of this book discusses this frequently made error.

Page 54: As explained earlier in this chapter, Miller received the Letter of Commendation from the Secretary of the Navy; he did not receive one from President Franklin Roosevelt.

Page 54: "On May 7, 1942, Doris was awarded the Navy Cross (Medal of Honor) [sic] and advanced to first class petty officer."

First of all, if the Navy Cross is the MOH, as one is led to believe by the parenthetical, then Miller was awarded a MOH. Therefore, what is the point of writing the book advocating that he receive a MOH?

Second, the Navy Cross is not the MOH; it is second to the MOH. For the author to confuse the decorations is indicative of her lack of understanding of the awards a Navy member may receive. This lack of understanding seriously undermines the author's overall credibility if she cannot distinguish the Navy Cross and the MOH.

Third, Miller was not advanced to first class petty officer, which is the grade just below chief petty officer (see Chapter 1 of this book for the navy's grades). At the time of the attack, he was a mess attendant second class, which was a grade below mess attendant first class. After initial training as a seaman third class (lowest grade), he began his Navy service, advanced to mess attendant second class, and then was promoted to mess attendant first class. He then changed rating and became a cook third class, which was his final grade. He was never a petty officer, first class or otherwise. Perhaps she cannot distinguish between (from lowest to highest) third, second, and first class grades in the basic seaman category and third, second, and first class among petty officers in the noncommissioned officer category, which is above the basic seaman ratings. In short, the Navy grade system (for nonpetty officers and for petty officers) began with third as the lowest step, not first, and first is the last or highest step.

Page 55: "The Navy Cross is the US Navy's highest award…And Doris was the first black to receive the navy's [sic] highest decoration in World War II." The preceding comments concerning the errors on page 54 address the errors on page 55 about the difference between the MOH and the Navy Cross.

Page 55: "Doris shot down four Japanese planes on December 7, 1941, so truly he was the first full-fledged US hero in World War II." This absurd statement returns the reader to the discussion earlier in this chapter about Miller being the first American hero of World War II and again to the discussion about the number of planes purportedly downed.

Page 58: "On June 1, 1943, his ratings [sic] changed to cook, third class." "Ratings" should be singular.

Chapter 9: "The Commissioning of the USS Miller"

The major problems with this Chapter (pages 60–68) follow:

Page 60: Again, the author cannot report basic facts correctly. She notes correctly that "American fighter planes" killed Admiral Isoroku Yamamoto in 1943 when Yamamoto was flying in a bomber that the fighters shot down. She then inexplicably writes that "American bombers [sic] intercepted the Japanese bombers..." No American bombers flew the mission. Chapter 3 of this book discusses Yamamoto's fate.

Page 64: "On June 3, 1972, the US Navy named the destroyer escort after Doris Miller: Ocean Escort USS Miller (DE-1091)." Page 65: "She was the fourteenth ship of the Joseph Hewew class of ocean escorts." The Navy did not have one destroyer escort as implied by "the" in front of "destroyer escort." The Navy does not have an "ocean escort" ship. The ship named for Miller was a fast frigate, not a destroyer escort, commissioned on June 30, 1973, as a ship in the Knox class of frigates.[45]

Chapter 11: "A Family Still Seeks Honor"

Finally, in the book's last Chapter (pages 74–79), the author avails herself of a final opportunity to destroy her credibility by illustrating her complete lack of familiarity with the military and its awards system:

Page 75: Again, "Day of Infamy" should be "a date which will live in infamy."

Page 75: "Doris never received the Congressional Medal of Honor, the nation's highest military award for bravery in combat in World Wars I and II...No blacks received the MOH." On page 54, the author inferred that Miller had received a MOH as indicated by the phrase "Navy Cross (Medal of Honor)." On page 55, the author stated that the Navy Cross was the highest award, yet on page 75, she writes that the MOH is the highest award. Also, the inference is that the MOH was restricted to the two World Wars; in fact, the MOH existed and was awarded numerous times before and after World War II. As explained in this chapter and in appendix D of the present book, seven blacks belatedly received the MOH in 1997, but perhaps the author did not know of the belated awards since her book is dated 1997.

Pages 76–77: The author discusses the efforts to obtain a MOH for Miller. She writes, "It is not a cry for public sentiment, but a cry for Doris to be honored in accordance to [sic] his citizenship." Citizenship is a separate matter from the MOH, so the sentence is meaningless. Perhaps the inference here is that Miller's American citizenship is a factor supporting a MOH for him, but citizenship is not in the statutory criteria governing the MOH. The correct grammatical construction is "in accordance with his citizenship."

Pages 77: "The Congressional Medal of Honor, however, is awarded through the actions of Congress, not the navy [sic]." As Chapter 14 and Appendix D of the present book explain, the role of Congress was and is passing legislation creating and governing the MOH; only in rare cases has Congress itself been involved in the award of MOHs to a specific individual by enacting legislation awarding a MOH to that individual. In all likelihood, Congress would direct the Department of Defense or the Navy to determine if Miller deserved a MOH; Congress itself would not make that determination, although for Miller to receive a MOH, Congress would have to enact legislation waiving the time limitation for MOH awards, which was the objective of the bill Congresswoman Johnson introduced in Congress, as mentioned earlier in this chapter.

Page 79: The author notes that the Miller MOH controversy continues. "It is stipulated that in order for Doris to receive the Congressional Medal of Honor, his recognition has to proceed in this chain of order: the president [sic], secretary of defense [sic], chairman of the chief of staff [sic], secretary of the navy [sic], Medal of Honor Legion of the US [sic], and the House Armed Services Committee."

Here the author shows perhaps her highest degree of ignorance and poor writing ability. The paragraph is simply stupefying:

What "stipulates" the purported "chain of order" for consideration of a MOH for Miller? The proper term is recommendation, not "recognition."

Today, the correct process for routing a MOH recommendation through the chain of "command" (not "chain of order") is the field command or commander recommending it; the military service of the member recommended for the MOH; the secretary of the military service; the Secretary of Defense; and the President. A MOH recommendation would end with Presidential action; the President would not be the first official to receive a MOH recommendation.

Also, the U.S. military has no "chairman of the chief of staff." A chief of staff superintends a commander's staff. The author probably intended "chairman of the joint chiefs of staff," the senior military advisor in the United States.

Congress, as has been noted before, is generally not involved in individual MOH awards, although it could enact legislation that, if approved by the President, would waive the time limitation on MOH recommendations so that Miller could receive a posthumous award.

The "Medal of Honor Legion of the US" (if such an organization exists) would not be involved in determining if a MOH should be awarded. The author probably intended "the Congressional Medal of Honor Society," which does not act on MOH recommendations.

Page 79: "Yet, of the 1.5 million black men who served, none have been awarded the Congressional Medal of Honor." Served when? For example, the MOH was awarded to black recipients during the Vietnam War. Again, as with page 75, perhaps the author did not know of the belated seven Black MOH awards for World War II in 1997 since her book is dated the same year.

In summary, the poor writing and the number of factual errors in the book Doris Miller: A Silent Medal of Honor Winner do a disservice to Doris Miller and fail to make even the weakest case for awarding him a MOH. Nowhere in her writing does she demonstrate that she reviewed the MOH awards for December 7 or that she knows the statutory criteria for a MOH award. She never cites a MOH statute. The book is simply an embarrassment to author and to subject.

At various times, from approximately 2009 to 2012, the author looked at the Vickie Gail Miller website and at her e-mail concerning the "awardance" of a MOH for Doris Miller. Rather than prolong the analysis of her poor writing style, grammar, and factual inaccuracies found on the website and in the e-mail, the author will simply say that the website and e-mail were written with those same characteristics as her book.

After all was said and done, one letter "resolved" the Doris Miller MOH matter for Vickie Gail Miller, but she continued her efforts notwithstanding the letter's "negative" reply. She wrote to the Department of Defense about a MOH for Doris Miller. For some reason, the response dated March 28, 1995, was from the "Military Awards Branch" but on Army letterhead. The letter explained the MOH process described in Chapter 14 of this book. First, Miller's actions had to meet the statutory requirements for the MOH. Second, a fully documented account of those actions had to be submitted to the chain of command for review within two years of the actions. If all members of the chain of command approved the recommendation, it was then sent to the President for his final approval. The letter also discussed a waiver of the time limitation that could be obtained, but the letter advised her that the waiver was irrelevant since the military had no evidence that Miller was ever recommended for a MOH.[46]

DORIS MILLER: IN SUMMARY AND IN PERSPECTIVE

An important point emphasized at the beginning of this chapter should be reemphasized: the intent of this chapter is not to criticize Doris Miller as a person or sailor and is not to question his bravery—no one questions the bravery or sincerity of his actions on December 7. Also, this chapter was not written to examine or to defend the racial segregation existing in the navy in World War II. Segregation was the way of life at the time and must be accepted as a historical reality, no matter how much segregation is detested today or how much present generations condemn the segregation in World War II. This chapter does not deny that racial prejudice existed in society or the Navy before and during World War II, a prejudice extending to Japanese-Americans as well as blacks.

Rather, the objectives of this chapter were to provide a factual account of the actions of Doris Miller on December 7 and of the events leading to his Navy Cross and to demonstrate that he does not deserve a MOH. In achieving these objectives, the mythical Doris Miller had to be eliminated. Elimination of the myth requires one to confront and to eliminate political correctness, speculation, and assertions and opinions unsupported by facts. Hero worship also had to be eliminated; perspective and context had to be restored.

With the facts known, one can uncover the actions of Doris Miller on December 7 and determine if he deserved a MOH or even a Navy Cross for those actions.

The facts are that officers and enlisted members, regardless of race and including Doris Miller, expended a vast amount of energy and effort and displayed great dedication to duty, trying to save and to move the mortally wounded and suffering Captain Bennion, energy and effort expended in the worst of circumstances aboard USS *West Virginia*. Those trying to help the captain persisted notwithstanding the smoke and fire and chaos of battle. One can only try to imagine the emotions they felt to the extent that the horrible circumstances and time pressure permitted them to feel or to access emotions to any degree or at all.

The question of an award for Doris Miller arises from his actions in these conditions. A mere assertion that he deserves a MOH is not a fact justifying a MOH. This point is especially true when the following is obvious: authors Buckley and Vickie Gail Miller and former Congress member Johnson have not examined facts or context in detail concerning Doris Miller and the December 7 MOH recipients. As was shown earlier in this chapter, Buckley cannot even recite the facts of the Doris Miller story correctly.

Buckley's carelessness with the facts resulted in an inaccurate account of Miller's actions at Pearl Harbor. A MOH based on a disregard for accurate facts and context would be a travesty and a slap in the face to those who in fact deserved MOHs. Facts are critical in the demanding process of determining if a MOH has been earned. Anyone questioning the importance of facts or the high standards used in evaluating MOH recommendations should read the account in Chapter 19 of the prolonged, thorough process involved in the MOH awarded to Jackson Pharris of USS *California* or the Congressional debate discussed in Chapter 20 over the propriety of awarding Billy Mitchell a MOH.

To award Miller a MOH would, in logic and fairness, lead to the ludicrous conclusion that everyone on December 7 who assisted the wounded or manned a machine gun should receive a MOH. This logic was the same logic, described in Chapter 16, that the Permanent Board of Awards used in recommending disapproval of a MOH for Lieutenant Colonel Daniel Fox of *Arizona*. In the Board's own words, "to award the Medal of Honor in this case would establish a precedent for awards to every one [sic] who has lost or subsequently may lose his life while at his battle-station…"[47]

One could also argue that the other men assisting Captain Bennion were unfairly treated since, as noted several times, they did not receive Navy Crosses for assisting their mortally wounded captain.

Moreover, to award a MOH unsupported by the facts would demean the value of the award. The award of a MOH is—as shown by the MOH for *California*'s Pharris—and should be a serious matter, requiring verified facts supporting the recommendation and meeting the statutory criteria for a MOH. Two of the December 7 MOHs—those awarded to Kidd and Van Valkenburgh—were unsupported by facts. To award another December 7 MOH unsupported by facts to placate Doris Miller advocates seems senseless. And to award him a MOH for other reasons—such as redress for racial grievances—would demean the MOH in general and Doris Miller as a person since the award would be based not on merit or facts but on politics and political correctness. The Army commissioned a study by Shaw University to review the records of black soldiers from World War II who were possible MOH candidates but who were not recommended due to racial prejudice. Congress also directed a review of various racial minority records of those who but for racial prejudice would have been awarded MOHs (see
Appendix D of the present book). A review of citations of the MOHs awarded belatedly to the minorities recite deeds much more extensive than what Miller performed on December 7; clearly the belated MOH awards had the factual bases justifying MOHs that any MOH awarded to Miller would lack.

Finally, whether the facts support a Navy Cross for his actions on December 7 is a moot point since President Roosevelt directed that he receive a Navy Cross, and he in fact received one. The fact that he received it is important and, really, a victory for Miller and his supporters since, as noted repeatedly, none of the others assisting Captain Bennion received a Navy Cross. One must imagine how they felt knowing that Miller received preferential treatment by being awarded a Navy Cross for the same actions they took but for which they received no award. Also, the Navy had initially determined that a Letter of Commendation was adequate recognition for Miller, and the Navy, as an institution, is the most recalcitrant military service insofar as changing its decisions and conclusions about events and people. President Roosevelt had to step in and direct the award of a Navy Cross to Miller.

In the final analysis, Miller was fortunate. He was the subject of a Presidential decision overriding the Navy's determination that the Letter of Commendation was sufficient recognition for his deeds on December 7. The result was a Navy Cross for those deeds, a Navy Cross that he did not deserve. To think that he did anything more extraordinary than the average crew member on *West Virginia* on December 7 is to engage in fantasy and to construct a mythical world of December 7, 1941.

He appears to have received as much or more public attention than the MOH recipients in this book with the exception of Billy Mitchell. He even had a postage stamp issued for him. The author bought a panel of stamps in 2010 titled "Distinguished Sailors." The stamps were forty-four-cent stamps with images of these men: William S. Sims, Arleigh A. Burke, John McCloy, and Doris Miller. In the author's opinion, Miller does not belong in the company of these men, but the Postal Service apparently must do its part to keep the myth alive. What is more distressing is that the author knows of no MOH recipient discussed in this book who has a postage stamp with his image, although the Postal Service has issued stamps with the images of MOH recipients from World War II, the Korean War, and the Vietnam War. A guide map sold at the Pearl Harbor Visitor Center for the "day of infamy," published by Franko Maps, has one person named as a "Pearl Harbor Hero," Doris Miller, chosen as an example of "many heroes." In a guidebook to Pearl Harbor, the section "Heroes of December 7, 1941" includes only two MOH recipients: Ensign Flaherty and Chief Petty Officer Finn. Why were they and they alone chosen? And as is de rigueur, Doris Miller is included.[48]

The objectives of this chapter were to provide a factual account of the actions of Doris Miller on December 7 and of the events leading to his Navy Cross and to demonstrate that he does not deserve a MOH. In achieving these objectives, the mythical Doris Miller had to be eliminated and a factually supportable conclusion had to be reached. That conclusion is that a black hero was demanded or needed for December 7, and President Franklin Roosevelt delivered one by directing that Doris Miller receive a Navy Cross, a political award to mollify those making the demands for a black hero for December 7. In doing so, he overrode the decision of his own secretary of the navy, who had determined that a Letter of Commendation was sufficient recognition of Miller's performance on December 7. Whether the facts supported a Navy Cross or even a MOH was an irrelevant concern.

And Miller did not receive a MOH due to Congressional direction to the services to review the cases of minorities who would have received MOHs but for racial prejudice. The congressional direction included certain minorities but not blacks, and the Army's review of the records of black soldiers would not affect Miller since he was in the Navy.[49]

In short, to use a sports analogy, Doris Miller is a football team ranked number one without reference to its won-lost record and without reference to other good teams.

But the myth will persist as long as Miller is considered the first hero of World War II or the first American hero of World War II or as a World War II icon. Paschall's summary of Miller in America's War Heroes: Unsung and Legendary is in the following section of the magazine.[50]

World War II Icons

And lunacy will prevail as long as people think Miller deserves a MOH for helping his captain, firing a machine gun, and saving some shipmates—unless that thought can be reversed by people who read the MOH citations for Jackson Pharris and Samuel Fuqua and think again in perspective, how Doris Miller compares to these two men.

Fate and Legacy

As mentioned earlier, Miller was lost at sea in 1943 when his ship sank. His tombstone is the inscription of his name at the Honolulu Memorial at the National Memorial Cemetery of the Pacific. He received a Purple Heart for death in combat.[51]

USS Miller was named for Miller; she was a fast frigate commissioned in 1973.

NOTES

1. Report from USS *West Virginia* (Subject: "Action of December 7, 1941—Report of") of December 11, 1941 (hereafter "*West Virginia* Report"); Enclosure (D): statement of Lieutenant Commander D. C. Johnson, U.S. Navy (taking Miller to the bridge with him); Enclosure (H): statement of Lieutenant (junior grade) F. H. White, U.S. Naval Reserve (manning machineguns with Miller).

2. Ibid.; paragraph 2 of the report mentions White and Miller saving lives by hauling men to the quarterdeck.

3. The process of identifying and rewarding Miller for his actions on December 7 is described in detail in two sources: Neil Sapper, "ABOARD THE WRONG SHIP IN THE RIGHT BOOKS: DORIS MILLER AND HISTORICAL ACCURACY," East Texas Historical Journal 28, no. 1 (1980); Richard Miller, The Messman Chronicles: African Americans in the US Navy, 1932–1943 (Naval Institute Press, Annapolis, MD, 2004), 285–318.

4. Letter to the author from the Department of the Navy of August 14, 2001, enclosing a copy of a card recording awards for Doris Miller (hereafter "Miller awards card").

5. Endnote 1, *West Virginia* report.

6. Letter to the author from the Department of the Navy of August 8, 2001, stating that none of the names the author submitted to the navy for review received Navy Crosses for helping Captain Bennion. As noted in chapter 6, the primary personnel trying to assist Bennion were, in addition to Miller, Lieutenant D. C. Johnson, Lieutenant (junior grade) F. H. White, Lieutenant C. V. Ricketts, and Chief Pharmacist's Mate L. N. Leak. Furthermore, their names were not among the names of officers and men recommended by the Fleet Board of Awards or the Permanent Board of Awards. See endnote 19 of Chapter 14 concerning the Third Endorsement of the Permanent Board of Awards on the report of the Fleet Board of Awards; the endorsement is in the Official Military Personnel File (OMPF) of Rear Admiral Isaac Kidd. The Third Endorsement and its accompanying summary are in Section 06 ("Awards, Decorations, and Correspondence") of the CD on pages 40–45 of the OMPF CD (CD page numbers). The Navy Cross recommendations are on pages 41 and 42 (CD page numbers); the page numbers on the endorsement itself are 1 and 2. The document makes no recommendation for Miller; his name does not even appear on it.

7. Endnote 3, Sapper, Doris Miller and Historical Accuracy, 7; Doris Miller Internet biographical information from the Naval History and Heritage Command (published April 20, 2015)(hereafter "Doris Miller Internet biographical information from the Naval History and Heritage Command").

8. The author has seen the inscription in person. The entry for Doris Miller can also be found by searching his name on the American Battle Monuments Commission

Internet site, where his grade is given as cook third class.

9. Gail Buckley, American Patriots: The Story of Blacks in the Military from the Revolution to Desert Storm (Random House, 2001), 275 (hereafter, "Buckley, American Patriots).

10. John White clay Chambers II, "The Long Thread of Black Valor," Washington Post, May 28, 2001.

11. Endnote 9, Buckley, American Patriots, xix.

12. Wil Haygood, "Courage in Full Color," Washington Post, August 17, 2008, section M, 1.

13. Endnote 2: Sapper, Doris Miller and Historical Accuracy.

14. Irwin H. Lee, Negro Medal of Honor Men (Dodd, Mead & Company, 1967, 1969), 107 (hereafter Lee, Negro Medal of Honor Men).

15. Vice Admiral Homer N. Wallin, US Navy (Retired), Pearl Harbor: Why, How, Fleet Salvage, and Final Appraisal (Washington, DC: Naval History Division, United States Government Printing Office, Washington, DC, 1968), 11 (the date the "European War" began, understood to mean World War II) (hereafter "Wallin, Pearl Harbor: Why, How, Fleet Salvage, and Final Appraisal").

16. Ibid., 114.

17. Endnote 9, Buckley, American Patriots, 275.

18. Rod Paschall, America's War Heroes: Unsung and Legendary (Primedia, 2002), 68 (hereafter "Paschall, America's War Heroes: Unsung and Legendary"); the Miller story is in the section "World War II Icons."

19. "Black History at Arlington National Cemetery" (Historical Information, printed from the Arlington National Cemetery Internet site on December 12, 2000) (hereafter "Black History at Arlington National Cemetery").

20. Francis Trevelyan Miller, History of World War II (The Publisher's Guild, New York, NY, 1945), 328.

21. Endnote 9, Buckley, American Patriots, 275.

22. Endnote 14, Lee, Negro Medal of Honor Men, 108.

23. Endnote 9, Buckley, American Patriots, 275.

24. Endnote 19, Black History at Arlington National Cemetery.

25. Endnote 18, Paschall, America's War Heroes: Unsung and Legendary, 68.

26. Endnote 14, Lee, Negro Medal of Honor Men, 109.

27. Endnote 3, Miller, The Messman Chronicles, 299. Endnote 3, Sapper, Doris Miller and Historical Accuracy, 3–4; endnote 7, Doris Miller Internet biographical information from the Naval History and Heritage Command.

28. Jonathan B. Parshall and Anthony P. Tully, Shattered Sword: The Untold Story of the Battle of Midway (Potomac Books, 2005); Zero speeds: page 479; Val speed: 483; Kate speeds: page 481.

29. Endnote 1, *West Virginia* report.

30. Endnote 3, Miller, The Messman Chronicles, 312–313.

31. Ibid., 312.

32. Catherine Cantwell, "Doris Miller Decorated 40 Years Ago," Waco Tribune-Herald, May 3, 1982. No ship named USS Virginia was present at Pearl Harbor on December 7. Miller did not stumble over Bennion while running to his battle station. He did not drag Bennion to a safer spot. He did not shoot down five Japanese aircraft. Nimitz awarded the Navy Cross less than one year after it was authorized. Miller was not promoted to first class petty officer, which is the highest noncommissioned officer grade before chief petty officer (see chapter 1 of this book). He was never a petty officer of any class. His terminal grade was cook third class.

33. Gregory Epps, "Bombs Away," Port Folio Weekly, June 5, 2001, 29.

34. Gordon W. Prange, Donald W. Goldstein, and Katherine V. Dillon, December 7, 1941: The Day the Japanese Attacked Pearl Harbor (McGraw Hill Book Company, New York, NY, 1988), 148–149; Walter Lord, Day of Infamy (Henry Holt and Company, New York, NY1957), 131–132; endnote 1, *West Virginia* report, Johnson's statement is Enclosure (D).

35. A description of the Johnson bill is found in a news release for Congresswoman Eddie Bernice Johnson (May 25, 2001); it was H. R. 1944, May 24, 2001, First Session of the 107th Congress; the resolution of the U.S. Conference of Mayors is from the US Conference of Mayors Internet site, printed on August 25, 2001, and October 30, 2001.

36. Lieutenant Colonel Jeffrey J. Gudmens and the Staff Ride Team, Combat Studies Institute, Staff Ride Handbook for the Attack on Pearl Harbor, 7 December 1941: A Study of Defending America (Combat Studies Institute Press, reprinted June 2009), 153–158; the Miller section is on page 158.

37. Navy Cross citation for Ensign Joseph K. Tausig, Jr.. In 2015, the author saw Tausig's name listed as a Navy Cross recipient on the memorial to USS *Nevada* at Hospital Point on Naval Station Pearl Harbor.

38. Leatrice R. Arakaki and John R. Kuborn, 7 December 1941: The Air Force Story (Pacific Air Forces, Office of History, Hickam Air Force Base, Hawaii, 1991), 76–80 and 135 (DSC awards).

39. Jane Blakeney, Heroes: US Marine Corps 1861 *1955 (Guthrie Lithograph Co., Inc., 1957), 228; endnote 15, Wallin, Pearl Harbor: Why, How, Fleet Salvage, and Final Appraisal, 306–307 (description of factual basis for Shapley's Silver Star, preventing a Marine corporal from drowning as the two men moved from *Arizona* to Ford Island).

40. Vickie Gail Miller, Doris Miller: A Silent Medal of Honor Winner (Eakin Press, Austin, TX, 1997).

41. Endnote 3, The Messman Chronicles, 365.

42. Colonel Charles A. Jones, US Marine Corps Reserve (Retired), Hawaii's World War II Military Sites (Mutual Publishing, Honolulu, HI, 2002), 27.

43. Endnote 15, Wallin, Pearl Harbor: Why, How, Fleet Salvage, and Final Appraisal, 85.

44. Endnote 3, Sapper, Doris Miller and Historical Accuracy, 5.

45. Endnote 7, Doris Miller Internet biographical information from the Naval History and Heritage Command.

46. Letter from the Chief, Military Awards Branch, to Vickie Gail Miller (March 28, 1995).

47. Letter from the Senior Member of the [Navy] Board for the Award of Medals of Honor, Distinguished Service Medal, Navy Cross, Distinguished Flying Cross, and Life Saving Medals ("Subject: Recommendation for the Posthumous Award of the Medal of Honor in the case of the Late Lieutenant Colonel Daniel R. Fox, U.S. Marine Corps") of June 3, 1942.

48. Richard A. Wisniewski, Pearl Harbor and the *Arizona* Memorial: A Pictorial History (Pacific Basin Enterprises, Honolulu, HI 2014).

49. See Chapter 5 and Appendix D of this book concerning review of minority service records.

50. Paschall, America's War Heroes: Unsung and Legendary, 68.

51. Endnote 7, Doris Miller Internet biographical information from the Naval History and Heritage Command.

Photograph: Doris Miller

Doris Miller receiving his Navy Cross from Admiral Chester Nimitz at an awards ceremony held on the flight deck of USS *Enterprise* (CV-6) at Pearl Harbor, May 27, 1942. (Photograph NH 80-G-23588 from the Naval History and Heritage Command.)

Chapter 18
Errors and Omissions concerning the Medals of Honor Earned in the Hawaiian Islands

Introduction and Perspective: Too Fat To Escape

The day the author began editing this chapter, he looked at a book, Pacific War Stories, an anthology of interviews of World War II Pacific War veterans. When looking for MOH information, he found an interview of a veteran describing *Oklahoma* capsizing on December 7. The veteran stated that the *Oklahoma*'s chaplain was a "portly little fellow" and that his size prevented him from escaping the ship. He was "too big to get out of the porthole." He stated that the chaplain stayed in a compartment, helping others to escape until he drowned there. "He [the chaplain] got a Medal of Honor for that."[1]

Not quite—this assertion is one of the most egregious errors in the December 7 MOH literature. No chaplain received a MOH for December 7. Chapter 5 of this book is the story of the two *Oklahoma* MOH men, a line officer and a seaman. The anthology's editor gave no indication that the story was inaccurate, leaving readers believing the chaplain received a MOH.

This example is one of many of the numerous errors found in the accounts of the MOHs earned in the Hawaiian Islands in World War II.

The accounting in this book of the many errors concerning the MOH recipients can be tiresome, but it is necessary to dispel myths and mistakes so the MOH recipients and the context of their deeds and lives can be portrayed accurately and honorably. Such an accounting reveals a disturbing lack of concern (intentional or unintentional) for historical accuracy. MOH recipients are omitted or portrayed inaccurately in private and governmental publications. MOH recipients are even fabricated from nothing, such as *Oklahoma*'s "chaplain" just mentioned. Also disturbing is the scope and the tenacity of the errors. Chapter 14 discusses the numerous erroneous assertions that John Finn or Donald Ross received the first MOH for World War II or for December 7. The statements seem immune to factual rebuttal.

Errors in the Accounts of MOH Recipients

While researching the subject matter of this book, the author found a staggering number of factual errors and omissions concerning the MOH recipients and their deeds in various publications, both traditional (books and magazines) and electronic (the Internet and DVDs). One wonders why accounts of two of the most important events in the history of the United States, the attack on Oahu on December 7, 1941, and the 1942 Battle of Midway, contain so many errors in the stories of the men whose actions during those events led to their MOHs. In the context of the importance of events and in the context of the MOH—the country's highest award for combat bravery—the degree of sloppy or incomplete research is truly remarkable and embarrassing.

Everyone makes mistakes, including the present author. Anyone pointing out the mistakes of others risks those others will find errors in his or her own work. The author is willing to take that risk when the number of errors is sufficient to comprise an entire chapter in this book, especially when those errors are basic factual errors that could have been avoided with minimal concern for checking assertions for truth and accuracy. The men in this book deserve no less care in having their stories told.

Perhaps the most interesting, if not puzzling, aspect of these errors is that two of the sources are the US Navy, the very organization whose members earned all but three of the nineteen MOHs discussed in this book (two marines and one army officer), and the Congressional Medal of Honor Society, which offered assistance with programs or publications.

Many of the errors are in publications dedicated exclusively or almost exclusively to topics concerning December 7 or Midway. But in many cases readers do not have to worry about finding errors concerning the MOHs in such publications; the authors have solved that problem for the readers by failing to include any information whatsoever about the MOHs. No errors can be made if the topic is not even addressed.

So the question becomes why the current author—who lacks classic academic credentials and media connections—can accurately convey information about these MOH recipients while other authors cannot.

WHY ARE SO MANY ERRORS MADE?

The errors seem to be due to four factors, but in short, what appears to be the case is that anyone can write anything about these men without regard to accuracy, omission, or context.

First is sloppy, incomplete, and inaccurate research by sloppy and lazy writers and commentators.

Second is the lack of critical thinking. Many Americans believe—without questioning or analyzing critically—that any information disseminated by the media (television, radio, Internet, or publication) is true. The information is ingested as provided; the power of discernment is disabled or weakened. Discernment is reading or hearing critically, asking if the information is correct or in context, and challenging incorrect information.

Third are the information outlets, primarily the written and electronic news media, which are notorious for disregarding or downplaying fact-checking, proofreading, and good editing. Also, context and history are jettisoned or minimized, and one cannot, in many cases, judge facts without considering history and context: if one does not know if history and context are accurate, then one has problems judging if a fact in that history or context is partially or fully accurate. Finding context and history requires research, which requires time, which is at a premium in the media-driven American society where information must be disseminated rapidly in a short format and dumbed down so that average citizens can be slammed with as much information as possible in the shortest time possible. Data or episodes are reported without regard to their place in historical or other context.

Chapter 17 of this book, about Doris Miller, is the classic example. He was the subject of a campaign to have a MOH awarded to him posthumously without reference to the entire story of the MOH for December 7 and examination of the facts of what happened aboard his ship, USS *West Virginia*, on that date. No one in this campaign asks if the facts support an award of a MOH to him for his actions on December 7.

In modern times, a primary danger is an Internet presenting its own challenges. Anyone can easily post any information—true or false, accurate or inaccurate, without or within context—on the Internet. The only safeguards are other Internet users who challenge the person providing the information, but the challengers themselves may provide inaccurate information. The Internet is also transitory. A site may be present one day and absent the next, and a site's content may change overnight.

Fourth is error due to conflicting information. The classic example seen later in this chapter involves John Finn.

Listed here are major errors from various sources the author encountered in conducting the research necessary to write this book. Undoubtedly, other errors exist. The number of errors is disturbing, especially given the forum in which some of the errors were made.

THE MOST FREQUENTLY MADE ERRORS

The errors most frequently made concern the following topics, all of which are related to the MOH or the attack on Oahu, which was the event leading to the awards of the majority of the MOHs that are the subject of this book. The errors are made by the general public, by self-appointed December 7 experts, by authors, and by the media. Many seem de rigueur.

- the inability to name correctly the first recipient of a MOH in World War II and the first recipient to receive a MOH for actions on December 7. Giving the incorrect name of the first MOH recipient of World War II is de rigueur mistake number 1. Chapter 14 (Overview) covers this topic in detail, so this chapter will not revisit it.

- the inability to give accurate information about the MOH recipients, such as the number of recipients and their names, duty stations, and actions leading to their MOHs, including the failure to count accurately posthumous and nonposthumous awards and the number of awards and places of those awards on Oahu. Authors simply cannot provide this information accurately. Giving the incorrect number and locations of the MOH recipients for and on December 7 is de rigueur mistake number 2. Again, Chapter 14 covered this topic in detail, so this chapter will only provide correct information where necessary.

- an incorrect number or identification of battleships at Pearl Harbor on December 7. Battleship quantity and identification are important since so many—twelve—MOHs went to battleship sailors: *California* (four), *West Virginia* (one), *Oklahoma* (two), *Arizona* (three), and *Nevada* (two).

- misunderstanding of the role of Congress in awarding a MOH. The two errors here are referring to the "medal of honor" (the term used in the statutes) as the "Congressional Medal of Honor" and stating that Congress is involved in the award of the typical individual combat MOH. Since Chapter 14 addresses these errors, this chapter will not revisit them except to note three examples showing the errors to be universal.

In a book about the raid to rescue General George Patton's son-in-law in 1945 (he was a captive of the Germans), the leader of the raid, who received a Distinguished Service Cross, purportedly said, "Congress investigates a Medal of Honor."[2] Congress would rarely if ever investigate a combat MOH awarded via the normal awards process by which the president approves the MOH. In a military historical journal, of all places, an author writing about the MOH awarded to Lieutenant (junior grade) Albert David for his role in capturing U-505 wrote, "Congress eventually designated Lieutenant…David to wear the Medal of Honor…"[3] Congress did not designate the MOH; it was awarded via the normal procedure used for combat MOHs. In Aviation History, an author wrote, "Congress authorized the award, which [then-General Douglas] MacArthur personally presented to Bong." While technically speaking the statement is correct (Congress "authorized" the MOH by creating it), the implication that can be drawn is incorrect (i.e., that Congress approved the Bong award).[4] Again, Congress was not involved in the award of the MOH. Congress does not review or approve the typical MOH awarded by the president in the name of Congress.

- errors involving Doris Miller. Chapter 17 of this book discusses errors concerning Miller.

- errors involving Billy Mitchell. Chapter 20 of this book discusses the errors concerning Mitchell

- referring to a MOH recipient as a MOH "winner." Winner implies that the MOH is an award for a contest; recipient is the correct term.

- omitting the MOH awarded posthumously to First Lieutenant George Cannon, U.S. Marine Corps, the only MOH recipient for December 7 who was not on Oahu (he was on Midway) Apparently with the focus on the morning attack on Pearl Harbor, the evening attack on Midway during which Cannon was mortally wounded is unknown. He was not at Pearl Harbor or on Oahu.

Discussion of Specific Errors
Errors in General

Errors are organized by source, not by type of error, since many sources have multiple errors. The organization by source in a numbered section as follows:

Organization of Errors

Section of this Chapter	Source
1	Newspapers
2	Books in General
2A	Books about the MOH
2B	Books about December 7th or World War II
2C	Magazine Articles, Phamphets, and Miscellaneous
3	Speech
4	Electronic Media

Errors Involving the Marine Recipients

At the end of this chapter is a discussion of the errors concerning the two marine MOH recipients included in this book.

The Errors

Section 1: Newspapers and News Releases

Honolulu Newspaper

The irony of a newspaper on Oahu—the Honolulu Advertiser—reporting MOH information erroneously cannot be missed. The Wednesday, December 7, 1966, edition of the newspaper marked the twentieth anniversary of the attack with a story titled "Medal of Honor to 15 at P.H." Above the headline reads "11 Killed in Dec. 7 Attack, One Later in War." In fact, as this book repeatedly stresses, only fourteen recipients were at Pearl Harbor; one was at Kaneohe Bay, and the other at Midway. Moreover, of the sixteen recipients (fifteen on Oahu and one on Midway), ten—not eleven—died on December 7. The mistake is repeated in the body of the article. It also notes that eight ships were named for the recipients; in fact, ships were named for all fifteen of the Oahu recipients except for Fuqua (see chapters 4 through 12 and 19 of this book).

The article's photograph labeled "Van Valkenburgh" is not a photograph of Franklin Van Valkenburgh. It appears to be a photograph of Isaac Kidd.[5]

The article omitted Lieutenant Cannon's MOH for Midway, which is part of the Hawaiian Islands.

THE WALL STREET JOURNAL ("WSJ")

The author of a WSJ article about the MOH Museum at Mount Pleasant, South Carolina, wrote, "The first World War II Medal of Honor was awarded to Navy Lt. John Flinn [sic] for action at Pearl Harbor." He also wrote, "Fourteen other sailors earned the medal that day, 10 posthumously."[6]

Chapter 14 of this book addresses the question of Finn not being first MOH recipient of World War II. Although he later became an officer and lieutenant, Finn was enlisted at the time of his MOH action and when he received the MOH (the MOH citation is addressed him as an "aviation chief ordnanceman," which is a chief petty officer, not an officer, such as lieutenant. Also, his name is "Finn," not "Flinn."

The statement "Fourteen other sailors earned the medal that day, 10 posthumously" is correct in number but misleading since "sailor" properly refers to an enlisted member of the navy, not to a Navy officer. Counting Finn, only four of the December 7 recipients were enlisted: Scott on *California*, Ward on *Oklahoma*, and Tomich on *Utah*.

Posthumous presents another problem; of the ten posthumous awards, one was to a Marine, Lieutenant Cannon, on Midway (Chapter 12). He was definitely not a sailor.

NAVY TIMES

Navy Times, a weekly newspaper devoted to Navy stories and news, had two stories about Finn. In the story in the December 10, 2007, edition, authors Robert F. Dorr and Fred L. Borch refer to Finn as a "chief ordnanceman." He was, in fact, a chief petty officer who was an aviation ordnanceman. In the story by Dorr in the December 10, 2001, edition, he makes the same mistake, although the headline reads "Aviation Ordnanceman…" Chapter 14 discusses the erroneous assertion in the 2001 article about Finn being the first World War II MOH recipient.

The 2007 article correctly notes that Finn's MOH was the only one for a recipient who shot at the Japanese, but it is misleading in stating that "other Medals of Honor were for heroic rescues that day." The statement is ambiguous. One could conclude that all the MOHs except Finn's were for rescues. In fact, only two involved rescues in the classic sense. Warrant Officer Jackson Pharris saved his ship and her crew, USS *California*, by ordering counterflooding. He also rescued and assisted many of the crewmen aboard the ship. Lieutenant Commander Samuel Fuqua maintained order as best he could on USS *Arizona* and organized rescue and firefighting parties. Warrant Office Ross could be considered to have rescued men by forcing them to leave the area of his station. Ensign Flaherty and Seaman First Class Ward assisted men in escaping a turret or turrets on *Oklahoma* but did not rescue anyone in the normal understanding of the word rescue.[7]

THE WASHINGTON POST

As Chapter 11 explains, John Finn died on May 27, 2010, at age one hundred, the oldest living MOH recipient at the time of his death and the last of the December 7 recipients living.

The Post's May 29, 2010, obituary for him was correct when it stated that his was the only MOH earned that day for combat. He was the only MOH recipient that date directly engaged in combat with the attacking Japanese aircraft (he shot at them with a machine gun). It was incorrect, however, when it stated, "Of the 15 Medal of Honor recipients from Pearl Harbor, 14 were for rescue attempts."[8]

First of all, only fourteen MOHs were earned at Pearl Harbor. The fifteenth, Finn's, was earned at Naval Air Station Kaneohe Bay, which is north of Pearl Harbor and is a separate installation from Pearl Harbor.

Second, fourteen MOHs were not awarded for "rescue attempts." This topic was just discussed in reviewing the 2007 article in Navy Times, but the Post article is even clearer in stating that all the other fourteen MOHs were for rescue attempts. Again, the only men effecting rescue in the classic sense were Pharris and Fuqua.

THE NEW YORK TIMES

The New York Times obituary for John Finn (May 27, 2010) has this headline: "John Finn, Medal of Honor Winner, Dies at 100." As is emphasized in this book, one who earns a MOH is not a "MOH winner" but a "MOH recipient" since "winner" implies that the person achieved the MOH via a contest.[9]

THE JOHN FINN MOH AWARD

John Finn's MOH is a magnet for errors. In addition to falsely asserting that John Finn was the first World War II MOH recipient, various publications err concerning the date of approval of the John Finn MOH and the date of presentation and by whom it was presented.

A 2010 news release from, of all places, Pearl Harbor's World War II Valor in the Pacific National Monument mistakenly states that Finn received his award from President Franklin Roosevelt on September 15, 1942.[10] A Public Broadcasting System item stated that President Roosevelt signed the MOH citation on September 15, 1942.[11] A news report from Channel 7 in San Diego, California, states that President Roosevelt approved the MOH on September 15, 1942, and repeated the mistake that Finn was the first man to receive a MOH in World War II.[12]

In fact, President Roosevelt signed the citation in June 1942, and it was presented to Finn on September 25, 1942, by Admiral Chester Nimitz.[13] A Navy photograph shows Finn wearing the uniform of a chief petty officer with his wife after he received the MOH; the caption states that they were "at Pearl Harbor" at the time the photograph was taken.[14]

SECTION 2: BOOKS IN GENERAL

Numerous books about December 7 contain errors and omissions concerning the December 7 MOH recipients. One reaches this conclusion fairly quickly when researching the MOHs that are the subject of this book. Soon the errors and omissions are no longer a surprise; errors and omissions become the general rule, not the exception. What is surprising, baffling, and ironic, however, are the errors and omissions in books specifically focusing on the MOH.

Section 2A: Books about the MOH

Above and Beyond: The Story of the Congressional Medal of Honor

At page 148, the author reports nine battleships in Pearl Harbor when in fact eight were present—seven on Battleship Row and USS Pennsylvania at the Navy Yard Shipyard. Perhaps he erroneously includes *Utah* as a battleship when she was in fact a target and training ship.

On that same page, he writes that "Fourteen Medals of Honor were awarded by the Navy [for December 7]." His count is eight for officers and six for enlisted men, which gives the erroneous total of fourteen. First of all, the correct total awarded by the Navy is fifteen (fourteen for Pearl Harbor and one for Kaneohe Bay). Second, the correct count is eleven for officers and four for enlisted men. He omits the Cannon MOH for Midway.

He writes on page 150 of two awards for *Arizona*, omitting the award for Lieutenant Commander Fuqua, the only survivor of the ship's three MOH recipients and the most deserving.[15] Chapters 4 through 12 and 19 of this book give the correct number of MOHs for December 7, including the correct number for *Arizona*.

Above and Beyond: A History of the Medal of Honor from the Civil War to Vietnam

This book discusses the December 7 awards—incorrectly, which is remarkable since the book was "Produced in cooperation with The Congressional Medal of Honor Society of the United States of America."[16]

Pages 196 to 198 discuss Fuqua, Kidd, Van Valkenburgh, Young, and Bennion. Page 198 correctly notes that Kidd, Van Valkenburgh, and Bennion received posthumous MOHs. Page 198 then states, "Eight others at Pearl Harbor were awarded the Medal of Honor posthumously." Thus, using the numbers on page 198, eleven posthumous MOHs were awarded. In fact, ten of the Pearl Harbor MOHs were posthumous. Therefore, the "eight" is incorrect; seven others in addition to the three named (Kidd, Van Valkenburgh, and Bennion) received posthumous MOHs (Jones, Reeves, and Scott aboard *California*; Flaherty and Ward aboard *Oklahoma*; Hill aboard *Nevada*; and Tomich aboard *Utah*).

Page 198 ends by noting that fifteen medals were awarded for bravery at Pearl Harbor. Fourteen were earned at Pearl Harbor; the fifteenth MOH for Oahu was John Finn's earned at Naval Air Station Kaneohe Bay, miles from Pearl Harbor.

The book's other error is on page 208, where it discusses the four medals awarded to men aboard USS San Francisco, "more than on any ship for a single action in World War II." This statement is incorrect; four men from USS *California* earned MOHs on December 7 (see Chapter 4 of this book).

0755: The Heroes of Pearl Harbor

Captain Donald Ross and his wife wrote this book. Since Ross received a MOH for December 7 (USS *Nevada*), one assumes this book, of all books, would lack the errors the average book or article would include. Such assumption is incorrect.[17]

On page 10, the book erroneously states that marine First Lieutenant George Cannon graduated from the Naval Academy (see Chapter 12 of this book (Midway) and 14 (Overview), Cannon simply did not attend the Naval Academy).

On page 8, Petty Officer Scott is listed as a "Machinist Mate" rather than a "Machinist's Mate First Class" (Ross himself was a warrant officer machinist). The page also includes Ensign Flaherty (*Oklahoma*) in the regular Navy, not the Naval Reserve; see Chapters 4 (*California*) and 5 (*Oklahoma*).

Medal of Honor Recipients 1863–1994

This book by Facts on File has an entry for Kidd, correctly listing his unit as Battleship Division One but has him serving as its "commanding officer," which is incorrect. Generally speaking, an officer above the grade of Navy Captain or Army or Marine colonel would not be a commanding officer" but would be a "commander" (Nnavy or Marine) or "commanding general" (Marine). Thus, Kidd was the "Commander [not Commanding Officer], Battleship Division One ."[18]

SECTION 2B: BOOKS ABOUT DECEMBER 7 OR WORLD WAR II

Air Raid—Pearl Harbor

At the end of this book, the reader learns that "Acclaimed Author Theodore Taylor…was also involved with the production of Tora! Tora! Tora!, a film about the air raid at Pearl Harbor." One wonders if that is an accomplishment about which to brag. And apparently "acclaimed" does not mean "accurate."[19]

On page 178 in Chapter 15 ("The Heroes and the Scapegoats"), he writes, "A total of fourteen officers and enlisted men received the Medal of Honor…" As noted so many times in this book, the correct number of MOHs for December 7 MOHs is fifteen for Oahu and sixteen total if Cannon's Midway MOH is included. From pages 173 to 177, Taylor only mentions six by name as MOH recipients: Finn, Jones, Scott, Hill, Tomich, and Bennion. He mentions Flaherty and Ward but does not state that they received MOHs.

On page 175, he mention's *Nevada*'s Chief Boatswain Edwin Hill. In the next paragraph, he discusses USS *Utah*, beginning the paragraph, "Another veteran chief petty officer, Peter Tomich…" The inference is that both men were chief petty officers.

As explained in chapter 1 of the present book, a chief petty officer is an enlisted grade (Tomich); a chief boatswain is an officer grade, specifically one type of chief warrant officer, a boatswain (Hill). An enlisted boatswain would be a chief petty officer (i.e., a "chief boatswain's mate").

One Day in History: The Days That Changed the World
December 7, 1941

The Smithsonian Institution sponsored this book, which is a collection of articles about various aspects of December 7. One expects accuracy from a Smithsonian-sponsored publication.[20] Such an expectation is unfulfilled.

One article is titled "Congressional Medal of Honor," which Chapter 14 and Appendix D of this book note is the incorrect term for the decoration: it is "medal of honor" in the statutes with no "Congressional" preceding it.

The article states that "Ten of the 15 Medals of Honor for actions at Pearl Harbor were posthumous. The recipients represented all ranks, from enlisted men to an admiral." Again, only fourteen of the MOHs were for action at Pearl Harbor; John Finn's action was at Kaneohe Bay, and Cannon is omitted. Chapter 1 of the present book explains correctly "enlisted" and "grade." "Enlisted men" is not a "rank" but a class, each member of which has a grade, such as "petty officer second class" or "sergeant." No "admiral" received a MOH; a rear admiral, Isaac Kidd, was the flag officer receiving a MOH on December 7. "Admiral" is not a class but a grade indicated by four stars; a rear admiral had two. The correct phrase would be "from the lowest enlisted man to a flag officer."[21]

Second, the article states that "Edwin Joseph Hill, also of the USS *Nevada*, swam back from safety to help keep his ship from sinking in the channel and was killed in the process." The inference is that the ship was in the channel. The author has confused Hill's two actions. First, he led men to the mooring quays so they could free the ship's mooring lines from the quays so she could move from her Battleship Row berth. He then had to swim back to the ship. Second, he was killed later, according to his MOH citation, when he was "attempting to let go the anchors..." Rather than keeping the ship from sinking in the channel the crew was trying to stop the ship before she reached the channel leading from Pearl Harbor to the Pacific Ocean so that it would not sink in the channel and block it (see chapter 9 of this book (*Nevada*)).

Third, the article states that Francis Flaherty and James Ward remained in "their compartment" to help others escape. As Chapter 5 (*Oklahoma*) of this book explains, they were in a gun turret or turrets, not a compartment or compartments.

As a "bonus error," the article following the MOH article ("Congressional Reaction") had a photograph of President Roosevelt signing the declaration of war on December 8, 1941. The title of the photograph is "A DAY THAT WILL LIVE IN INFAMY" [bold and quotations in original]. No citation of authority is required: the correct word is "date," not "day."

Dec. 7 1941, The Day the Japanese Attacked Pearl Harbor

This book is by the trio writing the famous book At Dawn We Slept: Gordon Prange, Donald M. Goldstein, and Katherine V. Dillon.

At pages 128 to 129, they mention Scott (footnote 19) and Jones, Reeves, and Pharris, and Scott (footnote 20). Footnote 20 correctly notes that the three officers received MOHs, but neither text nor footnote 19 states that Scott received a MOH. The authors also omit the Cannon Midway MOH award. Otherwise, in text or in footnotes, they (surprisingly) correctly report the number of December 7 MOHs.[22]

The USS Arizona

Should readers be informed that three men aboard of one of the most famous ships in history, USS *Arizona*, received MOHs for December 7, especially since one was awarded to the commanding officer and one was awarded to a rear admiral whose flagship was *Arizona*?

Apparently not.

The USS *Arizona* has no reference to the three MOHs but one reference in the index to "Purple Heart" on page 65, which has no mention of a Purple Heart.[23]

In the section with photographs is a photograph of Van Valkenburgh; beside it is a photograph with this caption: "Rear Admiral Isaac C. Kidd, US Navy, on the USS *Arizona*..." While the man in the photograph is Isaac Kidd, the photograph shows him in the uniform of a navy captain (four stripes on each of the cuffs of his uniform coat), not a rear admiral. The photograph is obviously of Captain Kidd when he was the ship's commanding officer.

Ironically, one of three authors (Jasper) is a journalist, (Delgado) is an underwater archaeologist who has dived on *Arizona*, and (Adams) is a National Park Service employee who formerly worked at, of all places, the *Arizona* Memorial as the cultural resources manager.

Pearl Harbor Fact and Reference Book, Everything to Know about December 7, 1941

Appendix C on page 123 of this book is titled, "Medal Of Honor Recipients December 7, 1941. The list is correct except that it includes navy diver Owen Hammerberg as a December 7 MOH recipient; he earned his MOH in 1945 in the West Loch of Pearl Harbor.[24]

History of World War II

An interesting book containing numerous factual errors regarding the MOH recipients for December 7 is History of World War II by Francis Trevelyan Miller, LittD, LLd. "with a board of historical and military authorities." The copyright for the book is 1945, and the content of the book indicates that it was written almost immediately after the war ended on September 1 or 2, 1945 (depending on one's position with reference to the International Date Line). The chapter "Day of Infamy" is remarkable for the number of errors, some of which have been dissected in other chapters of this book, including "day" for "date," yet another perfunctory error.[25]

- "Dorris" [sic] Miller aboard *Arizona* (see Chapters 6 (*West Virginia*) and 18 (Miller) of the present book)

- "Captain Bennion, as had Captain Van Valkenburgh on the *Arizona*, refused to be moved and ordered his subordinate officers to save the men and themselves." Bennion refused evacuation; no evidence exists other than the book's assertion that Van Valkenburgh did so (see Chapters 6 (*West Virginia*) and 7 (*Arizona*) of the present book.

- In discussing the capsizing of *Oklahoma*, the author(s) write that "Seaman James Richards, trapped with his mates in a gun turret in pitch-blackness when the lighting failed, and under water [sic], held a flashlight so the other men of the crew might escape through the emergency exit. There was no one left to hold the light for him." The enlisted MOH recipient who took such action was Seaman First Class James Ward, not Seaman James Richards (see Chapter 5 (*Oklahoma*) of the present book).

- The book notes that Cassin Young decided to beach *Vestal* to save the ship and that while he was doing so, "Warrant Officer Donald K. Ross was in the forward dynamo room which was rapidly filling with smoke, steam, and heat." The inference is that Warrant Officer Ross was aboard *Vestal*. Ross was aboard USS *Nevada* (see Chapter 9 of the present book).

- In discussing the fate of the battleships on December 7, the book states, "The *Arizona* remained a total loss, but the *Oklahoma* was righted and modernized in 1944—thirty years after she had been laid down…Eight battleships out of action; only one lost." In fact, *Oklahoma* was righted but never modernized, and she was one of two battleships lost, the other being *Arizona*, although *Oklahoma* was not lost until 1947 when she sank while being towed to *California* from Pearl Harbor (see Chapter 5 of this book).

The Battle of Okinawa

A book need not be about December 7 or Midway to contain errors about them.[26] In The Battle of Okinawa, a book about the battle for Okinawa in 1945, the author states that Japanese aircraft sank or "severely disable[d] 'five of the eight battleships nestled in 'battleship row.'" While eight battleships were present in Pearl Harbor on December 7, as stated throughout this book, only seven were on Battleship Row; the eighth, Pennsylvania, was in the shipyard at the navy yard.

Another interesting error in the Okinawa book is incorrectly stating that the twenty-three MOHs earned on Okinawa, "the largest number of any campaign in the war[.]" His assertion would be news to anyone who has studied the Battle of Iwo Jima; twenty-seven MOHs were awarded for that battle (twenty-two to Marines and five to Navy personnel).

The All Americans

The book is the story about the Army-Navy football game on November 29, 1941, just days before the December 7 attack on Oahu.

On page 109, the author writes that a Marine officer assigned to USS *Arizona* "approached the *Arizona*'s Captain, Van Valkenburgh…" Later on the same page, he writes, "Valkenburgh reluctantly agreed…"[27]

Unfortunately this error is a common one, here made more obvious by the comma after "Captain," writing as if the captain's first name is "Van" and last name is "Valkenburgh." Anyone with the slightest degree of knowledge about December 7 or anyone with a competent editor or fact checker would know that the captain's first name was "Franklin" and that his last name was "Van Valkenburgh." After all, he was the captain of one of the most, if not the most, famous ships in the US Navy on a very important day, a day leading to the beginning of World War II for the United States and a MOH for Van Valkenburgh.[27]

As an aside, errors in the name can be found in three other places. One was mentioned in chapter 21 ("Legacy—Men"), a street near Pearl Harbor named "Valkenburgh St."[28] In one of the investigations of the events of December 7, the organization of the Pacific Fleet is delineated. Under Task Force 2 is Battleship Division One, commanded by Rear Admiral Kidd and comprising *Arizona*, *Nevada*, and *Oklahoma*. The ship commanding officers' names are given; the name for *Arizona* is "Capt. F. Valkenburgh."[29] The website Home of Heroes has a page for the December 7 MOH recipients with photographs under which are first and last names; under the photograph for Franklin Van Valkenburgh is "Van Valkenburgh" as if it were his full name.[30]

Pearl Harbor

This book by Ernest Arroyo, at the time president of the Pearl Harbor History Associates, contains some key errors.[31]

The book mentions only thirteen of the fifteen MOH recipients for Oahu on December 7; it omits Scott and Pharris but of course includes Doris Miller.[32]

It states that Ross retired as a lieutenant commander, so one must wonder why one sees photographs of a retired Donald Ross wearing a Navy captain's uniform. He in fact achieved the grade of commander via the normal promotion process and would have retired as such, but because of his combat awards, he received a tombstone promotion to captain and retired in that grade (see Chapter 9 (*Nevada*) of the present book).[33]

A sentence in the sidebar about Chief Boatswain Edwin Hill begins, "Chief Hill, a warrant officer..." "Chief Hill" would be a chief petty officer (enlisted member), not a chief warrant officer, which is what Hill was (see Chapters 1 (Organization) and 9 (*Nevada*) of the present book).[34]

Dictionary of American Naval Fighting Ships

Although not a book specifically about December 7, it provides a history of the ships that were involved in the attack, including what happened to them during and after the attack. In the entry for USS *Nevada*, the author writes that being moored "singly" gave *Nevada* "a freedom of maneuver denied the other eight battleships present during the attack." The inference from "other eight battleships" is that nine battleships were in Pearl Harbor; the correct number, as stated repeatedly, is eight (seven on Battleship Row and USS Pennsylvania at the shipyard at the Navy Yard's Shipyard).[35]

American Caesar

In this book about Douglas MacArthur, one would expect such an esteemed author as William Manchester to "get it right."[36]

At page 203 in describing the Japanese task force sailing toward Oahu for the December 7 attack, he refers to "the carrier Kido Butai." In fact, the term referred to the strike force, not a specific aircraft carrier (no carrier had that name).[37]

At page 242, he refers to eight battleships lost at Pearl Harbor. The Navy did not lose eight battleships; it lost only two if "lost" means irreparable damage: *Arizona* (sank in place) and *Oklahoma* (capsized). The six other battleships were damaged but survived to fight another day (chapters 6 (*California*), 8 (*West Virginia*), and 11 (*Nevada*) of the present book. Add to the list battleships Pennsylvania, Maryland, and Tennessee.

SUBPART 2C: MAGAZINE ARTICLES, PAMPHLETS, AND MISCELLANEOUS

World War II

In the January 1998 edition of World War II magazine is the story "*Nevada*'s Heroic Run," referring to USS *Nevada* being the only battleship to get underway on December 7, sailing under attack from Battleship Row to Hospital Point.[38]

At page 46 of the issue is a photograph of Chief Boatswain Edwin Hill and Commander Joseph Tausig, a *Nevada* officer. The caption on page 47 reads, "Left: Two Medal of Honor recipients from *Nevada*: (from left) Chief Boatswain Edwin J. Hill and Commander Joseph K. Tausig, Jr..." In fact, Tausig was an ensign who received a Navy Cross; he was mentioned in chapter 17 (Miller) of this book (endnote 37). The other MOH recipient was Warrant Officer Donald Ross, who is unmentioned in the article (see Chapter 9 (*Nevada*) of the present book).

On page 49, Hill is referred to as "Chief Boatswain Edwin Hill" but then as "Chief Hill." On page 51, he is also referred to as "Chief Hill." As was just explained in the discussion of this same error in Arroyo's Pearl Harbor, "Chief Hill" is proper terminology for a chief petty officer, an enlisted man, but Hill was an officer—specifically a chief warrant officer—and would not have been called "Chief Hill."

In its issue commemorating the sixtieth anniversary of the attack, World War II Presents Pearl Harbor: The Day of Infamy, the magazine reprinted the *Nevada* article from the 1998 issue. On page 61 of the commemorative issue, Hill is again referred to as "Chief Boatswain Edwin Hill" but then as "Chief Hill." Also on the page are photographs of Hill, Tausig (correctly referred to as "Ensign"), and Ross, but the caption does not mention the Hill or Ross MOHs. On page 62, Hill is again referred to as "Chief Hill." No mention is made of the Hill or Ross MOH in the article.[39]

Flight Journal

As stated in the introduction and in chapter 14, all of the MOH recipients awarded MOHs for actions in the Hawaiian Islands during World War II were in the Naval service: the Navy, the Naval Reserve, the Marine Corps, or the Marine Corps Reserve. None were in the Army, the Army Air Forces (the Air Force did not exist as a separate service during World War II), or the Coast Guard. Whether members of other services should have received MOHs for actions in the Hawaiian Islands in World War II is a topic beyond the scope of this book.

The matter of the service of the recipients, however, gives rise to errors in the October 2013 issue of Flight Journal. Barrett Tillman's short article, "The Pearl Harbor Medal Battle," is incredible, providing some of the most incoherent, ill-informed commentary on the subject of the December 7 MOHs.[40] He cites "Internet rumors" insisting that two Army pilots, Second Lieutenants George Welch and Kenneth Taylor, were denied MOHs for December 7 actions because they took off "without permission." They were P-40 fighter pilots who engaged attacking Japanese aircraft and are credited with downing aircraft—seven between the two of them. They were mentioned in chapter 17 (Miller) at endnote 38.

Tillman writes that the men in fact took off with permission, "so the fact that they did not receive the nation's highest award needs to be seen in context." The context is "After the smoke cleared, the medal process began. Eventually, 15 Navy men received the Medal of Honor; Army personnel received none." He then explains the differences in the number of second-tier awards (Navy Crosses for Navy and Marine personnel and Distinguished Service Crosses (DSC) for Army personnel) as "Perhaps Rank Hath Its Privileges (RHIP)." He notes that Taylor and Welch, who received DSCs, were the highest-ranking Army members to receive awards (second lieutenants). "Contrarily, the Navy recipients included an admiral, three captains, and a commander. Some of the Navy citations were extremely nonspecific."

Tillman then takes the reader through a meandering discussion about the MOH and about ignoring or altering the rules governing the MOH. He notes that no living men had received the MOH in the first nine years of the global war on terror (Iraq and Afghanistan). "The cynical deduction is that politicians did not want to risk living heroes making impolitic statements." His conclusion is a one-word paragraph—

"Politics"—followed by a plea to alter the MOH rules so the two pilots could receive belated MOHs for "their deeds [that] remain etched in the Day of Infamy."

In the "meandering" is included the following statements: President Bill Clinton "handed out dated MoHs in wholesale lots…" He includes one given to Teddy Roosevelt's family for his service in the Spanish-American War, noting, "It's unclear how Roosevelt—a regimental commander leading his regiment—performed 'above and beyond the call of duty.'" He writes that Roosevelt's son, an army brigadier in World War II, received a MOH "for determining that his division landed at the wrong beach on D-Day and directing his forces inland. Again: a leader performing his expected role."

One hardly knows where to begin in dismantling such error-filled, sloppy rhetoric.

First of all, as Commander in Chief of the Pacific Fleet, Admiral Nimitz would convene a local board of awards only for personnel (generally Navy and Marine personnel) under his command since he was the Navy fleet commander. He would not have been involved in the award nomination or process for Army personnel not assigned to the Fleet, such as Welch and Taylor. The grades of Army versus Navy MOH nominees would have no bearing on whether they were nominated for MOHs; nomination for a MOH for December 7 between the services would depend on the nominee's service, not his grade. Navy and Marine nominations were a Naval service matter, regardless of grade. Army nominations were an Army matter, regardless of grade.

Second, one assumes that the term "navy recipients" refers to MOH recipients, not Navy Cross recipients, even though "Navy recipients" follows the statement that Welch and Taylor received DSCs and the context is second-tier awards. If this assumption is true, Tillman is wrong. No admiral received a MOH. The recipient was a rear admiral, Kidd. Three captains did not receive MOHs if he is referring to the grade of Navy captain; only two men in the grade of captain, Bennion and Van Valkenburgh, received MOHs. One commander MOH recipient is correct if he is referring to the grade of Navy commander (Young). Three "captains" in the sense of commanding officers of ships is correct—Bennion, Van Valkenburgh, and Young—but adding one "commander" is senseless if he means "captain" in the sense of commanding officer (see Chapters 6 (*West Virginia*), 7 (*Arizona*), and 8 (*Vestal*)).

And he omits context. If "rank" (grade) has its privileges, then why were most of the Naval service award recipients in lower grades—for the Marines, one first lieutenant, and for the Navy, one commander, two ensigns, one chief warrant officer, three warrant officers, and five enlisted men? Only three of the Navy recipients held senior grade: Kidd (rear admiral) and two captains (Bennion and Van Valkenburgh) (see Chapters 4 through 12, 14, and 19).

Third, President Clinton did not "[hand] out dated MoHs in wholesale lots…" What modern Presidents have done is to award MOHs to men denied MOHs in earlier wars because of their race. The well-earned MOH awards in 2000 presented by President Clinton to the Japanese American soldiers from World War II must be an example of Tillman's assertion about MOHs handed out in "wholesale lots" (see Appendix D).

Fourth, Tillman asserts that the global war on terror did not produce any living MOH recipients during its first nine years (2001 to 2010) because of "politics" or fear that a living recipient would say something "impolitic." A more ludicrous statement is difficult to imagine. Its lack of foundation in reality can be proved by one question. If such a policy existed, then why did it change such that living MOH recipients were suddenly "authorized" beginning with a MOH to the first living MOH recipient since the Vietnam War: Army Staff Sergeant Salvatore Giunta, who earned a MOH in 2007? President Barack Obama presented the award on November 16, 2010. Other MOHs followed to eleven more Army recipients, three Marine recipients, and three Navy recipients; any recipient could have said something "impolitic" (the numbers are as of the writing of this book). Since some of the MOHs were posthumous awards, perhaps Tillman's fear was the recipients' families would say something "impolitic."[41]

Fifth, the correct term is "date of infamy."

Sixth, Tillman implies for Theodore Roosevelt's MOH and states for his son's MOH that the MOHs were for doing what was expected (i.e., not extraordinary actions warranting MOHs). If such is the case, then his own opinion undermines his case for MOHs for Welch and Taylor. After all, they merely did was expected of them on December 7. Being fighter pilots, they took off and did what fighter pilots do— engage enemy aircraft in aerial combat. By doing what was expected of them, they did not warrant MOHs.

He correctly writes, "Some of the Navy citations were extremely nonspecific." Here one thinks of the Kidd and Van Valkenburgh citations not citing specific acts warranting MOHs. And he may be correct about "politics" regarding these MOHs (see chapter 15). But the other Navy and Marine December 7 citations cite at least one specific act that meets MOH criteria.

The Pearl Harbor History Associates, Inc. Pamphlet

Although it is not a magazine article, it is close to being one. It is a pamphlet the author obtained in the 1980s. In yet another irony, a 1987 pamphlet, issued by The Pearl Harbor History Associates, Inc. of Sperryville, Virginia, is titled What Happened at Pearl Harbor December 7, 1941. One would assume that such an organization would provide accurate information. Such an assumption would be incorrect. The pamphlet provides a summary of the attack, complete with "facts and figures" and lists the names of fourteen MOH recipients, omitting Cannon and Pharris.

National Park Service Brochures for Oahu

One would think that National Park Service brochures found at the World War II Valor in the Pacific Monument would mention the MOHs for December 7, at least for *Arizona*. No mention of the MOHs is made, however.

Subpart 3: Speech

Speech by Commander, US Pacific Command

One would think that a speech on September 2, 2000 (VJ Day) aboard USS Missouri in Pearl Harbor honoring the end of World War II by Admiral Dennis Blair, Commander, U.S. Pacific Command, would recite the story of the MOH recipients correctly. Not so as listeners were told they would hear about fifteen MOH recipients, but only fourteen were mentioned.[42]

Rear Admiral Kidd was named as a "commanding officer" (along with Bennion and Van Valkenburgh) who went down with his ship, the inference being he was *Arizona*'s commanding officer. In fact, he was in a billet higher than the ship's commanding officer, Captain Van Valkenburgh. He was a flag officer, commanding a battleship division comprising three battleships. He was not a commanding officer, a title reserved in this context for the commander of a ship, who is always in the grade of Navy captain or below. Bennion did not go down with his ship. The ship did not sink in the classic sense (submerge completely). She sank upright, so Bennion's body could be recovered, unlike the body of a commanding officer who truly goes down with his ship (see Chapters 6 (*West Virginia*) and 9 (*Arizona*).

These men from USS *California* were cited for supplying ammunition and air to antiaircraft guns: Herbert Jones; Thomas Reeves, and Robert Scott. The officer with the longest MOH citation of the ship's MOH recipients and the man most responsible for saving the ship by preventing capsizing, Jackson Pharris, was omitted (see Chapters 4 (*California*) and 19 (*Pharris*)).

Subpart 4: Electronic Media

Find A Grave

To determine if an "In Memory Of" Marker existed for Captain Ross, the author searched the Internet via a site titled Find A Grave, finding a Ross entry in 2015, which read as follows: "Burial: Beverly Cemetery, Beverly, Lincoln County, Kansas, USA. Specifically: ashes scattered over the USS *Nevada*, Pearl Harbor." In truth, as explained in chapter 9 (*Nevada*), his ashes were scattered over USS *Nevada*'s final resting place, which was not Pearl Harbor. The ship was used as a target for the atomic bomb tests at Bikini in 1946. Having survived the tests, she was later towed to an area near the Hawaiian Islands and sunk as a target ship—but not at Pearl Harbor.

"Find A Grave" has a page for an "In Memory of" marker for Captain Van Valkenburgh, located at Forest Home Cemetery in Milwaukee, Wisconsin. The page, as printed in 2009, has a photograph of the marker and the following narrative:

Burial:
Forest Home Cemetery
Milwaukee
Milwaukee County
Wisconsin, USA

The entry is misleading since the site is not the place of his burial. As noted in Chapters 15 and 21 and Appendix C, his body was not recovered, so the site in Forest Home is not a burial but is, as indicated by the inscription at the top of the stone, an "In Memory of" marker to mark an empty grave.

US Navy Publications and Internet Information

One would assume that the Navy would "get it right" in stories about its own heroes, its own MOH recipients. Such assumption would be erroneous.

USS *Utah* Error

As noted in Chapter 14 of this book, in 2006, the Navy presented Chief Tomich's MOH to members of his family. Two Internet stories on Navy Newsstand about the presentation note that Tomich was awarded the MOH for his actions on "the battleship" USS *Utah* (BB-31) on December 7. Chapter 10 explains that *Utah* was originally a battleship but was converted into a target ship and gunnery training ship in the 1930s and was such on December 7, not a battleship. Thus her designation changed from "BB-31" to "AG-16," with AG meaning "miscellaneous auxiliary ship."[43]

Ships Named for MOH Recipients

The Naval History and Heritage Command maintains on the Internet a list of ships named to commemorate men at Pearl Harbor on December 7. Most of the men are the MOH recipients listed in this book. The member's command is given. The command for Warrant Officer Reeves (USS Reeves, DE-156) was "Not Applicable" when the author saw the list. As noted in
Chapter 4, Reeves was aboard USS *California* on December 7, not USS Not Applicable. The basic fact of a MOH recipient's duty station should be easy for the recipient's military service to report accurately.[44]

To add confusion, for some reason, USS Reeves (DLG-24) is listed, named after Vice Admiral Joseph Mason Reeves. Two other Naval History and Heritage Command websites provide the histories of the two ships named after the two officers named Reeves. One is "Reeves (DE-156) i" and the other "Reeves (DLG-24) ii." The second ship, commissioned in 1964, was named for Vice Admiral Reeves, who according to the history of the ship, played no role at Pearl Harbor; his name does not seem to appear prominently in the December 7 literature. Incredibly, in the biography for Thomas James Reeves, who was at Pearl Harbor, each site states that the first Reeves (DE-156) was named for "Electrician's Mate, Third Class, Thomas James Reeves," yet each site also states that he was a "chief radioman," which is a chief petty officer radioman, an enlisted member. An electrician's mate third class is also an enlisted member. Reeves was in fact an officer: a warrant officer (radio electrician).[45]

Documentaries and Films
"The Unsung Heroes of Pearl Harbor"

The History Channel produced a documentary titled, The Unsung Heroes of Pearl Harbor. One might assume that a documentary produced by the prestigious History Channel would be an accurate, comprehensive story of the December 7 MOH recipients. Such an assumption would be incorrect. Of note:

About Kaneohe, it mentions "Chief Ordnanceman John Finn" but not his MOH and omits "Aviation" preceding "Ordnanceman."

About *Oklahoma*, her two MOH recipients are unmentioned.

About *West Virginia*, Bennion's MOH is mentioned. It also mentions Miller's Navy Cross without discussing any controversy about the Miller award (Chapter 17 of this book) and is misleading in that it shows blacks shooting water-cooled machine guns without stating whether any of the shooters are Miller. None are; to the author's knowledge, no movie coverage of Miller on December 7 exists (if any existed, the world would be thoroughly aware of it).

About *California*, it notes that one of the Navy's highest honors is to name a ship for someone fallen in battle, stating that *California* had no fewer than five men for whom ships were named. It names Jones, Reeves, Scott (without reference to their MOHs), and two others but not Pharris.

About *Utah*, it mentions the MOH for Tomich, stating, "The more moments he kept the ship from rolling over, the more shipmates could be saved." The statement is nonsensical. Tomich's actions, as reflected in Chapter 10 and his MOH citation in Appendix A, had no effect on the ship capsizing. He could not prevent the ship from capsizing or govern the speed at which she capsized.

It states *Arizona*'s commanding officer and the battleship division commander "Admiral Isaac Kidd" died instantly. If so, how did they have the time to take any action resulting in any award (other than a Purple Heart for combat death) much less a MOH? (see Chapter 15 (*Arizona*) for an extended discussion of what Kidd and Van Valkenburgh did between the beginning of the attack and the catastrophic explosion of the ship). Also, Kidd's grade was rear admiral, not admiral. It mentioned the ship's three MOH recipients, naming Fuqua as a recipient but not the other two.

In writing about *Nevada*, it mentions Hill but not his death. It does not mention Ross or either of the two MOHs.

It shows the gilded names of Kidd and Van Valkenburgh with their MOH symbols at Punchbowl without explaining the significance of the gilding, meaning the person earned a MOH. Appendix C explains gilding's importance.

Pearl Harbor: Tora! Tora! Tora!

The History Channel produced another documentary titled Pearl Harbor: Tora! Tora! Tora! It refers to Chief Finn as "Navigation Chief Ordnanceman Finn," a nonsensical designation (navigation and ordnance are two separate specialties); his correct title is "Chief Petty Officer (Aviation Ordnanceman) Finn. Near the end of the documentary, Finn is shown with his MOH, but the program does not give the total number of MOHs for December 7, does not mention any other MOHs for December 7, and does not mention that Finn was the last survivor of the four December 7 MOH recipients who survived the war.

In Harm's Way

Otto Preminger's opus on the Pacific War could have been named "How John Wayne's Character Won the Pacific War". Regardless, the film begins with the attack on Oahu. Actor Franchot Tone is Admiral Husband Kimmel, the Commander in Chief of the U.S. Pacific Fleet. After the attack starts, he asks how many ships have answered the "emergency sortie signal." He also asks how many battleships have answered. When told none, he incredulously asks out loud, "Out of nine battleships?" He had a similar problem as did the author of The Battle of Okinawa discussed earlier: naming the correct number of battleships at Pearl Harbor on December 7. Again, the correct count is eight—seven on Battleship Row and one at the Navy Yard's Shipyard.

Internet Information: The General Public as the Source

Genuine danger of gross inaccuracy lurks here.

The Internet has but one safeguard to ensure information posted on it by User A is historically accurate or in context: User B detecting errors in User A's content. Thus Internet sites, whether operated by private or public parties or organizations, can be filled with errors. Two examples of errors from private-party Internet sites follow.

A website found in 2002, written by Tenna Perry, was titled The battle ships [sic] of Pearl Harbor. First, "battleships" is one word. Second, she wrote that seven battleships and one "ex-battleship [*Utah*] which had been turned into a target ship" were moored along Battleship Row. As explained in chapter 2 ("The Attacks on December 7, 1941"), seven battleships were moored along Battleship Row, but *Utah* was moored on the opposite side of Ford Island on Carrier Row. Third, she identified *California* as the flagship of the Pacific Fleet (the Fleet's flagship was Pennsylvania). Finally, she wrote that both Captain Van Valkenburgh and Rear Admiral Kidd received MOHs "as did several other members of the *Arizona*'s crew." As noted in chapter 7 (*Arizona*), only one other *Arizona* officer received a MOH, Lieutenant Commander Samuel Fuqua. A site "eSSORTMENT [:] Information and advice you want to know" appeared in 2008, again written by Tenna Perry, with substantially the same errors) Unfortunately, "accurate" cannot be placed before "information." In the 2008 title, "battleships" is again misspelled as two words.

Don Feder wrote in a site titled The day America lost its innocence that "Of 15 Medals of Honor awarded that day, eight were posthumous." In fact eleven were posthumous, and sixteen were awarded for the day.

Internet Information: Official or Private Organizations as the Sources

The Writer's Almanac

In his short daily radio feature The Writer's Almanac, American Public Media commentator Garrison Keillor, the national "windbag" commentator, mentions important historical events occurring on the broadcast day in previous years. His programs for December 7, 2001, and December 7, 2007, both contained errors when he discussed the attack on Oahu. The errors appear in the transcripts, which listeners could print from the Internet.

In the December 7, 2001, program's transcript, he commits one of the most frequent errors, as noted at the beginning of this chapter: the wrong number of battleships. He said that three of the nine battleships at Pearl Harbor were destroyed that day and five more damaged. In fact, as noted ad nauseam in this book, only eight battleships were in Pearl Harbor on December 7 (perhaps he was including the former battleship *Utah* as the ninth battleship when in fact she was a target ship). Only two were destroyed: *Arizona* (blown apart) and *Oklahoma* (capsized). Of the remaining six, *California* and *West Virginia* sank in place; *Nevada* was damaged and was intentionally grounded; and Pennsylvania, Tennessee, and Maryland were damaged (see Chapters 4 through 12 and 14 of this book).

The 2001 transcript also states, "The next day, Franklin D. Roosevelt declared war against Japan." As explained in Chapter 3 of this book, although the President is the Commander in Chief of the Army and Navy, he cannot declare war; only Congress can do so. The correct history is that on December 8, President Roosevelt asked for and received from Congress a declaration of war against Japan because of the attack on December 7. The correct process for declaring war is important since the MOH is a combat award (i.e., usually earned during a war declared by Congress).

In the December 7, 2007, program's transcript, Keillor twice refers to the personnel at Pearl Harbor as "soldiers," who are members of the Army, which would mean, for example, Lieutenant Commander Fuqua was a member of the army on December 7, a ludicrous statement. While some soldiers may have been at Pearl Harbor on December 7, the vast majority of personnel present at Pearl Harbor were members of the Navy or Marine Corps since Pearl Harbor was a Navy installation and the Army's installations were elsewhere on Oahu. The transcript states that "*Arizona* was completely destroyed, killing more than 1,500 soldiers aboard." In fact, the ship's dead and missing were Navy and Marine crewmen. As a general rule, soldiers would not be aboard battleships, and the casualty list for the ship lists only navy and marine personnel. Also, the number of *Arizona* dead is incorrect; the number of dead and missing was 1,177 (1,104 Navy and 73 Marine) (see Chapter 7 (*Arizona*) of this book).

Marine Corps MOH Recipients

Lieutenant Cannon

The MOH award for Lieutenant Cannon at Midway for December 7 is omitted in almost all accounts of the attacks on December 7, perhaps because of ignorance of the Japanese shelling of Midway on the evening of December 7, an event overshadowed by the attack on Oahu that morning. He is truly a "hidden hero" although not one from Oahu.

Condition Red: Marine Defense Battalions in World War II

This monograph is one in a series of monographs in the World War II Commemorative Series, published by the Marine Corps History and Museums Division. The subject of Condition Red is Marine Corps defense battalions organized to defend naval bases in World War II. On page 1, it states that "[Lieutenant] Cannon, who died of his wounds, earned the first Medal of Honor awarded a Marine officer during World War II." On page 2, however, is Cannon's photograph with the following in the caption: "After the war he was awarded the Medal of Honor." Cannon was awarded a posthumous MOH awarded during the war (in 1942); he was not just the first Marine officer to earn a MOH during the war; he was the first Marine, officer or enlisted, to earn a MOH in World War II. He was the first and only Marine MOH nominee submitted to President Franklin Roosevelt for approval in March 1942 (see Chapters 12 (Midway) and 15 (Overview) of this book).[46]

Military Officer

A staff writer on the staff of the Military Officer Association of America (MOAA), wrote an article about Midway published in the December 2007 issue of MOAA's magazine, Military Officer. The author omitted the Cannon and Fleming MOHs (and any mention of the officers, period), which is especially interesting since the author was a retired Marine.[47]

Captain Fleming

As was noted in "Why I Wrote This Book," more than any other MOH recipient in this book Captain Richard Fleming, along with First Lieutenant Cannon, appears to be one of the most, if not the most, "hidden" heroes. He is the sole MOH recipient for a crucial battle, Midway 1942, yet he and his MOH are often omitted from various accounts of the battle. Many accounts that do mention him are filled with errors, as discussed here. Chapter 12 (Midway) discussed the errors concerning Captain Fleming's MOH action on June 5, 1942, including the erroneous identification of the ship he was attacking as a battleship, not a cruiser (his MOH citation is in chapter 12 and at appendix A of this book).

Midway Internet Site

A 2015 search on the U.S. Fish and Wildlife Service website for "Cannon" produced two references to Cannon, noting in each case that he was the first Marine to receive a MOH in World War II. A search for "Fleming" produced no result. Chapter 12 discussed the inclusion of Cannon and omission of Fleming in Midway history. The section "Midway Atoll in World War II" contains this sentence: "At the end of the Battle of Midway, all four Japanese carriers involved in the attack on Pearl Harbor had been sunk." The statement leads readers to believe that only four Japanese carriers attacked Oahu when the strike force in fact had six; the sentence should have read, "At the end of the Battle of Midway, all four Japanese carriers had been sunk; all four had participated in the attack on Oahu on December 7, 1941…" Also, the attack was not just on Pearl Harbor. As Chapter 2 explained, six Japanese aircraft carriers participated in the attack on Oahu, and numerous other military installations besides Pearl Harbor were attacked.

History of US Marine Corps Operations in World War II

One would think that a book written by the Marine Corps Historical branch would mention Fleming's MOH. Such thinking would be erroneous.

The history series is a set of five volumes covering the Marine Corps in World War II. Volume I am Pearl Harbor to Guadalcanal and cover the Battle of Midway. It discusses Fleming's attack on Mikuma but does not mention his MOH or that he was the sole MOH recipient for this crucial battle, but the book mentions the December 7 attack and Cannon being the first Marine to receive a MOH in World War II.[48]

Find a Grave

The Find a Grave website entry for Fleming (accessed in 2008 and 2015) revealed photographs of Captain Fleming and his "In Memory Of" marker at Fort Snelling, Minnesota. The biographical information contains basic errors. It states that Fleming's aircraft had 171 holes in it after his attack on June 4; the MOH citation states 179. It states that during Fleming's June 5 attack on Mikuma that Fleming's bomb hit the ship and then his aircraft did (see Chapter 12 of this book, which reached the conclusion that the aircraft did not hit the ship; the MOH citation in chapter 12 and at Appendix A states plainly that his bomb missed the ship).

World War II

World War II magazine's July 2002 issue has an interview with one of Fleming's fellow pilots. The article has a photograph of Fleming on page 51; the caption identifies him as "Francis M. Fleming." The name is "Richard E. Fleming" (see Chapter 12 of this book).

Vought Aircraft Website

The Vought Aircraft website has a section on the history of its SB2U-3 "Vindicator," the type of aircraft Fleming flew. The photographs are excellent, but—ironically since Vought built the aircraft that Fleming flew—the site contains several factual errors in the account of Fleming's June 5 action.

First, under the icon "Products" for the SB2U-3 is a statement that Zeros (misspelling the word as "Zero's") attacked Fleming's Vindicator on the second day of the battle, which would have been June 5 for Fleming. While fighters attacked Fleming's flight on June 4, the defense he faced on June 5 was antiaircraft fire from the ships, not fighters. Japanese fighters would themselves have been hit by the torrent of antiaircraft fire coming from the cruiser Fleming was attacking on June 5.[49]

Second, the site incorrectly names his June 5 target as Mogami, not Mikuma. The same mistake is made under the icon "Special Stories." Chapter 12 clarifies the identity of the ship Fleming was attacking.

Third, it states that Fleming was "the first Marine pilot to receive [a MOH]" but omitted context. The first Marine pilot to receive a MOH in World War II? The first Marine pilot to receive a MOH ever? Most accurately, it should have limited the statement to Fleming being the first Marine pilot to receive a MOH in World War II. Endnote 100 of Chapter 12 of this book confirms that Fleming was the first Marine aviator to receive a MOH in World War II.

Website for Fleming Field

Information about Fleming appears on a website for Fleming Field, an airfield in Minnesota named for him, also called South St. Paul Municipal Airport. The information is under "Fleming Field History." Unfortunately, a printing of the site in 2015 revealed several errors, many of them basic. The number and type of errors is indicative of the care or competence of high-school-level research and writing.

First and most unbelievably, the site states that South St. Paul—Fleming Field is named for Richard Fleming, a Navy pilot during World War II. The site later refers to him as a "Marine pilot." Several other places in the site refer to him being a Marine.

Second, it states that on June 4, Fleming "failed to drop a bomb on the aircraft carrier Akaqi." Does "failed to drop a bomb" mean that he did not drop a bomb due to mechanical malfunction or to enemy action? Or does it mean that the bomb missed the target? As explained in chapter 12, the carrier Fleming's squadron attacked was Hiryu. The Japanese had a carrier named Akagi but not one named Akaqi, a spelling that is ludicrous on its face.

Third, it has the same errors as noted above in the biographical information at the Find a Grave site. The beginning of the site erroneously states 171 instead of 179 holes after the attack on June 4 and that Fleming's bomb and aircraft hit Mikuma, a Japanese cruiser.

Ironically, the site has a link to his MOH citation, which clearly states that his bomb missed the target ship and that Fleming's aircraft crashed into the sea.

Time of the Aces: Marine Pilots in the Solomons

On page 14 of this monograph produced by the Marine Corps History and Museums Division is "Marine Corps Aviators Who Received the Medal of Honor in World War II." Again, the author cannot get it right. He writes that Captain Henry Elrod's MOH "award is chronologically the first Medal of Honor to be awarded to a Marine during the war." While Elrod's actions on Wake Island leading to the MOH were the first by a Marine aviator in World War II to lead to a MOH, they were not known until after the war.[50]

As noted in this chapter and in Chapters 12 (Midway) and 14 (Overview), the Cannon MOH was the first Marine MOH action in the war (ground or aviation, officer or enlisted) and the first Marine MOH approved and awarded during the war. The Elrod action on Wake was the first action by a Marine aviator to ultimately lead to a MOH, but Fleming's MOH award was the first received by a Marine aviator during the war, his mother receiving it on November 24, 1942, from President Franklin Roosevelt (see endnote 100 in Chapter 12, which states that Elrod's widow received the MOH on November 8, 1946).

SUMMARY: ERRORS

Everyone makes errors, but most of the errors in this chapter seem to have been, with simple due diligence and basic research, avoidable. Some show the authors simply do not know about the MOH. One last example will suffice.

On page 89 of Allen Seiden's book From Fishponds to Warships: Pearl Harbor, A Complete Illustrated History (Mutual Publishing, 2001)—billed as the book with the most sales at the Pearl Harbor Visitor Center—one finds a drawing of a MOH above the chapter title "The Phoenix Rises." The caption reads, "Medals of Honor (above) were issued to those in the attack." The main question coming to mind is, Did everyone receive a MOH, including American and Hawaiian civilians and Japanese combatants (they were in the attack)? No MOH recipients are listed, so readers are left with the erroneous belief that the MOH is a unit award when in fact it is for individual heroism.

One caring for historical accuracy must be stupefied at the statement that MOHs were issued to those in the attack without a qualifier as to the number of MOHs issued, especially since one should be able to assume—but assumption is fatal—that authors know that the MOH is an individual, not a command, award.

The Phoenix rose but not with everyone receiving MOHs.

NOTES

1. Rex Alan Smith and Gerald A. Meehl, Pacific War Stories (Abbeville Press, New York, NY, 2004), 34.

2. Richard Baron, Major Abe Baum, and Richard Goldhurst, Raid! The Untold Story of Patton's Secret Mission (G. P. Putnam's Sons, 1981), 199.

3. David Kohnen, "Tombstone of Victory: Tracking the U-505 from German Commerce Raider to American War Memorial 1944–1954, Journal of America's Military Past, 32, no. 3: 10, winter 2007.

4. Jon Guttman, "Richard Ira Bong: American World War II Ace of Aces," Aviation History (March 2007), 33.

5. The author has seen photographs of both men. The photograph in the newspaper purportedly of Kidd resembles strongly the photograph of Kidd in a newspaper article found in his Official Military Personnel File (see endnotes 7 and 113 in Chapter 9 (*Arizona*)).

6. Mark Yost, "A Museum Honoring Real Heroes," Wall Street Journal, November 8, 2007.

7. Robert F. Dorr, "Aviation Ordnanceman Led Valiant Defense at Pearl Harbor," Navy Times, (December 10, 2001); Robert F. Dorr and Fred L. Borch, "All I Did Was Shoot at Everyone One I Could," Navy Times, December 10, 2007.

8. T. Rees Shapiro, "Lt. John W. Finn, Medal of Honor Recipient, Dies at 100," Washington Post, May 29, 2010, B5.

9. Richard Goldstein, "John Finn, Medal of Honor Winner, Dies at 100," New York Times, May 27, 2010 (hereafter "Goldstein, John Finn Death").

10. "Passing of John Finn WWII Medal of Honor Recipient," National Park Service news release, May 27, 2010, citing the Associated Press.

11. "American Valor: John Finn," September 28, 2015, printing from Public Broadcasting System, WETA Internet site with information dated August 24, 2008.

12. "Lt. John Finn: A True Hero," news story by National Broadcasting System Channel 7 in San Diego, California, May 27, 2010.

13. The Roosevelt approval of the MOH citations is based on a copy of the citation provided to the author by the Franklin D. Roosevelt Presidential Library and Museum. The President's signature is undated, but the citation was prepared on June 6, 1942, and a handwritten notation states that the signed original was sent to the Navy Department on June 22, 1942; endnote 5, Goldstein, John Finn Death (correctly reporting the presentation by Nimitz).

14. Photograph of John Finn with his wife at Pearl Harbor (U.S. Navy file photograph dated September 28, 1942).

15. Joseph L. Schott, Above and Beyond: The Story of the Congressional Medal of Honor (G. P. Putnam's Sons, New York, NY, 1963); the correct number of battleships can be found in Vice Admiral Homer N. Wallin, US Navy (Retired), Pearl Harbor: Why, How, Fleet Salvage, and Final Approach (Naval History Division, U.S. Government Printing Office, Washington, DC, 1968) (hereafter "Wallin, Pearl Harbor: Why, How, Fleet Salvage, and Final Approach"). The seven battleships on Battleship Row are listed in the table of contents under Chapter 9 on page xiii with *Utah* being a target and gunnery training ship; pages 189 to 190 discuss Pennsylvania at the Navy Yard's Drydock Number 1.

16. Editors, Boston Publishing Company, A History of the Medal of Honor from the Civil War to Vietnam (Boston Publishing Company, Boston, MA, 1985).

17. Donald K. and Helen Ross, "0755," The Heroes of Pearl Harbor (Rokalu Press, Port Orchard, WA, 1988).

18. George Lang (MOH), Raymond L. Collins, and Gerald F. White (compilers), Medal Of Honor Recipients 1863-1994, Vol. II (Facts on File, Inc., New York, NY, 1995), 517 (see endnote 13 of Chapter 9 (*Arizona*)).

19. Theodore Taylor, Air Raid—Pearl Harbor (Gulliver Books, Harcourt, Inc., San Diego, 1971, 1991).

20. Rodney P. Carlisle, PhD, general editor, One Day in History: The Days That Changed the World: December 7, 1941 (HarperCollins Publishers, New York, NY, 2006); "Congressional Medal of Honor" is at page 39.

21. Ibid.

22. Gordon Prange, Donald M. Goldstein, and Katherine V. Dillon, Dec. 7, 1941: The Day the Japanese Attacked Pearl Harbor (McGraw-Hill Book Company, New York, NY, 1988).

23. Joy Waldron Jasper, James P. Delgado, and Jim Adams, The USS *Arizona* (Truman Talley Books, St. Martin's Press, New York, NY2001).

24. Terence McComas, Pearl Harbor Fact and Reference Book: Everything to Know about December 7, 1941 (Mutual Publishing, Honolulu, HI,1991).

25. Francis Trevelyan Miller, History of World War II (The Publisher's Guild, New York, NY, 1945), 328 (Miller), 329 (Bennion and Van Valkenburgh), 329 (Ward), 329–330 (Young and Ross), and 333 (*Oklahoma*).

26. George Feifer, The Battle of Okinawa (The Lyons Press, Guilford, CT, 2001). The

battleship error is on page 5. The MOH error is on page 220. Twenty-seven MOHs were awarded for Iwo Jima, five to Navy personnel and twenty-two to Marines; Hal Buell, Uncommon Valor, Common Virtue (The Berkley Publishing Group, New York, NY, 2006), 226–252.

27. Lars Anderson, The All Americans (St. Martin's Press, New York, NY, 2004); see Chapter 9 of the current book (*Arizona*) for the correct name of *Arizona*'s commanding officer.

28. Chapter 9 (*Arizona*), endnote 115.

29. PEARL HARBOR ATTACK: HEARINGS BEFORE THE JOINT COMMITTEE ON THE INVESTIGATION OF THE PEARL HARBOR ATTACK, SEVENTY-NINTH CONGRESS, Second Session, Part 21 (1946), 4557.

30. Home of Heroes Internet site, printing September 29, 2014.

31. Ernest Arroyo, Pearl Harbor (Metro Books, New York, NY, 2001).

32. Ibid., 69.

33. Ibid., 94.

34. Ibid., 69.

35. Naval Department, Dictionary of American Naval Fighting Ships, Vol. V (Naval Historical Center, Department of the Navy, 1981), 52 (*Nevada*).

36. William Manchester, American Caesar (Little, Brown and Company, Boston, 1978).

37. Colonel Charles A. Jones, U.S. Marine Corps Reserve (Retired), Hawaii's World War II Military Sites (Mutual Publishing, Honolulu, HI, 2002), 20; page 33 lists the names of the carriers in the strike force.

38. "*Nevada*'s Heroic Run," World War II (January 1998).

39. "*Nevada*'s Heroic Run," World War II (2001).

40. Barrett Tillman, "The Pearl Harbor Medal Battle," Flight Journal (October 2013), 60.

41. The MOH citations can be found by searching "Army MOH site" on the Internet and using the icons labeled "Iraq" and "Afghanistan" at the "Medal of Honor Recipients: Center of Military History" Internet site.

42. Admiral Dennis Blair, "Remarks Honoring the End of World War II," US Pacific Command, (September 2, 2000; VJ Day was postwar terminology for "Victory over

Japan."

43. Lieutenant Chris Servello, "Navy to Present Medal of Honor to Family of World War II Vet," Navy newsstand (May 11, 2006); Jason Thompson, Journalist Second Class, U.S. Navy, "Medal of Honor Presented to Family of Pearl Harbor Vet," Navy newsstand (May 19, 2006).

44. "US Navy Ships Named for Individual Sailors to Commemorate Their Actions during the Attack [December 7, 1941]," Naval Heritage and History Command, printed September 30, 2015.

45. The two sites "Reeves (DE-156) i" and "Reeves (DLG-24) ii" are found at the main Naval History and Heritage Command Internet site by searching "Joseph Mason Reeves."

46. Major Charles D. Melson, USMC (Retired), Condition Red: Marine Defense Battalions in World War II, (History and Museums Division, Headquarters, U.S. Marine Corps, Washington, DC, 1996).

47. Major Dale Robinson, US Marine Corps (Retired), "Moment of Truth," Military Officer (December 2007), 62–69.

48. Lieutenant Colonel Frank O. Hough, USMCR; Major Verle E. Ludwig, USMC; and Henry I. Shaw, Jr., Pearl Harbor to Guadalcanal: History of the U.S. Marine Corps Operations in World War II, Vol. I (Historical Division, Headquarters, US Marine Corps, Washington, DC, 1958, reprinted by the Battery Press, Inc., 1993). Cannon is mentioned on pages 79 to 80. Fleming is mentioned on page 229.

49. Endnote 43 of Chapter 14 (Midway) is the official report for Fleming's squadron's action at Midway for June 4–5. Paragraph 40 does not mention Zero opposition during the attack on June 5, but in paragraph 40 mentions "[v]iolent anti-aircraft fire" from the target ship.

50. Commander Peter B. Mersky, U.S. Naval Reserve, Time of the Aces: Marine Pilots in the Solomons, 1942–1944 (History and Museums Division, Headquarters, US Marine Corps, Washington, DC, 1993).

Part VI

Makeup Medals

Chapter 19
The Pharris Medal of Honor
(USS California)—Late and Lost

Warrant Officer (Gunner) Jackson Pharris, US Navy

USS California, December 7, 1941

Chapter 4 explained the attack on the battleship USS *California* on December 7 and the action of three MOH recipients who were members of her crew: Ensign Herbert Jones, Warrant Officer (Radio Electrician) Thomas Reeves, and Machinist's Mate First Class Robert Scott. President Roosevelt approved their posthumous MOHs on March 4, 1942.

The officer who would, more than six years after the attack, become the fourth *California* MOH recipient was Warrant Officer (Gunner) Jackson Pharris, who went from Navy Cross recipient in 1942 to MOH recipient in 1948. His story warrants a separate chapter because of the extent and nature of his actions on December 7, the effort made and "intrigue" involved to upgrade his Navy Cross to a MOH, and the physical loss of the MOH in a legal proceeding after his death. Also, the process of upgrading the Navy Cross to a MOH gives an excellent snapshot (or, really, a slow-motion movie) of the MOH process.

Background

Pharris was born in Columbus, Georgia, on June 26, 1912. He enlisted in the Navy on April 25, 1933; went to Naval Training Station Norfolk; and was honorably discharged on April 18, 1939, but immediately reenlisted. He rose through the lower enlisted ranks as an apprentice seaman, seaman second class, and seaman first class. He then rose through the petty officer ranks—gunner's mate third class (GM3), gunner's mate second class (GM2), and turret captain first class (TC1).[1] Gunner's mates maintained and repaired guns, gun mounts, and gun parts; they also fired the gun in action and stood signal gun watch. A turret captain commanded a gun turret and its crew, assembled and repaired naval guns, and handled ammunition. A turret captain also used periscopes and range finders and had to understand "electric fire-control and firing mechanisms."[2]

On January 29, 1941, his enlistment as a TC1 was terminated so that he could accept an appointment as a warrant officer (gunner). A warrant officer gunner was an assistant to the gunnery officer and was also responsible for caring for and preserving the ship's ordnance.[3]

He was on USS Mississippi as of April 19, 1939. He reported to USS *California* on March 28, 1941.[4]

Actions on December 7

Because Pharris was for some unknown reason awarded a Navy Cross for December 7 while Jones, Reeves, and Scott received MOHs and because of the prolonged process the Navy required to upgrade the Pharris Navy Cross to a MOH, Pharris's actions on December 7 are discussed in detail throughout this chapter as the essence of the chapter unfolds: the upgrade of the Navy Cross to a richly deserved MOH.

AFTERMATH OF DECEMBER 7

AFTER-ACTION REPORTS AND AWARDS RECOMMENDATION LETTER

Chapter 4 described the three documents Captain Joel W. Bunkley, the commanding officer of *California* on December 7, wrote after December 7. The first was an initial after-action report of December 13, addressed to the Commander in Chief, U.S. Pacific Fleet.[5] His second was a revised report dated December 22.[6] Both reports mentioned Reeves, Jones, and Pharris. Neither report letter mentioned Scott.

The third document was a letter Bunkley wrote dated January 10, 1942, to the "Commander in Chief, U.S. Fleet [sic]." The exclusive purpose of the letter was to recommend "appropriate awards" for Pharris, Jones, and Scott for their conduct on December 7. The letter summarized the action of each man on December 7 justifying the awards, with the summary for Pharris being the longest. The letter does not mention Reeves.[7]

THE THREE INITIAL MOH AWARDS FOR USS CALIFORNIA CREWMEN

Chapter 14 (Overview), Chapter 15 (Kidd and Van Valkenburgh undeserved MOHs), and Chapter 16 (Fox "non award") discussed the MOH process in detail. This chapter will also discuss it in detail as it concerns Jackson Pharris.

To recap for the reader at this point why only three men from *California* received MOHs when four should have, this paragraph will review briefly the MOH process described in the chapters just mentioned.

The original report of the Fleet Board of Awards submitted twelve names of officers and men recommended for the MOH. Nine of those recommended for MOHs were Bennion, Cannon, Flaherty, Fuqua, Hill, Ross, Tomich, Ward, and Young. When the three *California* men are included in the list of those recommended for MOHs—Jones, Reeves, and Scott—the total number of MOH recommendations is twelve. Pharris was omitted because the Fleet Board inexplicably recommended him for a Navy Cross, not a MOH.

The Navy Department Permanent Board of Awards reviewed the Fleet Board recommendations and added two more recommendations for MOHs for *Arizona* officers: Rear Admiral Isaac Kidd and Captain Franklin Van Valkenburgh. The name of Rear Admiral J. O. Richardson, as Senior member of the Permanent Board appears at the end of the Board's report; the Secretary of the Navy approved the recommendations on February 27, 1942.

Thus the letter of March 3, 1942, signed by Secretary of the Navy Frank Knox, forwarding MOH citations to President Roosevelt with a recommendation that he sign them included fourteen, not twelve, MOH citations for Presidential signature given the two additional citations (Kidd and Van Valkenburgh). Citations for the three *California* men were included—Jones, Reeves, and Scott. President Roosevelt signed all the citations on March 4, 1942.[8] As will be seen, Pharris would have to wait until 1948 to receive his MOH.

Overview of the Pharris Case

As the reader will see from the following discussion, the Pharris case is remarkable for three reasons.

First, Pharris arguably was one of the most deserving (if not the most deserving) MOH recipients for December 7—he saved numerous shipmates and kept his ship from capsizing—yet he received only a Navy Cross during the war for his actions that day. His Navy Cross citation, prepared March 3, 1942, is not only inadequate but insulting, a woefully short citation that in no way captures in full the conduct of Jackson Pharris on December 7, conduct described in detail in Captain Bunkley's awards letter of January 10, 1942.[9] What is beyond the author's understanding is how anyone could read Bunkley's January 10 letter and its detailed description of what Jones and Scott did—both of whom were recommended for and received MOHs—and also read the description of what Pharris did and not recommend him for a MOH also.

Second, while Pharris obviously deserved a MOH based on demonstrable proof of bravery warranting a MOH, he was recommended for and received a Navy Cross. At the same time, two MOH recipients, Kidd and VanValkenburgh, received MOHs for which no factual bases existed. Chapters 15 and 16 discuss this aspect of the MOH awards process.

Third, as will be seen, by the time the navy relented and decided to recommend that the president approve a MOH for Pharris, he would become the last recipient of a MOH for actions on December 7, receiving his MOH in 1948 from President Harry Truman at the White House—more than six years after December 7, 1941.

Actions on December 7 as Documented by Initial Reports and Letter

As previously mentioned, Captain Bunkley submitted three documents concerning the events of December 7 aboard USS *California*.

First Document

The after-action report dated December 13, 1941, was first the report Bunkley submitted concerning December 7. In his report, Bunkley mentioned Pharris under the heading "DISTINGUISHED CONDUCT PERSONNEL." He wrote, "Gunner J.C. Pharris, although injured, was outstanding in his work to continue ammunition supply in spite of fire and other hazards, during which he organized and reorganized able personnel and personally provided ammunition while men were dying in fuel oil and in rescuing many men from oil and vapors." He also noted that Pharris was injured.[10]

Second Document

The report dated December 22, 1941, was the second or revised report Bunkley submitted concerning December 7. Bunkley wrote that the ship lost light and power at approximately 8:10 a.m. Men in one section were supplying ammunition by hand until overcome with oil fumes; the men had to be evacuated. "Gunner J.C. Pharris, with replacements from the broadside guns, succeeded in removing the [men overcome by fuel oil fumes] and getting sixty-two rounds from the magazines to the guns." Under "DISTINGUISHED CONDUCT—PERSONNEL," he included "Pharris, J.C., Gunner, USN," following this sentence: "The following named men and officers were outstanding in their work during battle in the ammunition supply and in removing wounded."[11]

Third Document

The letter dated January 10, 1942, was the third document Bunkley submitted concerning December 7. Bunkley stated that Pharris suffered a painful back injury when knocked down by the impact of a torpedo hitting outboard of his compartment. Although he was injured and the compartment was flooding with water and oil, Pharris remained at his station, organizing ammunition supply until he could no longer obtain ammunition. Although the men around him became unconscious due to oil fumes, Pharris continued working the ammunition hoists until he was completely exhausted. He lost consciousness and had to be evacuated to the boat deck. After he revived, he went back into the ship to obtain more ammunition. He again lost consciousness and had to be carried to the deck. He was taken to the dispensary ashore, probably on Ford Island, where his clothes were cut off and he was put to bed. After reviving, he procured other clothing and returned to the ship. He again went below to a magazine area that was flooding and obtained a supply of ammunition. He concluded, "It is believed that Gunner Pharris displayed initiative, leadership, courage and pertinacity to an outstanding degree."[12]

In summary, Bunkley's after-action reports of December 13 and 22, 1941, cited Jones, Pharris, and Reeves for bravery but did not mention Scott; his letter of January 10 cited Jones, Pharris, and Scott for bravery but did not mention Reeves.

The question to which the answer must be "Unknown" is as follows: What did the personnel in the Navy, responsible for recommending awards, know about what Pharris did on December 7? Someone in command or on a staff had to know something about Pharris's bravery on December 7. After all, he was mentioned in three official documents generated by his commanding officer, reporting his outstanding performance, dedication, and bravery, documents resulting in MOHs for Jones, Reeves, and Scott but not for Pharris, who had done more to save the ship than Jones, Reeves, and Scott.

Regardless, and for whatever reason or reasons, Jones, Reeves, and Scott received posthumous MOHs; Pharris—the lone survivor of the four—whose deeds far exceeded those of the other three *California* MOH recipients, received a Navy Cross, the award second in precedence to the MOH for Marine Corps, Navy, and Coast Guard personnel. The equivalent award in World War II for the Army, including the Army Air Forces, was the Distinguished Service Cross (DSC).[13]

THE PHARRIS NAVY CROSS AND PURPLE HEART

In its 1942 Third Endorsement of the report of the Fleet Board of Awards, the Navy Department Permanent Board of Awards recommended various personnel receive Navy Crosses. One of those recommended was "GUNNER JACKSON C. PHARRIS." The Secretary of the Navy approved the Third Endorsement on February 27, 1942.[14]

A letter of March 18, 1942, from the Chief of the Bureau of Navigation transmitted the Navy Cross citation for Pharris, along with Navy Cross citations for other recipients, to the Commander in Chief of the U.S. Pacific Fleet (CINCPACFLT) for him to present to the recipients; the CINC was to present them on Oahu since transporting the recipients to Washington for presentation by the Secretary of the Navy was impractical. The Navy Crosses themselves were to be taken from the supply of Navy Crosses already sent to Pearl Harbor.[15]

By letter of April 16, 1942, CINCPACFLT advised *California's* commanding officer that the Secretary of the Navy had approved the recommendation by the Pacific Fleet Board of Awards that Pharris receive a Navy Cross. The letter also advised that CINCPACFLT would personally present the award on April 7, 1942, at an "appropriate ceremony."[16]

The Pharris Navy Cross citation, prepared March 3, 1942, is pathetic and insulting (including its typographical error). It mentions nothing about Pharris saving the ship from capsizing by ordering counterflooding. The citation reads as follows:

> For distinguished service in the line of his profession during the attack on the fleet in Pearl Harbor, Territory of Hawaii, by Japanese forces on December 7, 1941, during which he maintained the ammunition supply to the anti-aircraft guns on the USS *California* and for his extraordinary courage and disregard of his own safety in rescuing many men from ail [oil] and vapors.
>
> For the President,
>
> *FRANK KNOX*
>
> SEcretary [sic] of the Navy[17]

Pharris also received a Purple Heart since he was wounded on December 7.[18]

Thus until 1948, Pharris stood on the pier, so to speak, with his only awards for December 7 a Purple Heart and a Navy Cross with a pathetically worded citation—all for an officer who, at a minimum, singlehandedly saved his ship from the horrors of capsizing.

Wartime Life

Life after December 7 was at times difficult for Pharris because of his medical condition, as will be described in this chapter; up to now, readers should have a hint that he took a beating on December 7. In fact he certainly endured a physical beating on December 7, probably one from which he never fully recovered.

After December 7, Pharris continuously suffered medical problems and was hospitalized. The following chronology of his later life, wartime and postwar, is from two sources. One is Mindy Pharris, the wife of Pharris's son, Jackson Pharris II, who kindly provided a chronology.[19] The other source is corroborating documentation the Harry S. Truman Library and Museum provided the author in 2008.

A document thought to be the undated enclosure submitted with Rear Admiral Bunkley's letter of January 16, 1946 concerning Pharris, ended as follows: "At the present time Lieutenant Pharris is a patient in the U.S. Naval Hospital, Oakland, *California*, for a complete physical check-up due to combat fatigue…" The Bunkley letter and enclosure, as endorsed by the Navy, are discussed later in this chapter concerning the upgrade of the Pharris Navy Cross to a MOH.

From June 1947 to November 1947, Pharris wrote and received several letters at the US Naval Hospital in Long Beach, California, concerning the upgrade of his Navy Cross to a MOH. This correspondence is also discussed later in this chapter concerning the Navy Cross upgrade.

What is remarkable, as shown by the following chronology, is the amount of medical care and hospitalization Pharris required during and after the war. The medical care and hospitalization can also be seen from the postwar correspondence he sent from medical facilities to the Board of Review for Decorations and Medals concerning witness statements for upgrading his Navy Cross to a MOH. For example, one letter, dated November 3, 1947, was from "US Naval Hospital, Long Beach [4], California." At the time, he was living at a residence but being treated at the hospital.

- December 1941 to March 1942—Pharris was hospitalized at the U.S. Naval Hospital at Pearl Harbor for back injuries and double pneumonia.
- March 1942 to January 1943—Pharris returned to USS *California* as ammunition disposal officer. After the ship was salvaged, she was taken to Bremerton, Washington, for repair. During the salvage work, Pharris went back to his compartment and found his wallet, which still contained a twenty-dollar bill.
- August 15, 1942—Pharris was appointed an ensign (the next grade above chief warrant officer) for temporary service with a date of rank of June 15,

1942.
- October 27, 1942—Pharris began a period of leave (eighteen days).
- January to June 1943—Pharris was hospitalized at U.S. Naval Hospital Bremerton. He had collapsed because oil remaining in his lungs impeded oxygen flow to his body.
- February 2, 1943—Pharris was recommended for promotion from ensign to lieutenant (junior grade), but the recommendation was disapproved on February 28, 1943.
- June 8, 1943, to August 1944—Pharris returned to active duty aboard the USS *California* as a turret officer and division officer for turret number 2.
- May 1, 1943—Pharris was appointed a temporary lieutenant (junior grade).
- July 16, 1943—Pharris was found not physically qualified for the appointment to lieutenant (junior grade), so he retained his appointment as an ensign.
- July 22, 1943—Pharris was recommended for temporary appointment as a lieutenant (junior grade); the temporary status was apparently due to medical reasons. A medical report of June 10, 1943, was not immediately forwarded to the Bureau of Medicine and Surgery for notification to the Bureau of Naval Personnel.
- August to September 1943—Pharris attended Fire Control School, Washington, DC, for five weeks.
- July 1, 1944—Pharris was temporarily appointed a lieutenant.
- August 1944—Pharris detached from USS *California* and was assigned temporary duty at the office at the Bethlehem Steel Company in Massachusetts at the shipyard fitting out the heavy cruiser USS St. Paul (CA 73).
- February 17, 1945—Pharris reported for duty with USS St. Paul. He was wounded aboard ship on August 9, 1945, and received a second Purple Heart (Gold Star in lieu of second medal).[20]
- June 7, 1945—On this date, the homeport of St. Paul changed from Boston to Mare Island, California.

Postwar life
- September 12, 1945—Pharris detached from St. Paul and reported aboard USS Salamaua for medical transport to the United States.
- October 3, 1945—Pharris detached from Salamaua in Alameda, California, and was hospitalized for injuries received on August 9, 1945, while aboard St. Paul.
- February 18, 1946—Pharris began thirty days of convalescent leave at his home in Long Beach.
- March 25, 1946—Pharris was discharged from the US Naval Hospital at Long Beach.
- April 1, 1946—Pharris reported to Naval Ammunition and Net Depot, Seal Beach, California.
- September 17, 1946—Pharris detached from duty at Seal Beach and was granted three months' sick leave.
- December 30, 1946—Pharris was admitted for treatment, U.S. Naval Hospital, Long Beach.

- January 28, 1947, to March 6, 1947—Pharris was assigned to shore duty at U.S. Naval Base Terminal Island (San Pedro) while awaiting action of a Board of Medical Survey.
- March 1947—Pharris requested to remain on active duty until June 30, 1948, or longer.
- March 17, 1947—Pharris was assigned to U.S. Naval Training and Distribution Center, Construction Battalion Center, Point Hueneme, California, as the recreation officer. He had additional duty as the welfare and recreation officer of the US Naval School as of March 25, 1947.
- June 11, 1947—Pharris detached from duty at Port Hueneme, returning to U.S. Naval Hospital Long Beach, California, for treatment.
- September 1947—He appeared before a Survey Board at the Long Beach Naval Hospital, which recommended that he appear before the Naval Retiring Board.
- December 19, 1947—He appeared before the Naval Retiring Board, which found that he was "incapacitated for active service." He was ordered home on terminal leave to await final action in his case. The retiring board examined men to determine physical fitness to perform the duties of their grades, including examinations for physical incapacity retirements.[21] Given the Board's finding for Pharris, he was ordered home on terminal leave to await final action on the Retiring Board's proceedings concerning medical retirement.
- April 30, 1948—The President of the United States approved the findings of the Naval Retiring Board.
- May 1, 1948—Pharris was placed on the retired list in the grade of lieutenant commander.

THE CAMPAIGN TO UPGRADE THE NAVY CROSS TO A MOH

The following section describes the actions taken by Bunkley after the war to upgrade Pharris's Navy Cross to a MOH. It is extensive and detailed for two reasons. One is to show just how difficult the process can be for obtaining a MOH for a service member. Two is to show the politics that can influence the MOH award process and how they can lead to the following result: a deserving service member is denied a MOH while undeserving service members are awarded MOHs.

Specifically, the story is one of how a single officer, Jackson Pharris, was inadequately recognized for bravery by not receiving a MOH during the war, a MOH he clearly deserved and which was supported by an overwhelming amount of factual evidence of bravery. That evidence is documentation to be described in the remainder of this chapter. As will be seen, the standards the Navy imposed for the Pharris MOH were "incontestable justification" and "incontrovertible facts" to support the recommendation for the MOH. At the same time and as discussed at length in chapter 15, two other officers—Rear Admiral Isaac Kidd and Captain Franklin Van Valkenburgh of *Arizona*—received posthumous MOHs in 1942, awards lacking basis in fact. The addition by the Permanent Board of their names to the twelve names of men recommended for MOHs by the Fleet Board of Awards led to the Kidd and Van Valkenburgh MOHs. The standard by which the Navy Department Permanent Board of Awards judged their conduct worthy of a MOH is unknown. A reading of their MOH citations leads one to believe that they were awarded MOHs simply because of their status as senior officers killed in action: Commander, Battleship Division One (Kidd) and Commanding Officer, USS *Arizona* (Van Valkenburgh). For whatever these facts are worth, they were each KIA or MIA, perishing aboard *Arizona*, and were both Naval Academy graduates.

In any event, fortunately for Pharris and for anyone who seeks a just result in the awards process, Pharris eventually received a MOH.

As will be seen by the chronology of events below, the Bunkley letter began a dizzying spiral within the Navy's bureaucracy, generating extensive correspondence and much investigation, but one must remember that a MOH is not, and should not be, awarded without substantial proof that the statutory requirements for a MOH are met: the service member, "in action involving actual conflict with an enemy [must distinguish] himself conspicuously by gallantry and intrepidity at the risk of his life above and beyond the call of duty." If the MOH is to have any value as the nation's highest military award, it must be presented only to those whose deeds are proven by confirmed and corroborated facts. As will be seen, the implicit and explicit message in the correspondence from the Navy to Pharris and to the witnesses is that the MOH is a serious matter and that the Pharris Navy Cross would not be upgraded to a MOH absent very strong evidence supporting a MOH.

To recap, Pharris received a Navy Cross in 1942 for his actions on December 7 aboard *California*. *California's* Commanding Officer, Captain Bunkley, had summarized those actions in his after-action report of December 13, 1941; in his revised after-action report of December 22, 1941, and in his awards recommendation letter of January 10, 1942. His documents are a treasure trove of information documenting the actions of Jackson Pharris on December 7.

After reading Bunkley's wartime accounts of what Pharris did on December 7, one should ask who knew what and when he or they knew it about the actions Pharris took on December 7 in light of these three documents and especially in light of the MOHs awarded to three other *California* crew members: Jones, Reeves, and Scott.

What information about Pharris was known by the Fleet Board of Awards at Pearl Harbor? It must have known some information since it recommended him for a Navy Cross.

Why was information obtainable after the war to support the upgrade of the Navy Cross to the MOH apparently unobtainable during the war when one could assume that the witnesses providing the information postwar were still aboard ship after the attack? In other words, why was information sufficient to upgrade his Navy Cross to a MOH not available until after the war? In still other words, why was he not recommended for a MOH by the Fleet Board from the beginning? The statements of these witnesses are found in the chronology that follows in this chapter.

Was information sufficient to support a Pharris MOH available to the Navy

Permanent Board of Awards?

If either board knew about information that ultimately was used to upgrade his Navy Cross to a MOH, why was Pharris not recommended for a MOH?

The reader must ask if either board ever reviewed the two after-action reports Captain Bunkley submitted in December 1941 or the awards recommendation letter he submitted in January 1942. One would be hard-pressed to believe that Bunkley's reports and letter were ignored; after all, common sense dictates that the information in his reports and letter had to be the bases for the MOHs awarded to the three other *California* crewmen: Jones, Reeves, and Scott.

Regardless of what was or was not known during the war, apparently the effort to upgrade the Navy Cross to a MOH began in 1946 with Bunkley's submission to the Navy of a letter dated January 16, 1946 (with an enclosure), recommending that Pharris receive a MOH. With the letter unavailable, as is explained here, one cannot read it with a view to discerning Bunkley's reasons or motivation for writing the letter.[22]

The information about Harris's actions can be divided into two time periods: wartime and postwar.

Wartime (three documents)—the two 1941 *California* after-action reports and the January 10, 1942, letter submitted by Bunkley have already been summarized.

Postwar (five documents)—What follows is a discussion of five postwar documents concerning the attempt to upgrade the Pharris Navy Cross. As explained here, one document appears to be an enclosure to the January 16, 1946, Bunkley letter, the letter endorsed by the navy on February 1, 1946. The document is unsigned and undated, and the author is unknown. The other three documents are postwar statements from three *California* crewmen who witnessed Pharris's actions on December 7. These statements were submitted to support the postwar efforts by Bunkley and Pharris to upgrade the Pharris Navy Cross to a MOH. Two are from officers: Lieutenant Commander D. C. McCartin (the Board would receive McCartin's letter after the Secretary of the Navy approved the Board's recommendation that the Navy Cross be upgraded) and Lieutenant Samuel Killingsworth. Two were from enlisted men: Chief Petty Officer (Pay Clerk) J. O. Bussey and Chief Petty Officer (Gunner's Mate) H. F. Reynolds. The five postwar statements provide a picture of Pharris's actions on December 7, actions taken in the worst of circumstances and that would result in the MOH awarded him in 1948. They are summarized in detail to show that different crewmen witnessed actions by Pharris that, without question, warranted a MOH.

Before summarizing the wartime and postwar documents, an outline follows for the reader's orientation to categorize Pharris's actions on December 7, with the most important action listed first. The wartime and postwar correspondence will support the information in this outline.

1. Damage control and ordering counterflooding of the ship

California was listing dangerously to port because of torpedo hits on the port side of the ship. Men were unable to walk on the decks because of oil leaks and oil on their footwear; also, the list undoubtedly made walking difficult. Facing such conditions, Pharris, without awaiting orders, ordered counterflooding, which undoubtedly kept the ship from capsizing. Counterflooding permitted water to enter the starboard side of the ship, thus leveling the ship and preventing her from sharing the fate of *Oklahoma* and *Utah*: capsizing and its attendant problems and nightmares. Chapters 5 and 10, respectively, of this book discuss the ghastly conditions aboard *Oklahoma* and *Utah*, the only ships to capsize on December 7.

California was fortunate; *Arizona* was not. *Arizona*'s damage-control officer, Samuel Fuqua, faced catastrophic conditions beyond his remedy. Pharris, however, could perform effective damage control, such as counterflooding. Chapter 7 of this book describes the dreadful, hopeless situation that Fuqua faced on December 7 aboard *Arizona*.

2. Ensuring antiaircraft ammunition was supplied to the ship's antiaircraft guns

With the exception of the five midget submarines used in the attack, the Japanese attacked Oahu by naval aircraft, so antiaircraft guns and their ammunition were critical in defending battleships since their biggest guns in the main turrets were Useless in defending against air attack. When the ship lost power, thus stopping electric hoists from supplying ammunition to the guns, Pharris used the auxiliary system to supply the guns. To speed the supply of ammunition, he also organized ammunition "trains" by which crewmen supplied ammunition to the guns by hand.

3. Saving the lives of crewmen

Pharris, at risk to his own life and while he himself was suffering the debilitating effects of oil fumes, saved the lives of at least seventeen crewmen, most if not all of whom were incapacitated by oil fumes and covered with or submerged in oil

4. Clearing a misfire from one of the ship's guns

Pharris cleared a misfire in one of the ship's guns; apparently the misfire was a "hangfire," which is a shell that fails to discharge after the crew has attempted to fire the gun. The danger is that the hangfire can then discharge at any time, and thus the discharge is beyond the control of the gun's crew. He removed the shell from the gun and tossed the shell overboard, allowing the gun crew to resume firing.

The wartime information about Pharris, together with the postwar information about him, also show that Pharris's attitude and conduct on December 7 are distinctive in two ways. First, he distinguished himself by disregarding his own welfare. He was preoccupied with saving the ship and her crewmen while disregarding his own safety and welfare. As Bunkley stated in his January 10 letter recommending awards for Jones, Pharris, and Scott, at one point after losing consciousness from the oil fumes, Pharris was taken to the dispensary ashore and put to bed. After he revived, he left his bed and procured new clothing, which he needed since his uniform had been cut off, apparently when he reached the dispensary. He then returned to the ship. In short, Pharris continued his activity notwithstanding injury and revival after loss of consciousness. He paid a price for his bravery and actions; throughout the attack, he sustained several injuries, was rendered unconscious at least twice, and suffered exhaustion.

Second, he also distinguished himself by decisiveness. Pharris made several crucial decisions that kept the ship fighting. He helped to keep the antiaircraft guns in action by ensuring an uninterrupted ammunition supply, and his decision to counterflood kept the ship level, preventing capsizing.

The Correspondence Leading to the Navy Cross Being Upgraded to a MOH

To prevent repetitive endnotes, the author states at the outset that he obtained the documentation described in this section from the Harry S. Truman Presidential Library and Museum. The Truman Library was the source because Harry Truman was president during the time Bunkley and Pharris tried to have the Navy Cross upgraded. Correspondence is identified by date, sender, and addressee. The perhaps mind-numbing detail is offered to show just how much effort was expended to upgrade the Navy Cross, how seriously the navy took the matter, and how, in the finest tradition of the military, shipmate helped shipmate—the shipmates of Pharris came to his aid to help him upgrade the Navy Cross.

Apparently the effort to upgrade the Navy Cross began with a January 16, 1946, letter, with an enclosed or attached statement ("enclosure") from Bunkley to some section within the Navy; in Naval correspondence, a complete document is the basic letter with any enclosure or enclosures. Unfortunately the letter was not provided to the author by the Truman Presidential Library and Museum. The letter's existence, however, can be proven by referring to a February 1, 1946, memorandum from the senior member of the Board of Review for Decorations and Medals, Admiral F. J. Horne, US Navy. His memorandum is "End-1 on rear [sic] admiral J. W. Bunkley ltr of 16 Jan 1946" (Bunkley had been promoted to rear admiral and had retired during the war). The memorandum is the Navy's first endorsement ("End-1") of the Bunkley letter with its enclosure. The subject of the Board's memorandum is "Recommended [sic] for Medal of Honor for Lieutenant Jackson C. Pharris, US Navy, in lieu of Navy Cross." The body of the February 1 memorandum refers to "the basic correspondence [the Bunkley letter of January 16, 1946] *with enclosure...*" [Italics added for emphasis.] What had been the Navy Department Permanent Board of Awards was now the Board of Review for Decorations and Medals.[23]

To assist the reader in navigating the process resulting in the Pharris MOH, a chronology of events follows.

Correspondence: 1946

January 16

This date is the date of Rear Admiral Bunkley's letter just described. Although the Truman Library did not provide the author a copy of the Bunkley letter, it provided an unsigned and undated document believed to be the enclosure to the 1946 Bunkley letter. The document is titled "Actions of Lieutenant Jackson C. Pharris, USN. during the [attack] on Pearl Harbor, December 7th…by the Japanese." A summary of the document follows:

The attack completely surprised the crew.

Some of the officers, including the commanding officer, and crew were ashore in a nonduty status at the time of the attack.

When the first torpedo hit, Pharris and his men set "material condition ZED," the final damage-control condition for battle. Lieutenant Samuel Killingsworth's statement, mentioned later in this chapter, discusses ZED, noting that it meant hatches and openings were closed except for those required to remain open for combat purposes.

The torpedo's explosion threw the men to the overhead (ceiling).

Pharris, knowing that officer in charge of the antiaircraft ammunition supply was not aboard, acted without orders and began an ammunition train to supply the antiaircraft guns.

Soon a second torpedo hit, extinguishing the lights. Pharris ordered the men to use lanterns and flashlights, and he shifted the ammunition hoists to auxiliary power.

By then, oil was filling compartments, with oil vapors causing men to lose consciousness. Pharris contacted gun turrets to obtain replacement sailors for handling ammunition and to assist in removing the stricken men.

During the attack, oil fumes caused Pharris to pass out twice. After he revived from the first loss of consciousness, he realized that ammunition supply via the auxiliary system was too slow, so he began ammunition passage by hand.

As he moved about the ship, Pharris noticed men passing out from the oil vapor. Risking his own life, he saved six men completely submerged in oil that had flooded a compartment.

The ship was also listing, and with no damage-control officer aboard, Pharris ordered counterflooding, "which no doubt saved the ship from flooding."

Pharris, at the risk of his own life, saved eleven men trapped in an ammunition-handling room, men overcome by smoke and by oil vapor (Chief Petty Officer J. O. Bussey was one of these men and would submit a statement to assist Pharris in upgrading the Navy Cross to a MOH).

Upon Pharris reviving after his second loss of consciousness, he was topside (above or on the deck). Told that one of the guns had misfired, he unloaded the gun within the thirty-minute time limit for unloading misfires. While he was clearing the misfire, a Japanese torpedo aircraft was attacking USS *West Virginia*. *California's* guns were shooting at the aircraft, and the muzzle blast from one of the guns "almost tore the shirt from his [Pharris's] back" and burned his neck and hair from behind. After removing the undetonated shell from the gun, he threw it overboard. The gun was reloaded and continued firing.

Pharris went below decks again, and finding that the ammunition supply was moving too slowly, he began another passage by hand.

During this time, horizontal bombers were attacking the ship, dropping bombs that barely missed her. But one bomb did hit the ship, killing everyone in the vicinity of one of the ammunition supply trains and also killing men who had been brought topside to recover from oil fumes as well as crewmen on another deck.

Pharris was injured numerous ways: "flash burns on face, neck and hands; ruptured left eardrum; contusions to the lower back (lumbar region); contusions of the ligaments in the right knee; efection [sic] of fuel oil, (which affected his lungs, that he later developed pneumonia and pleurisy, spending approximately 9 1/2 months in hospitals."

The memorandum stated that at the time it was written, Pharris was a patient at the Naval Hospital, Oakland, California "for a complete physical check-up due to combat fatigue."

February 1

The Board of Review for Decorations and Medals endorsed Bunkley's January 16, 1946, letter by the February 1, 1946, memorandum previously described. The memorandum advised Secretary of the Navy James Forrestal that the board had reviewed Bunkley's letter "with enclosure" and had concluded that the Pharris Navy Cross was "sufficient recognition" for his actions aboard *California* on December 7, 1941. Captain P. W. Steinhagen was the recorder or administrative assistant for the board. Admiral F. J. Horne signed the letter as the Senior Member of the Board.

February 8

Forrestal approved the Board's endorsement. The "approved" block is dated February 8, 1946, with "Forrestal" typed in the signature block?

Correspondence: 1947

June 26

Pharris wrote the Board requesting that it review and reconsider the request by

Bunkley that his Navy Cross be upgraded to a MOH. He expressed his belief that "all additional facts and papers which were sent in [at] a later date were not included in the review of Admiral Bunkley's recommendation."

July 22

One must give the Navy—the most recalcitrant of the military services—credit for reopening the Pharris case. In its letter to Bunkley on this date, the board noted that Secretary Forrestal had approved the board's conclusion that the Navy Cross was sufficient recognition, but the letter stated that the Board was reopening the case; the reasons for reopening the case were not explained in the letter. The Board's letter stated that Bunkley's original letter of January 16, 1946, included an unsigned "memorandum" (the enclosure), citing the actions of Pharris on December 7. The Board requested that Bunkley provide the name of the source of the information in the memorandum since a MOH award must be based on "incontrovertible facts."

July 25

The Board letter to Pharris on this date asked Pharris if he knew the source of the information in the memorandum. It added that Bunkley had been requested by letter "to amplify his recommendation" although the Board's July 22, 1947 letter to Bunkley contained no reference to "amplification."

August 7

In Bunkley's letter to the Board of this date, he referenced a letter from the Board of July 28 and stated that he regretted he had misplaced his files and that he "[could] not furnish you with the requested information." He did not describe the information, and the letter of July 28 was not provided to the author.

August 9

Pharris wrote the Board stating that he thought that Rear Admiral Earl E. Stone could supply the information requested in the Board's letter of July 25 to Pharris. Pharris informed the Board that Stone was his executive officer (second in command) on *California*. Pharris sent the letter to the Board from the Navy Hospital in Long Beach.

October 14

Pharris or someone else provided the Board the name of Chief Petty Officer (Pay Clerk) J. O. Bussey. The Board wrote Bussey, advising it was considering a recommendation that Pharris receive a MOH in lieu of his Navy Cross and that it needed "incontestable justification" for a MOH. The board believed that Bussey was on the ship on December 7 and had personal knowledge of Pharris's heroism. Accordingly, it requested a statement about Pharris's actions on that date.

The Board wrote Pharris, asking him to furnish the names of anyone else other than Bussey who had firsthand knowledge of Pharris's actions on December 7.

November 3

Pharris wrote the Board, providing other names: Lieutenant Samuel "Killingswarth" [sic] and Lieutenant (junior grade) H. F. Reynolds. Pharris also mentioned that Rear Admiral Stone had written him. Stone's letter informed Pharris that Stone had spoken to Steinhagen, the Board's recorder, by telephone. It also informed Pharris that Stone, at Steinhagen's request, had forwarded to the Board an August 9, 1947, letter Pharris had written and also had forwarded to Steinhagen documents from Stone's own files concerning Pharris. Pharris also wrote that Stone had told him that he would help him in any way to upgrade the Navy Cross to a MOH. Pharris concluded by noting that both Killingsworth and Reynolds were "advanced to Chief Petty Officer for meritorious conduct on December 7." They had obviously been junior petty officers on December 7, and Killingsworth later became an officer. At the bottom of the letter is Pharris's name and "S.O.Q., (Patient)." Pharris sent the letter from the Navy Hospital in Long Beach.

A letter of this date from Bussey from his duty station (ironically, the cruiser USS St. Paul, the ship aboard which Pharris served in the war and aboard which he earned his second Purple Heart) described Pharris's actions on December 7.

Bussey stated that he saw Pharris save eleven men.

When the attack began, Bussey and ten other men went to their battle station, an ammunition-handling room. The hatch above them was closed. Soon thereafter a torpedo hit the ship and exploded in an adjacent compartment.

The men were sending antiaircraft ammunition by electric hoist up to the guns, but after the area lost electricity, the men passed the ammunition by hand. Soon, however, oil fumes entered the compartment and the men became unconscious. Blood ran from their noses and ears, and they fell to the deck.

The men could not open the upper hatch, and Bussey's calls for help went unheeded; each person he called said that everyone was dead. One person talking to Bussey was himself dying. Bussey finally reached Pharris. By this time, oil fumes were affecting Bussey as oil seeped into the compartment. Pharris opened the hatch and entered the compartment by himself. Pharris carried Bussey out since Bussey was too weak to exit by himself. Pharris then carried out the other ten men. During this process, the oil fumes affected Pharris himself, and he had to remain outside to breathe fresh air before entering the compartment again to remove a sailor.

Bussey concluded his letter as follows:

It is my most earnest belief that Lieutenant Pharris should be awarded the Medal of Honor in lieu of the Navy Cross for his heroic actions on December 7, 1941. He [risked] his life many times for his ship and shipmates and today his medical record will attest the fact that he has been a patient in various

Naval Hospitals over half the time since 7 December 1941 because of injuries received that day. He is at present in the US Naval Hospital, Long Beach, California, a total nervous and physical wreck all [caused] by his heroic actions far and beyond the call of duty on 7 December 1941.

November 14

As it did with Bussey, the Board wrote Killingsworth and Reynolds on this date, requesting statements about Pharris's actions on December 7 and noting that the Board had to have "incontestable justification" for a MOH award (the letter to Reynolds had a misspelling: "incontestavle").

December 15

A letter of this date from Chief Petty Officer (Gunner's Mate) H. F. Reynolds from his duty station (U.S. Naval Magazine, Adak, Alaska) provided the information summarized here.

He wrote, "It is impossible to remember all the facts concerning Lt. Pharris but…I do know that his performance was outstanding."

Pharris was securing a watertight door when the first torpedo hit the ship. The explosion threw Pharris into the air, injuring his back when he struck the overhead. The compartment began filling with oil, causing the ship to list to port. The ship also lost power.

Pharris directed the supply of antiaircraft ammunition, but almost immediately oil fumes rendered men unconscious. Reynolds estimated that Pharris rescued more than twelve crewmen. He named two of those rescued: Bussey and Raymond Nicholas, a member of the "gunner gang." Oil fumes overcame Pharris himself at least twice, but knowing the danger of sailors losing consciousness and drowning in oil, Pharris returned to the compartment to rescue them. Reynolds summarized the rescues as follows: "[Pharris] deliberately risked his life to save other sailors with complete disregard for his personal safety."

Pharris later unloaded a hot gun that had misfired; this must have been the hangfire previously described.

Reynolds concluded his letter as follows:

His performance was so outstanding that all the [ship's] company was discussing and praising him. He has earned, in my opinion, any honor that can be given him including the Congressional Medal of Honor.

Correspondence: 1948

January 19

Pharris wrote Captain Steinhagen, again providing information about Killingsworth and Reynolds. He also noted that Stone and Steinhagen had spoken by phone, with Stone offering to help Steinhagen in any way he could.

Pharris also summarized his medical status processing. As noted earlier in this chapter, Pharris appeared before a medical board (a Survey Board) in 1947 that had recommended he appear before the Naval Retiring Board, which he did on December 19, 1947, and was found "incapacitated for active service." He was sent home on terminal leave to await final Board action.

When he appeared before the Retiring Board as a lieutenant, he submitted to it a letter from him noting that he had received the Navy Cross and requested that if he were retired because of physical disability, he should, because of the Navy Cross, be advanced one grade upon retirement as was permitted by Article 1668(3) of Navy Regulations, thus making him a lieutenant commander when he retired. Article 1668(3) of Navy Regulations (1920) provided that Navy line officers "who have been specially commended for their performance of duty in actual combat" be retired in the next higher grade; this is language similar to the language found in the Fuqua retirement certificate that earned Fuqua a tombstone promotion from captain, his terminal grade, to rear admiral, his retirement grade. The basis for the Pharris commendation was, at that time, his Navy Cross since he did not receive his MOH until June 3, 1948. He also asked if the Navy Cross could be upgraded to a MOH while he was still on active duty. Finally, he stated that he was on terminal leave but still being treated at the Naval Hospital at Long Beach, California.[24]

Undated Letter

Pharris wrote Captain Steinhagen, providing the name of another witness: D. C. McCartin, who was at the Young Men's Christian Association (YMCA) in Green Bay, Wisconsin. McCartin was an ensign aboard *California* on December 7.

January 23

Steinhagen wrote Pharris, advising that the Board had sent inquiries to Killingsworth and Reynolds and that while his case was not completed "every effort will be made to expedite the proceedings."

March 8

A letter of this date from Lieutenant Samuel Killingsworth to the Board from his duty station (Naval Reserve Officers Training Corps, Oregon State College, Corvallis, Oregon) provided a long, detailed summary of his observations of Pharris on December 7.

On December 7, Pharris, as a warrant officer gunner, was Killingsworth's immediate superior. Killingsworth was then an enlisted man, a first class petty officer (gunner's mate). When the general quarters alarm sounded, both men went to the compartment that was their battle station. Pharris directed Killingsworth to assist in setting "material condition ZED," which meant preparing the ship for combat by sealing the ship, closing all hatches except those that had to be open to enable the ship to engage in combat.

A torpedo hit directly under their compartment, throwing Killingsworth across the compartment and Pharris up to the overhead and then back to the deck. Although the impact confused and stunned Killingsworth, he remembered Pharris directing the men to maintain watertight integrity. Oil and water poured into the compartment because of a rupture in the bulkhead; oil fumes caused men to retch and to lose consciousness.

Without awaiting orders, Pharris established an ammunition supply line. The ship then lost power and lights. Pharris ordered men to use lanterns and flashlights. The working conditions degraded as oil fumes entered the area, causing men to lose consciousness. Pharris himself lost consciousness because of the fumes and his back injury. Revived, he organized a second ammunition line on another part of the ship.

When he returned to his compartment, he noticed many men had lost consciousness and were in oil, which was flooding the compartment. He moved the men to a safer location. He went to another compartment upon learning several men were in danger, and there, without regard for his own safety, entered and rescued six unconscious men "who had been completely submerged in fuel oil."

Pharris ordered counterflooding since footing was difficult as the ship was listing to port—she had taken three torpedo hits on the port side—and oil made the deck and footwear slick. The counterflooding decreased the listing and righted the ship a few degrees.

Pharris was told that another group of men required rescue from a compartment. As Pharris left, Killingsworth passed out, regaining consciousness only a few moments on Ford Island and then at a hospital.

While he made no comment concerning the award Pharris deserved, he noted that he returned to the ship late on December 8 and reported to Pharris "who was still doing everything that could be done under the circumstances. During the following hectic and confused days, Lt. Pharris maintained order and discipline among his men and set an example which kept up my faith and morale."

March 10

The Board wrote McCartin asking him to furnish a statement concerning the actions of Pharris on December 7 since a MOH award must have "incontestable justification."

March 19

Killingsworth again submitted his statement, this time in a different format.

The Board's letter of this date to the Secretary of the Navy stated that it had "made a thorough and prolonged investigation of this case in review, and, in view of the additional incontestable evidence submitted" the Navy Cross awarded Pharris should be "withdrawn and cancelled" and that Pharris should receive in its place a MOH. One could hardly disagree with the Board in the face of overwhelming evidence of record supporting a MOH: the two reports submitted by Bunkley (December 13 and 22, 1941), his awards recommendation letter (January 10, 1942), the document that was likely the enclosure to Bunkley's letter (January 16, 1946), and the statements of Bussey, Reynolds, Killingsworth, and McCartin.

April 2

On this date, John L. Sullivan, the Secretary of the Navy, approved the Board's recommendation concerning a MOH for Pharris. He did so by signing a recommendation beginning with classic understatement advising him about the case: "The Board has made a *thorough and prolonged* investigation of this case in review, and, in view of the additional *incontestable* evidence submitted [recommends that the Navy Cross be withdrawn and a MOH awarded]" [Italics added for emphasis]

April 6

This is the date of the letter from McCartin, now a lieutenant commander in the Naval Reserve, to the Board he wrote from the YMCA in Green Bay. Although dated after the date of Sullivan's approval of the Board's recommendation, it corroborates the statements from the other witnesses.

McCartin went to his battle station on December 7, but since his station could not meaningfully participate in defending the ship, he was asked to assist with passing ammunition for the antiaircraft guns. He found Pharris organizing a hand supply of ammunition and asked Pharris if he wanted to go topside since Pharris seemed to have difficulty with his back and problems with oil fumes in his eyes and on his legs. McCartin then learned that Pharris alone had been responsible for organizing the ammunition supply passage.

After the power ceased, Pharris used auxiliary systems to deliver some ammunition to the antiaircraft guns. He found some crewmen passing out because of the oil fumes. Although he knew that he was himself in danger of passing out, Pharris assisted in saving some crewmen before he himself passed out. Pharris was discovered and moved topside.

Pharris recovered and went back down into the ship to attempt to speed up the ammunition supply; at this time, he was weak and choking. He discovered six men unconscious and submerging in the rising oil. "At the risk of becoming a victim of the [oil] himself, he saved the men."

Around this time, Pharris, without authority or orders from higher command, counterflooded the ship, "an act which certainly was the largest single measure which kept the *California* from capsizing."

McCartin was himself overcome by oil fumes and assisted topside. McCartin recovered sufficiently to discover that Pharris had again entered one of the ship's compartments and, continuing to risk his own life, saved eleven crewmen before Pharris again passed out.

After Pharris recovered, he unloaded a misfire from one of the ship's guns and, while doing so, was injured by the muzzle blast of a nearby gun. He then went below yet again to assist in ammunition handling until a bomb blast required his removal. McCartin was also hit, lost track of Pharris, and later learned that Pharris had been taken to the hospital on Ford Island.

While he made no comment concerning the award Pharris deserved, he concluded:

It is my own opinion that Gunner Pharris was the person most responsible for the stubborn resistance put up by the California on that eventful day. To him should go a great deal of the credit for keeping the ship afloat to fight again. Most of all, he should achieve suitable recognition for the lives he saved, directly and indirectly, by his tremendous courage and complete disregard for his own life. [Italics added for emphasis]

May 1

Pharris was transferred to the retired list as a lieutenant commander as he had requested in his January 19, 1948, letter to Captain Steinhagen.[25]

May 20

A memorandum for the President, signed by Secretary of the Navy Sullivan on this date, forwarded for President Truman's signature a MOH citation for Pharris. Sullivan made no recommendation; he simply asked the president to sign the citation if he approved it. Also included was the basic correspondence concerning the MOH.

May 21

A memorandum for the President signed by his Naval aide, Robert Dennison, summarized the Pharris case, noting that after detailed study, the Board recommended that the Navy Cross be upgraded to a MOH and that the Secretary of the Navy agreed that a MOH should be awarded. Dennison recommended approval of the MOH citation.

June 3

President Truman signed the Pharris MOH citation.

A MOH IN 1948—FINALLY

The seemingly unending spiral of bureaucracy and naval correspondence ended with the president's signature on June 3 and at a ceremony in the White House Rose Garden at 12:30 p.m. on June 25, 1948, when President Harry Truman presented a MOH to Lieutenant Commander Pharris, who had already retired but was present in uniform; the shoulder boards on his uniform coat were those of the grade of a lieutenant commander. The schedule for the presentation can be seen via the website for the Harry S. Truman Library by searching for the president's schedule for that day.

With this ceremony and presentation, the MOH for December 7 had been awarded more than six years after the events warranting the MOH, events that must have been known in 1941 or 1942 given the witness statements obtained after the war.

Three questions about why Pharris did not receive a MOH during the war can be asked. They should be asked when someone as deserving as Pharris did not receive a MOH in a timely fashion—he did not receive it until 1948—yet two officers who did not deserve MOHs, Kidd and Van Valkenburgh, were Permanent Board add-ons to the Fleet Board of Awards' recommendations and received posthumous MOHs in 1942, the same year the Permanent Board added their names to the Fleet Board's list of men recommended for MOHs.

One, why were statements concerning the actions of Pharris on December 7 not obtained from the witnesses (Killingsworth, Bussey, McCartin, and Reynolds) after the attack when their memory of events would be the strongest? After all, supporting documentation must have been obtained for the original twelve MOH recommendations made by the Fleet Board of Awards (Bennion, Scott, Jones, Flaherty, Ward, Young, Fuqua, Tomich, Hill, Ross, Cannon, and Reeves). After all, the Navy Board was adamant that a MOH—at least the Pharris MOH—be based on incontrovertible or incontestable facts.

Two, if information were known and sufficient for the Fleet Board of Awards to recommend MOHs for three *California* crewmen (Jones, Reeves, and Scott), why was sufficient information not known about Pharris to support a MOH when he had done far more to earn a MOH than any of the other men from *California* recommended for a MOH? One has to wonder if Captain Bunkley's letter of January 10, 1942, was lost or ignored. He recommended Jones, Pharris, and Scott for "appropriate awards." If Jones and Scott received MOHs in part because of this letter, one must wonder why Pharris only received a Navy Cross when the content of the letter demonstrated that his actions were deserving of the same or higher award as would be appropriate for Jones and Scott.

Three, to add insult to injury, why did the endorsement of the Navy Department Permanent Board of Awards on the fleet board of awards' report add Kidd and Van Valkenburgh to the list of men recommended for MOHs without citing any support for these two MOHs? The permanent board cited no evidence to support their inclusion in the list of MOH recommendations, yet Pharris had to submit "incontrovertible facts" or "incontestable justification" supporting his MOH. Chapter 15 discusses at length the "asymmetrical" treatment of the Kidd and Van Valkenburgh cases.

Thus, on the one hand, the permanent board's endorsement simply added Kidd and Van Valkenburgh to the list of men recommended for MOHs and included proposed citations for each of the two men without any reference to supporting documentation for the MOHs (i.e., no witness statements such as those that were the lifeblood of the Pharris Navy Cross upgrade). On the other hand, a universe of information about Pharris existed and should have been known to both boards. After the war, the Navy Department Board of Decorations and Medals held the Pharris recommendation to a standard of "incontrovertible facts" and "incontestable justification"; the standard, if any, to which the permanent board held Kidd and Van Valkenburgh during the war is unclear but was certainly less rigorous than "incontrovertible facts" or "incontestable justification."

The hidebound and recalcitrant traits of the Navy were at work, as illustrated by the Navy's initial response to Bunkley's attempt to have the Navy Cross upgraded; the first endorsement of the Board of Review for Decorations and Medals of Bunkley's January 16, 1946, letter advised the Secretary of the Navy that the Navy Cross was "sufficient recognition of Lieutenant Pharris's service aboard USS *California* (BB-44) on December 7, 1941." On February 8, 1946, Secretary Forrestal concurred with the Board's opinion. Again, this decision was adding insult to injury; his Navy Cross citation is embarrassingly short and does not mention his most important action—preventing his ship from capsizing.

Apparently the tenacity and persistence of Bunkley and Pharris were the essential factors leading to the upgrade of the Navy Cross to the MOH. Also crucial was the willingness of the Board of Review for Decorations and Medals to reopen the case for whatever reason and notwithstanding its earlier conclusion that the Navy Cross was sufficient recognition for Pharris, a conclusion with which the Secretary of the Navy concurred. The trifecta of Bunkley, Pharris, and the Board uncovering witnesses to the actions of Pharris on December 7 resulted in the recommendation of a MOH for Pharris.

The Navy's reluctance to alter course, once course is set, is well known. It probably did so in the Pharris case because it simply could not ignore the overwhelming amount of evidence supporting a MOH award for Pharris. The famous Marine General Holland M. "Howlin' Mad" Smith of World War II fame seemed to have had as many battles with the U.S. Navy has he did with the Japanese Navy. He wrote in his memoir, CORAL AND BRASS, about the Navy's reluctance to change, "In the Navy, tradition never dies while there is a shot left in the locker."[26]

Fortunately for Jackson Pharris, several factors emptied that locker of all its shots in his case, and President Harry S. Truman signed the long overdue MOH citation on June 3, 1948.

MOH Citation

For conspicuous gallantry and intrepidity at the risk of his life above and beyond the call of duty while attached to the USS *California* during the surprise enemy Japanese aerial attack on Pearl Harbor, Territory of Hawaii, December 7, 1941. In charge of the ordnance repair party on the third deck when the first Japanese torpedo struck almost directly under his station, Lt. (then Gunner) Pharris was stunned and severely injured by the concussion which hurled him to the overhead and back to the deck. Quickly recovering, he acted on his own initiative to set up a hand-supply ammunition train for the antiaircraft guns. With water and oil rushing in where the port bulkhead had been torn up from the deck, with many of the remaining crewmembers overcome by oil fumes, and the ship without power and listing heavily to port as a result of a second torpedo hit, Lt. Pharris ordered the shipfitters to counterflood. Twice rendered unconscious by the nauseous fumes and handicapped by his painful injuries, he persisted in his desperate efforts to speed up the supply of ammunition and at the same time repeatedly risked his life to enter flooding compartments and drag to safety unconscious shipmates who were gradually being submerged in oil. By his inspiring leadership, his valiant efforts and his extreme loyalty to his ship and her crew, he saved many of his shipmates from death and was largely responsible for keeping the *California* in action during the attack. His heroic conduct throughout this first eventful engagement of World War II reflects the highest credit upon Lt. Pharris and enhances the finest traditions of the U.S. Naval Service.

Purple Heart Award

Pharris had also earned a Purple Heart due to the injuries he sustained on December 7.[27]

He has a gold star (in lieu of a second Purple Heart award) for injuries sustained later in the war aboard USS St. Paul. Family history reports the circumstances for the second award as follows. As the war was ending, the Japanese discovered that St. Paul's defense system was vulnerable. Specifically, suicide aircraft could dive directly toward the bridge, but the ship's five-inch guns could not elevate sufficiently to hit the aircraft. The upper elevation of the guns was such that if they fired at oncoming aircraft, the shot would hit parts of the ship's superstructure, endangering men on the bridge. On August 9, 1945, as Japanese suicide planes were attacking the bridge, Lieutenant Pharris ordered part of the bridge cleared while he stayed at his post. The concussion from the firing of a five-inch gun broke his back and ruptured his eardrum. A medical report (signed by a Navy physician) confirms the August 9 injuries.[28]

Life after Receiving the MOH

Pharris earned a degree in real estate in 1956 from the University of Southern California, Los Angeles. He also worked with a pipeline construction company.[29] Another ironic incident in a lifetime of ironies in and out of the Navy occurred in 1959 when on a construction job, he saved the life of Marshal Weigand "from a flaming trench"; in a life full of coincidences and ironies, Weigand was at Pearl Harbor on December 7. His ship? USS *California*.[30]

In yet another instance of irony and bad luck, Pharris became ill at a MOH Society banquet on October 15, 1966, and died on October 17 at the Veterans Administration hospital in Los Angeles (also called "Sawtelle") from a heart attack.[31]

THE LOSS OF THE PHARRIS MOH: ESCHEATING

The Pharris MOH saga would be incomplete without one last irony and one last instance of bad luck, irony not involving Pharris personally but the MOH itself. The irony was the disappearance, albeit temporary, of his MOH, the very MOH that required so much effort and time to obtain and was the last December 7 MOH to be awarded.

The causes of the problem were two. First, the surviving family members did not know the location of the Pharris MOH or Navy Cross. Second, California state law and officials, rather than facilitating the discovery and return of safe deposit articles to the family, were impediments to the family's attempt to locate the MOH and the Navy Cross.

The following account of the disappearance and recovery is from information from various sources, including Mindy Pharris, the wife of Jackson Pharris II, son of Lieutenant Commander Pharris.[32]

After Lieutenant Commander Pharris died, his wife had his MOH and Navy Cross. When Mrs. Pharris became ill, one of the daughters (Janet) placed the medals in a safe deposit box in a bank. In 2002, Janet died; her mother died months later. Unfortunately, Janet's death triggered an ordeal for the family. The surviving children could not find the two medals among the family's possessions and did not know they were in the safe deposit box.

The medals remained in Janet's safe deposit box for three years at which time the bank, as state law required, surrendered its contents to the California state government as unclaimed property since, upon the death of the sister, the rental payments for the safe deposit box stopped. In addition to not knowing about the safe deposit box, the family did not know about the cessation of the payment of fees for the box, so the fees for the safe deposit box were not paid. Because of the fees were not paid, the contents of the box were surrendered to the California state government via a legal process termed "escheating."

Mindy Pharris eventually found and visited the bank that had the safe deposit box. The bank could not determine the location of the safe deposit box's contents, most likely because, in the process of "escheating," the contents were in transit to the state government.

Mindy Pharris contacted the state government to determine how the family could obtain the contents of the safe deposit box. The matter was dormant until early 2006, when Jack Pharris, son of Jackson Pharris, read an article in a local paper regarding unclaimed property held by the state government.

The Pharris family again attempted to contact the state government. The family found on the state government's website a safety deposit box listed under the name of Janet Pharris, but the contents were not listed.

Mindy Pharris attempted to complete the paperwork required to regain possession of the box's contents, but the process was so complicated that delay ensued. Months later, when she checked the state website, she did not find the safe deposit box listed. She contacted the state government and was told that after someone starts the process of claiming the property, the items are removed from the website. She was also told that since she was not entitled to the property, she would not be provided any information about the claim.

Even at this point, no one knew if the MOH was in the safe deposit box, so the family set the project aside. Until August of 2007, California law prohibited the state controller's office from contacting the owners of unclaimed property.

In 2007, a federal judge ruled that the state's efforts to contact the owners of unclaimed property were insufficient. The state controller, at a news conference in August 2007, announced that he was taking actions to contact owners of unclaimed property. He mentioned various items of such property, including one MOH.

The formal return of the MOH was on October 2, 2007, at a ceremony at Naval Amphibious Base, Coronado, California. The officer returning the MOH was Commander, Naval Surface Forces, Vice Admiral Terrance T. Etnyre.[33]

As a practical matter, one must ask how any bank or state official could be so unintelligent or naïve that he or she would not recognize or identify a MOH, especially when the name of the MOH recipient is engraved on the reverse of the MOH. The official, even if he or she did not recognize a MOH, should have seen, with the most cursory inspection, the engraved name, and one would think that the person would have sufficient intelligence to ask an expert what the object was and what its importance was.

But the author can empathize with the Pharris family since his own family almost lost property via escheatment when the fees for a safe deposit box were inadvertently unpaid.

Summary: The Pharris MOH

As can be concluded from the discussion of the upgrading of the Pharris Navy Cross to a MOH, the story of Pharris's MOH is noteworthy for five reasons. The context of the story is mystery, delay, bureaucracy, and bad luck. The context is also persistence and tenacity in the face of the famous recalcitrance for which the navy is known—an unwillingness to change a position or decision in the face of overwhelming facts proving the position or decision was or is wrong. Why the Navy Board did change its position that the Navy Cross was sufficient recognition and initiate investigation leading to the MOH is unknown. And the context is that Pharris is arguably one of the most deserving of all the December 7 MOH recipients, an officer who was the epitome of courage and cool, clear thinking in the worst possible circumstances.

One, he was the last December 7 recipient to receive his MOH. He did not receive it until July 25, 1948, a few months short of seven years after the attack.

Two, why he was not nominated for, and why he did not receive, a MOH during the war is a mystery. The January 10, 1942, letter from the ship's Commanding Officer praised Pharris and two other *California* crew members. The other two received posthumous MOHs in 1942, but Pharris's name was among the list of those recommended by the fleet board and permanent board in 1942 to receive a Navy Cross, not a MOH. Witnesses from the crew who saw what Pharris did on December 7 could be found after the war, long after they had transferred from *California* and moved to different places; once located, they could provide sufficient information to ensure that the Pharris Navy Cross was upgraded to a MOH. One wonders why this information could or was not obtained from these same witnesses in early 1942 when they were presumably still aboard the ship. In other words, if the witness statements could be obtained after the war, one wonders why they could not be obtained during the war. The result of not obtaining the statements until after the war led to the omission of Pharris from the list of the fourteen men recommended for MOHs for December 7 submitted to President Roosevelt in March 1942.

Three, he received a MOH only after his former commanding officer aboard *California* launched a postwar campaign, beginning in 1946, to obtain the MOH for him.

Four, the Navy is the most recalcitrant of the armed forces and the least likely to change a position or decision after making or adopting it. For the Navy to recommend a MOH to replace the Navy Cross originally awarded to Pharris is unusual. Why the Navy reopened the case is a mystery, especially after the Board of Review for Decorations and Medals initially stopped the Bunkley effort cold by advising the Secretary of the Navy that the Navy Cross was "sufficient recognition of Lieutenant Pharris's service aboard USS *California* (BB-44) on December 7 1941," an opinion approved by the Secretary of the Navy. An example of the Navy's recalcitrance is the removal of the court-martial conviction of Captain Charles McVey from his record; he was convicted in the (in)famous case of the loss of the USS Indianapolis. The Navy acted only after years of pressure and effort from politicians and members of the general public.

Finally, as explained previously, through the unique circumstances involving Pharris and the MOH, the MOH itself would be lost to the family from 2002 to 2007.

Unless visitors to Arlington National Cemetery have read this book, when they view the tombstone of Jackson Pharris—assuming they can find it—they will have no idea of the pain, sacrifice, and effort that led to the few, simple gilded inscriptions on the tombstone that they see before them, that of a man who was, to say the least, indefatigable on December 7, 1941: "MEDAL OF HONOR" and "PH & GS" for

Purple Heart and Gold Star (second award).

NOTES

1. The National Personnel Records Center, St. Louis, Missouri, furnished military and personal information from Pharris's Official Military Personnel File (OMPF) at the author's request (hereafter "Pharris OMPF").

2. Ibid.; endnote 18, J. W. Bunkley, Rear Admiral, United States Navy, Retired, MILITARY and NAVAL RECOGNITION BOOK (D. Van Nostrand Company, Inc., New York, NY, 1943) (hereafter "Bunkley, MILITARY and NAVAL RECOGNITION BOOK"). The duties of the gunner's mate and the turret captain are found at pages 141 and 144, respectively.

3. The National Personnel Records Center, St. Louis, Missouri, furnished military and personal information from Pharris's Official Military Personnel File (OMPF) at the author's request (hereafter "Pharris OMPF"); endnote 2, Bunkley, MILITARY and NAVAL RECOGNITION BOOK. The duties of a gunner warrant officer are at page 138.

4. Endnote 3, Pharris OMPF.

5. Report from USS *California* (Subject: Report of Raid, December 7, 1941) of December 13, 1941 (hereafter "*California* report").

6. Report from USS *California* (Subject: "Report of Raid (Revised), December 7, 1941") of December 22, 1941 (hereafter "*California* report (Revised)").

7. Letter from commanding officer, USS *California*, to Commander in Chief, U.S. Fleet (Subject: "Awards of Medals for Heroic Conduct during the Raid on Pearl Harbor, December 7, 1941; Recommendations Concerning) of January 10, 1942, paragraph 2 (hereafter "*California* awards letter").

8. The Roosevelt approval of MOH citations is based on documents provided to the author by the Franklin D. Roosevelt Presidential Library and Museum.

9. Endnote 7, *California* awards letter.

10. Endnote 5, *California* report.

11. Endnote 6, *California* report (Revised).

12. Endnote 7, *California* awards letter.

13. After the Army Air Forces became a separate service, the U.S. Air Force, after World War II, Congress established an Air Force Cross (AFC) for Air Force personnel, the equivalent of the Navy Cross for the Naval service.

14. Third Endorsement QB-4-OS from the Senior Member, Navy Department Permanent Board of Awards to the Secretary of the Navy, "Subject: Japanese Attack on US Pacific Fleet in Pearl Harbor 7 Dec. 1941—Recommendations for Awards for Gallant Conduct in Action of Naval and Civilian Personnel"; the Third Endorsement can be found in the Kidd OMPF on a compact disc (see endnote 7 in Chapter 7 (*Arizona*) and endnote 1 in Chapter 15 (Undeserved MOHs) for more details on the Third Endorsement); the Pharris Navy Cross recommendation is on page 2 of the endorsement (frame 41 of the CD).

15. Documentation provided by the Harry S. Truman Library to the author in 2008.

16. Ibid.

17. Ibid.

18. Endnote 3, the Pharris OMPF documents a Purple Heart with a Gold Star (second award).

19. E-mail from Mindy Pharris to the author of February 18, 2009, with an attachment, "Pharris MOH Clarification," containing a chronology and other information (hereafter "Mindy Pharris e-mail").

20. Ibid.; the OMPF confirms a Purple Heart with one Gold Star; endnote 19, Mindy Pharris e-mail.

21. Division of Public Inquiries, United States Government Manual (Office of War Information, Washington, DC, 1945), 297.

22. Letter from Rear Admiral J. W. Bunkley of January 16, 1946, with enclosure referenced in a memorandum from the Senior Member, Board of Review for Decorations and Medals to the Secretary of the Navy (Subject: "Recommended for Medal of Honor for Lieutenant Jackson C. Pharris, US Navy in lieu of Navy Cross") of February 1, 1946.

23. Ibid.; for the awards board name change, see Jane Blakeney, Heroes: US Marine Corps 1861 *1955 (Guthrie Lithograph Co., Inc., Washington, DC, 1957), 4.

24. "United States Navy Regulations" (1920, reprinted in 1941).

25. Endnote 3, Pharris OMPF.

26. General Holland M. Smith, U.S. Marine Corps (Retired), CORAL AND BRASS (The Battery Press, Inc. 2004, Nashville, TN, reprint of 1948 edition), 93.

27. Endnote 3, Pharris OMPF.

28. Endnote 19, Mindy Pharris e-mail.

29. "Lt. Cmdr. Pharris Dies; Medal of Honor Winner," Evening Star, October 25, 1966, B-4.

30. Ashley Ratcliff, "Medal of Honor Keeps Hill Family's Legacy Alive," Palos Verdes Peninsula News, October 8, 2007, printed from the Internet September 2, 2008; "Hill" refers to Rolling Hills Estates, where the Pharris family lived.

31. "…Winner Jackson Pharris Dies" [first part of title cannot be read], Los Angeles Times, October 18, 1966, Part I, page 21.

32. Endnote 19, Mindy Pharris e-mail; Alex Roth, "WWII Medal of Honor Winner's Family Finally Regains Decoration," San Diego Union-Tribune, October 3, 2007, printed from the Internet September 2, 2008; author's familiarity as a lawyer with the process of escheating (the author's family experienced a similar problem).

33. Mass Communication Specialist First Class Paula M. Ludwick, "COMNAVSURFOR Hosts Medal of Honor Ceremony," Navy.mil (October 4, 2007), printed from the Internet September 1, 2008.

Photograph
USS California MOH Recipient

Warrant Officer (Gunner) Jackson Pharris, U.S. Navy, as a lieutenant. (Photograph NH 106422 from the Naval History and Heritage Command.)

Presentation of MOHs on June 25, 1948, by President Harry S. Truman, with Jackson Pharris, a retired lieutenant commander, at far left having just received his MOH. (Photograph NH 80-G-705728 from the Naval History and Heritage Command.)

Chapter 20
The Mitchell Medal of Honor—
The Golden Apology

Brigadier General Billy Mitchell, U.S. Army

As mentioned in chapters 2 and 3, Brigadier General and then Mr. William (Billy) Mitchell was the leading advocate in the United States for military aviation beginning in World War I until his death in 1936. He was a veteran of World War I, having flown in combat as an Army officer and pilot (military aviation other than that of the Navy and Marine Corps was under the Army since the Air Force was not a separate service until 1947). He was promoted from colonel to brigadier general upon assuming the title of Assistant Chief of the Air Service; after leaving that billet, he reverted to his permanent grade of colonel. He resigned from the army in 1926 after being court-martialed in 1925 for making statements criticizing the military after an airship crashed, killing fourteen crewmen. Legislation in 1930 permitted him to bear the title of his highest grade in wartime, which was brigadier general, thus permitting him to be addressed by that grade.[1]

The Navy officers especially hated Mitchell (derisively calling him "Admiral" Mitchell) because of his idea that ships—especially the Navy's prized battleships—were vulnerable to air attack, an idea he proved with his aerial bombing trials in the 1920s, which successfully sank ships, trials that the navy tried to stop and, failing to do so, tried to impede.[2]

As mentioned in Chapter 3, the caption of the photograph of *Arizona* in the November 1941 program for the Army-Navy football game ironically captures the Navy's insulting intransigence and arrogance aimed at "air enthusiasts," such as Mitchell, although his name is not mentioned—it did not have to be. The caption? "It is significant that despite the claims of air enthusiasts no battleship has yet been sunk by bombs." Japan corrected the caption to read, "Billy Mitchell's assertion that battleships could be sunk by aerial bombs was proven to the Navy at Pearl Harbor."

Mitchell is included in this book because he spoke out about airpower as a danger to the United States and a danger to the enemies of the United States on the receiving end. He tried to warn the U.S. military that Japan would attack Oahu by air and that Oahu's defenses were inadequate. As to be explained, he also received a special MOH, in part a belated acknowledgment that his ignored warning and observation were correct.

Chapters 2 and 3 also noted how, long before December 7, Mitchell tried in two ways to warn a recalcitrant, hidebound military (particularly the Navy) that airpower was superior to naval power and that Oahu would be attacked, but he may as well have been talking to a wall—it would have paid more attention than the Army or the Navy.

The first warning was his ship-sinking tests in the 1920s proving the vulnerability of ships to aerial attack. The irony is that on December 7, the Japanese used Mitchell's precedent to attack ships by aircraft, and at Midway in 1942, U.S. Navy aircraft flying from aircraft carriers sank four Japanese aircraft carriers. Marine and Army aircraft from Midway also attacked Japanese ships. The Japanese in turn crippled one of two American aircraft carriers, but they failed to capture Midway. Mitchell did not sink ships in combat conditions, but in effect, December 7 and Midway were ship-sinking "trials" in such conditions.

The second warning was a result of his trip to the Far East and to Hawaii in the 1920s, resulting in a prediction (the United States would fight Japan in a war beginning with an aerial assault on Pearl Harbor carrier aircraft) and an observation (that the defense of Hawaii against aerial attack was inadequate).

If the military had heeded his warnings, would any difference have been made?

Answering a hypothetical question is dangerous. The or a correct answer can never be given with certainty. But one must wonder if more and better antiaircraft defenses on Oahu and on ships would have mitigated the attack, thus saving the lives of some or all of the ten of the fifteen Oahu MOH recipients who died on December 7 as well as other service members perishing that day.

While the Japanese attack was not in hypothetical conditions and was not an academic or practical exercise to prove the truth of Billy Mitchell's predictions or the value of his ideas about airpower, the attack vindicated him, in particular his predictions about a Japanese attack on Oahu, its weak defenses, and his adamant belief that aircraft could sink ships even in protected harbors. To think that the Japanese did not study his ideas before and during their planning of the December 7 attack is to live in a world of fantasy.

One thinks of that piercingly insulting caption in the Army-Navy football program, mentioned earlier in this chapter, printed just days before December 7, the caption ridiculing "air enthusiasts." One wonders what type of caption Mitchell would have written beside a photograph of a battleship attacked and sunk on December 7. One wonders what type of caption the Japanese would have written after December 7.

Finally, one must remember that the battleship's main reason for being was its big guns. Those guns, designed to slug it out with other ships at sea in classic naval surface warfare, were useless against air attack on December 7. As noted earlier, even if such guns could be elevated toward aircraft, the close proximity of the ships in Pearl Harbor would have made firing them impractical and dangerous. And such guns lacked ammunition made especially for use against aircraft, such as a "beehive" round (in effect, making the gun a huge shotgun).

But as Mitchell would have known, the most important guns on December 7 aboard ship were antiaircraft guns. The importance of keeping those guns firing can be seen in the MOH citations for three *California* MOH recipients: Pharris, Jones, and Reeves. As seen in Chapters 4 (*California*) and 19 (Pharris) and Appendix A, their MOH citations noted their efforts to ensure antiaircraft gun ammunition was supplied from below decks to the guns above decks, at times by hand when mechanical hoists were damaged or inoperable.

The Mitchell MOH: The Golden Apology

After House Subcommittee hearings on May 31, 1945, Congress enacted private legislation in 1946 authorizing a special medal for Mitchell. Germany had surrendered, but war with Japan continued. The title to the legislation read as follows:

An Act

Authorizing the President of the United States to award posthumously in the name of Congress a Medal of Honor to William Mitchell.

The first section of the legislation read:

Be it enacted by the Senate and House of Representatives of the United States of America in Congress assembled, That the President of the United States is requested to cause a gold medal to be struck, with suitable emblems, devices, and inscriptions, to be presented to the late William Mitchell, formerly a colonel, United States Army, *in recognition of his outstanding pioneering service and foresight in the field of American military aviation.*[3] [Italics added for emphasis.]

Although "Medal of Honor" is in the header of the legislation, the medal is not the classic MOH awarded for combat bravery (the legislation did not mention Mitchell's combat service in World War I) and does not resemble such MOHs. It was for presentation to his son since Mitchell died in 1936. It is generally considered an apology for the military ignoring Mitchell's ideas before the war concerning the importance of military aviation.

President Truman signed the act on August 8, 1946, ironically one day short of a year after the United States dropped a second atomic bomb on Japan, the ultimate demonstration of the power of an air force. The MOH was presented to his son, William, Jr., in 1948.[4]

The inscription on the obverse of the medal is "BRIGADIER GENERAL WILLIAM MITCHELL." The figure on the front is that of an aviator with leather cap, goggles, and scarf; the reverse is a star and an eagle with this inscription:

> AWARD OF THE CONGRESS
> AUGUST 8, 1946
> FOR OUTSTANDING
> PIONEER SERVICE AND
> FORESIGHT IN FIELD [SIC]
> OF AMERICAN MILITARY
> AVIATION[5]

Mitchell's medal differs in three respects from the MOHs awarded to the other men discussed in this book.

First, seventeen (fifteen on Oahu, one at Midway in 1941, and one at Midway 1942) men mentioned in this book received classic MOHs for combat bravery, MOHs the President approved based on recommendations from field commands; they were not the result of Congressional action. Although the eighteenth MOH was a noncombat MOH, Petty Officer Second Class Hammerberg's MOH was still a classic MOH approved by the President without Congressional action. The Congressional legislation just cited authorized Mitchell's MOH.

Second, as noted earlier, his medal is a special gold MOH that does not resemble the MOHs the other men discussed in this book received.

Finally, his MOH is generally considered an apology for the military ignoring Mitchell's ideas before the war concerning the importance of military aviation. The other MOH awards discussed in this book were not apologies or awards for general contributions to or for foresight in national defense. With the exception of the Kidd and Van Valkenburgh MOHs, they were MOHs recognizing proven combat bravery (or in the case of Hammerberg, noncombat bravery), the very reason for the classic MOH. No other conclusion than advocacy and apology concerning the reason for Mitchell's MOH can be reached from reading the record of the Subcommittee's hearing concerning the Mitchell MOH; the hearing is discussed later in this chapter.

It should be noted that, despite its title in the legislation heading as a MOH, it is also considered a Congressional Gold Medal, although that nomenclature is not used in the legislation.[6]

THE MITCHELL COURT-MARTIAL

It should be noted also that the MOH was not a corrective measure aimed at his 1925 court-martial conviction. In the next section, a member of the House of Representatives makes clear that the subcommittee hearings leading to the Mitchell MOH were not meant to relitigate his court-martial. But the court-martial looms in the background, and one may view it in one of two ways. One, it could be considered the means by which the military finally got Mitchell. Two, one could view it as a self-inflicted wound, the price of Mitchell shooting himself in the foot by publicly criticizing the military—he did so while a member of the military, thereby violating military law in the eyes of the members (military jurors) trying him at his court-martial. Regardless of viewpoint, after the court-martial, the military got what it wanted: Billy Mitchell out of the service, albeit by his own choice (resignation).

He was charged at the court with violating Article 96 of the Articles of War. The Articles of War, which were the criminal statutes governing the conduct of members of the Army, were the forerunner of the Uniform Code of Military Justice (UCMJ), the current military criminal law governing all the services.[7]

Article 96 was the general article, a catchall article, covering offenses not prohibited by a specific article (for example, spying has its own article in the Articles of War and in the UCMJ and therefore does not fall under the general article). Article

96, similar to today's UCMJ general article (Article 134), covered "all disorders and neglects to the prejudice of good order and military discipline" and all conduct that brought "discredit upon the military service." Crimes charged under either general article must be noncapital.[8]

Mitchell was charged under Article 96 for making statements criticizing the Navy Department and War Department concerning the crash of the dirigible Shenandoah. His statements were considered conduct prejudicing good order and discipline and insubordination, as well as contemptuous, disrespectful, and intended to discredit the service.[9]

The court-martial panel (jury) comprised six major generals (including Douglas MacArthur) and six brigadiers. Interestingly, one of the court-martial members (jurors) was Major General Charles Summerall, who was the Army commander in Hawaii when Mitchell issued his report criticizing the defenses in Hawaii. Summerall challenged the report. For that reason, Mitchell challenged Summerall's presence as a member of the court-martial on the grounds of bias; Summerall asked to be and was excused as a member of the panel.[10]

Mitchell was found guilty and suspended from duty, without pay or allowances, for five years. President Calvin Coolidge approved the findings of guilty but mitigated the sentence by suspending all allowances and restoring one-half of the forfeiture of pay for the five years, but Mitchell resigned in 1926, thinking he could campaign for airpower more effectively as a civilian.[11] The court-martial sentence did not affect his grade of colonel. He was a colonel at the time of the trial and resignation, which was his permanent grade. He had been a brigadier general until 1925, when he administratively reverted to his permanent grade of colonel. Since he may be properly addressed by his highest grade held, he would be addressed as a brigadier general.[12]

MacArthur is thought to have been the sole vote of the court-martial panel for acquittal. An irony and connection to Hampton Roads is that MacArthur, who himself would receive a MOH in World War II and was the son of a Civil War MOH recipient, is buried in downtown Norfolk at the MacArthur Memorial, not far from Hampton Roads, the site of the birth of naval aviation.[13]

Mitchell's son tried to have the court-martial conviction removed from his father's record by petitioning the Air Force Board for Correction of Military Records. Congress created for each service such a board to correct a military record to remove errors or injustices. The board recommended that the conviction be removed, but the board's action was just that: a recommendation for the Secretary of the Air Force, who by law makes the final decision on a petition to the board. The Secretary disapproved the Board's recommendation.[14]

The author has seen the 1955 movie made about the court-martial, starring Gary Cooper as Billy Mitchell, The Court-Martial of Billy Mitchell. In the Movies Unlimited catalog for March 2016, the movie is offered for sale and summarized in part, "By 1925, an enraged military brass saw to his demotion, as well as his secret court-martial for insubordination." The errors are as follows. He was reduced from brigadier to colonel as an administrative measure, not as punishment, and his court-martial was by no means secret (the movie itself reveals no effort to keep the trial a secret).

Congressional Hearings for the MOH for Mitchell, the Prophet without Honor, and the Bitterest Cup

Notwithstanding the court-martial conviction and sentence, Mitchell's supporters tried to obtain for him recognition for his advocacy of aviation; the recognition desired was a MOH. The record of Subcommittee Number Eight of the [House] Committee on Military Affairs gives insight into the MOH itself, the politics that can influence granting or denying a MOH, and the problems Mitchell encountered in advocating air power, the force that on December 7 devastated the fleet at Pearl Harbor and riddled Oahu.

Representative A. Willis Robertson, Mitchell's friend, spoke in favor of the bill, which he sponsored. He noted the importance of Mitchell's ideas about airpower and how the Japanese, whom the United States had regarded as militarily inferior, had struck Pearl Harbor by airpower the United States lacked and "it took us a year to get it."[15]

Robertson made two important points. One, although Congress delegated to the president the authority to award MOHs, it retained the power to itself award MOHs by legislation to honor noncombat aviation achievements, such as those by Captain Charles Lindbergh, U.S. Army Air Corps Reserve, for his solo flight from New York to Paris, and Commander Robert Byrd, U.S. Navy, for his flight over the North Pole.[16] Two, Robertson, himself an officer, "in the last war," did not want to relitigate Mitchell's court-martial, although he thought the sentence was harsh. As noted earlier, Mitchell had been convicted at a court-martial in 1925 for criticizing the military after and concerning a fatal airship crash.[17]

After reading a letter from Mitchell's aide during World War I supporting a MOH as an apology by the nation to Mitchell, Robertson said, "Mitchell was a prophet without honor in his day and time," and stated that his views on airpower had been "fully justified."[18]

Robertson said that "our boys" were being hurt on Okinawa in 1945 because the Japanese were in caves and had to be defeated in "a bloody undertaking." "So I am primarily interested in our frank acknowledgment of the value of airpower."[19]

Mr. E. G. B. Riley stated at the hearings that the author of the 1941 book *Winged Warfare*, General H. H. Arnold, commanding the Army Air Forces in World War II, wrote that only three well-known military leaders came away from World War I "with a conviction that a new weapon vital to modern warfare, had come into existence, and that the airplane was that weapon." One was Mitchell; one was Hermann Goering, the commander of Germany's air force in World War II; and one was Admiral W. S. Sims, U.S. Navy.[20]

The Subcommittee received numerous letters supporting the MOH, including a letter from World War I ace Eddie Rickenbacker, based on Mitchell's World War I service and his advocacy of airpower. Rickenbacker himself earned a MOH in World War I.[21]

The Subcommittee addressed opposition to a MOH for Mitchell not from the Navy Department but the War Department, which comprised the Army and the Army's air assets since the Air Force had not yet been created as a separate service. As expected, the War Department vehemently objected to a MOH for Mitchell, stating that the award should be limited, as prescribed by statute, to combat bravery and that an award without such basis would "alter the whole scheme of military decoration." The War Department report stated that statutes required combat bravery for a MOH award.[22]

But the Subcommittee, and rightly so, disagreed with the War Department's positions, citing other noncombat MOHs, including a MOH for Adolphus Greely for a "life of splendid public service" and two other MOHs for noncombat (Lindbergh and Byrd).[23]

The Subcommittee also disagreed with the War Department's position that an award to Mitchell would depart from the statutory requirements for a MOH and thus "alter the whole scheme of military decoration." The subcommittee felt that the noncombat awards Congress authorized for Lindbergh and Byrd did not "alter the whole scheme of military decoration."[24]

In summary, Riley stated,

Every day [of the war with Japan] serves to demonstrate more thoroughly that air power has been the determining factor in winning the European war and that if Gen. William Mitchell's repeated specific warnings had been heeded the disaster of Pearl Harbor would have been avoided and many lives lost in World War II would have been spared.[25]

The Subcommittee received a chronological history from J. V. McClintic for Mitchell spanning 1919 to 1942; much of it concerned the Navy's ridicule and dismissal of Mitchell's ideas. The entry for January 30, 1921, noted that the Navy had ridiculed Mitchell and called him "Admiral" Mitchell. Secretary of the Navy Josephus Daniels "said that if the 'admiral' can't drop bombs from the air more effectively than he explodes them in committee meetings, I would like to maneuver a battleship myself and let him try out dropping bombs on same." He also added that a later secretary of the navy, Curtis Wilbur, "said that he would be willing to stand on the deck of a battleship and let Mitchell drop a 2,000-bomb from the air on same."[26]

The McClintic statement also had this line: "The bitterest cup a person has to drink out of is the cup of defeat."[27]

At the end of the hearing documentation is a summary of the ship sinkings. The Army and Navy ridiculed Mitchell when he confidently told Congress he could sink any ship afloat with aircraft. When the Navy opposed the tests, Congress authorized the President to provide vessels obtained from Germany after World War I for bombing trials. The summary noted that the navy, in the written agreement governing the tests, made the tests as difficult as possible, placing the ships almost beyond the range of Mitchell's aircraft.[28]

A joint Army-Navy board observing the tests, headed by General of the Armies John J. Pershing of World War I fame, concluded that aircraft carrying adequate ordnance had the ability to sink or to damage seriously any ship then in service and that building any type of ship to withstand attack from the air, with the largest bombs aircraft could carry, would be difficult if not impossible.[29]

The hearings revealed that Mitchell had, to say the least, alienated the military establishment. For example, on May 22, 1927, he called "old-fashioned types of maneuvers and plans for war as sponsored by the Army and Navy as being representative of the 'bow and arrow' period."[30]

But the sentiment of those at the hearing and those submitting documents supported Mitchell. In written remarks, Robertson wrote that the committee knew better than him [Robertson] the role of aviation "in this war," so he thought pointless any explanation by him concerning "how much better prepared we would have been to fight and win this war [World War II] had we followed the advice given us by General Mitchell a quarter of a century ago." He later stated, "We know that we would have been far better off if we had adopted his views 25 years before we did."[31]

The chronology mentioned above stated that the press, after December 7, noted that two events made Americans take notice of what Mitchell had said twenty years earlier: Pearl Harbor and the sinking by Japanese aircraft of the British capital ships Prince of Wales and Repulse. The press headlines were screaming: "Mitchell's Air Prophecy Comes to Grim Fruition."[32]

Perhaps the best summary is in Mitchell's own words. In his 1925 book, Winged Defense, he made two observations that would prove true after December 7 for the United States; the Germans and British had already proven the first one true when fighting each other before the United States entered the war.

The first was "neither armies nor navies can exist unless the air is controlled over them."

The second was "changes in military systems come about only through the pressure of public opinion or disaster in war."[33]

Another of his opinions should be considered. In 1933, he said that "only air power can oppose air power."[34]

Finally, one should remember that a German Ju 87 Stuka, a dive bomber, dropped the first aerial bomb of World War II on September 1, 1939—while flying over Poland.[35]

The ultimate irony? The Navy named a ship for Mitchell but certainly not an aircraft carrier. USS General William Mitchell (AP-114) was a transport ship.[36]

More information about Mitchell is at the Billy Mitchell Addendum at page 548.

NOTES

1. Hearings [May 31, 1945] before Subcommittee No. 8 of the Committee on Military Affairs, House of Representatives, Seventy-Ninth Congress, First Session on H.R. 2227 and Other Bills [authorizing the president to award a posthumous MOH in the name of Congress to William Mitchell] (Washington, DC: US Government Printing Office, 1945) (hereafter "Mitchell hearings").
Combat service: Mitchell hearings, pages 15–16, of note are pages 35–36, remarks by General of the Armies John J. Pershing; resignation from army: Mitchell Hearings, page 30; promotion to colonel: Walter J. Boyne, "The St. Mihiel Salient," AIR FORCE MAGAZINE (February 2000), 78; promotion to brigadier general and finality of that grade: Roger G. Miller, Billy Mitchell: "Stormy Petrel of the Air (Office of Air Force History, Washington, DC, 2004), 53–54; airship crash and Mitchell statement and court-martial: "Statement of William Mitchell Concerning the Recent Air Accidents" (Brigadier General William Mitchell Statement to the Press, San Antonio, September 5, 1925); "The Keeper File," AIR FORCE MAGAZINE (July 2006); a summary of Mitchell's statement is at page 28, which gives instructions on accessing the complete statement.

2. Mitchell hearings, 29.

3. The legislation is Private Law 884, Seventy-Ninth Congress (Second Session), approved August 8, 1946.

4. Roger Burlingame, General Billy Mitchell: Champion of Air Defense (McGraw-Hill Book Company, Inc., New York, NY, 1952), 187–188.

5. Printing of photograph of front and back of Mitchell MOH from the U.S. Air Force Museum on February 26, 2003.

6. The Internet site maintained by the Office of the Historian, U.S. House of Representatives, lists Brigadier General William Mitchell as a recipient of a Congressional Gold Medal (CGM). E-mail of May 2, 2016, to the author from the Office of the Historian, U.S. House of Representatives, confirms that it is a CGM.

7. For an overall view of the court-martial, see John T. Correll, "The Billy Mitchell Court-Martial," AIR FORCE MAGAZINE (August 2012), 62–66 (hereafter, Correll, Mitchell Court-Martial); author's knowledge of military law.

8. John A. McComsey and Morris O. Edwards, The Soldier and the Law, Second Ed. (The Military Service Publishing Co., Harrisburg, PA, 1943), 438; author's knowledge of military law.

9. Endnote 1, Airship crash and Mitchell statement and court-martial.

10. H. Paul Jeffers, Billy Mitchell: The Life, Times, and Battles of America's Prophet of Air Power (Zenith Press, St. Paul, MN, 2005), 235. Correll erroneously writes in "Mitchell Court-Martial" (page 64) that the court comprised twelve senior generals. The correct term for the collective of officers in the grades of brigadier to general is "general officers." To have twelve "generals" would mean to have twelve four-star officers, which was clearly not the compostion of the Mitchell court-martial board.

11. Correll, "Mitchell Court-Martial," 66.

12. Endnote 1, Resignation from army and promotion to colonel.

13. Correll, Mitchell Court-Martial, 66; the author has visited the MacArthur Memorial in Norfolk, VA, numerous times.

14. Ibid., 66.

15. Mitchell hearings, 2–6.

16. Ibid., 3, 8, and 23.

17. Ibid., 3.

18. Ibid., 5.

19. Ibid.

20. Ibid., 10.

21. Ibid., 11 and 21.

22. Ibid., 28.

23. Ibid., 8.

24. Ibid., 23.

25. Ibid., 25.

26. Ibid., 29 (Daniels) and 31 (Wilbur).

27. Ibid., 32.

28. Ibid., 38.

29. Ibid.

30. Ibid., 30.

31. Ibid., 2 (written statement) and 6 (oral statement).

32. Ibid., 31.

33. William Mitchell, Winged Defense (G.P. Putnam's Sons, New York, NY, 1925), xv (armies) and xvii (changes).

34. Endnote 1, Mitchell hearings, 30.

35. Zaur Eylanbekov, "Airpower Classics" (Ju 87 Stuka), AIR FORCE MAGAZINE (April 2008), 88.

36. NavSource Online: Service Ship Photo Archive (accessed September 5, 2016). See also Appendix B.

Photograph: Billy Mitchell

Billy Mitchell (NavSource Online: Service Ship Photo Archive.)

Part VII

Memories–Lists of Names

Chapter 21
Legacy—Men

What was the fate of the MOH recipients who are the subjects of this book? Since none of them are alive today, how they are remembered and honored is important.

This Chapter is an overview of what happened to the MOH recipients and their legacies—how they are remembered or commemorated. The Chapter is intended for the average reader; readers desiring more detail should consult Appendix B for information about ships named for the MOH recipients and Appendix C for more detailed information about graves and memorials. Photographs of the graves and memorials are at the end of Appendix C.

The author has seen in person every grave and memorial mentioned in this chapter with the following exceptions: the graves of Bennion, Finn, and Hammerberg; the "In Memory of" markers for Flaherty, Fleming, Ross, Van Valkenburgh, and Young; and the inscription for Young at Manila American Cemetery in the Philippines.

The recipients and their legacies can be classified many ways. The author has chosen to divide the MOH recipients into two broad categories: men who survived the war and men who did not. Photographs of the ways they are remembered are at Appendix C.

Of the four men who survived the war, three were buried. These men have graves and tombstones. One was cremated and has an "In Memory of" (IMO) marker, which is in effect a tombstone marking an empty grave.

Those who did not survive the war can be further classified into two categories.

One is recipients whose bodies were recovered. These men have graves and tombstones. The other is the recipients whose bodies were not recovered. Universally, they are formally commemorated by having their names inscribed at memorials for the missing superintended by the American Battle Monuments Commission (ABMC), which supervises U.S. military cemeteries overseas. The ABMC's Courts or Tablets of the Missing commemorate those whose bodies were unrecovered because they were missing in action; they were killed or died of wounds, but their bodies were unrecovered; they were killed or died of wounds and buried at sea; or their bodies were donated to medical science. Their MOH status is indicated by the gilded lettering of their names and a gilded MOH symbol. The ABMC superintends only one site in the United States: the Honolulu Memorial at Punchbowl with its Courts of the Missing (the Veterans Administration superintends Punchbowl's cemetery).

Each of these men may also have an IMO as another means of remembrance.

Under each category are other means of remembering or honoring the MOH recipients.

★ ★ ★ ★ ★ ★ ★ ★ ★ ★

The Mechanics of Death Notification

In a sense, the documented legacy of the MOH recipients who were killed or lost in action began with the infamous death telegram, the telegram no family wanted to receive, the one with this phrase at the beginning: "deeply regret(s) to inform you..." A family was notified of the death of a service member by such a telegram delivered by a civilian messenger; today such notification would be like notifying a family by e-mail, a process which would be, to say the least, impersonal, barbaric, and horrifying.

But during the war, the number of casualties made impractical notification in person by service members of the deceased's service.

Two examples will suffice, showing that in death notification, the families of senior officers and junior officers were treated equally.

The first example is for Captain Franklin Van Valkenburgh, the Commanding Officer, USS *Arizona*; a carbon copy of the telegram is found in his Official Military Personnel File. The telegram was addressed to his widow and signed by Rear Admiral C. W. Nimitz, Chief of the Bureau of Navigation. The telegram stated the Navy Department

...DEEPLY REGRETS TO INFORM YOU THAT YOUR HUSBAND, CAPTAIN FRANKLIN VAN VALKENBURGH, UNITED STATES NAVY, WAS LOST IN ACTION IN THE PERFORMANCE OF HIS DUTY AND IN THE SERVICE OF HIS COUNTRY X THE DEPARTMENT EXTENDS TO YOU ITS SINCEREST SYMPATHY IN YOUR GREAT LOSS X TO PREVENT POSSIBLE AID OT YOUR ENEMIES PLEASE DO NOT DIVULGE THE NAME OF HIS SHIP OR STATION X IF REMAINS ARE RECOVERED THEY WILL BE INTERRED TEMPORARILY IN THE LOCALITY WHERE DEATH OCCURRED AND YOU WILL BE NOTIFIED ACCORDINGLY[.]

The second example is recorded in a Michigan newspaper (no name of the paper or date is given). The headline is "F. C. Flaherty Dies at Pearl Harbor." The article refers to a dispatch received by Flaherty's brother (Flaherty's parents were dead). The name of his ship was not provided, and the dispatch advised that if his remains were recovered that they would be buried temporarily locally and the brother would be notified. As with the Van Valkenburgh telegram, Rear Admiral C. W. Nimitz, the Chief of the Bureau of Navigation, signed it, and it came from Washington, DC.[1]

★ ★ ★ ★ ★ ★ ★ ★ ★ ★

BURIAL AND REMEMBRANCE: MOH RECIPIENTS WHO SURVIVED THE WAR

CHIEF PETTY OFFICER AVIATION ORDNANCEMAN JOHN FINN

Finn died on May 27, 2010, and was buried with full military honors at the Campo Reservation in Chula Vista, California, cemetery, where his wife is buried.[2]

LIEUTENANT COMMANDER SAMUEL FUQUA

Fuqua died at the Veterans Administration Medical Center in Decatur, Georgia, on January 27, 1987; at the time, he was a rear admiral (two stars) because of his tombstone promotion. He was buried in Arlington National Cemetery.[3]

WARRANT OFFICER (GUNNER) JACKSON PHARRIS

Pharris died on October 15, 1966, in Los Angeles; at the time, he was a lieutenant commander because of his tombstone promotion. He was buried in Arlington National Cemetery.[4]

WARRANT OFFICER (MACHINIST) DONALD ROSS

Ross died on May 27, 1992, at Bremerton, Washington; at the time, he was a captain because of his tombstone promotion. He was cremated, and his ashes were scatted over the site where *Nevada* sank. He therefore has no grave, but he has an "In Memory of" marker at Beverly Cemetery, Beverly, Kansas, the town of his birth.[5]

REMEMBERING OR HONORING THOSE WHO SURVIVED THE WAR

SHIP MEMORIALS

A destroyer was named for Ross. A destroyer escort was named for Pharris (she later became a fast frigate). The USS John Finn (DDG-113) is a guided missile destroyer launched on March 28, 2016; construction was begun on her in 2012 (see Appendix B). With a ship finally named for Finn, Fuqua remains the only December 7 recipient who never had a ship named for him; the author found no indication anywhere that a ship was named for Fuqua.

OTHER MEMORIALS

Today, Kaneohe Bay is home to Marine Corps Base Hawaii, including a Marine Corps Air Facility. Although the Naval Air Station was closed, the base is also home for Navy Patrol and Reconnaissance Wing 2.[6]

On June 29, 1999, the John W. Finn Building was dedicated on Marine Corps Base Hawaii. Finn attended the ceremony. Just inside the entrance to the building is a bust of Finn and a display with his decorations, including a replica MOH.[7]

White Navy motorboats transport tourists across the waters of Pearl Harbor from the landing at the *Arizona* Memorial's theater to the Memorial and return them to the landing at the theater. A boat is named for each of the four survivors: Finn, Fuqua, Pharris, and Ross.[8]

★ ★ ★ ★ ★ ★ ★ ★ ★ ★ ★ ★

Burial and Remembrance: MOH Recipients Who Did Not Survive the War

Captain Mervyn Bennion
First Lieutenant George Cannon
Chief Warrant Officer (Boatswain) Edwin Hill
Ensign Herbert Jones
Warrant Officer (Radio Electrician) James Reeves
Machinist's Mate First Class Robert Scott
Boatswain's Mate Second Class Owen Hammerberg

Captain Mervyn Bennion, who died on December 7 aboard *West Virginia* from wounds suffered during the attack, was buried in Salt Lake City Cemetery. He has two flat tombstones, one of which is a MOH stone with a MOH symbol at the top; the symbol and the inscriptions are gilded to indicate his MOH statUS.[9]

According to the official US Marine Corps casualty report for First Lieutenant Cannon, his mother requested that he be buried at an American military cemetery overseas, so he is buried on Oahu at Punchbowl, the National Memorial Cemetery of the Pacific.

The three *California* MOH recipients who died on December 7 are buried: Ensign Herbert Jones at Fort Rosecrans National Cemetery, Warrant Officer James Reeves in Punchbowl, and Machinist's Mate First Class Robert Scott in Arlington National Cemetery.

Chief Warrant Officer (Boatswain) Edwin Hill, who died on December 7 aboard or near *Nevada*, is buried in Punchbowl.

Petty Officer Second Class Hammerberg, who died on February 17, 1945, was buried on Oahu with a simple wooden cross marking his grave (his name is misspelled as "Hammerburg") (see the photograph at the end of this chapter).[10] His final resting place is Holy Sepulchre Catholic Cemetery, Southfield, Michigan, where he was buried on October 24, 1947.[11] The inscriptions on his grave are gold to indicate his MOH status.

Ship Memorials

A destroyer was named for Bennion. Destroyer escorts were named for the other recipients in this section (see Appendix B).

Other Memorials

Hammerberg Hall is at Naval Magazine Pearl Harbor, Oahu, Hawaii.

★ ★ ★ ★ ★ ★ ★ ★ ★ ★ ★ ★

Remembrance: MOH Recipients Whose Bodies Were Not Recovered

Ensign Francis Flaherty
Captain Richard Fleming
Rear Admiral Isaac Kidd
Chief Watertender Tomich
Captain Franklin Van Valkenburgh
Seaman First Class James Ward

The National Memorial Cemetery of the Pacific ("Punchbowl"): The Courts of the Missing at the Honolulu Memorial

The author has seen the names of various MOH recipients on the Courts of the Missing at the Honolulu Memorial at Punchbowl, the National Memorial Cemetery of the Pacific in Honolulu, most recently in 2015. The ABMC superintends the Honolulu Memorial. Each name is gilded and has a MOH symbol beside it. The following names are on the Courts of the Missing because their bodies were not recovered:

Rear Admiral Isaac Kidd and Captain Franklin Van Valkenburgh of Arizona.

No identifiable remains were found for either officer. As recounted in chapter 15, Lieutenant Commander Fuqua stated that the crew found Kidd's body, or what was thought to be his body, at the foot of the ladder leading to the flag bridge, the area from which a flag officer directs operations. Fuqua said that Van Valkenburgh's body was never found although he said that his ring and some coat buttons were found on the flag bridge. He did not identify the type of ring.

The strongest conclusion about the ultimate fate of Kidd and Van Valkenburgh is that they perished in the catastrophic explosion that killed the ship. This conclusion cannot be doubted given Fuqua's testimony and written statements, the statements of junior officers, and the circumstances of the ship's destruction. That testimony and those statements were summarized in Chapter 15.

Ensign Francis Flaherty and Seaman First Class James Ward of Oklahoma

They perished after staying behind in a turret or turrets aboard *Oklahoma* to provide light to others who were escaping as the ship was capsizing. As can be imagined, the nearly complete capsizing of a battleship and the subsequent rescue and salvage operations were, to use the phrase used by the famous war correspondent Robert Sherrod in describing the first night on Iwo Jima, "a nightmare in hell."[12] The remains of Flaherty and Ward were not recovered from *Oklahoma*. Locating them would have been impossible since the ship capsized and water flooding the ship was pumped out during the recovery process (who knows what was in the water?). Also, the ship sank while being towed back to the United States.

Chief Watertender Peter Tomich of Utah

His body was not recovered from the capsized *Utah*; capsizing of his ship would have presented the same horrors and conditions as with *Oklahoma*.

Captain Richard Fleming, USMCR

His body was not recovered after his aircraft crashed into the Pacific Ocean at the end of his diving attack on a Japanese cruiser near Midway. When the author saw the Fleming inscription before his latest viewing in 2015, it was clear and clean. When he saw it in 2015, Fleming's name and MOH symbol had weathered and deteriorated. While the author was at Punchbowl in 2015, he found a large construction site at the Courts of the Missing at which workmen were improving the site, including the Fleming inscription.

In Memory of Markers (IMO)

Rear Admiral Kidd

In 2014, the author visited the cemetery at the U.S. Naval Academy in Annapolis, Maryland, and saw an inscription on the Kidd family tombstone for the Isaac Kidd who died on December 7. The inscription is in effect an IMO marker.

Captain Van Valkenburgh

He has two IMO markers at Forest Home Cemetery, Milwaukee, Wisconsin. One is a stone monument; the other is the classic VA IMO.[13]

Ensign Flaherty

His IMO marker is in Charlotte, Michigan (Eaton County), at Maple Hill Cemetery, but the phrase "In Memory of" is not inscribed in the stone. He also has a large monument at the Eaton County Courthouse.[14]

Seaman First Class Ward

In 2002, the author visited the Ward IMO marker at Ferncliff Cemetery in Springfield, Ohio. It was a classic horizontal metal IMO.

Captain Fleming

The Fleming IMO is at Fort Snelling National Cemetery, Minneapolis, Minnesota[15] (see appendix C for more details).

Ship Memorials

Destroyers were named for Kidd and Van Valkenburgh. Destroyer escorts were named for the other recipients in this section (see Appendix B).

Other Memorials, Finds, and Tributes

During his many visits to the *Arizona* Memorial, the author saw the Kidd and Van Valkenburgh inscriptions among the many names inscribed on the stone wall of the memorial that is the remembrance of the dead and the missing.

In 2014, the author saw, at the U.S. Naval Academy, a monument near the cemetery with the names of graduates who are missing in action; the names of Kidd and Van Valkenburgh are on the monument under their class years (1906 and 1909, respectively), but Young's name is not, presumably because he was buried at sea and thus is not missing in action.

A salvage crew found Kidd's Naval Academy ring, class of 1906, "fused to the steel on the top of the *Arizona*'s conning tower." Cassin Young, *Vestal*'s commanding officer on December 7 and fellow Naval Academy graduate and MOH recipient for December 7, received the ring and sent it to Kidd's widow.[16]

In Kidd's Official Military Personnel File (OMPF) are a newspaper article about him and a tribute to him. The newspaper was the Times Herald of Washington, DC; its article of December 11, 1941, is titled, "Admiral Kidd, DC Resident, Killed in Attack on Hawaii." The article stated that Kidd was the first American "admiral" to be killed in action in the history of the United States. The article mentioned that his son, Isaac Kidd Jr. was soon to graduate from the Naval Academy. The article noted that a classmate of Kidd's, Rear Admiral Chester Nimitz, was on duty in Washington in the Navy Department. The tribute was in the Army and Navy Register of March 7, 1942. The unnamed author of "Tribute to Admiral Kidd" wrote about his life and death; his comments about Kidd and Japanese treachery were mentioned in Chapter 3 of this book. The author referred to Kidd by two nicknames: "Ike" and "Cap" with the latter assumed to be short for the famous pirate "Captain Kidd."[17]

In Honolulu near the Naval Station Pearl Harbor is "Valkenburgh St.," which intersects Nimitz Highway (Highway 92) near an overpass. The author saw the site in 2015. Apparently the person naming the street thought that "Van" was the captain's first name and wanted to name the street using only the last name. The author has seen this error before, a person thinking that "Van" is Van Valkenburgh's first name (see Chapter 18 of this book (Errors)).

In addition to inscriptions at Punchbowl, Flaherty and Ward are remembered at the USS *Oklahoma* Memorial near USS Missouri on Ford Island, completed in 2007, which the author saw in 2015. It has the names of Flaherty and Ward on it, each in two places, with indication of MOH status: one, on the reverse of the large black stone that is the front of the monument and that has a list of the names of the dead and mission, and two, each has a white standard with his name and MOH status inscribed on it.

At Naval Station, Newport, Rhode Island, the author saw and visited the U.S. Navy Senior Enlisted Academy Building, which is named "Tomich Hall."

A white motorboat at the *Arizona* Memorial is named for Tomich.[18]

★ ★ ★ ★ ★ ★ ★ ★ ★ ★ ★ ★ ★

Burial and Remembrance: MOH Recipient Buried at Sea

Commander Cassin Young

As recounted in Chapter 8, Young was promoted to captain and assigned to command the cruiser USS San Francisco. He was killed aboard her on November 13, 1942, at the Naval Battle of Guadalcanal, and according to the service record obtained by the author, Young was buried at sea. He is remembered in two places.

One is the inscription of his name on the Tablets of the Missing at the Manila American Cemetery and Memorial in the Philippines. In Manila, the names of the missing are inscribed on one of two hemicycles (East and West) comprising the Memorial Court. Each hemicycle contains twenty-four pairs of "fin" walls (for a total of forty-eight fins); upon the four faces of each fin wall are inscribed names of the missing. Young's inscription, in the West Hemicycle, is gilded, and to the left of his name is a gilded upside-down star that looks similar to a MOH emblem.[19]

The other is a flat "In Memory of" marker at Mount Pleasant Memorial Gardens, Mount Pleasant, South Carolina, near Charleston and, ironically, near the Congressional Medal of Honor Society Headquarters at Mount Pleasant aboard USS Yorktown. At the top of the marker is a MOH symbol, and it and the lettering are gilded to indicate his MOH status.[20]

Ship Memorial

A destroyer was named for Young (see appendix B).

Other Memorial

A white motorboat at the *Arizona* Memorial is named for Young.[21]

Notes

1. The National Personnel Records Center, St. Louis, Missouri, furnished military and personal information from Van Valkenburgh's Official Military Personnel File (OMPF)

at the author's request. The material came in two formats. Initially, it was in selected pages copied from his OMPF; later, it came in the form of a compact disc with his entire OMPF. The death telegram is on the CD (Section 04, Service Documents, page 45).

2. Chapter 11 (Kaneohe Bay).

3. Chapter 7 (*Arizona*).

4. Chapter 19 (Pharris MOH).

5. Chapter 9 (*Nevada*).

6. Chapter 11 (Kaneohe Bay); author's many visits to Marine Corps Base Hawaii at Kaneohe; Internet site for Marine Corps Base Hawaii.

7. Program from Commander, Patrol and Reconnaissance Force, US Pacific Fleet, for the dedication ceremony of the John W. Finn Building: "John W. Finn Building Dedication Ceremony"; author's visit to the John W. Finn Building.

8. Information provided to the author from Navy personnel in 2015 after he noticed the name "Peter Tomich" on the stern of one of the tour boats as the boat was leaving the dock to take visitors to the *Arizona* Memorial in Pearl Harbor (hereafter "White Boat information"). Robert Stirrup, Mass Communication Specialist Second Class, U.S. Navy, "Medal of Honor Recipient Lt. John Finn Visits Namesake *Arizona* White Boat," press release by Commander, Navy Region Hawaii Public Affairs (December 9, 2009).

9. Cemetery information courtesy of Brandi Madrill, Salt Lake City Cemetery, Salt Lake City, *Utah*.

10. Photograph of original grave provided to the author by Mr. Stan Bozich of Michigan's Own Military and Space Museum.

11. Attorney Robert E. Sullivan, Jr., of Southfield, Michigan, provided information about the cemetery and the burial.

12. George W. Garand and Truman E. Strowbridge, Western Pacific Operations: History of the U.S. Marine Corps Operations in World War II, Vol. IV (Historical Division, Headquarters, US Marine Corps, 1971, reprinted by The Battery Press, Inc., 1994), 527.

13. Cemetery information courtesy of Jan Van Rens, Executive Director, Forest Home Cemetery, Milwaukee, Wisconsin.

14. Cemetery information and photograph of Flaherty's "In Memory Of" marker and courthouse monument courtesy of Sherry Copenhaver and Charles Brandon of Charlotte, Michigan.

15. Cemetery information courtesy of Ken Everson of the Fort Snelling National Cemetery in Minneapolis, Minnesota.

16. Paul Stillwell, Battleship *Arizona* (Naval Institute Press, Annapolis, MD, 1991), 271–272.

17. Endnote 7, Kidd OMPF (CD), described in detail at endnote 7 of Chapter 7 (*Arizona*), section 08 ("Newspaper Clippings"); the newspaper article is at pages 1 and 2, and the tribute is at page 3.

18. Endnote 8, White Boat information.

19. Photographs of the Young inscription at Manila American Cemetery taken for the author by Sergeant Major Hubert O. Caloud, U.S. Marine Corps (Retired), the assistant superintendent of the cemetery. He supplied the photographs and information by e-mail to the author, dated July 8, 2015; Manila American Cemetery and Memorial (The American Battle Monuments Commission), 11–12.

20. Photographs taken for the author of the Young "In Memory Of" marker by the author's parents, the late Lieutenant Colonel Elmer C. and Aileen M. Jones and by Mr. Patrick J. Mallard of Mount Pleasant Memorial Gardens, a cemetery in Mount Pleasant, South Carolina.

21. Endnote 8, White Boat information.

Chapter 22
Legacy—Ships and Stations

The fates of the ships aboard which MOHs were earned on December 7, 1941, were varied.

Only two ships present on December 7, 1941, in Pearl Harbor remain there today: *Arizona*, which sank upright in place, and *Utah*, which capsized and was partially righted. Both are wrecks and nautical graves for the crewmen who perished aboard them.

The Battleships

Arizona's MOH recipients were Rear Admiral Isaac Kidd, Captain Franklin Van Valkenburgh, and Lieutenant Commander Samuel Fuqua. The ship remains in Pearl Harbor because of extensive and irreparable damage. She suffered a deathblow on December 7—the catastrophic explosion on the forward powder magazine, resulting in the famous ghastly photograph showing the ship's forward mast bent forward as if some prehistoric creature. The ship sank in place, as did *West Virginia* and *California*, but the damage was so great that the ship, unlike those other two ships, could not be restored to service, so no attempt was made to raise her. Much of her superstructure was salvaged and removed.[1] Two of her fourteen-inch guns were mounted at Battery Pennsylvania at Mokapu Point at Naval Air Station, Kaneohe Bay, for coastal defense.[2] Other parts of the ship were placed on the Waipio Peninsula, where some of them remain today.[3] (See Appendix C, concerning the ship, her Memorial, and visiting the Memorial and shore facilities related to the ship and to December 7).

California's MOH recipients were Ensign Herbert Jones, Warrant Officer (Gunner) Jackson Pharris, Warrant Officer (Radio Electrician) Thomas Reeves, and Petty Officer (Machinist's Mate) First Class Robert Scott. The ship was repaired after December 7 and returned to serve in the Pacific. In 1944, her port bow was damaged in a collision with USS Tennessee. In 1945, a kamikaze airplane hit her, killing 44 and wounding 155 of her crew. She survived the war and was sold for scrapping on July 10, 1959.[4]

Nevada's MOH recipients were Chief Boatswain Edwin Hill and Warrant Officer (Machinist) Donald Ross. The ship was repaired and returned to service in both the Atlantic, where she shelled France during the Normandy invasion, and the Pacific, where she shelled Iwo Jima and Okinawa. A kamikaze airplane hit the *Nevada* on March 27 off Okinawa, killing eleven members of her crew. She survived the war and survived being a target ship during the atomic bomb tests in 1946 at Bikini Atoll. She was sunk by naval gunfire and aerial torpedoes off Hawaii in 1948.[5]

Oklahoma's MOH recipients were Ensign Francis Flaherty and Seaman First Class James Ward. The ship was righted in 1943 by cables connecting her hull to winches on Ford Island that pulled her over toward Ford Island. Although she was pulled fully upright, the damage was so great that she could not be returned to service. Her guns and superstructure were removed, and she was sold for scrap. As she was being towed from Pearl Harbor to the mainland United States in 1947, problems developed. The tug turned back to Pearl Harbor, but during the return trip, the towline parted and the ship sank in the Pacific Ocean on May 17, 1947.[6]

West Virginia's MOH recipient was Captain Mervyn Bennion. The ship was repaired and served in the Pacific, enjoying a measure of revenge for Pearl Harbor; she was in Tokyo Bay on September 2, 1945, for the Japanese surrender. She was sold for scrapping in 1959.[7]

Other Ships

Utah's MOH recipient was Chief Petty Officer Watertender Peter Tomich. Since *Utah* was, like *Oklahoma*, capsized, cables were attached to the ship to connect the ship to winches on Ford Island, winches that pulled the ship toward Ford Island to attempt to right her. Unlike *Oklahoma*, she was never fully righted, so she remains off Ford Island tilted in her final resting place. As with *Oklahoma*, a decision was made not to salvage the ship, especially given her age. Thus she is a ghastly, rusting, red-and-brown metal hulk, a reminder of the attack, much as *Arizona* is a reminder of the attack and the rusting hulk of LST-480 is a reminder of the West Loch Disaster (Chapter 13 and Appendix C). More of the wreckage of *Utah* can be seen than that of *Arizona*[8] (see Appendix C concerning the ship and her Memorial).

Vestal's MOH recipient was Commander Cassin Young. The ship was repaired and returned to service, serving throughout the Pacific during the war. She was decommissioned in 1946, sold in 1950, and ultimately scrapped.[9]

Stations

As has been explained in earlier chapters, not all the MOHs in the Hawaiian Islands were earned on ships. One was earned on Midway Atoll by a Marine: First Lieutenant George Cannon. Another was earned by a Marine flying from his station on Midway: Captain Richard Fleming. Midway is now a National Wildlife Refuge and Battle of Midway National Memorial superintended by the US Fish and Wildlife Service (see Chapter 23).[10]

Chief Petty Officer Aviation Ordnanceman John Finn earned his MOH on December 7 at what was then Naval Air Station Kaneohe Bay, which is now Marine Corps Base Hawaii.[11]

Notes

1. Vice Admiral Homer N. Wallin, U.S. Navy (Retired), Pearl Harbor: Why, How, Fleet Salvage, and Final Appraisal (Naval History Division, United States Government Printing Office, Washington, DC, 1968), 267–269.

2. Paul Stillwell, Battleship *Arizona* (Naval Institute Press, Annapolis, MD, 1991), 280–281.

3. Brian M. Sobel, "The Sacred Relics of Pearl Harbor," THE WALL STREET JOURNAL, December 4, 2007; Joe Dovener, "Exploring the World War II Secrets of Hawaii," After the Battle (Battle of Britain International, Ltd., Number 127, 2005), 30–31.

4. The Navy Department, Dictionary of American Naval Fighting Ships, Vol. II (Naval History Division, Department of the Navy, Washington, DC, 1976), 14–15 (hereafter "DANFS").

5. DANFS, Vol. V, 52.

6. Ibid., 148.

7. DANFS, Vol. VIII, 222–227 (Naval Historical Center).

8. Ibid., Vol. VII, 421–424; Vice Admiral Homer N. Wallin, US Navy (Retired), Pearl Harbor: Why, How, Fleet Salvage, and Final Approach (Naval History Division, US Government Printing Office, Washington, DC, 1968), 262–267; the author has visited the *Utah* Memorial numerous times, most recently in 2015.

9. DANFS, Vol. VII, 494–498 (Naval Historical Center).

10. See the Internet site for Midway Atoll.

11. The author has many times visited what is now Marine Corps Base Hawaii (Kaneohe Bay).

Chapter 23
Legacy—Places

Pearl Harbor and Ford Island

Chapter 3, "Aftermath," discussed the status of Pearl Harbor and Ford Island today. To recap, the large white mooring quays remaining in Pearl Harbor just off Ford Island serve as memorials to the ships moored there on December 7. The author visited the area and saw the quays numerous times, the most recently in 2015. As explained here, some quays were removed.

F-3: California (Alone)

The mooring quays for berth F-3 at Ford Island can still be seen and are the quays closest to the channel leading from Pearl Harbor to the Pacific Ocean; on one of them in large black letters is USS *California* BB 44, but the letters and numbers can only be seen looking at the quay from Pearl Harbor. The letters cannot be seen by looking at the back of the quay from Ford Island. Near the quays on Ford Island is a monument memorializing the action there on December 7.[1]

F-5: Oklahoma and Maryland

The mooring quays for berth F-5 at Ford Island no longer exist. In the berth used by *Oklahoma* and Maryland on December 7 is a new berth, Pier 5, for the battleship USS Missouri, a battleship that is now a "floating museum"; she was not at Pearl Harbor on December 7.[2] Years ago, the author saw a plaque about *Oklahoma* and Maryland on December 7 on the outside of a firehouse on Ford Island near USS Missouri.[3] The USS *Oklahoma* Memorial on Ford Island is near Pier 54 (see Appendix C for details).

F-6: West Virginia and Tennessee

The mooring quay for berth F-7 at Ford Island can still be seen and is marked USS *WEST VIRGINIA* BB 48 in large black letters as seen from Pearl Harbor. The quay is just in front of the port bow of USS Missouri.[5] Also near the bow is a marker about *West Virginia* and December 7. Looking from Pearl Harbor at *Missouri*'s starboard side, one would see the *West Virginia* quay near the bow; to the right of the *West Virginia* quay is a quay marked USS TENNESSEE BB 43.[6]

F-7: Arizona and Vestal

Two mooring quays can be seen when approaching the *Arizona* Memorial from Pearl Harbor by boat. To the left of the memorial is the quay for *Vestal*: USS *Vestal* AR 4. To the right of the memorial is the quay for *Arizona*: USS *Arizona* BB 39.[7]

The most obvious reminder of *Arizona* is the white stone Memorial straddling the ship (Appendix D describes the memorial in more detail). The Memorial's wall facing Ford Island has inscribed on it all the names of the navy personnel lost on the ship. The names of the Marines assigned to the ship who were lost on December 7 are identified as Marines and inscribed in a separate section in the lower right corner of the wall.⁸

Arizona survivors who died after the war and who were cremated have had their urns placed inside the ship during ceremonies conducted by the Navy and the National Park Service; divers place the urn inside the ship. The names of the men so interred are inscribed on a stone bench in front of the wall with names of those lost on December 7 (at the corner in front of the Marine names of *Arizona* casualties).⁹

Arizona is no longer a ship commissioned in the Navy but is a grave holding the remains of those lost on the ship. To honor them, Navy ships passing *Arizona* between sunrise and sunset must render "passing honors consisting of sounding 'Attention' and rendering the hand salute by all persons in view on deck and not in ranks shall be executed by that ship."¹⁰ The attack on *Arizona* caused the greatest single loss of life aboard a ship in the history of the US Navy: 1,177 crewmen (1,104 Navy members and 73 Marines). Among the thirty-six sets of brothers on the ship, sixty-one brothers died on December 7. Both brothers died in twenty-two sets (only in one set of two brothers did both survive); one brother survived in each of three sets of brothers.¹¹

Arizona is one of the only two ships left in Pearl Harbor from December 7. The other is *Utah*, on the opposite side of Ford Island on Carrier Row. The ships share another connection. They were in Norfolk in June 1931 when a large fire consumed part of downtown Norfolk. The local newspaper (the price of the paper was three cents) reported a fire in its June 8, 1931, edition, noting that the Navy helped to battle the fire: "Besides the contingents sent in from the USS *Arizona*, the USS *Utah*, and the Naval Operating Base ["NOB" or now "Naval Station Norfolk"], dozens of sailor boys, all decked out in white and on liberty, hopped to the task with a will." The fire chief was "particularly high in his praise" of these men.¹²

The City of Norfolk issued *Arizona* a large certificate of appreciation, which sank with the ship at Pearl Harbor. It was salvaged, however, after December 7, and is at the Naval Shipyard Museum at Portsmouth, Virginia, having been presented to the Museum by a former commanding officer of the ship.¹³

F-8: NEVADA (ALONE)

The mooring quay for berth F-8 at Ford Island can still be seen: it is between the *Arizona* Memorial and the bridge connecting Ford Island and Highway 99 (Kamehameha Highway) near Aloha Stadium. Looking at the quay from Pearl Harbor, the *Arizona* Memorial is to the left; the bridge is to the right. The quay is marked USS *Nevada* BB 36 in large black letters.14 The area on Ford Island near berth F-8 and behind the quay is now officer housing. In the back yard of one of the houses behind the mooring quay for *Nevada* at berth F-8 is a small monument memorializing *Nevada*'s action on December 7.¹⁵

A monument with an American flag at Hospital Point, in officer housing near the shipyard at Naval Station Pearl Harbor, commemorates the grounding of USS *Nevada* on December 7, first at Hospital Point then at a point across the channel leading to

Pearl Harbor from Hospital Point. The point of the second grounding, which is on the Waipio Peninsula, is known as known as "*Nevada* Point." The monument has tablets with information about the ship's December 7 action as well as a list of the dead. It also lists *Nevada* personnel who received MOHs and Navy Crosses.[16]

F-11: UTAH

Utah and *Arizona* are the only two ships at Pearl Harbor that were there on December 7, and like *Arizona*, *Utah* is also a grave since most of the bodies of the crew members lost were not recovered. *Utah* does not receive the attention *Arizona* receives since she rests opposite *Arizona* and Battleship Row off Ford Island, an active military installation inaccessible to members of the general public unless they are on a tour. Also, while *Utah* has a Memorial, it does not have a visitor's center. To the author's knowledge no tours go to *Utah*'s Memorial; they go to USS Missouri and the nearby *Oklahoma* Memorial.

Today, *Utah* is a study in contrasts and paradox, in beauty and in ugly reminder. At Ford Island is a beautiful white monument, complete with pier, flag, and plaques, commemorating *Utah*. One plaque has the names of the crewmen lost aboard the ship, including Tomich. A wayside exhibit has been added in recent years (since the author first saw the *Utah* Memorial in 1999) explaining what happened to the ship with a photograph showing the capsized ship and her two mooring quays. The wayside exhibit mentions Tomich as follows: "The ship capsized, trapping dozens of men inside. They included Medal of Honor recipient Chief Watertender Peter Tomich, who stayed at his post to make sure the ship's boilers were secured and all fireroom personnel had left their stations." The casual reader would not know if (a) he already had a MOH before the attack or if (b) he earned the MOH for his actions during the attack (b) is the correct choice).

Just beyond the white monument is a ghastly sight: the canted, exposed, red and brown rusted remains of the ship—an observer sees the upper starboard side of the ship tilted up with most if not all of the deck and port side of the ship in the water. *Utah*'s rusting hulk is a gruesome reminder of the attack, the ship's fate, the loss of life, and her status as a tomb.[17]

WEST LOCH

West Loch remains the site of an active navy installation, a munitions depot: Naval Magazine Pearl Harbor. The author has seen in person, at Naval Magazine Pearl Harbor, the four reminders of the 1944 West Loch Disaster.[18]

The first is Hammerberg Hall, near the magazine's main entrance. Inside on the second floor in a lounge is a plaque commemorating Hammerberg and reciting his MOH citation.

The second is a stone memorial outside a building near the channel leading from Pearl Harbor to the Pacific Ocean.

The third is a wayside exhibit erected in 1994 by the National Park Service, a superb, comprehensive exhibit with photographs, diagrams, and text. It is just off First Street near Power Point and the West Loch Dock. Unfortunately, it does not mention Hammerberg or his MOH.

Fourth is the only tangible, visible reminder of the disaster: the bow of LST-480, a hulk of metal protruding from West Loch just off Hanaloa Point. Its red rust is at once a haunting but spectacular and a stark reminder of the disaster.

In typical government or military fashion, for a site as interesting as West Loch, all of the reminders (LST-480 and the wayside exhibit) are off limits or inaccessible to the public since they are on the premises of the Naval Magazine, a high-security area. One wonders why a duplicate wayside is not outside the main entrance to the magazine or why a duplicate wayside is not at the Pearl Harbor Visitor Center.

MIDWAY

Midway Atoll is "Midway Atoll National Wildlife Refuge and Battle of Midway National Memorial" under the jurisdiction of the US Fish and Wildlife Service.[19]

On Midway, First Lieutenant Cannon has a beautiful memorial stone, complete with US and Marine Colors flying from it. His is the only Marine Memorial on Midway; incongruously, Captain Fleming, the other Midway MOH recipient, does not have a memorial on Midway.[20] Repeated attempts by the author to interest Midway or the Marine Corps League in erecting a monument to Fleming on Midway have gone unanswered (MCL) or met with bureaucratic indifference (the Fish and Wildlife Service on Midway). An official at Midway did not even know about Fleming until the author informed him by e-mail of Fleming and his MOH.

At one time, the official Fish and Wildlife Midway Internet site for Midway had a "virtual" walking tour. Stop 13 was a photograph of Cannon's command post as it looks today. The site's history of Midway in World War II mentions Cannon.[21]

In 2015, a search for "Cannon" on the Midway Internet site leads to a section titled "Preparing for War." Under the heading of "A day that will live in infamy" is Cannon's story and mention of his MOH and that he was the first Marine to receive a MOH in World War II. A street on Sand Island bears his name. Of course, by now, the reader knows that the correct phrase is "a date which will live in infamy." The site also has photographs of monuments commemorating the Battle of Midway; a viewing from the Internet reveals no mention of the Fleming MOH.[22] Nothing is seen about Fleming, who, ironically, is still "missing in action" literally and figuratively.

The author finds this situation intolerable: one MOH Marine has a memorial on Midway, yet the other—who participated in the most important battle of the Pacific War and was the sole MOH recipient for that battle—has no memorial on Midway. From the author's experience as a Marine, he finds the lack of a memorial on Midway for Captain Fleming inexplicable—the U.S. Marine Corps usually does not ignore its heroes—but suspects that the lack of a memorial is due to the senior U.S. Marine

Corps leadership not even knowing about Captain Fleming. The true surprise is that anyone connected to the Marine Corps even knew about First Lieutenant Cannon such that he was given a memorial on Midway.

Wartime information about the 1942 Battle of Midway can be found in the documentary film The Battle of Midway, made by the famous director John Ford. It won an Academy Award for Best Documentary in 1943. During the film, the narrator identifies one officer as "Colonel Shannon," the officer who wrote the report of the 1941 attack, including the narrative about MOH recipient First Lieutenant George Cannon (Chapter 12). He also identifies "Major Roosevelt," the president's son who was a Marine on Midway. The red US Marine Corps colors (flag) of the Sixth Defense Battalion can be seen beside the U.S. flag as a color guard is seen marching. First Lieutenant Cannon was part of this command, and Shannon was its commander.

NOTES

1. The author saw the *California* quay in 1999.

2. The author has visited the F-5 area numerous times, most recently in 2015.

3. The author saw the *Oklahoma* plaque in 1999.

4. The author first saw the *Oklahoma* Memorial in 2015.

5. The author has visited the F-6 area numerous times, most recently in 2015.

6. The author saw the *West Virginia* plaque in 1999.

7. The author has visited the F-7 area numerous times, most recently in 2015.

8. The author's numerous visits to the Memorial, the most recent in 2015.

9. The author attended such a ceremony at the *Arizona* Memorial on March 26, 2004, for Jerome H. Garfield, who was an ensign aboard *Arizona* on December 7, 1941.

10. Colonel Charles A. Jones, USMCR (Retired), Hawaii's World War II Military Sites (Mutual Publishing, Honolulu, HI, 2002), 91 (*Arizona* no longer commissioned and Article 1282 of Navy Regulations requires passing ships to pay honors to *Arizona*); endnote 2, Stillwell, Battleship *Arizona*, 279 (ship is no longer commissioned).

11. "Casualties on the USS *Arizona* on December 7, 1941" (document from USS *Arizona* Memorial, National Park Service, U.S. Department of the Interior).

12. "$3,000,000 Fire Checked," Virginian-Pilot and the Norfolk Landmark, June 8, 1931 (hereafter "1931 Fire"), 1 and 2.

13. E-mail to and photograph for the author sent by Diane Cripps at the Portsmouth Naval Shipyard Museum, Portsmouth, Virginia, of September 20, 2015; endnote 13,

1931 Fire, 1 and 2. The author saw the certificate of appreciation on display years ago, which is how he knew about it.

14. The author has visited the F-8 area numerous times, most recently in 2015.

15. The author saw the *Nevada* plaque in 1999.

16. The author visited *Nevada* Point in 1999 and 2015.

17. The author has visited the *Utah* Memorial numerous times, most recently in 2015.

18. The author toured West Loch in 2001 and again in 2004 (the 2004 visit was for the commemoration of the sixtieth anniversary of the disaster).

19. Midway Atoll Internet site viewed February 8, 2016.

20. The author has photographs of the Cannon Memorial sent to him by U.S. Government personnel on Midway. E-mail between the author and US Government personnel on Midway indicated a lack of knowledge on the part of those personnel about Captain Fleming. One reply from the refuge manager at Midway Atoll National Wildlife Refuge (April 15, 2008) reads as follows: "I must admit that I am ashamed that I knew nothing of Captain Fleming. We obviously need to do something here on Midway to tell his story as we do with Lt. Cannon." To the author's knowledge, no memorial for Captain Fleming was erected on Midway.

21. Author's access of the Midway Internet site.

22. Viewing of current Midway Internet site.

Chapter 24
Conclusions and Observations -
Clanging Halyards and the Last Light in the Turret

The subject of this book is, for me, the story of eighteen noble men who were noble because they risked and sacrificed their well-being and often their lives to do what they had to do in the worst of circumstances during World War II. They exhibited a single-minded drive to confront and to mitigate the damage done by an enemy who had been underestimated but who had proven to be more than formidable. That all but two of them deserved the MOHs they received is a testament to the high standard of valor they displayed.

The stories have no happy endings—one thinks of Captain Fleming perishing in the Pacific Ocean in a flaming Vindicator—except for the five men who survived their individual ordeals, escaping with their lives to fight another day and to enjoy a full life, although Cassin Young, who survived December 7, would die all too soon in November 1942.

As for the December 7 recipients, all were ordinary officers and enlisted men thrust by surprise into tremendously challenging, tense, and stressful situations. They met and conquered extraordinary anxiety, tension, and pressure. Those who survived did so by sheer willpower, by focusing on the problems at hand, by dedication, by concentration, and by disregard for their own discomfort and the danger surrounding them. For example, on December 7, a wounded and injured Jackson Pharris left the hospital on Ford Island and returned to *California* to continue rendering assistance aboard his gravely damaged ship. Samuel Fuqua supervised the dying moments of *Arizona*, a ship whose name became a rallying cry for defeating the Japanese in World War II. Many would know the name *Arizona*, but few would know the name Fuqua.

On December 7, these men had to meet rapidly changing, sudden, and unpredictable conditions full of various dangers, known and unknown, and to face fear, fear of the unknown and the fear of uncertainty: what calamity was going to happen next? On December 7, they found themselves in a world not operating according to the rules they expected would obtain in combat and lead to a fair fight. As can be seen from the comments in Chapters 2 and 3, the men on Oahu were angry not only at the attack but at its nature; it was a sneak attack lacking the warning required by international law that deprived them of the opportunity to meet the enemy in a "fair fight." A fair fight would be like a baseball game. both sides know that conflict is about to occur and are ready for it. And when the men were surprised, the luxury of choice vanished. They had no time to consult the playbook; they could only react, not act.

The other three recipients also faced danger of a different kind. Captain Richard Fleming was in traditional combat; he did not face the surprises that the December 7 recipients did.

The one man who received a noncombat MOH confronted a different enemy—wreckage and nature, nature that had become an enemy because of the conditions of war.

Finally, the one man who received from Congress a special MOH or Congressional Gold Medal had risked his life in World War I and his status and reputation after that war to argue for ideas about airpower that were ahead of his time. Perhaps the Navy did not like his ship-sinking trials in the 1920s because they were afraid he would succeed and thus kill the Navy's sacred cows, its surface ships with naval guns and the belief that they were immune to attack from the air. His "surprise attack" that caused Navy resentment was to prove what he said was right, that the sacred cows could be sunk by aerial bombardment.

In the face of fear, one can fight, flee, or freeze. Fortunately, I had the population of men just described who unhesitatingly chose to fight.

★ ★ ★ ★ ★ ★ ★ ★ ★ ★ ★ ★

A final comment about terminology.

Many would say this book is about heroes. I believe firmly that it was only partially about heroes. Sadly, the word hero is used today almost universally to describe anyone who does anything in an average or above-average manner. Someone who handles insurance claims well can be a "hero" today. I reserve the word for a narrower sense: heroes act in the face of danger to render aid or to stop or to mitigate disaster or attack, usually at the risk of their own lives and in the face of some type of enemy, human or natural. But combat veterans I have spoken to narrow the definition even more so; to them, the heroes are those who do not return home. So in that sense, the only heroes in this book are the men who died during or after the action leading to their MOHs. But whether they perished or survived, they are all great men.

Many would say that the men in this book who died during the war gave their lives for their country. I knew for many years a very wise combat veteran, Colonel J. Shelton Scales, US Marine Corps Reserve (Retired). He was a battalion commander at Iwo Jima and has been in all of Fourth Marine Division's actions preceding Iwo. He bristled when he heard "gave"; he was adamant that the lives of men killed in combat were taken from them. I agree.

★ ★ ★ ★ ★ ★ ★ ★ ★ ★ ★ ★

I reluctantly stopped writing this book because I suffered a writer's problem: falling in love with the subject matter. I came to know and to respect these men, and I with hesitation request their leave to depart their company.

I regret that more of them did not survive the war; most of their stories are not works of fiction with happy endings. The only happy endings, with "happy" meaning "survival," were for Finn, Fuqua, Pharris, and Ross, who survived the war. The other characters, except for Billy Mitchell, perished in ghastly circumstances.

But the end comes down to two aspects of warfare.

One, as expressed in Parts 2 and 3 of this book, was that much of the world's history from 1930 to 1945 was, in the words of Reed G. Landis, "written in such dark ink…"

Two, and a corollary of one, are the many lists of the names of the dead, names initially recorded on paper rosters in that "dark ink" to which Mr. Landis referred before being transferred to monuments: names on a wall at the *Arizona* Memorial; names on plaques of the *Utah* and the *Nevada* Memorials at Ford Island and Hospital Point, respectively; names on blue tablets at Remembrance Circle at the Pearl Harbor Visitor Center; names on the memorial on Ford Island to USS *Oklahoma*; and names on the Courts or the Tablets of the Missing at American war cemeteries on Oahu or in foreign countries or at the Naval Academy.

One clue to the presence of a list of names is a US flag flying over the monument that is the repository of the names, its halyard clanging in the wind.

And locally, the reminders continue. In my neighborhood, I go for bike rides in March 2016. I see two signs in yards for two candidates seeking office in a primary election. Their names could only be: Ross and Kidd (Kidd for School Board and Ross for US Senate). I am sorry I did not see one reading Pharris.

Lessons Learned

No military exercise I experienced while in the Marine Corps or Reserve was complete until commanders submitted lessons learned or after-action reports. Although I did not write this book for the military, I think I should list lessons learned in writing a book about men such as these hidden heroes, the eighteen recipients of the MOH for bravery in the Hawaiian Islands during World War II—seventeen for combat and one for noncombat. I will add the Mitchell medal since he was so closely connected with Oahu and airpower.

Lesson 1: I hope I have exposed the stories of these men, making them no longer hidden heroes. They should be known for what they did. They exhibited bravery that for some cost them their lives. The bravery of all but two of the recipients (Kidd and Van Valkenburgh) was proven by facts supporting their MOHs.

Lesson 2: Along those lines, the price of bravery is high—loss of life, physical wounds and injuries, and psychological "damage" from seeing the horrors of stationary, trapped ships unable to maneuver while under unrelenting aerial attack (except for *Nevada*'s short sortie). Combat involving ships has its own set of unique horrors, including men drowning in water engulfed with burning oil and debris, men trapped in capsized ships, men blown apart—disintegrated—by explosions of ship ammunition magazines or fuel tanks, and men in confined spaces, gasping for air and desperately seeking light and a means of escape, maybe tapping on a hull of a capsized ship, hoping someone will hear their cries for rescue.

Lesson 3: Many of the MOH recipients showed a much-needed willingness and ability to take charge, to think quickly and clearly, and to set examples for junior personnel in the worst of conditions and in environments of chaos—all without regard to their own welfare.

Lesson 4: The most telling comment illustrating a sense of sacrifice among these men is the comment in Marine First Lieutenant Cannon's MOH citation that he was, while mortally wounded and resisting evacuation, "forcibly removed" from his CP. He simply would not leave his men until they were cared for before him. This tenacity and concern for the welfare of others while disregarding one's own welfare is leadership at its finest.

Lesson 5: The awards system can reward the undeserving and not reward the deserving. Arguably the most deserving December 7 MOH recipient, Jackson Pharris, received his MOH only after receiving a Navy Cross that was upgraded to a MOH via a lengthy, torturous process and ordeal involving the navy's awards bureaucracy with the end result being a MOH awarded more than six years after December 7, 1941, the date of the actions justifying a MOH. Ironically, he, a warrant officer, was required to produce "incontestable justification" and "incontrovertible facts" to support the recommendation for his MOH while MOH awards for two senior officers—Kidd and Van Valkenburgh—were approved without adequate factual support. Doris Miller received a political Navy Cross, yet visitors who see his images plastered all over the Pearl Harbor Visitor Center will only know that he was the first black sailor to receive a Navy Cross; they will not be told that it was a political award directed by the President himself to placate one segment of society or that his fellow crewmen who did as much or more than he did received no Navy Crosses.

SURPRISE

The story of the MOHs earned in the Hawaiian Islands in World War II is a story of surprise and intrigue, aspects I certainly did not expect to find when I began work on this book or my earlier book, Hawaii's World War II Military Sites (2002). In particular are the following:

First, perhaps the biggest surprise is the lack of publicity accorded these men, excluding Billy Mitchell, who received mostly adverse publicity during his lifetime. Absent physically on December 7 and at Midway in 1942, he was certainly at both battles in spirit. Nowhere on Oahu did the author ever see a display with a complete listing of the December 7 MOH recipients. Nowhere did he see a reference to the Midway 1942 MOH recipient or the West Loch recipient.

Second, the unexpected stories were Billy Mitchell and Jackson Pharris. As a veteran of the US Marine Corps from 1981 to 2009, I saw and heard firsthand how the military could mistreat its members. Mitchell and Pharris are the classic examples of how the military mistreats its members.

Perhaps the final irony involving Billy Mitchell is the first strike by the United States against the Japanese mainland in World War II was a Pearl Harbor in reverse.

On April 18, 1942, army aviators flying sixteen B-25 medium bombers (ironically named "Mitchell" bombers), launched not from land but from the aircraft carrier *Hornet*, surprised the Japanese by bombing Japan. The leader of the raid, Lieutenant Colonel James Doolittle, earned a MOH for leading the raid. He received it in 1942 from President Roosevelt at the White House when Doolittle was a brigadier general (he had been promoted from lieutenant colonel directly to brigadier); it was issued by General Orders Number 29 of June 9, 1942. The citation is as follows:

> For conspicuous leadership above the call of duty, involving personal valor and intrepidity at an extreme hazard to life. With the apparent certainty of being forced to land in enemy territory or to perish at sea, Gen. Doolittle personally led a squadron of Army bombers, manned by volunteer crews, in a highly destructive raid on the Japanese mainland.

Of note is that the citation omits the details of the raid, such as the bombers flying from an aircraft carrier; the general nature of the citation is obviously out of concern for OPSEC or "operational security."

The Mitchell was not a carrier aircraft (it was designed to be land-based), but the pilots trained such that they were able to launch successfully from Hornet and make the first strike by the United States on mainland Japan. Although the raid inflicted minor damage, it alarmed the Japanese and raised morale in the United States, morale that had slumped after Japan's strike on Oahu and elsewhere in late 1941 and early 1942. Ironically, the Air Force Museum's fact sheet about the B-25 does not mention that it was named for Billy Mitchell.[1] And a B-25 is featured in season 2 of The Twilight Zone (the episode is " King Nine Will Not Return"). The pre–December 7 military certainly was in a "twilight zone" when it ignored Mitchell's warnings and advocacy of airpower—specifically, its dominance over sea power—notwithstanding his proving in the 1920s that aircraft could sink ships.

Billy Mitchell was a public figure, a lightning rod in the macro world for ridicule, censure, and dismissal of his ideas. Jackson Pharris was different; he was an officer unknown to the public living in the micro world of his command—battleship *California*—risking his life in "hands-on" efforts to save his shipmates and his ship in the worst and foulest of conditions. To label his heroism above and beyond what is expected is a gross understatement.

His reward? While two senior officers, Kidd and Van Valkenburgh, received wartime MOHs based on _____ (fill in the blank with supportable facts), Pharris received the navy's second highest award for heroism and was in effect told to go away satisfied. But he would not go away and neither would his commanding officer, Captain then Rear Admiral Joel Bunkley, who did what any good commanding officer would do; he went to bat for a deserving shipmate and subordinate with tenacity and drive to obtain for him what he deserved: the nation's highest award for combat bravery. Pharris had the added burden of supplying the navy with sufficient information to justify a MOH while battling ill health because of his injuries from December 7. The Navy, which originally told him that the Navy Cross was sufficient recognition, should be given credit for reopening his case, an action that led to his MOH presentation approximately six and one-half years after the deeds warranting the MOH.

Were Bunkley not so determined, Pharris would have died with a Navy Cross instead of a well-deserved MOH. Bunkley's postwar efforts initiated a process of investigation and witness statements that finally led to the MOH. One wonders why these witnesses, who served with Pharris on December 7, could not have been located during the war so that Pharris would have received a MOH when the other December 7 recipients received theirs.

To add insult to injury, the MOH obtained through such an ordeal was almost lost because of a mishap involving the lockbox in which it was kept. One could ask why an official from the *California* state government, which received the contents of the lockbox via the escheating process, did not realize that the item was a MOH, a MOH means something rather important, it belonged to a man named "Jackson Pharris" because the name of the recipient is inscribed on the medal, and Pharris probably had family who could be found easily. How difficult can elementary recognition of an object's value and basic fact finding be?

Third, I did not expect to find so much intrigue and so many interesting aspects involving the MOH recipients and their individual MOHs. Examples include the following:

I did not expect to learn that one of the two MOHs for Owen Hammerberg had been stolen—from, of all places, the Congressional Medal of Honor Society—but that luckily his family had received two MOHs since the parents were divorced. The original MOH remains safe in a museum in Michigan.

I did not expect to find that Cassin Young had two MOHs.

I did not expect to learn of the great difficulty in placing Tomich's MOH.

I did not expect to conclude that two MOHs, those awarded to Kidd and Van Valkenburgh, were unsupported by factual bases and thus undeserved.

I did not expect to encounter the story of Jackson Pharris and the time required and torturous path taken to upgrade the Navy Cross he received in 1942 to a MOH he received in 1948, the last December 7 MOH awarded.

Fourth, I did not expect to find the staggering amount of erroneous and omitted information and outlandish statements about the recipients, the partial accounts of their deeds, or the complete omission of these MOHs or the recipients from publications, especially Fleming, the sole MOH recipient in the Pacific War's most important battle. Many of the errors and omissions can be traced to unexpected sources: books prepared with the assistance of the Congressional Medal of Honor Society and books written by so-called and self-appointed Pearl Harbor experts. Astonishingly, few people or organizations seem capable of determining who the first MOH recipient was for World War II and who the first December 7 MOH recipient was.

Fifth, superstition exists. I found thirteen involved in the stories of two of the recipients. In one case, thirteen was bad luck for the MOH recipient; in the other case, it was bad luck for me. Cassin Young survived December 7 but was killed on Friday, November 13, 1942, at the Naval Battle of Guadalcanal. Jackson Pharris is buried in Section 13 of Arlington National Cemetery. As I explained in the acknowledgments and Appendix C, his grave was by far the most difficult grave to find because of my incompetence at land navigation and the layout of Section 13.

I found irony in the case of Cassin Young. He survived the attack on December 7, an emphatic announcement that airpower was now dominant over sea power, yet he was killed in surface combat between ships at the Naval Battle of Guadalcanal: a naval gun shell exploded on his ship, the cruiser San Francisco, killing him with the very weapon that had lost its first-place standing on December 7 when airpower took first place from naval guns. Thus the old standby of naval guns still had their place in modern combat although airpower would be the dominant military force during and after the war.

And war is about having and not having second chances; unlike his fellow MOH recipients for December 7 who had no second chance to get back at the enemy in that fair fight so many December 7 survivors wanted, he had one as his cruiser's commanding officer, but he was killed during that second chance.

What These Men Did and What Their MOHS Represent

This book is about nineteen men who received MOHs, seventeen of whom received MOHs for combat actions and one of whom for noncombat actions. The nineteenth was Billy Mitchell's special Congressionally authorized MOH.

Mitchell did not receive a classic combat MOH. But he did engage an enemy—ironically, the military establishment of his own country. He fought for the recognition and development of airpower; his enemy was an arrogant U.S. military, whose leaders were wed to conventional thinking that focused on sea power and armies in the belief that they, not airpower, were the dominant factors in warfare. One cannot overemphasize that photograph of *Arizona* and the accompanying caption from the November 29, 1941, Naval Academy football game program—"It is significant that despite the claims of air enthusiasts no battleship has yet been sunk by bombs." Ironically it captured that arrogance by its demeaning reference to "air enthusiasts," an obvious slap at Mitchell.

But at 7:55 on a Sunday morning in December 1941, Japanese airpower rewrote that caption. It was the weapon Japan used so effectively to start the war that led to the actions resulting in the eighteen MOHs that are the subject of this book. It made a mockery of the *Arizona* photograph and caption just mentioned, and coincidentally, *Arizona* would be the ship suffering the most damage and largest loss of life.

Mitchell died before he could see his predictions about the attack on Oahu come true and before he could see his theories about airpower and the necessity of controlling the air vindicated during World War II.

The MOH recipients who lived for a period of time sufficiently long to take actions truly warranting MOHs faced two hardships. First, many suffered loss and anguish as they saw their comrades perish in combat. Second, they had to act with a sense of urgency based on incomplete information. They had to be decisive immediately, in the worst of circumstances. One is reminded of a postwar quotation from Audie Murphy, himself a MOH recipient: "Once you accept the fact that you are going to get it [killed], your mind clears up. You become decisive. That's important, because indecision kills people in war more often than anything else."[2]

One is left with the question: what do these MOHs represent? For both officers and enlisted men, the MOHs reflect the highest degree of courage in the worst of circumstances: fifteen men on the morning of December 7 who were executing tasks essential for their ships to repel a surprise attack or to save fellow crewmen, one man mortally wounded on the evening of December 7 who had to be "forcibly removed" from his duty station, one man in 1942 who aimed his obsolete aircraft at a Japanese cruiser, and one man in 1945 who saved two fellow divers at the cost of his own life, dying an excruciating death.

For officers in particular, their standard of conduct and performance was "special trust and confidence" in action. Officer recipients who earned their awards put meaning into that phrase.

The reader is left with—

- Captain Mervyn Bennion, disemboweled and dying on the deck of *West Virginia*, caring only for the condition of his ship and crew and resisting evacuation

- Ensign Herbert Jones and Warrant Officer Reeves passing ammunition by hand aboard *California* until Jones was killed and Reeves died

- Warrant Officer (Gunner) Jackson Pharris assisting his fellow crewmen aboard *California* and saving his ship from capsizing by ordering counterflooding, preventing the gruesome fate suffered by *Oklahoma* and *Utah*, a man who left his hospital bed on Ford Island on December 7 to return to his ship to continue aiding his shipmates

- Ensign Francis Flaherty and Seaman First Class James Ward, the latter a member of his ship's baseball team who held the Pacific Fleet batting championship, in a turret or turrets aboard *Oklahoma*, holding flashlights so that others could escape

- Lieutenant Commander Samuel Fuqua prominently setting the example aboard *Arizona* by calmly superintending firefighting and the care for and evacuation of the wounded until forced to abandon ship

- Chief Warrant Officer (Boatswain) Edwin Hill casting the lines off so *Nevada* could get underway, having to swim back to the ship, and later dying—blown off his ship and killed by bombs while attempting to let go the ship's anchor so it could ground at Hospital Point to prevent blocking the entrance to Pearl Harbor

- Warrant Officer Donald Ross remaining at his station aboard *Nevada* notwithstanding loss of consciousness and revival

- Chief Petty Officer (Watertender) Peter Tomich remaining at his station aboard the capsized *Utah*, securing (turning off) his boilers so that they would not explode in the cold waters of Pearl Harbor

- Chief Petty Officer (Aviation Ordnanceman) John Finn firing, from an exposed position, a machinegun at Japanese aircraft attacking the Naval Air Station at Kaneohe Bay

- Commander Cassin Young, blown off the ship he commanded, *Vestal*, by the catastrophic explosion that doomed the ship next to his, *Arizona*, swimming back to his own ship, managing to get back aboard, and being decisive by exercising the judgment to move his ship away from *Arizona* and to ground her (he would later perish on a Friday 13 during the Naval Battle of Guadalcanal)

- First Lieutenant George Cannon, U.S. Marine Corps, refusing to be evacuated from his command post on Midway until other wounded men were evacuated, all the while suffering two broken legs, a broken pelvis, and later dying from loss of blood

- Captain Richard Fleming, U.S. Marine Corps Reserve, who was in two days of ferocious, hair-raising aerial combat, facing the withering fire of antiaircraft guns, unrelenting buzz saws of projectiles coming at him and shredding his aircraft as he dive-bombed his targets—the second time as he flew his plane to his death, and the death of his gunner, in a diving attack on a Japanese cruiser

- Petty Officer Second Class (Boatswain's Mate) Owen Hammerberg, saving two fellow divers in the dark, dangerous waters of the West Loch of Pearl Harbor, and dying an agonizing death over a period of eighteen hours after he rescued them

- Billy Mitchell, a World War I veteran with a DSC for bravery in combat and a MOH (or Congressional Gold Medal) for bravery not in combat but in the arena of ideas, awarded for his courage in spreading his ideas about airpower in a military world that hated him for challenging its most sacred ideas and weapons (the battleship and naval guns) (he also rewrote a caption for a photograph of a battleship in the program of an army-navy football game, a caption that was a slap in the face until the Japanese attacked Oahu on December 7, 1941).

THE WHY: EVENING POSTMARKS AND LIVES CUT SHORT

Two themes haunt the author. One is why, addressed in the next section. The other is evening postmarks showing a life cut short.

As the author was finishing this book, he received by chance from the Eaton County Historical Society information about Ensign Francis Flaherty. One item was an undated, unsourced newspaper article: "F. C. Flaherty Dies at Pearl Harbor." A report of a war death is a report of a war death, but this article reported something poignant. It noted that "the young ensign had been in Honolulu the night before the surprise raid as his Christmas cards—received by a dozen friends Saturday—were postmarked at 6:20 p.m. December 6th and carried air mail postage."

Flaherty was born on March 15, 1919. He was dead by the time the postcards were received.

THE WHY: LAST LIGHT IN THE TURRET

One last question can be asked: "Why?" An observer could ask why the men who truly earned their MOHs did what they did. A certain amount of foreboding or resignation must be present; some of these men must have known they were going to die or that death was not only possible but also probable, yet they showed no concern for themselves. Acting completely selflessly, they showed concern only for their shipmates (comrades), their commands, and their missions.

Fleming, when diving his obsolete aircraft on a Japanese cruiser near Midway, had to know he would die but attacked anyway. Remaining in his capsized or capsizing ship to ensure his boilers were secured so they would not explode, Tomich had to know that he would die, but he stayed aboard ship anyway. Flaherty and Ward, remaining behind in a turret or turrets of a capsizing ship with flashlights, had to know they would die, but they remained in place holding the last lights so that others could escape.

Perhaps they were so dedicated to their duties and actions or to their comrades that they did not have the time to consider their own personal fates.

Regardless of what they may have thought, they acted according to the words of John Adams: "Our obligations to our country never cease but with our lives."[3] And as the famous Union commander William T. Sherman said, "War is hell," or to that effect. But he followed that line with, "I look upon war with horror, but if it is to come I am here."[4]

Perhaps the best reflection on why comes from an actor portraying a lieutenant in a Baltimore homicide unit in the television series Homicide: Life on the Street. A junior detective, who during interrogation tricks a suspect into implicating himself in a deadly arson, later asks the lieutenant why an otherwise ordinary person, the suspect, would go around killing people. He said, "Why did he do it?…What's that about? I don't get it."

The lieutenant responds emphatically and without hesitation as follows: "You don't have to get it. You'll sleep better if you don't know. Give me the where, the what, the when, the how. Why is a thing we can live without..."⁵

This book has attempted to provide the where, the what, the when, and the how for eighteen men who received MOHs for combat and noncombat actions and one man who received a special MOH for his advocacy of an idea that would prove crucial to modern warfare.

The why remains elusive. Thus the man whose life was saved by the sacrifice of one of these MOH recipients—whether the MOH recipient survived or not—may have slept or may sleep better at night jUSt appreciating his own survival; he did or does not need to know the why, the reason that a very brave man saved his life and afterward his savior, or his savior's family, received his country's highest award for combat heroism, the Medal of Honor.

NOTES

1. The story of the Doolittle Raid and the B-25 Mitchell bomber can be found in three fact sheets published by the National Museum of the U.S. Air Force and found on the Internet: "Doolittle Raid," "America Strikes Back: The Doolittle Tokyo Raid," and "North American [manufacturer of the] B-25B Mitchell." Information about Doolittle is also found in an Air Force pamphlet: George M. Watson, Jr., "General James H. Doolittle: The Air Force's Warrior-Scholar," Air Force History and Museums Program (Washington, DC, 2008); page 13 has a photograph of the MOH presentation. The Doolittle MOH citation can be found by searching "army MOH site" on the Internet and using the icon labeled "World War II (A-F)" at the "Medal of Honor Recipients: Center of Military History" Internet site.

2. Thomas B. Morgan, "The War Hero," Esquire (December 1983), 603.

3. John Adams, Letter to Benjamin Rush (April 18, 1808).

4. Andrew Roberts, "For Love of Country," *THE WALL STREET JOURNAL*, December 11, 2014, A15.

5. "Fire, Part 2," Homicide: Life on the Street, Season Four (October 27, 1995).

Appendix A
Biographical Sketches of the Medal Recipients in the Hawaiian Islands

Captain Mervyn Bennion, U.S. Navy

Born: May 5, 1897; Vernon, Utah
Source of military status: Appointed an ensign at the Naval Academy, Class of 1910; promoted to captain June 20, 1938
Grade and component: Captain, US Navy
Command and location: USS *West Virginia*, Pearl Harbor
Age: 44
Fate: Died aboard *West Virginia* in Pearl Harbor on December 7 of wounds sustained that morning
Buried: Salt Lake City Cemetery, Salt Lake City, *Utah*
MOH citation: For conspicuous devotion to duty, extraordinary courage, and complete disregard of his own life, above and beyond the call of duty, during the attack on the Fleet in Pearl Harbor, by Japanese forces on December 7, 1941. As Commanding Officer of the USS *West Virginia*, after being mortally wounded, Capt. Bennion evidenced apparent concern only in fighting and saving his ship, and strongly protested against being carried from the bridge.
Citation: Signed by President Franklin D. Roosevelt, March 4, 1942
Presentation of MOH:
    When: March 17, 1942
    Where: Salt Lake City, *Utah*
    By whom presented: By registered mail to the widow
    Who received the MOH: The widow, Mrs. Mervyn Bennion
Other awards and decorations: Purple Heart, Nicaraguan Campaign Medal (1912), Mexican Service Medal (1914), American Defense Service Medal with Fleet Clasp, Victory Medal with Atlantic Fleet Clasp (1918)
Ship named in his memory: Destroyer USS Bennion (DD-662)

First Lieutenant George Cannon, U.S. Marine Corps

Born: November 15, 1915; Webster Groves, Missouri
Source of military status: Appointed a Marine Corps second lieutenant June 25, 1938; appointed a first lieutenant August 13, 1941
Grade and component: First Lieutenant, U.S. Marine Corps
Command and location: Battery H, Sixth Defense Battalion, Midway Atoll (Sand Island)
Age: 26
Fate: Died on Midway December 7, 1941, of wounds sustained that evening
Buried: National Memorial Cemetery of the Pacific (Punchbowl)
MOH: For distinguished conduct in the line of his profession, extraordinary courage and disregard of his own condition during the bombardment of Sand Island, Midway Islands, by Japanese forces on December 7, 1941. First Lt. Cannon, Battery Commander of Battery H, Sixth Defense Battalion, Fleet Marine Force, U.S. Marine Corps, was at his command post when he was mortally wounded by enemy shellfire. He

refused to be evacuated from his post until after his men who had been wounded by the same shell were evacuated and directed the reorganization of his command post until forcibly removed. As a result of his utter disregard of his own condition, he died from loss of blood.
Citation: Signed by President Franklin D. Roosevelt, March 4, 1942
Presentation of MOH:
    When: March 1942
    Where: Ann Arbor, Michigan
    By whom presented: By registered mail to the mother
    Who received the MOH: The mother, Mrs. B. B. Cannon
Other awards and decorations: Purple Heart, American Defense Service Medal with base clasp, Asiatic-Pacific Campaign Medal, World War II Victory Medal
Ship named in his memory: Destroyer escort USS Cannon (DE-99)

AVIATION ORDNANCEMAN CHIEF JOHN FINN, U.S. NAVY

Born: Born July 24, 1909; Los Angeles, California
Source of military status: Enlisted July 29, 1926; date of promotion to chief petty officer unknown
Grade and component: Chief Petty Officer (Aviation Ordnanceman), US Navy
Command and location: Naval Air Station, Kaneohe Bay, Kaneohe Bay, Oahu
Age: 32
Fate: He survived December 7. He died on May 27, 2010.
MOH: For extraordinary heroism, distinguished service, and devotion above and beyond the call of duty. During the first attack by Japanese airplanes on the Naval Air Station, Kaneohe Bay, on December 7, 1941, Lieutenant Finn promptly secured and manned a fifty-caliber machine gun mounted on an instruction stand in a completely exposed section of the parking ramp, which was under heavy enemy machine-gun strafing fire. Although painfully wounded many times, he continued to man this gun and to return the enemy's fire vigoroUSly and with telling effect throughout the enemy strafing and bombing attacks and with complete disregard for his own personal safety. It was only by specific orders that he was persuaded to leave his post to seek medical attention. Following first-aid treatment, although obviously suffering much pain and moving with great difficulty, he returned to the squadron area and actively supervised the rearming of returning planes. His extraordinary heroism and conduct in this action were in keeping with the highest traditions of the U.S. Naval Service.
Citation: Signed by President Franklin D. Roosevelt (June 1942)
Presentation of MOH:
    When: September 15, 1942
    Where: USS Enterprise, Pearl Harbor, Oahu, Territory of Hawaii
    By whom presented: Admiral Chester Nimitz
    Who received the Medal: Chief Petty Officer Finn
Other awards and decorations: Purple Heart, Navy Unit Commendation, Good Conduct Medal (four stars), Asiatic-Pacific Campaign Medal (two stars), Yangtze Campaign, American Theatre, American Defense Medal (one star), World War II Victory Medal

Ensign Francis Flaherty, U.S. Naval Reserve

Born: March 15, 1919; Charlotte, Michigan
Source of military status: Appointed an ensign December 12, 1940
Grade and component: Ensign, U.S. Naval Reserve
Command and location: USS *Oklahoma* (BB-37), Pearl Harbor
Age: 22
Fate: Perished aboard *Oklahoma* in Pearl Harbor on the morning of December 7
Buried: Not buried since his remains were unrecovered
MOH citation: For conspicuous devotion to duty and extraordinary courage and complete disregard of his own life, above and beyond the call of duty, during the attack on the Fleet in Pearl Harbor, by Japanese forces on December 7, 1941. When it was seen that the USS *Oklahoma* was going to capsize and the order was given to abandon ship, Ens. Flaherty remained in a turret, holding a flashlight so the remainder of the turret crew could see to escape, thereby sacrificing his own life.
Citation: Signed by President Franklin D. Roosevelt, March 4, 1942
Presentation of MOH:
When: March 6, 1946
Where: Lompoc, California
By whom presented: Unknown
Who received the MOH: His brother, John J. Flaherty
Other awards and decorations: Purple Heart, American Defense Service Medal with Fleet Clasp, Asiatic-Pacific Campaign Medal, World War II Victory Medal, and the Honorable Lapel Button
Ship named in his memory: Destroyer escort USS Flaherty (DE-135)

Captain Richard Fleming, U.S. Marine Corps Reserve

Born: November 2, 1917; St. Paul, Minnesota
Source of military status: Appointed lieutenant September 10, 1940; appointed captain May 16, 1942
Grade and component: Captain, U.S. Marine Corps Reserve
Command and location: Marine Scout-Bombing Squadron 241, Midway Atoll
Age: 24
Fate: Perished when his aircraft crashed at sea while attacking the Japanese cruiser *Mikuma*.
Buried: Not buried since his remains were unrecovered
MOH citation: For extraordinary heroism and conspicuous intrepidity above and beyond the call of duty as flight officer, Marine Scout-Bombing Squadron 241, during action against enemy Japanese forces in the battle of Midway on June 4 and 5, 1942. When his squadron commander was shot down during the initial attack upon an enemy aircraft carrier, Captain Fleming led the remainder of the division with such fearless determination that he dived his own plane to the perilously low altitude of 400 feet before releasing his bomb. Although his craft was riddled by 179 hits in the blistering hail of fire that burst upon him from Japanese fighter guns and antiaircraft batteries, he pulled out with only two minor wounds inflicted upon himself. On the night of June 4, when the squadron commander lost his way and became separated from the others, Captain Fleming brought his own plane in for a safe landing at its base

despite hazardous weather conditions and total darkness. The following day, after less than four hours' sleep, he led the second division of his squadron in a coordinated glide-bombing and dive-bombing assault on a Japanese battleship [cruiser]. Undeterred by a fateful approach glide, during which his ship was struck and set afire, he grimly pressed home his attack to an altitude of 500 feet, released his bomb to score a near miss on the stern of his target, and then crashed to the sea in flames. His dauntless perseverance and unyielding devotion to duty were in keeping with the highest traditions of the U.S. Naval Service.

Citation: Signed by President Franklin D. Roosevelt, November 10, 1942
Presentation of MOH:
    When: November 24, 1942
    Where: White House
    By whom presented: President Franklin D. Roosevelt
    Who received the MOH: His mother, Mrs. Michael E. Fleming.
Other awards and decorations: Purple Heart, American Defense Service Medal with Fleet Clasp, Asiatic-Pacific Campaign Medal, World War II Victory Medal
Ship named in his memory: Destroyer escort USS Fleming (DE-32)

Lieutenant Commander Samuel Fuqua, US Navy

Born: October 14, 1899; Laddonia, Missouri
Source of military status: U.S. Naval Academy, Class of 1923; appointed lieutenant commander June 23, 1938
Grade and component: Lieutenant Commander, US Navy
Command and location: USS *Arizona*, Pearl Harbor
Age: 42
Fate: Survived December 7; died January 27, 1987
Buried: Arlington National Cemetery
MOH citation: For distinguished conduct in action, outstanding heroism, and utter disregard of his own safety, above and beyond the call of duty during the attack on the Fleet in Pearl Harbor by Japanese forces on December 7, 1941. Upon the commencement of the attack, Lt. Commdr. rushed to the quarterdeck of the USS *Arizona*, to which he was attached, where he was stunned and knocked down by the explosion of a large bomb that hit the quarterdeck, penetrated several decks, and started a severe fire. Upon regaining consciousness, he began to direct the fighting of the fire and the rescue of wounded and injured personnel. Almost immediately, there was a tremendous explosion forward, which made the ship appear to rise out of the water, shudder, and settle down by the bow rapidly. The whole forward part of the ship was enveloped in flames, which were spreading rapidly, and wounded and burned men were pouring out of the ship to the quarterdeck. Despite these conditions, his harrowing experience, and severe enemy bombing and strafing, at the time, Lt. Commdr. Fuqua continued to direct the fighting of fires in order to check them while the wounded and burned could be taken from the ship and supervised the rescue of these men in such an amazingly calm and cool manner and with such excellent judgment that it inspired everyone who saw him and undoubtedly resulted in the saving of many lives. After realizing that the ship could not be saved and that he was the senior surviving officer aboard, he directed that it be abandoned but continued to remain on the quarterdeck and directed abandoning ship and rescue of personnel until satisfied that all personnel

that could be had been saved, after which he left the ship with the (last) boatload. The conduct of Lt. Commdr. Fuqua was not only in keeping with the highest traditions of the naval service but characterizes him as an outstanding leader of men.
Citation: Signed by President Franklin D. Roosevelt (March 4, 1942)
Presentation of MOH:
    When: March 19, 1942
    Where: U.S. Naval Training Station, Newport Rhode Island
    By whom presented: Vice Admiral Royal E. Ingersoll
    Who received the Medal: Lieutenant Commander Fuqua
Other awards and decorations: Legion of Merit, China Service Medal, American Area Campaign Medal, American Defense Service Medal with Fleet Clasp (one star), European Area Campaign Medal (two engagement stars), Pacific Area Campaign Medal (one battle star), Philippine Liberation Medal (one engagement star), Philippine Independence Ribbon, Occupation Medal (Pacific Area) with Asia Clasp, World War II Victory Medal, World War I Victory Medal, National Defense Service Medal

Petty Officer Second Class (Boatswain's Mate) Owen Hammerberg, U.S. Navy

Born: May 31, 1920; Daggett, Michigan
Source of military status: Enlisted July 16, 1941, promoted to second class petty officer October 1943
Grade and component: Petty Officer Second Class (Boatswain's Mate), US Navy
Command and location: Salvage Unit, Service Force, Pacific, Pearl Harbor
Age: 24
Fate: Died on Oahu on February 17, 1945, from injuries sustained while saving fellow divers
Buried: Holy Sepulchre Cemetery, Southfield, Michigan
Medal of Honor citation: For conspicuous gallantry and intrepidity at the risk of his life above and beyond the call of duty as a diver engaged in rescue operations at West Loch, Pearl Harbor, February 17, 1945. Aware of the danger when two fellow divers were hopelessly trapped in a cave-in of steel wreckage while tunneling with jet nozzles under an LST sunk in forty feet of water and twenty feet of mud, Hammerberg unhesitatingly went overboard in a valiant attempt to effect their rescue despite the certain hazard of additional cave-ins and the risk of fouling his life line on jagged pieces of steel embedded in the shifting mud. Washing a passage through the original excavation, he reached the first of the trapped men, freed him from the wreckage, and, working desperately in pitch-black darkness, finally effected his release from fouled lines, thereby enabling him to reach the surface. Wearied but undaunted after several hours of arduous labor, Hammerberg resolved to continue his struggle to wash through the oozing, submarine, subterranean mud in a determined effort to save the second diver. Venturing still further under the buried hulk, he held tenaciously to his purpose, reaching a place immediately above the other man just as another cave-in occurred and a heavy piece of steel pinned him crosswise over his shipmate in a position that protected the man beneath from further injury while placing the full brunt of terrific pressure on himself. Although he succumbed in agony eighteen hours after he had gone to the aid of his fellow divers, Hammerberg, by his cool judgment, unfaltering professional skill, and consistent disregard of all personal danger in the face

of tremendous odds, had contributed effectively to the saving of his two comrades. His heroic spirit of self-sacrifice throughout enhanced and sustained the highest traditions of the U.S. Naval Service. He gallantly gave his life in the service of his country.
Citation: Signed by President Harry Truman, November 26, 1945
Presentation of MOH:
    When: February 16, 1946
    Where: Grosse Ile (ILE) Naval Air Station, Gross Ile, Michigan
    By whom presented: Captain G. R. Fairbanks
Who received the MOHs: One MOH for his father, Mr. Jonas Hammerberg; one MOH for his mother, Mrs. Elizabeth Moss (the parents were divorced)
Other awards and decorations: Asiatic-Pacific Campaign Medal, World War II Victory Medal
Ship named in his memory: Destroyer escort USS Hammerberg (DE-1015)

CHIEF WARRANT OFFICER (CHIEF BOATSWAIN) EDWIN HILL, U.S. NAVY

Born: October 4, 1894; Philadelphia, Pennsylvania
Source of military status: Appointed warrant officer (boatswain, temporary) November 3, 1918; appointed chief boatswain October 21, 1924
Grade and component: Chief warrant officer (Boatswain), U.S. Navy
Command and location: USS *Nevada*, Pearl Harbor
Age: 47
Fate: Killed at Pearl Harbor on the morning of December 7
Buried: National Memorial Cemetery of the Pacific (Punchbowl), Oahu
Medal of Honor citation: For distinguished conduct in the line of his profession, extraordinary courage, and disregard of his own safety during the attack on the Fleet in Pearl Harbor by Japanese forces on December 7, 1941. During the height of the strafing and bombing, Chief Boatswain Hill led his men of the line-handling details of the USS *Nevada* to the quays, cast off the lines, and swam back to his ship. Later, while on the forecastle attempting to let go the anchors, he was blown overboard and killed by the explosion of several bombs.
Citation: Signed by President Franklin D. Roosevelt, March 4, 1942
Presentation of MOH: No information available.
Other awards and decorations: Purple Heart, Victory Medal with Mobile Base Clasp, Mexican Service Medal, American Defense Service Medal with Fleet Clasp
Ship named in his memory: Destroyer escort USS Hill (DE-141)

ENSIGN HERBERT JONES, U.S. NAVAL RESERVE

Born: December 1, 1918; Los Angeles, California
Source of military status: Appointed ensign November 14, 1940
Grade and component: Ensign, U.S. Naval Reserve
Age: 23
Command and location: USS *California* (BB-44), Pearl Harbor
Fate: Died on December 7 of wounds sustained that morning aboard *California*
Buried: Fort Rosecrans National Cemetery, San Diego, California
Medal of Honor citation: For conspicuous devotion to duty, extraordinary courage,

and complete disregard of his own life, above and beyond the call of duty, during the attack on the Fleet in Pearl Harbor by Japanese forces on December 7, 1941. Ens. Jones organized and led a party, which was supplying ammunition to the antiaircraft battery of the USS *California* after the mechanical hoists were put out of action when he was fatally wounded by a bomb explosion. When two men attempted to take him from the area, which was on fire, he refused to let them do so, saying in words to the effect, "Leave me alone! I am done for. Get out of here before the magazines go off."
Citation: Signed by President Franklin D. Roosevelt, March 4, 1942
MOH presentation: No information available.
Other awards and decorations: Purple Heart, other awards and decorations unknown
Ship named in his memory: Destroyer escort USS Herbert C. Jones (DE-137)

Rear Admiral Isaac Kidd, U.S. Navy

Born: March 26, 1884; Cleveland, Ohio
Source of military status: Appointed an ensign at the Naval Academy, Class of 1906; appointed rear admiral July 11, 1940
Grade and component: Rear Admiral, U.S. Navy
Command and location: Commander, Battleship Division One (aboard USS *Arizona*), Pearl Harbor
Age: 57
Fate: Perished aboard *Arizona* on the morning of December 7
Buried: Not buried since his remains were unrecovered
MOH citation: For conspicuous devotion to duty, extraordinary courage, and complete disregard of his own life, during the attack on the Fleet in Pearl Harbor by Japanese forces on December 7, 1941. Rear Adm. Kidd immediately went to the bridge and as commander Battleship Division One, courageously discharged his duties as Senior Officer Present Afloat until the USS *Arizona*, his Flagship, blew up from magazine explosions and a direct bomb hit on the bridge, which resulted in the loss of his life.
Presentation of MOH:
    When: March 1942
    Where: Annapolis, Maryland
    By whom presented: Sent by registered mail to his widow
    Who received the MOH: The widow, Mrs. Inez Kidd
Other awards and decorations: Purple Heart, Cuban Pacification Medal, Mexican Service Medal, Victory Medal with Clasp, American Defense Service Medal, Asiatic-Pacific Campaign Medal, World War II Victory Medal
Ships named in his memory: Destroyer USS Kidd (DD-661); guided-missile destroyer USS Kidd (DDG-993)

Warrant Officer (Gunner) Jackson Pharris, U.S. Navy

Born: June 26, 1912; Columbus, Georgia
Source of military status: Appointed warrant officer on January 30, 1941
Grade and component: Warrant Officer (Gunner), U.S. Navy
Command and location: USS *California* (BB-44), Pearl Harbor, Oahu
Fate: Survived December 7; died October 17, 1966

Buried: Arlington National Cemetery
MOH citation: For conspicuous gallantry and intrepidity at the risk of his life above and beyond the call of duty while attached to the USS *California* during the surprise enemy Japanese aerial attack on Pearl Harbor, Territory of Hawaii, December 7, 1941. In charge of the ordnance repair party on the third deck when the first Japanese torpedo struck almost directly under his station, Lt. (then Gunner) Pharris was stunned and severely injured by the concussion, which hurled him to the overhead and back to the deck. Quickly recovering, he acted on his own initiative to set up a hand-supply ammunition train for the antiaircraft guns. With water and oil rushing in where the port bulkhead had been torn up from the deck, with many of the remaining crewmembers overcome by oil fumes, and with the ship without power and listing heavily to port as a result of a second torpedo hit, Lt. Pharris ordered the shipfitters to counterflood. Twice rendered unconscious by the nauseous fumes and handicapped by his painful injuries, he persisted in his desperate efforts to speed up the supply of ammunition and at the same time repeatedly risked his life to enter flooding compartments and drag to safety unconscious shipmates who were gradually being submerged in oil. By his inspiring leadership, his valiant efforts, and his extreme loyalty to his ship and her crew, he saved many of his shipmates from death and was largely responsible for keeping the *California* in action during the attack. His heroic conduct throughout this first eventful engagement of World War II reflects the highest credit upon Lt. Pharris and enhances the finest traditions of the U.S. Naval Service.
Citation: Signed by President Harry S. Truman, June 3, 1948
Presentation of MOH:
    When: June 25, 1948
    Where: The White House
    By whom presented: President Harry S. Truman
    Who received the MOH: Lieutenant Commander Pharris
Other awards and decorations: Purple Heart with one gold star, American Campaign Medal, American Defense Service Medal, Asiatic-Pacific Campaign Medal with four bronze stars, Navy Good Conduct Medal with one bronze star, Navy Expert Rifle Medal, Navy Occupation Service Medal with Asia Clasp, World War II Victory Medal, Pearl Harbor Commemorative Medal, Honorable Service Lapel Button
Ship named in his memory: Fast frigate USS Pharris (FF-1094)

WARRANT OFFICER (RADIO ELECTRICIAN) THOMAS REEVES, U.S. NAVY

Born: December 9, 1895; Thomaston, Connecticut
Source of military status: Appointed warrant officer November 13, 1941
Grade and Component: Warrant Officer (Radio Electrician), U.S. Navy
Command and location: USS *California* (BB-44), Pearl Harbor
Age: 45
Fate: Died on December 7 of injuries sustained on that morning aboard *California*
Buried: National Memorial Cemetery of the Pacific (Punchbowl)
MOH: For distinguished conduct in the line of his profession, extraordinary courage, and disregard of his own safety during the attack on the Fleet in Pearl Harbor, Territory of Hawaii, by Japanese forces on December 7, 1941. After the mechanical ammunition hoists were put out of commission in the USS *California*, Reeves, on his

own initiative, in a burning passageway, assisted in the maintenance of an ammunition supply by hand to the antiaircraft guns until he was overcome by smoke and fire, which resulted in his death.
Citation: Signed by President Franklin D. Roosevelt, March 4, 1942
Presentation of MOH: No information available other than his brother, Fred Reeves, receiving the MOH
Other awards and decorations: Purple Heart, American Defense Service Medal, Asiatic-Pacific Campaign Medal, World War II Victory Medal
Ship named in his memory: Destroyer escort USS Reeves (DE-156), later converted to APD-52, an auxiliary high-speed transport

WARRANT OFFICER (MACHINIST) DONALD ROSS, U.S. NAVY

Born: December 8, 1910; Beverly, Kansas
Source of military status: Appointed a warrant officer (machinist) in October 1940
Grade and component: Warrant officer (Machinist), U.S. Navy
Command and location: USS *Nevada*, Pearl Harbor
Age: 30
Fate: Survived December 7; died May 27, 1992
Buried: Ashes scattered over the site of the sunken USS *Nevada*; memorial marker in Beverly, Kansas
MOH citation: For distinguished conduct in the line of his profession, extraordinary courage, and disregard of his own life during the attack on the Fleet in Pearl Harbor, Territory of Hawaii, by Japanese forces on December 7, 1941. When his station in the forward dynamo room of the USS *Nevada* became almost untenable due to smoke, steam, and heat, Lieutenant Commander Ross forced his men to leave that station and performed all the duties himself until blinded and unconscious. Upon being rescued and resuscitated, he returned and secured the forward dynamo room and proceeded to the after dynamo room, where he was later again rendered unconscious by exhaustion. Again recovering consciousness, he returned to his station where he remained until directed to abandon it.
Citation: Signed by President Franklin D. Roosevelt, March 4, 1942
Presentation of MOH:
    When: April 18, 1942
    Where: Pearl Harbor
    By whom presented: Admiral Chester Nimitz
    Who received the MOH: Warrant Officer Ross
Other awards and decorations: American Defense Service Medal with Fleet Clasp, Asiatic-Pacific Campaign Medal, European-African-Middle-Eastern Campaign Medal, World War II Victory Medal, Navy Occupation Service Medal with Asia Clasp, China Service Medal, National Defense Service Medal, Korean Service Medal, United Nations Service Medal, and Good Conduct Medal with one bar.
Ship named in his memory: Guided-missile destroyer USS Ross (DDG-71)

Petty Officer First Class (Machinist's Mate) Robert Scott, U.S. Navy

Born: August 13, 1915; Massillon, Ohio
Source of military status: Enlisted in the Navy on April 18, 1938; date of promotion to first class petty officer unknown
Grade and component: Petty Officer (Machinist's Mate) First Class, U.S. Navy
Command and location: USS *California* (BB-44), Pearl Harbor, Oahu
Age: 26
Fate: Died on the morning of December 7 aboard *California*
Buried: Arlington National Cemetery
MOH citation: For conspicuous devotion to duty, extraordinary courage, and complete disregard of his own life, above and beyond the call of duty, during the attack on the Fleet in Pearl Harbor, Territory of Hawaii, by Japanese forces on December 7, 1941. The compartment, in the USS *California*, in which the air compressor to which Scott was assigned as his battle station, was flooded as a result of a torpedo hit. The remainder of the personnel evacuated that compartment, but Scott refused to leave, saying words to the effect, "This is my station, and I will stay and give them air as long as the guns are going."
Citation: Signed by President Franklin D. Roosevelt, March 4, 1942
Presentation of MOH:
    When: Most likely March 1942
    Where: Massillon, Ohio
    By whom presented: By registered mail
    Who received the MOH: Mrs. Lena Scott (mother?)
Other awards and decorations: Purple Heart, American Defense Service Medal, Asiatic-Pacific Campaign Medal, World War II Victory Medal
Ship named in his memory: Destroyer escort USS Scott (DE-214)

Chief Petty Officer (Watertender) Peter Tomich, US Navy

Born: June 3, 1893; Prolog, Austria
Source of military status: Enlisted in the Navy on January 23, 1919; promoted to chief petty officer June 1930
Grade and component: Chief Petty Officer (Watertender), US Navy
Command and location: USS *Utah*, Pearl Harbor, Oahu
Age: 48
Fate: Perished aboard ship on December 7
Buried: Not buried since his remains were unrecovered
Memorials: Tomich Hall at Naval Station, Newport, Rhode Island, is named for him.
MOH citation: For distinguished conduct in the line of his profession and extraordinary courage and disregard of his own safety during the attack on the Fleet in Pearl Harbor by the Japanese forces on December 7, 1941. Although realizing that the ship was capsizing, as a result of enemy bombing and torpedoing, Tomich remained at his post in the engineering plant of the USS *Utah* until he saw that all boilers were secured and all fireroom personnel had left their stations, and by so doing lost his life.
Citation: Signed by President Franklin D. Roosevelt, March 4, 1942
First Presentation of MOH:

When: January 4, 1944
Where: Aboard USS Tomich
By whom presented: Rear Admiral Monroe Kelly
Who received the MOH: The ship
Second Presentation of MOH:
When: Upon decommissioning of the ship, September 20, 1946
Where: Aboard USS Tomich
By whom presented: The ship
Who received the MOH: The Navy Department
Third Presentation of MOH:
When: May 25, 1947
Where: *Utah*
By whom presented: Rear Admiral Mahlon Tisdale
Who received the MOH: The State of *Utah*
Fourth and final presentation of MOH:
When: May 18, 2006
Where: USS Enterprise, Split, Croatia
By whom presented: Admiral Harry Ulrich
Who received the MOH: Croatian Army Lieutenant Colonel Srecko Tonic (Retired)
Other awards and decorations: Purple Heart, American Defense Service Medal with Fleet Clasp, Asiatic-Pacific Campaign Medal, World War II Victory Medal
Ship named in his memory: Destroyer escort USS Tomich (DE-242)

CAPTAIN FRANKLIN VAN VALKENBURGH, U.S. NAVY

Born: April 5, 1888; Minneapolis, Minnesota
Source of military status: Appointed an ensign at the Naval Academy, Class of 1909; promoted to captain December 23, 1937
Grade and component: Captain, U.S. Navy
Command and location: USS *Arizona*, Pearl Harbor, Oahu
Age at time: 53
Fate: Perished aboard ship on the morning of December 7
Buried: Not buried since his remains were unrecovered
MOH citation: For conspicuous devotion to duty, extraordinary courage, and complete disregard of his own life during the attack on the Fleet in Pearl Harbor by Japanese forces on December 7, 1941. As commanding officer of the USS *Arizona*, Captain Van Valkenburgh gallantly fought his ship until the USS *Arizona* blew up from magazine explosions and a direct bomb hit on the bridge, which resulted in the loss of his life.
Citation: Signed by President Franklin D. Roosevelt, March 4, 1942
Presentation of MOH:
When: March 1942
Where: Long Beach, California
By whom presented: Sent by registered mail to the widow in Long Beach
Who received the MOH: Mrs. Marguerite Van Valkenburgh, his widow
Other awards and decorations: Purple Heart, Haitian Campaign (1915), World War II Victory Medal with Atlantic Fleet Clasp
Ship named in his memory: Destroyer USS Van Valkenburgh (DD-656)

Seaman First Class James Ward, US Navy

Born: September 10, 1921; Springfield, Ohio
Source of military status: Enlisted in the Navy November 25, 1940; date of promotion to seaman first class unknown
Grade and component: Seaman First Class, U.S. Navy
Command and location: USS *Oklahoma* (BB-37), Pearl Harbor
Age: 20
Fate: Perished aboard *Oklahoma* in Pearl Harbor on the morning of December 7
Buried: Not buried since his remains were unrecovered
MOH citation: For conspicuous devotion to duty, extraordinary courage, and complete disregard of his own life, above and beyond the call of duty, during the attack on the Fleet in Pearl Harbor by Japanese forces on December 7, 1941. When it was seen that the USS *Oklahoma* was going to capsize and the order was given to abandon ship, Ward remained in a turret, holding a flashlight so the remainder of the turret crew could see to escape, thereby sacrificing his own life.
Citation: Signed by President Franklin D. Roosevelt, March 4, 1942
Presentation of MOH:
When: March 1942
Where: Springfield, Ohio
By whom presented: By registered mail
Who received the MOH: The parents, Howard and Nancy Ward
Other awards and decorations: Purple Heart, Asiatic-Pacific Campaign Medal, American Defense Medal, World War II Victory Medal
Ship named in his memory: Destroyer escort USS J. Richard Ward (DE-243)

Commander Cassin Young, U.S. Navy

Born: March 6, 1894; Washington, District of Columbia
Source of military status: Appointed an ensign at the Naval Academy, Class of 1916; promoted to commander April 14, 1937
Grade and component: Commander, U.S. Navy
Command and location: USS *Vestal*, Pearl Harbor, Oahu
Age: 47
Fate: Survived December 7; killed November 13, 1942, aboard USS San Francisco at the Naval Battle of Guadalcanal
Buried: At sea
Memorials: Name appears on the Tablets of the Missing, Manila Cemetery in the Philippines; "In memory of" marker at Mount Pleasant Cemetery, Mount Pleasant, South Carolina
MOH citation: For distinguished conduct in action, outstanding heroism, and utter disregard of his own safety, above and beyond the call of duty, as commanding officer of the USS *Vestal*, during the attack on the Fleet in Pearl Harbor, Territory of Hawaii, by enemy Japanese forces on December 7, 1941. Comdr. Young proceeded to the bridge and later took personal command of the three-inch antiaircraft gun. When blown overboard by the blast of the forward magazine explosion of the USS *Arizona*, to which the USS *Vestal* was moored, he swam back to his ship. The entire forward part of the

USS *Arizona* was a blazing inferno with oil afire on the water between the two ships; as a result of several bomb hits, the USS *Vestal* was afire in several places and was settling and taking on a list. Despite severe enemy bombing and strafing at the time and his shocking experience of having been blown overboard, Comdr. Young, with extreme coolness and calmness, moved his ship to an anchorage distant from the USS *Arizona* and subsequently beached the USS *Vestal* upon determining that such action was required to save his ship.

Citation: Signed by President Franklin D. Roosevelt, March 4, 1942

Presentation of MOH:
    When: April 18, 1942
    Where: USS *Vestal*
    By whom presented: Admiral Chester Nimitz
    Who received the MOH: Captain Young

Other awards and decorations: Purple Heart, Navy Cross, Presidential Unit Citation, Victory Medal, Atlantic Fleet Clasp, American Defense Service Medal, Asiatic-Pacific Area Campaign Medal, World War II Victory Medal

Ship named in his memory: Destroyer USS Cassin Young (DD-793)

NOTES

1. In World War II the status of Hawaii, including Oahu, was a US Territory.

2. The location of Pearl Harbor—Pearl Harbor is a harbor in Oahu, Hawaii.

3. The Naval Academy—The United States Naval Academy is in Annapolis, Maryland. Midshipmen who graduate are appointed as ensigns in the Navy or second lieutenants in the Marine Corps.

4. Memorials for MOH recipients whose remains were unrecovered—See Chapters 14, 21, and Appendix C for information about memorials for the MOH recipients whose remains were not recovered.

5. Good Conduct Medals—While only enlisted members can earn Good Conduct Medals (officers cannot earn them), an officer man have one if he was an enlisted man before becoming an officer. Officers may wear the medals on their officer uniforms.

6. Sources: Chapters 4–15 and 19 of the main text discuss the recipients in detail; Appendix B is a list of ships named to honor the recipients; Chapter 21 and Appendix C discuss burials and memorials for the recipients. Information on other awards comes from information in a recipient's Official Military Personnel File or in the official biography (one or two pages) his service prepared for him due to his MOH status.

APPENDIX B
SHIPS NAMED FOR THE HAWAIIAN ISLAND MEDAL OF HONOR RECIPIENTS

The ships in this chapter were named for eighteen of the nineteen MOH recipients discussed in this book. The Navy even named a ship after Billy Mitchell but certainly not an aircraft carrier: the transport ship USS General William Mitchell. Knowing the "acidic" history of Billy Mitchell's bouts with the Navy, one must wonder why the Navy named a ship for him.

Only one of the Navy and Marine MOH recipients in this book does not have a ship named for him: Rear Admiral Samuel Fuqua. The author can find no indication of any ship by that name. The failure to name a ship for Fuqua is incongruous since he deserved a MOH more so than two of his fellow *Arizona* crewmen for whom ships were named: Isaac Kidd and Franklin Van Valkenburgh (see Chapters 4 and 15). He was one of the most deserving 7 December MOH recipients.

Construction began in 2012 for the guided-missile destroyer USS John Finn, DDG-113. In 2011, the navy awarded the builder the contract to build the ship. The ship was launched March 28, 2016.[1]

The following table reiterates designations from Chapter 2:

Ship	Designation
Battleship	BB
Cruiser	CA
Destroyer	DD
Guided Missle Destroyer	DDG
Destroyer Escort	DE
Fast Frigate	FF

The ships named for the MOH recipients commissioned during the war were DDs or DEs. The DDG and FF were developed after World War II.

The primary role of the DD was to protect and to screen larger ships, protecting them from attack from submarines and aircraft. The primary role for the DE was to escort convoys and to detect and to destroy enemy submarines. They could also screen and protect other ships. For examples, see the histories of Flaherty and Fleming. They were roughly the equivalent of Great Britain's corvettes.

Today, two destroyers, Kidd and Cassin Young, are "floating museums" in Baton Rouge and Boston, respectively. I visited both of them; they are well worth touring, especially Kidd where the display on kamikaze attacks is harrowing.

The commissioning date is the date the ship was placed in service; the decommissioning date is the date the ship was removed from service.

The tradition of naming ships for MOH recipients continues. The USS Michael Murphy, a guided-missile destroyer (DDG-112), was commissioned in Manhattan, New York, on October 6, 2012.[2] Lieutenant Murphy was a Navy SEAL awarded a posthumous MOH for bravery in Afghanistan in 2005.

USS BENNION (DD-662)

Commissioned: December 14, 1943
Sponsor: Mrs. M. S. Bennion, the widow of Captain Bennion
Service: The ship served in various campaigns in the Pacific during the war.
Decommissioned: June 20, 1946
Disposition: Sold for scrapping on May 30, 1973[3]

USS CANNON (DE-99)

Commissioned: September 26, 1943
Sponsor: Mrs. E. H. Cannon, mother of Lieutenant Cannon
Service: The ship escorted convoys in the Atlantic.
Decommissioned: November 19, 1944
Disposition: Transferred to the Brazilian Navy and renamed Baependi.[4]

USS FLAHERTY (DE-135)

Commissioned: June 26, 1943
Sponsor: Mrs. J. J. Flaherty, sister-in-law of Francis Flaherty
Service: The ship conducted convoy escort and antisubmarine operations in the Atlantic.

She was in two operations in 1944 of note as part of a "hunter-killer" group, comprising the escort carrier USS Guadalcanal and five destroyer escorts. On April 9, she assisted two other destroyer escorts, USS Pillsbury and USS Pope, in destroying U-515. On June 4, she assisted the hunter-killer group in the famous capture of U-505 at sea. Coincidentally, one of the officers from the destroyer escort Pillsbury, Lieutenant (junior grade) Albert David, received a posthumous MOH for leading Pillsbury's boarding party, capturing the U-boat, which was the first foreign man-of-war captured by the Navy since 1815 (U-505 is displayed at the Chicago Museum of Science and Industry). His was the sole MOH for the Battle of the Atlantic.

On April 23, 1945, Flaherty bombed U-546 with "Hedgehog" explosive devices and forced her to surface, where other ships sank her with gunfire.

Decommissioned: June 17, 1946
Disposition: Sold for scrapping on November 4, 1966.[5]

USS Fleming (DE-32)

Commissioned: September 18, 1943
Sponsor: Mrs. W. E. Rutherford
Service: The ship initially escorted convoys in the Pacific. On January 14, 1944, she sank the Japanese submarine RO-47. In 1945, she screened escort carriers in the Pacific, including service at Okinawa. In May 1945, she downed two of three Japanese kamikaze planes trying to hit or to bomb her. During the Okinawa campaign, she also rescued crewmen from two ships sunk by kamikazes.
Decommissioned: November 10, 1945, ironic since the US Marine Corps "Birthday" is celebrated on November 10 each year
Disposition: Sold on January 29, 1948[6]

USS Hammerberg (DE-1015)

Commissioned: March 2, 1955
Sponsor: Mrs. Elizabeth Moss, Petty Officer Hammerberg's mother
Service: The ship served in various peacetime operations and during the crisis in the Dominican Republic in 1961 and the Cuban Missile Crisis in 1962.
Decommissioned: 1973
Disposition: Sold for scrapping on July 17, 1974[7]

USS Hill (DE-141)

Commissioned: August 16, 1943
Sponsor: Mrs. Catherine J. Hill, Chief Boatswain Hill's widow
Service: The ship performed convoy escort and antisubmarine operations in the Atlantic.
Decommissioned: June 7, 1946
Disposition: Sold for scrapping on January 18, 1974[8]

USS Herbert C. Jones (DE-137)

Commissioned: July 21, 1943
Sponsor: Joanne Jones, widow of Ensign Jones
Service: The ship served in the Atlantic, escorting convoys and conducting antisubmarine patrols. The ship was also fitted with radio-jamming equipment to counteract German radio-controlled glider bombs.
Decommissioned: May 2, 1947
Disposition: Sold for scrapping on July 19, 1973[9]

USS Kidd (DD-661)

Commissioned: April 23, 1943
Sponsor: Mrs. Isaac Kidd, Rear Admiral Kidd's widow
Service: The ship served initially in the Atlantic. She moved to the Pacific in 1943, where the ship, given its namesake, was called the "Pirate of the Pacific"; she had a pirate painted on her forward funnel (stack). The ship saw extensive combat and shot

down several Japanese aircraft. On April 11, 1945, while participating in the Okinawa campaign, a kamikaze plane hit the ship, inflicting great damage; the crew casualties were thirty-eight dead and fifty-five wounded. The ship was decommissioned on December 10, 1946, but recommissioned on March 28, 1951, for the Korean War.
Decommissioned: June 19, 1964
Disposition: The ship is a museum in Baton Rouge, Louisiana.[10]

USS KIDD (DD-993 AND DDG-993)

Commissioned: June 27, 1981
Sponsor: Mrs. Angelique Kidd Smith, granddaughter of Rear Admiral Kidd
Service: The ship was built for Iran but delivered to the US Navy in 1979 after the exile of the Shah of Iran and converted from DD-993 to DDG-993.
Decommissioned: March 12, 1998
Disposition: Transferred to Taiwan on May 30, 2003[11]

USS PHARRIS (DE-1094; FF-1094)

Commissioned: January 26, 1974
Sponsor: Mrs. Jackson C. Pharris, widow of Jackson Pharris
Service: The ship was originally a destroyer escort but was reclassified as a fast frigate on June 30, 1975
Decommissioned: April 15, 1992
Disposition: Sold to Mexico on June 15, 1999[12]

USS REEVES (DE-156)

Commissioned: June 9, 1943
Sponsor: Mary Ann Reeves, niece of Radio Electrician Reeves
Service: The ship escorted convoys in the Atlantic until 1944, when she was converted to an auxiliary high-speed transport (APD) with the designation APD-52. As an APD, she served in the Pacific.
Decommissioned: July 30, 1946
Disposition: Transferred to the government of Ecuador for use as an electrical generator plant[13]

USS ROSS (DDG-71)

Commissioned: June 28, 1997
Sponsor: Mrs. Helen Ross, Captain Ross's widow
Service: The ship deployed in the fall of 2001 in response to the attacks on the United States on September 11, 2001.
Decommissioned: Still in service.[14]

USS SCOTT (DE-214)

Commissioned: July 20, 1943
Sponsor: Mrs. George McBride, who had five sons in the Navy

Service: She escorted convoys in the Atlantic and assisted with training.
Decommissioned: March 3, 1947
Disposition: Sold for scrapping January 20, 1967[15]

USS TOMICH (DE-242)

Commissioned: December 28, 1942
Sponsor: Mrs. O. L. Hammonds, who had three sons in the Navy and one in the Army
Service: She served in various Pacific campaigns.
Decommissioned: September 20, 1946
Disposition: Sold for scrapping on January 18, 1974[16]

USS VAN VALKENBURGH (DD-656)

Commissioned: August 2, 1944
Sponsor: Mrs. Marguerite Van Valkenburgh, Captain Van Valkenburgh's widow
Service: The ship served in various Pacific campaigns and was decommissioned on April 15, 1946. She was recommissioned on March 8, 1951.
Decommissioned: October 21, 1953
Disposition: On February 28, 1967, the ship was transferred to the Turkish Navy and served until the early 1970s before decommissioning in 1986 and scrapping in 1987.[17]

USS J. RICHARD WARD (DE-243)

Commissioned: July 5, 1943
Sponsor: Marjorie Ward, Seaman First Class Ward's sister
Service: She served on antisubmarine patrol duty in the Atlantic.
Decommissioned: June 13, 1946
Disposition: Sold for scrap on April 10, 1972[18]

USS CASSIN YOUNG (DD-793)

Commissioned: December 31, 1943
Sponsor: Mrs. Cassin Young, Captain Young's widow
Service: The ship served in various Pacific campaigns. In October 1944, she rescued 120 survivors from the carrier USS Princeton. Like USS Kidd, the ship participated in the Okinawa campaign. On April 6, she rescued survivors from two other destroyers that were sunk. On April 12, a kamikaze plane hit the ship's foremast, exploding fifty feet from the ship. One crew member was killed; one was wounded. She was decommissioned on May 28, 1946, but recommissioned September 8, 1951, for service during the Korean War.
Decommissioned: April 29, 1960
Disposition: She is a museum in Boston, Massachusetts.[19]

USS GENERAL WILLIAM MITCHELL (AP-114)

Commissioned: January 19, 1944.
Sponsor: Mrs. William Mitchell, Brigadier General Mitchell's widow

Service: During World War II, this ship (an "AP," which is a transport ship) sailed in the European-African, China-Burma-India, and Pacific Theaters of Operations. The ship also sailed in support of United Nations forces in the Korean War. In 1950 she was redesignated USS General William Mitchell T-AP-114.
Decommissioned: Date unknown.
Disposition: Sold for scrapping on June 29, 1987 and scrapped in 1988.[20]

NOTES

Note for Dictionary of American Naval Fighting Ships: James L. Mooney was the editor for volumes VII and VIII. The publisher for DANFS is the Naval History Division or the Naval Historical Center of the Department of the Navy.

1. Contract and construction—"Fabrication Begins on the Future USS John Finn, Naval Sea Systems Command (September 11, 2012); launching—"Future USS John Finn (DDG 113) Launched," Team Ships Public Affairs, Naval Sea Systems Command, (March 30, 2015).

2. "USS Michael Murphy Departs for Maiden Deployment," Flagship, Pilot Targeted Media (October 29, 2014).

3. Bennion—Dictionary of American Naval Fighting Ships, Vol. I (Naval History Division Center, Department of the Navy, Washington, DC, 1959), 118 (hereafter "DANFS").

4. Cannon—Ibid., Vol. II (1963), 26.

5. Flaherty—Ibid., 410.

6. Fleming—Ibid., 414–415.

7. Hammerberg—Ibid., Vol. III (1968), 225–226.

8. Hill—Ibid., 331.

9. Jones—Ibid., 310–311.

10. Kidd (DD-661)—Ibid., 641–642.

11. Kidd (DDG-993)—"Navsource Online: Destroyer Archive" (printed from the Internet October 15, 2015); "USS Kidd (DDG-993)," Louisiana Naval War Memorial Commission, printed from the Internet October 15, 2015.

12. Pharris—"Navsource Online: Destroyer Escort Photo Archive," printed from the Internet October 15, 2015.

13. Reeves—DANFS, Vol. VI (1976), 58–59.

14. Ross—Information from the "History" icon under "About US" on the ship's official Internet site (printed from the Internet October 15, 2015).

15. Scott—DANFS, Vol. VI (1976), 388.

16. Tomich—Ibid., Vol. VII (1981), 230–232 (Naval Historical Center).

17. Van Valkenburgh—Ibid., 450–453.

18. Ward—Ibid., Vol. III (1968), 477 (Naval History Division).

19. Young—Ibid., Vol. II (1963), 48–49 (Naval History Division).

20. Mitchell—DANFS and NavSource Onlline: Service Ship Photo Archive; both sources accessed on the Internet on November 9, 2015.

APPENDIX C
VISITING GRAVES, MEMORIALS, AND MUSEUMS RELATED TO THE HAWAIIAN ISLAND MEDAL OF HONOR RECIPIENTS

1. Warnings

a. Before visiting historical sites related to the MOHs mentioned in this book, readers should read the last two paragraphs of this Appendix (paragraphs 26 and 27) concerning visiting MOH graves and memorials and taking photographs. Both activities can be tricky and distressing. Visitors should use their own judgment in accessing sites and taking photographs; they may have opinions on these matters different from mine, and I assume no liability for any problems visitors may encounter, especially on military bases. I am merely reporting my own experiences.

b. The goal of this section is to prevent readers from spending hundreds or thousands of dollars and hours and days traveling to various places in the world only to find to their surprise one or more of the following circumstances: (1) having great difficulty finding the site or sites, (2) access to the sites is denied or restricted for any reason or number of reasons, or (3) photography at the site or sites is forbidden. I have been in all three circumstances, so I can report firsthand that no reader wants to experience any of them. For example, when I visited Punchbowl in April 2015, I found part of the Courts of the Missing closed for construction work, which appeared to be necessary to restore some of the walls to good condition (after all, the Hawaiian sun and weather must take a terrific toll on the courts, which are outside). As an illustration, at the end of this chapter, one can compare the slide I took of Captain Richard Fleming's inscription in 1999 with the photograph I took of it in 2015. A very kind construction foreman escorted me in 2015 to the areas under construction that had the names I wanted to photograph (nothing like traveling to Oahu only to find that the precise parts of the Honolulu Memorial I wanted to photograph were blocked to access because of construction).

c. Also, this chapter will assist readers in obtaining the most fulfilling and informative visit possible to a site related to a MOH mentioned in this book—if the site is accessible. Much of the information in this chapter is practical, based on what I learned the hard way from experience and spending time and money. And much of this information will not be found elsewhere. So this chapter is my personal, unvarnished message to the reader.

d. The "rule of last resort" is that if you cannot find a grave or an IMO ("In Memory of" marker) in a civilian cemetery, go to the veterans' section. In a military cemetery, obviously, a military grave or marker may be anywhere, but a civilian cemetery may have a veterans section for military dead.

2. Introduction

a. **Scope of sites.** Numerous relics, sites, graves, and memorials concerning the Hawaiian Island MOH recipients exist on Oahu and on the mainland United States, including both the MOH recipients whose bodies were recovered (or who died natural deaths) and those recipients whose bodies were not recovered. Locating all of them is difficult, since they are scattered all over the continental United States, Oahu, and Midway, so I do not guarantee I found every memorial for these men since I did not travel to all their hometowns or home states. The average member of the public will not know about these graves or memorials or many of the ones I did find. Listed in this appendix are the major sites and memorials I found through extensive research, persistence, oral history, stray remarks, stray glances, numerous visits to sites of MOH actions, chance, and being in the right place at the right time or the wrong place at the right time. Incredibly, Oahu lacks a "single source" memorial or plaque listing all the MOH recipients who earned MOHs in the Hawaiian Islands during World War II, especially a memorial on Oahu at or near Pearl Harbor.

b. How to find MOH sites. My book, *Hawai'i's World War II Military Sites* (2002) is the best guide for information on these and other military historical sites on Oahu. It is no longer in print but can be purchased via the Internet. Buyer beware: it was published in 2002 and is outdated. For example, it does not mention the USS *Oklahoma* Memorial and the Pacific Aviation Museum (both on Ford Island) since they were established after the book was printed. Also the *Arizona* Memorial Visitor Center has changed markedly since the book's publication and is now called the Pearl Harbor Visitor Center at the World War II Valor in the Pacific National Monument. The book does, however, contain good background information that is timeless. Its focus on MOH recipients is also timeless. Maps and general guidebooks for Oahu can be purchased, but free maps and booklets on Oahu may be as or more helpful than items purchased.

c. Sources for this chapter. I have personally seen these tombstones: Cannon; Fuqua, Hill, Jones, Pharris, Reeves, and Scott. I have personally seen the Kidd tombstone that is in effect an "In Memory Of" (IMO) marker for him. I have not seen the graves of Bennion, Finn, and Hammerberg or the IMO markers for Flaherty, Fleming, Ross, Van Valkenburgh, and Young. I have not seen personally the inscription for Young at Manila American Cemetery in the Philippines, but I have seen the inscriptions at Punchbowl for Flaherty, Fleming, Kidd, Tomich, Ward, and Van Valkenburgh. To my knowledge, Tomich lacks a formal IMO marker. For places I have not seen, I have put the source of information in the acknowledgments or the captions of photographs.

3. Author's notes on visiting MOH recipient graves and memorials

I can offer some crucial advice for visiting cemeteries. Unless visitors already know grave or memorial locations, they should either visit on weekdays when cemetery personnel are on duty and can be asked the locations of graves or memorials or call during the week and obtain the information if the visit will be on a weekend; cemetery personnel may not be present on weekends. I can attest to the following based on personal experience. Without knowing the exact location of a grave or memorial from cemetery staff or a good map, the visitor (me) can waste hours looking for a grave or memorial. Some cemeteries, however, such as Arlington National Cemetery, are open on weekends with staffs available to help visitors. For the convenience of the reader and because of the massive amount of process and material presented in this chapter, it is divided into the four sections listed here. For obvious reasons, Oahu sites have their own section.

Section 1—Personal Markers

Section 2—Group Memorials

Section 3—Sites on Oahu

Section 4—Museum

Section 5—Miscellaneous Memorials and Sites

Section 6—Guidance for Visiting Sites

★ ★ ★ ★ ★ ★ ★ ★ ★ ★ ★ ★

SECTION 1—PERSONAL MARKERS

4. Disposition and memorials. The disposition of deceased MOH recipients varies. The following abbreviations describing combat fate may be seen:

Abbreviation	Meaning
KIA	Killed in Action
DOW	Died of Wounds
MIA	Missing in Action
MIA / PD	Missing in Action / Presumed Dead
WIA	Wounded in Action

a. **Natural or combat death: body recovered.** If a MOH recipient was killed in combat or if he died a natural death, he was buried in a public or private cemetery, cremated, or buried at sea. Ross was the only recipient cremated. Young was the only recipient buried at sea.

b. **Combat death: missing in action or killed but body unrecovered.** If a MOH recipient was MIA, he simply vanished or was known to be killed in combat but his body was not recovered. He is memorialized in one or two ways.

(1) **Inscriptions on the Courts or the Tablets of the Missing.** The names of MIAs are inscribed on stone walls called Courts or Tablets of the Missing found at cemeteries for American war dead outside the United States. The American Battle Monuments Commission (ABMC) superintends American war dead cemeteries and their Courts or Tablets of the Missing outside the United States. For example, Cassin Young's name is inscribed on a Tablet of the Missing at Manila American Cemetery, which the ABMC superintends. The Honolulu Memorial and its Courts of the Missing are

an exception; they are at the National Memorial Cemetery of the Pacific (commonly called "Punchbowl") on Oahu and thus in the United States, but the ABMC superintends them. For example, the names of all the December 7 MOH recipients whose bodies were not recovered are found on the Courts of the Missing at Punchbowl as is the name of Captain Richard Fleming (Midway). Punchbowl comprises two separate sections: the cemetery, managed by the Veterans Administration (VA), and the Honolulu Memorial, just described, managed by the ABMC even though it is in the United States. A name can also be found on the Courts or Tablets of the Missing by using the ABMC Internet site.

(2) **In Memory of markers**. Many recipients have "In Memory Of" (IMO) markers, tombstones in a cemetery marking an empty grave. A government-issue IMO looks like a standard Veterans Administration (VA) headstone or footstone but will have "In Memory Of" inscribed at the top. Other tombstones not issued by the VA look different, such as the Kidd family tombstone and one of the Van Valkenburgh IMO markers, both described later in this chapter. They function as IMOs since they mark empty graves—empty for one of several reasons: the deceased is MIA, he was killed but his body was not recovered, he was buried at sea, his body was donated for science, or he was cremated.

c. **Gilding and MOH symbol.** Whether the MOH recipient has a tombstone, an inscription on the Courts or Tablets of the Missing, or an IMO, the inscriptions on the stone (the name and a MOH symbol) are usually gilded to indicate MOH status.

5. **Marked graves: wartime deaths.** The bodies of these MOH recipients, who were KIA or DOW, were recovered, identified, and buried in marked graves. Included is Hammerberg, who died a noncombat death.

    a. **Punchbowl.** I found all three graves easily by using a cemetery map available at the Visitors' Center near the large flagpole in a circle found just after entering Punchbowl.

    (1) First Lieutenant George Cannon, USMC: Grave C-1644.

    (2) Chief Warrant Officer (Boatswain) Edwin Hill, USN: Grave A-895

    (3) Warrant Officer (Radio Electrician) Thomas Reeves, USN: Grave A-884.

    b. **Arlington National Cemetery.** Petty Officer (Machinist's Mate) First Class Robert Scott, USN, grave number 34-3939. I found this grave easily. After leaving the Visitors' Center, turn left on Eisenhower Drive heading toward Section 60. Section 34 is on the right of and up a hill from Eisenhower Drive.

    c. **Salt Lake City Cemetery, Salt Lake City, Utah.** Captain Mervyn Bennion USN, grave number West-3-148-1-E (west plot, block three, lot 148, grave 1, tier E). Captain Bennion has two markers in the same plot.

    d. **Fort Rosecrans, San Diego, California.** Ensign Herbert Jones, USNR, grave

G-7G. The grave was easy to find with assistance from cemetery personnel.

  e. **Holy Sepulchre Cemetery, Southfield, MI.** Petty Officer (Boatswain's Mate) Second Class Owen Hammerberg, USN, grave 01, section 4, lot 145.

6. **Marked graves: natural deaths.** The two graves here are in Arlington National Cemetery, Arlington, Virginia:

  a. **Rear Admiral Samuel Fuqua, USN, grave 59-485.** I found this grave easily. After leaving the Visitors' Center, turn left on Eisenhower Drive, heading toward Section 60. Section 59 is on the left of Eisenhower Drive.

  b. **Lieutenant Commander Jackson Pharris, USN, grave 13-16281.** Finding this grave, which I did on May 31, 2015, was a three-hour nightmare due to a combination of my incompetent land navigation and the layout of section 13, the site of the Pharris grave. I had found the tombstone years ago only to find it canted, as is typical of the Pharris bad luck. I was unable to find it again during my trip to Arlington several years ago, and I was not about to miss it in 2015. Even having a map with step-by-step directions did not help. Two cemetery employees confirmed to me in 2015 that finding a grave in section 13 is difficult—even for them. I only found it with the help of one of the employees. My recommendations follow. First, obtain a map of the cemetery at the Visitors' Center. Second, use the locator to obtain a map and directions to the Pharris grave. Third, by any way possible, go to the James Tanner Amphitheater. Fourth, at the amphitheater, look for the white chapel at the intersection of Meigs Avenue and Wilson Avenue. Fifth, stand with your back against the back of the chapel and look away from the chapel for a square fenced area with two Cutis graves inside it. The square makes a diamond behind the chapel. The square's sides of the Custis site are not parallel with the back of the chapel. One point of the diamond points to the back of the chapel (my point "A") and one point of the diamond (my point "B" directly opposite point "A") points toward the Pharris grave out in section 13, away from the chapel and the Custis site. Fifth, walk to point "B" and continue into section 13 to the Pharris grave. To reach the grave, walk between two trees and head away from the chapel and the fenced area. Finally, look for the Pharris grave just beyond the two trees. You will see the back of the Pharris grave first if you follow my directions; on the back is the name of his wife ("ELIZABETH LEE").

7. **Names on the Courts or Tablets of the Missing**

  a. **Punchbowl.** These MOH recipients are memorialized by inscriptions on the Courts of the Missing at the Honolulu Memorial at Punchbowl on Oahu. Courts are organized by service and by war; each court also has a number.

Recipient, Unit, Date Became Missing	Location of Inscription
Ensign Francis Flaherty: USS Oklahoma, MIA December 7, 1941	Court Number 3
Captain Richard Fleming: VMSB-241, Midway, MIA June 5, 1942	Court Number 2
Rear Admiral Isaac Kidd: USS Arizona, MIA December 7, 1941	Court Number 3
Chief Petty Officer (Watertender) Peter Tomich: USS Utah, MIA December 7, 1941	Court Number 2
Captain Franklin VanValkenburgh: USS Arizona, MIA December 7, 1941	Court Number 2
Seaman First Class James Ward: USS Oklahoma, MIA December 7, 1941	Court Number 2

b. **Names on the Tablets of the Missing: Manila American Cemetery**—The name of one Hawaiian Island MOH recipient is on the Tablets of the Missing at Manila American Cemetery in the Philippines:

Recipient, Unit, Date Became Missing	Location of Inscription
Captain Cassin Young: KIA, USS San Francisco, November 13, 1942	Name inscribed on the West "Hemicycle"

8. **"In Memory Of" Markers**

a. **Combat deaths.** The bodies of these MOH recipients were unrecovered, so the men are memorialized by "In Memory Of" markers of various types (see notes below the table).

Recipient, Unit, Date Became Missing	In Memory of Marker (IMO) Location
Ensign Francis Flaherty: USS Oklahoma, MIA December 7, 1941	Maple Hill Cemetery, Charlotte, MI (Section F, Lot 12)
Captain Richard Fleming: VMSB-241, Midway, MIA June 5, 1942	Fort Snelling National Cemetery, Minneapolis, MN (Section F-1, Marker 111)
Rear Admiral Isaac Kidd: USS Arizona, MIA December 7, 1941	Naval Academy Cemetery, Annapolis, Maryland (Section 5)
Chief Petty Officer (Watertender) Peter Tomich: USS Utah, MIA December 7, 1941	Ferncliff Cemetery, Veterans' Section, Springfield, OH
Captain Franklin VanValkenburgh: USS Arizona, MIA December 7, 1941	Forest Home Cemetery, Milwaukee, WI (Section 25, Block 6, Lot 12)
Seaman First Class James Ward: USS Oklahoma, MIA December 7, 1941	Mount Pleasant Memorial Gardens, Mount Pleasant, SC (Garden E, Lot 58, Space A-3)

b. **Nature of markers.**

(1) Fleming and Flaherty have classic upright stone "In Memory Of" markers.

(2) Ward and Young have "In Memory Of" markers that are metal and flat. These markers would be difficult to find without assistance from cemetery personnel. I made the mistake of visiting Ferncliff Cemetery to see the Ward IMO on a weekend without having talked to the cemetery staff during the week. Fortunately, a burial was held on the day of my visit and a cemetery staff member was by chance available to help me.

(3) VanValkenburgh has two markers in Section 25, Block 6, Lot 12 of the Forest Home Cemetery in Milwaukee, Wisconsin. One is a tall vertical memorial, not the classic VA "In Memory Of" marker, with the following lettering, which is difficult to read on the stone:

IN MEMORY OF
FRANKLIN
VAN VALKENBURGH
CAPTAIN U.S.USN.
KILLED WHILE COMMANDING
HIS SHIP USS ARIZONA
AT PEARL HARBOR, T.H.
DECEMBER 7, 1941

The marker does not indicate his MOH status. "T.H." is Territory of Hawaii. The other marker for him is a classic footstone MOH "In Memory Of" marker, indicating his MOH status.

(4) Kidd does not have a formal "In Memory Of" marker. On the grounds of the US Naval Academy in Annapolis, Maryland, is a cemetery that in Section 5 has a large tombstone for the Kidds. On it are inscriptions for five members of the Kidd family, including the Kidd killed aboard *Arizona*. I found the tombstone by entering the Naval Academy through Gate 8, following Bowyer Road from the gate a short distance, and then turning left onto Phythian Road toward the cemetery and continuing until I reached the cemetery sign. At the sign, I turned right, drove a very short distance, and turned right onto Cushing Road. I followed it to the top of a hill. At the top of the hill, Cushing bears left; just after bearing left, I looked into the cemetery and saw the Kidd tombstone in the distance near a tall monument atop of which is a cross and an anchor. Among the inscriptions for five Kidds is the following inscription:

ISAAC CAMPBELL KIDD
REAR ADMIRAL, US NAVY
KILLED IN ACTION, USS ARIZONA
AWARDED THE MEDAL OF HONOR
MAR. 26, 1884 – DEC. 7, 1941

One is led to believe by reading the inscription for Rear Admiral Kidd that he is buried there (no "In Memory Of" inscription is on the stone) when in fact, as discussed in chapter 15, his body was never positively identified. Also, as noted in this chapter, his name appears on the Courts of the Missing at Punchbowl.

b. **Noncombat death.** Captain Donald Ross, USN, died in 1992 and was cremated. His ashes were scattered over the site of the sunken USS *Nevada*. At Beverly Cemetery in the town of his birth (Beverly, Kansas) is an "In Memory Of" marker for him in Lot 309.

Section 2—Group Memorials

9. **The Naval Academy monument for graduates missing in action (MIA).** Below the Naval Academy cemetery is Ramsay Road on which, near the columbarium, is a monument to Naval Academy graduates missing in action; the names are listed by class year. The front of the monument looks in part as follows:

--------- CLASS OF 1906 ---------

Isaac Campbell Kidd

--------- CLASS OF 1909 ---------

Franklin Van Valkenburgh

Kidd is the only MIA from his class; Van Valkenburgh is one of two members of his class who are MIA. Cassin Young's name is not on the monument; an educated guess is the omission is due to his burial at sea: his remains were recovered but those of Kidd and Van Valkenburgh were not, so he was not formally missing in action as were Kidd and Van Valkenburgh.

10. **Congressional Medal of Honor Memorial in Indianapolis.** I visited the very large and impressive Congressional Medal of Honor Memorial in downtown Indianapolis, Indiana. It was dedicated on May 28, 1999. Indianapolis Power and Light Company (IPALCO) sponsored construction of the memorial. Information about the memorial was in "IPALCO Presents Champions of Courage," a special supplement to the newspaper the Indianapolis Star and News (May 1999). How I got the supplement I do not know.

Section 3—Sites on Oahu

11. **Sites on Oahu: Overview.** On Oahu, the MOHs were earned at three places: around Ford Island, which is inside Pearl Harbor; in the West Loch of Pearl Harbor; and at Kaneohe Bay. But any visit should start at the Pearl Harbor Visitor Center at the World War II Valor in the Pacific National Monument. Oddly, the title contains "valor," yet as noted, earlier no "single source" listing exists of the men who earned MOHs in the Hawaiian Islands in World War II. Only two ships and memorials are actually in the waters of Pearl Harbor: USS *Arizona* with her memorial over her middle (perpendicular to the ship lengthwise) and USS *Utah*, still capsized, with her memorial extending from the shore of Ford Island into the waters of Pearl Harbor. That memorial

does extend over the remains of the ship.

12. **World War II Valor in the Pacific National Monument.** The three most important components of the monument on Oahu are memorials for *Arizona, Oklahoma,* and *Utah.* The most popular ship and memorial is USS *Arizona.* The visitors area, known as the Pearl Harbor Visitor Center (formerly the *Arizona* Visitor Center), is open to the public and comprises various museums, plaques, and artifacts. The area is usually crowded with tourists, especially during the morning. Visitors should know that the area has various security rules, such as prohibitions against entering the site with such dangerous items as backpacks, purses, fanny packs, luggage, diaper bags, shopping bags, camera bags, and large cameras (what is a "large" camera?). These ultra-hazardous items may be stored at a nearby storage trailer while visitors tour the area.

    a. **The blue tablets: Remembrance Circle.** At the rear of the visitor center and close to the water's edge is a semicircular monument, comprising blue tablets with the names of the dead from December 7 except for the names of *Arizona* dead, which are found on a wall at *Arizona* Memorial in Pearl Harbor. The tablets are easily overlooked in the excitement of being at the Pearl Harbor complex. Names, organized by ship or by station, are in white; MOH recipient names are in brown. The names are only for those lost on Oahu on December 7 and do not include three of the MOH dead discussed in this book: the two Midway MOH recipients (Cannon and Fleming) and the West Loch MOH recipient (Hammerberg).

    b. **The Arizona Memorial.** As noted in the text, *Arizona* is the only ship on Battleship Row that was there on December 7 and is one of only two ships that was there on December 7 (the other is *Utah*).

    (1) **Access.** The Memorial is in the waters of Pearl Harbor over the sunken ship, which remains on Battleship Row. The ship sank in place; the memorial spans the middle of the ship, so visitors walk over the middle of the ship from port (left) to starboard (right). White buoys mark the stern (closest to *Nevada*'s quays) and bow of the ship (between *Arizona* and USS *Missouri*). Visitors reach the Memorial by taking a tour boat from the theater at the visitor center to the Memorial. Visitors must obtain free tickets at the ticket counter just beyond the entrance to the Pearl Harbor Visitor Center. Arrive early, since tickets may be distributed quickly with none left for those arriving too late. Also, allow for a time gap between the time a ticket is issued (for example, 10:00 a.m.) and the time for the movie (2:00 p.m.). Before boarding the white boats that take visitors to the Memorial, visitors must watch a movie about the Memorial. Six boats are named for December 7 MOH recipients: Samuel G. Fuqua, Peter Tomich, Cassin Young, Jackson Pharris, John Finn, and Donald Ross. The names are on the sterns (rear) of the boats. Tourists do not step on Ford Island during this tour. Boats go from the landing outside the theater to the memorial and back to the landing and do not go around or land at Ford Island. The best place to sit in a tour boat is in the left rear, which is the best place for taking photographs. By the way, do not take anything into the theater other than a camera and a small water bottle.

    (2) **While on the Memorial.** Because of the large number of visitors, visits only last approximately twenty minutes, which pass quickly, so to have the most efficient and

best experience, the visitor should know what sites to look for and should find them quickly: the mooring quays described in subparagraph (3) here, the names of the dead and missing on the wall facing Ford Island, and the diagrams of the ship—both in normal and destroyed conditions—in the middle of the Memorial. My advice is to go quickly to the wall with the names of the dead and missing; this wall is on the opposite end of the Memorial as the entrance. The back of the wall faces Ford Island. By going there quickly, one can reach it before other visitors and can photograph the wall without other people standing in the way. Most of the names are those of Navy officers and men; the Marine officers and men who perished on the ship are listed in the lower right corner of the wall in their own section and are identified as Marines. They were members of the ship's Marine detachment or of Rear Admiral Kidd's staff. The MOH names to look for are Kidd and Van Valkenburgh; their MOH status is not indicated, but their command statuses are. They appear as follows:

I. C. KIDD RADM
BATTLESHIP DIV. COMMANDER

F. VAN VALKENBURGH CAPT
COMMANDING OFFICER

Alternatively, the visitor can wait to visit the wall until near the end of the visit when visitors are being rounded up to leave the Memorial. At that point, most people are in the line, waiting for the return boat, so the space in front of the wall is open for photography without having to consider the presence of other visitors—until the next boat of visitors arrives, so move quickly. Another highlight is to look upward when in the center of the memorial to see the U.S. flag atop the memorial.

(3) **What to Look for during Trips to and from the Memorial.** During the boat trip to the Memorial, visitors will not be told to look to the left of the Memorial to see the white mooring quays between the bows of Missouri and *Arizona* (the quays were used to secure lines to moor the ships to Ford Island). They are from Missouri to *Arizona* (left to right): *West Virginia*, Tennessee, and *Vestal* closest to the *Arizona* Memorial. To the right of the *Arizona* Memorial is one quay for *Arizona* and two for *Nevada*. The visitor will not be told about the MOHs awarded for men on nearby ships. They are Rear Admiral Isaac Kidd, Captain Franklin Van Valkenburgh, and Lieutenant Commander Samuel Fuqua (*Arizona*); Chief Boatswain Edwin Hill and Warrant Officer Donald Ross (*Nevada*); and Commander Cassin Young (*Vestal*).

These are the mooring quays that can be seen during the boat trip across Pearl Harbor to the memorial:

Berth Number	Marking as Seen from the Pearl Harbor Side
F-6	USS WEST VIRGINIA BB 48
F-6	USS TENNESSEE BB 43
F-7	USS VESTAL AR 4
F-7	USS ARIZONA BB 39
F-8	USS NEVADA BB 36

Unfortunately, the visitor traveling to *Arizona*'s Memorial cannot easily see the two mooring quays for *California*, which are behind Missouri's stern. Looking at the two quays from Pearl Harbor's water, one finds the right quay marked "USS CALIFORNIA BB 44."

c. The Exhibit Halls

(1) At the Pearl Harbor Visitor Center at the World War II Valor in the Pacific National Monument are two exhibit halls; the first is Road to War, the second is Attack. They are politically correct in that they warn visitors that some of the content of the halls may be offensive, yet I found nothing at all offensive except the exhibition on "Valor" in the second exhibit hall, which is truly pathetic and embarrassing as explained later in this chapter. No blood and guts are seen, but God forbid visitors (and many are Japanese) may hear or read the word "Jap."

(2) While "Valor" has a sign stating that fifteen MOHs were earned during the attack on Pearl Harbor (one was actually earned at Kaneohe Bay), the names of the recipients are not listed. The only other MOH information is a partial citation for Jackson Pharris with a Navy MOH and ribbon above the citation, but the MOH and ribbon are unidentified, so the viewer does not know if it is the Pharris MOH and ribbon or not. Pharris is the only MOH recipient identified by name. Although the MOH is the country's highest military honor, the display's focus is not the MOH. The display is politically correct by focusing on Doris Miller, who is black and who received a Navy Cross, the second-highest award for valor next to the MOH. The "Attack" exhibit hall includes a large photograph of him receiving his undeserved Navy Cross (see Chapter 17) from Admiral Chester Nimitz, and large photographs of Miller can be seen at the entrance to the first exhibit hall and at the exit of the second exhibit hall, but no photographs of MOH recipients are displayed. Tourists, not knowing the material presented in this book, could easily and incorrectly conclude that Doris Miller was the most important sailor or one of the most important at Pearl Harbor on December 7. I thought the exhibit was politically correct due to its focus on Doris Miller (first black to receive a Navy Cross) and dumbed down. He was, by all the attention accorded him, made larger than life both by narrative and the large photographs of him. The MOH recipient information disgusted me. These men who did so much more than Miller, including sacrificing life in eleven cases, were grossly and disrespectfully shortchanged (see Chapter 17 concerning Doris Miller).

13. Ford Island

a. **Access.** Ford Island is an active military installation, so a military or proper government identification card or visitor's pass is required to gain entrance. I make no representation regarding visitor policy. Tourists gain limited access by buying a tour package at USS Bowfin, the World War II submarine on display near the Pearl Harbor Visitor Center. Tourists travel by bus across the bridge linking Ford Island and the mainland and can see the *Oklahoma* Memorial, USS Missouri, and the Pacific Air Museum. Although Ford Island is an active military base, I know of no prohibition against taking photographs on Missouri, at the *Oklahoma* Memorial, or in or around the museum.

b. **USS *Oklahoma* Memorial.** As mentioned in Chapter 7 (*Oklahoma*), a memorial to the ship was dedicated on December 7, 2007, on Ford Island near USS Missouri, which is in the berth (F-5) occupied by *Oklahoma* on December 7. A memorial for *Oklahoma* at Pearl Harbor was long overdue, especially since only *Arizona* lost more crewmen than *Oklahoma*, which lost 429 officers and men—415 Navy personnel and 14 Marines (officer and enlisted). As noted here, the names of Flaherty and Ward with MOH status indicated can be found in two places: among the list of the names of the dead and missing on a black panel and each man has a white panel or "standard" with his name and MOH symbol on it.

(1) **The front of the Memorial.** The front of the Memorial is a black stone panel with "USS *OKLAHOMA* BB 37" inscribed on it. On the back side of the panel are lists of names of the dead and missing by section number with Flaherty and Ward listed with asterisks to indicate MOH status.

(2) **The "Heart" of the Memorial.** Behind the black stone panel are 429 upright white marble pillars ("standards") arranged in four rows with each pillar representing one of the 429 men lost on December 7. Each Navy member or Marine lost on December 7 has a marker with his service emblem at the top; under it is his name and grade or rating. The names and grades read vertically down the markers. The pillars are arranged in four rows; the rows begin closest to Missouri and at some point turn at an angle to the right. The pillars in each row continue until they end at large black stones on which are engraved quotations from famous men. The pillars for Flaherty and Ward have MOH symbols at the top to indicate their MOH status. A separate black stone with the title "MANNING THE RAILS" explains the symbolism of the memorial: the pillars represent ship crewmen "manning the rails" of the ship (crewmen standing near the edge of the deck).

(3) **Wayside exhibit.** A wayside exhibit is also part of the Memorial. In part, it reads, "The marble standards represent the 429 crewmen lost. Each standard bears a name beneath a Navy eagle or Marine insignia. Gold stars on two standards mark Medal of Honor recipients." Unfortunately the wayside does not identify the MOH recipients by name, so to find them, one either has to know who they are before arriving at the Memorial or know to look on the back side of the black panel (the front is marked "USS *OKLAHOMA* BB 37"), find the list of names organized by numbered columns, and know that Flaherty and Ward have asterisks beside their names to

indicate MOH status. Otherwise, the visitor must look at all 429 standards in a search for their names (organized alphabetically). The insignia above their names on the standards are not "gold stars" but are MOH symbols, which resemble stars but are not classic stars.

(4) Mooring quays and other memorials not visible to the public. The main inaccessible-to-the-public attraction is the *Utah* Memorial described here, an important part of the history of December 7. Numerous historical markers are on Ford Island, but the average tourist would not know where to find them; many of them are "off limits" since they are in officer housing. The three types of markers or reminders are described here. They do not indicate that MOHs were earned at the sites.

(a) One: mooring quays. The first type of reminder is the unmarked backs of the mooring quays in Pearl Harbor close to Ford Island along Battleship Row for *California*, *West Virginia*, Tennessee, *Vestal*, *Arizona*, and *Nevada*. Inboard ships, when ships were moored in pairs, were moored to the quays (outboard ships were then moored to the inboard ships). The mooring quays in front of Missouri's bow are for *West Virginia*, the ship on which Captain Mervyn Bennion earned his MOH (this is the quay closest to Missouri's bow) and for Tennessee. The quays for Maryland and *Oklahoma* at berth 5 no longer exist; in that space is a pier to which USS Missouri is moored (to state the obvious, Missouri was not at Pearl Harbor in 1941). Maryland was the inboard ship in the space now occupied by Missouri; the outboard ship was *Oklahoma*, the ship aboard which Ensign Francis Flaherty and Seaman First Class Ward earned their MOHs.

(b) Two: metal plaques. The second type of reminders are small metal plaques indicating where ships were moored on December 7 and what happened near the location of the monument. These monuments are near the mooring quays for *California*, *West Virginia*, and Tennessee, *Vestal* and *Arizona*, and *Nevada*. *Nevada*'s plaque is in the backyard of an officer's quarters near the waters of Pearl Harbor. No such monument exists for Maryland and *Oklahoma*, but years ago, I saw the plaque for the two ships mounted on the front of the fire station near Missouri. The *Utah* plaque is on the wreckage of the ship and visible only from the Pearl Harbor side of the wreckage.

(c) Three: *Arizona* monuments. Various monuments concerning *Arizona* are on Ford Island behind the *Arizona* Memorial. Looking from the monuments to the memorial, one would look across the waters of Pearl Harbor toward the back side of the large wall of the Memorial on which the names of the dead are inscribed.

(c) USS *Utah* Memorial

(1) Access. The other ship and memorial in Pearl Harbor is USS *Utah*, in the waters of Pearl Harbor on the opposite side of Ford Island from *Arizona*. While the public can see *Arizona* by the tour just mentioned, Ford Island is still an active military base and, sadly, generally inaccessible to the general public. Those with military or government identification cards or visitor passes can cross the bridge to Ford Island to see *Utah* and her Memorial. To my knowledge, the Memorial is not part of the tour

package for Ford Island, so access is only by government identification card or visitor's pass.

(2) **Memorial**. As noted in the text, *Utah* is the only ship on Carrier Row (Carrier Row is on the opposite side of Ford Island as is Battleship Row) that was there on December 7 and is one of only two ships that was in Pearl Harbor on December 7. Much more wreckage can be seen at *Utah* than at *Arizona*, but *Utah*'s Memorial is in the officer housing area, so most visitors will not see it or the surrounding piers where other ships were moored forward and aft (back) of *Utah* on December 7. The Memorial is a large, flat, white structure on Ford Island with a walkway that extends into Pearl Harbor, permitting the visitor to see the remains of the ship. Unlike *Arizona*, the *Utah* Memorial stops short of, and does not extend over, the ship herself. Most of *Arizona* is underwater; much of *Utah* is above water—a large reddish-brown rusting hulk, a ghastly reminder of a ship never fully righted after she capsized. A U.S. flag flies at the Memorial. The Memorial has a tablet listing the names of those lost aboard the ship (see photo on the cover of this book). Tomich's name is on the tablet but with no indication that he received a MOH. A memorial marker is on the wreckage of the *Utah* but can only be seen from Pearl Harbor; it cannot be seen from the *Utah* Memorial on Ford Island side. White buoys mark the stern (to the left of the Memorial) and bow of *Utah* (to the right). The wayside exhibit mentions that Tomich is a MOH recipient but does not clarify that he earned the MOH on December 7 aboard *Utah*. A memorial marker is on a modern pier where Raleigh was moored in front of *Utah*, but it is inaccessible and unreadable at a distance.

14. Naval Station Pearl Harbor (Joint Base Pearl Harbor/Hickam Air Force Base, "PHH")

a. **Overview**. Naval Station Pearl Harbor and Hickam Air Force Base were separate active military installations for decades. They were separate in World War II when they were Navy Yard Pearl Harbor and Hickam Field, but metamorphosis hit, and they later became Naval Station Pearl Harbor and Hickam Air Force Base. But with the military's fixation and obsession with names and joint service everything, the two bases were, by that magic and hocus-pocus only known to the U.S. military, joined and transformed into one base, "PHH" (Pearl Harbor-Hickam). Making any activity or anyplace "joint" is magic for the military; the military places a premium on joint places and activities. In any event, a military or proper government identification card or visitor's pass is required to gain entrance to one or both members of this couple. I make no representation regarding visitor policy.

b. **Ward Field**. Ward Field at Pearl Harbor and was named for Seaman First Class James Ward, who earned a posthumous MOH aboard USS *Oklahoma*. It comprises two athletic fields and remains in use today. The program for the field's dedication, held on April 7, 1953, referenced his MOH and stated, "Baseball was his prime interest and the batting championship of the Pacific Fleet was among his achievements." The program included the "Introduction of Mr. and Mrs. Howard Ward, parents of honored hero." It also included the "Unveiling of [a] bronze plaque by Mrs. Ward." I unsuccessfully looked for the plaque several times on or near Ward Field, but I did see a large blue sign reading "Ward Field" (see Chapter 5 (*Oklahoma*)).

c. **Sites at or near Naval Shipyard Pearl Harbor.** Luckily for the public, it cannot see two important sites at or near the Naval Shipyard.

(1) **Cryptology plaques.** One if the most important events in U.S. history occurred in the basement of an administrative building at the Shipyard; cryptologists working there broke the Japanese naval code, enabling the United States to win the Battle of Midway, a somewhat important event in U.S. history leading to the activities of and MOH for Marine Captain Richard Fleming, one of the MOH recipients discussed in this book. Attached to an outside wall of the building are two plaques concerning the operations of the code breakers working in the basement of the building. Unfortunately, since the building is in the Naval Shipyard, a high-security area, inspection of the plaques by the general public or photography by anyone would run afoul of regulations governing photography on base and in the Shipyard. The large plaque, which I call "the secret sign," so essential to current national security that one cannot photograph it, reads as follows; it is a great, concise summary of the Battle of Midway and the crucial events leading to it. It is "Midway 101" or "Midway for Dummies."(The Fourteenth Naval District was not a combat command; it was a commend having jurisdiction over the installation (primarily the Navy Yard) that was the base for the Fleet and the various arms of the Navy that supported the Fleet.)

DEDICATED TO THE OFFICERS AND MEN
OF THE 14TH NAVAL DISTRICT
COMBAT INTELLIGENCE UNIT

COMMANDING OFFICER: LCDR JOSEPH J. ROCHEFORT USN

IN THE EARLY MONTHS FOLLOWING THE SURPRISE ATTACK ON PEARL HARBOR (DECEMBER 7, 1941), A GROUP OF DEDICATED MEN IN THE COMBAT INTELLIGENCE UNIT LABORED IN THIS BASEMENT OF THIS 14TH NAVAL DISTRICT HEADQUARTERS TO DECIPHER THE JAPANESE NAVAL CODE. THIS UNIT IS KNOWN AS "HYPO" BUT A MORE PROPER DESIGNATION IS "FLEET RADIO UNIT PACIFIC" (FRUPAC). CODE NAME "HYPO", THEN THE STANDARD NAME FOR THE "H" FLAG IN THE INTERNATIONAL SIGNAL CODE, WAS SOMETIMES USED LOOSELY FOR THE WHOLE ACTIVITY AND THUS APPLIED HERE.

UNDER THE INSPIRATIONAL LEADERSHIP OF LCDR JOSEPH J. ROCHEFORT, USN, THESE CRYPTANALYSTS HAD DECODED A FEW KEY WORDS IN THE JAPANESE NAVAL CODE (JN-25), AND CONCLUDED THAT THE LETTERS "AF" STOOD FOR MIDWAY ATOLL. WHEN MIDWAY SENT OUT A BOGUS MESSAGE THAT THE ATOLL HAD EXPERIENCED A SERIOUS CASUALTY IN THE FRESH WATER SYSTEM, THE JAPANESE SIGNALED THAT "AF" WAS HAVING TROUBLE WITH ITS FRESH WATER DISTILLATION SYSTEM. ARMED WITH THIS INTELLIGENCE REPORT AND DEEP CONFIDENCE IN ROCHEFORT'S TEAM, NIMITZ PLACED THREE AMERICAN AIRCRAFT CARRIERS 240 MILES NORTHEAST OF MIDWAY TO AMBUSH THE JAPANESE TASK FORCE AND REINFORCED MIDWAY WITH MEN, PLANES AND EQUIPMENT. AIDED BY THIS PIVOTAL INFORMATION, THE UNITED STATES NAVY ON JUNE 4, 1942 WROTE A "GLORIOUS PAGE IN OUR HISTORY" AND TURNED THE TIDE OF WAR IN THE PACIFIC.

HONORED BY THE
INTERNATIONAL MIDWAY MEMORIAL FOUNDATION
30 JUNE 1999

An "authorized" photograph of this plaque I took in 1999 appears at the end of Chapter 12. I lacked the guts to take an unauthorized photograph of it in 2015.

(2) *Nevada* **Memorial.** The other site is the *Nevada* Memorial at Hospital Point just beyond the Shipyard area and in officer housing (one must pass through the shipyard to reach the site). The Memorial is near the site where the ship was ordered to ground on December 7 so she would not be sunk in the channel leading from Pearl Harbor to the Pacific Ocean (see chapter 9). One must travel through the Shipyard and

another sensitive area, officer housing, to reach the memorial at Hospital Point. A U.S. flag flies at the Memorial, which has plaques about *Nevada* getting underway during the December 7 attack. It also has a plaque listing the ship's dead and the ship's MOH recipients (Hill and Ross).

15. **The National Memorial Cemetery of the Pacific ("Punchbowl")**

    a. **Overview.** MOH recipients killed during or missing after the December 7 attack are memorialized at Punchbowl, the National Military Cemetery of the Pacific, described earlier in this Appendix. To recap, Punchbowl comprises two areas: the cemetery, supervised by the Veterans Administration, and the Courts of the Missing, supervised by the ABMC or American Battle Monuments Commission. The Courts of the Missing have the names of those who are missing in action from World War II, the Korean War, and Vietnam. Visitors who have the good fortune to be there on Memorial Day will see that each grave has a U.S. flag and lei, and each MOH recipient grave will have a light-blue MOH flag. Boy and Girl Scouts and other volunteers place these items on the graves. To say that the sight of Punchbowl on Memorial Day is breathtaking is an understatement. Punchbowl's Visitors' Center can provide two lists of MOH names: those MOH recipients buried in the cemetery and those whose names are on the Courts of the Missing. As far as MOH recipients in this book are concerned, the graves of Cannon, Hill, and Reeves are at Punchbowl, and on the Courts of the Missing at the Honolulu Memorial are the names Flaherty, Fleming, Kidd, Miller, Tomich, Van Valkenburgh, and Ward. Because Cassin Young was killed near Guadalcanal, his name is on the Tablets of the Missing at Manilla American Cemetery and not at the Honolulu Memorial.

    b. **Finding graves or names at Punchbowl.** Punchbowl is not on a military installation, so it is open to the public. I never had any problems at Punchbowl finding or photographing graves or names on the Courts of the Missing except when some of the courts were inaccessible in 2015 because of rehabilitation and construction (a friendly foreman escorted me to an off limits area I wanted to photograph). Graves can be found by using maps available at the visitors' center, and names on the Courts of the Missing can be found by looking at the top of the courts for identifying data (war and military service). Also the courts are numbered with small numbers in front of them (the numbers can be easily overlooked if the visitor does not know to look for them). The easiest way to find a name is not by court number but by war and military service. Fortunately, the names are in alphabetical order. A quick look at a court will rapidly and easily orient visitors about how and where to find names.

16. **Marine Corps Base Hawaii (Kaneohe Bay).** The base is an active military installation with an airfield, so a military or government identification card or visitor's pass is required to gain entrance. I make no representation regarding visitor policy. The base was Naval Air Station Kaneohe, the site where Chief Petty Officer John Finn earned his MOH on December 7. At Kaneohe Bay, one can see the hangar near which Finn earned his MOH. A building on the base is named for him; just inside the front of the building is a display about him.

17. **Naval Magazine Pearl Harbor (West Loch).** The Naval Magazine is a special case, very similar to the shipyard at Pearl Harbor; it is a high-security area, and as such, even military or government identification cards do not guarantee entry or access. A member of the public would be unable to see anything concerning the 1944 West Loch Disaster or Petty Officer Second Class Owen Hammerberg, the Navy diver who earned his MOH at West Loch in 1945. A building inside the front entrance is named for Hammerberg, and inside it is a plaque inscribed with his MOH citation. I was twice among the fortunate few who managed to reach the magazine's docks to see a National Park Service wayside exhibit, large panels describing the 1944 West Loch Disaster. Hammerberg and his MOH are not mentioned on the wayside. The rusted wreckage of LST-480 (one of the ships involved in the 1944 disaster) can still be seen, a colorful but grim reminder of the "Second Pearl Harbor."

18. **Midway.** The U.S. Fish and Wildlife Service based in Honolulu manages Midway and can provide information about it. Visiting Midway is very difficult, which is tragic since the Memorial to Lieutenant George Cannon is on Midway as is his command post where he earned his posthumous MOH in 1941. The Marine Corps League erected the memorial to Cannon on Midway. Those seeking symmetry can forget it. Midway lacks a monument to Captain Richard Fleming, the Marine aviator who earned the sole MOH around Midway in 1942. My repeated attempts to ignite interest in a memorial for Fleming flamed out, meeting the usual default governmental and bureaucratic "ho-hum" response (i.e., no interest and no action). The U.S. Fish and Wildlife representative on Midway with whom I corresponded did not even know about Fleming, and the amount of interest he exhibited in honoring Fleming was despicably and bureaucratically tepid. The closest the average person can come to visiting Midway and seeing its memorials is to access the official government Internet site for Midway (see Chapter 12 (Midway)).

Section 4—Museum

19. **The National Naval Aviation Museum in Pensacola, Florida.** This museum is first class and on par with the Smithsonian. Period. I have visited it four times, and three of those four times I spent entire days in the museum. During my fourth and most recent visit (2015), I spent almost two full days touring the museum. It is on Naval Air Station Pensacola, where Navy, Marine Corps, and Coast Guard pilots are trained. The following aspects of the museum are relevant to this book:

   a. **Captain Fleming and Chief Finn.** They are on the museum's MOH wall with their citations and their facial images. I found Fleming easily but did not think to look for Finn; fortunately, by chance, I saw him above Fleming (thank goodness both last names began with "F" and were in sequence with Finn above Fleming). The connections with naval aviation? Fleming was a Marine Corps pilot, and Finn was an aviation ordnanceman. Incredibly, the docent leading my tour of the museum, a retired Marine aviator of all people, did not know that Fleming flew a SBD and a Vindicator or that his was the sole MOH recipient for 1942's Battle of Midway.

   b. **Midway aircraft.** The Museum has the only SB2U Vindicator in existence; Captain Fleming, stationed at Midway, flew a Vindicator to his death during one of his MOH actions. The museum has a SBD Dauntless that was at Pearl Harbor on December 7; she also flew at Midway. She was riddled with over 200 bullet holes after flying from Midway on June 4, 1942, and attacking the Japanese. Fleming's SBD, flown on that date, had 179 bullet holes. Other aircraft of interest are Wildcat and Zero fighters. These types of aircraft were at Oahu on December 7 and at Midway in 1942.

Section 5—Miscellaneous Sites

20. **Floating museums: USS Cassin Young and USS Kidd.** Two of the MOH recipients in this book have floating museums that are ships named for them. USS Cassin Young is a destroyer moored near USS Constitution in Boston, Massachusetts. USS Kidd is a destroyer in Baton Rouge, Louisiana (see appendix B).

21. **U-505.** The German World War II submarine U-505, in whose capture USS *Flaherty* participated, is displayed at the Museum of Science and Industry, Chicago, Illinois. The ship was named for posthumous MOH recipient Ensign Francis Flaherty of USS *Oklahoma*.

22. **Tomich Hall: Naval Station, Newport, Rhode Island.** Tomich Hall is a building with a display on Tomich in its foyer, complete with a replica of his MOH.

23. **The Congressional Medal of Honor Society.** The Congressional Medal of Honor Society (CMOHS) and its museum are aboard the USS Yorktown at Patriots Point, near Charleston, South Carolina. Contact the Congressional Medal of Honor Society, 40 Patriots Point Road, Mt. Pleasant, South Carolina 29464. The telephone number is (843) 884-8862. The society also has an informative Internet site with recipients organized alphabetically; clicking on a name produces the citation. To find recipients and citations by wars in which they fought, access a separate list of recipients: the army's master list of MOH recipients on the Internet. Search for "army MOH site," which takes you to the US Army's Center of Military History Internet site. The citations may contain typographical errors or misspellings. These are two separate entities: the CMOHS and the Army Center of Military History.

24. **The Marine Corps War Memorial.** Popularly known as the Marine Corps Iwo Jima Monument, it has a chiseled "1941 PEARL HARBOR" but not one for Midway 1941.

25. **MOH memorial at Eaton County, Michigan.** This impressive memorial on the grounds of the courthouse was dedicated in 2000 and includes markers for the county's two MOH recipients, one of whom is Ensign Francis Flaherty, lost on *Oklahoma*.

Section 6—Guidance for Visiting Sites

26. **Access to MOH sites**

   a. **Off limits.** Unfortunately for the casual visitor or the expert history enthusiast, some of the markers and memorials concerning the MOHs that are the subject of this book are inaccessible to the general public. In a sense, visitors to Oahu are unable to view certain crucial aspects of the history of their own country. In particular, the sites involving December 7 and some of the most crucial events in World War II history are on active military bases and thus inaccessible to the general public, thus depriving it of viewing the sites where World War II history was made. Perhaps the most important such site is the codebreaker site described earlier in this chapter.

b. **How to see what is off limits.** The average person can see some off-limits areas in one of two ways. One is to have a friend or family member with a military or government identification card that permits entry onto a base. The other is by reading one of my books and looking carefully at the pictures in them: this book focusing on the MOH or my other book described earlier in this Appendix, Hawai'i's World War II Military Sites, if a copy can be found on the Internet. Sadly, casual visitors to Oahu are ignorant of many aspects of December 7 and the two Battles of Midway (1941 and 1942) unless they read one or both of my books.

c. **No duplicate memorials or signs.** The author, having served in the Regular and Reserve Marine Corps, understands the need for military security but fails to understand why duplicate signs or monuments concerning historical sites in secure areas cannot be made and placed in areas to which the general public has access. For example, copies of the code breaker plaques at the Shipyard or the wayside at West Loch could be made and placed outside an entrance to the Naval Station or at the Pearl Harbor Visitor Center at the World War II Valor in the Pacific National Monument.

27. Taking photographs of MOH recipient graves and memorials

a. **Private cemeteries.** Private cemeteries may have policies about photography. I generally just take photographs, and if accosted, I explain what I am doing; the person generally goes away satisfied that I am not a foreign agent or vandal. After all, I am trying to capture the history of my own country.

b. **Public cemeteries.** Public cemeteries may have policies about photography. I generally just take photographs; if accosted, I do what I do at private cemeteries, and the person generally goes away secure in the knowledge that my intent is pure.

c. **On military bases**

(1) Military bases generally have policies prohibiting photography even of historical sites. The policies seem to be more about control than security, and personnel enforcing the policy can be hypervigilant, bordering on hysterical and paranoid attitudes and actions. The policies appear to be leftovers from the Cold War, combined with a gross overreaction to the attacks on September 11, 2001. Banning photography of a secret SEAL facility is one thing and of no interest to me; banning photography of a historical marker or place is another thing and seems ludicrous. Although military personnel should be given some credit for realizing on their own what to photograph and what not to photograph, security personnel are apt to overheat or to slip into overdrive at the site of a camera or someone taking pictures. At Naval Station Guam in 2015, I was even accosted by a sailor obviously assigned to security for taking photographs of a rack of SPAM (the atrocious meat product) in an Navy Exchange. I explained that my father served on Guam in World War II and hated SPAM, hence the

reason I was taking the photograph—because my father mentioned SPAM frequently and not very positively. The sailor told me he had noticed me taking photographs days earlier. (I was either alone or part of a tour group when previously taking pictures.) I wondered why, when I was part of a tour group, I could take all the photographs I wanted, but suddenly when alone and taking pictures of a rack of SPAM, obviously a secret military site, I was some kind of enemy agent (perhaps SPAM's taste could be used to disable an enemy). But the real question is what harm is done by taking photographs of historical sites on a military base, such as the codebreaker plaques at Naval Shipyard Pearl Harbor and other subjects that probably have been shown in other books or on the History Channel?

(2) So one can either (a) take photographs without asking and risk being caught and having the camera confiscated or (b) ask permission and be told to contact Public Affairs, which is the default bureaucratic answer. Asking permission risks triggering a bureaucratic wave of reaction or overreaction with the result being Public Affairs machinery moving about as fast as a three-legged dog. The end product is extended delay in obtaining permission to take photographs or possibly being denied permission to take photographs of the most benign sites—sites that probably can be seen on the History Channel or the Discovery Channel. In summary, nothing attracts notice of military police or other military officials more than someone taking photographs; while a gang of terrorists is crashing the gate, the police would be focusing on the lone retired reserve colonel taking a photograph of some innocuous, nonsecret historical site.

(3) I can state three absolutes unequivocally: unless photographers have permission, they should never take photographs of entrances or exits of military bases; in or around a naval shipyard; or of flight lines, as if the enemies of the United States have never seen our aircraft or runways (try Google map). For example, I was forbidden in 2015 from taking photographs in the Pearl Harbor Shipyard of the two historical plaques just mentioned concerning the famous World War II navy code breakers who worked in the building to which the plaques were attached (their work ensured success at the Battle of Midway). I asked to take the photographs and was told to contact Public Affairs and that the approval process could take weeks, which seemed insane and typically bureaucratic. I asked the bureaucrat if he could escort me and allow me to take photographs, but like a broken record, I heard, "Contact Public Affairs," as if I would live sufficiently long to receive an answer. But I left happy; I already had a photograph of the plaques taken on an earlier visit courtesy of a friendly security manager who escorted me around the building after I asked him politely if I could photograph the area. As another example, on Guam, I drew fire photographing the Andersen Air Force Base sign several yards away from the main entrance to the base. I was photographing the sign, not the entrance, but I had to show a friendly air policeman my digital photographs so he could rest easy that I had not photographed the entrance but just the sign.

(4) In summary, my advice is to check with the base's military police before taking pictures notwithstanding the chances of being caught in a bureaucratic "loop" or being referred to Public Affairs. I recommend contacting the base's military police or Public Affaris BEFORE visiting the base. Additional advice: if I feel queasy about photographing any subject on a military base, I will identify myself to a friendly-

looking law enforcement person (almost always a young one), talk shop so he or she will know I am not a terrorist or a mobster, and then ask if I can take a picture. Generally if I am nice and explain what I want to photograph, the answer is "yes." This approach works much better than anger or pulling rank.

Photographs:
MOH Graves and Memorial Markers

Captain Mervyn Bennion, U.S. Navy.

The Bennion grave site with two markers. (Photograph courtesy of Kevin Dolan, 2002)

Close-up of bottom marker at the Bennion grave site. (Photograph courtesy of Brandi Madrill, 2016)

First Lieutenant George Cannon, U.S. Marine Corps

The Cannon grave site at Punchbowl. (Author's photograph, 2015)

The Memorial on Midway Atoll to First Lieutenant Cannon. The flag on the right is that of the Marine Corps. (Photograph courtesy of Barry Christenson of the Fish and Wildlife Service, 2008)

Ensign Francis Flaherty, U.S. Naval Reserve

The Flaherty inscription at Punchbowl. (Author's photograph, 2015)

The Flaherty marker at the USS Oklahoma Memorial on Ford Island. Note the MOH symbol at the top above the Navy eagle. (Author's photograph, 2015)

The Flaherty IMO. (Photograph courtesy of Chuck Brandon, 2016)

The MOH Memorial at the Eaton County, Michigan, Courthouse; Ensign Flaherty's inscription is at left. (Photograph courtesy of Chuck Brandon, 2016)

Captain Richard E. Fleming, U.S. Marine Corps Reserve

The effect of time and weather on inscriptions at Punchbowl. The Fleming inscription in 2001 (author's slide)

The Fleming inscription in 2015 (author's photograph)

The Fleming In Memory of Marker in 2015 at Fort Snelling National Cemetery. (Photograph courtesy of Ken Everson)

Lieutenant Commander Samuel Fuqua, U.S. Navy

The Fuqua tombstone in Arlington in 2015. (Author's photograph)

Petty Officer Second Class (Boatswain's Mate) Owen Hammerberg, U.S. Navy

The original grave on Oahu. (Photograph courtesy of Stan Bozich, 2002.)

The Hammerberg final resting place. (Photograph courtesy of Robert Sullivan, 2002)

Chief Boatswain Edwin Hill, U.S. Navy

The Hill grave at Punchbowl in 2015. (Author's photograph.)

Ensign Herbert Jones, U.S. Naval Reserve

The Jones grave in 2003. (Author's slide)

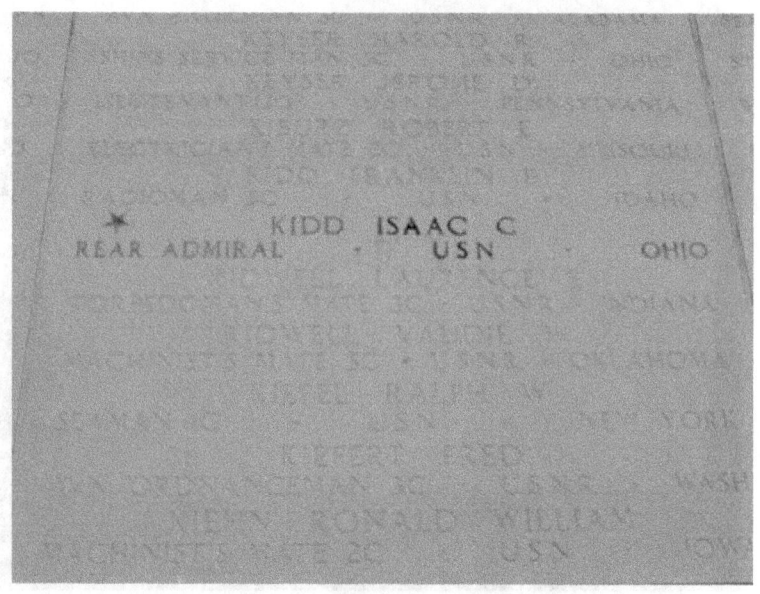

The Kidd inscription at Punchbowl in 2015. (Author's photograph)

The Kidd family tombstone at the cemetery at the US Naval Academy in 2014. (Author's photograph)

WARRANT OFFICER (GUNNER) JACKSON PHARRIS, U.S. NAVY

The Pharris tombstone at Arlington National Cemetery in 2002. (Author's slide)

The Pharris tombstone at Arlington in 2015. (Author's photograph)

WARRANT OFFICER (RADIO ELECTRICIAN) THOMAS REEVES, U.S. NAVY

The Reeves grave at Punchbowl in 2015. (Author's photograph)

WARRANT OFFICER (MACHINIST) DONALD ROSS, U.S. NAVY

The Ross IMO in 2015 at Beverly Cemetery, Beverly, Kansas. (Photograph by Joan Detmer)

Petty Officer First Class (Machinist's Mate) Robert Scott, U.S. Navy

The Scott grave in Arlington in 2015. (Author's photograph)

Chief Petty Officer Watertender Peter Tomich, U.S. Navy

The Tomich inscription at Punchbowl in 2015. (Author's photograph)

Tomich's name on the list of the dead and missing (the "Honor Roll") at the USS Utah Memorial in Pearl Harbor, sixth from the top. "CWT" following his name is Chief Watertender," his grade. (Author's photograph, 2015)

Captain Franklin Van Valkenburgh, U.S. Navy

The Van Valkenburgh inscription at Punchbowl in 2015. (Author's photograph)

One of two Van Valkenburgh IMO at Forest Home Cemetery, Milwaukee, WI. (Photograph courtesy of Jan Van Rens, 2015)

The other Van Valkenburgh IMO. (Photograph courtesy of Jan Van Rens, 2015.)

Seaman First Class James Ward, U.S. Navy

The Ward IMO in 2002. (Author's slide)

The Ward inscription at Punchbowl in 2015. (Author's photograph)

Captain Cassin Young, U.S. Navy

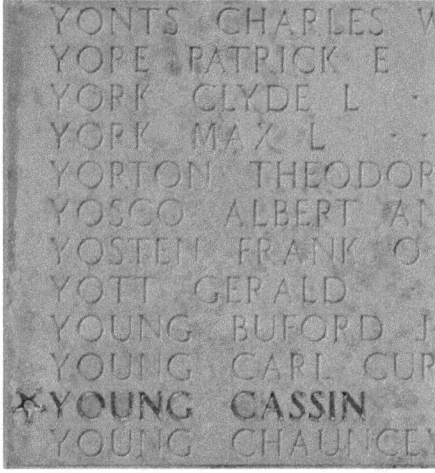

The left side of the Cassin Young inscription on the Tablets of the Missing at Manila American Cemetery, the Philippines in 2015. (Photograph courtesy of Hubert Caloud)

The entire Cassin Young inscription on the Tablets of the Missing at Manila American Cemetery, the Philippines in 2015. (Photograph courtesy of Hubert Caloud)

The Young IMO in 2002. (Photograph courtesy of the author's father, Lieutenant Colonel Elmer C. Jones, U.S. Air Force Reserve (Retired))

Photographs Part II: Ship Memorials

USS Arizona

Memorial to the USS Arizona in Pearl Harbor along Battleship Row. Note the ship's mooring quay to the far right. The vegetation to the right is on Ford Island. (Author's photograph, 2015)

USS Utah Memorial

Memorial to the USS Utah in Pearl Harbor along Carrier Row. Wreckage of the ship can be seen at left beyond the left side of the white memorial. (Author's photograph, 2015)

USS Oklahoma Memorial

Memorial on Ford Island in Pearl Harbor to the USS Oklahoma. (Author's photograph, 2015)

USS Nevada Memorial

Memorial at Naval Station Pearl Harbor to the USS Nevada at Hospital Point. Across the water at approximately the eleven o'clock position is "Nevada Point." (Author's photograph, 2015)

Appendix D
A Brief History of the Medal of Honor and the Awards Process

Introduction: The Medal of Honor

The Medal of Honor (MOH) has been awarded to two categories of men: those earning the MOH in combat and those not earning it in combat.

The Role of Congress: Overview

Congress is involved or uninvolved in the MOH in one of four ways, discussed in more detail throughout this chapter, with the different subjects in different parts of this chapter.

Part 1: Legislation Creating and Governing MOHs

Congress created the MOH by legislation, created time limits for MOH awards, and amended MOH legislation. Congress may do so under Section 8 of Article 1 of the Constitution, which authorizes Congress to make rules governing the country's land and naval forces.

Part 2: Permitting the Executive Branch to Award MOHs

Second, the general rule is that Congress is uninvolved in a MOH award; the language of the MOH statutes permits the President to present MOHs in the name of Congress. Thus the executive branch, not the legislative branch, normally awards combat MOHs. In World War II, the executive branches processing awards were the War and Navy Departments. Today, the executive branch doing so comprises first the individual military services; second the Departments of the Air Force, Army, and Navy; and third the Department of Defense, which was not created until 1947 and which is the superior organization for all the services and their departments.[1] Each military service falls under a department (the marine corps is under the Department of the Navy).

Part 3: Congressionally Awarded MOHs

Congress did not, by authorizing the President to award MOHs, relinquish its power to enact legislation awarding a MOH to specific individuals, although such awards are rare.[2]

Part 4: Policing the MOH

Congress can pass and has passed legislation requiring the military to examine service records to determine if service members receiving awards less than MOHs should have received MOHs. If such cases are discovered, Congress enacts legislation waiving the time limits to permit the belated MOH awards.[3]

Part 1: Legislation Creating and Governing MOHs

In different years, Congress passed legislation concerning different aspects of the MOH. The approach was piecemeal, as will be seen later in this appendix. One would have thought that a MOH would have been created for all services and for officers as well as enlisted from the beginning, but such a one-step process did not happen. Modern (current) MOH statutes finally established uniformity among the services and among grades. (MOHs are not limited to officers or to enlisted personnel.)

Congress also created an award that was the second highest decoration for combat bravery: the Distinguished Service Cross (DSC) for the army, the Navy Cross (NC) for the "naval service" (Marine Corps, Navy, and Coast Guard), and the Air Force Cross (AFC) for the Air Force, which became a separate service after World War II. The cross decorations are included in this book because Jackson Pharris and Doris Miller received Navy Crosses.

In short, the path of the MOH is from creation during the Civil War to the statutes currently governing MOHs. Until Congress put everything in one place in the current statutes, creating a MOH for each service and establishing various time limits, MOH legislation comprised various laws passed in various years.

Creating the MOH for Enlisted Men

First, in 1861, Congress created a MOH for Marine Corps and Navy enlisted members. During the Civil War, Congress enacted legislation on December 21, 1861, authorizing the Secretary of the Navy to prepare two hundred "medals of honor" for award to "petty officers, seaman, landsmen, and marines [sic] as shall most distinguish themselves by their *gallantry in action* and other seamanlike qualities during the present war..." (Italics added for emphasis in quotation.) No eligibility for officers was created.[4]

Second, in 1862, Congress created a MOH for Army enlisted members. This legislation was enacted on July 12, 1862, authorizing the President to present medals of honor in the name of Congress, a qualifier not in the Navy legislation, to "noncommissioned officers and privates as shall most distinguish themselves by their *gallantry in action* and other solider-like qualities, during the present insurrection [the Civil War]" (Italics added for emphasis in quotation). No eligibility for officers was created.[5]

Creating the MOH for Officers

Third, in 1863, Congress authorized MOHs for Army officers. On March 3, 1863, Congress enacted legislation permitting Army officers to receive MOHs by including "officers" in the following legislative wording. It permitted the President to present MOHs to "such *officers*, noncommissioned officers, and privates as have most distinguished or who may hereafter distinguish themselves in action" (Italics added for emphasis in quotation).[6]

Fourth, in 1915, Congress authorized awards of MOHs for Naval service officers (Marine Corps, Navy, and Coast Guard). On March 3, 1915, Congress enacted legislation permitting such officers to receive MOHs, again by including the word officer in the legislation: the "officer" had to "distinguish himself in battle or display extraordinary heroism in the line of his profession" (Italics added for emphasis in quotation).[7]

THE ARMY MOH: 1918

Fifth, in 1918, Congress created a MOH, DSC, and Distinguished Service Medal (DSM) for the Army. Congress enacted legislation on July 9, 1918, authorizing the President, in the name of Congress, to present a MOH to a member of the Army (officer or enlisted) who, in actual conflict with an enemy, "distinguish[es] himself conspicuously by gallantry and intrepidity at the risk of his life above and beyond the call of duty."[8]

The same legislation established two other awards for the Army:

The Distinguished Service Cross (DSC) was for extraordinary heroism "in connection with military operations against an armed enemy." The DSC was for heroism not meeting MOH standards.

The Distinguished Service Medal was for "exceptionally meritorious service to the Government in a duty of great responsibility."

The DSC and DSM were not presented in the name of Congress.

THE NAVY MOH: 1919

Sixth, in 1919, Congress created a MOH, NC, and Navy Distinguished Service Medal (NDSM) for the Naval service. Congress enacted this legislation on February 4, 1919, for a MOH for the Naval service (Marine Corps, Navy, and Coast Guard), permitting the President, in the name of Congress, to present a MOH to a member of the Naval service who, in actual conflict with an enemy, "distinguish[es] himself conspicuously by gallantry and intrepidity at the risk of his life above and beyond the call of duty and without detriment to the mission or to the command to which attached" (Italics added for emphasis). The emphasized qualifier was not in the Army MOH legislation.[9]

The same legislation established two other awards for the Marine corps and the Navy, in this order:

The Navy Distinguished Service Medal was for "exceptionally meritorious service to the Government in a duty of great responsibility."

The Navy Cross was for "extraordinary heroism or distinguished service in the line of his profession." The award was for heroism or service insufficient to justify a MOH.

The NDSM and the NC were not presented in the name of Congress.

Confusion arose over when the Navy Cross and when the Navy Distinguished Service Medal should be awarded.

The Navy MOH: 1942

Seventh, in 1942, Congress amended the 1919 legislation creating the Naval service awards (MOH, NC, and NDSM).

On August 2, 1942, Congress amended the 1919 act governing the Navy MOH to change the award and its design. The MOH was for all members of the "naval service." It was awarded by the President in the name of the Congress to a member of the naval service who, in actual conflict with an enemy, or in the line of his profession, "distinguish[es] himself conspicuously by gallantry and intrepidity at the risk of his life above and beyond the call of duty without detriment to the mission or to the command to which attached." (Italics added for emphasis in quotation.) The italicized language is not in the 1919 legislation for the army MOH. The Navy MOH could be awarded for noncombat bravery as can be seen by including the following language: "or in the line of his profession."[10]

Because of the confusion over the circumstances justifying awards of the NC and the NDSM, in the 1942 legislation, Congress restricted the NC to awards for extraordinary heroism in combat. Thus, it established the two awards, in this order, with the Navy Cross listed first and with the following criteria:

The Navy Cross was for extraordinary heroism "in connection with military operations against an armed enemy."

The Navy Distinguished Service Medal was for "exceptionally meritorious service to the Government in a duty of great responsibility."

Again, the Navy Cross and the Navy Distinguished Service Medal were not presented in the name of Congress.

The legislation did not affect the Army MOH, so the standards for the Army MOH during World War II were based on the 1918 legislation. The standards for Navy MOHs in World War II were those in the 1919 legislation until the 1942 legislation was enacted.

Current MOH Legislation: Creation of MOHs

The current statutes for the MOH for each service centralize the law for each service. The following legislation is found in the following sections of Title 10 of United States Code, a compilation of laws enacted by Congress:

Service	Statue Creating the Service's MOH
Navy, Marine Corps, and Coast Guard	Section 6241
Army	Section 3741
Air Force	Section 8741

Current MOH Legislation: Time Limitations and Delegation of Presentation

In addition to statutes creating a MOH for each service, two related statutes exist for each service's MOH: one imposing time limitations on the award (from deed to award) and one permitting the president to delegate authority to present the MOH to certain commanders in the field. These sections are in Title 10.

Service	Time Limitation	Delegation of Presentation Authority
Navy, Marine Corps, and Coast Guard	Section 6248	Section 6251
Army	Section 3744	Section 3745
Air Force	Section 8744	Section 8745

Additional guidance is in regulations for the Department of Defense (DoD Manual 1348.33-M, *The Manual of Military Decorations and Awards*) and the different branches of service.

What is noteworthy is that the statutes do not mention a standard of proof (i.e., how strong the evidence must be to support a MOH). By what standard is the evidence judged? A preponderance of the evidence? Beyond a reasonable doubt? In addition to the absence of a standard of proof in the MOH statutes, a "plain reading" of the statutes reveals no requirement concerning the number or status of witnesses to the action for which the MOH is recommended.

The Distinguished Service, Navy, and Air Force Crosses

As noted previously, Congress realized that some extraordinary combat heroism did not warrant a MOH but was sufficiently outstanding to warrant some award, so it created the Distinguished Service Cross and the Navy Cross and, after the air force became a separate service, the Air Force Cross (before the separation of Army and Air Force, Army aviators could receive DSCs). The current statutes in Title 10 creating the cross medals are as follows:

Service	Decoration	Statue Creating the Cross Decoration
Navy, Marine Corps, and Coast Guard	Navy Cross	Section 6242

| Army | Distinguished Service Cross | Section 3742 |
| Air Force | Air Force Cross | Section 8742 |

In short, the service member must be engaged in combat with the enemy and must exhibit extraordinary heroism not justifying a MOH.

Part 2: Permitting the Executive Branch to Award MOHs

Chapter 14 discussed the process for awarding MOHs to the men who earned them in the Hawaiian Islands. Additionally, Chapter 19 discussed the process by which the Pharris Navy Cross was upgraded to a MOH.

In the statutes, the MOH is the "medal of honor" (lowercase), not the "Congressional medal of honor." Again, the role of Congress was limited. It created the MOH by legislation and amended that legislation. None of the legislation gave Congress any role in awarding individual MOHs. The legislation states that the President, not Congress, presents the MOH in the name of Congress. In other words, when a MOH recommendation passes through the chain of command for action, the recommendation is not routed through Congress; it is routed through the military chain of command to the President for final action. Many people, including experts in military history, mistakenly believe that Congress must approve an individual MOH. Examples were provided in Chapter 18 (Errors).

Congress, however, retained the inherent power (no legislation exists authorizing Congress itself to award MOHs) to award, in special and rare cases, a MOH to an individual by legislation authorizing a MOH for that individual.[11]

Part 3: Congressionally Awarded MOHs

Although the usual role of Congress is enacting legislation governing MOHs the President presents in the name of Congress, exceptions to its limited role do occur and are described in this section.

One was just mentioned. Congress retained the power to award MOHs to individuals in special cases. Examples include MOHs for Lieutenant Commander Richard E. Byrd (flight over the North Pole) and Colonel Charles Lindbergh (nonstop flight from New York City to Paris). These could be called "adventure," "exploration," or "first achievement" MOHs. The Lindbergh MOH was by an act of Congress on December 14, 1927.[12]

Perhaps the most questionable such award, an award with a short and dubious citation, was the posthumous award for Major General Adolphus Greely "for his life of splendid public service." The Greely MOH was by an act of Congress of March 21, 1935.[13]

In contrast to these MOHs, Congress passed no legislation awarding MOHs to any of the recipients of traditional combat MOHs described in this book. These MOHs were awarded via the normal MOH award process. The Billy Mitchell award, however, was by congressional legislation.

PART 4: POLICING THE MOH

Perhaps the most prominent example of Congressional involvement in individual awards was redressing the military's failure to award MOHs to minorities because of racial prejudice. Congress directed the military to review cases of minority service members to determine if MOHs were warranted when lesser awards were presented. Along with the directive to review cases is legislation waiving the time limits for making MOH awards so if a case warranted a MOH, the award could be made without regard to the time limitations that ordinarily apply.[14]

What is important to note is that Congress did not direct that certain individuals receive MOHs; it only directed review of records to determine if MOHs, absent prejudice, would have been awarded following the normal awards process.

In addition, the army, on its own, acted to address the prejudice problem in awarding MOHs.

The MOHs awarded after examination of minority cases are summarized as follows:

- **Army Review of Records**

Since no blacks received MOHs in World War II, in 1993, the Secretary of the Army, without Congressional direction, contracted with Shaw University in Raleigh, North Carolina, to review the records of certain black soldiers to determine why no black soldiers had received MOHs in World War II. Shaw recommended that the Army consider ten blacks for MOHs, nine who had received Distinguished Service Crosses and one who had received no decoration for an action that may have warranted a MOH. The Army recommended seven of the ten for MOHs. In 1996, Congress passed legislation waiving the time limitations for MOH awards in these cases, and the President awarded the seven MOHs in 1997. Six of the awards were posthumous (four of the soldiers had been killed in their MOH action and two had died after the war). Only one black veteran was alive to receive his MOH; he received it from President Bill Clinton on January 13, 1997.[15]

- **Congressional direction to review records: Asian American, Native American, and Pacific Islander veterans**

In 1996, Congress, by legislation, directed the Secretary of the Army to review the records for members of these two populations who had received DSCs in World War II to determine if the DSCs should be upgraded to MOHs. It also directed review for those members who had received NCs. After such review, twenty-two Japanese Americans received MOHs in place of awards they had received (twenty-one had received DSCs and one a Silver Star). Congress passed legislation waiving the time limitations for MOH awards so that MOHs could be presented in these cases (one Japanese American had received a posthumous MOH in 1946).[16]

- **Congressional direction to review records: Jewish and Hispanic veterans**

In 2001, Congress, by legislation, directed the Secretary of each military department to review the records of Jewish and Hispanic veterans to determine if they should have been awarded MOHs. The population to be reviewed comprised Jews and Hispanics who had received DSCs, NCs, or Air Force Crosses or any other Jew or Hispanic whose name was submitted to a secretary for consideration. Again, Congress passed legislation waiving the time limitations so that MOHs could be presented in these cases. As a result, for example, two MOHs were awarded to Jewish soldiers (one posthumous award for World War II presented in 2002, one living recipient for the Korean War presented in 2005).[17]

Miscellaneous MOH Matters

Medal of Honor Design

Each service has its own MOH design. The basic design is the same: a metal star with five points with one point pointing directly downward. The medal is attached to a light-blue ribbon worn around the neck. On the ribbon just above the Medal is a section that is a field of thirteen stars, representing the original thirteen colonies of the United States. The Marine Corps and Navy MOH (the two services have the same MOH) is suspended from the ribbon by a hook shaped like an anchor; the Army MOH is suspended by an eagle; and the Air Force MOH is suspended by small flight wings. Nothing surrounds the star for the Marine Corps and Navy MOH. The Army and Air Force MOHs have green wreathes around the metal star; the Air Force's wreath is the largest.

On a military uniform, a recipient not wearing the MOH itself wears a light-blue ribbon with five stars (two at the top of the ribbon, three on the bottom of the ribbon). If the recipient is wearing civilian clothes, he or she may wear a small blue device (rosette) on the coat lapel indicating a MOH award.

A citation signed by the President is issued with each MOH, although some MOHs may be signed by Service secretaries on behalf of the President.[18]

The First MOH Recipient

Although the Marine and Navy MOH was the first MOH created, the first recipient of any MOH was Army Private Jacob Parrott of the Thirty-Third Ohio Infantry Regiment, who was one of the soldiers participating in "The Great Train Robbery" (also called "Andrews' Raid" and "the Great Locomotive Chase"). During the raid, Union soldiers dressed as civilians—led by James Andrews, a civilian and Union spy—hijacked the Confederate train the General in 1862 (the incident is the basis for the famous Buster Keaton silent movie The General).

Parrott was captured, but in 1863, he was exchanged (returned to the Union in exchange for a Confederate held by the Union). When he and some of his compatriots went to Washington after the exchange, they met the Union secretary of war, Edwin Stanton, who presented them with MOHs on March 25, 1863. Parrott received the first.[19]

Presenting a MOH

Presentation may be at the White House by the President in person to the recipient or, if the recipient is deceased, to the family.

The current MOH statutes permit a field commander to present a MOH, codifying a wartime practice; during wartime, not every recipient or family of a recipient can travel to the White House for presentation. Examples are the MOH presentations by Admiral Nimitz in 1942 to Cassin Young, Donald Ross, and John Finn.

In World War II, posthumous MOHs could be sent to families by registered mail (see chapter 14 and Appendix A).

The MOH Is an Individual Award

Some people erroneoUSly think MOHs can be awarded to everyone in a command, but the plain language of the statutes clarifies that the MOH is an individual award, not a command or unit award.

Terminology

Terminology is important.

The MOH's Correct Name

The name used in the older and modern statutes creating it is "medal of honor" (lowercase), not the "Congressional Medal of Honor," a term used repeatedly by the public, the media, and authors. Prefacing "Medal of Honor" with "Congressional" is misleading since "Congressional" implies that Congress is involved in individual awards of combat MOHs. As explained earlier, Congress is rarely involved in the award of a MOH.

A Person Who Receives the MOH

MOH recipients are properly called "MOH recipients" not "MOH winners," which implies some type of contest where one "wins" the nation's highest combat award.

Everyone Salutes a MOH Man

By tradition, everyone salutes a MOH recipient regardless of grade, so a colonel would salute a sergeant who had a MOH. Even Hollywood movies acknowledge this tradition and practice. For example, in the movie Twelve O'Clock High, Brigadier General Frank Savage (portrayed by actor Gregory Peck) salutes a junior officer pilot who reports to him, saying that the pilot should become accustomed to seniors saluting him since the pilot was nominated for the MOH.

NOTES

1. Hearings [May 31, 1945] before Subcommittee No. 8 of the Committee on Military Affairs, House of Representatives, Seventy-Ninth Congress, First Session on H.R. 2227 and Other Bills [authorizing the President to award a posthumous MOH in the name of Congress to William Mitchell] (Washington, DC: US Government Printing Office, 1945). Statement by Representative John J. Sparkman, page 8: Congress authorized the President to present MOHs in its name but kept the inherent power to award MOHs by legislation (hereafter "Mitchell Hearings"). The modern MOH statutes listed at endnote 12 follow the same scheme: Congress authorizes the President to present a medal of honor in the name of the Congress.

2. Ibid.

3. See Endnotes 14 and 15 of this chapter.

4. Public Acts of the Thirty-Seventh Congress, Second Session, Chapter 1, Section 7 (December 21, 1861).

5. Joint Resolution of the Thirty-Seventh Congress, Second Session, Chapter 1, Section 7 (July 12, 1862).

6. Public Acts of the Thirty-Seventh Congress, Third Session, Chapter 79, Section 6 (March 3, 1863).

7. Public Acts of the Sixty-Third Congress, Third Session, Chapter 83 (March 3, 1915).

8. Public Acts of the Sixty-Fifth Congress, Second Session, Chapter 143 (July 9, 1918).

9. Public Acts of the Sixty-Fifth Congress, Third Session, Chapter 14 (February 4, 1919).

10. Public Acts of the Seventy-Seventh Congress, Second Session, Chapter 551 (August 7, 1942).

11. Endnote 1, Mitchell Hearings, 8.

12. The Byrd and Lindbergh MOH citations can be found by searching the Internet for "Army MOH cite" and accessing the citations by choosing the icon "Interim 1920–1940" at the "Medal of Honor Recipients: Center of Military History" Internet site.

13. The Greely MOH citation can be found by searching the Internet for "Army MOH

site" and accessing the citation by choosing the icon "Interim 1920–1940" at the "Medal of Honor Recipients: Center of Military History" Internet site.

14. Congress directed a review of service records of the following minorities (hereafter "Minority MOHs"):

    a. Jewish and Hispanic service members of all services who received Air Force Crosses, Distinguished Service Crosses, Navy Crosses—Public Law 107-107, Division A, Title V, Section 522 (2001).

    b. Asian Americans and Native Americans and Pacific Islanders for World War II service in the Army and Navy who received Distinguished Service Crosses or Navy Crosses—Public Law 104-106, Division A, Title V, Section 524 (1996). In 2000, twenty-two Asian Americans received MOHs due to this review. The author has a copy of the program for the White House presentation of these twenty-two MOHs.

15. Karel Margy, "Medals of Honor Awarded—50 Years After," After the Battle (Battle of Britain Prints International, Ltd., Number 96, 1997), 32–39.

16. Endnotes 14 and 15, Minority MOHs.

17. Ibid.; for example, the waiver of time limitations for Jewish and Hispanic service members is in Section 552(f) of the law cited in endnote 15a.

18. Secretary of War Henry Stimson signed Audie Murphy's MOH certificate; Harold B. Simpson, Audie Murphy, American Soldier (The Hill Jr. College Press, 1975), 190.

19. Headquarters, Department of the Army, The Soldier's Guide (FM 7-21.13, October 15, 2003), 2–19; printing of the Parrott citation from the Congressional MOH Society Internet site on October 8, 2015.

Acknowledgments

My acknowledgements are similar to those in my first book, Hawaii's World War II Military Sites. I began collecting data about December 7 in 1999, including about the Medal of Honor (MOH) recipients but did not begin researching the MOH recipients in detail until after I had completed Hawaii's World War II Military Sites.

★ ★ ★ ★ ★ ★ ★ ★ ★ ★ ★

To recap, my interest in the events of December 7, 1941, began when I spent time on Oahu and learned about December 7 and Midway. I was on Oahu serving three brief tours of duty as a lawyer in the U.S. Marine Corps Reserve. I worked at the Office of the Staff Judge Advocate (SJA), U.S. Marine Corps Forces, Pacific, at Camp Smith, Hawaii. The first tour was in 1999 when Colonel Lewis Bumgardner, U.S. Marine Corps (Retired), was the SJA. The second and third tours were in 2001 and 2004, when my good friend Lieutenant Colonel Robert E. Pinder, U.S. Marine Corps (Retired), was the SJA. Mahalo ("thank you" in Hawaiian) to both officers.

★ ★ ★ ★ ★ ★ ★ ★ ★ ★ ★

As I recount in "Why I Wrote This Book," I met Daniel Martinez of the National Park Service, who worked at what was then the USS *Arizona* Visitors' Center. He is widely recognized as an expert on the attacks on December 7, 1941. He wrote the foreword to my book Hawaii's World War II Military Sites. In my never-ending quest to learn about the MOH recipients, I asked Dan who knew the most about them. He surprised me by looking at me directly and saying, "You do." For that answer, I thank him; it motivated me in great part to write this book to prove the truth of his answer.

★ ★ ★ ★ ★ ★ ★ ★ ★ ★ ★

My Norfolk, Virginia, connections served me well.

When I lived in Norfolk—where I did most of my research and writing about December 7—Dr. Gail Nicula was chief of the Library Division at Norfolk's Joint Forces Staff College (JFSC). She allowed me access to the JFSC's superb library, which includes a great Pearl Harbor collection and many older books and manuals—including those printed during World War II—explaining Navy and Marine traditions, personnel, and procedures. As they did for my Hawaii's World War II Military Sites, she and her staff offered me superior assistance. The information available from the JFSC was essential in writing this book.

Living in nearby Virginia Beach is Colonel Dennis Clancey, U.S. Marine Corps (Retired). I thank him for his suggestion for this book's title. He served at times as my mentor in the marine corps and has taken a great interest in my work on December 7. The "hidden" in the title conveys the general lack of attention the Pearl Harbor MOH recipients have received, a fact I found surprising and explain in detail in the book. Most attention they receive is limited to publications concerning December 7. None, except Lieutenant John Finn, appear to receive, as a group or individuals, the wider attention given more prominent or recent MOH recipients.

★ ★ ★ ★ ★ ★ ★ ★ ★ ★ ★

I necessarily had to request various types of assistance from people who lived in cities other than Norfolk. I appreciate the help from the following people, many of whom did not know me and kindly responded to my "cold" calls or e-mails.

On Oahu, Joanne Maluotoga of Naval Magazine Pearl Harbor provided me an invaluable article from Naval History magazine about the 1944 "West Loch Disaster," which is important background for 1945's West Loch of Pearl Harbor that led to the MOH for Petty Officer Second Class Owen Hammerberg. While West Loch was one of the few sites I missed on Oahu in 1999, its staff kindly arranged a tour for me when I returned to Oahu in 2001. I learned much from Petty Officer Third Class Todd Richard, US Navy, who was an outstanding tour guide and escort. He showed me Hammerberg Hall and the National Park Service wayside or historical exhibit for the West Loch Disaster.

I was lucky at West Loch during my third tour on Oahu (2004), which was the year of the sixtieth anniversary of the West Loch Disaster or, as it is often called, the "Second Pearl Harbor." I traveled up West Loch on a Navy vessel to attend the memorial for the disaster. For that trip, I thank the person who issued me the invitation: the Public Affairs Officer of Navy Region Hawaii, Lieutenant Commander Jefferson Davis, U.S. Navy.

From her office at the Fish and Wildlife Service in Honolulu, Barbara Maxfield assisted me with information about Midway and in 2004 provided the photographs from Midway Island of the Cannon Memorial, honoring MOH recipient First Lieutenant George H. Cannon, U.S. Marine Corps, and of the power plant where he earned the MOH. Due to computer problems, I lost the photographs, so I thank Mr. Barry Christenson of the Fish and Wildlife Service, who lived on Midway and e-mailed me in 2008 the same photographs that Barbara had sent me.

Not living on Oahu, I depend on those who do live there for updates and other information. In May 2008, Beverly Au of the *Arizona* Memorial Association told me of a new memorial of which I had no knowledge and that was not on Oahu when I was there: a memorial to the USS *Oklahoma* dedicated on December 7, 2007. Without her telling me about it, I would not have known. It is crucial to the story of USS *Oklahoma*, especially since the only ship losing more crewmen than *Arizona* was *Oklahoma*.

Carol Cepregi at the Congressional Medal of Honor Society (CMOHS) in Mount Pleasant, South Carolina, provided me information in 2002. When I visited the CMOHS in 2000, Sherry Russell, who worked there at the time, provided invaluable assistance. In 2015, Victoria Kueck and Laura Jowdy of the CMOHS kindly provided me assistance.

National Park Ranger Vincent M. Kordack sent me information from the Charlestown Navy Yard in Boston, home of the destroyer USS Cassin Young.

From the U.S. Naval Academy (USNA) in Annapolis, Maryland, James Cheevers provided helpful information on Naval Academy graduates who received MOHs for December 7. He provided copies of the academy's yearbook, The Lucky Bag, entries for each of the December 7 MOH recipients who graduated from the USNA. In 2015, Claude Berube and James Cheevers provided me information about the Cassin Young MOH on display at the USNA Museum.

In the 1990s, I had visited the superb Nimitz Museum in Fredericksburg, Texas. I asked Richard Koone of the Museum (now the National Museum of the Pacific War) for any information he had about the MOH recipients. He had a member of the staff, Reagan Grau, contact me. She sent me the four photographs of the Cassin Young MOH on display at the Museum. I thank Mr. Mike Lebens, the curator of collections at the National Museum of the Pacific War for updating me in 2015, confirming that his Museum had a Cassin Young MOH.

I visited the guided-missile destroyer USS Ross (DDG-71) on December 12, 2005, and received first-class treatment and information about the ship's namesake, Captain Donald Ross, US Navy (Retired), who received a MOH for his bravery on USS *Nevada* on December 7. In particular, I thank Commander Dan Shaffer and my "tour guide," Ensign S. C. Robbins, whose assistance was invaluable. One of the recipients for whom I found the least information was Machinist's Mate First Class (MM1) Robert Scott, who died aboard USS *California* on December 7, 1941. Fortunately, when I was aboard USS Ross, Petty Officer Second Class Michael Harwig overheard me and Ensign Robbins discussing the MOH. Petty Officer Harwig suggested that I contact the Ohio Military Museum in MM1 Scott's hometown, Massillon, Ohio. By using the Internet, they had the museum's phone number for me in seconds. I called the Museum and spoke to Mike Bardin, who graciously sent me a package of very informative material about MM1 Scott.

In 1995, when I went to Iwo Jima for the fiftieth anniversary commemoration, I had the great fortune of meeting many men from an infantry company who fought on the island: Fox Company, Second Battalion, Twenty-sixth Marine Regiment, and Fifth Marine Division. One of the members was a corpsman, Bob DeGeus. I became very close to these men—I became an associate member of the company—and attended most of their reunions beginning in 1995. At one reunion, Bob, a very kind gentleman, surprised me by giving me The Bluejackets' Manual (1940 edition) he used in basic training in World War II. It has been a treasure trove of information about the Navy circa 1941. I referred to it frequently; it was indispensable in writing this book.

★ ★ ★ ★ ★ ★ ★ ★ ★ ★ ★

One of my goals was to locate tombstones for the World War II Hawaiian Island MOH recipients whose bodies were buried on land and any "In Memory Of" (IMO) markers for those whose bodies were not recovered, who were buried at sea, or who were cremated. A special "thank you" to all of those mentioned here who helped me obtain these photos.

I appreciate the assistance from my mother, Aileen M. Jones, and my late father,

Lieutenant Colonel Elmer C. Jones, U.S. Air Force Reserve (Retired), who flew thirty missions in a B-29 in World War II. They assisted me in two cases. In March 2002, they visited Mount Pleasant Memorial Gardens Cemetery, Mount Pleasant, South Carolina, near the Congressional MOH Society offices. They obtained information about Cassin Young and photographed his "In Memory Of" marker and his wife's grave. Ironically, I was close to this site in 2000 while visiting the MOH Museum but did not read my own information about Cassin Young, so I missed the marker. Ms. Terri K. Freeland of the cemetery staff helped my parents find it. In 2015, Patrick J. Mallard of Mount Pleasant Memorial Gardens kindly gave me the marker location and sent me a photograph of it.

In September 2002, my parents and I drove from my father's Thirty-Ninth Bomb Group reunion in Miamisburg, Ohio, to Springfield, Ohio, where, with the assistance of Assistant Cemetery Superintendent Stanley Spitzer, we found the "In Memory of" marker for Seaman First Class James Ward, the youngest December 7 MOH recipient, earning a posthumous MOH aboard USS *Oklahoma*.

Mindy Pharris, the daughter-in-law of Jackson Pharris, provided me a mother lode of information about Jackson Pharris by e-mail in 2009. We lost contact, and I could not contact her when I began work anew on the book in 2015. She kindly consented to let me use all the information she had previously provided me, information that made complete the telling of the saga and ordeals of Jackson Pharris.

Don Morfe's dedication to preserving the history of the MOH is impressive, an example of a citizen who, upon his own initiative, assumes the role of honoring our greatest heroes. His dedication to finding and documenting MOH graves and "In Memory of" markers is impressive. Through him, I learned of the Kidd family tombstone at the USNA's cemetery, which includes the name of Rear Admiral Isaac Kidd, who died aboard USS *Arizona* and received a posthumous MOH. Since his body was never recovered, the tombstone is in effect an "In Memory of" marker. Because Don had informed me of the Kidd tombstone, I knew about it and found it when I visited the Naval Academy in 2014.

Don's information about the Kidd tombstone led me to check Find A Grave for Captain Franklin VanValkenburgh, *Arizona*'s commanding officer who received a posthumous MOH. Through that search, I found an "In Memory of" marker for him in Wisconsin. In 2015, Jan Van Rens, executive director of Forest Home Cemetery, Milwaukee, Wisconsin, provided me information about and photographs of the memorial markers for him in Forest Home Cemetery.

The Naval Academy Alumni Association led me by great fortune to Kevin Dolan, a Naval Academy graduate who took photos of Captain Mervyn Bennion's grave in Salt Lake City Cemetery, Salt Lake, *Utah*; he earned a posthumous MOH aboard USS *West Virginia* on December 7 when he was the ship's commanding officer. Through Kevin, I found Ronald and Robin Reedy, who took photos of the grave of December 7 recipient Ensign Herbert Jones at Fort Rosecrans National Cemetery in San Diego. Fortunately in 2003, I visited San Diego and the Jones grave myself and could take additional slides of his grave.

In 2015 and 2016, I received the following assistance. Brandi Madrill of Salt

Lake City Cemetery in *Utah* provided me information about the location of Captain Bennion's tombstone in the cemetery. Ken Everson of the Fort Snelling National Cemetery in Minneapolis, Minnesota, provided me photographs of the "In Memory of" marker for Marine Captain Richard Fleming, the sole MOH recipient for 1942's Battle of Midway. Sergeant Major Bert Caloud, U.S. Marine Corps (Retired) of the American Battle Monuments Commission, kindly sent me photographs of and information about Cassin Young's inscription at the Manila American Cemetery; he earned a MOH as the commander of USS *Vestal* on December 7. His name appears here as well as at Mount Pleasant since he was killed at the Naval Battle of Guadalcanal in 1942 and was buried at sea. Photographer Joan Detmer of Lincoln, Kansas, provided the photographs and the location of the Donald Ross marker at Beverly Cemetery at Beverly, Kansas. Curt Lawson, a library research volunteer at the National Naval Aviation Museum, assisted me with the abbreviation "VF." Doug Misner of the Research Center of the *Utah* State Archives and *Utah* State History sent me information about the MOH awarded posthumously to Captain Mervyn Bennion.

A heat-exhausted, dehydrated, and tired retired Marine Reserve colonel looking for the grave of Jackson Pharris in Arlington National Cemetery on a very hot May 30, 2015, was extremely fortunate to encounter a very conscientious cemetery employee, Michael Springs, who helped him find the grave in Section 13, the section presenting the most difficulty for those trying to find a grave inside it. After his fifteen-minute search, he found the grave and took the exhausted colonel to it. The colonel was not about to leave without finding the grave since during his previous visit he could not find it although he had found it years ago when it was partially sunken and leaning to the side.

Several contacts in Michigan were of invaluable assistance.

Stanley Bozich, director of Michigan's Own, Inc., Military and Space Museum in Frankenmuth, Michigan, provided information, photographs, and correspondence concerning two MOH recipients who were Michigan natives. One was Ensign Francis Flaherty, who earned a MOH aboard USS *Oklahoma*. The Museum has the Flaherty MOH. The other was Petty Officer Second Class Owen Hammerberg, who earned his MOH in Pearl Harbor's West Loch in 1945. The Museum has one of two MOHs the Hammerberg family received (see Chapter 15).

Also in Michigan, Mark Pawelczak graciously answered my inquiries concerning Ensign Flaherty and provided me photographs of a memorial in Charlotte, Michigan, and of the Flaherty "In Memory of" marker in Maple Hill Cemetery, Charlotte, Michigan. Attorney Robert Sullivan, Jr., provided information about and numerous sharp photographs of the Petty Officer Second Class Hammerberg grave.

From Eaton County, Michigan, I received information about Ensign Francis Flaherty from Sherry Copenhaver of the Eaton County Historical Society. Charles Brandon kindly sent me photographs of the county's memorials to Ensign Flaherty.

Mr. James R. Hall, the circulation and advertising assistant at Michigan History magazine, sent me a magazine article mentioning Ensign Flaherty.

★ ★ ★ ★ ★ ★ ★ ★ ★ ★

Closer to home, I received various forms of assistance from numerous people and agencies.

From Washington, DC, Janea Milburn and Daniel Finney of the Naval Historical Foundation assisted me in obtaining historical photographs for my first book, Hawaii's World War II Military Sites, photographs that I could also use in this book.

The late Gary A. Lavalley of the U.S. Naval Academy sent me the photograph of USS *Arizona* from the program for the Army-Navy game held November 29, 1941, just days before the Japanese attack on Oahu; the irony of the photograph and caption cannot be missed
(Chapter 3).

Captain Stephen T. Dexter, Supply Corps, U.S. Navy (Retired), and I swam frequently at the naval station pool. He reminded me that the attacks on December 7, 1941, were not the first by aircraft launched from aircraft carriers. In May 1941, a torpedo launched from a British torpedo plane based on a carrier disabled the German battleship Bismarck such that the British fleet could sink her.

Intellectual property attorney Blake Hurt of Greensboro, North Carolina, assisted me as well as my counsellor, Scott Lineberry. In early 2015, Scott dragged me out of the horrors of 2014—the year my father died from cancer in April followed by my own diagnosis of lymphoma in August—and encouraged me to start writing this book again.

My cousin, Lindsay Mateer, is as obsessive and detail oriented as I am. For Lindsay, nothing is valid in a Museum unless he inspects every rivet; for me, noting is valid unless it is photographed. So thanks to him, I spent close to two days in the wonderful Naval Aviation Museum in Pensacola, Florida, taking hundreds of photographs, many of which were actually relevant to this book: Captain Fleming and Chief Petty Officer Finn, both MOH recipients who were connected to naval aviation (Fleming as a pilot and Finn as an aviation ordnanceman). I took photographs of the types of aircraft Fleming flew at Midway in his MOH actions: the Dauntless and the Vindicator.

★ ★ ★ ★ ★ ★ ★ ★ ★ ★ ★ ★

Finally, I thank the following people and institutions.

Major General Thomas Wilkerson, US Marine Corps Retired, was of invaluable assistance in helping me to complete this project; he provided me contact with the CMOHS. I was greatly fortunate to have served in the US Marine Corps Forces Reserve when he was its commander. He was and is the epitome of an officer and gentleman and a marine leader who cared for his marines on active duty and in retirement.

Two teachers mercilessly decorating my English compositions with red ink directly led to the improvement in my writing that produced this book (I trust the reader will find that their efforts were successful). The primary credit goes to my twelfth-grade English teacher at Oak Ridge Academy, Ms. Betty Hobbs. Without her guidance, I would not be writing at a level that could produce a book. In 1977, I was responsible for much of the red ink used by my freshman English professor at Wake Forest University, Edward Lob.

One institution is Campbell University School of Law, where my professors—especially Bill Martin—taught the importance of checking facts and conducting thorough research. I hope that I followed their instruction well in this book. The other institution is the US Marine Corps. Beginning in Officer Candidate's School, I was taught (often painfully) the importance of attention to detail. I hope I executed that principle in writing this book and honoring the men who are the subjects of it.

And Semper Fidelis.

Notes about Illustrations and Maps

I. Photographs and Slides

A. Thousands of photographs of the attack on December 7 are available, and numerous photographic histories of December 7 can be purchased. My focus is on photographs of the Medal of Honor (MOH) recipients and the stations and sites where they earned their MOHs and not on photographs of the December 7 attack itself.

B. Sources of photographs are indicated by the following abbreviations:

Source of Photograph	Abbreviation or Identification
National Archives	NA
Naval History and Heritage Command (Internet postings of photographs)	NH
US Marine Corps	Marine Corps Historical Division or HD
US Navy	USN
Author	Author's photograph or slide

C. For those interested in photography, I used slide film in the dark ages before digital photography made slides obsolete. I used Kodak Elite Slide Film or Fuji film, 200 speeds, with an Olympus point-and-shoot camera. In 2015, I reluctantly made the switch to digital photography, using a Nikon COOLPIX P600, obtaining excellent results.

D. My photographs or slides may represent what I saw when I took the photograph or slide, but the site or subject may have changed by the time of publication of this book.

II. Maps

Composited from Google Maps and artistically styled by Timothy Cox at Stir Creative Group in Greensboro, North Carolina.

III. Typesetting

Typesetting was done by Josh Grabiec at Stir Creative Group.

Bibliography

Organization of Bibliography

Part A: General Comments

Part B: Personally Visiting the Sites Relevant to the MOH Recipients

Part C: Information about the MOH Recipients

Part D: Information about the MOH Awards Process

Part E: Miscellaneous Aspects of the MOH

Part F: William ("Billy") Mitchell

Part G: Doris Miller

Part H: Information about Ships

Part I: The Attack on Oahu

Part J: Salvage Operations at Pearl Harbor

Part K: Aftermath of Attack

Part L: The West Loch Disaster

Part M: Military Organization, Grade, Customs, and Organization

Part N: Errors in MOH Literature

Part O: Guide to Military Sites on Oahu

Part P: Miscellaneous

Part A: General Comments

I. Substantive Information

    A. To my surprise, I made three discoveries about many of the MOH recipients who are the subject of this book. One, little information is available about some of them. Two, the information available was often difficult to locate and to obtain. Three, important information was incomplete, inaccurate, or omitted.

    B. Thus, one of my goals in writing this book is not only to uncover more information about them—and to ensure that it is complete, accurate information—

but also to organize the information and to have it in one place (i.e., this book). The following is an overview of the sources of information used to write this book.

II. Endnotes

A. Nature of endnotes. Endnotes are at the end of each chapter so readers do not have to keep fingers on a page while looking in the back of the book for an endnote.

B. "Author's knowledge, observation, and experience." In some cases, an endnote will read to this effect: "Author's knowledge, observation, or experience." This phrase means the information cited is known to me firsthand from one of my four visits to Oahu or from my visit to a site on the mainland. That citation also includes the knowledge I acquired from serving a combined total of thirty years (1981 to 2011) as a judge advocate (lawyer) in the Regular and Reserve Marine Corps.

III. Note on Internet Research

A. Necessity. Internet research is essential and provides information previously unavailable or available but difficult to obtain.

B. Dangers. Internet research is dangerous in three respects because of the Internet's ephemeral nature. One, sites change locations or disappear completely after information has been retrieved from them. Two, information on sites may change or disappear. Three, the information on Internet sites must be subjected to the same level of critical review as any other source. In fact, information on the Internet, even from sites operated by recognized or official organizations, can be false, misleading, or incomplete. This danger exists especially on the Internet because the public can place information on it at will without any formal fact checking or screening for accuracy. At least with a commercially published book, editors and fact checkers will usually, but not always, detect false, misleading, or incomplete information supplied by the author.

PART B: PERSONALLY VISITING THE SITES RELEVANT TO THE MOH RECIPIENTS

I. Oahu

A. Time on Oahu. I had three tours of duty on Oahu as a Marine Corps Reservist at Camp Smith: 1999, 2001, and 2004. When not working at Camp Smith, I visited most, if not all, of the sites where the MOH recipients described in this book earned their MOHs. I revisited many of the sites again when I visited Oahu in 2015.

B. Scope of in-person information gathering. I visited all the sites where MOHs were earned on Oahu in 1941 and 1945. I did not visit Midway.

(1) Sites visited. I spent hours visiting the following sites: Naval Station Pearl Harbor, Hickam Air Force Base, the *Arizona* Memorial, the Pearl Harbor Visitor Center at the World War II Valor in the Pacific National Monument (formerly the *Arizona* Visitors' Center), and Ford Island, including the *Oklahoma* Memorial.

(2) Boat tours. I also took at least two of the special boat tours offered by the *Arizona* Visitors' Center around Ford Island given on special days such as Memorial Day or Pearl Harbor Day. The normal tour takes visitors by boat to and from the Visitors' Center to the memorial; the special tours circle Ford Island and pass by the Naval Shipyard.

(3) West Loch. Naval Magazine Pearl Harbor at West Loch is a highly secure area inaccessible to the public. Such inaccessibility is unfortunate because the National Park Service wayside (sign or exhibit) concerning the West Loch Disaster is well inside the compound. I was, however, able to tour the area with a navy petty officer in 2001 and again in 2004 with a group commemorating the sixtieth anniversary of the disaster. Those arranging these tours were listed in the "Acknowledgments" section of this book.

II. The Mainland. I also visited sites in the continental United States relevant to the MOH recipients, including cemeteries and museums.

A. The Congressional Medal of Honor Society—I visited it in 2000.

B. Arlington National Cemetery—I visited it many times, most recently in 2015, when I saw the graves for Rear Admiral Samuel Fuqua, Lieutenant Commander Jackson Pharris, and Machinist's Mate First Class Robert Scott.

C. Ferncliff Cemetery in Springfield, Ohio—I visited it and saw the "In Memory of" marker for Seaman First Class James Ward.

D. Fort Rosecrans National Cemetery in San Diego, California—I visited it twice and saw the grave of Ensign Herbert Jones.

III. Midway. I did not visit Midway.

Part C: Information about the MOH Recipients

I. **Information from Official Military Personnel Files (OMPF).** The National Personnel Records Center (NPRC) at St. Louis, Missouri. The NPRC is the repository of military service records. I obtained limited biographical and military career information from the OMPFs at the National Personnel Records Center (NPRC), St. Louis, Missouri, by submitting Standard Form 180 (Request Pertaining to Military Records). While service members themselves or next of kin are entitled to all of the member's service record, privacy considerations severely limited the amount of information the center provides the public (with three exceptions noted here).

A. Differing results. I received responses to all my NPRC requests for information for the MOH recipients with two exceptions: I did not file a request for Billy Mitchell, and in 2004, a staff member at the NPRC called me, informing me that the personnel file for Seaman Ward had been misplaced, so I never received any information from his OMPF.

B. Form of information in most cases. Most of the OMPF material from St. Louis was copies of various documents in the OMPF in no special order; these pages were the result of my initial requests long ago and included Kidd, Van Valkenburgh, and Fuqua. Generally the amount of information provided was minimal.

C. Special cases: "Individuals in whom there is significant public interest, 10 years after their death" (the Kidd, Van Valkenburgh, and Fuqua OMPFs).

(a) Compact disc OMPFs. I obtained what appeared to be the complete service records for Rear Admiral Isaac Kidd, Rear Admiral Samuel Fuqua, and Captain Franklin Van Valkenburgh on compact discs (CD) for $90.00 each since each of these men were judged to be of "significant public interest." In short, they are prominent individuals whose complete or nearly complete OMPFs are now "public records" releasable to the public.

(b) Compact disc organization. The CDs had the information in an organized format, thus making the CDs the only OMPF material that can be given a "fixed" location; it is on CDs I received for Kidd and Van Valkenburgh (in 2014) and for (Fuqua 2015). The CDs, which were unavailable at the time of my initial OMPF requests, contain the entire OMPFs and are available because of the status of these three service members (persons of public and historical interest). The sections are numbered, such as "05 Correspondence.pdf," and within the sections, the documents are at various page (or really screen) numbers. I found the number of the page or screen by placing my cursor at the bottom of the page or by hitting print for the current page, which shows the number of the current page. The document itself may have its own numbers, such as pages 1 through 4 with a cover page. I cited to the OMPF page or screen number.

D. MOH recommendations. Despite my notations on SF 180s that I specifically requested information about MOHs, I received only copies of MOH citations or indications in service records that the member had received a MOH. I never received what I wanted: witness statements and command recommendations for MOHs except for the chance find of the Third Endorsement in the Kidd OMPF discussed in section II of part C of this bibliography. Of all OMPFs I have requested for MOH recipients, only one had detailed information about the MOH action, command recommendations, and witness statements (Larry Maxim, a Marine who received a posthumous MOH for bravery in Vietnam).

E. Timeliness of responses. Also, obtaining NPRC information can take months. For example, I requested information about Rear Admiral Samuel Fuqua in 2001; the NPRC received my request on March 15, 2001. I received its reply on March 25, 2001, which was unusually fast. I received printed copies of a few of the documents in his Official Military Personnel File (OMPF). Taking a chance that I may obtain more information about him, I submitted a second request on August 31, 2014; I received a reply on March 9, 2015, which informed me that the OMPF was now a public record and that I could obtain a compact disk (CD) of the OMPF for $90.00. I mailed my request on March 9, 2015; I received the CD on March 23, 2015 (see discussion in the preceding paragraph about the OMPFs of prominent individuals).

II. Official Biographies. I obtained one- or two-page official biographies prepared by the Navy or the Marine Corps for these recipients; for the Navy: Hill, Reeves, Ross, Scott, Tomich, Ward, and Young; for the Marine Corps, Cannon and Fleming.

III. Official Reports from Commands. Generally commanders submit reports in letter format after an event or combat action. I have termed these reports "after-action reports" although the subject lines of the reports may read otherwise. Reports generally include enclosures, which are documents or witness statements supporting the content of the letter reports or offering additional information. Reports may or may not mention MOH recipients.

    A. *Arizona*. Report from USS *Arizona* (Subject: Action Report of USS *Arizona*, December 7, 1941) of December 13, 1941.

    B. *California*. The ship's commanding officer submitted two reports and one letter.

        1. Report from USS *California* (Subject: Report of Raid, December 7, 1941) of December 13, 1941.

        2. Report from USS *California* (Subject: Report of Raid (Revised), December 7, 1941) of December 22, 1941.

        3. Letter from Commanding Officer, USS *California*, to Commander in Chief, U.S. Fleet (Subject: Awards of Medals for Heroic Conduct during the Raid on Pearl Harbor, December 7, 1941, recommendations concerning) of January 10, 1942.

    C. *Nevada*. Report from USS *Nevada* (Subject: Report of December 7, 1941, Raid) of December 15, 1941, paragraph 3 (hereafter "*Nevada* report").

    D. *Tennessee*.Report from USS Tennessee (Subject: "Narrative of event of action in Japanese Air Raid on Pearl Harbor, December 7, 1941") of December 11, 1941.

    E. *Utah*. Commanding Officer's Report, "USS *Utah*—Loss by Enemy Action," dated December 15, 1941, paragraph 2 of Lieutenant Commander Isquith's report, which is Enclosure (A) to this report (hereafter *Utah* report).

    F. *Vestal*. Report from USS *Vestal* (Subject: Report of Action on December 7, 1941, in Accordance with References (a) and (b)) of December 11, 1941.

    G. *West Virginia*

        1. Report from USS *West Virginia* (Subject: "Action of December 7, 1941—Report of") of December 11, 1941 (hereafter "*West Virginia* Report").

        2. First Endorsement dated December 13, 1941, to *West Virginia* BB48/A

16-3 of December 11, 1941, by Commander Battleships, Battle Force Rear Admiral W. S. Anderson.

H. Kaneohe Bay

1. Attack on Naval Air Station Kaneohe Bay: Report attack on Kaneohe Bay from ("Subject: Report of Japanese Air Attack on Kaneohe Bay, T.H. [Territory of Hawaii]—December 7, 1941").

2. Attack on Naval Air Station, Pearl Harbor: Report from Commander Patrol Wing 2 (Subject: Operations on December 7, 1941) of December 20, 1941.

I. Midway

1. Cannon. Report of action on night of December 7, 1941" of December 12, 1941, by Lieutenant Colonel H. D. Shannon, US Marine Corps, Commanding Officer, Sixth Marine Defense Battalion on Midway found in The Roberts Commission investigation of 7 December 1941, included in the report of the 1945 Congressional investigation of the attack found in PEARL HARBOR ATTACK: HEARINGS BEFORE THE JOINT COMMITTEE ON THE INVESTIGATION OF THE PEARL HARBOR ATTACK, SEVENTY-NINTH CONGRESS, FIRST SESSION, Part 24 (U.S. Government Printing Office, Washington, DC, 1946).

2. Fleming

(a) Group report (commanding officer)—Report of Marine Aircraft Group 22 (Subject: Battle of Midway Islands, Report of) of June 7, 1942.

(b) Group report (executive officer)—Report of Executive Officer, MAG-22 (Subject: Marine Aircraft Group 22, Second Marine Aircraft Wing, Midway Islands T.H.) of June 7, 1942.

(c) Squadron report—Report of Marine Scout-Bombing Squadron 241 (Subject: Report of Activities during June 4 and June 5, 1942.) of June 12 1942.

E. *Nevada*. Report from USS *Nevada* (Subject: Report of December 7, 1941, Raid) of December 15, 1941.

F. *Oklahoma*. Report from USS *Oklahoma* (Subject: Action Reports) of December 18, 1941, concerning the attack on the ship on December 7, 1941.

G. *Vestal*. Report from USS *Vestal* (Subject: Report of Action on December 7, 1941, in Accordance with References (a) and (b)) of December 11, 1941.

H. *West Virginia*

   1. Action of December 7, 1941—Report of. After-action report from Lieutenant Commander R. H. Hillenkoetter, the senior surviving officer, USS *West Virginia*. The report and its enclosures discuss the actions of Captain Mervyn Bennion (Medal of Honor) and Petty Officer Doris Miller (Navy Cross).

   2. First Endorsement of December 13, 1941, by Commander Battleships, Battle Force, Rear Admiral W. S. Anderson on *West Virginia* BB48/A 16-3 [report] of December 11, 1941.

I. Anderson reports

   1. Report from Rear Admiral W. S. Anderson (Subject: Distinguished Conduct—Report of—Pearl Harbor Raid, December 7, 1941) of December 19, 1941.

   2. Rear Admiral W. S. Anderson, Commander Battleships, Battle Force (Subject: Attack at Pearl Harbor by Japanese Planes on December 7, 1941) of December 19, 1941.

IV. Congressional Investigations Involving MOH Recipients

   A. *Arizona*: Kidd and Van Valkenburgh. Testimony of Lieutenant Commander Fuqua on January 2, 1942, before the Roberts Commission, included in the report of the 1945 Congressional investigation of the attack found in PEARL HARBOR ATTACK; HEARINGS BEFORE THE JOINT COMMITTEE ON THE INVESTIGATION OF THE PEARL HARBOR ATTACK, SEVENTY-NINTH CONGRESS, FIRST SESSION, Part 23 (U.S. Government Printing Office, Washington, DC, 1946).

   B. Midway

   (1) See the item under section 1 of part III of this bibliography ("Report of action on night of December 7, 1941" of December 12, 1941, by Lieutenant Colonel H. D. Shannon, US Marine Corps).

   (2) PEARL HARBOR ATTACK: HEARINGS BEFORE THE JOINT COMMITTEE ON THE INVESTIGATION OF THE PEARL HARBOR ATTACK, Part 1 (US Government Printing Office, 1945).

V. MOH Citations

   A. Presidential libraries. The author obtained copies of MOH citations as follows:

   1. Franklin D. Roosevelt Presidential Library and Museum provided MOH citations for all MOH recipients except for Pharris and Hammerberg.

2. Harry S. Truman Presidential Library and Museum provided the MOH citations for Pharris and Hammerberg.

B. Internet access. MOH citations were also found by searching the Internet for "Army MOH site" and accessing the citation by choosing the correct icons at the "Medal of Honor Recipients: Center of Military History" Internet site.

VI. Secondary Sources for the MOH

A. Books in general

1. Garand, George W., and Truman E. Strowbridge. Western Pacific Operations: History of the US Marine Corps Operations in World War II, Volume IV ("Nightmare in Hell"). Historical Division, Headquarters, U.S. Marine Corps, Washington, DC, 1971, reprinted by The Battery Press, Inc., Nashville, TN, 1994.

2. Jones, Colonel Charles A., US Marine Corps Reserve (Retired). Hawaii's World War II Military Sites. Mutual Publishing, Honolulu, HI, 2002.

3. Lang, George (MOH), Raymond L. Collins, and Gerald F. White (compilers), Medal of Honor Recipients 1863–1994, Volume II. Facts on File, Inc, New York, NY, 1995.

4. Miller, Francis Trevelyan. History of World War II. The Publisher's Guild, New York, NY, 1945. Captain Donald Ross, U.S. Navy Retired, and Helen Ross. 0755: The Heroes of Pearl Harbor. Rokalu Press, Port Orchard, WA, 1988. Captain Ross was a December 7 MOH recipient.

6. Schuon, Karl. US Navy Biographical Dictionary. Franklin Watts, Inc, New York, NY, 1964. This book has biographical summaries of famous Navy personnel, including Medal of Honor and Navy Cross recipients.

7. Stillwell, Paul. Battleship *Arizona*. Naval Institute Press, Annapolis, MD, 1991.

8. Young, Stephen Bower. Trapped at Pearl Harbor, Escape from Battleship *Oklahoma*, Naval Institute Press, Annapolis, MD. The book mentions Flaherty and Ward aboard USS *Oklahoma* on December 7.

B. Books and Magazines about Midway

1. Blakeney, Jane. Heroes: US Marine Corps 1861 * 1955. Guthrie Lithograph Co., Inc., Washington, DC, 1957.

2. Fuchida, Mitsuo, and Masatake Okumiya. Midway, The Battle That Doomed Japan: The Japanese Navy's Story. Naval Institute Press, Annapolis,

MD, 1992.

3. Guttman, Jon. "A Marine at Midway." World War II, July 2002.

4. Heinl, Lieutenant Colonel Robert D., Jr. Marines at Midway. Historical Section, Division of Public Information, Headquarters, U.S. Marine Corps, Washington, DC, 1948.

5. Hough, Lieutenant Colonel Frank O., Major Verle E. Ludwig, and Henry I. Shaw. History of U.S. Marine Corps Operations in World War II, Volume I. Historical Branch, G-3 Division, Headquarters, U.S. Marine Corps, Washington, DC, 1958. Reprinted by The Battery Press, Inc., Nashville, TN.

6. Parshall, Jonathan B. and Anthony P. Tully. Shattered Sword, The Untold Story of The Battle of Midway. Potomac Books, Washington, DC, 2005.

7. Prange, Gordon W. At Dawn We Slept. Penguin Books, New York, NY, 1982.

8. Prange, Gordon W., Donald M. Goldstein, and Katherine V. Dillon. Miracle At Midway. McGraw-Hill Book Company, New York, NY, 1982.

9. Lord, Walter. Incredible Victory. Harper & Row, Publishers, New York, NY, 1967.

10. Melson, Major Charles D. USMC (Retired). Condition Red: Marine Defense Battalions in World War II. History and Museums Division, Headquarters, US Marine Corps, Washington, DC, 1996.

11. Mersky, Commander Peter B., US Naval Reserve. Time of the Aces: Marine Pilots in the Solomons, 1942–1944. History and Museums Division, Headquarters, US Marine Corps, 1993.

12. Naval Analysis Division. United States Strategic Bomb Survey [Pacific], Washington, DC. Volume II, Interrogation Number 83.

D. Magazines and Newspapers Concerning MOH Recipients

1. Bennion

"Congressional Medal Arrives in S. L. [Salt Lake] for Late Captain Bennion," Deseret News, March 17, 1942.

2. Finn

(a) "Dec. 7 Hero at Kaneohe Is honored." Honolulu Star-Bulletin, June 30, 1999.

(b) Associated Press. Finn Obituaries, May 27, 2010, on the Internet. One was by Julie Watson; the other listed no author.

(c) "American Valor: John Finn." Public Broadcasting System, WETA Internet site (August 24, 2008), printed September 28, 2015.

3. Flaherty.

Colizzi, Don, "Charlotte's Medal of Honor Recipients." Michigan History. May 7, 1999.

4. Fleming

(a) Goodspeed, Hill. "Always Faithful." Naval Aviation News, May–June 2003.

(b) "Slain St. Paul Hero Given Highest Tribute." St. Paul Dispatch. November 24, 1942.

5. Fuqua

Bennett, Tom. "Adm. Samuel Fuqua, 87, Honored for Heroism at Pearl Harbor, Dies." Atlanta Constitution. January 28, 1987.

6. Hammerberg

Allen, Florence. "Detroit Salutes Hero in Tribute to War Dead." Detroit Free Press. Undated.

7. Pharris

(a) "Lt. Cmdr. Pharris Dies; Medal of Honor Winner." Evening Star. October 25, 1966. Page B-4.

(b) Ratcliff, Ashley. "Medal of Honor Keeps Hill Family's Legacy Alive." Palos Verdes Peninsula News. October 8, 2007. Story printed from the Internet September 2, 2008. "Hill" refers to Rolling Hills Estates, where the Pharris family lived.

(c) "...Winner Jackson Pharris Dies" [First part of title cannot be read]. Los Angeles Times. October 18, 1966. Part I, 21.

(d) Roth, Alex. "WWII Medal of Honor Winner's Family Finally Regains Decoration." San Diego Union-Tribune. October 3, 2007. Printed from the Internet September 2, 2008.

(e) Ludwick, Mass Communication Specialist First Class Paula M. "COMNAVSURFOR Hosts Medal of Honor Ceremony." Navy.mil. October 4, 2007. Printed from the Internet September 1, 2008.

8. Ross

Palmer, Vorina. "It's Taps for the Captain." Port Orchard Independent. June 3, 1992.

9. Scott

(a) "Gave His Life to Keep Guns Firing." Massillon Independent. Author and date unknown.

(b) "Service Held for War Hero." Massillon Independent. Date and author unknown, sent to the author from the Ohio Military Museum in 2006.

(c) Untitled newspaper article caption printed in the Massillon Independent for a photograph of Scott's mother unveiling a memorial during the war. Author and date unknown, sent to the author from the Ohio Military Museum in 2006.

(d) "Hall Names [at Ohio State University] Reflect Honor of Past Students." The Lantern. Story posted November 13, 2001, at the Lantern website and printed by the author February 21, 2007. The Lantern is the student newspaper at Ohio State.

10. Tomich

(a) O'Brien, Thomas. "Pearl Harbor's Forgotten Ship." Naval History. August 2001.

(b) Thompson, Jason, Journalist Second Class (Surface Warfare), US Navy. Navy Newsstand. May 19, 2006. Printed from the Internet June 26, 2006.

(c) "USS *Utah*: The Forgotten Memorial," VFW (Veterans of Foreign Wars). December, 1985, 18. The letter to the editor is from the February 1986 issue of the magazine at page 8.

11. Ward

(a) "Recipient Data Sheet" for James Ward completed by the Ward family.

(b) Program "Dedication of Ward Field." April 7, 1953.

(c) Ward, Mr. and Mrs. Howard J. Letters to and from:

(1) Letter of March 7, 1974, from Mr. Howard J. Ward and Mrs. Nancy M. Ward to Mr. Carl A. Robin, North Carolina State Director, Medal of Honor History Roundtable.

(2) Letter of March 7, 1974, from Mr. Howard J. Ward and Mrs. Nancy M. Ward to the Department of the Navy.

(3) Letter of March 17, 1942, from Mr. Howard J. Ward and Mrs. Nancy M. Ward.

(4) Letter of March 23, 1942, from Captain John L. McCrea, Naval Aide to the President, to Mr. Howard J. Ward and Mrs. Nancy M. Ward.

12. Naval Academy graduates

Jones, Colonel Charles A. USMCR (Retired). "Men of Honor." Shipmate (December 2001).

E. Letters and Other Documents

1. Cannon

Letter of March 22, 1942, from Mrs. Estelle Ham Cannon to President Franklin D. Roosevelt.

2. Finn

Program from Commander, Patrol and Reconnaissance Force, US Pacific Fleet, for the dedication ceremony of the John W. Finn Building: "John W. Finn Building Dedication Ceremony."

3. Hammerberg

(a) Letter by Commander Henry Foss, US Naval Reserve, Deputy Fleet Salvage Officer letter of March 8, 1945, to Mrs. Elizabeth Hammerberg.

(b) Letter from Secretary of the Navy James Forrestal of March 30, 1945, to Mr. Jonnes Hammerberg.

(c) Letter from Lieutenant W. J. McNicol, Jr. Navy Department, Bureau of Naval Personnel of May 4, 1945, to Mr. Jonnes Hammerberg. McNicol was the Assistant Officer in Charge of the Casualty Notification and Processing Section.

(d) Story from America's Most Wanted website: "Congressional Medals of Honor Stolen." February 12, 2007. E-mail of October 7 from the Congressional Medal of Honor Society to the author.

4. Hill

   (a) Press release (1942).

   (b) Letter of April 2, 1970, from an official in the city of Cape May, New Jersey to US Representative Charles W. Sandman, Jr.

   (c) Letter of May 19, 1970, from Lieutenant Commander J. C. Gilbert, US Navy, Assistant Director, Personal Affairs Division to Representative Sandman.

5. Ross

   Document appearing to be a typed obituary of Donald Kirby Ross (undated and with no source) provided to the author by the crew of USS Ross. The public relations department of Litton Ingalls Shipbuilding had telefaxed the document to the ship's PCO (Prospective Commanding Officer) on March 24, 1995.

6. Pharris

   The Harry S. Truman Presidential Library and Museum sent the author documents concerning the attempt to upgrade the Pharris Navy Cross to a MOH:

   (a) Letter from Rear Admiral J. W. Bunkley of January 16, 1946, with enclosure referenced. The author did not receive a copy of the Bunkley letter—only what appears to be the enclosure.

   (b) Endorsement (Subject: "Recommended for Medal of Honor for Lieutenant Jackson C. Pharris, U.S. Navy in lieu of Navy Cross") of February 1, 1946, by the Board of Review for Decorations and Medals of the January 16, 1946, Bunkley letter and enclosure.

   (c) Pharris letter June 26, 1947, to Board.

   (d) Board letter July 22, 1947, to Bunkley.

   (e) Board letter July 25, 1947, to Pharris.

   (f) Bunkley letter August 7, 1947, to Board.

   (g) Pharris letter August 9, 1947, to Board.

   (h) Board October 14, 1947, letter to Chief Pay Clerk J. O. Bussey.

   (i) Board letter October 14, 1947, to Pharris.

(j) Pharris letter November 3, 1947, to Pharris.

(k) Bussey letter November 3, 1947, to Board.

(l) Board letters November 14, 1947, to Lieutenant Samuel Killingsworth and Chief Gunner's Mate H. F. Reynolds.

(m) Reynolds's letter December 15, 1947, to Board.

(n) Pharris January 19, 1948, letter to Board.

(o) Pharris letter (undated) to Board.

(p) Board letter January 23, 1948, to Pharris.

(q) Killingsworth March 8, 1948, letter to Board.

(r) Board letter March 10, 1948, to Lieutenant Commander D. C. McCartin.

(s) Killingsworth letter March 19, 1948, to Board.

(t) Board letter June 26, 1947, to the Secretary of the Navy.

(u) McCartin letter April 6, 1948, to Board.

7. Tomich. Correspondence and other documents concerning the Tomich MOH:

(a) Letter October 30, 1946, from Mr. J. M. Steele to Vice Admiral A. S. Carpender, USN.

(b) Letter February 11, 1985, from then-Senator Jake Garn (*Utah*) to Mr. J. B. Vaessen.

(c) Letter of June 23, 1987, from Mr. Paul Bucha to Rear Admiral J. Robert Lunney, NYNM (New York Naval Militia).

(d) Letter of October 15, 1997, from David Sanders, Public Affairs Officer at the Naval Education and Training Center in Newport, Rhode Island, to Chief Warrant Officer Donald H. Chavark, U.S. Navy (Retired).

(e) Letter of November 4, 1997, from Chief Warrant Officer Donald H. Chavark, U.S. Navy (Retired) to the Naval Historical Center in Washington, DC.

(f) Letter of November 3, 1997, from Senior Chief Machinist Mate

Richard Moore, US Navy, to Chief Warrant Officer Donald H. Chavark, U.S. Navy (Retired).

(g) Letter of November 13, 1997, from Chief Warrant Officer Donald H. Chavark, U.S. Navy (Retired) to the Congressional Medal of Honor Society.

(h) Letter of November 19, 1997, from Mr. Normal M. Cary Jr., Head, Curator Branch, Naval Historical Center, Washington, DC, to Chief Warrant Officer Donald H. Chavark, U.S. Navy (Retired).

8. Midway

(a) Who's Who in Marine Corps History, "Major Henry Talmage Elrod, USMC (Deceased), a fact sheet produced by the Marine Corps History Division and accessible via the Internet.

(b) Official US Marine Corps casualty reports for Lieutenant George Cannon, Captain Richard Fleming, Private First Class George Toms, and Majors Lofton Henderson and Benjamin Norris.

F. Military museums and societies. I obtained information about the following MOH recipients from the following military museums:

1. Flaherty and Hammerberg. Stan Bozich of Michigan's Own Military and Space Museum provided information about Flaherty and Hammerberg.

2. Scott. Mike Bardin of the Ohio Military MUSeum provided me information about Scott.

3. Young. Reagan Grau and Mike Lebens of the National Museum of the Pacific War provided information about the Young MOH.

G. The United States Naval Academy. Mr. James Cheevers provided information as follows:

1. Copies of the entries in the Academy's yearbook, The Lucky Bag, for Bennion, Fuqua (1923), Kidd (1906), Van Valkenburgh (1909), and Young (1916).

2. Information about the duplicate Young MOH in the Academy's museum.

VII. The Nininger MOH (The first awarded in World War II)

A. War Department General Orders Number 9 (February 5, 1942), Section V.

B. The Officer's Guide. 9th edition. The Military Service Publishing Company, Harrisburg, PA, 1943.

VIII. Ships Named for MOH Recipients

    A. Dictionary of American Fighting Ships. Naval Historical Center, Department of the Navy, Volumes I (1959), II (1963), III (1968), VI (1976), and VII (1981).

    B. Other

        1. Kidd (DDG-993): "Navsource Online: Destroyer Archive." Printed from the Internet October 15, 2015. "USS Kidd (DDG-993)." Louisiana Naval War Memorial Commission. Printed from the Internet October 15, 2015.

        2. Pharris: "Navsource Online: Destroyer Escort Photo Archive." Printed from the Internet October 15, 2015.

        3. Ross: Information from the "History" icon under "About US" on the ship's official Internet site. Printed from the Internet October 15, 2015.

        4. "USS Michael Murphy Departs for Maiden Deployment." The Flagship. Pilot Targeted Media. October 29, 2014.

IX. Purple Hearts. General Order 186 of January 21, 1943, authorized the Secretary of the Navy to award a Purple Heart posthumously, in the name of the President, to anyone in the Navy, Marine Corps, or Coast Guard who, since December 6, 1941, was killed in action or who died of wounds received in action with an enemy of the United States.

PART D: INFORMATION ABOUT THE MOH AWARDS PROCESS

I. For the December 7 recipients: The Theobald Board, the missing report

    A. The Theobald Board. I remain convinced that the most valuable insights into the awards process and the MOH awards for December 7 would be the formal report, if such were compiled and still existed, of the "Board of the Awards," headed by Rear Admiral Robert A. Theobald, US Navy. Paragraph (D) of Part IV of the February 15, 1942, report by Admiral Chester Nimitz. The report states in Part IV(D), "A Board of Awards, headed by Rear Admiral Robert A. Theobald, U.S. Navy, is currently in session for the purpose of making recommendations for awards incident to the Pearl Harbor attack." I assume that, in typical military fashion, the Board would have issued a written report with recommendations for awards, including MOHs, and that this report was the basis for the original twelve MOH recommendations sent from Pearl Harbor to the Department of the Navy.

    B. Attempts to obtain report. I attempted unsuccessfully to obtain such a report from the Naval Historical Center, the Naval Academy, the National Archives, and the National Museum of the Pacific War (formerly the Nimitz Museum) in Fredericksburg, Texas.

II. For the December 7 recipients: The Third Endorsement

A. The Kidd OMPF. In 2014, the author ordered the Kidd OMPF from the National Archives. The OMPF was $90.00 each copy and was delivered in compact disc format.

B. The Third Endorsement

(1) Fortunately, the absence of any report from the Fleet Board of Awards is mitigated by the material in the Kidd OMPF (CD). It has a summary of a February 23, 1942, meeting of the Navy Department Permanent Board of Awards; the recorder (administrative assistant to the Board) did not sign this summary in the space for his signature, so the document is unsigned. Behind the summary is a document at the top of which reads "Third Endorsement," which is critical not only because it lists all the recommendations for awards but shows how the Kidd and Van Valkenburgh MOH recommendations were added by the permanent board (the fleet board report had not recommended either officer for an award). When military correspondence is sent up the chain of command, each office reviewing the correspondence adds an "endorsement" stating its views regarding the basic correspondence that is being forwarded.

(2) The subject of the Third Endorsement is "Japanese Attack on US Pacific Fleet in Pearl Harbor 7 Dec. 1941—Recommendations for Awards for Gallant Conduct in Action of Naval and Civilian Personnel." An educated guess is that the "Fleet Board of Awards" report is the correspondence being endorsed by the Third Endorsement of the permanent board since paragraph 4 of the Third endorsement references "The Fleet Board of Awards." Logically, the "Fleet Board of Awards" report would be the report of the Theobald Board of Awards since the term "Fleet" is used, indicating that the basic correspondence being endorsed originated from the Fleet (i.e., the Pacific Fleet whose commander had mentioned in his 1942 report a "Board of Awards" headed by Rear Admiral Theobald).

III. Presidential Approval of All the MOH Awards

A. December 7 MOHs. The author obtained documents from the Franklin D. Roosevelt Presidential Library and Museum for all December 7 MOH approvals except for Pharris's. The author obtained documents concerning the Pharris MOH award (upgrading the Navy Cross and approving a MOH) from the Harry S. Truman Presidential Library and Museum.

B. Midway 1942 MOH. The author obtained documents from the Franklin D. Roosevelt Presidential Library and Museum concerning the Hammerberg.

C. West Loch 1945 MOH. The author obtained documents concerning the Pharris MOH award (upgrading the Navy Cross and approving a MOH) from the Harry S. Truman Presidential Library and Museum.

Part E: Miscellaneous Aspects of the MOH

I. The Legal Bases for the MOH, MOH Criteria, and Time Limits for MOH Awards

    A. MOH legislation: historical. Congress and the President, via legislation, created the MOH and have amended that legislation over the years. I obtained copies of the various statutes establishing MOHs over the years:

        (1) MOH for enlisted members of the Marine Corps and Navy—Public Acts of the Thirty-Seventh Congress (Session II), Chapter I, Section 7 (December 21, 1861).

        (2) MOH for enlisted members of the Army—Joint Resolution of the Thirty-Seventh Congress (Session II), Chapter I, Section 7 (July 12, 1862).

        (3) MOHs for Army officers—Public Acts of the Thirty-Seventh Congress (Session III), Chapter LXXIX, Section 6 (March 3, 1863).

        (4) MOH for Naval service officers (Marine Corps, Navy, and Coast Guard): Public Acts of the Sixty-Third Congress (Session III), Chapter 83 (March 3, 1915).

        (5) MOH for the Army (1918)—Public Acts of the Sixty-Fifth Congress (Session II), Chapter 143 (July 9, 1918).

        (6) MOH for the Naval service (1919)—Public Acts of the Sixty-Fifth Congress (Session III), Chapter 14 (February 4, 1919).

        (7) MOH for the Naval service (1942)—Public Acts of the Seventy-Seventh Congress (Session II), Chapter 551 (August 7, 1942).

    B. MOH legislation: modern. The statutes for the current MOH are as follows:

        (1) Navy, Marine Corps, and Coast Guard—Section 6241, Title 10, US Code.

        (2) Army—Section 3741, Title 10, US Code.

        (3) Air Force—Section 8741, Title 10, US Code.

II. Congressional or Service Mandated Review of Lesser Awards for Minorities

    A. Congressional mandates. Legislation mandated review of service records of minorities who possibly received lesser awards than the MOH due to racial prejudice:

        (1) Jewish and Hispanic service members of all services who received Air Force Crosses, Distinguished Service Crosses, Navy Crosses—Public Law 107-107, Division A, Title V, Section 522 (2001).

(2) Asian-Americans and Native American Pacific Islanders for World War II service in the Army and Navy who received Distinguished Service Crosses or Navy Crosses. Public Law 104-106, Division A, Title V, Section 524 (1996).

B. Army review. On its own, the Army reviewed records of black veterans to find men who received lesser awards than the MOH due to racial prejudice. Margy, Karel. "Medals of Honor Awarded—50 Years After." After the Battle. Battle of Britain Prints International, Ltd., Number 96 (1997), 32–39.

Part F: William ("Billy") Mitchell

Army-Navy game program, November 29, 1941. Provided by the United States Naval Academy.

Burlingame, Roger. General Billy Mitchell: Champion of Air Defense. McGraw-Hill Book Company, Inc., New York, NY, 1952.

Correll, John T. "Billy Mitchell and the Battleships." AIR FORCE MAGAZINE (June 2008), 62–68.

DeSeversky, Alexander P. Air Power: Key to Survival. Simon and Schuster, New York, 1950.

Frisbee, John L. "Warrior, Prophet, Martyr." AIR FORCE MAGAZINE (September 1985), 162 (predictions; report suppressed). National Museum of the U.S. Air Force.

"Gen. Billy Mitchell." U.S. Air Force Fact Sheet accessed from the Internet May 11, 2008 (prediction) (hereafter "Mitchell Air Force Fact Sheet").

Hurley, Alfred, USAF. Billy Mitchell: Crusader for Air Power. Indiana University Press, Indianapolis, IN, 1975.

Hearings [May 31, 1945] before Subcommittee No. 8 of the Committee on Military Affairs, House of Representatives, Seventy-Ninth Congress, First Session on H.R. 2227 and Other Bills [authorizing the President to award a posthumous MOH in the name of Congress to William Mitchell]. Washington, DC: US Government Printing Office, 1945.

Private Law 884, Seventy-Ninth Congress, Second Session. Approved August 8, 1946 (Mitchell MOH).

Part G: Doris Miller

Arakaki, Leatrice R., and John R. Kuborn. December 7, 1941: The Air Force Story (Pacific Air Forces, Office of History, Hickam Air Force Base, Hawaii, 1991), 76–80 and 135 (DSC awards).

Awards record for Doris Miller. Letter to the author from the Department of the Navy of August 14, 2001, enclosing a copy of the card.

"Black History at Arlington National Cemetery." Historical Information. Printed from the Arlington National Cemetery website on December 12, 2000).

Blakeney, Jane. Heroes: US Marine Corps 1861–1955. Cited in part C of this bibliography.

Buckley, Gail. American Patriots: The Story of Blacks in the Military from the Revolution to Desert Storm. Random House, New York, NY 2001, 275.

Cantwell, Catherine. "Doris Miller Decorated 40 Years Ago." Waco Tribune-Herald. May 3, 1982.

Chambers II, John Whiteclay. "The Long Thread of Black Valor." Washington Post. May 28, 2001.

Epps, Gregory. "Bombs Away." *Port Folio Weekly*. June 5, 2001, 29.

Gudmens, Lieutenant Colonel Jeffrey J. and the Staff Ride Team, Combat Studies Institute. Staff Ride Handbook for the Attack on Pearl Harbor, December 7, 1941: A Study of Defending America (Combat Studies Institute Press). Reprinted June 2009.

Haygood, Wil. "Courage in Full Color." Washington Post. August 17, 2008.

Jones, Colonel Charles A., USMC Reserve (Retired). Hawaii's World War II Military Sites (Mutual Publishing, Honolulu, HI, 2002).

Lee, Irwin H. Negro Medal of Honor Men. Dodd, Mead & Company, 1967, 1969, 107 (hereafter Lee, Negro Medal Of Honor Men).

Letter to the author from the Department of the Navy of August 8, 2001, stating that none of the names the author submitted to the navy for review received Navy Crosses for helping Captain Bennion.

Letter from the Chief, Military Awards Branch, to Vickie Gail Miller (March 28, 1995).

Lord, Walter. Day of Infamy. Henry Holt and Company, New York, NY, 1957.

Miller, Francis Trevelyan. History of World War II. The Publisher's Guild, New York, NY, 1945. Cited in parts C and F of this bibliography.

Miller, Richard E. The Messman Chronicles: African Americans in the US Navy, 1932–1943. Naval Institute Press, Annapolis, MD, 2004.

Miller, Vickie Gail. Doris Miller: A Silent Medal of Honor Winner. Eakin Press, Austin, TX, 1997.

News release for Congresswoman Eddie Bernice Johnson (May 25, 2001). It was H.R. 1944, May 24, 2001, First Session of the 107th Congress.

Parshall, Jonathan B., and Anthony P. Tully. Shattered Sword: The Untold Story of the Battle of Midway (Potomac Books, Washington, DC, 2005).

Paschall, Rod. America's War Heroes: Unsung and Legendary. Primedia, 2002, 68

Prange, Gordon W., Donald W. Goldstein, and Katherine V. Dillon. December 7, 1941: The Day the Japanese Attacked Pearl Harbor. McGraw Hill Book Company, New York, NY, 1988.

Report from USS *West Virginia* (Subject: Action of December 7, 1941—Report of) of December 11, 1941 (hereafter "*West Virginia* Report"). Enclosure (D): statement of Lieutenant Commander D. C. Johnson, U.S. Navy (taking Miller to the bridge with him). Enclosure (H): statement of Lieutenant (junior grade) F. H. White, U.S. Naval Reserve (manning machine guns with Miller).

Resolution of the U.S. Conference of Mayors is from the U.S. Conference of Mayors website. Printed on August 25, 2001, and October 30, 2001.

Sapper, Neil. "Aboard the Wrong Ship in the Right Books: Doris Miller and Historical Accuracy." East Texas Historical Journal. 28, no. 1, 1980, 3–11.

Wallin, Vice Admiral Homer N., US Navy (Retired). Pearl Harbor: Why, How, Fleet Salvage, and Final Appraisal. Washington, DC: Naval History Division, United States Government Printing Office, 1968.

PART H: INFORMATION ABOUT SHIPS

Dovener, Joe. "Exploring the World War II Secrets of Hawaii." After the Battle. Battle of Britain International, Ltd., Number 127 (2005).

Dictionary of American Naval Fighting Ships. Naval Historical Center, Department of the Navy. Volumes I, II, III, VI, and VII.

Sobel, Brian M. "The Sacred Relics of Pearl Harbor." THE WALL STREET JOURNAL. December 4, 2007.

"$3,000,000 Fire Checked." Virginian-Pilot and the Norfolk Landmark. June 8, 1931.

PART I: THE ATTACK ON OAHU

I. General Reference

Altfield, Bess (publisher). Air Raid, Pearl Harbor. This Is Not Drill! O. S. B. MapMania, Phoenix, AZ, 1999 (map and pamphlet showing moorings on December 7).

Arakaki, Leatrice R., and John R. Kuborn. December 7, 1941: The Air Force Story. Cited in Part G of this bibliography.

Army-Navy game program. November 29, 1941. Cited in part F of this bibliography.

Blakeney, Jane. Heroes: US Marine Corps 1861 * 1955. Cited in part C of this bibliography.

Correll, John T. Billy Mitchell and the Battleships. Cited in part F of this bibliography.

DeSeversky, Major Alexander P. Victory through Airpower. Cited in part F of this bibliography.

Frisbee, John L. "Warrior, Prophet, Martyr." AIR FORCE MAGAZINE (September 1985). Cited in part F of this bibliography.

"Gen. Billy Mitchell." US Air Force Fact Sheet. Cited in part F of this bibliography.

Hague Convention No. III, "Relative to the Opening of Hostilities" (1907), Article 1. Headquarters, Department of the Army. International Law (Department of the Army Pamphlet 27-161-2, October 1962), 36.

Morison, Samuel Eliot. History of United States Naval Operations in World War II (Little, Brown and Company, 1948).

Nimitz, Chester. Report from Commander in Chief, Pacific Fleet (Subj: Report of Japanese Raid on Pearl Harbor, December 7, 1941) of February 15, 1942.

Prange, Gordon W. At Dawn We Slept. Cited in part C of this bibliography.

Scott, Commander Roger D. Judge Advocate General's Corps, US Navy. "Kimmel, Short, McVay: Case Studies in Executive Authority, Law, and the Individual Rights of Military Commanders." Military Law Review, Department of the Army Pamphlet 27-100-156, Volume 156. June 1998.

US Army Air Forces. Impact: Air Victory Over Japan (Assistant Chief of Air Staff, 1945). The section of the report cited was part of Impact excerpted in the publication "Flying."

Stillwell, Paul (editor). Air Raid: Pearl Harbor! Recollections of a Day of Infamy. Naval Institute Press, Annapolis, MD, 1981.

Hearings [May 31, 1945] before Subcommittee No. 8 of the Committee on Military Affairs, House of Representatives, Seventy-Ninth Congress, First Session on H.R. 2227 and Other Bills [authorizing the President to award a posthumous MOH in the name of Congress to William Mitchell]. Cited in part F of this bibliography.

Hurley, Alfred USAF. Billy Mitchell: Crusader for Air Power. Cited in part F of this bibliography.

PEARL HARBOR ATTACK: HEARINGS BEFORE THE JOINT COMMITTEE ON THE INVESTIGATION OF THE PEARL HARBOR ATTACK, SEVENTY-NINTH CONGRESS, FIRST AND SECOND SESSIONS (U.S. Government Printing Office, Washington, DC, 1946):

    a. Part 1 (Fuchida described the aircraft and the targets in a 1945 postwar "questionnaire").

    b. Part 6 (Kimmel and oil tanks).

    c. Part 21: Item 12 (anchorage plan for Pearl Harbor) and Item 17 (attack plane routes).

    d. Part 24:

        (1) Narrative of Events, December 7, 1941.

        (2) Damage to Ships, December 7, 1941.

    e. Part 26 (attack by air anticipated).

    f. Part 24: Numbers of Navy and Marine personnel assigned to ships and locations of ship captains, December 7, 1941.

    f. Part 25: Item 35 (Oahu military installations) and Item 85 (ships in Pearl Harbor).

    g. Part 33: Antitorpedo baffles for Pearl Harbor.

    h. Part 33: Damages Sustained by Ships, December 7, 1941.

"The Japs Hear Things, Too. Collier's Weekly. August 1945, 82.

"This Day in History" at the History.com Internet site. Accessed October 12, 2015.

II. Reports

Report by Rear Admiral W. S. Anderson. Cited in part C of this bibliography.

Reports from USS *California*, December 13, 1941, and December 22, 1941. Cited in part C of this bibliography.

Report from Commander Patrol Wing 2. Cited in part C of this bibliography.

Report from USS Cassin (Subject: Report of Action with Japanese Aircraft during

Attack on Pearl Harbor, T.H., December 7, 1941, of December 13, 1941).

Report from USS Downes (Subject: Report of Action with Japanese Aircraft during Attack on Pearl Harbor, T.H., December 7, 1941) of December 17, 1941.

Report from USS Pennsylvania (Subject: USS Pennsylvania's Report of Action during Enemy Air Attack Morning of Sunday, December 7, 1941) of December 16, 1941.

III. Other

"Casualties on the USS *Arizona* on December 7, 1941" (document from USS *Arizona* Memorial, National Park Service, US Department of the Interior).

The number of dead and missing from USS *Oklahoma* is from the National Park Service Brochure "USS *Oklahoma* Memorial" (obtained online in 2010) and from the author's visitation of the Memorial in 2015.

IV. The Marine Corps

Cressman, Robert J., and J. Michael Wenger. Infamous Day: Marines at Pearl Harbor December 7, 1941. History and Museums Division, Headquarters, US Marine Corps, Washington, DC (1992). This pamphlet is one in a series of pamphlets published by the Marine Corps History and Museums Division to commemorate the fiftieth anniversary of World War II.

Furer, Julius A., Rear Admiral, US Navy (Retired). Administration of the Navy Department in World War II. Washington, DC: Department of the Navy, Washington, DC (1959). Chapter XIV discusses the status of the US Marine Corps in World War II.

PART J: SALVAGE OPERATIONS AT PEARL HARBOR

Wallin, Vice Admiral Homer N. Pearl Harbor: Why, How, Fleet Salvage, and Final Appraisal. Cited in part G of this bibliography.

PART K: AFTERMATH OF ATTACK

"Admiral's Week." Time. July 24, 1944, 28.

Anderson reports. Citied in part C of this bibliography.

Associated Press item (in newspaper with no identification) of August 11, 1945 (treachery).

Barber v. Sheila Widnall (U.S. Ninth Circuit Court of Appeals, No. 93-36200, 1996).

Bunkley, J. W., Rear Admiral, US Navy (Retired). MILITARY and RECOGNITION

BOOK (D. Van Nostrand Company, Inc., 1943).

Burlingame, Roger. General Billy Mitchell: Champion of Air Defense. Cited in part F of this bibliography.

Bureau of Naval Personnel. SEAMANSHIP. NAVPERS 16118. U.S. Navy, Training, Standards, and Curriculum Division (June 1944).

Dictionary of American Naval Fighting Ships. Cited in part C of this bibliography.

Furer, Rear Admiral Augustus Furer, US Navy (Retired). Administration of the Navy Department in World War II. Cited at part I of this bibliography.
"Paragraphics." Greensboro Daily News. June 28, 1945.

Hearings [May 31, 1945] before Subcommittee No. 8 of the Committee on Military Affairs, House of Representatives, Seventy-Ninth Congress, First Session. Cited in part F of this bibliography.

Iwo Jima reports. Regimental Combat Team 21 (Subject: Action Report, Iwo Jima Operation) of April 10, 1945. Action Report of Combat Team 28, Iwo Jima (no subject, undated), Annex Baker. Commanding Officer, Third Battalion, Twenty-First Marines, Third Marine Division, (Subject: Action Report) of April 11, 1945.

Jones, Colonel Charles A. US Marine Corps Reserve (Retired). Hawaii's World War II Military Sites. Cited in part C of the bibliography.

"Kimmel, Short, McVay: Case Studies in Executive Authority, Law, and the Individual Rights of Military Commanders." Military Law Review. Cited in part I of this bibliography.

Tactics and Technique of Infantry. The Military Service Publishing Company, Harrisburg, PA, 1942.

Mitchell, William. Winged Defense. G.P. Putnam's Sons, New York, NY (1925).

Nimitz report. Cited in part I of this bibliography.

Pacific Fleet Notice 45N-41 (Subject: Surprise Attack, Sundays and Holidays) of December 28, 1941.

Prange, Gordon W. At Dawn We Slept. Penguin Books, 1982. Cited in part C of this bibliography.

Printing of photograph of front and back of Mitchell MOH from the U.S. Air Force Museum on February 26, 2003.

Private Law 884, Seventy-Ninth Congress, Second Session. Cited in part F of this bibliography.

Roosevelt, Franklin D. "Address to Congress Requesting a Declaration of War with Japan. December 8, 1941. Printed from the Franklin D. Roosevelt Presidential Library and Museum October 9, 2015.

Spencer, Murlin. Associated Press. July 28, 1945 (cities). Greensboro Daily News. United Press. August 23, 1945.

Stillwell, Paul (editor). Air Raid: Pearl Harbor! Recollections of a Day of Infamy. Naval Institute Press, 1981. Cited in part I of this bibliography.

The Story of the 73rd: The Unofficial History of the 73rd Bomb Wing. Reprinted by the Battery Press, Nashville, TN, 1980, no page number.

War Department, Military Intelligence Division. THE PUNCH BELOW THE BELT, JAPANESE RUSES, DECEPTION TACTICS, AND ANTIPERSONNEL MEASURES. August 1, 1945. The photographs precede page 1.

Wallin, Vice Admiral Homer N., US Navy (Retired). Pearl Harbor: Why, How, Fleet Salvage, and Final Appraisal. Cited in part G of this bibliography.

PART L: THE WEST LOCH DISASTER

"Investigation Report," Fourteenth Naval District, United States Intelligence Service (Subject: Destruction of Six LST's by Explosions and Fire, West Loch, Oahu, T.H., 21 May 1944) of July 24, 1944.

Report of U.S. Navy Court of Inquiry (Subject: Destruction of Six LST's by Explosions and Fire, West Loch, Oahu, T. H. [Territory of Hawaii]) of May 21, 1944.

Salecher, Gene Eric. The Second Pearl Harbor: The West Loch Disaster, May 21, 1944. University of Oklahoma Press, Norman, OK (2014).

Schuman, Howard E. "The Other Pearl Harbor Disaster." Naval History (Summer 1988).

PART M: MILITARY ORGANIZATION, GRADE, CUSTOMS, AND ORGANIZATION

Bureau of Naval Personnel. SEAMANSHIP. Cited in part J of this bibliography.

Bunkley, J. W., Rear Admiral, US Navy, Retired. MILITARY and NAVAL RECOGNITION BOOK. Cited in part J of this bibliography.

Callandar, Bruce D. "When Is a Major Not (Exactly) a Major?" AIR FORCE MAGAZINE. November 1996. This article discusses "tombstone" promotions.

"Dictionary.com." Accessed October 6, 2015 (definition of "mister" in the military context).

Fuqua, Lieutenant Commander Samuel. Testimony on January 2, 1942, before the Roberts Commission, included in the report of the 1945 Ccongressional investigation of the attack found in HEARINGS BEFORE THE JOINT COMMITTEE ON THE INVESTIGATION OF THE PEARL HARBOR ATTACK (U.S. Government Printing Office, Washington, DC, 1946), Part 23. Fuqua describes the duties of the damage control officer and first lieutenant.

George, James L. History of Warships. Naval Institute Press, Annapolis, MD (1998). This book has a discussion of post–World War II destroyer developments and modifications.

Grier, Peter. "The Highest Ranking." AIR FORCE MAGAZINE (March 2012). This article discusses the six- and five-star grades.

Heinl, Colonel Robert D, US Marine Corps (Retired). The Marine Officer's Guide (Naval Institute Press, Annapolis, MD, 1977). This book is a manual for Marine officers.

Munson, Kenneth G. Aircraft of World War Two. Doubleday and Company Inc., 1968. This book has summaries of World War II aircraft.

Reynolds, Clark G. Famous American Admirals. US Naval Institute Press, Annapolis, MD, 2002. This book contains a discussion of the grade of commodore.

Roscoe, Theodore. United States Destroyer Operations in World War II. United States Naval Institute, Annapolis, MD, 1953, page 297. This book describes destroyer escorts.

Rottman, Gordon L. U.S. Marine Corps World War II Order of Battle. Greenwood Publishing Group, Westport, CT (2002), page 578. This book describes enlisted grades in World War II.

US Code, Title 10, Section 101(b) (7) ("grade") and (8) ("rank").

US Code, Title 10, Section 5501 (4) and (5) (current officer grade structure).

United States Information Service. United States Government Manual. Executive Office of the President, Office of Government Reports, Washington, DC (March 1941).

Division of Public Inquiries. United States Government Manual. Office of War Information, 1945.

The Bluejackets' Manual: United States Navy, 10th edition. United States Naval Institute, Annapolis, MD (1940). This is a manual for those just entering the Navy in World War II.

U.S. Marine Corps History Division. Biographies of World War II Marine Corps Commandants General Thomas Holcomb, U.S. Marine Corps, and General Alexander Vandegrift, U.S. Marine Corps. Accessed on the Internet October 6, 2015.

PART N: ERRORS IN MOH LITERATURE

Anderson, Lars. The All Americans. St. Martin's Press, New York, NY, 2004. See Chapter 9 of this book (*Arizona*) for the correct name of *Arizona*'s commanding officer.

"American VALOR: John Finn." (September 28, 2015.) Printed from Public Broadcasting System, WETA Internet site with information dated August 24, 2008.

Arroyo, Ernest. Pearl Harbor. Metro Books, New York, NY (2001).

Baron, Richard, Major Abe Baum, and Richard Goldhurst. Raid! The Untold Story of Patton's Secret Mission. G. P. Putnam's Sons, New York, NY, 1981.

Blair, Admiral Dennis. "Remarks Honoring the End of World War II." US Pacific Command. September 2, 2000. "VJ Day" was postwar terminology for "Victory over Japan."

Buell, Hal. Uncommon Valor, Common Virtue. The Berkley Publishing Group, New York, NY 2006.

Carlisle, Rodney P. PhD. (General Editor). One Day in History: The Days That Changed the World: December 7, 1941. HarperCollins Publishers, New York, NY 2006.

Dorr, Robert F. "Aviation Ordnanceman led valiant defense at Pearl Harbor." Navy Times, December 10, 2001. Dorr, Robert F., and Fred L. Borch. "All I did was shoot at everyone I could." Navy Times. December 10, 2007.

Editors, Boston Publishing Company. A History of the Medal of Honor from the Civil War to Vietnam. Boston Publishing Company, Boston, MA, 1985.

Feifer, George. The Battle of Okinawa. The Lyons Press, Guilford, CT, 2001.

Dictionary of American Naval Fighting Ships. Naval Historical Center, Department of the Navy, 1981. Cited in part C of this bibliography.

Goldstein, Richard. "John Finn, Medal of Honor Winner, Dies at 100." New York Times. May 27, 2010 (hereafter "Goldstein, John Finn death").

Guttman, Jon. "Richard Ira Bong: American World War II Ace of Aces." Aviation History (March 2007).

Home of Heroes Internet site, printing September 29, 2014.

Jasper, Joy Waldron, James P. Delgado, and Jim Adams. The USS *Arizona*. Truman Talley Books, St. Martin's Press, New York, NY 2001.

Jones, Colonel Charles A. US Marine Corps Reserve (Retired). Cited in part C of this bibliography.

Kohnen, David. "Tombstone of Victory: Tracking the U-505 from German Commerce Raider to American War Memorial 1944–1954. Journal of America's Military Past. Volume 32, no. 3, winter 2007.

Lang, George (MOH), Raymond L. Collins, and Gerald F. White (compilers), Medal of Honor Recipients 1863–1994. Facts on File, Inc. Volume II, 517. Cited in part C of this bibliography.

"Lt. John Finn: A True Hero." News story by National Broadcasting System Channel 7 in San Diego, California, May 27, 2010.

McComas, Terence. Pearl Harbor Fact and Reference Book: Everything to Know about December 7, 1941 (Mutual Publishing, Honolulu, HI, 1991).

Manchester, William. American Caesar. Cited in part M of this bibliography.

Melson, Major Charles D. USMC (Retired). Condition Red: Marine Defense Battalions in World War II. History and Museums Division, Headquarters, U.S. Marine Corps, 1996. Cited in part C of this bibliography.

Miller, Francis Trevelyan. History of World War II. The Publisher's Guild, 1945. Cited in parts C and F of this bibliography.

"*Nevada*'s Heroic Run." World War II (January 1998).

"*Nevada*'s Heroic Run." World War II (2001).

"Passing of John Finn WWII Medal of Honor Recipient." National Park Service news release, May 27, 2010, citing the Associated Press.

Photograph of John Finn with his wife at Pearl Harbor (US Navy file photograph dated September 28, 1942).

Prange, Gordon, Donald M. Goldstein, and Katherine V. Dillon. Dec. 7 1941, The Day the Japanese Attacked Pearl Harbor (McGraw-Hill Book Company, New York, NY, 1988).

Robinson, Major Dale U.S. Marine Corps (Retired). "Moment of Truth." Military Officer (December 2007), 62–69.

Ross, Donald K. and Helen. 0755: The Heroes of Pearl Harbor. Cited in part C of this bibliography.

Schott, Joseph L. Above and Beyond, The Story of the Congressional Medal of Honor. G. P. Putnam's Sons, New York, NY 1963.

Servello, Lieutenant Chris. "Navy to Present Medal of Honor to Family of World War II Vet." Navy newsstand. May 11, 2006. Thompson, Jason Journalist Second Class. "Medal of Honor Presented to Family of Pearl Harbor Vet." Navy newsstand. May 19, 2006.

Shapiro, T. Rees. "Lt. John W. Finn, Medal of Honor Recipient, Dies at 100." Washington Post. May 29, 2010, page B5.

Smith, Rex Alan and Gerald A. Meehl. Pacific War Stories. Abbeville Press, New York, NY 2004.

Taylor, Theodore. Air Raid—Pearl Harbor. Gulliver Books, Harcourt, Inc., San Diego, 1971, 1991.

Tillman, Barrett. "The Pearl Harbor Medal Battle." Flight Journal (October 2013).

"US Navy Ships Named for Individual Sailors to Commemorate their Actions during the Attack [December 7 1941]." Naval Heritage and History Command. Printed September 30, 2015.

Yost, Mark. "A Museum Honoring Real Heroes." THE WALL STREET JOURNAL. November 8, 2007.

Hough, Lieutenant Colonel Frank O., USMCR, Major Verle E. Ludwig, USMC, and Henry I. Shaw Jr. Pearl Harbor to Guadalcanal: History of the U.S. Marine Corps Operations in World War II. Historical Division, Headquarters, U.S. Marine Corps, Washington, DC, 1958. Reprinted by the Battery Press, Inc., Nashville, TN, 1993. Volume I. Cannon is mentioned on pages 79–80. Fleming is mentioned on page 229.

Mersky, Commander Peter B. US Naval Reserve. Time of the Aces: Marine Pilots in the Solomons. Cited in part C of this bibliography.

Part O: Guide to Military Sites on Oahu

Jones, Colonel Charles A., USMCR (Retired). Hawaii's World War II Military Sites. Cited in part C of this bibliography. Part tour book and part history book, this guide gives a detailed overview of the December 7 attack and the various military sites and bases found on the island of Oahu. The book is outdated, but it continues to be a good reference for the attack and the World War II historical sites on Oahu, subjects that, in general, will not change over time.

Part P: Miscellaneous

Adams, John. Letter to Benjamin Rush (April 18, 1808).

Chang, Iris. The Rape of Nanking. BasicBooks, New York, NY, 1997.

deKay, James Tertius. Monitor. Ballantine Books, New York, NY, 1997, 180–198.

DeSeversky, Alexander P. Air Power: Key to Survival. Cited in part F of this bibliography.

Eylanbekov, Zaur. "Airpower Classics." AIR FORCE MAGAZINE. Ju 87 Stuka: April, 2008, 88; SBD Dauntless, October 2009, 80.

Fox, Daniel R. Lieutenant Colonel MOH recommendation documentation from the Fox OMPF:

    a. Letter from Headquarters, Marine Forces, Fourteenth Naval District, Navy Yard, Pearl Harbor, T. H. (Subject: Lieutenant Colonel Daniel R. Fox, Report of) of March 27, 1942.

    b. First endorsement from Headquarters, U.S. Marine Corps (Subject: Information Regarding the Service of the Late Lieutenant Colonel Daniel R. Fox, USMC., on December 7 1941) of April 14, 1942.

    c. Third endorsement from Major Alan Shapley (Subject: Information Regarding the Service of the Late Lieutenant Colonel Daniel R. Fox, USMC., on December 7, 1941) of April 14, 1942.

    d. Fifth endorsement from Major General Thomas Holcomb (Subject: Recommendation for the Posthumous Award of the Medal of Honor in the Case of the Late Lieutenant Colonel Daniel R. Fox, USMC., on December 7, 1941) of May 4, 1942.

    e. Second Endorsement from Major General Thomas Holcomb (Subject: Non award of the Medal of Honor in the Case of the Late Lieutenant Colonel Daniel R. Fox, USMC) of June 18, 1942.

    f. Letter from the Senior Member of the [Navy] Board for the Award of Medals of Honor, Distinguished Service Medal, Navy Cross, Distinguished Flying Cross and Life Saving Medals (Subject: Recommendation for the Posthumous Award of the Medal of Honor in the Case of the Late Lieutenant Colonel Daniel R. Fox, US Marine Corps) of June 3, 1942.

"Fire. Part 2." Homicide: Life on the Street (Season 4, October 27, 1995).

Hough, Lieutenant Colonel Frank O., USMCR, Major Verle E. Ludwig, USMC, and Henry I. Shaw Jr. Pearl Harbor to Guadalcanal: History of the U.S. Marine Corps Operations in World War II. Historical Division, Headquarters, US Marine Corps, Washington, DC, 1958. Reprinted by the Battery Press, Inc., Nashville, TN, 1993. Volume I.

Lamothe, Dan. "Modern Medals of Honor and the Time They Take to Award." Washington Post. July 21, 2014.

Manchester, William. American Caesar. Little, Brown and Company, Boston and Toronto, 1978.

Morgan, Thomas B. "The War Hero." Esquire (December 1983), 603.

Morison, Samuel Eliot. History of United States Naval Operations in World War II. Atlantic Monthly Press. Little, Brown, and Company, 1949. Volume V.

Munson, Kenneth. Aircraft of World War II. Doubleday & Company, Inc., New York, NY, 1962.

Potter, E. B. Nimitz. Naval Institute Press, Annapolis, MD, 1976.

PEARL HARBOR ATTACK: HEARINGS BEFORE THE JOINT COMMITTEE ON THE INVESTIGATION OF THE PEARL HARBOR ATTACK, SEVENTY-NINTH CONGRESS, SECOND SESSION (U.S. Government Printing Office, 1946), Part 21.

The Roberts Commission investigation of December 7, 1941, included in the report of the 1945 Congressional investigation of the attack found in PEARL HARBOR ATTACK: HEARINGS BEFORE THE JOINT COMMITTEE ON THE INVESTIGATION OF THE PEARL HARBOR ATTACK, SEVENTY-NINTH CONGRESS, FIRST SESSION (U.S. Government Printing Office, 1946), Part 39.

Roberts, Andrew. "For Love of Country." THE WALL STREET JOURNAL, December 11, 2014.

Roscoe, Theodore. United States Submarine Operations in World War II. Naval Institute Press, Annapolis, MD, 1949.

Scherman, David E. (editor). Life Goes to War. Pocket Books, New York, NY 1997, 50.

Simpson, Harold B. Audie Murphy, American Soldier. The Hill Jr. College Press, 1975.

Smith, General Holland M. USMC (Retired). Coral and Brass. The Battery Press, Inc., Nashville, TN, 2004. Reprint of 1948 edition.

Sullivan, Robert (editor). Pearl Harbor: America's Call to Arms. Life Books, 2000, 2011.

Steere, Edward, and Thayer M. Boardman. Final Disposition of World War II Dead 1945–51. Historical Branch, Office of the Quartermaster General, 1957. QMC Historical Studies, Series II, No. 4, page 625 to 626.

Tibbets, Paul W. Flight of the Enola Gay. Mid Coast Marketing, Columbus, OH, 1989.

United States Navy. United States Navy Regulations. Washington, DC: United States Government Printing Office, Washington, DC, 1990.

United States Navy. United States Navy Regulations. Washington, DC: United States Government Printing Office, Washington, DC (1920, reprinted 1941).

The Virginian Pilot. Hampton Roads Naval Aviation: A Centennial Retrospective, Norfolk, VA. 2011, pages 8–10.

Truman, President Harry S. Statement of August 6, 1945, announcing the atomic bombing of Hiroshima, Japan printed in AIR FORCE MAGAZINE (September 2006).

Zanger, Jack. "A Perspective in Leadership: Rear Adm. Herbert E. Schonland." Surface Warfare 23, no. 6 (November /December 1998).

BILLY MITCHELL ADDENDUM

The purpose of this addendum is to advise the reader of four sites at which Billy Mitchell is mentioned. Photographs follow the text of this addendum.

The first site is the Air Force Memorial in Arlington, Virginia. The Memorial comprises granite panels with names and information as well as tall metallic structures pointing to the sky to simulate flight. One section of the granite panels is titled, "AIRMEN MEDAL OF HONOR RECIPIENTS." Beside "PEACETIME" is the following:

Col. WILLIAM 'BILLY' MITCHELL
Milwaukee, Wisconsin

He should be listed as a brigadier general. See Chapter 20 of this book.

The second site is a historical marker outside the Virginia Air and Space Center in Hampton, Virginia. The marker reads as follows:

LANGLEY FIELD:
CREATING AN AIR FORCE
In Dec. 1916, the U.S. Army purchased land four miles north of here to build an airfield to use jointly with the National Advisory Committee for Aeronautics. During World War I, the Army trained aircrews and tested aircraft there. In 1921, Brig. Gen. William "Billy" Mitchell led bombing trials from Langley to demonstrate that air power could destroy battleships. On 1 March 1935, Air Corps combat units were realigned nationwide under the GHQ Air Force. Led from Langley by Maj. Gen. Frank Andrews, that combat air command was the forerunner of the Army Air Forces of World War II and marked the first real step toward the U.S. Air Force.

The third and fourth sites are on the North Carolina Outer Banks.

The third site is at the town of Frisco on Highway 12. Visitors turn off Highway 12 at Billy Mitchell Road and drive toward the beach to reach Billy Mitchell Airstrip, which apparently is under the joint control of the Cape Hatteras National Seashore (the National Park Service under the U.S. Department of the Interior) and the North Carolina Department of Transportation (Division of Aviation). At the airport buildings are various placards telling the story of Billy Mitchell's aircraft, flying from Langley Field in Virginia, sinking the battleships USS Virginia and USS New Jersey. In the Hatteras area is a roadside historical marker aside North Carolina Highway 12 reading as follows:

BILLY MITCHELL Brigadier General of the Army Air Service, demonstrated air power by bombing battleships off coast, Sept. 5, 1923. Landing field was here.

The fourth site is at the Graveyard of the Atlantic Museum at Hatteras. One wall has photographs and text concerning the Mitchell bombing trials in 1923 off the North Carolina Outer Banks. A panel in the display titled "1923 The Birth of Strategic Bombing" mentions the Mitchell sinkings of the battleships USS Virginia and USS New Jersey.

PHOTOGRAPHS

A granite panel at the Air Force Memorial at Arlington, Virginia lists Billy Mitchell as a Medal of Honor recipient. (Author's photograph)

This historical marker at Hampton, Virginia (see text at the beginning of this Mitchell addendum) mentions Billy Mitchell and his 1921 bombing trials during which his aviators sank ships. (Author's slide)

The Billy Mitchell Airstrip at Frisco, North Carolina on the Outer Banks. (Author's photograph)

Billy Mitchell historical marker in the Hatteras area aside North Carolina Highway 12. (Author's photograph)

"1923 The Birth of Strategic Bombing" panel that is part of the Mitchell display at the Graveyard of the Atlantic Museum in Hatteras, North Carolina on the Outer Banks. (Author's photograph)

The original caption reads as follows: "This final picture shows a Martin MB-2 dropping four 100 lb Phosphorus bombs, one striking the crows [sic] nest of the [battleship] *Alabama* [in 1921]. Military men of the times were amazed that such small fabric covered wooden flying devices could do so much harm to the mighty battleships." (Photograph courtesy of Adam Hebert of AIR FORCE Magazine)

About the Author
Colonel Charles A. Jones, USMCR (Retired)

Charles A. Jones is a native of Greensboro, North Carolina. He graduated from Oak Ridge Military Academy, Wake Forest University, and Campbell University School of Law. In high school, he was active in Junior Achievement, winning numerous awards, and in Scouting, where he attained Eagle Scout.

He joined the U.S. Marine Corps in 1980 and in 1981 completed Officer Candidates School, The Basic School (TBS), and Naval Justice School. Due to his high class standing at TBS (fifth of 151 lieutenants), he earned a regular commission. He served on active duty in the Marine Corps as a lawyer from 1981 until 1992, at which time he left active duty to write, primarily about military history. While in the Regular component, he served as a review officer, prosecutor, counsel, and legal assistance attorney. From 1982 to 1983, he was the legal advisor to the commander of the Thirty-Second and Twenty-Second Marine Amphibious Units and was ashore in Beirut, Lebanon. He also served a tour as in Washington, DC, at Headquarters, Marine Corps, answering letters from the public and from Congress as well as preparing legal research projects. Beginning in 1993, he became active in the U.S. Marine Corps Reserve, serving on inactive duty as a drilling Reservist as well as on extended periods of active duty. He retired from the reserve in 2009. His last duty station was the Marine Corps Historical Division. He served a combined total of thirty years in the Regular and Reserve Marine Corps.

His first commercial book, Hawaii's World War II Military Sites, was published by Mutual Publishing in 2002 but is no longer in print. It was a 250-page, comprehensive, very detailed unique combination of guidebook and history book, guiding the reader on tours of sites of importance during World War II—not just December 7 sites but also all major sites involving the Pacific War.

His articles have appeared in numerous magazines, such as Air Force Magazine, Proceedings, World War II, After the Battle, Shipmate (the magazine U.S. Naval Academy alumni), and the Marine Corps Gazette. His articles and letters to the editor have also appeared in numerous newspapers, such as Air Force Times, Navy Times, Marine Corps Times, Washington Post, Washington Times, Virginian-Pilot, Greensboro News and Record, Rhinoceros Times, and Port Folio Weekly. His articles about Iwo Jima have also appeared in the Fifth Marine Division newsletter, Spearhead NEWS, and in the Fourth Division newsletter, The Fighting Fourth Marine Division of WWII.

He wrote a 101-page self-published biography of his great-great grandfather, a Confederate lieutenant from North Carolina who survived the war.

He has presented several classes on Iwo Jima and on the Oahu attack on December 7, 1941, to various organizations, including adult education classes at Old Dominion University.

He is a member of Greensboro Masonic Lodge 76 and a Third-Degree (Master) Mason.

He lived in Norfolk, Virginia, from 1988 to 2012. He now lives in Greensboro, North Carolina, his hometown.

www.ingramcontent.com/pod-product-compliance
Lightning Source LLC
Chambersburg PA
CBHW050247170426
43202CB00011B/1584